Insid

Dan Ablan

Inside LightWave v9
by Dan Ablan

New Riders
1249 Eighth Street
Berkeley, CA 94710
510/524-2178
510/524-2221 (fax)

Find us on the Web at: www.newriders.com
To report errors, please send a note to: errata@peachpit.com

New Riders is an imprint of Peachpit, a division of Pearson Education.

Editors
Victor Gavenda and Rebecca Gulick

Development Editor
Jim Akin

Copy Editor
Liz Welch

Technical Reviewer
Deuce Bennett

Production Coordinator
Myrna Vladic

Compositors
Deborah Roberti, Rick Gordon

Indexer
James Minkin

Cover Design
New Riders

Front Cover Image
William C. Vaughan and Alejandro Parrilla

Back Cover Images
Dan Ablan

ISBN-13: 978-0-321-42684-0
ISBN-10: 0-321-42684-3

9 8 7 6 5 4 3 2 1

Printed and bound in the United States of America

Contents at a Glance

Table of Contents

Acknowledgments

Just as it was with my *Inside LightWave [8]* book, I cannot express my gratitude to my friend, Deuce. He, in many ways, has made this book possible. Without his help and sincere friendship, this book would be nothing more than a paperweight. Thanks, Deuce, for all of your help and direction. But it goes further, maybe even more than Deuce (just kidding!)—thank you so much, William Vaughan, for your insight, help, models, and cover image. Your expertise, years in the field, and general good nature have made working on this book more enjoyable than I expected. Thank you also to Alejandro Parrilla, who worked on the image for our cover along with William.

Of course, I'd probably still be writing this tome at this very moment if it weren't for Victor Gavenda and Rebecca Gulick. You really lit the fire under my you-know-what to get this book done. Thank you for your support and words of encouragement! Thank you Jim Akin, my editor extraordinaire, who really put me to the test, making sure we got everything just right. Thanks to Ellen Cavalli for stepping in at the last minute to help edit and meet our printer deadline. Thank you to Myrna Vladic, Liz Welch, Sara Jane Todd, Eric Geoffroy, and Charlene Will for putting the polish on this book.

To the team at NewTek—Jay, Deuce, William, Donetta, Jim, and, of course, Chuck Baker—you guys have been a tremendous help to this book. Also thank you to Kurtis Harris for your excellent support. Your efforts and concern are sincerely appreciated. The LightWave v9 development team is often left in the shadows, but I know how hard you've worked getting this new, and clearly the best version of LightWave out the door. Congrats to all of you, and thanks!

To my wonderful wife, Maria. Your support while writing three books back to back has been amazing. I can't thank you enough for everything you do. You're the best. And to little Amelia, thanks for being the best little girl anyone could ask for.

Finally, to all LightWave users around the globe who read my books and use my 3D Garage.com training materials—thanks. Your feedback, on all levels, is greatly appreciated. All of you are the reason I lose sleep writing these books, so keep in touch and let me know what you're doing with your newfound knowledge.

Foreword

The beginning of knowledge is the discovery of something we do not understand.
–Frank Herbert

Throughout my life I have been lucky enough to have some of the most passionate instructors that helped to shape the person I am today. In high school, Von Kwallak instructed me for four years on everything from design, illustration, sculpture, art history, and more. He was a quiet man but had a lifetime of experience that he shared with the classes he taught. There wasn't a project I could throw at Kwallak that he didn't suggest several paths I could take to meet my goals. I became the problem solver I am today through his instruction.

Mary Knape taught private art classes in my area, and, on a whim, I signed up for one of her night classes about 15 years ago. Little did I know her teachings would send my understanding of color into overdrive. She had a real gift for making even the most hard-to-grasp concepts a walk in the park.

Shortly after my classes with Knape, I went off to college, where my luck continued and I received training from some of the best designers and illustrators. Then I was off to join the workforce, where I thought my training would come to an end. I couldn't have been more wrong! I had a real thirst for knowledge and found that my education had just begun.

I started working in new areas like interactive design and multimedia, which required that I pick up new skills—which of course meant new things to learn. It was also at this time that I caught the 3D bug and purchased my first copy of LightWave 3D. At this time, 3D was still new territory, so there were no classes being offered that I could take to get a jumpstart. Having never really worked in 3D, I moved pretty slowly until 1996, when I was introduced to my first 3D instructor, Dan Ablan.

Dan was the author of *LightWave Power Guide*, which was the first in a series of LightWave books that later became the *Inside LightWave* series. Like Von Kwallak, Mary Knape, and my college professors, Dan has played a role in advancing my skill set as an artist. He was there in the beginning, lighting the way for hundreds of artists who now make up the rich talent pool in the LightWave community. Dan's education work can be seen in studios in Hollywood, the game industry, and many other areas of digital content creation. He has a solid understanding of how to train artists and has helped many take their first step into 3D.

With every new release of LightWave comes the countdown to Dan's book, and *Inside LightWave v9* is no exception. The entire LightWave community has waited for what I'm sure will become another must-have resource for any LightWave user. If this is your first book by Dan, prepare to add him to your favorite instructor list, as I did 10 years ago. I'm happy to say Dan is still on my list, and I continue to learn from his teaching.

–William "Proton" Vaughan, NewTek's LightWave 3D Evangelist

About the Author

Before I entered the glamorous and fascinating world of 3D animation, I worked in a not-as-much-fun world of video production. After graduating college with a Bachelor's degree in broadcast journalism, I promptly went to work for a very small CBS affiliate. If your idea of experience is standing in the center of Indiana with a 70-pound camera on your shoulder in the 20-degree Midwest cold, then I've got the referral!

For me, I wanted more, and moved up to a program manager position for a large cable television outfit. There, I discovered 3D animation via NewTek's LightWave 3D and an Amiga computer. Now, you have to remember, today 3D is everywhere. In 1989, 3D was only prevalent in hugely expensive systems in the top video production studios, and mostly in an experimental state. Either way, one look at a small red apple rendering one pixel at a time (I think it took an hour or so) and I was hooked. From there I produced corporate video for a couple of years, and along the way emmersed myself in 3D.

In 1994, I went to work for an Amiga dealership, selling and training Video Toaster and LightWave systems. Also in 1994, I was fired from the Amiga dealership because Commodore stopped making Amigas. However, I had started doing 3D work on the side, and with the help of unemployment checks from the state of Illinois, I was able to forge ahead with my own business, AGA Digital Studios.

While creating 3D animations for corporate accounts like Bosch and Kraft Foods, I also began submitting articles to the only LightWave publication at the time, *LightWave Pro*. From there, I wrote tutorials every month, and also contributed to their sister publication, *Video Toaster User*. I was "Dr. Toaster" and would answer questions for readers (I did not choose the name of the column, by the way). Avid Media Group, publishers of *Video Toaster User* and *LightWave Pro*, were bought out by Miller Freeman Publishing, and so I started writing for a new magazine called *3D Design*. Around 1995, I met with a representative from Macmillan Publishing and we discussed the idea of LightWave book. They knew who I was through my articles in the trade magazines, and in 1996, the first book on LightWave was published, *LightWave Power Guide* from New Riders Publishing. *Inside LightWave v9* is my eleventh book and follows the popular *Inside LightWave [8]*, *LightWave [8] Killer Tips*, *Inside LightWave [7]*, *Inside LightWave [6]*, *LightWave 6.5 Magic*, and *Inside LightWave 3D* books. In addition to the LightWave books, I've also written *Digital Cinematography & Directing*, the *Official Luxology modo Guide*, and *Digital Photography for 3D Imaging and Animation*.

Now, more than a decade later, AGA Digital Studios, Inc., is located in the Chicago area; we create animations for corporate and industrial clients such as United Airlines, NASA, Lockheed Martin, the FAA, Blue Cross and Blue Sheild, AllState, McDonald's, and many others. In addition to daily animation work, in 2003 I founded a new division to AGA Digital dedicated to 3D learning courses. 3D Garage.com is a training source with material that is presented as project-based courses. Visit www.3dgarage.com for more information and free samples.

For more information on my other books and photography, visit my Web site, www.danablan.com.

About the Cover

The *Inside LightWave v9* cover image was created in LightWave by William C. Vaughan and Alejandro Parrilla. Quincy is the star of the cover and was modeled with subdivision surfaces using the box modeling technique. He has 118 bones and 26 endomorphs used to pose and animate him. The scene that was used for this illustration uses a basic three-point light setup taking advantage of LightWave's area lights. Render time for the print resolution image was just under 14 minutes.

Introduction

Welcome to the next installment of *Inside LightWave*. This book represents more than seven years of LightWave® books written and published by myself, a few good friends, and New Riders. Inside books—a staple in the ever-growing digital image creation industry and your own personal library—are present in bookstores and online retailers around the globe. I personally want to thank you for your continued support, suggestions, and comments, which have helped make this new version of *Inside LightWave* the best the series has ever seen. To give you the most complete and up-to-date information, *Inside LightWave* was written in conjunction with the development of the LightWave v9® software (including v9.2) from NewTek, Inc. No other book can offer you as much comprehensive information. With *Inside LightWave*, you will take your favorite 3D application to the next level. LightWave v9 is a major release for NewTek, Inc., and I've made this book as informative as possible while keeping it more organized and to the point. Every tutorial and task you will create is straightforward to you can get up to speed with this powerful program quickly. Every project and note will give you a clear and concise understanding of the powerhouse of tools LightWave v9 has to offer through simple and easy-to-follow tutorials.

Getting the Most from *Inside LightWave*

Although we have a set format for the Inside books, I had a situation while planning the *Inside LightWave [8]* book in 2004 that forced me to change how I approached these books. I was at my favorite Borders bookstore in Chicago, looking for ideas to create a cool and modern Web site. Using my suite of tools from Macromedia and Adobe Photoshop 7, I had built a decent Web site but I still needed some excitement. Perhaps some of those cool animated Macromedia Flash header bars, some animated buttons, and a few little gizmos to spice up the site. But I found that there wasn't a book that just showed me how to do what I wanted. All the books I looked at were good, informative, well thought-out, and so on. But I just wanted to get going! I didn't want to sift through page after page of making curves and animating little clip art bumblebees and the like. This experience got me thinking! Afterward, I went back to the office and jotted down some notes on how I wanted to refocus the *Inside LightWave* books.

The formula for the Inside books has worked well since the first *Inside LightWave* edition in 1997, and I don't want to change that. Many of the longtime readers look for this same format because of its proven track record. However, I did not want you to be in the situation I was in, especially when trying to learn a complex 3D application, not just a Web-creation program. Therefore, I created the Inside LightWave [8] "Quick-Start" for Chapter 1. This was a not-too-involved type of tutorial that got you up and running with LightWave [8]. To continue the tradition for *Inside LightWave*, I've gone a step further and provided the Quick-Start as a free training video on the book's DVD. This will help you get to speed even faster with LightWave. The Quick-Start certainly doesn't inform you about all the tools and features in LightWave v9, but it does help familiarize you with the software and its workflow. Then, you can move into the chapters and learn about the panels, modeling, texturing, layout, animation, and rendering.

About the Creation of This Book

Inside LightWave was written entirely on Macbook Pro Core2 Duo laptop computer. This is a testament to the performance of computer systems in today's marketplace, as many desktop systems couldn't support 3D applications a few years ago. There are few differences between LightWave on the Mac and LightWave on Windows. The biggest difference is the use of a three-button mouse. If you are a Mac user, you probably know that Macs shipped with single-button mice for years, and only recently started shipping with the two-button Mighty Mouse. Many programs, and the Mac OS X operating system itself, employ right-mouse button functions, however, and I highly recommend you get a two-

or three-button mouse if you're working on the Mac. This will benefit you greatly working in LightWave v9 as well as other programs. Logitech-brand optical mice work well from my experience. For you Mac users who cannot part with the one-button mouse, simply hold your Command key (often called the Apple key) in conjunction with the mouse button to achieve right-mouse button functions. We'll provide reminders to you throughout this book.

Your choice of using Mac or Windows is strictly up to you. There is no benefit or drawback from either. It's merely a matter of preference.

Using the LightWave v9 Software with This Book

LightWave v9 has many differences from LightWave 7.5 and [8]. I recommend that you use the latest revision of LightWave with this book to maximize your learning. Many of the tutorials in this book use tools only available in version v9, such as the Node Editor for advanced surfacing, and consequently those tutorials won't work with previous versions of LightWave. However, if you happen to have the *Inside LightWave 6, Inside LightWave 7*, or *Inside LightWave [8]* books, you can take advantage of the tutorials in those books with the LightWave v9 software. Although some buttons and panels may have changed, the core workflow and key functions of LightWave v9 work the same as with previous versions. Additionally, you can change LightWave's menus back to [8] mode through the Edit Menu Layout panel, found in the Edit drop-down lists in the program.

Always Use the LightWave v9 Manuals

People always criticize software manuals. I think it's almost a preconceived notion that they are not the best learning tools; and in some cases, they are not. However, they do serve a strong purpose: to introduce and offer reference material on the current version. The LightWave manuals, both printed and electronic, provide great reference information when you need to find out about a key function or tool. The current manuals from NewTek are the best they've been in years, so refer to them often for specific technical information. For learning beyond what you find in the manual, use *Inside LightWave*. This book takes you to the next level by walking you through the toolset with projects and tasks. However, I've created this new *Inside LightWave* book as a manual replacement, and you can start learning LightWave with the Quick-Start tutorial video, then move right into Chapter 1. From there, learn about cameras, lights, texturing, and utilize that information in projects throughout this book.

Where Should You Start?

As I mentioned earlier, it kills me to buy a big new book on a software application and be forced to sift through page after page of information that doesn't provide the answer I'm looking for. In the past, I've written the *Inside LightWave* books as "start to finish" guides. With this version, I've tried to make a collection of little books, with each chapter being self-contained. When you're comfortable with the workflow of LightWave v9 and ready to go further, pick up this book and do one of two things. You can either start at the beginning with Chapter 2, learning about 3D basics, then move to Chapter 3, Chapter 4, and so on. Or you can hop over to a chapter of your choice and start working through a project right away. The benefit of this is time efficiency—if you're short on time, you can get in, learn something and get out, then come back later for more. It's totally up to you. Some chapters will use projects from other chapters. For example, you might model in one chapter, and then animate that object in another. If you would like to just learn about animation, you can load the finished object from this book's DVD, without having to complete the modeling chapter first.

Explore the Software

When learning LightWave, or any other software application, technical skill, keen insight, forethought, and clever deduction are always helpful, but there's another ingredient that's far more important to your success: experimentation. As you work through the exercises in this book, don't get hung up on being a mathematical wizard or a serious traditional artist. These skills may help, but they are not necessary to create beautiful 3D animations and graphics. Explore the software on your own terms. Experiment with buttons and tools, and don't be intimidated. There is no substitute for practice, whether it's a musical instrument, athletic ability, or 3D animation. I've said it before, and I'll say it again: Don't wait until you have a paid project or assignment to work in LightWave! All the extra time you spend modeling and animating will give you an extra edge.

No Method Is the Best Method

If you've ever read any of the 3D forums on the Internet, you might have seen some discussions about what is "the best" modeling method, or "the best" renderer, and so on. Do yourself a favor; read those posts and then forget them. They are nothing more than opinion. What matters is what works for you. Perhaps you like to model with splines? Great. Perhaps you would never like to see a spline curve for the rest of your life. That's great, too.

Have you ever watched the Fox Television show "American Idol"? If you've ever heard its judges tell young hopefuls to take a song and "Make it your own," you've heard some good advice—advice that applies to 3D design and animation as well as pop stardom. When a prospective Idol sings her guts out on live television with a rendition of a popular tune, raw talent can make a performance stand out, but to really wow the judges, she must invest the song with her own personal feeling, style, and creativity. Make it her own. You can do the same with 3D modeling and animation. Find what works for you and run with it.

Use Other Books with This Book

People often ask me how I write these books. Sometimes, I ask myself the very same question! Whether I'm completing my daily animation work, writing another book, or creating courseware for 3D Garage.com, I find that using other books is a huge help. Books on topics such as architectural design, photography, anatomy, and many other subjects can be significant resources for 3D modeling, texturing, lighting, and animation. Don't limit yourself to only books and magazines focused on LightWave, computers, or 3D. Go beyond the scope of what you're doing by referencing other books. You can find many resources for character study, sculpture, and even drawing that will help you understand foundations 3D models and animations are based on—or simply inspire you to create. As a little shameless plug, be sure to check out a new book I wrote called *Digital Photography for 3D Imaging and Animation.* It's designed to teach you how and what to shoot with your digital camera, for use in 3D. This can be texturing, panoramas, or HDR (high-dynamic range) imaging.

The Organization of This Book

Inside LightWave is organized differently than our previous versions. This book starts with the basics, then moves to intermediate projects, and then walks you through a few advanced concepts.

The new LightWave Quick-Start video on this book's DVD will get you up and running fast with LightWave's workflow and toolset. In the book, you'll also find a chapter overview on the new tools and enhancements available in LightWave v9 for both Modeler and Layout (Chapters 1 and 2). From here, you can learn about texturing, following that up with an overview of both working with cameras, lights, and motions.

In the next part of this book, you'll model with just about all possible methods, allowing you to decide which method is right for you. You'll start with simple modeling using text, then move to the intermediate with real-world objects, and then finish with the organic, such as characters, and more. These chapters will instruct you in the process, tools, and organization needed to create literally anything you can think of.

After you have modeling mastered, along with some texturing and animation, you can educate yourself on more powerful texturing and lighting techniques, while explaining how to put everything in motion. You'll learn how to make LightWave's character tools bring your 3D models to life, while incorporating compositing.

Toward the end of this book, you'll learn to get your animations rendered and into playable formats. You'll learn about LightWave's powerful rendering engine, network rendering, and new render options. You'll also learn how to use LightWave to create cool effects with the system's new dynamics engine. You'll see how easy it is to use real-world physics to collide objects, push them around, and make smoke.

In the appendixes, you'll find details where you can go for further learning. The final appendix contains important information on using this book's DVD. Please read this appendix before you insert the DVD into your computer.

As you read this book, you'll find helpful Notes. These will be noticeably marked with a small icon.

Control areas throughout the program will be referred to as panels. Fields in which you enter values are called requesters, and buttons that have downward-pointing triangles are drop-downs. Be sure to go through Chapters 1 and 2 for clear overviews of Modeler and Layout control areas.

When working in LightWave, specifically Modeler (LightWave is comprised of two programs, Modeler and Layout), be sure the Caps Lock is off. Keyboard shortcuts are first programmed in lowercase keys, whereas more complex, less-used commands are programmed with uppercase keys. Should you be following a tutorial in this book and are instructed to press a keyboard function and do not see results, there's a good chance you've got your Caps Lock on.

System Considerations

Inside LightWave has had a boost in performance over previous versions. In addition, a good amount of display options have been added, which can be great for your animation setup but taxing on your system. Obviously, the better your video card, the better the performance that you'll see, and more memory is always good. But you don't need to have a multithousand-dollar system to run LightWave efficiently. On the contrary, LightWave can run exceptionally well on systems costing just a few hundred dollars. Of course, this is all dependent on the type of work you're doing. Simply put, the more detail you put into a 3D model and animation, the more system resources you'll need. If there is one thing I cannot stress enough, it's memory. Do not go out and get the fastest processor and skimp on the memory. You are better off with a 1GHz processor and 1GB of RAM than a 3.0GHz processor and 256MB of RAM. You may render a little slower, but you'll be able to work faster. Many system crashes are attributed to lack of memory, so try to make your absolute minimum 256MB. Your NewTek manual can also instruct you on the optimal system requirements. You can also work directly with your LightWave dealer or computer dealer to assist you.

One thing to remember when working in a computer-based field: Don't wait. There will always be an upgrade, always a faster system and cheaper parts. But if you wait too long, you'll put aside valuable hours in which you could have been learning and creating, as well as earning! Buy a computer that is comfortably within your budget but as powerful as it can be, and get to work.

Video Memory

Don't think that because you have the latest processor on the market, or the fastest Mac available, you'll have the best computer for animation. Processing power is only one part of the computing process when it comes to creating with LightWave. Your system memory—in this case, 256MB of RAM or more—is important to a productive system. However, your video memory is just as important.

With LightWave v9's expansive interface enhancements, you should have a decent OpenGL-compatible video card with at least 32MB of RAM or more. Personally, I wouldn't go less than 64MB. LightWave's Modeler and Layout allow great control over viewports, shading, and interface color, and there are brand-new OpenGL controls in Layout, all of which will rely heavily on your video memory.

You can view images projected through lights, fog, reflections, and multi-textures, and view them more directly in Layout. Because of the popular video-game market, graphic cards have become ridiculously fast and cheap. And, the Macintosh market finally has some powerful graphics cards. It's highly recommended that you get a decent video card, which by the way, shouldn't cost you more than $150 US.

Any video graphics card you use should be fully OpenGL compliant. Also, video cards change often, so be sure to check with NewTek about any new card recommendations the company may have.

Dual Monitors

Even though they are commonly seen these days, you might not be familiar with dual monitors. Essentially, many video cards now allow you to connect two, or even three, computer monitors to a single card. You can also add a secondary video card and put your monitors side-by-side for an expanded, wide desktop. This is a wonderful way to work with LightWave and many other graphics programs that require a great deal of onscreen real estate. With LightWave, you can keep panels such as the Graph Editor open and move them to the secondary monitor for constant control over your keyframes for timing and motion.

Installing LightWave 3D®

Installing LightWave 3D is as easy as putting the software disc into your PC or Mac. Follow the instructions that NewTek, Inc. has provided in its software manual. If you have any LightWave 3D installation problems, please direct those questions to NewTek's Technical Support (www.newtek.com). However, it's often best to let the installer do its job—that is, don't be clever and try to install different parts of the application to different parts of your hard drive.

Using the Book's DVD

The DVD that comes with this book contains all the necessary project files for you to follow along with the examples. Additionally, you can load finished project scenes and dissect them for your interest and reference.

What's on the DVD?

In addition to the project files on the book's DVD, you'll find materials to take your LightWave v9 learning further than you can with any other LigthWave book you'll find:

- Free video tutorials from 3D Garage.com, which will take you further with many of the book's chapters
- Full-sized color images of this book's figures
- Free textures
- A 30-Day Trial version of LightWave v9

See Appendix B, "What's on the DVD," for more detailed information.

Installing the Practice Files

Too often, readers install a book's DVD into their drive and then try to open scenes. Sure enough, an error appears that LightWave "can't find" a necessary object or image. This is not a defective DVD, but rather has to do with LightWave's Content Directory. You'll learn more about this as the chapters progress. Basically, the Content Directory tells LightWave 3D where to look for files. If you press the **o** key (not zero) in LightWave Layout or Modeler, you'll get the General Options panel. Click to the Paths tab. At the top of that tab, you can click the Content Directory button. Set the Content Directory to point to yourDVDdrive://Projects. That's it!

Note

For your convenience, we've put the necessary project files from this book online, just in case you have trouble with your DVD. Go to www.danablan.com and click the Books page for download. Unzip or unstuff the file, and you'll find a Projects folder. Simply put this folder somewhere on your hard drive and point LightWave's Content Directory to that folder.

Within the Projects folder is an Images folder for necessary textures and images, an Objects folder containing LightWave 3D objects, and finally a Scenes folder that is home to this book's LightWave scenes. When you load a scene into LightWave Layout (you cannot load scenes into Modeler, only objects), the Scene file looks to the Content Directory for the necessary objects. The objects loaded look to the Content Directory for the necessary images. It sounds complicated, but it's not. All you're doing is telling LightWave where to find its files. By default, the Content Directory should point to yourdrive://LightWave.

Throughout these chapters, if you're called upon to "load an object," simply selecting the Load Object command in Layout or Modeler automatically opens the Objects folder within your set Content Directory. The same goes for images or scenes, so be sure to keep this set while working through the projects.

Words to Work By

The 3D market has changed since I got into this business. In the beginning, it was like a little club, and everyone got along. Anything we did, and I want to stress anything, was just cool as hell. In a small LightWave user group in Chicago that met monthly, each month's 3D creations were crude and generally of poor quality, but great to look at nonetheless. Now, some 16 years later, it's a different world. 3D is everywhere—in movies, television, video games, the Internet, even cell phones. Our likes and dislikes have changed, and the market has grown beyond belief. Not everything is cool to look at anymore, but that's OK. No matter what, it's always great to see someone's work because you can learn from it. The 3D world we live in is no longer a small club of enthusiasts, but rather a world full of 3D artists all working toward that ultimate render. It has become a competitive industry, but an industry built on passion and the love of 3D art. To this day, I've never met anyone that just "had" to do 3D. They "wanted" to, and I'm pretty sure you are one of those people. That hunger for 3D animation is what makes your digital creations better each time you sit down in front of the computer. You're striving to learn more and to make it better, perhaps convey a message and portray your artistic style. That is what it's all about, after all.

The tools you have at your fingertips seemed inconceivable 14 years ago, even 6 years ago. Some of you are students; some of you are professionals; and some just hobbyists, young and old. You have the ability to create anything you can imagine. Do not feel that you need additional plug-ins, or other four-lettered software applications to do "better" work. You don't. LightWave, like any other application, is nothing more than code. It is buttons and an interface. It is simply a machine that you are driving, and your job is to finish the race. Now, turn the page and start working through the Quick-Start tutorial video as I help you steer down the course.

Chapter 1

LightWave v9 Modeler

Imagine that LightWave is a virtual television studio and 3D models are your actors. Although some animations can be created with animated textures or photographs, most include 3D models. These models are made up of points, edges, and polygons. This chapter takes you on a tour of LightWave Modeler. Along the way, I'll explain points, edges, and polygons and show you how to use them to create 3D objects—which you will then animate and render in LightWave Layout.

LightWave Modeler is where your 3D animations begin. That's not to say you can't start animating right away. NewTek Inc., the makers of LightWave, have included a terrific amount of prebuilt content for you to use and explore. In fact, you can load a sample scene in LightWave v9 Layout and click the Render button to create your very first animation without ever launching Modeler. But to really know your software, you must first understand what a 3D model is all about.

Note

If you only plan to animate, and never plan to model, you might wonder if you should even read this chapter. The answer is yes! Even if you never plan to model in your career, it's still important to understand LightWave Modeler for a couple of reasons. You may at some point need to import a model from another program. Or, at the very least, you'll need to assign a surface to parts of your model. You can only do that in Modeler.

Understanding Modeler

LightWave Modeler has evolved into one of the most advanced tools of its kind, and enhancements in version 9 take it to a new level of power and sophistication.

Consistent with its complex abilities, Modeler has many buttons, panels, and menus, but there's no need to be intimidated if you stay focused on the task you want to accomplish. All the tools are useful, but many tasks require only a few of them at once. You've probably heard this before: You'll use only 20 percent of the tools 80 percent of the time. As with any fully equipped software program, some general-purpose tools get used every day; more specialized ones get pulled out once in a while—so you should always know what's in your toolbox.

Note

Please, by all means, before you go any further, read the info in the front of the book about the Content Directory and how to set it up. In fact, stop now, and do it. We'll wait.

This book will explain all of LightWave's tools, and help you find the ones you need to get your work done. This chapter begins by covering the features of Modeler. And speaking of Modeler, did you read about the Content Directory in the front of the book? Make sure you do!

There are practically no limits to what you can create using 3D animation, which means a virtually unlimited number of variables to manage—and a vast number of tools within LightWave to control them all. However, I want you to ignore the overall cluster of buttons in LightWave and concentrate instead on the tools and what you are trying to do. In other words, don't get overwhelmed by the buttons. I can't stress this enough. There are times when you will use only half a dozen buttons and tools for an entire project. Often, your particular type of work may never even unwrap some of the tools and panels LightWave has to offer. And there's nothing wrong with that. The goal of this book, and more specifically this chapter, is to help you understand how to use LightWave Modeler and work with its toolset. Even with so many improvements in LightWave over the years, version 9 includes some of the most complex changes to date. LightWave Modeler has been touted as one of the best 3D modelers in the industry, and the latest update makes it a more efficient, powerful tool, with much enhanced workflow. This chapter introduces you to that workflow. Here are some of the key areas discussed in this chapter:

- LightWave v9 Modeler interface navigation
- Viewports

- Simple objects
- Points, edges, and polygons
- Selection and deselection
- Splines and subdivisional surfaces

Proper construction of 3D models and animations takes discipline, focus, and a keen sense of direction. And, just as if you were building a cabinet in your garage or redoing the tile in your own bathroom, it also requires careful planning and a full understanding of the tools involved. This is because you want your 3D models to be efficient. That is, you have to construct the models properly so that you can animate them correctly. When you know your tools and methods, the goal is not difficult to accomplish. Your focus should be clear and your work environment should be comfortable. There's nothing worse than working on a complex model without a plan and in an uncomfortable workspace. Be prepared, both mentally and physically.

3D Modeling in LightWave

Before we start using Modeler, you should become familiar with the medium that is 3D animation. You should understand how the X-, Y-, and Z-axes relate to one another and your LightWave workspace. If you don't, please refer to the QuickTime movie "3D Animation Basics" on the book's DVD for a primer.

Note

Too often when people work in 3D, either in modeling or animation, they only consider the flat screen in front of them. Do not make this mistake! Remember that your 3D models are more than just what's visible in front of you—they have sides, a top, a bottom, and a back, even if you can't see them.

3D modeling is like interactive geometry. You can begin creating models with simple points and connect them with curves or straight lines. LightWave also gives you a slew of basic geometric shapes such as boxes and spheres to work with, and you'll see throughout this book just how those basic shapes can be used to create complex 3D models. Before you concern yourself with building complex 3D models, however, let's take a look at how the LightWave interface is laid out.

LightWave v9 Modeler Interface

If you're new to LightWave with version 9, the interface (**Figure 1.1**) will obviously look unfamiliar. Initially, working through the interface might be frustrating, but if you understand the tools and their arrangement and keep in mind what you want to do, you'll find using the program simpler than you might think.

If you're an experienced LightWave user and have just upgraded to LightWave v9, you'll notice at first a similarity to previous versions. With version 9, LightWave adds some great new tools and rearranges some preexisting ones to bring them closer to the surface. Both LightWave Layout and Modeler have been significantly streamlined and navigation has never been easier, but the changes may require some adjustment.

Although much of this book focuses on the modeling tools in action, this section highlights the features of LightWave v9 Modeler. You'll be able to try them out in just a few steps to gain a strong working knowledge of their functions.

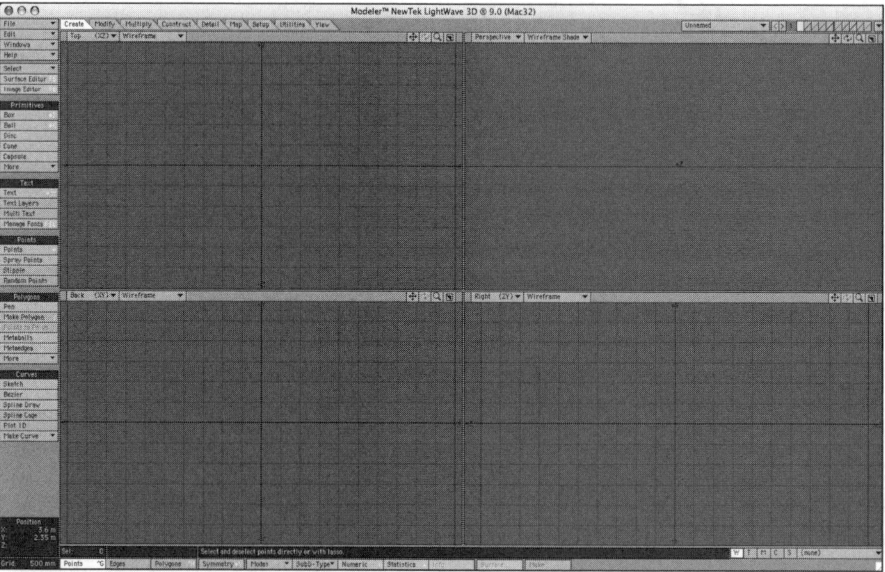

Figure 1.1 The LightWave 3D Modeler interface.

Modeler Viewports

To begin working with LightWave v9 Modeler, you should understand the viewports first. These four windows are the areas that will be your work environment, and by default, they show all sides of your 3D model.

Take a look at **Figure 1.2**, which shows the same full Modeler interface as Figure 1.1, but this time with a 3D model loaded. By default, LightWave Modeler assigns the viewports Top, Back, and Right views of your model, along with a Perspective view. Each is a little awkward at first, but try to remember this:

- Top view (XZ) provides a view along the Y-axis. You are looking down at the top of your object.
- Back view (XY) looks down the Z-axis. You are looking from the back of your object toward its front.
- Right view (ZY) looks down the X-axis. You are looking at the left side of your object, toward its right.

Yes, this may sound confusing, but after you get used to the concept, it will make more sense. And eventually, it'll even become familiar. For instance, when you get to Layout later, you'll find that the Back view you see in Modeler is the default view that the LightWave camera sees. The LightWave camera looks toward the back of the object, forward in the scene.

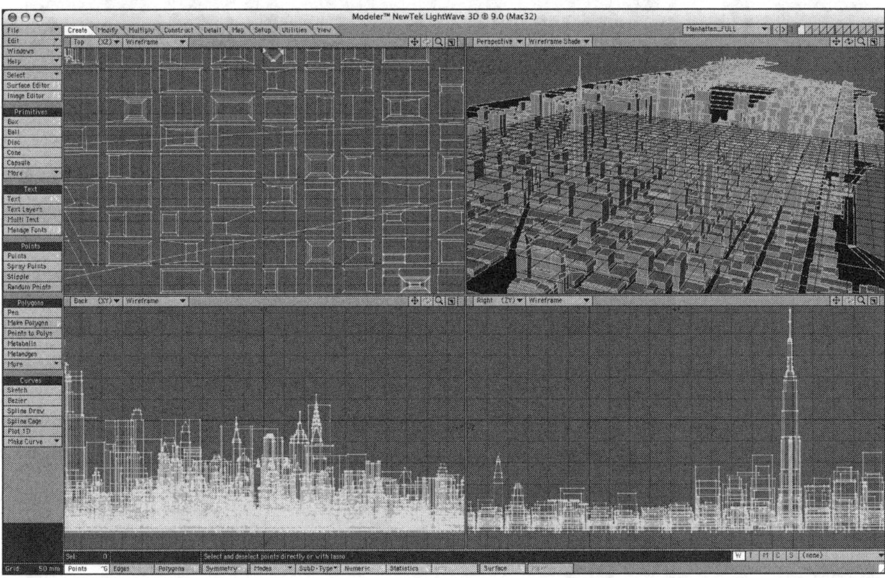

Figure 1.2 A 3D model of Manhattan loaded into LightWave Modeler can be seen from all sides, and the default layout also shows a solid color version.

Don't let this layout of viewports make you feel constrained. You can change any viewport to look any way you like. Check out **Figure 1.3**, where a close-up of the top-left viewport is shown.

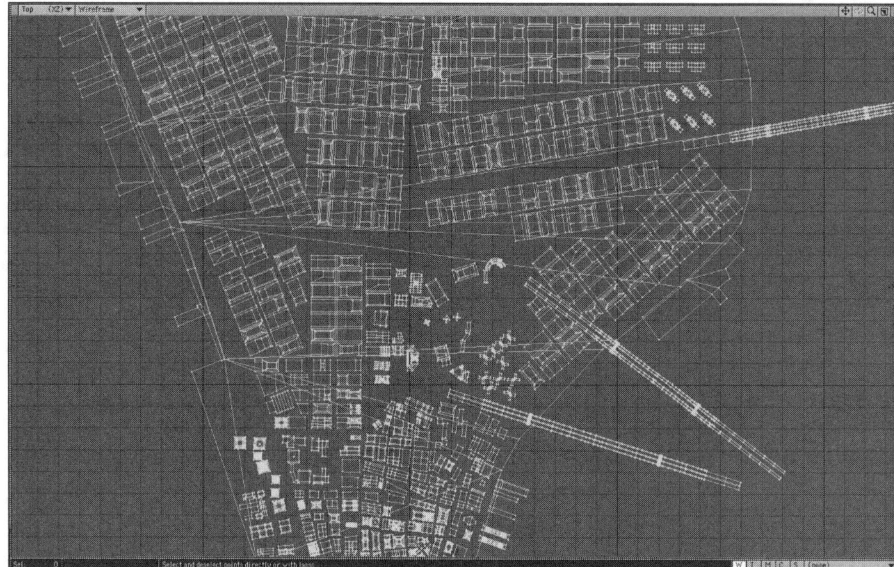

Figure 1.3 A close-up of the upper left viewport, with some geometry loaded.

This top-left viewport is called Top by default, and it shows the 3D object from above—you're looking at the "top" of the object. Notice that at the top of the viewport there are buttons labeled Top (XZ) and Wireframe. This tells you that the particular viewport is set to Top. The XZ means these are the two axes you have control over. Because you're looking down the Y-axis, you can't move your object along that axis in this view.

Figure 1.4 The four small icons at the top right of each viewport enable you to move, rotate, zoom, and maximize the viewport.

At the top right of the viewport, you'll see four small icons. These are your viewport position controls. **Figure 1.4** shows the buttons up close.

Note

Depending on viewport settings, certain position control icons may be dimmed to indicate they are unavailable. In the Top viewport, for instance, the Rotate icon is dimmed because you can only rotate in a Perspective view, not an orthogonal (X, Y, Z) view.

Click, hold, and drag on these buttons to use them. Too often, people click them and release, but that's not how they work. Click and hold to use! The first button is Move, the next is Rotate, the third is Zoom, and the last is the Maximize viewport button. Click this one, and your viewport will become full screen. This is great for getting up close to your model for fine-tuning point position or measurements. To return from a full-screen viewport, just click that icon again.

Note

If your keyboard has a numeric keypad (most nonlaptop models do, and some laptops sport them, too) you can use its 0 key in place of the Maximize viewport button. (That's 0, as in zero, and in the numeric keypad only; you'll use the number keys at the top of your keyboard to change layers.) Be sure your mouse cursor is in the viewport you want to maximize before pressing the 0 key. Press 0 again to return from full-screen mode.

Viewport Customization

You can customize each of the four viewports in Modeler any way you like. In **Figure 1.5**, you can see that you can assign any or all viewports a Back, Top, Right, or Perspective view. You can make all four viewports Top views if you like, although it might not help your modeling process too much.

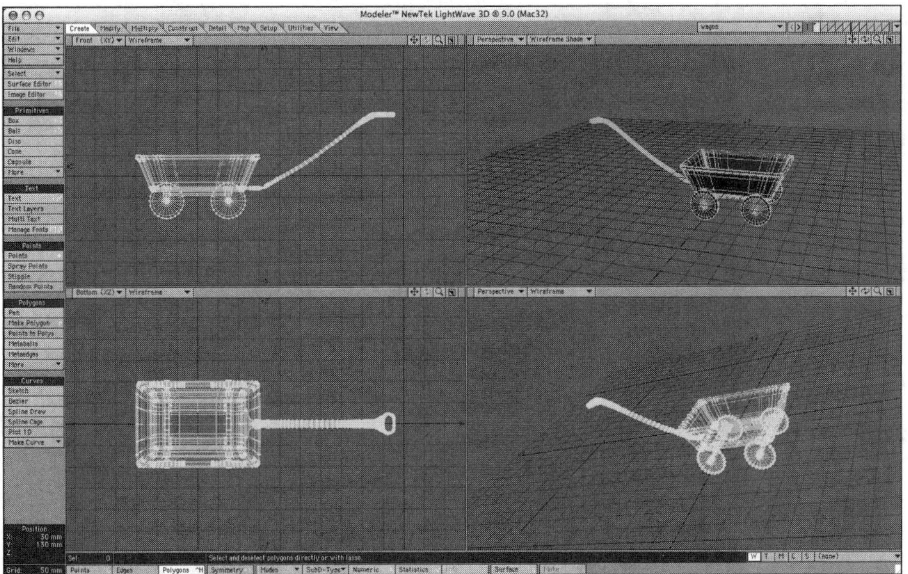

Figure 1.5 Each viewport can be set to any view you like. Here, with a simple wagon object loaded, the Top left is a Front view now, the Back is set to Bottom, while the Right view is now a Perspective view.

Note

Although LightWave v9 is extremely customizable, the projects in the book will use the default configurations for Modeler and Layout, for the sake of consistency.

Something you might change more often than the viewport view is the viewport *style*—its method of drawing the objects it depicts. Choosing any of the 10 settings from the drop-down menu shown in **Figure 1.6** lets you visualize models using styles, including Wireframe, Smooth Shade, and Textured Wire. Different styles are better suited to various modeling tasks, as we'll see later in the book.

Figure 1.7 shows each viewport set to a different style with a different model loaded, so you can see how flexible the options are.

Wireframe
Color Wireframe
Hidden Line
Sketch
Wireframe Shade
Flat Shade
Smooth Shade
Weight Shade
Texture
Textured Wire

Figure 1.6 Each viewport can also have a unique viewport style, such as Wireframe or Textured Wire.

Note

Your choice of viewport style will be based on the model you are creating. Often, a good way to work is with the default settings—Wireframe style in the X, Y, and Z viewports, while a Smooth Shade or Textured Wire style is used in a Perspective view. It's totally up to you.

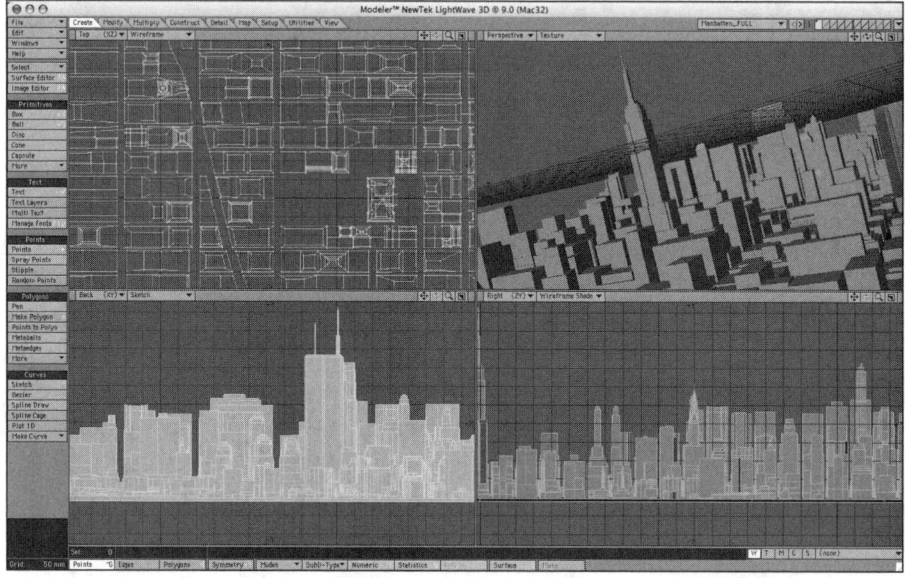

Figure 1.7 Here, each viewport is set to a different style. There are a total of 10 viewport style choices.

Working with Objects and Layers

Now, take a look at how LightWave works with objects. From there, you'll learn about points, edges, polygons, selection, and deselection, while making a few simple objects along the way. LightWave objects are unique to the program, and have the file extension .lwo. You can load existing objects from LightWave's content directory simply by pressing Ctrl+o for open (that's the letter o). But also take a look at the File drop-down menu at the top left of the Modeler interface. Click it, and you'll see all your common load and save functions, plus a few extras. **Figure 1.8** shows the panel.

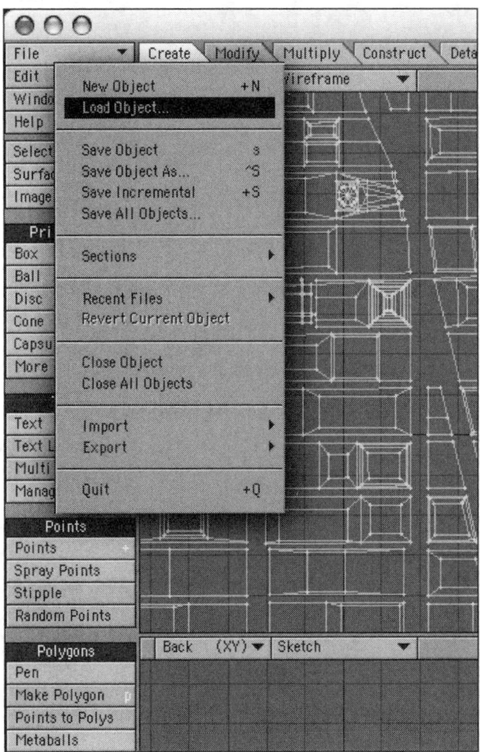

Figure 1.8 Using the File drop-down menu in Modeler, you can load, save, and perform similar operations.

If you use Photoshop, you are probably familiar with the concept of layers and how they are used if, say, you're building a billboard ad: You might put a color gradient in the background layer, add text in a new layer, a picture in another, and so on. Why do you do all this in layers? So that each layer's contents can have its own set of parameters, such as size, position, effect settings, and so on. If all the components lived on the same layer, you'd have a tough time applying effects to any individual element. LightWave Modeler works in much the same way. Each item that you need to control individually, for purposes of modeling or animation, should be in its own layer.

This means that if your car model has four wheels (and I hope it does), and you want each wheel to be able to roll separately, each wheel must live on its own layer. If a wheel were placed in the same layer as the rest of the car, you'd have to animate the entire layer to make the wheel turn. You will also learn later in the book how layers are used to perform various modeling actions. For now, take a look at the top right of the Modeler interface, and you'll find a set of 10 buttons (**Figure 1.9**), each representing a layer within a model.

Figure 1.9 At the top right of the Modeler interface are the layer buttons.

Note

An object can have multiple layers. You can work with multiple layers at one time if you like (just hold the Shift key to select multiple layers). By the same token, you can also have multiple objects loaded at once.

At first glance, if you start clicking on the layer buttons, they look like they do nothing. However, they are crucial to properly setting up and building certain types of models. And don't think that because there are 10 buttons you're limited to 10 layers. Layers are infinite in LightWave. Press **F7** and the Layers panel opens (**Figure 1.10**). You can also open this panel from the Windows drop-down menu in Modeler, as shown in **Figure 1.11**.

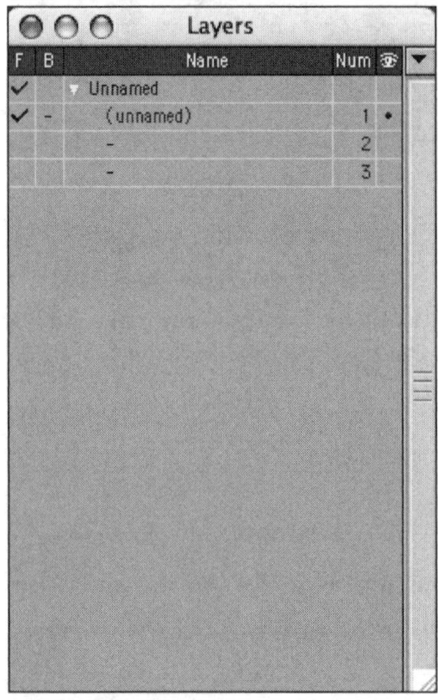

Figure 1.10 Pressing F7 opens the Layers panel, which gives you access to Modeler layers. Here you see a blank Layers panel, because no objects are loaded.

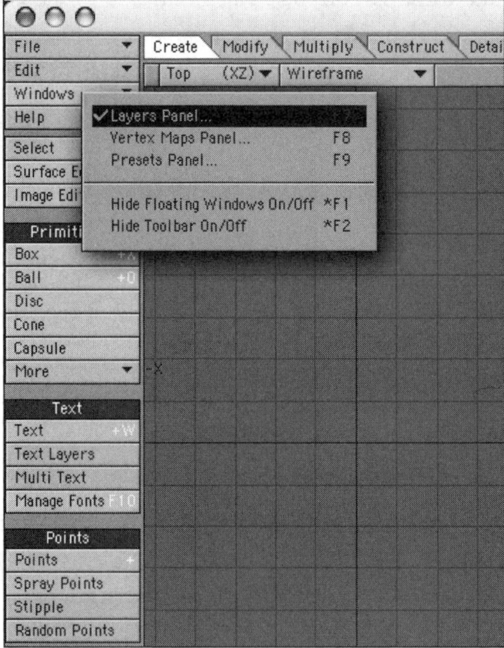

Figure 1.11 Use the Windows drop-down menu to access the Layers panel if you don't like the F7 key.

Note

If you are working on a Mac laptop and nothing happens when you press a function key such as F1 or F9, you need to open System Preferences and tell your computer to allow software applications to use the function keys, rather than the system. If you're on a desktop Mac, select Keyboard & Mouse in System Preferences, and under Keyboard Shortcuts, uncheck the function keys, such as F9, that you wish to use in LightWave. F9 on a desktop Mac defaults to Exposé's All Windows command. F9 in LightWave is Render Current Frame. Note that you can change the shortcut for render in LightWave, but the tutorials in this book will use the default settings.

To demonstrate how LightWave Modeler works with existing 3D models, you'll work with simple models that ship with your LightWave software. These will be located in the Objects folder. This folder is typically located in yourdrive://NewTek/Applications (Mac) or Program Files\LightWave 3D\Content\Objects (Windows). Be sure you have set up the content directory as instructed in the "Content Directory" movie on this book's DVD (in the "3D_Garage_Videos\Please_Start_Here" directory), and make sure to read the Read Me section of the disc contents.

Note

One more plea: Before you do anything else, learn about the Content Directory! It will save you from lots of headaches. This is the number one problem reported by new LightWavers.

Loading Objects and Naming Layers

The procedure for loading single-layer and multiple-layer objects is the same. Layer information is stored within each LightWave object file, and it's not something you need to worry about. LightWave object files retain data about changes you apply to them, such as colors and textures.

Note

The sample content included with LightWave v9 comes on a DVD that's separate from the program installer CD. Look for it in your LightWave software case, and install these files as instructed. You'll use them in this chapter.

Exercise 1.1 Loading Objects and Naming Layers

1. Press Ctrl+o (PC), Cmd+o (Mac) or choose Load Object from the File drop-down menu and load the Anime_Zombie object from the Objects folder, which

is within the Content folder, in your LightWave version 9 install folder. Once it loads, press **a** to maximize the object within the window. You'll use this keyboard shortcut quite a bit throughout this book.

Note

When working with keyboard equivalents, it's best to always keep your Caps Lock off. Many basic LightWave functions are assigned to lowercase keyboard shortcuts, while more complex functions are set to capital letters. These complex functions can create problems if you use them accidentally. For example, pressing **q** as lower case allows you to set a surface name. Pressing **q** with Caps Lock on will quit the program!

2. **Figure 1.12** shows the object-selection pull-down and the layer buttons as they appear after the model is loaded into LightWave Modeler. You'll see that the first layer button is depressed by default, and it contains a small dot.

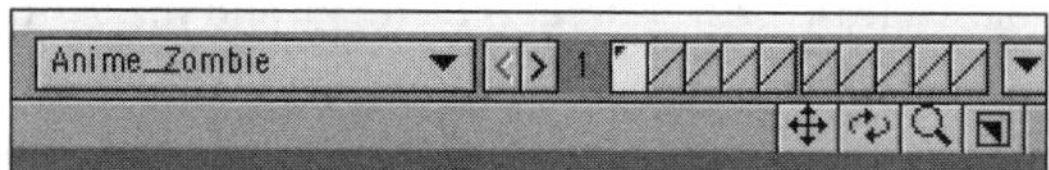

Figure 1.12 Modeler's object-selection pull-down shows the name of the loaded object, Anime_Zombie, and the layer buttons indicate that just one layer is associated with this object.

These dots inform you that there is geometry in that layer, such as points, edges, or polygons. Open the Layers panel (**F7**) and look at what the listings show. You'll see the name of the object, and if you click the small white triangle to expand the object's layers, you'll see a listing that reads "unnamed." Unnamed refers to the geometry in the layer, which you've yet to name.

3. Double-click the last "unnamed" listing, and you'll see a panel pop up that reads Layer Settings. If you had multiple layers—that is, objects in other layers—selecting any one of these layers instantly would change your view to that selection.
4. In the Layer Settings panel, enter **Zombie** as the Name. If you had another layer with geometry, you could also tell one layer to be "parented" to another. Parenting means that the selected object becomes a child and "belongs" to the parent. Whenever you move, rotate, or scale a parent object in LightWave Layout, objects in its child layers will follow. You'd use this for wheels on a car, letters in a logo, and more. **Figure 1.13** shows the operation.

Note

Just to the left of the 10 layer buttons at the top left of Modeler is a number with a left- and right-arrow button. When you open a model, you'll see the number 1. This means you're working with the first set of 10 layers. You can click the right arrow to get to another set of 10, and the number changes to 2. Click again, and you're in the third tier of layer buttons, and so on. However, this is cumbersome, and the Layers panel is often a better way to go. Open the panel and put it aside while you work. Unlimited layers, baby!

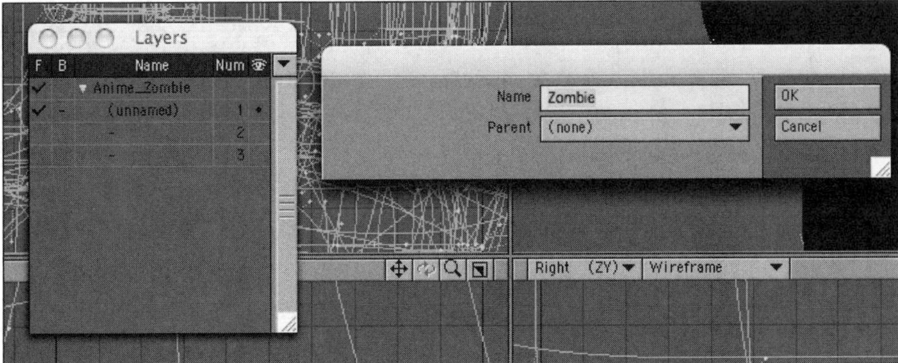

Figure 1.13 By double-clicking a chosen layer in the Layers panel, you can rename it and parent it to other layers.

When you loaded the Zombie object, you saw that the layer 1 button was selected. If you wanted to add parts to the model, or perhaps build a set of some sort, you would do so in another layer. To accomplish this, you select another layer by clicking on it. And as you did earlier, simply double-click the layer listing in the Layers panel to name that layer.

So, what's the point of all this, you ask? Even though this is a simple object, all of your 3D objects will be handled in this way. The purpose of naming each layer is so that when animating later, you're not guessing which layer is which. Given that, naming your object layers is not necessary, but it's an efficient way to work and organize. When you save your object, its layers and their names are saved with it. What's great about this is that you can send just this one single object to a coworker or client, and all of its parts (such as the wheels), as well as the parenting hierarchy, are contained within.

Note

You can load multiple objects into Modeler at the same time. However, unless you specifically cut and paste those objects together in some fashion, you can view only one object at a time. Figure 1.12 shows the layer buttons at the top right of the interface, and to the left of the layer buttons is the Current Object selection list. Any objects loaded into Modeler can be selected from this drop-down list. It's important to note that each loaded object retains its own layers. Choosing to load multiple objects will not load them into individual layers within the same model.

Foreground and Background Layers

There are a few more things to note about the Layers panel. Looking at **Figure 1.14**, you can see some additional labels in the Layers panel. The F at the top left of the panel stands for Foreground, while the B stands for Background.

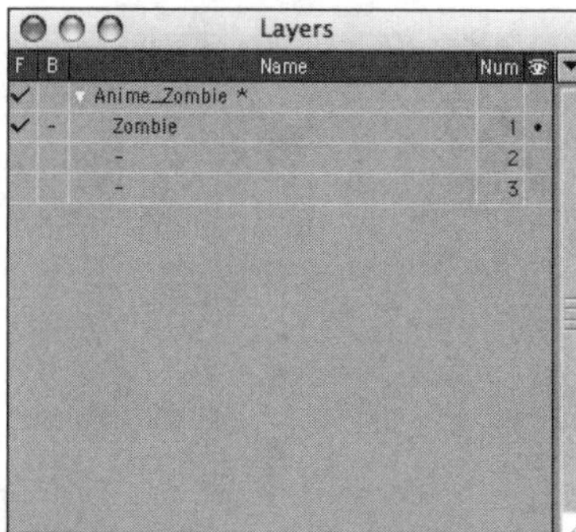

Figure 1.14 Additional controls are available in the Layers panel.

As you get into more complex projects, you'll use these commands in the Layers panel to place objects in both the foreground and the background. To try this out, follow these steps:

1. Load the Bae_Hawk_T1A object from your LightWave installation folder. This object has many layers, and when first loaded, all are seen in the foreground, as in **Figure 1.15**.

Figure 1.15 Selecting a layer in the Layers panel brings that layer to the foreground.

2. Press **F7** to open the Layers panel. Don't click any individual layer itself, but click the check box beneath the B column (B for background) next to the Fuselage layer. If you only see the name of the model, click the white expansion triangle to the left of its name to reveal all the layer names, as in **Figure 1.16**.

Figure 1.16 By selecting a layer under the B column in the Layers panel, you can put layers in the background for reference.

Take a close look at the top right of the Modeler interface, and you'll still see the body fuselage of the plane, but in a dark outline. You'll see the wheels and other parts still in a foreground layer. You've now defined foreground and background layers. The reason for this is threefold—objects in background layers are used for reference, as separate animation elements, or as modeling tools.

You can hold the Shift key and select multiple background layers as well. On the right side of the Layers panel, you'll see numbers. These are the layer numbers for each layer, and unlike Photoshop layers, their order does not affect the appearance of the model.

Note

Layer order becomes important when you use foreground and background layers as modeling tools. This topic will be covered later in the book.

Layer Visibility

To the right side of the Layers panel, at the top, is a small eyeball icon. Beneath that, next to each layer is a little dot. Let's say you've placed an object in a background layer and used it as a reference to build a new object. If you save your LightWave object and load it into Layout, all layers will be visible. However, if you click that little dot in the Layers panel in Modeler, when the object is loaded into Layout, the layer will not be visible. Load it back into Modeler, and it will be there. This is great when you use objects as modeling tools.

Finally, there's one more area you should be aware of in the Layers panel, and that's the Hierarchy view option. It's easy to miss, but at the very right top corner of the Layers panel, there's a small drop-down arrow. Select it and you see the option for List or Hierarchy. So far, you've been seeing the Layers panel in List view. **Figure 1.17** shows the Layers panel in Hierarchy view. This is useful for more complex objects like characters or mechanical creations.

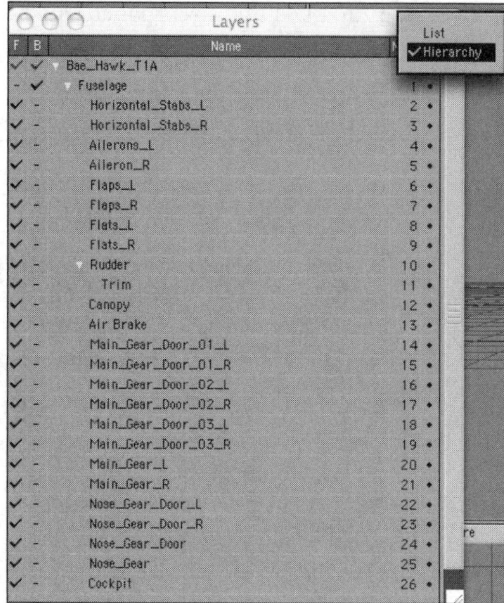

Figure 1.17 You can also choose to view your object layers as a List or Hierarchy.

There are many more panels in LightWave v9 Modeler, but it's important to understand how to navigate before you get more involved. Working with the layers is essential to any model you create, which is why it's covered first in this chapter. Now, to the menus!

Tabs and Menus

Across the top of the Modeler screen, you'll see nine tabs, each representing a different group of modeling tools. This section guides you through the different tabs and explains how they are organized. **Figure 1.18** shows the tabs across the top of Modeler.

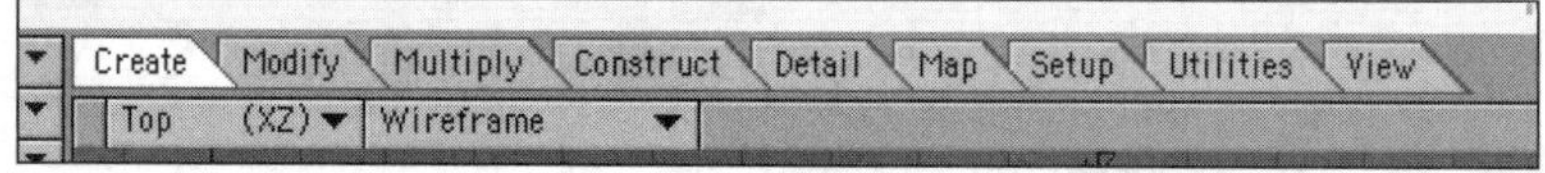

Figure 1.18 The LightWave v9 menus are tabbed across the top of the interface. Selecting any of these brings up various tools on the left side of the screen.

When you select different tabs, different toolsets become available. Think of a toolset simply as a group of tools. Years ago, tools were just floating around in LightWave Modeler, some of them hidden deep within menus. Now, version 9 has significantly streamlined the tools and grouped them quite well. The LightWave Modeler toolset works similarly throughout the program, with slight variations depending on which tool you are using. This next section guides you through the toolset categories within each of the Modeler tabs.

Note

On the top left of the Modeler interface, you'll find a set of drop-down menus that will always appear, no matter what tab you've clicked. These include File, Edit, Window, Help, Surface Editor, and Image Editor. These selections are the same in Layout and are covered in detail in Chapter 2, "LightWave v9 Layout."

When working in LightWave Modeler, really think about the process, and you'll have a much easier time locating the proper tool. For example, say you've just started up Modeler and want to build a 3D television set. You want to create something and need basic geometry to get started. OK, head on over to the Create tab. Choose the box tool, and go. Then, let's say you want to change it in some way, perhaps rotate it or move it. What are you doing? You're modifying it, right? You'd go to the Modify tab to find the necessary tools. What if you need to add to this, perhaps by beveling it a bit? Think about a bevel, and you might realize that this operation will add to the geometry of your object, so look under the Multiply tab. Many tools in LightWave v9 have been rearranged in ways that make even more sense than in previous versions. If some tools are no longer where you're used to finding them, keep the task at hand in mind and you'll probably see that they've been moved to a location that makes more sense.

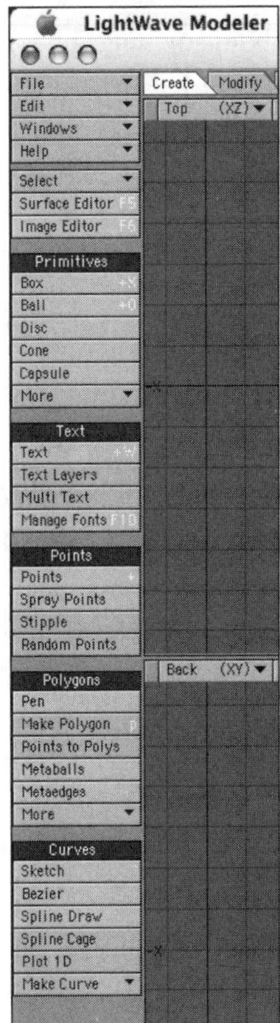

Figure 1.19
The Create tab is home to many basic tools that you'll need in the course of most modeling projects.

Create Tab

The Create tab calls up the basic tools you need to create geometric shapes such as boxes, balls, discs, and more. Additionally, you'll find tools to create points and curves. **Figure 1.19** shows the tools under the Create tab.

The first thing you'll see when you click the Create tab is that the toolset starts at the top of the screen on the left side and pretty much runs down the entire left side of the interface! The first seven buttons at the top will always be there, no matter what menu you've chosen (unless you customize your interface and change their location, as described later in the book). These key tools are the File menu, Edit menu, Windows menu, Help menu, Select menu, Surface Editor, and Image Editor. These are important areas that you will access often, which is why they're always accessible from every tab in Modeler.

Primitives

At the top of the toolset under the Create tab is the Primitives category, as shown in **Figure 1.20**. Here you'll find the tools for creating geometric shapes such as a Box, Ball, Gemstone, and Capsule. These basic (and some not-so-basic) geometric shapes are key building blocks for just about anything you want to create. Think about it—the forms of nearly everything around you are based on geometric shapes: a television, a couch, a kitchen sink! A vast number of 3D models start out as primitives, which are multiplied, cut, shaped, and formed into final objects.

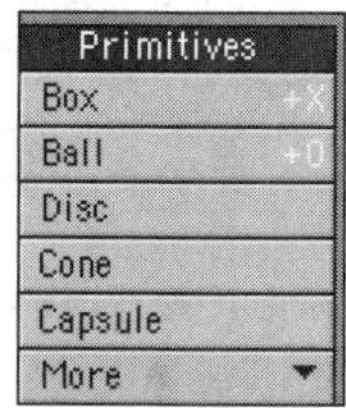

Figure 1.20 The Primitives category within the Create tab offers a wide range of basic (and some not-so-basic) shapes you can use to create 3D models.

Text

LightWave is famous for generating spaceships and animated characters but, believe it or not, 3D text is one of its most popular and in-demand applications. As you'll see in Chapter 7, "Text and Logo Creation," you can make some pretty outstanding broadcast-style animations and graphics with these tools. But what's more, text objects can also be used as building blocks. For example, you can take the letter C, turn it on its side, extrude it, and you have a slide you can put into a 3D playground. Or how about using the letter E as a building block for creating a 3D maze?

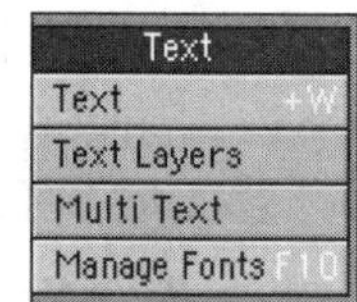

Figure 1.21 The Text tool category is where you'll find the Manage Fonts command, Text Layers, Multi Text tool, as well as the Text creation tool.

In previous versions of LightWave, to use the text tools properly you needed to first select the Manage Fonts button, shown in **Figure 1.21**. This tool enables you to load fonts into Modeler. But LightWave v9 has made text creation even easier: It allows you to choose any font on your system by opening the numeric panel for the Text tool. The Text Layers tool in LightWave v9 is so easy to use, it's just silly. Here, you can instantly create a string of text or a simple logo and have the program instantly add surfaces, while putting each word or letter on its own individual layer. This means you get to animating even faster!

Points

Often you'll need to build an object from scratch, starting not with a box or a ball, but rather a point. Later in this chapter, you'll read about points, edges, and polygons, but essentially, points make up polygons, sort of like connect the dots. The Points category gives you the tools to create points one at a time, in clusters with the Spray Points tool, or with the Random Points generator. **Figure 1.22** shows the category.

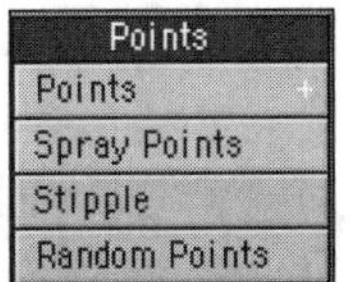

Figure 1.22 The Points category offers tools to create single points or clusters of points. Points, as you know, make up objects.

Polygons

Many 3D shapes you'll create in Modeler begin as simple 2D polygonal shapes. And just because primitive shapes make basic objects and points create individual points doesn't mean that you can't create simpler polygonal objects. The Polygons category has a tool called Pen, for example, which is similar to the Points tool except that as you create with this tool, polygonal lines are automatically generated between each point; the dots are connected automatically. You can convert selected points to polygons, or use the Make Polygon command, which you can apply after you've used the Points tool from the previous category. Additionally, you can create some organic objects with the Metaedges and Metaballs tools. **Figure 1.23** shows the category.

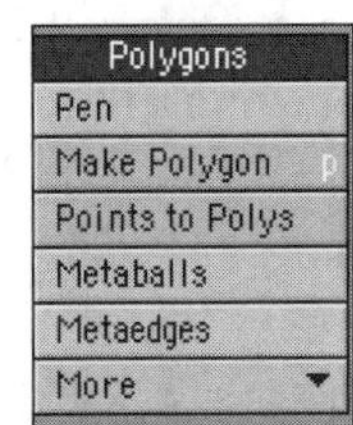

Figure 1.23 The Polygons category offers polygonal creation tools.

Curves

The last category in the Create tab is Curves. This category includes tools for generating curves from points you've created. Curves are used for many things, such as motion paths and extrusion paths as well as shaping models. The Sketch tool enables you to just click and draw, and when you release the mouse button, you have a 3D curve! You can use curves to build objects with splines. As you'll learn later in this book, splines are useful for building organic objects such as boats, curtains, or sometimes characters. Another key tool in this category is Spline Draw, with which you can precisely create curves, not only for models, but even text or custom shapes. **Figure 1.24** shows the tools in this category.

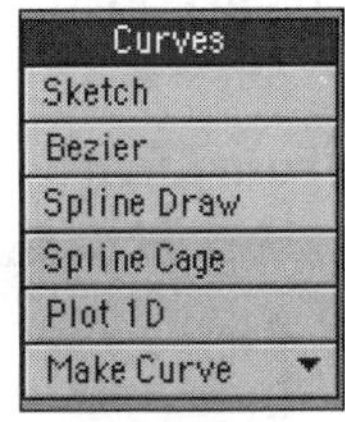

Figure 1.24 You can use curves for text, characters, motion paths, and more.

Modify Tab

The Modify tab—sounds simple enough, right? Well, it is. Anytime you want to modify your object in some way that does not require adding or removing points or polygons, you need to use a modify function. Click this tab and at the top left you'll see the seven tools available in every tab. Below them, you'll see three toolset categories: Translate, Rotate, and Transform (**Figure 1.25**).

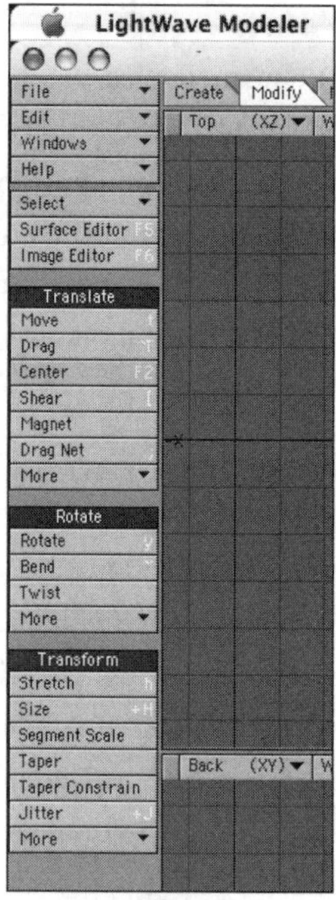

Figure 1.25 The Modify tab is used when you need tools to move, rotate, or size your object.

Translate

No, this category doesn't contain tools to make objects fluent in foreign languages. Its tools are used to move objects in 3D space (**Figure 1.26**). Typically, the 3D industry calls a move function a *translation*. The Translate category contains tools like Move, Drag, Magnet, and a few others. Each tool repositions your object in some way.

Rotate

This category (**Figure 1.27**) is almost self-explanatory. Of course, you can rotate points or polygons with the Rotate tool, but there's much more! You can also bend, twist, and even use the cool Vortex tool (in the category's More drop-down). Other tools like Rotate to Ground or Rotate to Normal provide extra control for precise rotations.

Transform

Transform is a sizing function, so anytime you hear a seasoned animation veteran talk about "transforming the object," they're not talking about a Saturday morning cartoon. The

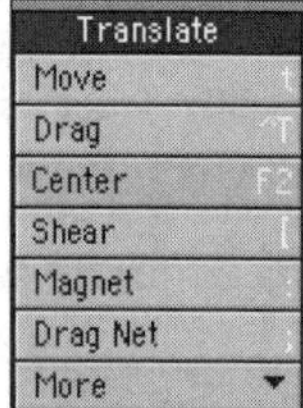

Figure 1.26 Tools in the Translate category let you move your geometry around—both points and polygons.

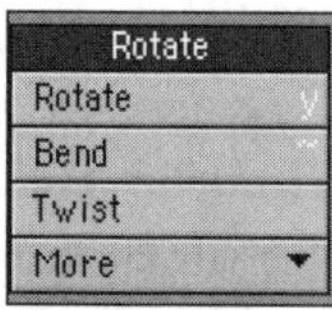

Figure 1.27 The Rotate category contains your basic rotation tools, as well as some cool extras like Vortex.

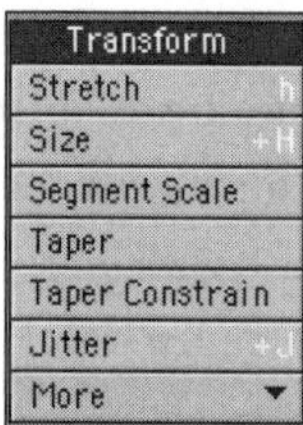

Figure 1.28 The Transform toolset is the place to find Size/Scale tools.

Transform category includes modification tools such as Size, Stretch, Pole, and others (**Figure 1.28**). Every tool in this category controls object size in some way. For example, Size scales your object or selection equally on all sides. Stretch sizes your object or selection on a specific axis. Use the Transform tools when you want to scale or distort objects or selections.

Multiply Tab

Tools in the Create and Modify tabs are generally easy to wrap your brain around. When you get into the Multiply tab (see **Figure 1.29**), things get more complex. Within LightWave, *multiply* means add onto a selection, and the tools within this tab do so in a variety of ways. You'll use these tools often in later chapters. For now, read on to find out what the categories in the Multiply tab can do for you.

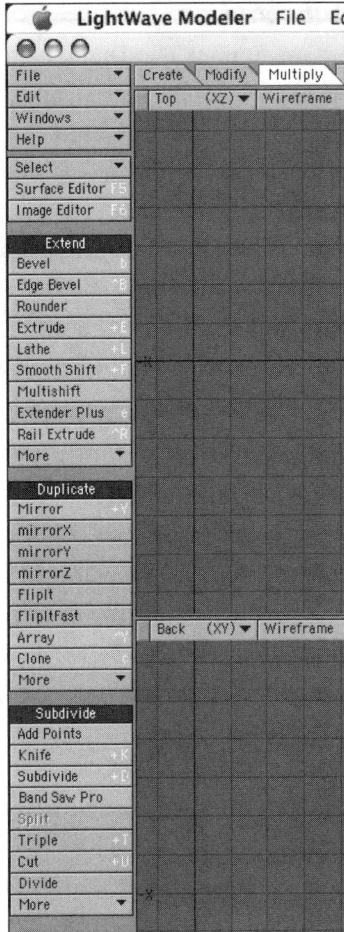

Figure 1.29 The Multiply tab contains some complex tools that enable you to build up your object in a variety of ways.

Note

Some tools throughout LightWave v9, especially these within the Multiply tab, are not available until there is geometry in a specific layer.

Extend

Extend is the first category of the Multiply tab, and it contains tools you'll probably use often (**Figure 1.30**). The Extend tools "grow" your selection in different ways. The Extrude and Bevel tools, for example, provide different ways of "stretching" polygons into 3D shapes. The category also includes more complex tools, such as Rail Bevel (located in the More drop-down), which enable you to build a bevel from a curve placed in a background layer. When we discussed layers earlier, we mentioned that foreground and background layers are used for modeling as well as reference. Rail Bevel takes advantage of this.

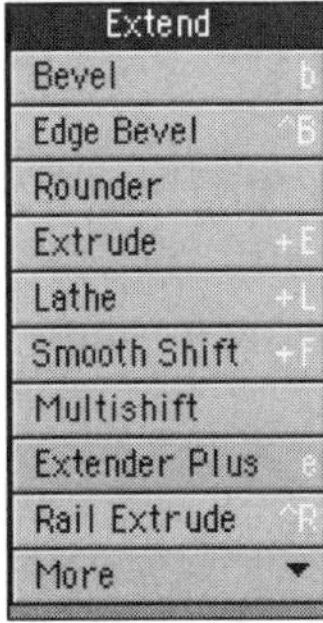

Figure 1.30 The Extend category of tools within the Multiply menu tab offers tools to add to your objects or selections, such as bevel tools.

Duplicate

You might think that Duplicate tools (**Figure 1.31**) would be under the Modify tab, but think again! Creating a new object by mirroring, cloning, or otherwise copying another one is a form of multiplication. The Duplicate tools create variant copies of selections or objects, but these copies are not attached to your original object or selection, the way points and polygons created with the Extend tools are.

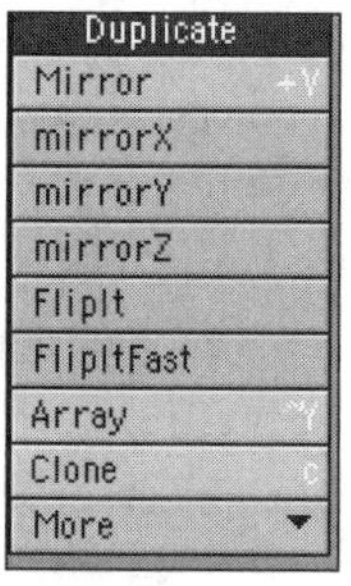

Figure 1.31 Duplicate tools add to your object or selection by mirroring, cloning, or otherwise copying it.

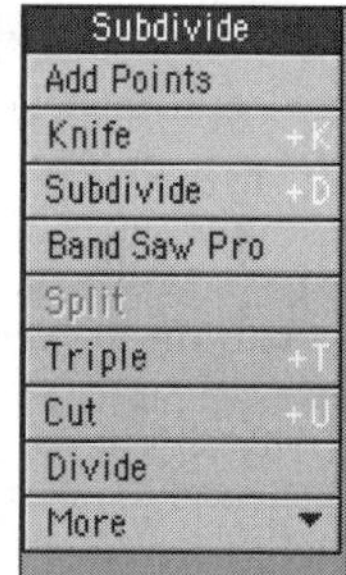

Figure 1.32 The Subdivide tools enable you to break up your model for added detail and animation control.

Subdivide

Ah, the Subdivide category. It's a deep, dark secret set of tools that can enhance your object or selection in a variety of ways. The Subdivide tools (**Figure 1.32**) perform very cool operations to slice up your object or selection, add to it, or split it up in some way. Let's say you built a cool character and soon realize that you can't bend the character's leg because it's just one long "solid" object. To make the leg bend at the knee, you would use the Knife tool in this category to slice the leg and add a segment so it can bend. Another cool set of Subdivide tools is the QuickCut tools in the category's More drop-down. These enable you to quickly slice up an object evenly, which helps you create additional detail for animation.

Construct Tab

When you have geometry that needs to be changed in terms of structure, you'll work with the Construct tab. Its tools handle tasks such as Boolean operations (which you'll perform later in the book) and reducing or converting various types of geometry. When you're building

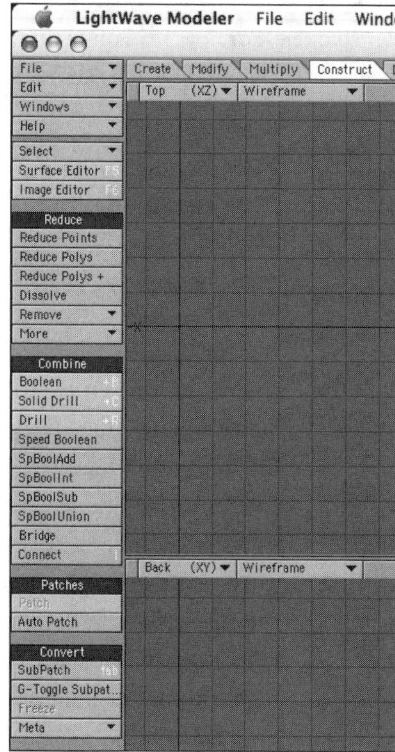

Figure 1.33 Using the Construct tab tools, you can add or subtract points and polygons to and from your models.

3D models, it's easy to confuse the tools in the Construct tab with those in the Detail tab. The main difference between them is one of scale; when you're working with multiple objects or sizable portions of objects, Construct is the tab you want. Use the Detail tab for fine-tuning at the level of individual points, curves, and polygons. **Figure 1.33** shows the Construct tab tools.

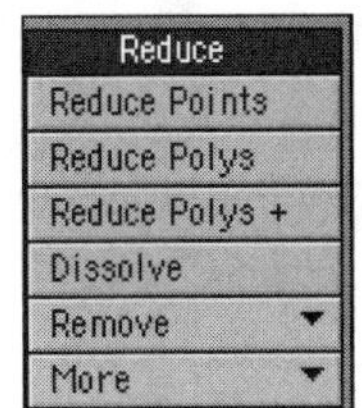

Figure 1.34 You can use tools in the Reduce category to decrease the number of points or polygons in an object or selection.

Reduce

The Reduce category contains tools that enable you take away geometry (points or polygons) from your model without changing its appearance (**Figure 1.34**). Why would you do this? You could be creating a model for a video game that requires a low number of polygons for speedy animation. Or perhaps you realize you've overbuilt a model and added more detail than you need. Why not just leave it detailed? Simple—the more detail you have in an object, the longer it takes LightWave to calculate and render. As mentioned at the beginning of this chapter, you need to work efficiently from the ground up. Planning is key, and making models that are not too simple but not too complex is essential to 3D animation. The Reduce category enables you to reduce or remove points or polygons from models while keeping them intact with tools like Bandglue (found in the category's More drop-down).

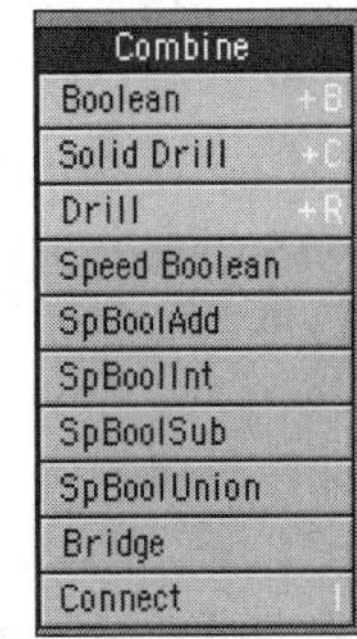

Figure 1.35 The Combine tools offers ways to cut holes in objects, merge and stencil objects, and bridge connections between them.

Combine

From time to time, it's useful to merge objects, or to "subtract" the shape of one object from another to create a hole or cavity. These operations, called *Boolean functions*, are performed using Combine tools (**Figure 1.35**), and they are another example of how foreground and background layers are used for modeling purposes. Typical Boolean operations involve placing an object you want to add or subtract in a background layer so that it overlaps the foreground object. LightWave v9 also features new Speed Booleans, clever tools that permit Boolean operations between objects within a single layer. The Combine tools also include Bridge, which lets you select points on two objects and "bridge" or connect them.

Patches

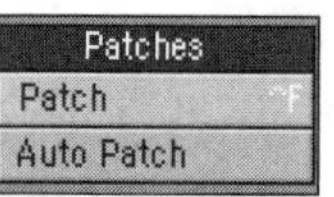

Figure 1.36 Use the tools the Patches category to build a skin over a group of curves.

The tools in the Patches category (**Figure 1.36**) are useful for applying surfaces, or skins, to curves called *splines*. Splines are curves that can be put together in multiple ways to build objects. After you group enough curves together, you can patch them to create a surface. Think of an umbrella's ribs as splines, and its cloth covering as a skin. Patching joins splines together and controls skin characteristics.

Convert

The Convert tools (**Figure 1.37**) turn curves into polygons, and polygons into curves—a function that's more helpful than you might think. Let's say you've built the ultimate 3D logo, using curves to surround the client's name. All is cool until you're ready to render it out. Curves do not render, but polygons do. So, head on over to the Convert tools and use Freeze to convert your curves into polygons. Other tools in here include the popular SubPatch command, which converts three- or four-point polygons into curves, to help create smooth organic objects. There's also the G-Toggle Subpatch, which works primarily in Layout as a way to turn a model's subpatch subdivisions on and off. In Modeler, it works like the normal subpatch mode, which you access by pressing the Tab key. You'll use this feature extensively in various modeling sections of this book.

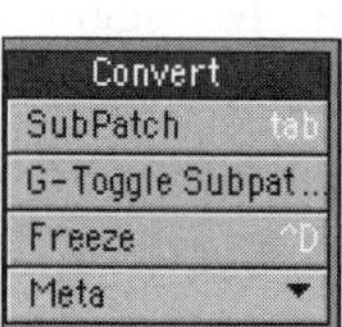

Figure 1.37 The Convert tool category within the Construct tab gives you the freedom to change—including the ability to change curves to polygons and vice versa.

Detail Tab

It's all about the details, isn't it? The Detail tab provides the tools that are useful for, and sometimes essential to, creating decent 3D models (**Figure 1.38**).

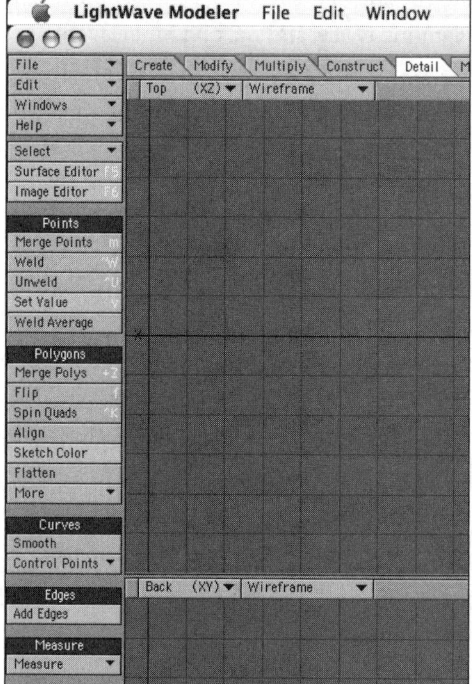

Figure 1.38 The Detail tab provides quite a few tools that let you make specific changes to points and polygons within your models.

Tools in the Detail tab are typically used to tweak a model once it's constructed, by fine-tuning one or more points or polygons. Their specific uses include adding and remove edges from models, adjusting the "grain" or "flow" of object surfaces, and cleaning up extra points that sometimes appear along the seams where objects are merged or mirrored. Check out the tool categories!

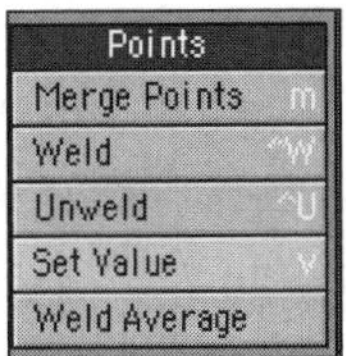

Figure 1.39 Tools in the Points category give you the power to control the detail of selected points within your models.

Points

Not to be confused with the Points tools in the Create tab, which are used to create points, the Detail tab's Points tools are used to adjust point details within an existing model (**Figure 1.39**). For example, the Weld tool lets you reduce a cluster of points down to one, in the position of the last point you selected, and the Weld Average tool joins irregular groups of adjacent points into smooth seams. The category's Set Value command also lets you precisely reposition groups of selected points.

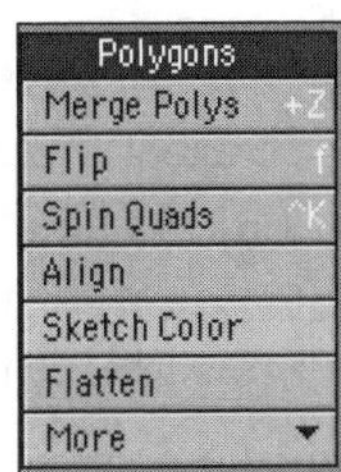

Figure 1.40 Tools in the Detail tab's Polygons category, such as Fix Poles (found in the category's More drop-down), give you great control over those nasty polygons.

Polygons

The Detail tab's Polygon category contains smart tools you can use to add polygons to models in spots where you need finer detail, merge polygons where you don't, and flip or perhaps just align them (**Figure 1.40**). Again, these are detail controls that help you fine-tune your models. So anytime you need to make detailed, specific polygon changes, this is the place to be.

Curves

There are just a few tools in the Curves category (**Figure 1.41**), which enable you to quickly smooth out curves or control a curve's start and end points. When spline modeling, for instance, you'll probably use the Smooth function often to massage curves before skinning them, to make sure the resultant surface is clean and even.

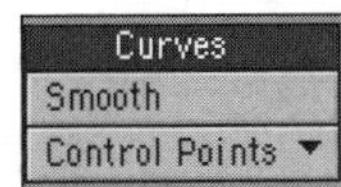

Figure 1.41 Tools for creating details for curves can be found in the Curves category of the Detail tab.

Note

Curves and splines can be used interchangeably for many tasks, and the choice of which to use is often a matter of user preference. Note that neither curves nor splines can be rendered in Layout, so curves and splines used in model construction must be converted to polygons for final output. Splines and curves are used in Layout for motion control, modeling, and deformation.

Edges

Tools in the Edges category (**Figure 1.42**) help you control fine polygon detail within your model or selection. The Add Edges tool, for example, lets you divide a polygon precisely by creating a new edge within it. Click a point on one edge of a selected polygon, then a point on another edge, and a new edge segment is added, connecting the clicked points. Don't confuse this command category with the Edges button at the bottom of the Modeler interface, which is used in Edges-selection mode.

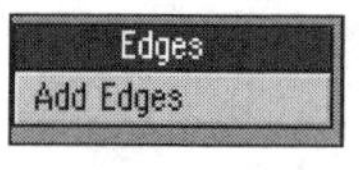

Figure 1.42 Tools for creating detailed polygon edges can be found in the Edges category of the Detail tab.

Figure 1.43 When you need to measure an object, find its center point, or generate a bounding box representation, use the Measure tools.

Measure

The last tool category in the Detail tab is Measure (**Figure 1.43**). It contains several measurement tools you can use to click and drag within selections for precise measurement readouts in the lower left info panel. You can measure angles, object lengths, and perimeters. But wait, there's more! You can use other Measure tools to locate the centers of objects, or create *bounding-box* representations, which can act as placeholders for complex objects within a model.

Map Tab

The Map tab is home to all the tools you'll need for working with vertex and weight maps in Modeler. Vertex maps control attributes of vertices, or points, in your models, and LightWave uses them to characterize the weights of different objects, control morphs, and more. You'll learn about setting these later in the book. In **Figure 1.44**, you can

Figure 1.44 The Map tab group of tools is home to a lot of interesting commands, some of which are very powerful.

see that there are a lot of tools, but don't worry, they're not all used all the time, and they are easy to understand when you break them down into categories. When you begin working with vertex maps, you can edit and control them through the tools in the Map tab.

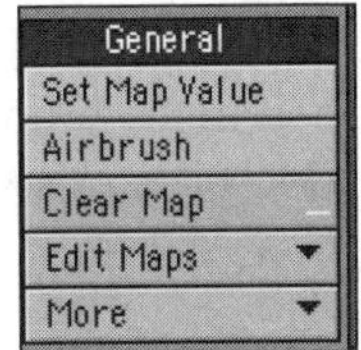

Figure 1.45
The General category of the Map tab offers basic tools for setting and editing values within vertex maps.

General

Multiple vertex maps may be applied to any given model, and the Map tab's General tool category (**Figure 1.45**) is useful for setting or adjusting map values for any point or set of points. You can also use its Airbrush tool to create new vertex maps.

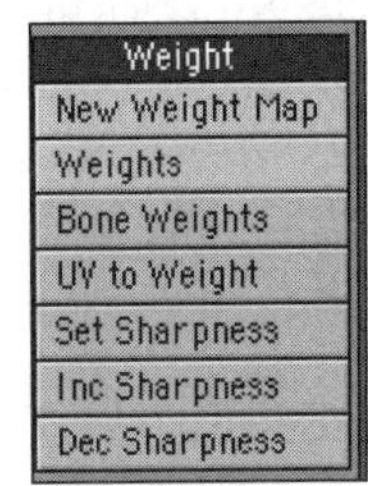

Figure 1.46
To control weights in LightWave Modeler, head on over to the Map tab's Weight tools.

Weight

Weights are a big deal in LightWave, and not just because you gain weight sitting in front of the computer while adding weights to your 3D models. You work with weights throughout the modeling process to control the flow of curves, and you can also use them in Layout later during animations. You'll use the tools in the Weight category to create new weight maps, to apply weights to bones for character animation, and to generate weights from certain UV maps, which are described later in the Texture tool category. **Figure 1.46** shows the Weight tool category.

Figure 1.47
The Color category gives you access to tools that can help you manipulate the color of an object's vertices, or points.

Color

Now don't confuse this category with the surface color of your object. Again, be aware of what you are doing and which panel and button you're working with. You're in the Map tab, which governs points, not the Surface Editor, which controls, well, surfaces. The Color tools within each have distinctly different applications. You use the Map tab color tools to create color vertex maps, which you can then use for specific surface control later in Layout. These tools also include Vertex Paint, which lets you paint color onto your model's vertices. Vertex colors blend with any polygonal surface textures you apply separately, and they are great for skin, landscapes, or just about anything. **Figure 1.47** highlights the tools.

Texture

Tools in the Texture category are used for creating and working with UV maps, which you can think of as the unwrapped skins of 3D models, flattened out on a grid with coordinate axes *U* and *V*. You can "paint" colors and textures onto a UV map in a third-party programs like Adobe Photoshop, then rewrap the model with it. UVs are often used in video games because one image can be used to surface an entire object. Have you ever put together a model of a car when you were a kid? Do you remember that huge sheet of stickers that you would apply to the model after building it? In a way, a UV map is like that big sheet of stickers. It's your entire model's texture maps, laid out. However, the map contains data unique to the specific model and it effectively will apply itself around the model the way you specify. Later in this book, you'll learn about working with UVs and create them yourself. When you do, you'll be guided to this Texture category of the Map tab. Here, you can edit the UVs, create them, set UV values, and more. **Figure 1.48** shows the category of tools.

Figure 1.48 The Map tab's Texture tools don't affect the actual surface textures of your models; instead, they control UV maps, which "wrap around" your model and anchor at the points on its surface.

Morph

LightWave morphs are much misunderstood. People often think they change one object into another at the push of a button. In fact, a morph (technically called an *endomorph*) is an operation that changes the position of one or more points in an object. Moving points changes an object's shape without adding new polygons or geometry. You'll use morphs later in the book to make a character move. LightWave uses vertex maps to store the point-position information used in morphs, and the Map tab's Morph tools (**Figure 1.49**) control those maps. Also note the M button down at the bottom right of the Modeler interface, which is where you can access any morphs that might be applied to your model.

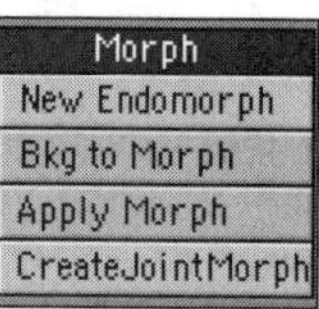

Figure 1.49 The Morph tools within the Map tab let you change objects' shapes by repositioning points on their surfaces.

Setup Tab

This tab is where you'll find all the necessary tools to create Skelegons. What's a Skelegon? No, it is not an evil cartoon character (that's Skeletor), it's a deformation tool. Skelegons are skeletal structures that you build along with your model to define how it bends and moves. Later, when you take the model into LightWave Layout, you convert the Skelegons to bones, and use them to deform and animate your object.

The Setup tab also includes tools for creating Luxigons and Powergons. Luxigons are polygons you turn into lights. Powergons are even more powerful. These are polygons to which you attach tiny command scripts, which will be executed when the model is moved into LightWave Layout for animation and rendering. You might use a Powergon to instantly add lights to a polygon for placement, like the headlights on a car. You can also define the properties for the light as well. **Figure 1.50** shows the tab and its tools.

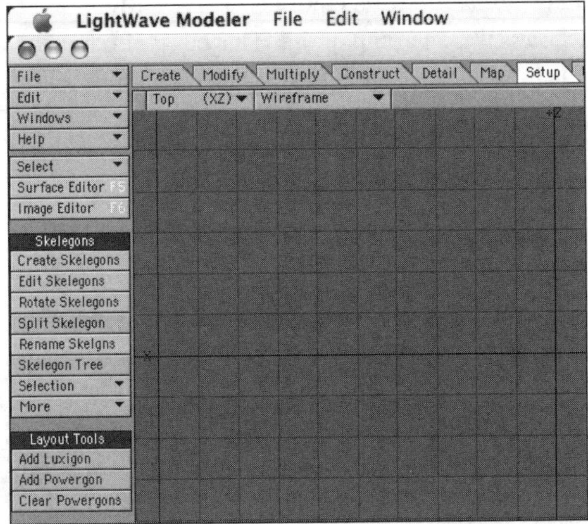

Figure 1.50 The Setup tab contains the tools you need for working with Skelegons as well as Luxigons and Powergons.

Skelegons

Naturally enough, the Skelegons category (**Figure 1.51**) is the area where you'll find all the Skelegon tools. Here, you can create Skelegons, edit them, rotate them, and so on.

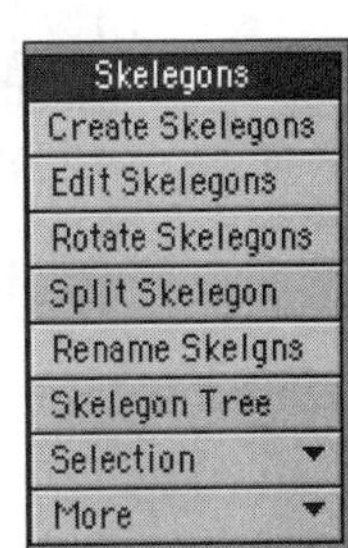

Figure 1.51 The Skelegons category houses all the tools you need to create and edit Skelegons, which you'll convert to bones in the LightWave Layout application.

Layout Tools

Layout tools are the tools that you set up in Modeler whose direct effect comes to light (pun intended) in LightWave Layout. Since Layout is the portion of LightWave in which you render and see your final image, the Luxigons and Powergons tools won't show their effects right away. Luxigons and Powergons are tools that allow you to create multiple lights and lights from polygons, for things like stage lighting, large architectural interiors, or even disco balls. John Travolta, watch out!

Because the end result of creating Luxigons and Powergons in Modeler happens in Layout, commands for creating them are found in the Layout Tools category (**Figure 1.52**).

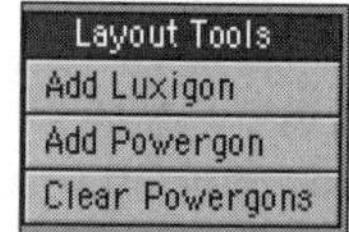

Figure 1.52 When creating Luxigons or Powergons, you access the tools from the Setup tab.

Utilities Tab

The Utilities tab contains tools for extending Modeler's features and giving you greater control over them (**Figure 1.53**). These tools are used to install and access third-party plug-ins. This tab is also home within Modeler to LightWave's custom scripting language, LScript. If you've added a third-party plug-in but don't know where it went, just look at the Additional drop-down list within this tab.

Figure 1.53 The Utilities tab is home to various commands, LScript tools, and plug-in controls.

Commands

You use tools in the tools in the Commands category (**Figure 1.54**) to create and edit instructions, or commands, for LightWave Modeler. Say you want to always perform the same string of events on an object. You can create a custom command to do so with the Edit Command tool. Or perhaps upon startup, you like to have a Luxigon created from a ball. You can do this and much more with the Edit Startup tool.

Figure 1.54 The Commands tool category lets you create your own custom actions for Modeler.

LScript

LightWave's custom scripting language enables you to create your own plug-ins and scripts, and the tools in the LScript category (**Figure 1.55**) let you create scripts of your own and manage ones you make or obtain elsewhere. Even if you never write a line of script, you may need these tools occasionally in order to tweak LScripts generated automatically by other LightWave tools or plug-ins, or to compile and load LScripts you exchange with friends or obtain free online at sites such as Flay.com.

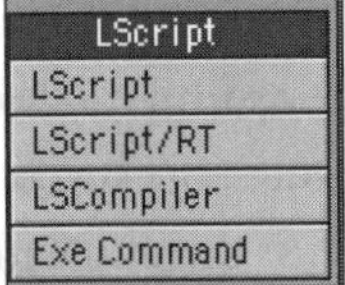

Figure 1.55 The LScript category gives you the tools to load and compile LScripts.

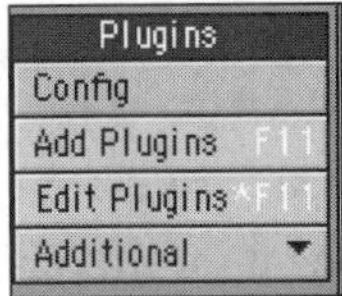

Figure 1.56 Use the tools in the Plugins category to manage software add-ons to LightWave.

Plugins

Last in the Utilities tab is the Plugins category (**Figure 1.56**). Here, you can add a single plug-in or edit your existing plug-ins. You'll also find the Additional list, which contains LightWave's plug-ins, many of which are already assigned to buttons and keyboard equivalents with the default configuration. If you choose to add third-party plug-ins, you can find them here as well. You can also create custom buttons for those added plug-ins using the Edit Menu feature in LightWave's Edit drop-down lists.

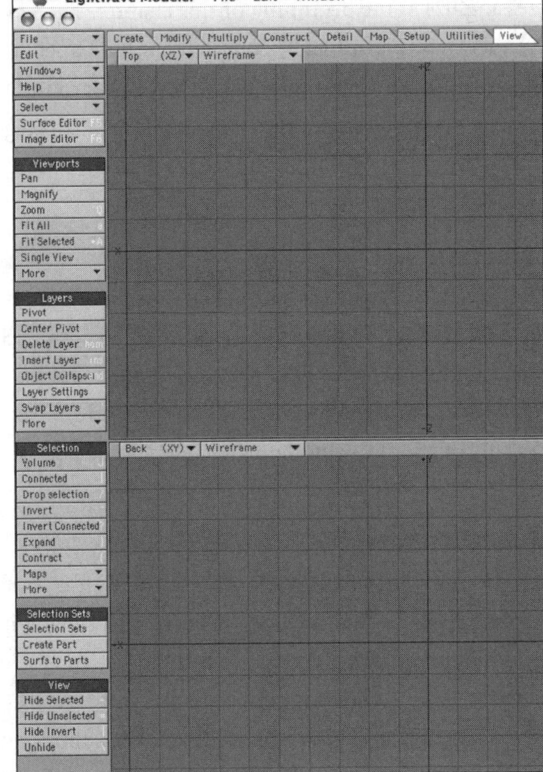

Figure 1.57 The View tab includes tools that help you effectively utilize the LightWave modeling environment.

View Tab

Earlier in this chapter, we discussed LightWave's viewports, but we have not yet talked about the other view options available to you. In the View tab (**Figure 1.57**), you'll find many tools designed to help you maximize your modeling experience, including Magnify tools, various Layer tools, and cool selection tools.

Viewports

Much of the viewport control you'll access on a regular basis is done through the keyboard (like pressing **0** for maximize), or directly within each view. However, the Viewports tool category (**Figure 1.58**) gives you all those controls and more, such as Fit and Fit All, as well as various zoom controls. So, anytime you want to adjust what you're seeing in your viewports, look here.

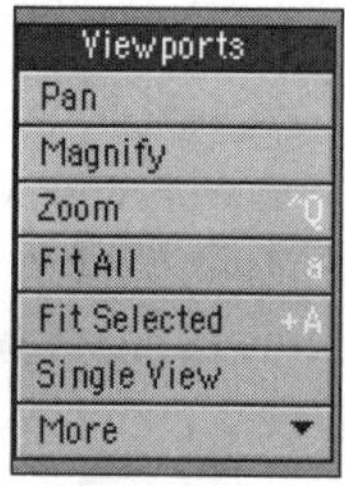

Figure 1.58
Take control of what you see with tools in the Viewports category.

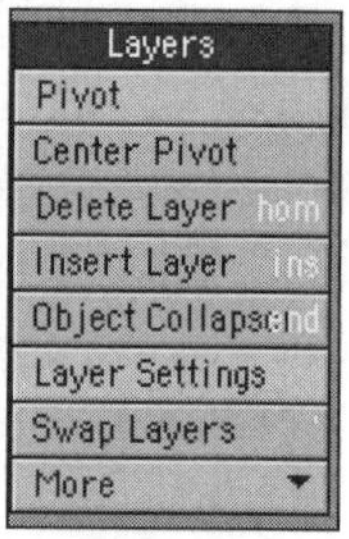

Figure 1.59
Work with your layers effectively by employing the Layers category tools in the View tab.

Layers

We talked about layers and the Layers panel (which you access by pressing **F7**) at the beginning of this chapter. The Layers tools within the View tab (**Figure 1.59**) complement the panel. Use these tools to add and remove new layers, swap layers (foreground to background), or even flatten all layers into one. Look to this category for specific layer control in addition to the Layers panel.

Selection

The Selection category (**Figure 1.60**) contains a host of tools for selecting and deselecting points and polygons, including Select Loop and Select Outline. In the next section, "Points, Edges, and Polygons," you'll learn about these key operations in Modeler. You'll employ these tools throughout the modeling chapters in this book.

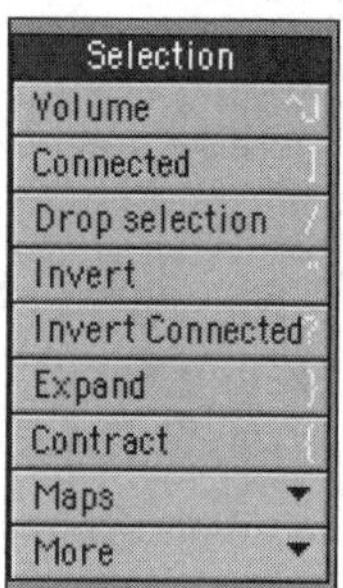

Figure 1.60
LightWave v9 Modeler offers a wide range of selection tools, all found under the View tab.

Selection Sets

Selection sets are often overlooked by animators, but they are quite helpful. Tools in this category (**Figure 1.61**) make it easy to select groups of points or polygons and combine them as selection sets. The benefit of this is twofold—not only can you easily select those same points or polygons again whenever you need them, you can also use them as specific controls in LightWave Layout.

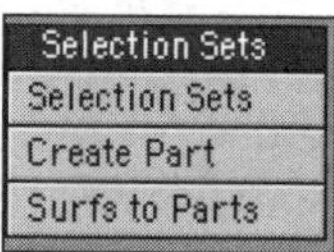

Figure 1.61
The View tab provides controls for grouping selections, small or large.

View

Last in the View tab is the View category (**Figure 1.62**). Use these tools to hide and unhide items you've selected. They're handy when you want to work on a specific part of a model without touching neighboring parts, or to better see what you're doing when working in Wireframe mode. Just remember that if you hide some geometry, you'll need to unhide it again—don't forget it's there!

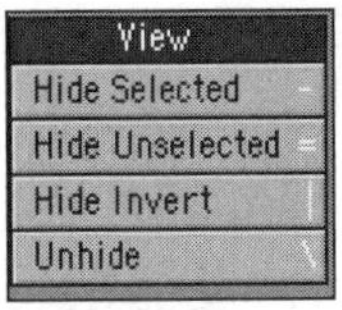

Figure 1.62 Find your way to the View category of the View tab, and you can hide or unhide selections.

So, there you have it: all the LightWave v9 Modeler menus in a nutshell. When you break them down and understand how they are organized, it will be much easier not only to find them but also to understand what they do. The next section shows you how to work more specifically with geometry in Modeler through point and polygon selection and deselection processes.

Points, Edges, and Polygons

For everything you create in Modeler, you'll need select or deselect points, edges, and polygons. As mentioned earlier, you create points to make polygons. A polygon can't exist without at least three points. (It's like connect-the-dots, remember?) When points are connected to form polygons, the lines between the points become edges. With that said, take a look at **Figure 1.63**. Here, you can see the Points, Edges, and Polygons selection and modeling modes.

Figure 1.63 At the bottom of the Modeler interface are the Points, Edges, and Polygons selection and modeling modes. Select the appropriate mode you want to work with.

Choose a selection mode simply by clicking on it, or you can rotate among them by simply pressing the spacebar. Essentially, all you need to do is think about what you want to extend, move, rotate, and so on, and then choose the appropriate mode.

Selection Modes

Let's say you have a project you've created for your best client. They come to you and say it's great, but they would like you to move some of the model slightly. For something like this, you might want to move points, or perhaps adjust the edges. Whichever the case, selection and deselection work the same no matter what mode you're in. This next project will help you understand further.

Exercise 1.2 Selecting and Deselecting in Modeler

Follow these steps to get a feel for selection, deselection, and the various options available to you when working with points, edges, and polygons.

1. From your LightWave install directory on your computer, load the Antique_Chadwick object. This is an old-fashioned lamppost.
2. **Figure 1.64** shows the object loaded into Modeler. Notice that the lamppost is very tall. Select the Points mode at the bottom of the interface in the Back view. The Back view is the bottom-left quadrant of the interface, and looks toward the back of the object. The Back view is an XY view, meaning that you only have control over those two axes; the Z-axis is not a factor in that viewport.

   Note that you should be working with a wireframe viewport style. Doing so will allow you to select the points in the front and back of the object.

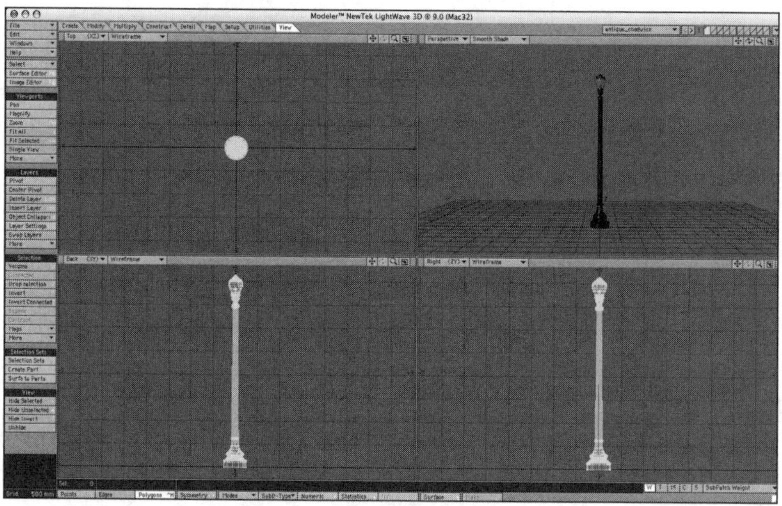

Figure 1.64 The simple lamppost object loaded into Modeler.

3. With Points selection mode enabled, you can select points of the object. You can do this in one of two ways. The first option is to click on any point directly to select it, so click around the top of the lamp. Your point should become highlighted as in **Figure 1.65**.

   When you release the mouse button, you automatically enter Deselect mode. Click on the point again, and it will be deselected. This is exactly how the Polygons selection mode works. Now that there is nothing selected, you can begin selecting points again. If you click on a point and then realize you want to select more, just hold the Shift key down and continue your selection.

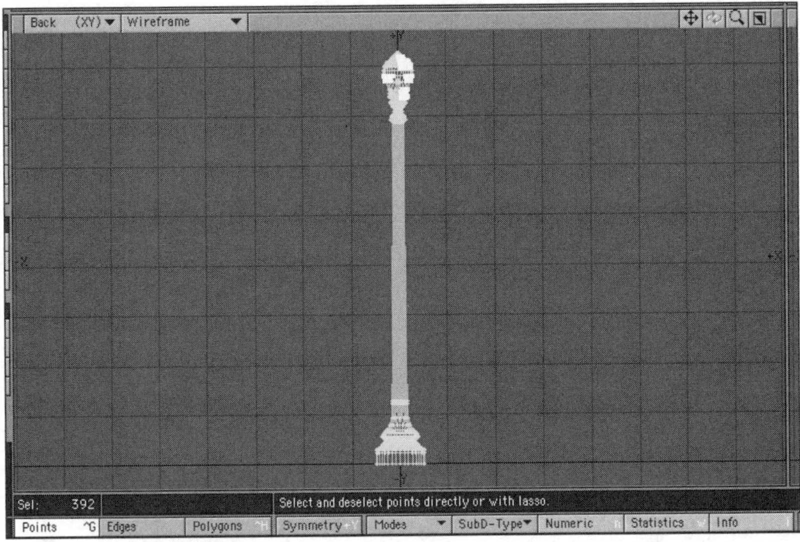

Figure 1.65 Directly clicking on a point with the left mouse button selects it. Let go of the mouse, click again, and you deselect.

4. The second option for selecting points uses Lasso select mode, which is a better choice for selecting all of the points around the top of the lamp. Press the slash key (/) to deselect the points. With the right mouse button held down, run your mouse around the points of the top of the lamp, as in **Figure 1.66**.

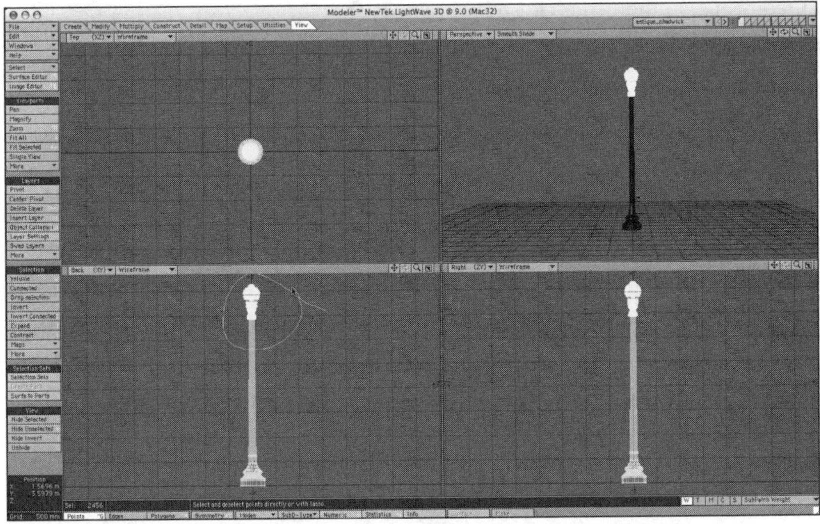

Figure 1.66 Use the right mouse button to select a range of points in Lasso mode.

Note

Mac users, if you're not working with a two-button mouse (even though you should be), use Cmd-click to accomplish right mouse button functions in LightWave 3D. But, go get a two-button mouse already, OK?

5. With the points of the top of the lamp selected, press **t** to select the Move tool from the Modify tab. Click and drag the points down in the Back view. You can hold the Ctrl key as you move to constrain the movement to an axis.

   Congratulations! You just edited points. That's all there is to it! After the points are adjusted to your liking, deselect them by pressing /.

Note

To properly deselect points, edges, or polygons, first turn off any tool you're using by clicking its button in the LightWave toolset, or simply press the spacebar. Then, press / to deselect. It's important to get in the habit of performing this process. Know what you're actually doing before you click the mouse or press a button. You can use only one tool at a time. Your process should be as follows. First, select points, edges, or polygons. Turn on a tool. Use the tool. Turn off the tool. Deselect the geometry. It sounds like a lot of steps, but learning this process will save you time in the long run.

Too often, people learning LightWave (or even those who already know it) jump the gun and forget to deselect their points or polygons and move on, only to accidentally get unwanted results in their model. And remember that the selection methods are identical whether you're working with points, edges, or polygons.

Symmetry Mode

Every once in a while, you might find that working on the same thing twice is a real pain. Perhaps you're building a character—why build one side of the body and then do it again for the other side? Sure, you could build half and then mirror it over. But there are times when creativity suffers when you can't see your how your entire model is coming along. If you turn on Symmetry mode, using the button to the right of the Points, Edges, and Polygons mode-selection buttons, whatever action is performed on the positive X-axis will also take place on the negative X-axis. Note, however, that whatever point, edge, or polygon you modify on the positive X-axis must live in the same space on the negative X-axis.

Note

If you have no need for Symmetry, always turn it off. Keeping it on can really mess you up because actions are mirrored across the X-axis!

Modes: Action Center

Figure 1.67 The Modes selection area enables you to change how tools react to the mouse.

To the right of the Symmetry button is another button, a drop-down list labeled Modes, which is used to set the *Action Center* for tools in Modeler. Settings in this list (**Figure 1.67**) determine how tools behave with respect to the mouse pointer, and you'll use them often in Modeler.

The Modes options enable you to change how certain tools work with the mouse or how their "action" is centered. The Action Center for your mouse is where a tool action happens. For example, by default the mode is set to Action Center: Mouse. This means that if you select the Rotate tool from the Modify tab, you can click and rotate in any viewport, and the spot you click will be the point around which your object or selection will rotate. If you change the Action Center to say, Selection, the selected object, polygon, or point will become the center around which other objects rotate.

You'll use these varying modes depending on what you're creating. If you're sizing an object within another object, it can be difficult to size perfectly in place using the Action Center: Mouse setting. Instead, with Action Center set to Selection, the Size tool works perfectly, and the object or selection is sized without shifting toward the mouse location.

Modeler General Commands

Now take a look at the rest of the buttons along the bottom of the interface, as in **Figure 1.68**. Here you can see a series of buttons and tools. These are key to working in Modeler, which is why they are always visible on the interface.

Figure 1.68 The LightWave v9 Modeler Interface keeps key tools accessible along the bottom of the screen, no matter which tool tab is selected.

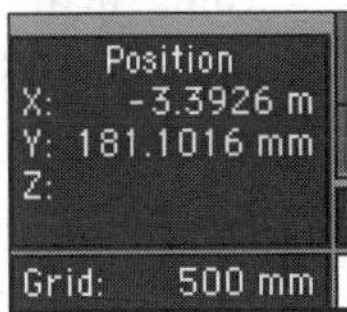

Figure 1.69 The info area at the bottom left of the Modeler interface shows key information about your tools.

At the bottom left of the interface is a small information area (**Figure 1.69**). This is the "info" area to which you'll be referred throughout this book. It shows you many properties, depending on the tool at hand, such as the size of objects, point position, and more.

You'll use the info area sometimes just as a reference and at other times to measure and control the movement of objects.

SubD-Type

SubD-Type stands for subdivision type. A subdivided object is one in which each polygonal patch is subdivided *x* number of times. You can tell Modeler (and Layout) how much subdivision to apply. The benefit of this feature is that you can create very simple geometry, manipulate it in the software, and then render it out as a detailed high-resolution model. There are two SubD-Type options in Modeler: the original Subpatch mode that existed in earlier versions of LightWave, and a new option called Catmull-Clark.

To work in Subpatch mode, select it from the SubD-Type drop-down and press the Tab key. You'll see your model change into curved surfaces, and a representative cage will appear around it. To revert to standard model view, press the Tab key again. In order to use the Subpatch SubD-Type, your object must have three or four vertices. That means a polygon can't be made up of five sides or more. For that matter, it can't be made up of one or two sides either.

Every once in a while, however, there's no way to reduce your entire model to polygons with just three or four vertices. It's for just those occasions that LightWave v9 added the SubD-Type called Catmull-Clark. Because this SubD-Type allows you to subdivide objects with more than three or four vertices, why even bother with the original Subpatch method at all? Backward compatibility is one reason. Those of you who have used LightWave in the past will appreciate that you can still use your existing models. Another reason is that the Catmull-Clark SubD-Type is more complex and a bit more demanding of your system resources. Applying it to one or more complex models might bring your system to its knees. That's not to say Catmull-Clark is bad—but use it only when needed and not as a default.

Numeric Panel

Vital to most modeling tools is the Numeric panel. Although many tools will be used just by turning them on and clicking and dragging, most tools have added control through the Numeric panel. **Figure 1.70** shows the Numeric panel open with the Capsule tool selected. You can press **n** on your keyboard, or just click the Numeric button at the bottom of the interface to open the panel.

Note

The Numeric panel can stay open all the time. Adjust your interface to give the Numeric panel its own space on your screen. It's useful for determining whether a tool is active. If the Numeric panel is blank, no tool is active.

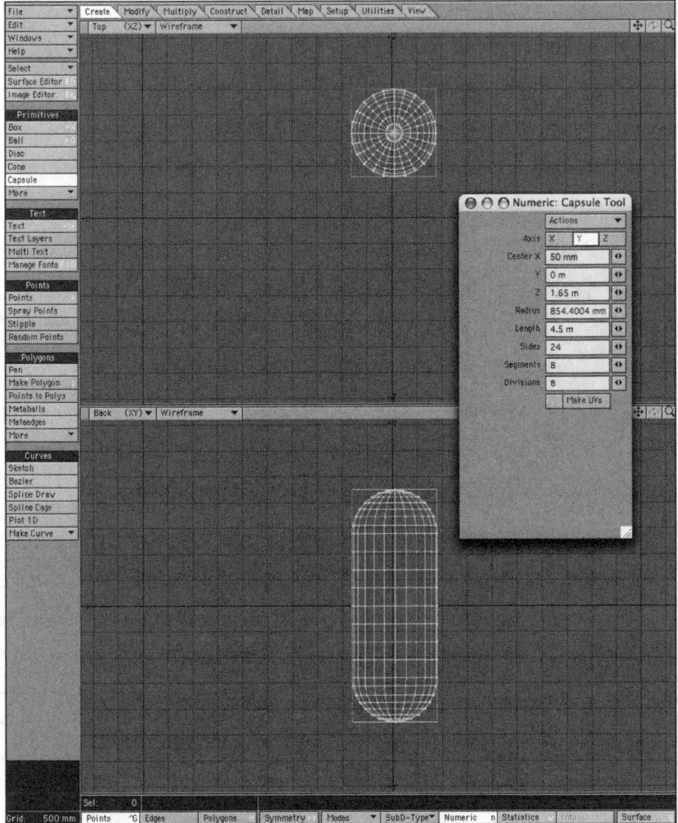

Figure 1.70 The Numeric panel, accessible by pressing **n** on the keyboard or by choosing it from the bottom of the interface, is useful for specific tool control.

Use the Numeric panel often, as both a reference and a control center for your tools.

Statistics

The Statistics panel (**Figure 1.71**) is another key panel you should keep open. It lets you view information about your points, polygons, surfaces, and much more. You'll employ this panel throughout the book. Note that it will change statistical information for both points and polygons based on which selection mode you're working in. You can also use this panel to select specific surfaces you've set up and even subpatched polygons.

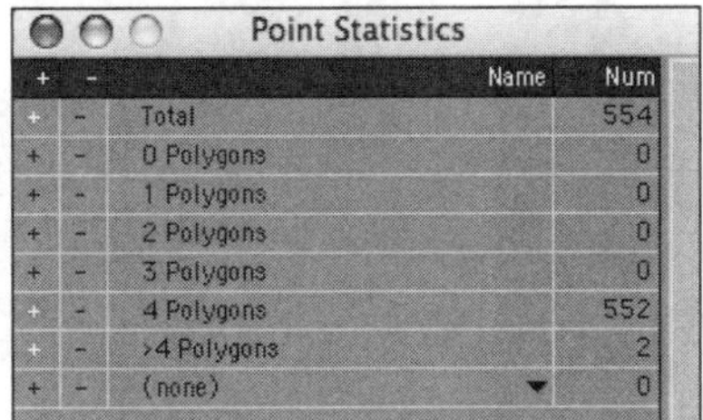

Figure 1.71 The Statistics panel, accessible from the bottom of the LightWave Modeler interface (also by pressing the w key), holds key information for points, polygons, surfaces, and more.

Info Panel

The Info panel (**Figure 1.72**) was a little-known feature in past versions of LightWave. Version 9 brings this panel to the forefront, with an access button at the bottom of the LightWave interface. This panel displays specific information about the points or polygons you have selected; the panel does not work in Edges selection mode. You can color wireframes with this panel, view surface names and groupings, and more.

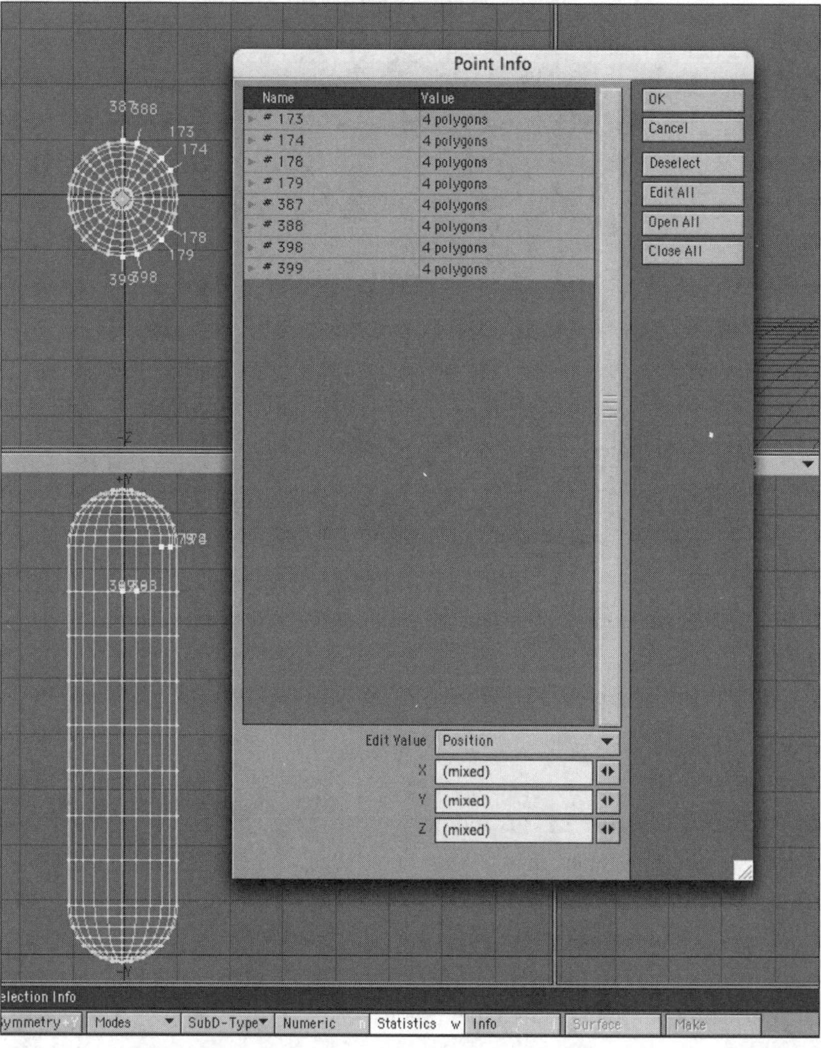

Figure 1.72 The Info panel, accessible from the bottom of the Modeler interface, shows you information about point and polygon selections (but not edges).

Surface

Another important button in Modeler is the Surface button located at the bottom of the interface. Be sure not to confuse this with the Surface Editor. Clicking the Surface button opens the Change Surface requester panel, which lets you define any polygon selection as a distinct *surface* within your model and assign it a name and a basic color. You'll do most of your surfacing and texturing in Layout, but you use this panel to tell LightWave that the eyeballs on your character are white, that the polygons that make up the fingernails are green, and so on. If you don't use this panel, your object will have only one surface to which colors and textures can be applied. **Figure 1.73** shows the Change Surface panel.

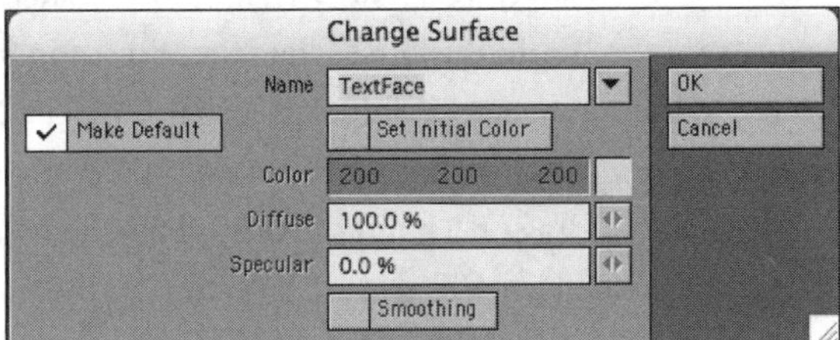

Figure 1.73 The Change Surface panel, accessible from the bottom of the Modeler interface (or by pressing **q**), enables you to name and assign colors to polygonal regions.

Make

The Make control does not have a panel but just a single button at the bottom of the Modeler interface. Say you created a few points to build an object. After your points are laid down, you can click the Make button (or press the Enter key on your keyboard) to "make" the polygon.

Using and Understanding W, T, M, C, S

To the far right of the bottom of the interface is a set of tool buttons with single-letter labels W, T, M. C and S, plus an associated drop-down list (**Figure 1.74**). These tools are part of LightWave's vertex map system, and you'll use them regularly as your work progresses in Modeler.

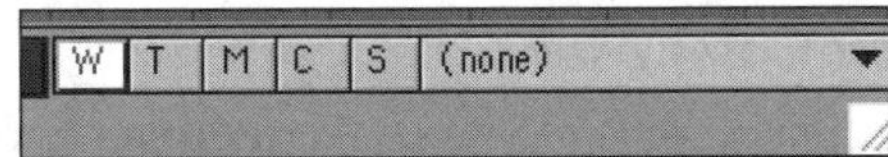

Figure 1.74 The W, T, M, C, and S function controls.

The vertex map tools all work in a similar fashion, but each has a different function. To use one of these tools, click its button, select New from the drop-down list to the right, and the appropriate panel will appear. But what are these tools? They are simpler than you might think.

W, for Weights

The Weights tool's main job, which we'll discuss later in the book, is to assign information to points or polygons in your model so that you can apply specific controls later in Layout. When you're first learning to create 3D models, you won't have much need of these functions. However, you can apply a SubPatch Weight to subpatched objects as well to change the shape of its curves. To do this, first select the W button for Weights. Then from the drop-down list to the right, choose SubPatch Weight. Go the Map menu tab at the top of the interface, and then on the left toolbar, select the Weights tool from the Weight category. Simply click and drag on a point of your subpatched object, and you can sharpen or smooth the curve. You'll use this feature later during the modeling chapters.

T, for Texture

The Texture mode enables you to create a new UV map for your objects. By first clicking the T button and then selecting New from the drop-down list, you can access the Create UV Map panel. UV maps are great for texturing complex objects, especially those with curves. Later in the texturing tutorials in this book, you'll see this panel in action.

M, for Morph

Morph (or endomorph) is a powerful feature in LightWave that enables you to move a point or set of points from one position to another over time. By first clicking the M button and then choosing New from the drop-down list to the right, you'll be able to create a new endomorph. This endomorph simply records the position of points or polygons. You can make multiple endomorphs and then use the Morph Mixer in Layout to access this data, which is saved with the object. You'll use this feature to change the shape of an object over time, such as a character talking or a car suddenly crashing and bending.

C, for Create Vertex Color Map

Create a new color vertex map with the C button. Vertex color maps tell Modeler to label specific point (vertices) selections so you can access them in Layout to apply additional surfacing and details. If you press **F8** or go to the Edit drop-down menu, you can open the Vertex Map panel and see which vertex maps are applied to your objects.

S, for Selection Set

Finally, the last button in the row at the bottom of the Modeler interface is S, for Selection Set. This handy option enables you to select any collection of points and define them as group—a selection set. It's like taking a bunch of points you've selected and giving them a group name. This group name can be accessed later in Layout for things like animated dynamics, cloth, and more. It's also handy for creating selection sets around areas of your models to create endomorphs. For example, you can create a selection set of points around the eye area of a character. By opening the Statistics panel (press **w**), you can quickly select this group anytime and adjust it, changing the shape of the eye for example, and then move on. This is a handy feature. Don't confuse it with the Surface button, which affects appearance and surfacing.

Modeler Options

There's one final area you should be aware of in LightWave Modeler: the Display Options panel (**Figure 1.75**), which you access by pressing **d** on your keyboard.

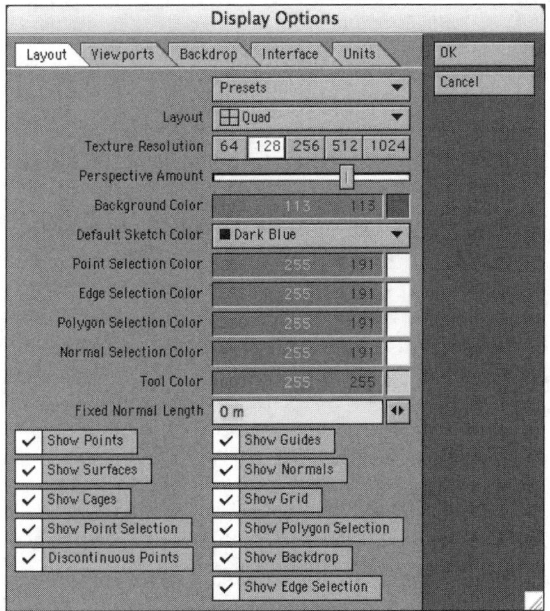

Figure 1.75 Pressing d calls up the Display Options panel, which controls settings that determine how the LightWave interface is organized.

Here, you can tell Modeler to change the way the layout of the viewports looks or change what's visible in the views. You can also use this panel to hide all your tools from view. What's more, in this panel you can specify background images and place them in Modeler's backdrop. Doing this enables you to work over a template, helping you build 3D models to real-world objects. You'll do this in the character modeling section of the book. Also in the Display Options panel, you can tell Modeler to work in English, Metric, or SI. The default is SI (System International), a common unit of measurement. This book uses all default settings for tutorials.

Now, if you press **o** on your keyboard (that's the letter o), you get the General Options panel (**Figure 1.76**). Here, you can set LightWave's content directory as well as Subpatch level and the number of undo operations you would like.

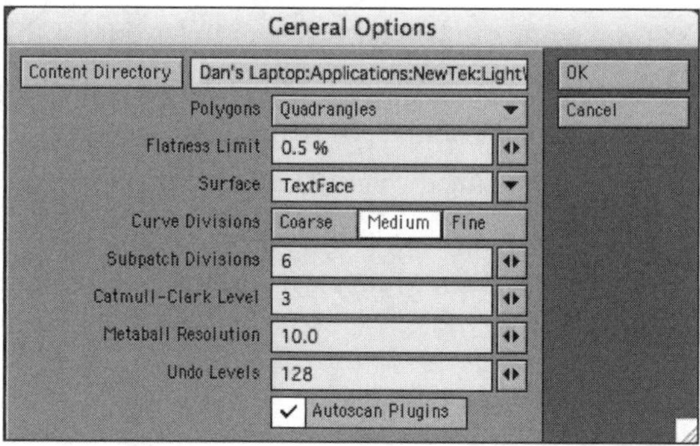

Figure 1.76 The General Options panel lets you set number of undos, content directory location, and more.

Note

The maximum number of undo operations available is 128. It's a good idea to set this value to the max and leave it. The only reason it should be lower is if you have limited resources and are working with very large amounts of polygons. Undoing too many times on large objects can bring down even the best of systems.

Any value you set in the General Options panel will become the default once you quit Modeler because the program writes that information to LightWave's configuration file.

The Next Step

This chapter has taken you on a tour through LightWave Modeler. And although it's not the most exciting chapter in this book, it is a chapter you can come back to often when you ask yourself, "What was that tool for?" Throughout this chapter, we mentioned that certain tools are used later in the book. Be sure to go through every chapter so that you can see how all these tools come together and so that you can learn just why they are included with your 3D software. There are a few other customizable areas that you should be aware of, but these tools work the same way in LightWave Layout, so we'll cover them in that discussion. We'll look at tools that enable you to edit your menus and set up custom keyboard shortcuts.

The next step is to take a tour of LightWave Layout in Chapter 2. As the book progresses, we'll ramp up the complexity and get you into even bigger and cooler projects.

Chapter 2

LightWave v9 Layout

Along with Modeler, which we met in the previous chapter, LightWave v9 includes another application called LightWave, which is commonly referred to as Layout. Layout is where all of your hard work in Modeler pays off. In Layout, you apply textures to models; assemble scenes, complete with lighting and motion; and see the final animated results.

Just about everything in Layout can be animated, from textures to lights to cameras to (of course) objects. There are plenty of tools for you to harness; in fact, many people spend more time in Layout than they do in Modeler. This chapter guides you through a tour of the LightWave 3D Layout interface, its workflow, panels, and possibilities. You'll learn about these topics:

- LightWave v9 Layout interface navigation
- Simple motions
- Viewports
- New cameras
- Surfacing enhancements
- Render Globals overview

Understanding Layout

3D animation is about geometry and movement. You create 3D geometry in Modeler, and Layout is where you put things in motion. LightWave's animation program is appropriately referred to as Layout, because that's where you lay out your scene. A scene consists of 3D models, lights, and cameras. Think of Layout as your stage. The 3D models you build in Modeler are your actors. You are the director. Oh, and if you haven't figured it out yet, you're also the gaffer, taking care of lighting, and you're the production designer. Keep this in mind as you learn about navigating the Layout interface.

LightWave v9 Layout Interface

When you first start up Layout, you see a large empty workspace. This workspace, however, is a three-dimensional space, rather than a flat grid as in most other programs. The view you're looking through is a Perspective view—sort of a bird's-eye view of your virtual set. After all, Layout is your virtual television studio, and if you noticed, there is a camera and a light already in place for you. **Figure 2.1** shows the Layout interface upon startup.

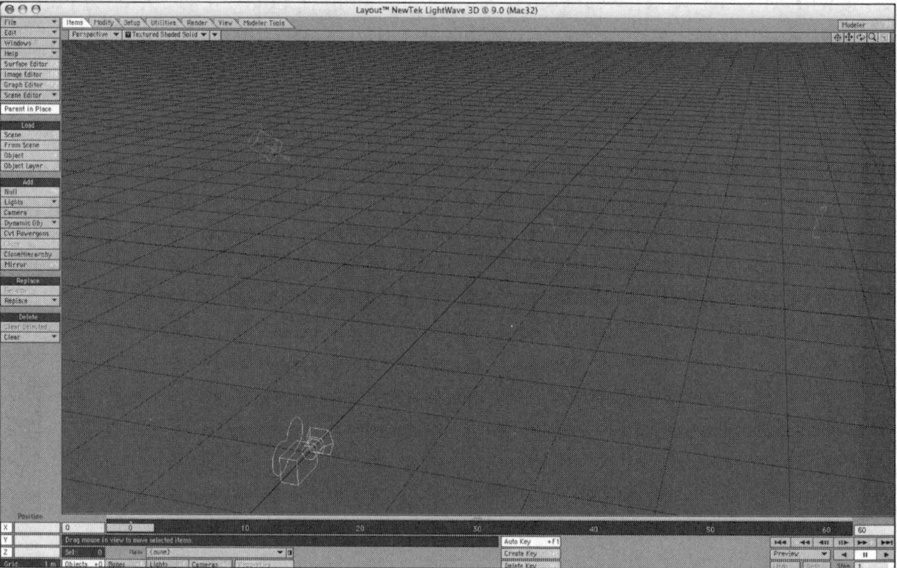

Figure 2.1 The LightWave v9 Layout interface.

This view is the default, and there is always one light and one camera. The interface will look familiar, because it resembles LightWave Modeler in its organization and workflow.

To understand how the LightWave 3D world works, consider this: LightWave Layout is a big 3D space. When you're working in Layout, you're inside a big invisible sphere, and everything you do in that sphere can react in various ways with everything else, such as reflections, shadows, and even dynamics such as gravity.

Across the top of the interface are tabbed menus, each containing key tools for object editing, animating different items, compositing, and more. Before you learn about the different menus, take a look at the bottom of the Layout interface. Here, you'll find your timeline.

The Timeline

Animation is all about timing. It's about telling items such as lights, cameras, objects, or even textures to occupy a specific point in space at a specific time. **Figure 2.2** shows the LightWave Layout timeline.

Figure 2.2 The LightWave v9 Layout timeline.

By default, Layout works in frames rather than seconds or minutes. This is because 3D animation, and even 2D animation, is a frame-by-frame process. Although the computer automatically interpolates motions, it's still up to you to create the "key" frames. A *keyframe* is nothing more than a marker in time. At the left side of the timeline, the value is 0, representing the first frame of the animation.

Note

Just because the front of the timeline defaults to 0, you are not locked into this value. You can start an animation at frame 6 or frame 40. You can also start an animation before 0 by entering a negative value. You would do this for certain animations that need a head start, for example. Let's say our object needs to already be in motion. If it starts at frame 0, then ramps up to speed, you could start the animation at the point of when it's in full motion. Similarly, you could keyframe the motion before frame 0, and then when your animation starts at 0, the item is already in full motion. It's all about control!

At the right side of the timeline is the ending frame number, which defaults to 60. Because LightWave defaults to the National Television System Committee (NTSC) video standard, 60 frames is 2 seconds, at a 30 frames per second rate. You can change this easily by pressing **o** (that's the letter o) and opening the General Options panel. Here, you can change the Frames Per Second setting to anything you like. Later in this chapter, you learn about all of LightWave Layout's preferences.

For example, the last frame of your animation can be changed just like the first frame. Most likely, many of your animations will go well beyond 60 frames, or 2 seconds. To change your current animation's overall time, it's just a matter of changing one value:

1. Double-click in the end frame window, which should read 60 by default. You can also just click and drag over the number.
2. Enter a new value—for example, 250—and be sure to press the Enter key on your PC or Return on your Mac.

After you enter the value, you'll see that the timeline looks a little different—this one's busier because it's now displaying keys for 250 frames rather than 60. If you need more frames for your animation, just change that value.

Selecting Items

You'll see that beneath the timeline on the left are four interesting buttons labeled Objects, Bones, Lights, and Cameras. Above the buttons is a drop-down list called Item. When an object is loaded and the Objects button is selected, you'll see the selected item here. Conversely, you can choose different items with this list, as well as bones, lights, and cameras. To the right of the Item list is a tiny button. If you click this, you'll be presented with LightWave v9's Current Item selector. **Figure 2.3** shows the item selection buttons with the Current Item panel open.

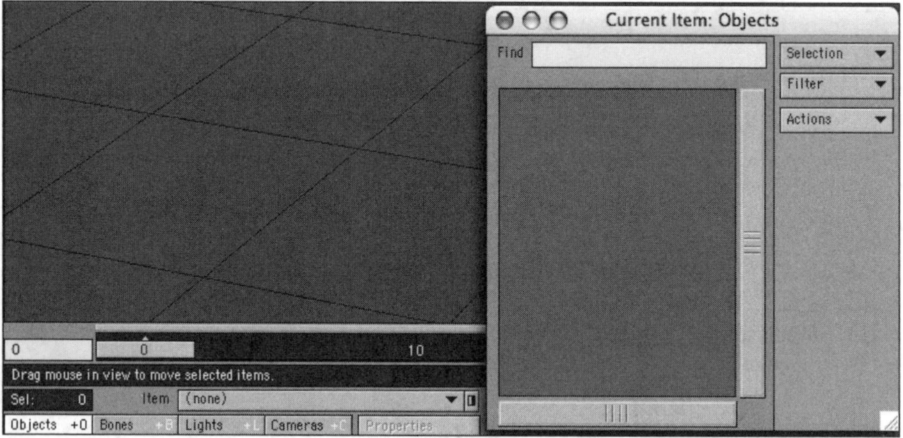

Figure 2.3 The item selection buttons allow you to choose which type of item you want to work with; click the button to the right of the Item list to open the Current Item window.

The Current Item Selector will be your friend in complex scenes as it allows you to easily organize your items, especially when you're using numerous objects in your scene. You'll employ this feature later in the book.

Here's your goal: Do not be confused by the buttons. Think about what you're doing before you click. Too often, animators click the mouse, press the spacebar, or press the Esc key until something happens. Usually, something does happen, but not what they intended. Do yourself a favor and think about your actions just as you do in Modeler. Select an item, turn on a tool, use it, and turn off the tool. Think about the process. Then, by paying attention to the buttons at the bottom of the interface, you'll know whether you are working with Layout's Objects, Bones, Lights, or its Cameras. After you've selected an item category, simply choose the Current Item from the drop-down list. Then, pick a tool, such as Move, and have at it.

Of course, there's more to animation than point, click, move—so much more! What's great about LightWave's vast toolset is that some things, such as the timeline, stay the same no matter what you're doing. Take a look at the bottom right. Those VCR-like buttons you see are your playback buttons (**Figure 2.4**). Don't confuse these with a final animation or real-time reference. These give you a pretty good idea of how your animation will play back.

Figure 2.4 The playback controls in LightWave v9 Layout.

Note

Never judge your animation entirely by the Layout playback buttons. This applies to motions, timing, shadows, textures, and so on. Always save judgment until the animation has been properly rendered out.

Keyframes

The best way to understand timing is to work with it, every day, all day. Timing is truly the hidden art of animation. Without it, nothing works. Sure, you can make pretty images, print ads, and the like. But if you're putting anything in motion, the timing needs to be dead on. It needs to "work." With that said, follow this next simple tutorial to set up some keyframes of your own, and see how LightWave interpolates motion.

Exercise 2.1 Creating Keyframes

1. Open LightWave Layout and make sure that nothing is in the scene. The scene is like your current project, so if you've loaded any objects, or sample scenes, be sure to save your work, and then choose Clear Scene from the File drop-down menu (or press Shift+n).

2. With a nice new default blank scene, all you're going to do is animate the camera. Click Cameras at the bottom of the Layout interface, as shown in **Figure 2.5**.

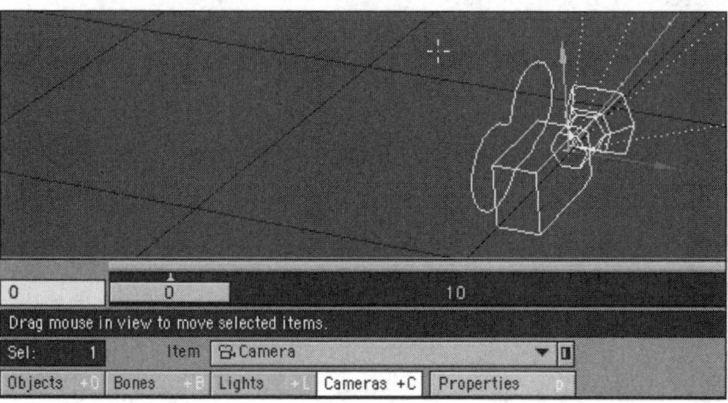

Figure 2.5 Tell LightWave Layout that you want to work with cameras by selecting the Cameras button at the bottom of Layout.

3. Because there is only one camera in the scene, it is automatically selected and highlighted after you choose to use Cameras. If you had multiple cameras in the scene, you would select which camera you want from the Current Item drop-down list, just above the Cameras button.

Note

To add multiple cameras to a scene, go to the Items tab at the top of Layout; then from the tools on the left side of the interface, choose Camera from the Add category of tools. You can name this camera anything you like. Multiple cameras are great for scenes in which you need to show your client different views. Rather than always moving the camera, it's better to switch between multiple cameras.

4. Make sure that the Auto Key button is on, beneath the timeline.

   Layout's Auto Key function provides a great way to get started with keyframing. When activated, it creates a keyframe to mark the position and rotation of an object, camera, or light any time you move it within a scene. As your animations get more sophisticated, you won't always want this turned on, but it's great for blocking out a basic scene.

5. You can grab the slider in the timeline to make sure it's at frame 0 all the way to the left. This is the start of your animation.

6. Make sure the camera is still selected (it should be highlighted in yellow) and press **t** on the keyboard. This calls up the Move tool from the Modify tab. Move the camera slightly to test.

7. Drag the timeline slider down to frame 60, and then click into the Layout and move the camera to a new position (**Figure 2.6**).

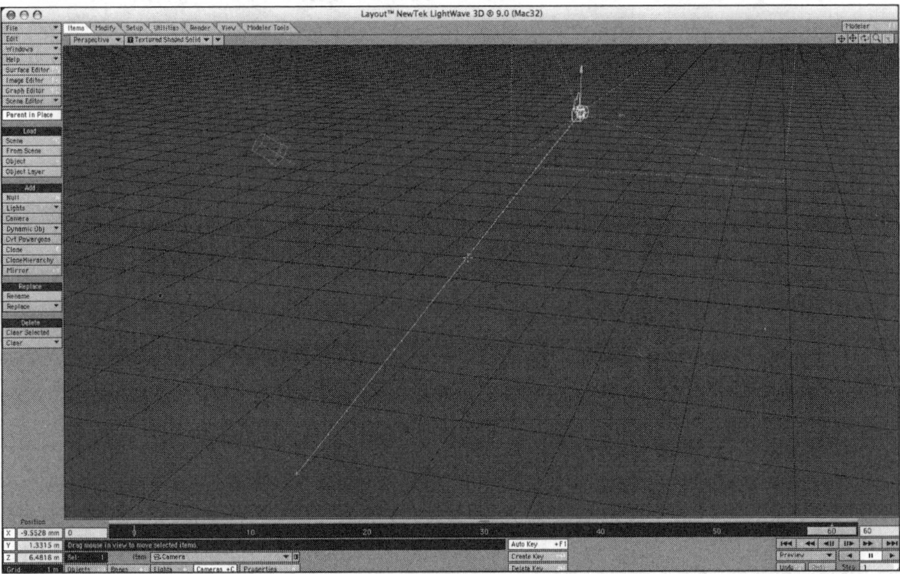

Figure 2.6 When the Auto Key button beneath the timeline is active, moving the frame slider automatically creates a new keyframe for the camera.

Note

A good way to keep track of your keyframes is to simply look at the timeline. When a keyframe is created, LightWave puts a small yellow dash at that point in time, like a marker. If you're wondering how many keyframes you've created, look to see how many markers are in the timeline.

8. Click the Rewind button at the bottom-right of the Layout, beneath the timeline, as shown in **Figure 2.7**. This quickly jumps your timeline slider back to 0.

Figure 2.7 The Rewind button in the timeline quickly brings your timeline slider back to 0.

9. Press the play button in the timeline, and you'll see your camera move from its 0 keyframe position to its 60 keyframe position.

   LightWave Layout calculates frames 1-59, and you might notice that after a keyframe at 60 is created (automatically with Auto Key), a motion path appears. That's the white line you see connecting the camera's first- and last-frame positions.

LightWave has interpolated the motion of the frames in between. If you do not see the motion path, press **d** to open the Display Options panel and under the OpenGL tab, make sure Show Motion Paths is selected. Of course, this motion path is just a straight line. So, try what is suggested in this next step.

10. Move your timeline slider to frame 30. Then, move the camera in some way, perhaps off to the side. You should see the motion path now curve, to accept the new keyframe. LightWave interactively updates the motion path, as shown in **Figure 2.8**.

Note

A quick way to jump to specific keyframes without dragging the timeline slider is to press **f**, which calls up the Go To Frame requester. Enter a value and press the Enter key, and your timeline slider jumps to the keyframe.

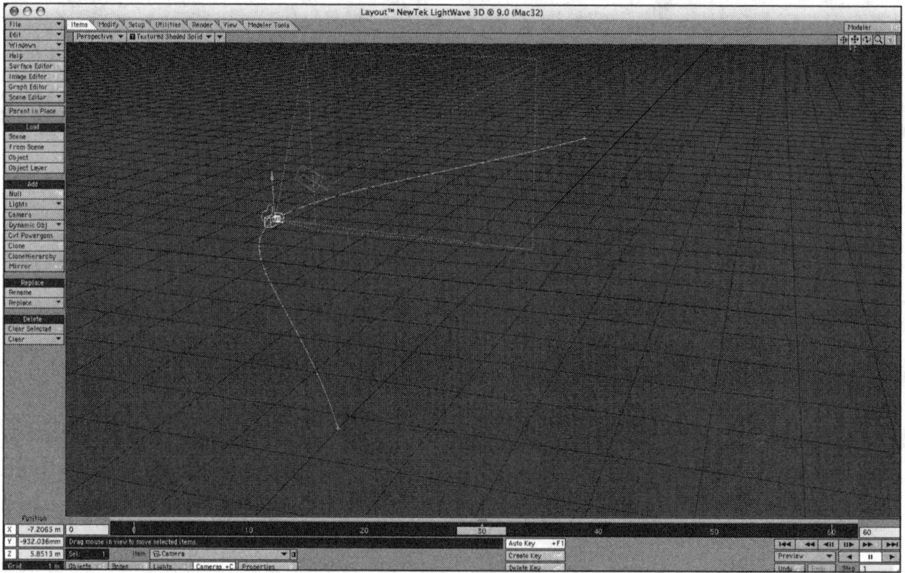

Figure 2.8 LightWave interactively updates motion paths with the Auto Key button active.

This example shows keyframing in the simplest form. Throughout this book, you'll be creating more advanced keyframing—and more precise keyframing. The Auto Key button you turned on to automatically create keyframes is on by default in LightWave; but as helpful as it is, it can be quite destructive too. There are times when you should use it—

for example, when tweaking character animation. Other times, you shouldn't use it—for example, when doing precise mechanical animations. You'll see how this use (or non-use) of Auto Key plays a part in your keyframing actions throughout the book.

The Dope Track

There's a hidden feature in the Layout timeline that you may or may not have found. If you move your mouse just above the timeline, right in the center, a small arrow appears, as shown in **Figure 2.9**.

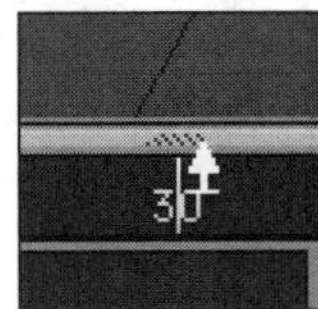

Figure 2.9 Just above the timeline in Layout, you can click to open the Dope Track.

When you see the arrow, click the bar that separates the Layout view and the timeline. The LightWave 9 Dope Track appears, offering additional control over your keyframes. See, it's all about control—the more you have, the better!

A Dope Track is a short or mini version of a *dope sheet*. What's a dope sheet, you ask? It is a page that outlines all of your keyframes, motions, and timing. LightWave v9 has its own Dope Sheet feature, which we'll get to later in this chapter. For now, the Dope Track is a simplified version of the Dope Sheet that offers you enhanced control over your keyframes. You'll use this during animation tutorials later in this book.

Exercise 2.2 Working with the Dope Track

To get an idea of how the Dope Track works, do the following:

1. Click the top center of the timeline to pop open the Dope Track.
2. You should still have your three-keyframe animation in Layout from the previous exercise, and you can use that. This scene is nothing more than one camera with three keyframes applied at 0, 30, and 60.
3. You'll see what looks like a second timeline appear above the first timeline, as in **Figure 2.10**.

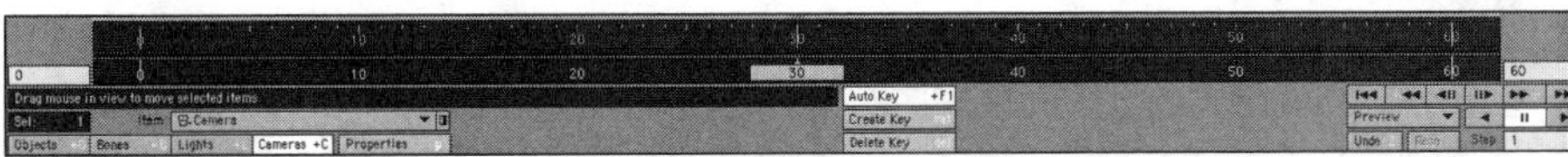

Figure 2.10 When the Dope Track is opened, you'll see what appears to be an additional timeline, above the standard timeline.

4. With just three keyframes applied to the camera, you can see their representations in the Dope Track.

5. If you right-click on one of the keyframes in the Dope Track, you get a list of commands available to you, as in **Figure 2.11**.

Note

Mac users! Remember to Cmd-click key to simulate right mouse button functions. Hey, did you go out and get a two-button mouse yet?

Figure 2.11
Right-click on one of the keyframes in the Dope Track, and you are greeted by a list of tools.

Some of these commands are ghosted with such a simple scene. However, as you build more complex animations, you'll find these tools very useful. Here are some tips to demonstrate the power of the Dope Track:

- The Dope Track shows keyframes for objects based on their individual X-, Y-, and Z- axes, as opposed to those of the overall scene. If you create a keyframe for an object when its axes are aligned with those of the main scene, and then use the Rotation tool to change the object's heading, pitch, or bank, the keyframe you made will still be there, but you'll no longer see it in the Dope Track. That's because the object's relative axes will be different from those of the scene.
- The Dope Track enables you to adjust objects' X, Y, and Z positions independently, for any given keyframe.
- In the Dope Track, the left mouse button selects keyframes.
- Hold down the Alt key and click-drag in the Dope Track to select a range of frames called a *local zone*. In this zone, you can *bake* keyframes for Move and Rotate operations. Baking is the process of converting frames interpolated by LightWave into actual keyframes. Conversely, holding down both the Alt and Shift keys sets a zone, allowing you to bake a keyframe for all objects in the scene.
- If you hold the Alt key and click-drag to select a range of keyframes in the Dope Track, you can make copies of those keyframes while leaving the originals untouched.
- To delete a zone you might have created with the previous step, hold down the Ctrl and Alt keys and drag.
- You can grab the arrows on either end of a zone to make it longer or shorter. Or, grab in the center to move a zone.

- You can snap keyframes in the Dope Track. LightWave's General Options (press o in Layout) allow you to turn on a feature called fractional keyframes. With this feature enabled, you can snap the selected keyframe to the closest whole keyframe, such as 1, 2, or 5. A fractional keyframe is in between a whole keyframe, such as 1.3 or 2.7.
- A really cool feature of the Dope Track is support for copying and pasting keyframes. When you paste copied keyframes in the dope track, their placement is determined by the slider in the timeline: The first pasted frame is inserted at the slider position.

Note

Don't worry about all of the details of the Dope Track right now. Review the information here, then when it's time to animate later in the book, you'll see this section in action.

Layout Viewports

Like Modeler, Layout has multiple viewports. Look at **Figure 2.12**. Here, you can see the viewport controls at the top of the Layout window, as you did in Modeler.

Figure 2.13 shows the viewing options available for each viewport you're working in, such as Light view or Camera view.

Figure 2.14 shows the viewport render-style pull-down, which allows you to view objects in Layout as bounding-box or wireframe forms or as solids, even with textures applied.

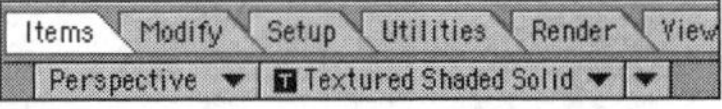

Figure 2.12 The default Perspective view in Modeler can be changed to any other viewport style from the drop-down at the top of the interface.

(none)
Top (XZ)
Bottom (XZ)
Back (XY)
Front (XY)
Right (ZY)
Left (ZY)
Perspective
Light View
Camera View
Schematic

Figure 2.13 Click the list at the top of the Layout viewport to change which view you work in.

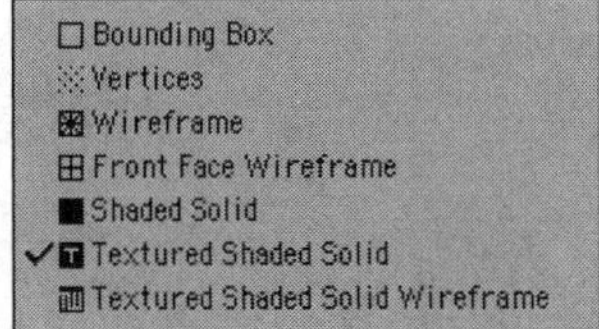

Figure 2.14 You can also choose how the objects in the viewport will be drawn.

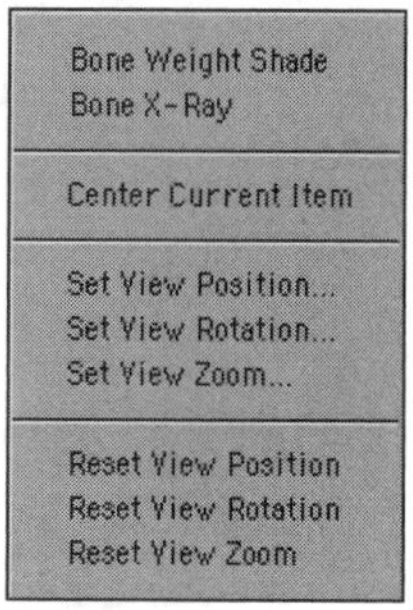

You'll find that you change these views often, depending on the project at hand. Just to the right of the viewport styles drop-down at the top of the frame are additional view options (**Figure 2.15**), such as Bone X-Ray mode. This mode enables you to see any bones applied to an object, even if the object is solid, hence the X-Ray title.

Bone Weight Shade
Bone X-Ray

Center Current Item

Set View Position...
Set View Rotation...
Set View Zoom...

Reset View Position
Reset View Rotation
Reset View Zoom

Figure 2.15 Additional view options are available directly to the right of the viewport render styles drop-down, at the top of LightWave Layout.

Multiple Viewports

You might be one of the select few who can work in multiple viewports while animating. If you're not sure whether that's your style, press **F3**, and you'll see a quad view just like LightWave Modeler (**Figure 2.16**).

But wait, there's more! Press **F3** again, and again. You cycle through all of LightWave Layout's available viewport arrangements. You can press F4 to go back. Let's say you have a quad view in Layout set, as shown in Figure 2.16. You can set any view to any style you want—for example, you can make two views a Perspective view, one view a Top view, and the other a Camera view. Many animators like to make the Layout viewports match that of Modeler. However, you might find that working in large single views, one at a time, is quite useful.

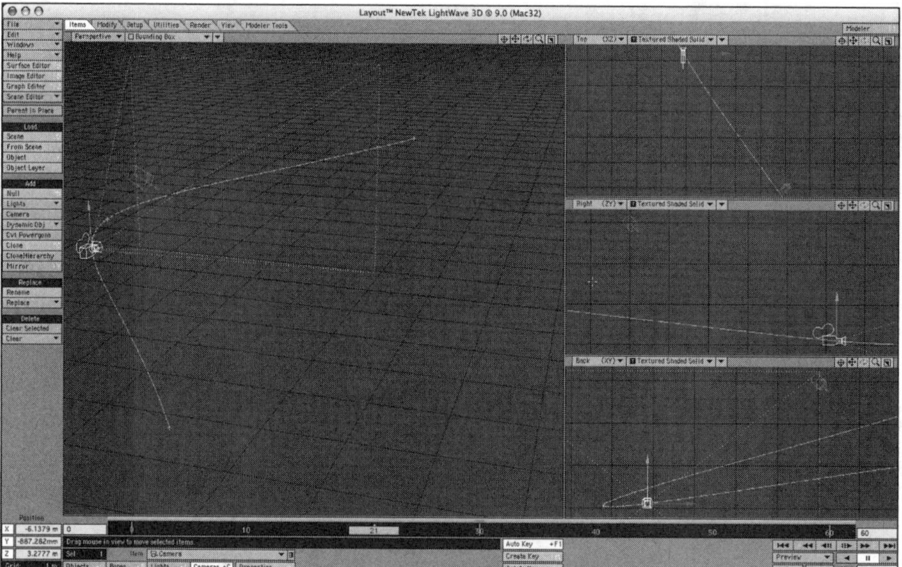

Figure 2.16 Pressing the F3 key cycles you through LightWave Layout's available viewport arrangements.

Note

A great way to work in Layout is to employ your numeric keypad or use the number keys across the top of your keyboard. Press **1** to jump to the Back view looking down the Z-axis; press **2** for the Top view looking down the Y-axis. As you can guess, pressing **3** takes you to the Right view looking down the X-axis. Press **4** to get to a Perspective view, **5** for a Light view, and **6** to switch to a Camera view. Do this as you work, and you'll be flipping back and forth between views without thinking about it.

Viewport Movement Control

To the top right of any Layout viewport are the viewport movement controls, just as you found in Modeler (**Figure 2.17**).

Figure 2.17
At the upper-right side of the Layout interface are the viewport movement controls. Click, hold the mouse button down, and drag the mouse to use them.

It's important to note that you cannot use these controls all the time, in every view. Their availability varies depending on which view you're working in. In Perspective view, the default viewport, these tools are all available. The five buttons are as follows:

- **Center Current Item.** This first button stays on when clicked. Click it again to turn it off. It keeps the currently selected item—be it a camera, light, or object—centered at all times.
- **Move.** The Move button enables you to move your view around in the Perspective, Top, Side, and Back/Front viewports.
- **Rotate.** Click, hold, and drag to rotate your viewport in the Perspective view only.
- **Zoom.** The Zoom viewport tool is useful for all views except Light view and Camera view.
- **Expand.** The Expand view control is great to quickly maximize any viewport. For example, let's say you're using LightWave Layout with a Quad viewport style like Modeler. Click this button in any viewport to maximize it to full screen. Click it again to return to your Quad view.

Use these viewport controls to properly take a look at your scene. They can help you stay aware of what's going on, and controls like the Center Current Item button can help you quickly find an item you've misplaced in the scene: Click the Center Current Item button, then select the missing item from the Selected Item list (see Figure 2.3), and the lost item will instantly jump into view. Zoom out slightly, and you can see where it is in relation to the rest of your scene.

Menus and Tabs

Across the top of the Layout interface are seven tabs. As in Modeler, each tab reveals a menu of tools. When you click on one of these tabs (**Figure 2.18**), the toolset on the left side of the interface changes accordingly.

Figure 2.18 The LightWave Layout tab set, across the top of the interface.

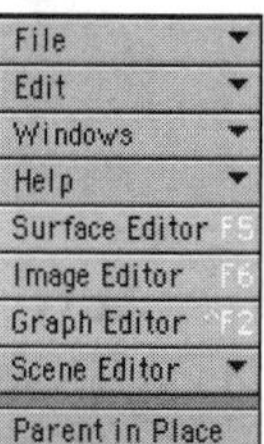

Figure 2.19 The nine buttons at the top left of LightWave Layout always appear, no matter what tab or menu you're working in.

It's important to note that the nine buttons at the top left of Layout (starting with the File drop-down) always appear, no matter what tab you've selected. These are key tools and commands you'll use throughout LightWave, both in Modeler and Layout (**Figure 2.19**).

Note

Remember that we're using the default LightWave tabs and menus throughout this book. Although you can change the menus to look like anything you want, the default setup keeps these nine tool buttons at the top left of LightWave Layout.

File Menu

Let's talk about the first of these buttons: the File drop-down menu. When we say *drop-down menu* (or just *drop-down*), we're talking about a button that has a small tiny downward-pointing arrow. Click this button and you'll find additional tools (**Figure 2.20**). Note that you do not need to click on the arrow to expand the menu; just click anywhere on the button.

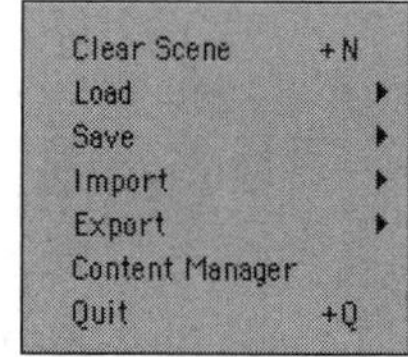

Figure 2.20 The File menu drop-down always appears at the top left of the Layout interface.

The File drop-down menu allows you to load and save scenes, and use the new Save Scene Increment feature. Using this feature adds 001, 002, and so on to the end of your scene name each time you save. You can also export scenes through LightWave's Content Manager.

Note

Pressing Ctrl+s (Mac or PC) on your keyboard tells LightWave to Save Scene As, whereas pressing Shift+s automatically saves a scene in increments.

Clear Scene

As the name implies, you can select Clear Scene, or press Shift+n, to clear your scene. After you perform this command, all that is left is a light and a camera. Be warned: You will not have an opportunity to save after you do this, and LightWave does not inform you that data might be lost. It asks you if you're sure you want to clear the scene, but that's it. So, save often!

Additionally, simply loading a new scene overrides your current scene. Therefore, using Clear Scene before you use Load Scene is a wasted step.

Load

The Load submenu in the File drop-down allows you to load scenes, load recent scenes, and load an item from a scene, which is a cool feature. You can also load objects and revert the current scene to its previously saved state.

The Load Items from Scene command in the Load submenu is especially handy for character animation. It allows you to load one scene into your current scene. For example, let's say you create a cool-looking giraffe and set up a workable bone structure for it. Of course, you've saved that scene so that you can work with it later. Then, you've built a huge safari scene with textures, landscapes, and lighting. Now all you have to do is use Load Items from Scene and choose the giraffe scene. The giraffe and all of its motions and bones will be imported into your existing scene. This allows you to set up scenes on their own for both speed and productivity, but use them together for final results.

Import

This submenu provides access to LightWave add-on modules called plug-ins, which can be used to convert models and animations created in other programs. LightWave ships with just one such plug-in, Mocap_BVH_Setup, which lets you apply BioVision motion-capture data to your animations.

Export

Certain third-party applications still work very well with LightWave. However, LightWave's core structure changed with version 6 in the year 2000, and many scenes were no longer compatible with third-party applications. Because of this, NewTek has added the ability to export your scene to LightWave version 5.6 with the Export command, which is also found under the File drop-down menu. And, you can export files in VRML (Virtual Reality Markup Language) and Shockwave 3D formats, used for displaying 3D objects on the Web. You can also export a list of your scenes images, either for later reference or for sharing scene information.

Content Manager

LightWave's Content Manager is extremely handy for backing up your scenes and sending them to coworkers or clients. You see, LightWave's scene file consists of objects or 3D models you create in Modeler. The objects in your scene hold surfacing data, whereas the scene file itself holds motion data. These data files can sometimes be located in various folders around your hard drive. The Content Manager gathers all of the files associated with the current scene and copies them to a directory you specify.

Edit Menu

The Edit drop-down menu (**Figure 2.21**) is home to quite a few useful tools that enable you to edit menu and keyboard layouts, change window configurations, and even choose your Content Directory. The main features you'll use in this drop-down list are the Edit Keyboard Shortcuts and Edit Menu Layout commands.

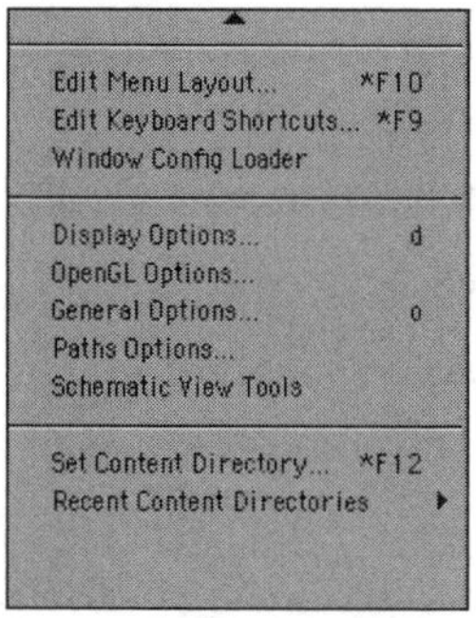

Edit Menu Layout... *F10
Edit Keyboard Shortcuts... *F9
Window Config Loader
Display Options... d
OpenGL Options...
General Options... o
Paths Options...
Schematic View Tools
Set Content Directory... *F12
Recent Content Directories

Figure 2.21 The Edit drop-down menu gives you access to key tools like Edit Menu Layout and Edit Keyboard Shortcuts.

Undo and Redo

In most circumstances, you'll use Ctrl+z to undo and the **z** key by itself to redo within LightWave. However, if you want, you can use toolset buttons to do so, too; they are found in the Edit drop-down list. Remember that you can set unlimited undos in LightWave Layout by pressing **o** for General Options.

There are a few warnings to note about using undo. First, too many undos can kill your system resources! Also, remember that undos don't apply to everything—that is, if you accidentally turn off a texture editor layer on your surface, there's no going back. However, if you create some bad keyframes, undo is an easy way to set them up again.

Edit Keyboard Shortcuts

Everyone likes things customized to their liking, right? LightWave 3D gives you this freedom by allowing you to assign keyboard equivalents to commands throughout the program. This next exercise shows you how to use these Edit features. **Figure 2.22** shows the Edit Keyboard Shortcuts selection.

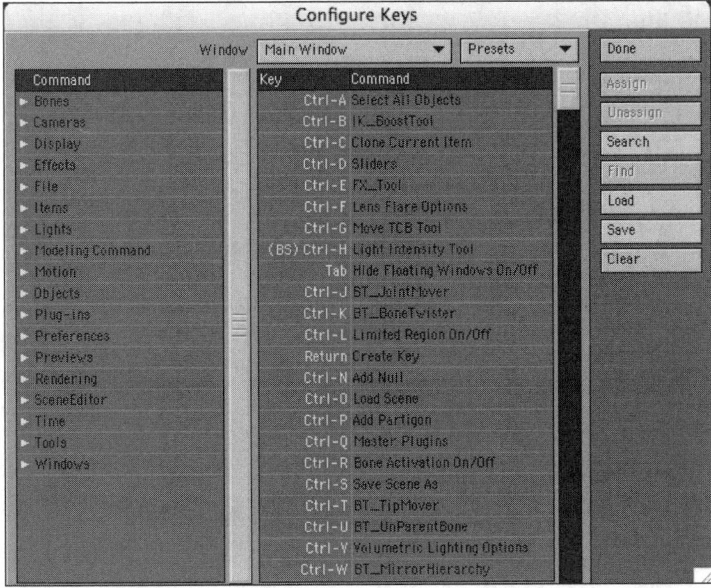

Figure 2.22 The Edit Keyboard Shortcuts panel enables you to rearrange existing keyboard shortcuts as well as create new ones.

Exercise 2.3 Editing Keyboard Shortcuts

1. Click the Edit drop-down menu and choose the Edit Keyboard Shortcuts command, or press Alt+F9 (Option-F9 on the Mac).
2. A panel appears where you can choose any of LightWave's tools and apply your own keyboard shortcut (see Figure 2.22).

Note

You can see any existing keyboard shortcut right on the Layout button. Any keyboard shortcut you apply will become visible on the buttons as a helpful reminder.

3. On the left side of the panel are the various commands Layout offers. On the right are keyboard shortcut listings. Scroll down the left side and select the Rendering listing. Click it to expand.
4. Within the Rendering commands, you find Render Globals, LightWave v9's new global control panel. Select it, as shown in **Figure 2.23** (on the following page).

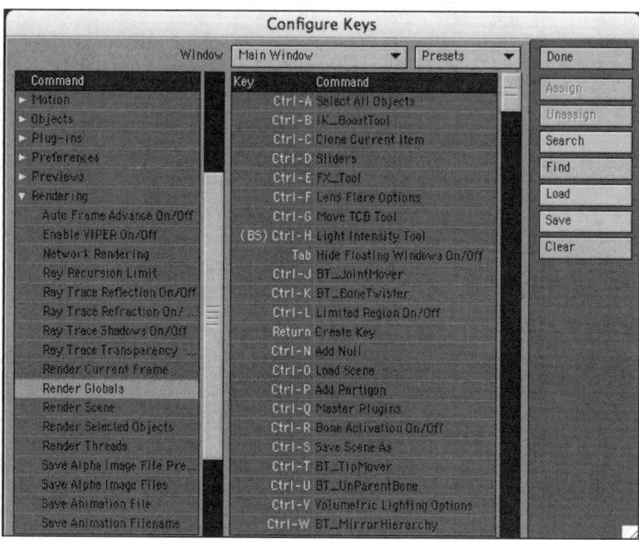

Figure 2.23 It's easy to select various commands from the categories. Here, the Render Globals command is selected.

5. Scroll down the right column to choose a keyboard equivalent to assign the Render Globals command to, perhaps Shift-T.
6. Select the Shift-T keyboard shortcut in the window, and on the right, click the Assign button, as shown in **Figure 2.24**. Click the Save button to keep your changes.
7. Assign more keys to your liking, saving each as you go, and click Done.

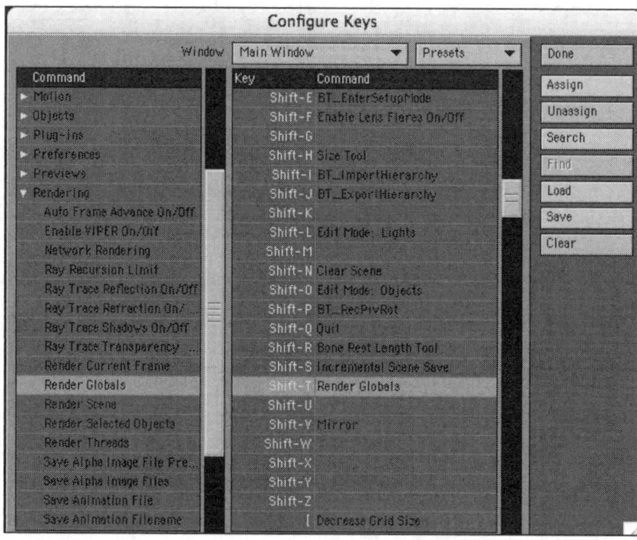

Figure 2.24 Assigning keyboard shortcuts is easy. Just pick a command, pick a key, and click Assign.

You can always go back to LightWave's default keyboard shortcuts by choosing the appropriate preset in the Configure Keys panel. Just click and select from the Presets drop-down at the top right of the panel. You can also set up keyboard shortcuts for the Graph Editor by choosing the option from the Window drop-down.

Another thing to remember is that you can apply these keyboard shortcuts in LightWave's Modeler in the same way. Just select the Edit drop-down in Modeler and repeat the preceding steps.

Note

Be sure to use the Save button within the Configure Keys panel to save your keyboard setups. Should you choose to select the default preset, your changes are gone forever.

Edit Menu Layout

Changing keyboard equivalents is great, no question. But if you want to go one step better and really make LightWave your own, try editing the menus!

Exercise 2.4 Editing Menus

1. From the Edit drop-down list, select Edit Menu Layout or press Alt+F10 (Option-F10 on a Mac). You are greeted with a panel that looks very similar to the Configure Keys panel from the previous exercise (**Figure 2.25**).

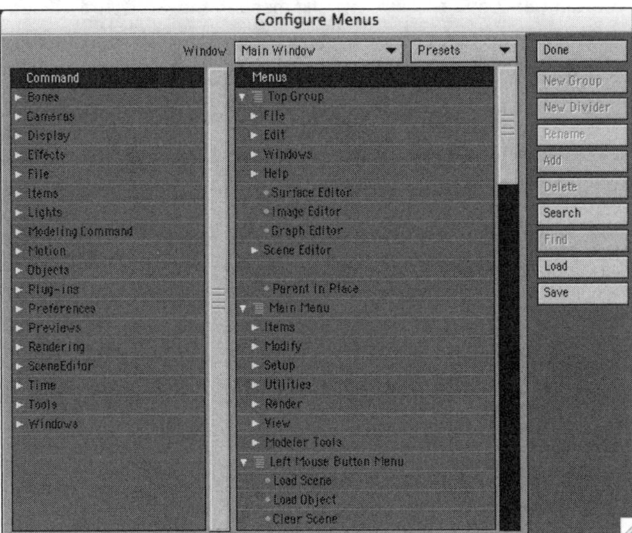

Figure 2.25 The Configure Menus panel, chosen from the Edit drop-down list's Edit Menu Layout command.

2. You'll use the panel the way you did editing keyboard shortcuts. Most tools are already out on the interface, but this panel is great for moving buttons, adding new menus, or creating buttons for your third-party plug-ins. Select the Parent in Place listing from the Menus column on the right, as shown in **Figure 2.26**. This determines the location of your new button; it will appear just beneath the Parent in Place button in the Top Group of toolset buttons.

Figure 2.26 You can select and edit any existing menu in the Configure Menus panel.

3. To the left of the panel, select the Rendering category. Expand it, and select Render Current Frame. This will be dimmed because it's already assigned to the F9 key and has a button, but you can still create another button for it. Once it's selected, click the Add button at the right of the panel and you'll see the command added to the LightWave interface. **Figure 2.27** shows the new Render Frame tool button, just below the Parent in Place tool.

Figure 2.27 Adding a custom interface button is as easy as the click of a button.

By adding the Render Current Frame command to the Top Group, you've assigned it to every tab, so it will always be visible within Layout. If you'd created this button within the Main Menu listings, it would apply only to the selected tab. You can select various tools from the command window on the left and select your new group. Then, click the Add button. You've now added buttons for commands in your own custom group. Feel free to select your new group and choose the Rename button to customize it. You can also drag entries up or down in the Menus column to reorder buttons within toolsets.

You should know a few things about using these configuration panels. When a command is dimmed, that means it's already assigned. However, it does not mean that you can't assign it again. Also, if you ever dislike the menus you've created, you can always choose Default from the Presets drop-down menu in the panel. To follow along with the rest of the book, go ahead and choose the default presets.

Windows Menu

Beneath the Edit menu drop-down list is the Windows menu (**Figure 2.28**). Here, you can access various windows or panels throughout LightWave. These windows are controls for Motion Options, including access to LightWave's nonlinear animation controller; Backdrop Options; Compositing Options; and the Image Processing tab.

You'll be employing all of these windows throughout this book's tutorials. Note the keyboard shortcuts to the right of the listings for quicker access.

Motion Mixer F2
Presets... F8
Backdrop Options... ^F5
Volumetrics and Fog Options... ^F6
Compositing Options... ^F7
Image Processing... ^F8
Motion Options... m
Hide Floating Windows On/Off tab
Scene Statistics... w

Figure 2.28
The Windows drop-down menu gives you access to many key panels throughout LightWave Layout.

Help Menu

LightWave's Help menu (**Figure 2.29**) can be found directly in Layout all the time. This is helpful (pun intended) for accessing LightWave's Web-based help system.

Additionally, you can enter your valid license key in this panel, as well as access LightWave's About section to check your version number, including information about your system's graphic card.

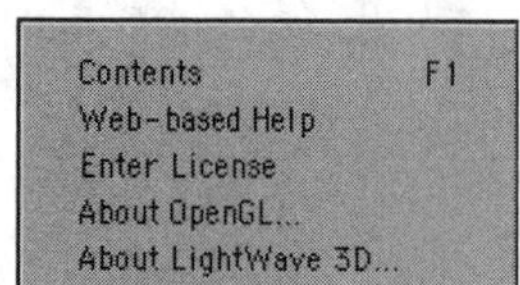

Figure 2.29
The LightWave v9 Help menu gives you quick access to online help and licensing.

Surface Editor

Beneath the Help menu is the Surface Editor. Here, you can apply all of the texturing to your objects. Within the Surface Editor is the Node Editor, new for LightWave v9. We'll explore its powerful network of surface functions later in this book. **Figure 2.30** shows the surface list for a loaded object in the Surface Editor; also, the Node Editor is open.

The Surface Editor is easier to work with than you might think. Again, if you think about the process you can easily navigate through the panel. First, you tell the Surface Editor which surface you want to work with. Where did you get that surface? You created it in Modeler with the Change Surface requester, accessed via the Surface button at the bottom of the Modeler interface. After choosing a surface, you work your way down the panel from color to luminosity to transparency and more.

Texturing can be a painstaking aspect of 3D animation and art, but as you'll see in the next chapter, applying basic surfaces and textures is easier than you might think.

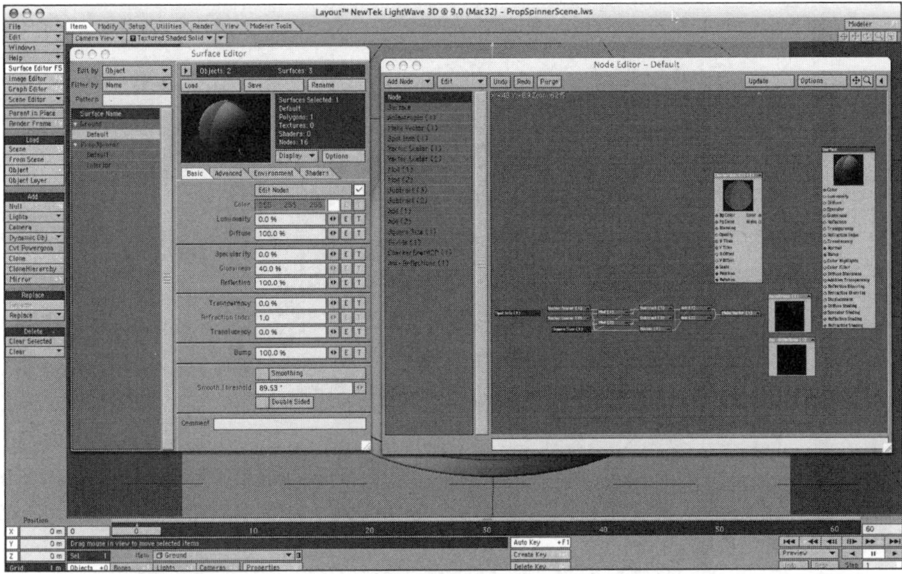

Figure 2.30 The Surface Editor in LightWave is your home for all surfacing.

Note

Throughout the Surface Editor and LightWave, you'll see little E and T buttons. These are important. The E allows you to create an Envelope for the given parameter. What's an envelope? It's a change in value over time. The E button opens the Graph Editor, which lets you animate that change. The T button allows you to apply textures—spatial variations in value, distributed over a surface. Pressing a T button opens the Texture Editor. If you click on an E or a T accidentally, simply hold the Shift key and click the button again to release. Undo does not work for this.

Image Editor

Below the Surface Editor button is the one for the Image Editor (**Figure 2.31**), which is used to load and manage image and movie files within LightWave.

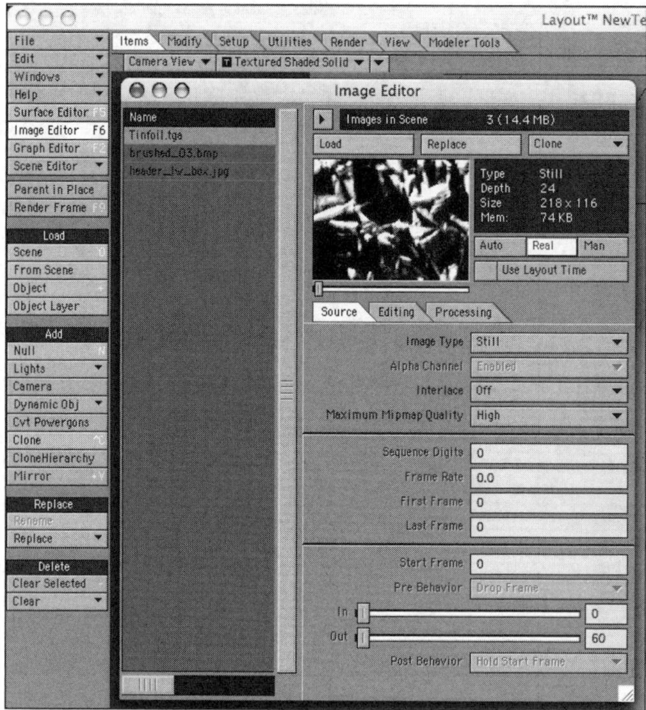

Figure 2.31 The Image Editor in LightWave 9 allows you to load images and movies, as well as edit them and apply effects.

You can do more than just load images in the Image Editor; you can edit them! The Processing tab allows you to apply simple enhancements to your images and movies. Additionally, you can apply textures to your images with the T buttons. You'll use the Image Editor in the next chapter to load reflection maps.

Graph Editor

Also part of the eight key menus in Layout is the LightWave Graph Editor (**Figure 2.32**). This panel gives you specific control over the motion channels of your Layout items. Each item, such as a light, camera, bone, or object, has nine motion channels. There is a specific channel of motion for the X-, Y-, and Z-axes for Movement, Scale, and motion on the H, P, and B (heading, pitch, and bank) for Rotation. You can control all of these channels in the Graph Editor.

In the Graph Editor, you can adjust the timing of specific channels. For example, say you've created a spinning top. You have rotated the top over 30 frames, but you need it to continue for 300. Rather than re-keyframing it, you can use the Graph Editor to "repeat" the past behavior of that specific motion channel. But you can do so much more, such as edit keyframes or create them. You can apply various motion plug-ins, such as a texture environment to the Y (up and down) motion channel to simulate an earthquake. As you work through tutorials in this book, you'll use the Graph Editor to perform these functions as well as learn how to navigate the panel.

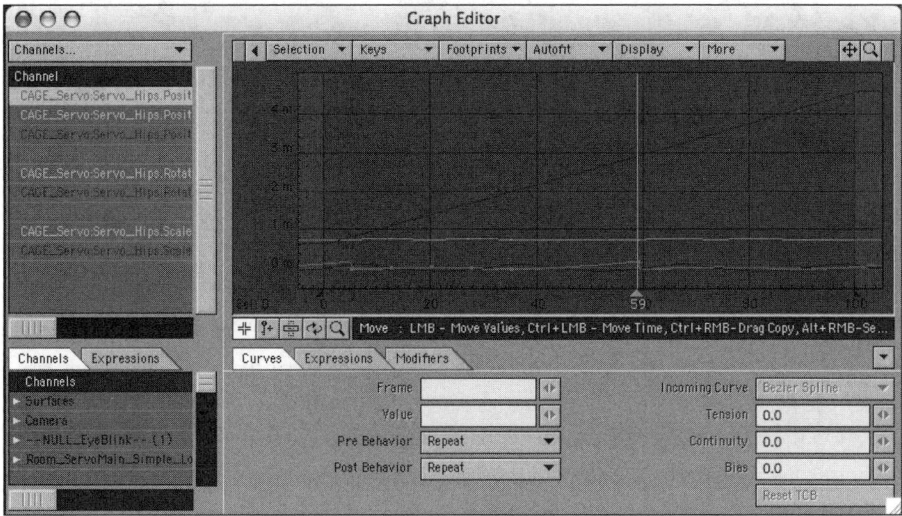

Figure 2.32 The LightWave Graph Editor offers specific control over motion channels for your Layout items.

Scene Editor

In the past, you accessed the Scene Editor by clicking a button. Now LightWave offers a drop-down menu for opening different versions of the Scene Editor—the newer version of the Scene Editor or the classic version you may know and love (**Figure 2.33**).

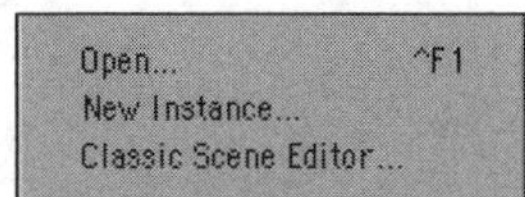

Figure 2.33 The Scene Editor menu gives you access to both the classic LightWave Scene Editor and the newer version.

The LightWave v9 Scene Editor is quite powerful, incorporating spreadsheet capabilities, a Dope Sheet, and overall editing of various scene parameters. It does not give you control over every aspect of LightWave, but it can significantly improve workflow by allowing control of multiple items at once. There are five main areas within the Scene Editor: Items, Surfaces, Channels, Property, and Dope Sheet. Exercise 2.5 guides you through a quick overview of the tool.

Exercise 2.5 Working with the Scene Editor

1. From the File drop-down menu, select Clear Scene.
2. From the Scene Editor drop-down menu, select Open. Because of the design of the Scene Editor, you can have multiple instances of the panel open at the same time; to do so, simply select New Instance. **Figure 2.34** shows the Scene Editor panel.

Figure 2.34 A new instance of the LightWave Scene Editor is created, and the panel appears.

3. On the left of the panel are the items in your scene, currently just one camera and one light. **Figure 2.35** shows that by clicking the small mark in front of an item, you can expand it to see its channels.

Figure 2.35 The left side of the Scene Editor contains the items you want to control.

4. At the top left of the Scene Editor are three tabs: Items, Surfaces, and Channels. Click the Surfaces tab, and the list changes, giving you access to any surfaces in your scene.
5. After you've selected certain surfaces to work with, you can select them on the right and make changes. This is useful for quickly seeing and editing all of your surfaces outside of LightWave Surface Editor. **Figure 2.36** shows a simple scene loaded so you can see the surfaces.

Figure 2.36 With a simple scene loaded, you can quickly see controls for enabling group editing of surfaces.

Dope Sheet

Within the Scene Editor is the Dope Sheet. You can find it in a tab on the right side of the panel. After you set up keyframes and complex motions, especially for characters, the Dope Sheet will be your best friend. The Dope Sheet allows you to see all of your keyframes for multiple items at once. You use it to set the times and numeric offsets, and even to erase keyframes. When you select specific keyframes in the Dope Sheet, you can change their settings values and edit them in the Graph Editor. **Figure 2.37** shows Dope Sheet contents for a character scene loaded from the LightWave Content Directory.

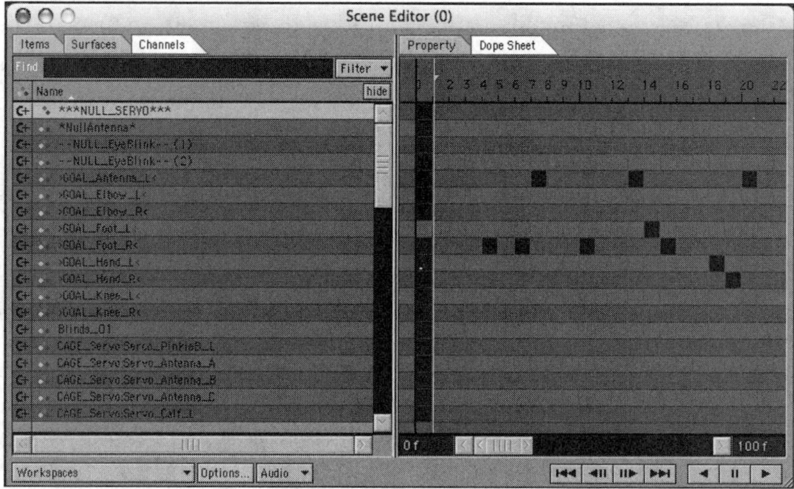

Figure 2.37 When a scene with keyframes is loaded, the Scene Editor's Dope Sheet gives you enhanced control over time, movement, and other parameters.

The Scene Editor is powerful, and to show its uses, we're going to dive right into it in some tutorials later in this book. This chapter's coverage should give you a quick overview of the power behind this cool new addition.

Parent in Place

The Parent in Place button is an on-off switch. When activated, it lets you parent (or unparent) items (objects, lights, etc.) to other items, while preserving their keyframed positions and rotations. Parenting and unparenting with this option disabled can cause items to move in unwanted ways.

You'll access and use these key tabs and menus often, which you'll see as you work your way through various tutorials in this book. First, read on to learn about the tool categories of the six main menu tabs in Layout.

Items Tab

Across the top of the Layout interface are the six key menu tabs you'll also find yourself accessing often. The first is the Items tab (much like Modeler's Create menu tab), which is where you can find the simple item controls, as shown in **Figure 2.38**. Here, you find one-click load tools, which replace, add, and delete functions. In previous versions of LightWave, it took a number of clicks to access these tools, and after a while, it became a bit annoying.

Load

The first category you see within the Items tab is labeled Load. Tools within the category let you load a scene, which is an entire project containing lights, motions, and objects. You can also just load an object into your scene with the Load Object button. Loading an object is the way to begin creating a scene. Loading new content overwrites whatever you have in Layout, so be sure to save before you load. The category also contains a button for the previously discussed Load Items from Scene command, found under the File drop-down menu, and the Object Layer button. This allows you to load just a specific layer of an object. Let's say you create a complex living room, with 12 layers. Layer 5 contains that awesome flat panel plasma television you modeled (because your spouse won't let you buy it!). To load it, select Object Layer and choose the object, and then choose the layer in the requester that appears.

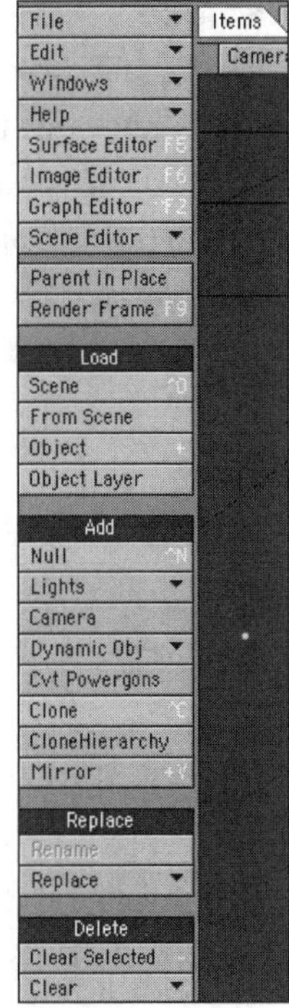

Figure 2.38
Layout's Items menu tab and its toolset, which allows you to load scenes and replace, add, and delete objects.

Note

When working in Layout, you'll often reload work you've already created. When you apply textures to your objects, you need to be sure to use the Save All Objects command from the File drop-down menu. This saves any textures or surface settings to your objects. Saving the scene alone does not save the surfaces on objects. Saving the scene only saves motion data, light data, and whatever elements you've added to the scene. Colors and textures are saved with objects. Therefore, when you reload your objects, the textures and surfaces you've applied will load as well.

Add

With the Add category of the Items tab, you can easily add items to your scene. These items include Null objects—single points that do not show up in the render but rather help facilitate control throughout your animations—which are useful for parenting, grouping, and effects. Tools in the category also make it easy to add dynamic objects, such as particle emitters, wind, gravity, and collision items. Also within the Item's tab's Add category are tools with which you can mirror and clone selected items at the click of a button.

Replace

Replacing objects is easier than ever before with the Replace category under the Items menu. Perhaps you need to replace a simple stand-in object with a high-polygon model for final rendering. Not a problem; just select the item and choose Replace. Also, tools here let you rename any item, including lights, cameras, and other objects.

Delete

The Delete category within the Items tab can be used to quickly clear a selected item or group of items all at once. Use this category for quick-click deletions.

Modify Tab

You might find that you visit the Modify tab often while working in Layout. Of course, you'll see the same familiar eight menus at the top, starting with the File menu. But if you look further down as in **Figure 2.39**, you'll see five categories of tools.

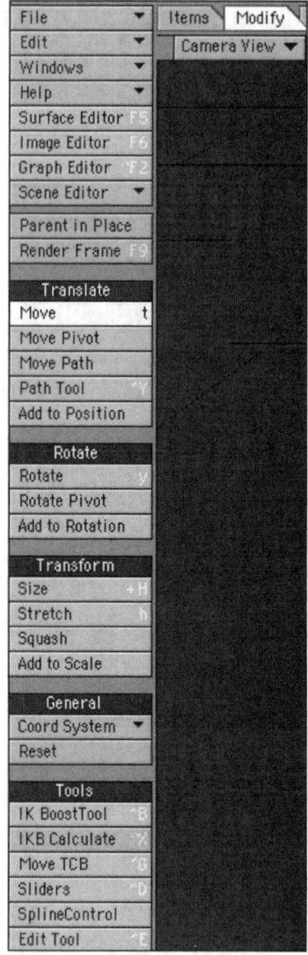

Figure 2.39
The Modify tab contains some of Layout's most frequently used tools.

Translate

The first category, Translate, houses several Move tools. These are all translate-type functions, as in Modeler. Use them for any item in Layout from bones to objects to lights. It's best to learn their keyboard equivalents too, such as the t key for Move.

Rotate

You'll find the Rotate tools just below the Translate tools. You can rotate any item and specify its pivot point. You'll learn about pivot points during the tutorials in the book.

Transform

Not to be confused with Translate, the Transform category offers various sizing tools, including Squash and Stretch.

General

The next tool category under the Modify tab is quite important to your workflow. Although the category title says General, the options within this category are anything but! They're more global than they are general. You'll find options for the Coordinate System, which determines how an item in Layout is controlled in relationship to the 3D world that is Layout. Earlier in the chapter, we characterized LightWave Layout as a big, invisible sphere in which you work. When you change the Coordinate System, you tell LightWave to adjust the relationship between the world's coordinates and the items. **Figure 2.40** shows the Coordinate System selections. You'll also find the Reset button. This is handy for keeping track of your items.. Let's say you move your camera around, and then at some point, lose track of it. This can happen with any item, even a light. If you first select Rotate (also from the Modify tab) and then click Reset, the rotation resets to the 0,0,0, setting. The same applies for Move. Keep this in mind when you're ready to scrap what you've done and start again without redoing your entire scene.

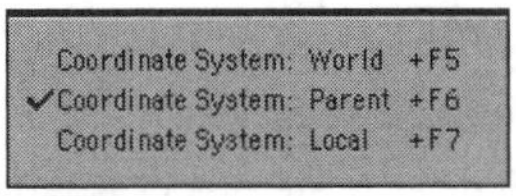

Coordinate System: World +F5
✓Coordinate System: Parent +F6
Coordinate System: Local +F7

Figure 2.40
The Coordinate System tool category within the Modify tab enables key changes used in animation.

To better understand the Coordinate System, look at **Figure 2.41**. This is the default LightWave layout, where the X-axis is left and right, the Y-axis is up and down, and the Z-axis is forward and back.

The object in the scene, the zombie, has default coordinates set to Parent in the Modify tab. That means the object's coordinate axes, represented by the arrow-shaped red, green and blue *handles* you use to move it along each axis, align with those of the overall layout. The object's green Y-axis handle stands vertically; its red X-axis handle lies down to the side, for left and right; and its blue Z handle points toward the back of the Layout interface.

Figure 2.41 LightWave Layout, with the default Coordinate System set to Parent.

Now look at **Figure 2.42**. in which the Coordinate System is set to Local. This makes the object's control handles align with *its own* X- Y- and Z-axes, rather than those of the scene. The zombie object is rotated so that it's leaning forward within the scene; if you use its green Y-handle to move it upward, it will rise at an angle relative to the overall scene, rather than straight up and down.

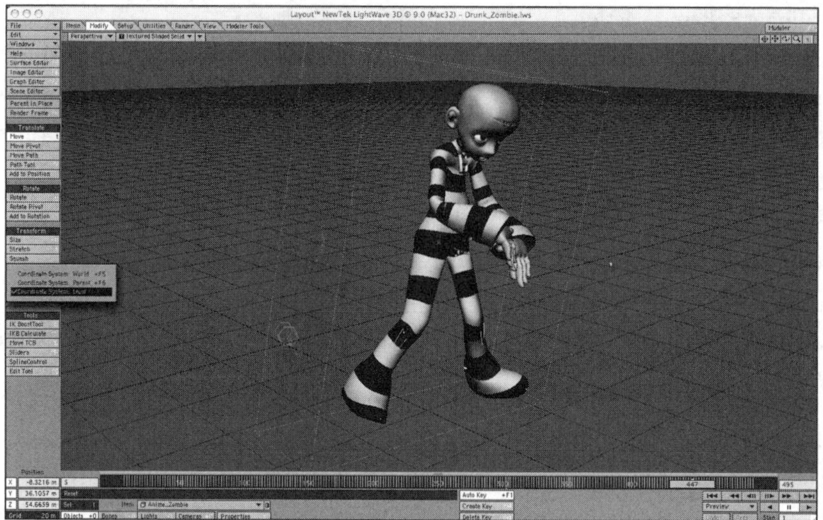

Figure 2.42 The object is rotated, and the Coordinate System is set to Local.

You'll use this feature often when working with bones for character animation, as well as mechanical animations. Many times, when setting up hierarchies of parented objects you'll need to change between Parent, World, and Local. Parent and World coordinates are essentially the same thing, except that if your object is parented to another item, it takes on that item's coordinates.

As you work through the tutorials, you'll see how this all comes into play. But remember: As you're setting up your animations, if something does not rotate or move the way you want it to, look to the Coordinate System in the Modify tab.

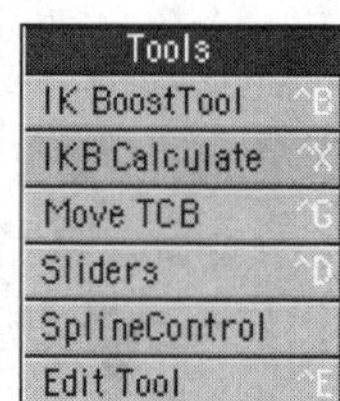

Figure 2.43 The Tools category is home to the IK Boost Tool, as well as Move TCB and others.

Tools

Finally, the Tools category found under the Modify tab is the location of some very powerful tools. As you can see in **Figure 2.43**, these tool names aren't as self-descriptive as the Translate or Rotate tools. These commands are some of LightWave's most important features.

IK Boost Tool

The "IK" in IK Boost Tool stands for inverse kinematics. It is a powerful new system primarily used for, but not limited to, character animation. What is inverse kinematics? In the simplest explanation, it is a system for determining how characters move based on the positions of their limbs and joints, much like a marionette on strings: When you move the string attached to a puppet's hand, its arm follows, moving in a specific way based on the length of the forearm and upper arm and position of its wrist, elbow, and shoulder joints. That's it! You'll be setting up your own IK in the upcoming character animation chapters.

The IK Boost Tool applies IK to a hierarchy of joined objects or bones, and allows you to instantly set parameters, limits, and controls for every aspect of your hierarchy.

IKB Calculate

After you've set up inverse kinematics and bone options with the IK Boost Tool, you can simply click the IKB Calculate button to "capture" movements generated through inverse kinematics in the form of animation keyframes. This is used for bone dynamics especially. You'll see this in full action later in the dynamics chapters of this book.

Move TCB Tool

The Move TCB command is sort of a new incarnation of an old feature. When you create a motion path with an object, LightWave creates a curve. Tension, Continuity, and Bias (TCB) are settings you can adjust for each keyframe on a motion curve. A common application is to set a positive tension for the keyframe at the end of a motion, to make the moving object "ease into" place. If this has always been possible in LightWave, then what's the big deal about the Move TCB button? Up until now, you had to open the Graph Editor, select the specific channel(s) to edit, and apply the appropriate T, C, or B settings. Now, you can use the Move TCB tool directly in Layout. You can see your settings down at the bottom left of the Layout interface in the Info area. All you need to do is press Ctrl+g for the selected item to activate, then click and drag in the Layout to set Tension, hold Ctrl and drag to set Continuity, then right-click for Bias.

Sliders

The Sliders tool lets you attach slider controls to items in your scene for specific control over their behaviors. This is helpful during character animation or precise movements where you only want an item to move between two specific ranges. A slider allows you to set minimum and maximum values for a specific action or behavior. Then, as you work out the details of your animation, you can simply drag the slider to adjust the attribute within that range. This works on move, rotate, size, and so on.

Spline Control

Spline Control is a tool that, when active, allows you to see a visible and controllable motion path for a specific item. Select the item and turn on Spline Control, and you can click and drag on the control handles that appear in Layout to change the shape of the object's motion path.

Edit Tool

Click this little bugger and you'll find that it seems to disable any movements in Layout. But wait! It is actually a very cool little tool. Let's say you added a particle emitter to Layout. Click the Edit Tool, and your particles will be identified numerically. You can then select any one of those particles and move it or delete! This is great for those annoying particles that won't behave or that just don't belong. Get rid of them, we say!

Setup Tab

The Setup tab in Layout is your pit stop for all things skeletal—that is, this is where you find controls for bones. **Figure 2.44** shows the menu with its tools.

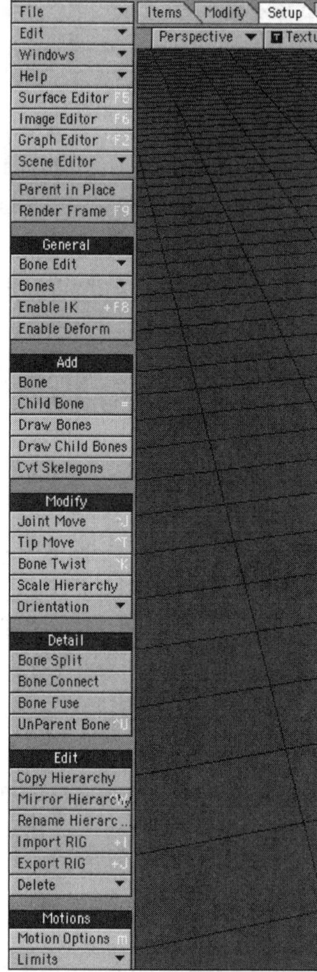

Figure 2.44 The Setup tab in Layout is where you find all the tools needed to work with bones, LightWave's deformation tools, and the Layout equivalent of Skelegons.

General

Yes, there is another General category—this time it's under the Setup tab, and we're talking about deformation tools. The General category offers bone tools such as Bone Edit functions, and global settings for activating (or deactivating) bones and inverse kinematics.

Note

Bones are deformation tools, meaning they deform your objects—not only animated characters but also such items as a curtain blowing in the wind, or the pages of a book curling. Throughout the character animation chapter, you'll find yourself guided to these tools for adding bones, editing bones, splitting them, and much more. In Chapter 1, "LightWave v9 Modeler," we introduced Skelegons. When you create Skelegons in Modeler for an object, they are converted to bones in Layout. You control, edit, and adjust those bones in the Setup tab.

Add

The Add category in the Items tab was all about objects, but in the Setup tab, the Add tools concern all things bones. Tools in this category can be used to add a bone, add a child bone, draw bones in Layout, and draw child bones. But another important tool is labeled Cvt Skelegons. This is the Convert Skelegons command that you'll use to change Skelegons (created in Modeler) into bones for use in Layout. Without this, Skelegons in Modeler are useless.

Modify

Once you've added bones to your scene, at some point, you'll need to modify them. The Modify tool category provides all that's necessary to adjust your bones. These powerful tools let you move bones' joints and tips, twist bones, and scale them. They are handy for properly setting up a perfect character rig.

Detail

Modifications are great, but sometimes when working with bones, you need to control more specific details. The Detail tab offers tools to split bones, and not just once. You can take one bone, for example, and cut it into four without destroying the hierarchy of your setup. This is useful when you've put a bone into a foot, for example, and then realize you need another one so the foot can bend! You'll also find Bone Fuse, which allows you to put two split bones back together, just in case you didn't want to split them after all. And, you can use the UnParent Bone tool here to remove a bone from its hierarchy.

Edit

Again, all of the tools within the Setup tab relate to bones. Use tools in the Edit category to copy hierarchies, rename them, save them, and load them.

Motions

One small category within the Setup tab relates to bones but also, potentially, to every other item in your scene. You can use the Motion Options tool in the Motions category to access a variety of motion tools and plug-ins. This can be for bones, lights, cameras, objects, or any effect item in your scene. Additionally, you can record minimum and maximum joint angles with the Limits drop-down selection.

Utilities Tab

Whenever you need to add plug-ins, edit them, or work with LightWave's LScript scripting language, you can click over to the Utilities tab. **Figure 2.45** shows the menu tab and its tools.

Figure 2.45 The Utilities tab is home to command tools, LScript programming tools, and plug-in tools.

Commands

The Commands category offers controls for looking up your command history or entering specific commands for LightWave to follow. Additionally, if you want to keep track of commands you've used, use the Save Cmd List option. Refer back to this for similar projects.

LScript

The LScript category is home to LightWave's custom programming language. Here, you can load preexisting LScripts, use the LScript compiler to build your own, and use LScript/RT to preview how they'll run. (Note that the LightWave v9 documentation incorrectly describes a fourth tool in this category, LScript Commander. This powerful tool is found in the Additional drop-down of the Plugins category (described below), under the name "LS Commander". It lets you create your own plug-in that loads an object, saves it, and then saves the scene, all in one button!

Plugins

The Plugins category is where you find the tools to add individual plug-ins, load multiple plug-ins with the Edit Plugins tool, and quickly find the last used plug-in. Within this category is the Master Plugins panel, which is where you can load Master class plug-ins, such as the LScript Commander. You also see the Additional list, where you can find additional plug-ins and any third-party plug-ins you might have added.

Render Tab

Rendering is the process by which LightWave generates the final output of a scene, using all of the lighting, surfaces, textures, animations, and environmental effects (wind, gravity, and so on) that you create in Layout. If a scene is animated, of course, the process can yield anywhere from hundreds to millions of rendered frames.

In earlier versions of LightWave, rendering tools were sort of hidden—kind of unusual for something so critical to the 3D animation process. If you are a veteran user of LightWave, you'll love the new Render menu tab (**Figure 2.46**). When it's time to render, LightWave v9 put the tools you need right in front of you.

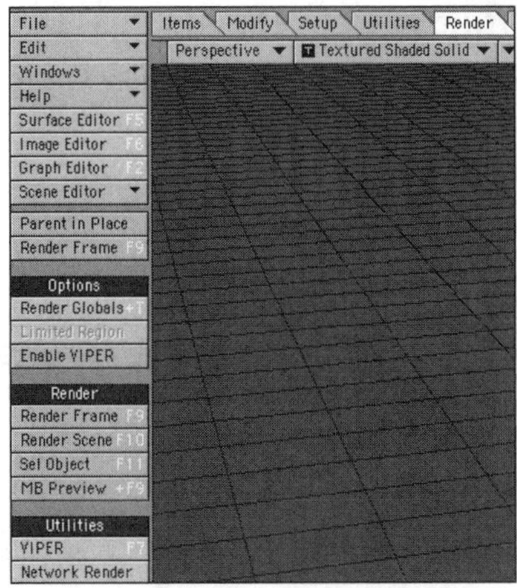

Figure 2.46 The Render tab encompasses all of your necessary render tools. Without these, you see nothing!

Options

The Options tool category houses the Render Globals menu button, where you'll find tools for setting up all of your animation characteristics. Use this panel to set camera resolution for single-frame renders, arbitrary renders, and full-frame animations. You can also set filtering methods, global illumination, and more, all from this one panel (**Figure 2.47**). You'll work through this panel and see how to render locally and over a network in Chapter 15, "Advanced Cameras and Rendering." This category also is where you'll find the Enable VIPER button. This is sort of an on/off switch for VIPER, LightWave's virtual preview render system, which we discuss shortly.

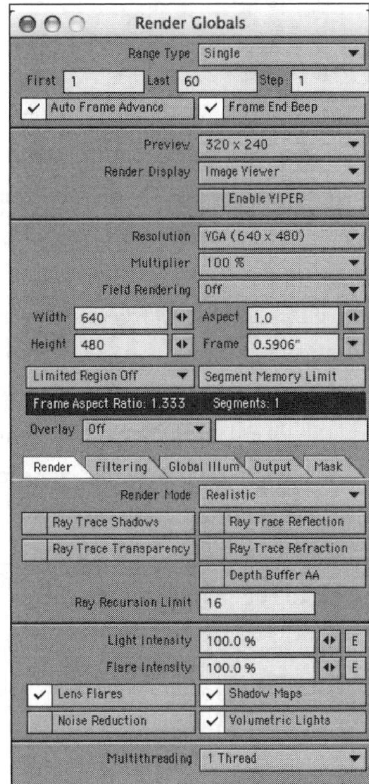

Figure 2.47 The Render Globals panel, accessible from the Render tab's Options tools.

Render

The presence of a Render tool category within the Render tab might seem confusing—or at least redundant—but it all makes sense: The Render tools let you click a button to render a single frame, a scene, a selected object, or preview a motion blur right in Layout. Click MB Preview to see any motion blur your scene might be using. You can also see that there is a Render Frame button. This is why the tool was dimmed earlier in the chapter when you edited menus.

Utilities

The Utilities category of the Render tab is where you find the tools for additional render options. First is VIPER, short for Virtual Interactive Preview Renderer. You can use VIPER to instantly see changes to surfaces, particles, and volumetrics, without performing a formal render. This saves time! You'll use VIPER in the next chapter's tutorials. The other Utilities tool is Network Render, which enables you to tie other computers on your network into your rendering. This is especially valuable because it doesn't require copies of LightWave to be installed on the other computers that help yours with rendering.

View Tab

The next menu tab across the top of Layout is the View tab. Here, you can find necessary tools to control your Layout viewports (**Figure 2.48**).

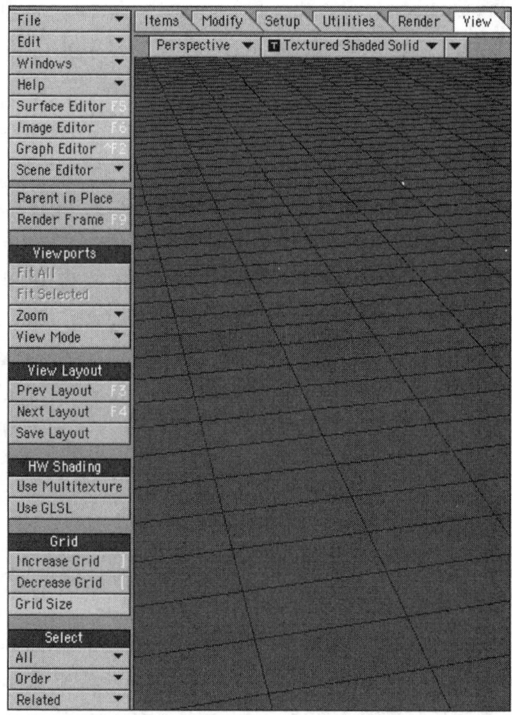

Figure 2.48 The View tab and its associated tools manage Layout's viewports.

Viewports

The sets of tools available in this menu give you additional control when working in Layout. Earlier in this chapter, we discussed the viewports, and you saw how to set up multiple viewports. The Viewports category in the View tab gives access to buttons that control those views. You can also use the Fit All and Fit Selected commands to quickly bring your items to view. Note, however, that these tools only work in certain viewports, such as the Top or Side views.

View Layout

The View Layout tools let you jump between preset layout views, such as single, quad, and so on. If you set up your own view, and perhaps click and drag the center of the windows to adjust, you can save that particular layout with the Save Layout button.

HW Shading

The HW Shading, or hardware shading, option enables computers with certain video cards to display multiple textures within Layout. It also enables supported cards to use a high-level shading option known as GLSL. Not all video cards support these options, so check the specifications for your particular video card before applying these.

Grid

Also within the View menu, you can find the Grid Size control in the Grid category. If you recognize that LightWave is a big 3D universe that you work within, it should be easy to understand that the Grid Size is the default unit of measurement you work with. In Layout (and Modeler, too), Grid Size is always displayed in the lower left corner of the LightWave workspace. By default, this measurement is 1 meter in size, as you can see in **Figure 2.49**.

Grid: 1 m

Figure 2.49
LightWave Layout's default unit of measurement, Grid Size, is 1 meter. The Grid Size can be increased or decreased as needed.

This means that every grid square you see in Layout, from any view, is 1 meter in size. Count three squares, and that's 3 meters, and so on. The reason you can increase and decrease the Grid Size in the View menu is because not all objects are scaled equally. For example, if you load in a Mars rover spacecraft, your unit of measurement automatically adjusts to the fit the size of the craft. You should be able to move and rotate the object just fine. If you load in the planet Mars, and it is built to scale, the Layout Grid Size might jump to 5 kilometers, and your rover will essentially disappear! This is because LightWave's grid adjusts itself to fit this large object. If you find your rover and move it, it will shoot off the screen with the slightest mouse movement. If this happens, you need to decrease the grid size.

Note

Adjusting the grid appears to change the size of the camera and lights, but it really doesn't. It only changes the relationship of those items to LightWave's world.

Select

The last category in the View tab contains the Select tools. Here, you can choose from various ways to select objects, lights, and cameras. You can choose to select by name or search by name. You can also select related parent or child items here, in addition to selecting in order, from one item to the next. A quicker way to select, however, is to click directly on the item in Layout and then use the up or down arrow on your keyboard to select the next or previous item.

Modeler Tools Tab

New to LightWave v9 is the Modeler Tools tab in Layout (**Figure 2.50**). This provides some basic modeling tools within Layout. While nowhere near as powerful as the tools in Modeler, these are mostly useful for setting up simple objects as placeholders.

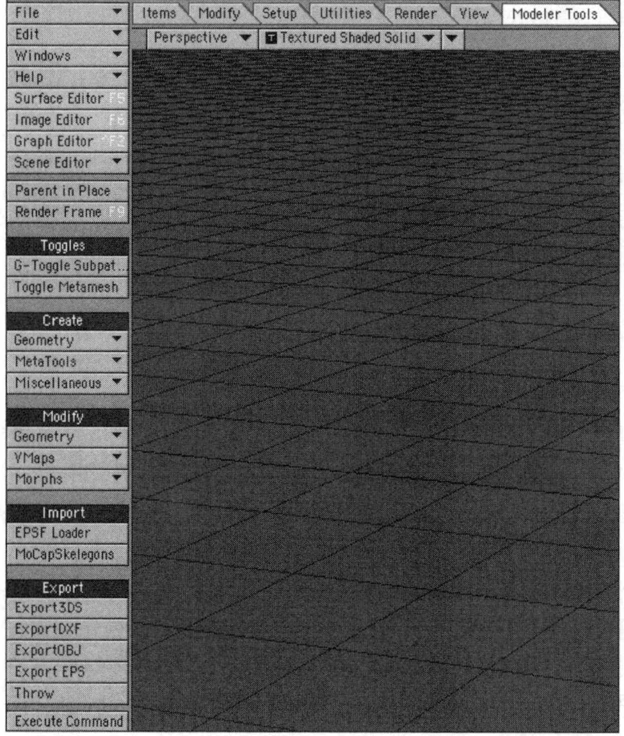

Figure 2.50 The Modeler Tools tab makes basic modeling possible within Layout.

Toggles

Tools in the Toggles category are really switches that turn on and turn off useful functions that were available only in Modeler in previous versions of LightWave. G-Toggle Subpatch globally activates and deactivates subpatch objects you create in Modeler. You might turn subpatches on in Layout when fine-tuning surface attributes, then turn them off to speed up animation previews. The Metamesh toggle works the same way on objects built using Modeler's metamesh tool; you can turn this feature on and off here as well, allowing you to work with simpler objects.

Create

In this category, you can create simple geometric shapes, including wedges, toroids (doughnuts), and other primitives. But in order to do so, you need to first create a null object. Do this from the Items tab, under the Add category.

Modify

In this area, you can modify the geometry you've created, with tools such as squash and stretch. You can also work with VMaps (vertex maps) that you might have setup in Modeler, or use the Apply, Rotate, and Scale Morph commands.

Import

In this section you have tools that allow you to import EPS and motion capture files.

Export

Animators often work with more than one program, and LightWave has set up tools that allow you to save 3DSs, OBJs, and other popular formats for use in other applications.

Preferences

LightWave, like many programs, has its own set of preferences. However, because LightWave is not native to particular operating systems and utilizes its own custom interface, accessing these options is not as easy as finding an Edit button at top of your computer screen. Instead, press **d** or **o**. The d key calls up Display Options, as shown in **Figure 2.51**.

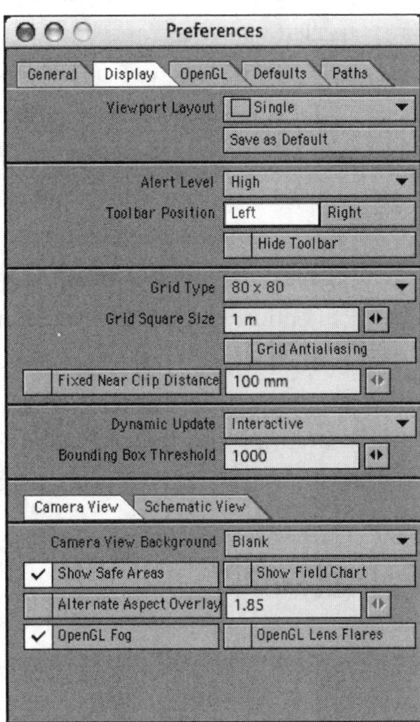

Figure 2.51 Open LightWave's Preferences panel by pressing the d or o key. Here, you can see the Display Options tab, which opens when you press **d**.

If you had pressed **o**, the General Options tab would have appeared, but both panels are embedded in the Preferences panel. Within the Display Options tab, you have specific control over settings that pertain to what you see in Layout. These are options concerning grid size, overlay colors, and many OpenGL options. The OpenGL, or Graphics Library, is the color shaded and textured views you see in Layout. Your video card determines how many OpenGL options you can support, but these days, even the simplest gaming cards work tremendously with LightWave. You can tell LightWave to turn on many OpenGL options concerning lens flares, textures, reflections, and even transparency. The new Preferences panel in LightWave v9 is extensive, but there are a few key areas you can read about here. For the rest, check out the video on the book's DVD.

Note

The new Preferences panel is quite robust, so to learn more about this updated LightWave v9 panel, be sure to view CH2_Prefs.mov in the 3D_Garage_Videos\ Chapter_Videos directory on the book's DVD.

Bounding Box Threshold

An important value in the Display Options tab is Bounding Box Threshold. You might have installed LightWave and hopped right into Modeler. The model you have created ended up being made up of 5,000 points and 5,200 polygons. When you send your object to Layout for animating, you see the object, but as soon as you move it, it turns into a wireframe box. What's going on? This is LightWave's way of saving system resources. If your object is made up of too many points and polygons, it can significantly slow down your system when you try to move or rotate it. This is because LightWave needs to redraw the object in real time on every frame. If it can't keep up, it stalls. The Bounding Box Threshold option allows you to set a limit of when LightWave has enough, so to speak. A basic 64 MB video card can have a bounding box threshold set to about 40,000. In other words, if your object is 35,000 polygons, it stays drawn all the time. If it's more than 40,000 polygons, it turns into a bounding box upon any movement. Set this one time, and you can leave it. Note that this does not affect rendering in any way.

General Options

If you press **o** for General Options, you see a tab with a tad fewer variables than are found in Display Options, but nonetheless important (**Figure 2.52**). You can use these settings to change LightWave's Input Device from a mouse to a tablet, and to set how your frame slider is viewed. By default, the LightWave timeline shows frames, but you can change this to show SMPTE (Society of Motion Picture and Television Engineers) time code units, film time code, or time in seconds. The most common setting is frames, as in frames per second.

LightWave also offers its own custom color picker, which you can turn on in this panel. When picking colors for backgrounds or surfaces, for example, this causes LightWave to calls up its own custom color picker rather than the one built into your Windows or Mac system software.

Finally, as mentioned previously, Layout offers multiple undo levels, which can be accessed in this category. Be careful with this. You can't undo everything; primarily, this command is useful for undoing keyframe motions. Let's say you add a few keyframes to your animation and decide you don't like them. Press Ctrl+z a few times to undo. Again, if you accidentally click Remove Texture in the Surface Editor rather than Use Texture, there is no undo for that! So be cautious.

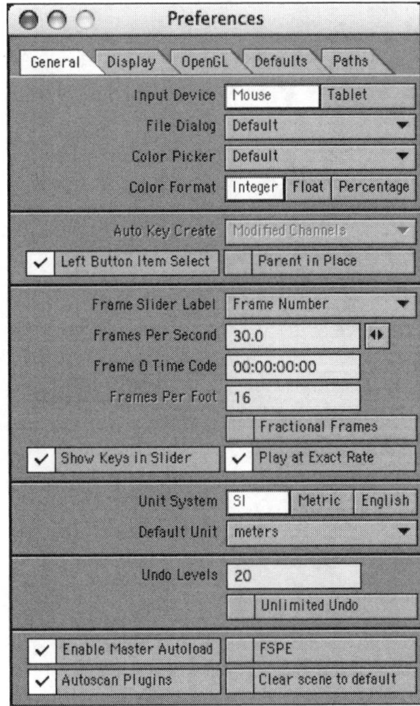

Figure 2.52 The General Options tab within the Preferences panel contains key settings for LightWave Layout.

The Next Step

This chapter has taken you on a brief overview of Layout and how it's organized. You have seen how the menus are arranged and how they work, and you took a tour of the tools available to you.

There is more to learn, and it's about to get more exciting. Soon, you'll be working completely on tutorials, learning firsthand the tools and how they work. What's more, you'll learn why you're instructed to do what you're doing. Subsequent chapters guide you through the basics of lighting, textures, and motions. Then, you'll take this knowledge into longer, full-blown projects.

Too often, books just click you through, leaving the figuring out up to you. *Inside LightWave v9*'s tutorials are designed to ramp you up from beginner to intermediate to advanced tutorials, offering clear explanations along the way.

We have a big journey ahead of us, so take a break, get some caffeine, and get ready to rumble!

Chapter 3

Understanding Basic Textures

The realism of 3D animation can be very eye-catching, and a good part of this realism comes from two key factors: lighting and surfacing. In your 3D career, professional or otherwise, you'll find that achieving this realism is a never-ending battle. Note, however, that this struggle is a blessing in disguise. You see, your mission, should you choose to accept it, is to continually better your work. Once you create a fantastic piece of 3D art, it's time to make a better one! Without forgetting that lighting setups play a big role in determining the realism of your scenes (we'll get to that in Chapter 4), this chapter will introduce you to LightWave's texturing capabilities. This chapter helps you take the next step with LightWave by introducing you to the powerful Texture Editor and teaching you how to navigate and use its interface. You'll learn about these topics:

- Using the Surface Editor
- Organizing surfaces
- Setting up surfaces
- Understanding the Node Editor

Note

The word *surface* is used three different but related ways in this chapter—to denote a specific group of polygons on the skin of a 3D object; to describe a collection of attributes (color, reflectivity, bumpiness, and so on) applied to a region to determine its appearance and behavior in a 3D scene; and as a verb ("to surface"), meaning the process of applying those attributes to polygon regions.

Perhaps one of the best things about LightWave's Surface Editor is that it puts everything you need to set up simple-to-complex surfaces in one location. The Surface Editor gives you control over everything you need to create a blue ball, an old man, or a modern city. If you are familiar with the Surface Editor in previous versions of LightWave, you'll find the updated Surface Editor works in much the same way but is definitely improved. Most notably, LightWave v9 brings a completely new way of texturing to the table with the Node Editor. **Figure 3.1** shows the Surface Editor interface at startup, with the Node Editor open.

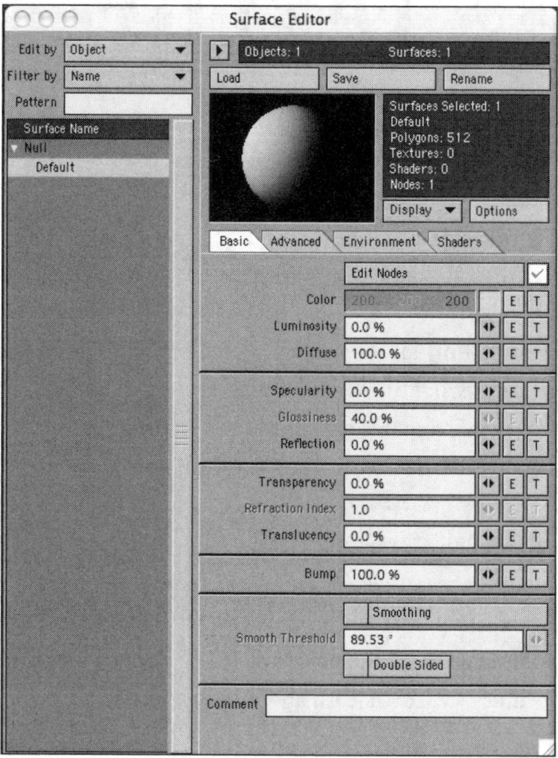

Figure 3.1 LightWave's Surface Editor at startup.

You'll get a brief introduction to the Node Editor in this chapter. Later, in Chapter 11 you'll be guided through node-based projects.

It's important to understand how basic texturing works, and the Surface Editor is the place to start. In early versions of LightWave, the process of setting up a model's surfaces began during construction, in Modeler. However, you could make only basic surface changes in Modeler—essentially, you could only select a group of polygons and name them as a surface. Defining and applying surface attributes such as color and shininess, or adding more complex textures, required moving over to Layout. In LightWave v9, the Surface Editor is accessible in both Modeler and Layout, so you can set up surfaces in either part of the program. This chapter applies to both Modeler and Layout, except for the section on the Node Editor, which is available only within Layout. The Surface Editor button is sixth from the top in Modeler (**Figure 3.2**) and fifth from the top in Layout (**Figure 3.3**, on the following page). The F5 key also opens the Surface Editor in both Modeler and Layout.

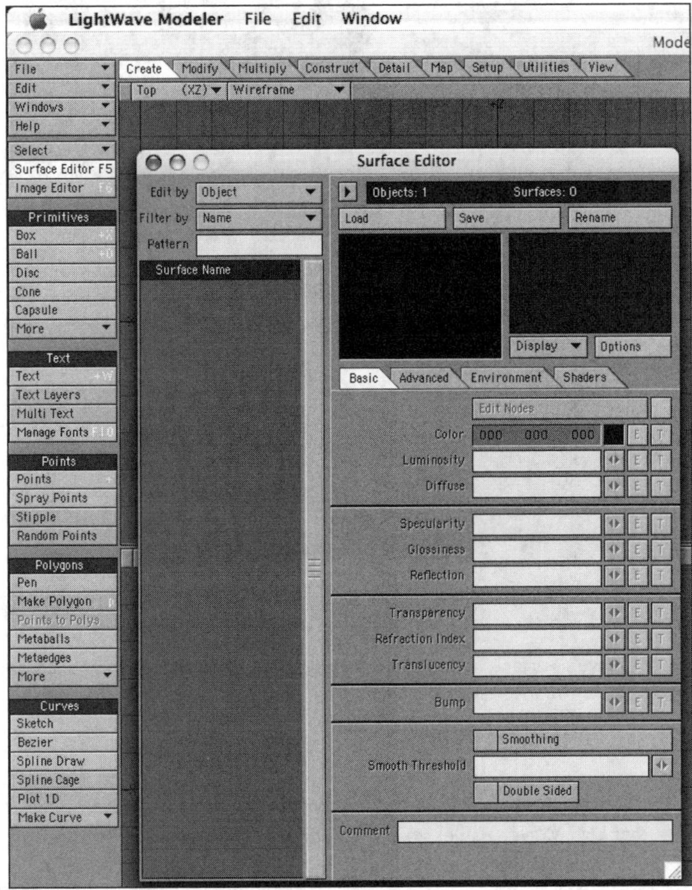

Figure 3.2 LightWave's Surface Editor can always be accessed at the top left in Modeler.

Note

Using the Surface Editor in Modeler does not give you access to LightWave's VIPER, discussed in detail later in this chapter, nor does it provide access to v9's powerful Node Editor. So for major surfacing projects, use the Surface Editor in Layout and take advantage of VIPER and the nodes. VIPER requires rendered data to work, and you can only render in Layout. VIPER uses information stored in LightWave's internal buffers for instant feedback. (Actually, it really works by magic. Honest!)

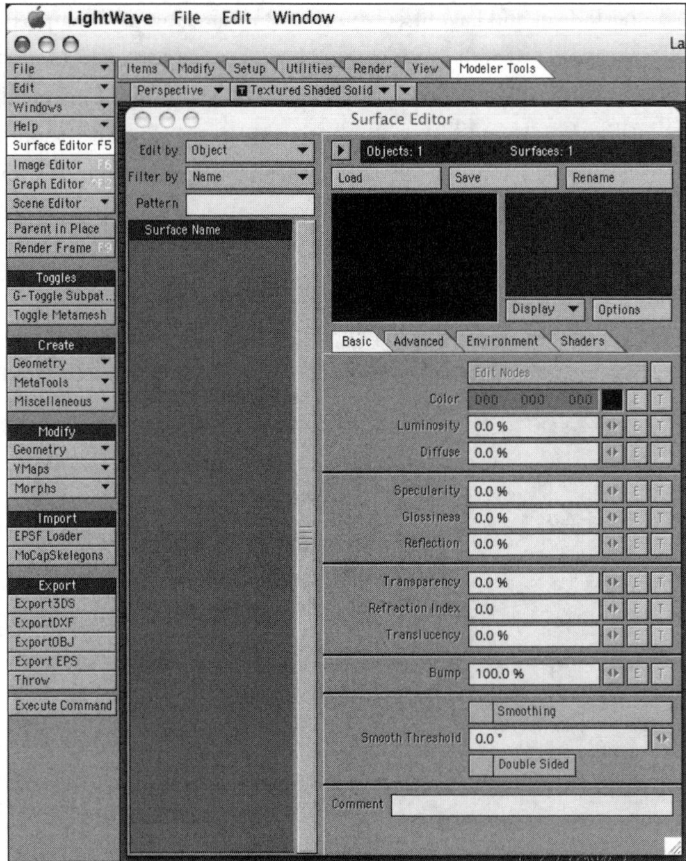

Figure 3.3 LightWave's Surface Editor is the same in Layout, and it's always accessed at the top left of the interface.

Note

Remember that LightWave enables you to completely customize the user interfaces of both Modeler and Layout. However, you should be working with the LightWave default Configure Keys (Alt+F9) and Menu Layout (Alt+F10) settings throughout this book.

Using the Surface Editor

As mentioned earlier, all of your surfacing needs can be accomplished within the Surface Editor, so you should be familiar with its features. This section guides you through its uses and helps you make sense of the panel. It's much easier than you might think! As with any task, you start by getting organized.

Organizing Surfaces

Good management of your 3D work, from models to keyframes to surfaces, will help you become a better artist. The Surface Editor makes it easy for you to manage your surfaces. **Figure 3.4** shows the Surface Editor as it appears when an object with multiple surfaces is loaded into Layout.

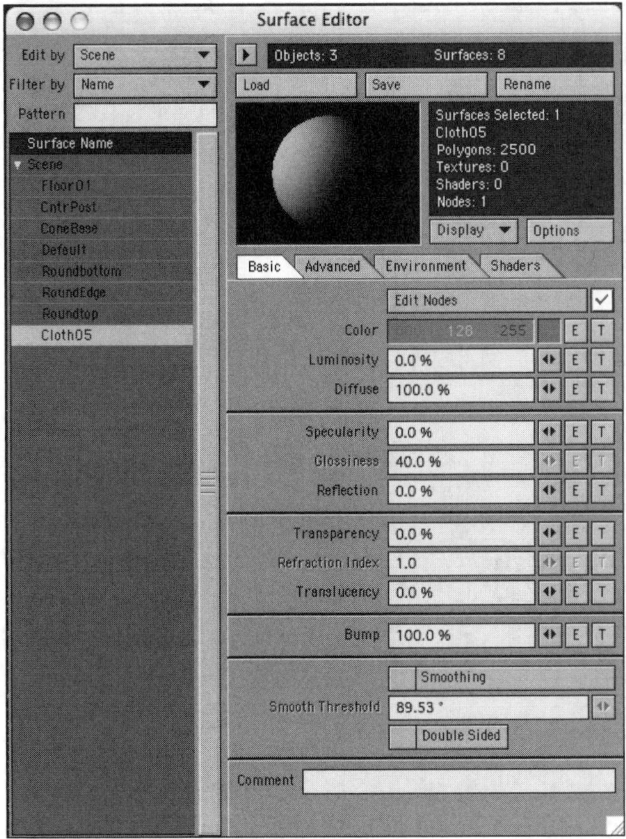

Figure 3.4 The Surface Editor enables you to manage your surfaces easily on an object or scene basis. You also can use filters to organize your surfaces by name.

When you open the Surface Editor after a scene has been loaded, the scene's surfaces are listed in the Surface Name list, as you can see in Figure 3.4. The Surface Name list contains information on every surface in the scene; by default it groups surfaces by object. Clicking the small triangle next to an object's name reveals a list of all the surfaces associated with that object. Note that by default, if an object is selected in Layout when you open the

Surface Editor, its first surface will be opened in the Surface Editor. **Figure 3.5** shows the same scene as Figure 3.4, but with a surface of the first object selected. Note that this setup is using the Edit By Object selection from the top left of the Surface Editor, which lists the surfaces with their appropriate objects.

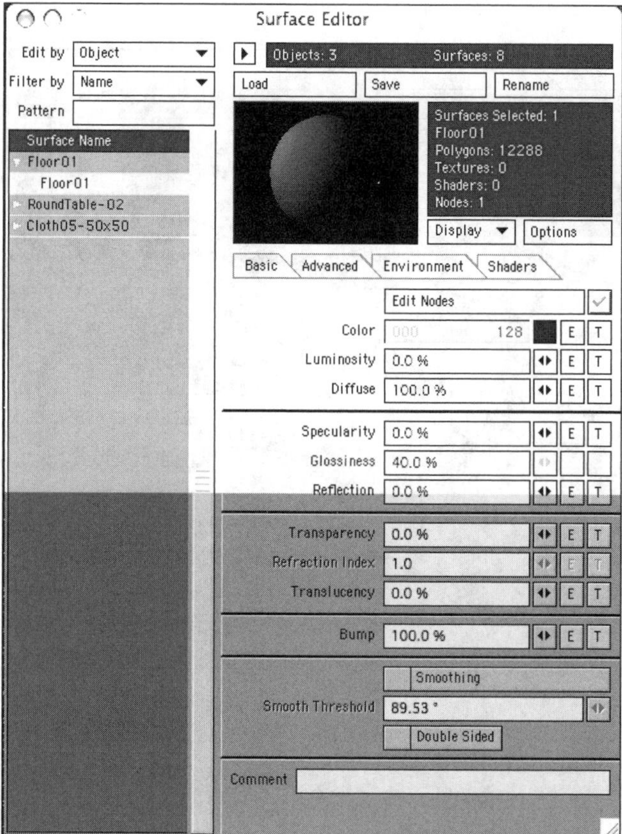

Figure 3.5 Surfaces are grouped with their respective objects if Edit By Object is selected.

When you click the small white triangle next to a surface name in the surface list, your surface settings, such as color, diffusion, or texture maps, won't be available until you click on a surface name. You must select one of the surfaces in the list before you can begin to work with it. When you select a surface, you see the surface properties change. Working with a hierarchy like this is extremely productive and enables you to quickly access any surface in your scene.

To save screen space, LightWave's Surface Editor allows you to collapse the Surface Name list by clicking the button marked with a right-pointing triangle above the Load button at the top of the panel. **Figure 3.6** shows the Surface Editor with the collapsed Surface Name list. Click the button again (it now points left) to expand the list, or choose a surface using the Surface drop-down at the top of the panel, as in **Figure 3.7**.

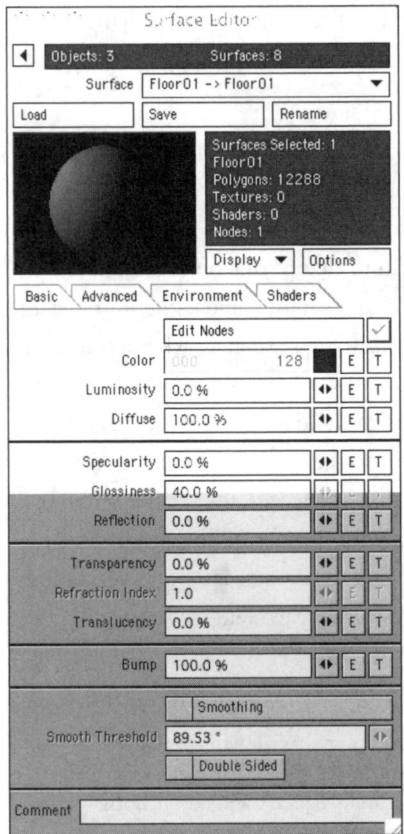

Figure 3.6 We clicked the small triangle at the top of the Surface Editor panel to collapse the Surface Name list.

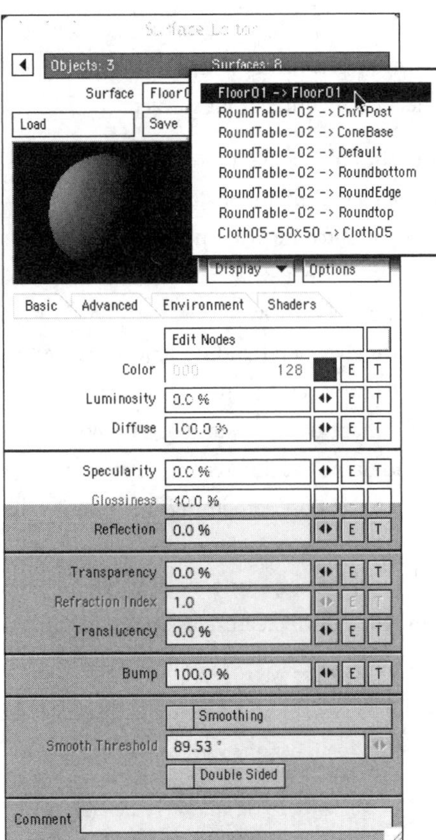

Figure 3.7 You select surface names in a collapsed view by using the Surface drop-down list.

Selecting Existing Surfaces

Take control of your surfaces, and you'll have a better time navigating through the Surface Editor panel. You have three modes to assist you in quickly selecting the surface or surfaces you want:

- Edit By
- Filter By
- Pattern

The Edit By drop-down, found at the top-left corner of the Surface Editor panel, has two options: Object and Scene. Here, you tell the Surface Editor to control your surfaces within just that, an object or the scene. For example, say you have 20 buildings in a fantastic-looking skyscraper scene, and eight of those buildings have the same surface on their faces. Using Edit By Object, adjusting that surface's characteristics would mean applying surface settings eight times; with Edit By Scene, changes to surface settings apply globally to all objects that contain that surface.

You should always be aware of the Edit By mode when you're tweaking surfaces. (LightWave remembers the Edit By setting when it saves models and scenes, so check each time you start the program to make sure you're in the mode you think you're in.) Applying and saving scene-wide changes when you only mean to change one object can have grim consequences. To avoid this, always make each surface name unique, and name your surfaces accordingly when building objects. For example, let's say you created a slick interior for an architectural render. In it, there are lots of white marble surfaces. (Why? Who knows, but that's what the client wanted.) Anyway, to properly isolate and organize those surfaces, you should name the different surfaces so they are unique to the geometry but familiar to you. You could choose something like "interior_marble_stairs" then "interior_marble_columns," and so on. This way, there is no confusion when using the Surface Editor. In addition, creating and naming surfaces properly in Modeler makes surfacing easier, and you end up using the Edit By feature as an organizational tool, not as a search engine.

Note

As a reminder, any surface settings you apply to objects are saved with those objects. Remember to select Save All Objects as well as Save Scene. Objects retain surfaces, image maps, color, and so on. Scenes retain motion, items, lighting, and so on. Both objects and scenes should always be saved before you render. This is a good habit to get into!

At the top-left corner of the Surface Editor panel, you'll see a Filter By listing. Here, you can choose to sort your surface list by Name, Texture, Shader, or Preview. Most often, you'll select your surfaces by using the Name filter. However, say you have 100 surfaces, and out of those 100, only 2 have texture maps. Instead of sifting through a long list of surfaces, you can quickly select Filter By and choose Texture from the drop-down list. This displays only the surfaces that have textures applied. You also can select and display surfaces that use a Shader, or you can use Preview. Preview is useful when working with VIPER because it lists only the surfaces visible in the render buffer image.

Note

You won't have access to the Edit By, Filter By, and Pattern sorting commands with a collapsed Surface Name list. Expand the list to access these controls.

Just beneath the Filter By setting, you have a field available to type in a pattern name. The Pattern field enables you to limit your surface list by a specific name, and it works in conjunction with Filter By. Think of this as an "include" filter. Only surface names that "include" the pattern will show up in the Surface Name list. For example, suppose you created a scene with 200 different surfaces, and 6 of their names include "carpet." Type **carp** into the Pattern field and your list will narrow to surfaces whose names contain that letter sequence—the six carpet surfaces, and possibly others related to carports, escarpments, carp (the fish), and so on. Continue typing the full word **carpet** and your list will probably narrow to just the six surfaces you seek. Handy feature, isn't it? Just remember that if you don't see your surface names, check to see whether you've left a word or phrase in the filter area.

Working with Surfaces

After you decide which surface to work with and select it from the Surface Name list, LightWave provides you with four commands at the top of the Surface Editor panel that are fairly common to software programs: Load, Save, Rename, and Display.

The first command, Load, does what its name implies. It loads surfaces. You can use it to load a premade surface for modification or application to a new surface.

The second command, Save, tells the Surface Editor to save a file with all the settings you've specified. This includes all color settings, texture maps, image maps, and so on. The ability to save surfaces lets you build an archive of useful surfaces you can use again and again.

Note

Storing surfaces in LightWave's Preset Shelf, which organizes samples in a visual browser, is often more useful than using the Surface Editor Save command. We discuss the Preset Shelf in detail later in this chapter.

With the third command, Rename, you can rename any of your surfaces—a habit you should get into from the start in your work with 3D surfaces. If you apply preset surface settings called "rusty_steel" to part of a Jeep model, for instance, you might rename that surface "jeep_rusty steel" to keep things orderly. With a few objects, surface names that really don't mean anything are fine. You could name a rusty surface "Lobesha" and you'd still be able to work without skipping a beat. But as your scenes grow, so do your objects and surfaces. This is why properly identifying surfaces is a good habit to practice right from the start. If you find that a surface name created in Modeler is not exact, you can use the Rename option to clarify or to give a more specific name to a surface.

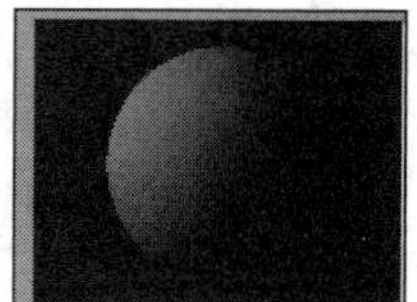

Figure 3.8 Use the Display window within the Surface Editor to preview the results of your surface-attribute settings.

The fourth command, Display, and its companion Options button determine what you see in the Display window at the top of the Surface Editor panel (the one that contains the sphere in **Figure 3.8**). As you assign and adjust surface attributes in the Surface Editor, you'll see them applied to that sphere, so you can gauge your progress without having to render your scene or model.

By default, the preview window (**Figure 3.9**) shows how your surface will look with all your surface settings applied collectively. You can use the Display drop-down to switch from this mode (which is called Render Output) to preview the effects of each attribute setting in isolation.

When you need to focus only on color, for instance, choose Color Channel from the Display drop-down (**Figure 3.10**) and you'll see only the color component of the surface, rather than a complex surface with specularity, bumps, and more.

You can change this display to any surface aspect you want to concentrate on, such as the transparency of the surface, glossiness, or reflection. If you are using a procedural texture for luminosity, for example, you might want to display just the Luminosity Channel. The choice is up to you. Most commonly, this value can stay at Render Output, but you have the control if you need it.

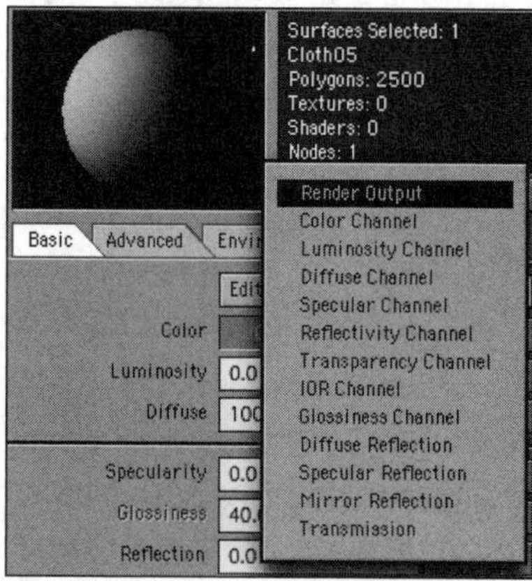

Figure 3.9 The Display drop-down list's default option, Render Output, shows the collective results of all surface-attribute settings in the preview window.

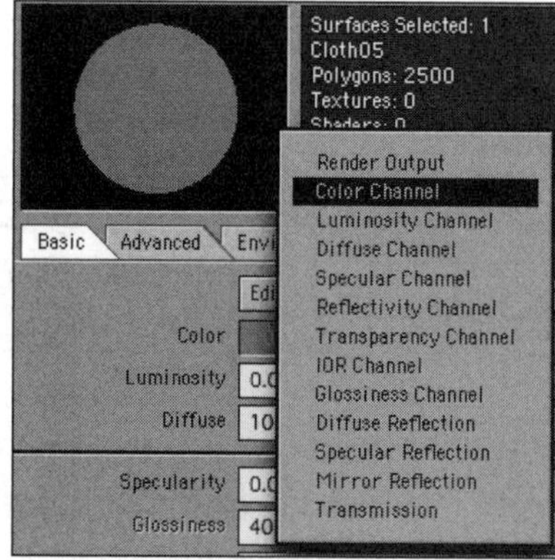

Figure 3.10 The same surface in the Display window with the Color Channel selected. Notice that the bump texture and specularity do not display as in Figure 3.9.

Note

Except for Render Output and Color, all the channels are grayscale, with pure white representing 100 percent of that surface attribute and black being 0 percent.

Click the Options button to the right of the Display drop-down to display a panel that lets you use a cube instead of a sphere as the preview object. The Options button also allows you to change the preview window's background and lighting effects.

The Preset Shelf

Building surfaces is fun, no doubt, but seeing results right away can be even better. The LightWave v9 Preset Shelf, a visual browser for surfaces, comes loaded with hundreds of prebuilt surfaces you can apply instantly to your models. (It also holds other types of preset attributes, such as camera handlers and environment handlers, along with surfaces).

To sample the prebuilt surfaces in the Preset Shelf, make sure the Surface Editor panel is open and choose Presets from the Windows drop-down, or just press **F8**. In the Surface Preset window that appears (**Figure 3.11**), click the Library drop-down (labeled WorkSpace, the default name for a new empty library) and choose any of the listed surface libraries.

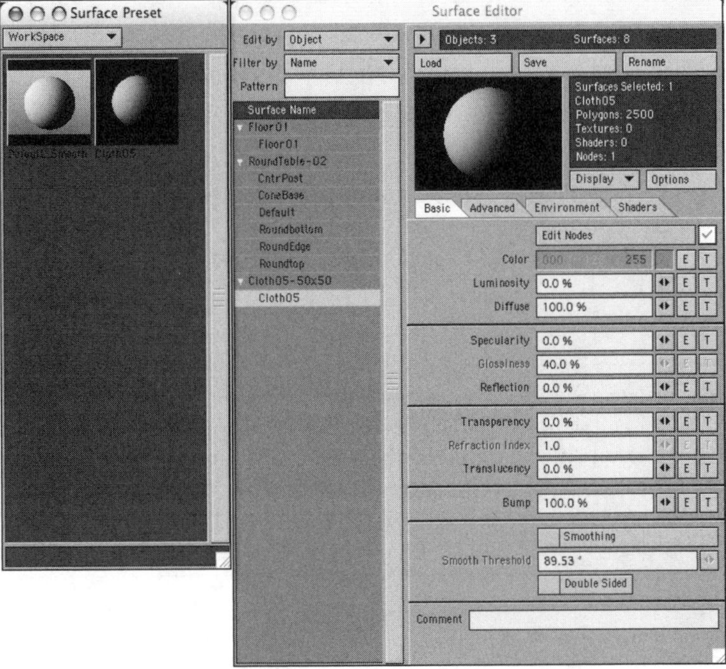

Figure 3.11 The Surface Preset panel is home to hundreds of readymade surfaces, as well as any you decide to add.

To copy a surface setting from the Surface Preset panel to another selected surface, first select the new surface name in the Surface Editor panel and then double-click in the preset surface in the Surface Preset panel. Also, double-click in the preview window to use the Save Surface Preset function. Be sure to have the Preset window open to see the saved surface. Double-click that surface preset to load it to a new surface. Similarly, you can right-click on the preview window for additional options such as Save Surface Preset. To save a surface to the Preset Shelf, double-click the Display window in the Surface Editor, and the currently selected surface will be added to the library.

Note

OK, if you've opened the Preset Shelf and don't see anything, make sure the Surface Editor panel is open. If it is, you may have moved LightWave's Presets folder, which belongs inside a folder named programs, in your main LightWave application folder.

If you right-click in the Surface Preset panel, you can create new libraries for organizing your surface settings. You also can copy, move, and change the parameters.

Setting Up Surfaces

The main functions you use to set up and apply surfaces in the Surface Editor occupy four tabs: Basic, Advanced, Environment, and Shaders (**Figure 3.12**). Each controls specific aspects of a selected surface. This chapter introduces you to the most commonly used tabs, Basic and Environment.

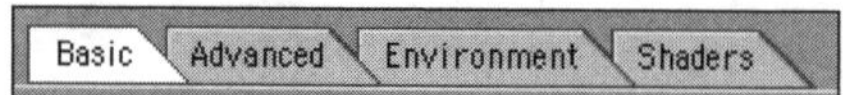

Figure 3.12 Surface Editor controls are organized in four tabs.

Note

At this point, it's a good idea to assign LightWave's Content Directory to this book's DVD if you haven't already. Insert this book's disc into your computer. Either install the project files, or click the Cancel button if the DVD auto-starts in order to work from the DVD. Press **o** in Layout to access the General Options tab of the Preferences panel. At the top, click Content Directory and set it to the Projects folder on the DVD. Now, LightWave knows where to look for this book's tutorial files.

Basic Tab

Aptly named, the Basic tab is home to all your basic surfacing needs. It's here that you start most surfacing projects (**Figure 3.13**).

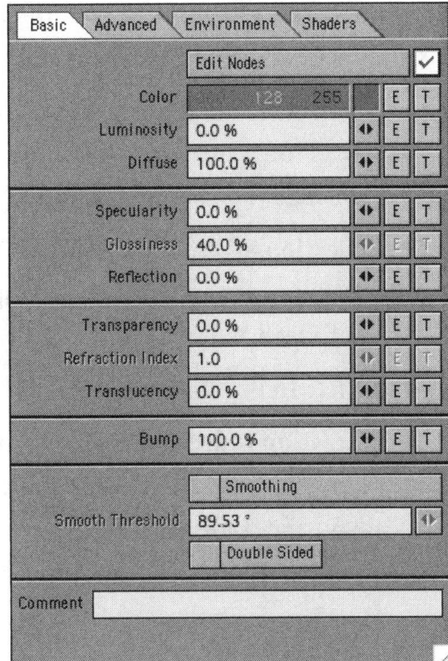

Figure 3.13 The Basic tab in the Surface Editor is home to the most commonly used surface settings.

Within the Basic tab, you'll find the following controls arranged from top to bottom:

- **Edit Nodes**. This new feature in LightWave v9 allows you to control surfaces in an entirely new way. You would click this button and use it instead of the basic Surface Editor. This feature will be introduced shortly, and you'll see it used later in the book as well.
- **Color**. Here, you can set the color of the selected surface by entering values from 0 to 255 for each of three RGB (red-green-blue) or HSV (hue-saturation-value) color channels. Right-click in the number field to toggle RGB and HSV modes. Click and hold your mouse button on a channel's numerical setting and slide the mouse right to increase the value or left to reduce it. Or just click the swatch to the right of the numerical field to open the standard color picker for your operating system.

  To the right of the Color control, as well as the remaining controls in the Basic tab, you'll find buttons marked E and T. Recall that E stands for Envelope—a function that enables a given surface-attribute value to vary over time. T stands for Texture, a function that lets you vary an attribute's setting spatially, over the area of the surface. We'll cover envelopes and textures later in the chapter.

The rest of the controls in the Basic tab all work the same way. Each contains a number field you can click and type into in order to enter a setting. To the right of each number field is a LightWave adjuster called a mini-slider. To use one, click on it, and holding down the mouse button, move your mouse left or right to change the setting value. The range of each mini-slider generally covers the observed values for that attribute in natural materials. Many controls let you type in values outside those naturally occurring ranges to achieve special effects.

- **Luminosity**. This controls the brightness, or self-illumination, of a surface.
- **Diffuse**. This is the amount of light the surface receives from the scene. You'll learn more about this shortly.

- **Specularity**. This value specifies the amount of shine on a surface. High specularity settings are appropriate for surfaces such as glass, water, and polished metal.
- **Glossiness**. Often confused with specularity, glossiness determines how shine spreads on a surface. A surface with high glossiness exhibits tight highlights or "hot spots"; this option is dimmed if specularity is 0.
- **Reflection**. If you want a surface to reflect light, you specify how much with this control; a mirror would have a high reflection setting. When you want to control what's reflected in a reflective surface, you'll use the Environment tab.
- **Transparency**. This controls the degree to which you can see through a surface.
- **Refraction Index**. This value controls the amount that light bends as it passes through a transparent surface. Material with an index of 1 doesn't bend light at all; the index for glass is about 1.5, and for water, about 1.3. This control is dimmed on surfaces with zero transparency.
- **Translucency**. This value specifies the degree to which light can pass through a surface from behind, as it might a thin leaf or piece of paper.
- **Bump**. This controls a function that makes surfaces look irregular. It gives an illusion of surface bumpiness, but doesn't actually cause any elevation or depression of the surface geometry. The default setting is 100%.
- **Smoothing**. This shading routine, which is activated by default, makes surfaces consisting of polygons appear smooth. Uncheck the box to turn it off.
- **Smoothing Smooth Threshold**. When smoothing is turned on, this specifies the sharpest angle between polygons that LightWave should try to smooth out. Generally, the default of 89.5° is too high. A typical beveled surface on a logo should have a threshold of about 30°.
- **Double Sided**. Check the box next to this option if you want selected polygons to exhibit surface attributes on both their front and back sides. Ideally, you don't want to use this unless you have to. All models created in LightWave Modeler have their surfaces facing in one direction. This option fakes it and forces the surface to face the opposite way as well.
- **Comment**. Use this field to enter notes on your surface as reminders or to include more detailed descriptions. This is a great feature when you're sending objects to colleagues and clients.

Environment Tab

Reflect for a moment about reflection. (Wow, that was lame!) But if you look at an object and see a reflection, its contents aren't determined by the object itself but by its surroundings, right?

In a 3D setting, surface reflections often include other models within a scene, and those reflections typically are created via a process called *ray tracing*, which generates reflections and shadows based on the location of objects and light sources within a scene. Reflections can also include images of objects that don't exist as models in a scene; reflections of "off-stage" objects or backdrops are created as 2D images, which you then overlay onto the reflective surface, a technique known as *reflection mapping*.

The Reflection attribute in the Basic tab controls how reflective a given surface will be; settings in the Environment tab (**Figure 3.14**) control what appears in reflections generated by the surface. When you're dealing with a transparent surface, the tab provides comparable control over how the surface refracts objects placed behind it in a scene.

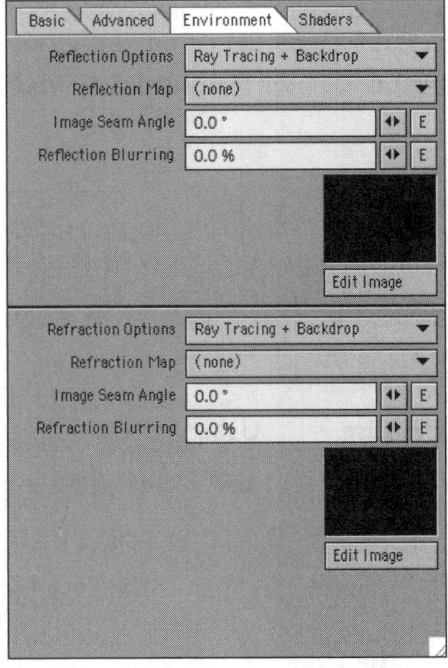

Figure 3.14 The Environment tab gives you access to reflection and refraction controls.

On the Environment tab, you can assign the following:

- **Reflection Options**. The type of reflection applied to a surface: spherical, ray trace, or backdrop
- **Reflection Map**. What image will be reflected
- **Image Seam Angle**. Where the seam of a reflected image will appear
- **Refraction Options**. The type of refraction applied to a surface, either spherical or ray trace
- **Refraction Map**. The image file used (if any) for refraction
- **Image Seam Angle**. Where the seam of a reflracted image will appear
- **Reflection Blurring**. The amount of blur your reflections will have
- **Refraction Blurring**. The amount of blur your refractions will have

The best way for you to get a feel for using the Surface Editor and the Basic and Environment tabs is to try them out for yourself. An excellent way to observe the effect of the settings you choose is to use LightWave's VIPER feature.

Working with VIPER

VIPER stands for Versatile Interactive Preview Render, and it gives you a previews of certain types of adjustments you can make to your scene in Layout, such as volumetric settings and surface settings. It's important to point out that because VIPER does not do a full-scene evaluation, some aspects of your surfacing are not calculated, such as UV mapping and shadows. This means that VIPER is limited in what it can show. However, it is very useful for most of your surfacing needs, such as specifying color and texture. As you adjust your surfaces, VIPER shows you what's happening and how the surface will look in your scene, without the need to re-render the whole scene. VIPER is available in Layout only.

Note

VIPER's ability to preview surface attributes and other effects extends only to changes made using LightWave's built-in editor panels. VIPER cannot display effects or changes made using third-party plug-ins such as FPrime from Worley Labs (www.worley.com).

Exercise 3.1 Using VIPER with Basic Surfacing

To get an idea of how useful VIPER is, try this quick tutorial.

1. Start Layout, or if it's already running, save any work you've completed so far and choose Clear Scene from the File drop-down menu (keyboard equivalent: Shift+n).

Note

You don't always need to clear the scene before loading a scene. Simply loading a scene overrides your current scene. This two-step process familiarizes you with the available tools and Layout's workflow.

2. Choose Load Scene from the Load drop-down and open Planet_Anim.lws (located in the Gradients folder, inside the Scenes folder provided to you with the NewTek LightWave v9 content). You'll see a green blob.
3. Press **F5** to open the Surface Editor panel.

   You'll use VIPER to preview changes made in the Surface Editor, which must be open for VIPER to render and display the surfaces you set.

4. Click Layout's Render tab, and then click the VIPER button in the Utilities tool category. When you do, the VIPER preview window opens and the Enable VIPER button (in the Render tab's Options tool category) is activated automatically (**Figure 3.15**). (Press **F7** in any Layout tab to accomplish the same thing.)

   When you click VIPER in the Render tab or press **F7** to open the VIPER window, VIPER is enabled automatically. Repeating either of those operations closes the window, but leaves VIPER active until you toggle it off using the Enable VIPER button—something you may want to do before running full frame or scene renders.

Figure 3.15 The VIPER command is found in Layout only, on the Render tab.

> **Note**
>
> Here's the lowdown on the two VIPER-related buttons in Layout's Render tab. The Enable VIPER button makes VIPER pay attention to the rendering buffer, which allows it to preview surface changes in its Display window. The VIPER button opens and closes, the VIPER window. Disabling VIPER with the toggle button allows you to leave the VIPER preview window open but frees up system resources to speed frame and scene renders.

5. With the VIPER window now open, click the Render button at the bottom of the VIPER panel. An error appears stating that VIPER has no surface data to render. Click OK to close the error window.

This is normal. For VIPER to work, it needs you to render a frame so that it can store information from a buffer. Otherwise, VIPER has no idea what's in your scene.

6. Click OK to close the error window, and then press **F9** to render the current frame.

   This renders the current frame and stores the information in LightWave's internal buffer and lets you see surface-setting changes through VIPER.

7. After the frame renders, press the Escape key (**Esc**) to close the Render Status window. If it's in your way, move the Image preview window to one side. Then, in the VIPER window, click the Render button again. Do you see anything? The render you just created is now appearing in the VIPER window. **Figure 3.16** shows the VIPER window once it has loaded and stored render settings such as Specularity, Diffuse, and Color. The previews in the VIPER window and Surface Editor's preview window differ somewhat because Surface Editor's preview uses a standard perspective or orthographic view of your object, while VIPER previews the scene from the viewpoint of your selected camera (thereby mimicking your intended results more closely).

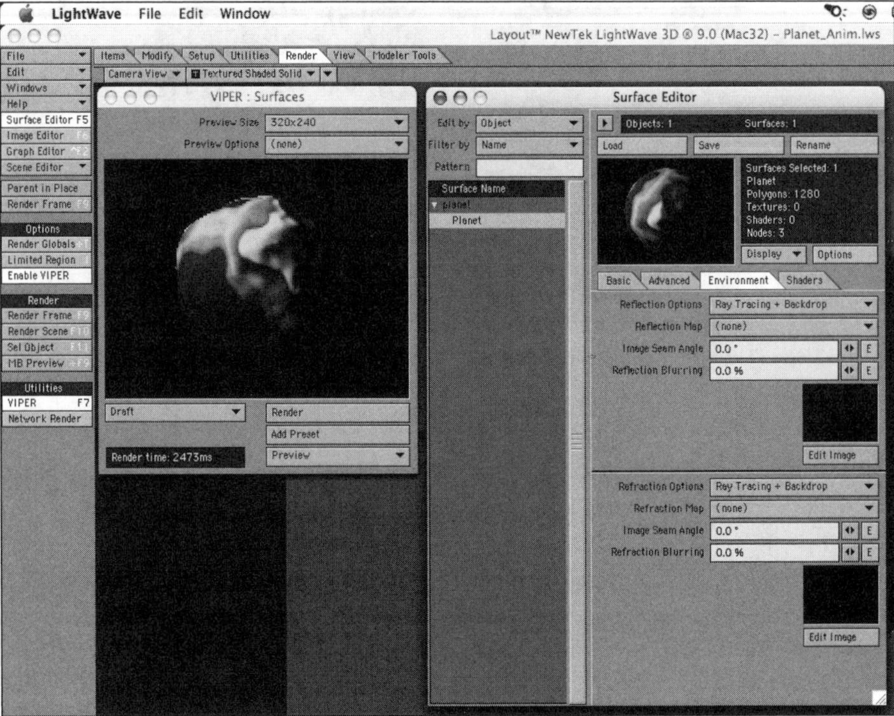

Figure 3.16 Pressing **F9** on the keyboard renders the current frame and lets you preview surface changes through VIPER.

Note

It doesn't matter with a simple "scene" like this, but for more complicated scenes, you might want to disable VIPER while rendering the frame, then turn it back on before continuing.

8. In Surface Editor, choose Planet from the Surface Name list. It's the only surface in the scene, and it belongs to the only loaded object, called planet. (To see the surface name, you may need to click the white triangle to the left of the object's name.)
9. To quickly see VIPER's interactivity, click the mini-slider to the right of Diffuse in the Surface Editor's Basic tab. Hold down the mouse button and slide your mouse to the left to take the value down to 0, and then release the mouse button. You'll see the VIPER window update, to make the planet appear black. What you did was tell the surface not to receive any light from the scene, essentially turning off the lights for that surface.

Note

You may think to yourself, "But Dan, I didn't set up any lights for this scene, so how can the object receive or not receive light?" Remember, Grasshopper: Every default LightWave scene has one camera and one light. Ah ha!

10. Now, restore the Diffuse value to 100% and continue.

    You'll see various surface settings appear throughout the commands on the right, on the Basic tab.
11. Click the T button to the right of the Color control to open the Texture panel for the planet object (**Figure 3.17**).

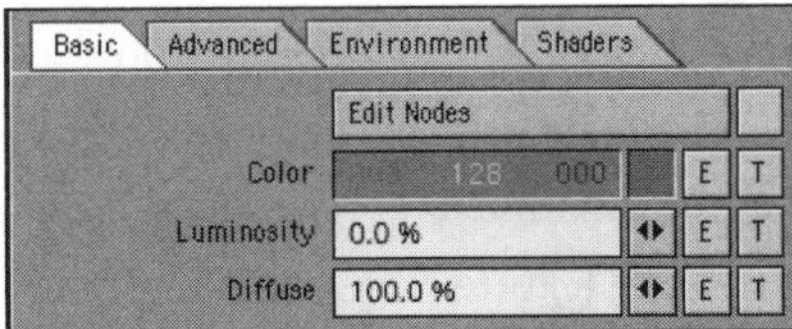

Figure 3.17 Clicking any of the T buttons throughout LightWave, including the Surface Editor, opens the Texture Editor.

Note

If the T button to the right of the Color control is dimmed, uncheck the Edit Nodes box located immediately above it.

You'll see that the Layer Type at the top of the commands is set to Image Map—a setting that lets you apply images to a surfaces and much more, as we'll see later in the book. For now, change the Layer Type to Procedural Texture, as in **Figure 3.18**.

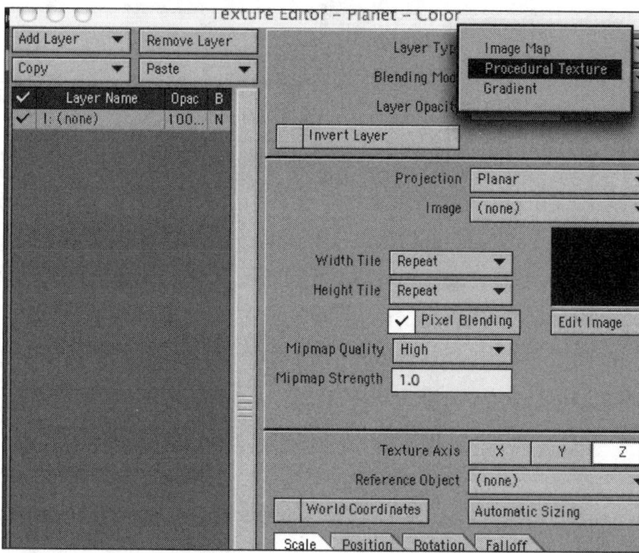

Figure 3.18 The default Texture Editor Layer Type is Image Map. Change this to Procedural Texture instead.

Procedural textures have no seams, and are often just what the doctor ordered for organic-looking surfaces. They vary surface attributes via mathematical *procedures*; each *procedural type* yields a different effect. By changing procedure settings within the Texture Editor and combining procedural textures in various ways, you can create a limitless range of organic surfaces.

The Procedural Type is set to Turbulence, a variation of fractal noise that has been used by LightWave animators for years. Adding Turbulence as the Procedural Type to the current surface color of the planet, which is a bright green, adds variances to the surface.

The Blending Mode is set to Normal, which tells LightWave to add this procedural texture to the selected surface. (Other Blending Mode settings are used when you apply multiple textures to a surface; they determine how textures combine with each other.)

The Layer Opacity is set to 100%, telling LightWave to use this procedural texture to the fullest extent.

12. Make sure the VIPER window is open and visible to the side of the Texture Editor.

    If VIPER is not open, click the VIPER button (not Enable VIPER) in Layout's Render tab. You rendered the scene in step 5, and LightWave remembers that by storing the data in its internal buffers.

13. With the Texture Editor and VIPER open, you can make changes to surface settings and see your changes in real time. **Figure 3.19** shows the VIPER panel.

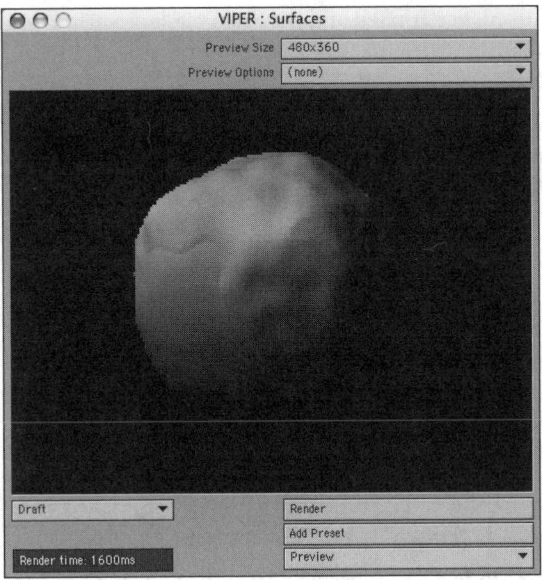

Figure 3.19 Once you've made a render of a frame (by pressing **F9**), VIPER can now display the render, and you can make surface changes in the Texture Editor (among other places) and see them in real time.

Note

The VIPER preview window has default size of 320×240 pixels. In Figure 3.19, we've expanded it to 480×360 pixels using the Preview Size drop-down. Adjust the preview window to suit your screen size. When you do so, there's no need to re-render your image. However, if you change scene lighting or object position, or add or remove objects in the scene, you need to re-render by pressing **F9**.

14. Make certain that the Texture Editor is still open (you got to the Texture Editor by clicking the T button next to Color in the Surface Editor).

    You can see from the VIPER preview window that the beautiful green surface is now sort of dusty-looking. This is because the basic default procedural texture was applied when you chose Procedural as the Layer Type.

15. Because the procedural turbulent noise texture was a little too heavy, change some of the parameters, such as Size, found at the bottom of the Texture Editor panel on the Scale tab. Click and drag the X, Y, and Z values and watch VIPER redraw your image with the surface changes.
16. Experiment with the other procedural type settings such as Underwater or Crumple. From there, try to use other procedurals and adjust their properties as well. **Figure 3.20** shows the Texture Editor and VIPER with a default Procedural Texture of Turbulence applied and the Scale made smaller.

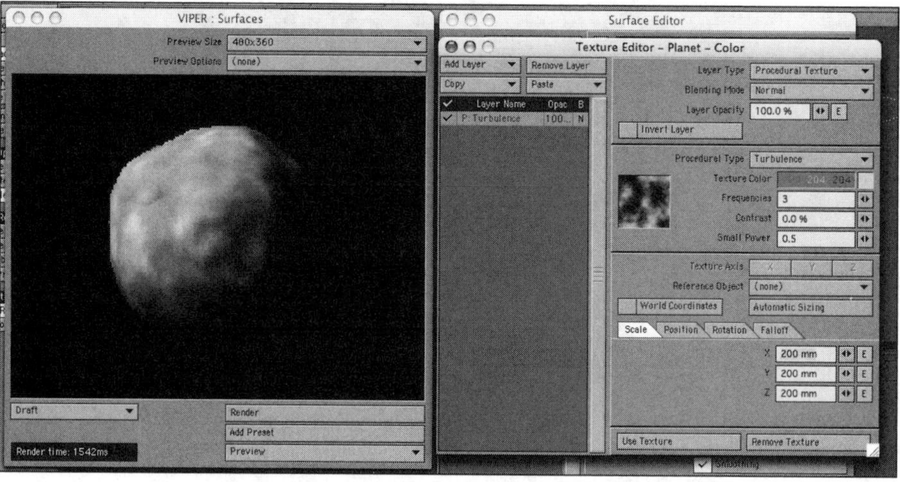

Figure 3.20 Changes to texture-property values such as Color, Scale, and Contrast are easy to see with the VIPER window open.

To the left of the Texture Color setting in the Texture Editor window is a small square display. This area shows your procedural pattern. The base background color for the procedural is black. When combined with a dark texture color, this makes a hard-to-see swatch. To remedy this, right-click on the swatch and set a new background color. In addition, you can left-click on the Display window and drag the preview around. Doing this helps you see more of the procedural pattern. **Figure 3.21** shows a close-up. Mac users with single-button mice, remember to Cmd-click for right-mouse button commands.

Figure 3.21 You can change the base background color for your procedural texture display by right-clicking in the Display window.

VIPER will quickly become one of your best friends when you're working with LightWave Layout because it saves you time. Not only that, many of you may not be mathematical wizards and do not care to calculate every value within the surface settings. Using VIPER can answer many of your questions when it comes to surfacing because you can instantly see the results from changed values. It's guaranteed that during your practicing, you'll utter a loud "Oh, *that*'s what that does!" from time to time.

VIPER Tips

Here are a few more VIPER tips before you move on:

- Never trust VIPER as your final render. If something looks odd, always make a true render (by pressing **F9** or **F10**) to check final surfacing.
- You can use VIPER to see animated textures by selecting Make Preview from the Preview drop-down list in the VIPER window.
- Press **Esc** to abort a VIPER preview in progress.
- Click Draft Mode in the VIPER window to reduce redraw time (and render quality).
- Clicking on a particular surface in the VIPER window instantly selects it in the Surface Editor's Surface Name list. This is a great feature and can save you a lot of time on complex textured scenes.
- VIPER is available only in Layout, not Modeler.
- To move beyond VIPER, visit www.worley.com and check out the FPrime plug-in. This killer LightWave plug-in allows real-time previews of just about everything in Layout, including reflections, ray-tracing, and transparency.

Common Surface Settings

To take you even further into the LightWave Surface Editor, try Exercise 3.2.

Exercise 3.2 Applying a Reflection to a Surface

You may sometimes have a project that requires you to use a building, vehicle, machine, toilet, or something completely different from what you're used to working with. This could be an object that you've created yourself, purchased, or downloaded from public archives on the Internet. Follow these steps to apply a simple reflection to a surface:

1. Be sure to save any work you've completed thus far. Start Layout, or if it's already running, choose File > Clear Scene.

2. From the DVD that accompanies this book, load the Basic scene from the Chapter 3 projects folder in \Projects\Scenes\CH3\. To load the scene, go to the Items tab, and then on the left side of the interface, click the Scene button under the Load category, as in **Figure 3.22**.

   Here's a very handy tip: You can hide all the toolbars and menus in Layout and work with just the keyboard and mouse. Press **d** on the keyboard to access the Display Options tab of the Preferences panel. Select Hide Toolbar (see **Figure 3.23**). Now when in Layout, you can access the Surface Editor (or any other panel) by Ctrl+Shift +clicking in the Layout window (using either the left or right mouse button).This pops up the list of commands and menus you've just hidden away (see **Figure 3.24**)! Press **d** again to access the Display Options panel to unhide the toolbar. Now that you know where things are located, just use Alt+F2 to hide and unhide the toolbar. You can also open the Surface Editor quickly by pressing **F5**.

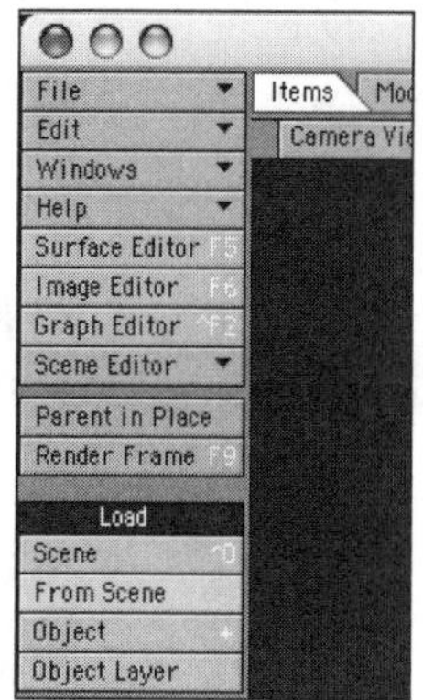

Figure 3.22 Load a basic scene into LightWave to set up some surfaces.

Figure 3.24 Display Load Scene and other valuable commands in this contextual menu by Ctrl+Shift+ clicking in the Layout window,.

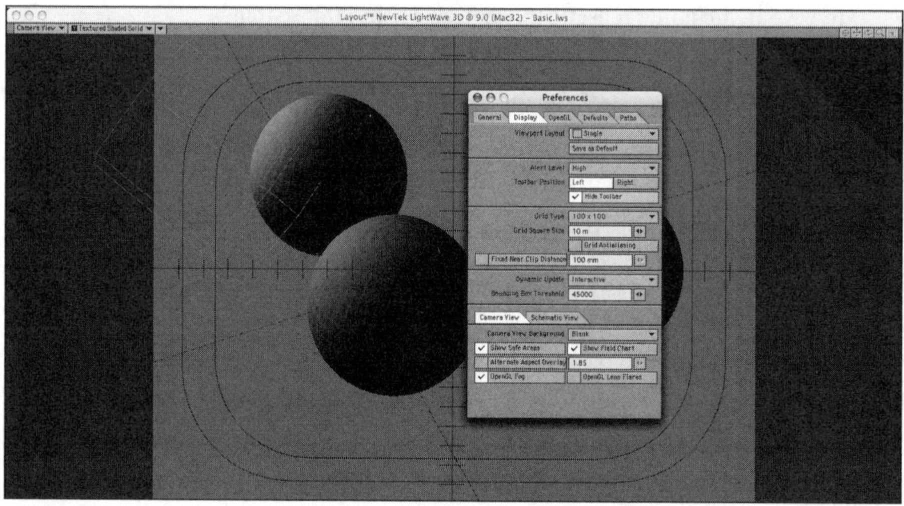

Figure 3.23 You can use the Display Options tab to hide Layout's toolbars.

Note

Remember that you should be using LightWave's default interface configuration for all tutorials in this book. To make sure you are, press Alt+F10 on the keyboard to call up the Configure Menus panel. Click the Default button from the Presets drop-down list at the top-right side of the panel's interface. If it is dimmed, you already have the default interface set. Click Done to close the panel.

3. After the scene has been loaded, click the Surface Editor button on the left side of the interface to open the Surface Editor panel.

   You can see that by default, the object name appears in the Surface Name list.

4. Clicking the small triangle to the left of the BasicBalls filename opens and closes the Surface Name list for that particular object.

   All the surfaces associated with the BasicBall object appear, as shown in **Figure 3.25**.

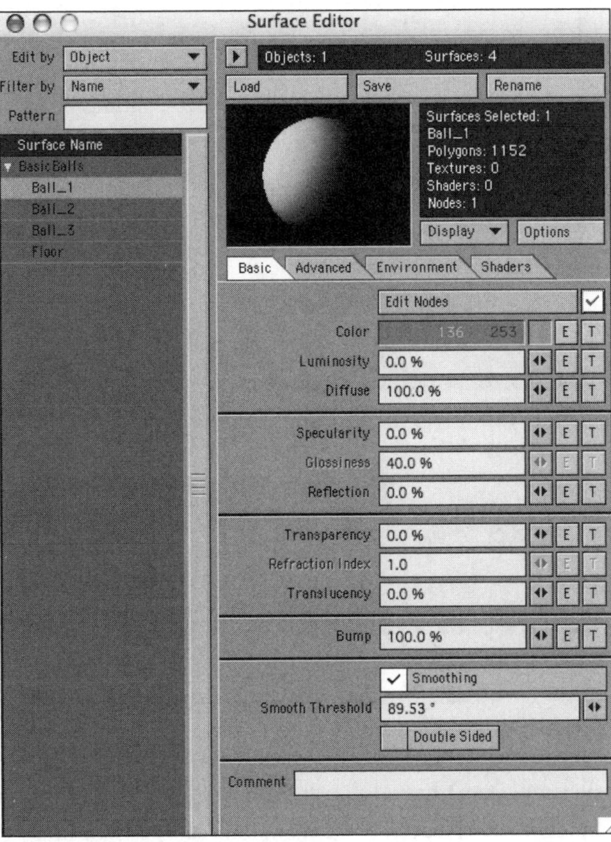

Figure 3.25 When an object is selected in Layout and the Surface Editor is opened, the selected object's surfaces are listed.

Note

If you have more surfaces than you do space in the Surface Name list, a scroll bar appears. Simply click and drag to view the entire surface list.

5. LightWave enables you to resize the Surface Editor panel simply by clicking and dragging on the edge of the panel. Click and drag the bottom edge to stretch out the panel. Conversely, you can collapse the panel by clicking the small triangle centered at the top of the interface, and you can simply select your surfaces from the Surface drop-down list.

Note

Naming your surfaces is half the battle when building 3D models. If you name your surfaces carefully, you'll save oodles of time when you have many surface settings to apply. Organization is key! You name your surfaces in Modeler, as explained in previous chapters.

6. In Layout, make sure you're in the Camera view. You should be already, because the scene was saved this way before you loaded it. If not, switch to Camera view by selecting the drop-down list at the top-left side of the viewport title bar. Then, select the Backing surface from the list within the Surface Editor.

   When a surface is selected, the name appears in the information window to the right of the surface preview. The number of polygons associated with that surface also appears. In this case, the selected surface, Ball_1, has 1,152 polygons, as shown in **Figure 3.26**. You'll also see a display at the very top of the surface panel that indicates the number of objects and surfaces in the scene.

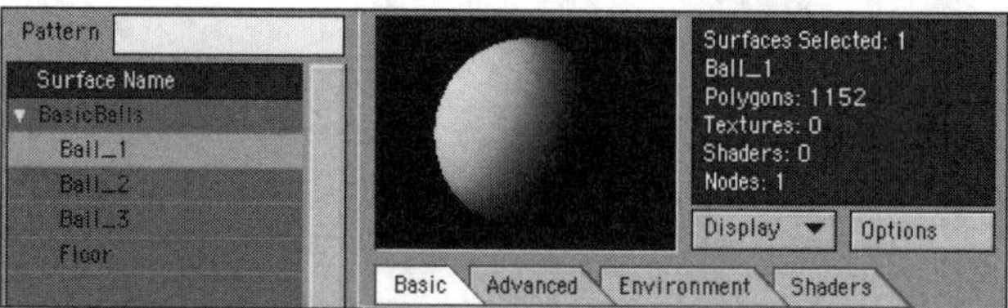

Figure 3.26 Summary information on the selected surface is displayed at the top right of the Surface Editor panel.

7. Because you simply can't have dull balls, you need to shine them up a bit. Make them look pretty. You can even make them look like glass, or brass! First, you want the color of the glass to be a soft grayish blue color, so set the RGB value to 180, 180, 200.

There are a few ways to set a color to the glass surface of the watch. Under the Basic tab within the Surface Editor, you'll see the Color listing at the top. There is an RGB value indicator with a small color sample. This small area offers you a lot of control:

- Left-clicking on the small, colored square next to the RGB values makes the standard system color palette appear. Here, you can choose your color in RGB (red, green, blue), HSV (hue, saturation, value), or from custom colors you may have set up previously.
- Right-clicking and dragging on the small colored square next to the RGB values in the Surface Editor changes all three values at once. This is great for increasing or decreasing the color brightness.
- Clicking the left mouse button on either the red, green, or blue numeric value and dragging left or right increases or decreases the color value. You will instantly see the small color square next to the RGB values change. You'll also see the sample display update.
- If you're not keen on setting RGB values and prefer HSV values instead, rest easy. Clicking once on the RGB values with the right mouse button changes the selection to HSV (**Figure 3.27**).

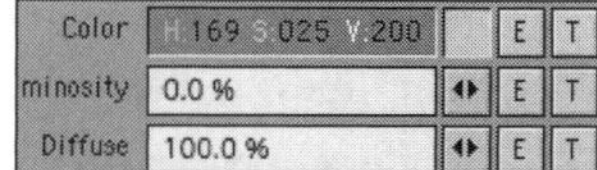

Figure 3.27 Right-clicking on any RGB value in the Surface Editor's Basic tab changes the color-selection tool to HSV mode, and vice-versa.

Note

HSV represents hue, saturation, and value. It describes colors directly by their overall color, unlike RGB values, which are three discrete subcolors. HSV is another way to change color values. However, you might have more flexibility using RGB values.

- Make sure you're using the display preview options as you like them. Right-click on the surface preview window to show more controls and options (**Figure 3.28**).

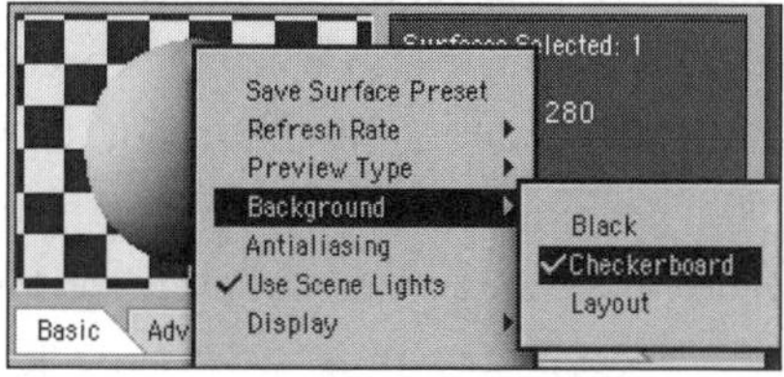

Figure 3.28 Right-clicking on the surface preview window in the Surface Editor offers more control over how the surface is displayed. Here, you can set a checkerboard background, which is great for transparent surfaces.

With the Glass surface set to the soft gray color, you still need to see what's under it! You'll need to make the glass transparent and shiny. This next tutorial discusses surfacing the glass while introducing you to the rest of the Surface Editor. Remember that you will create many more surfaces throughout the chapters in this book, and that this is a brief introduction to just some of the features.

Exercise 3.3 Surfacing Glass

1. Make sure VIPER is opened and set off to the side of the Surface Editor so you can see your changes in real time. You can press **F7** to open it.

   With the Ball_1 surface still selected as the current surface in the Surface Editor, go down the list of options and set each one accordingly.

2. Make sure that the value of Luminosity (the option just underneath Surface Color) is 0.

   Luminosity is great for objects that are self-illuminating, such as a lightbulb, candle flame, or laser beam. Note though that this does not make your surface cast light unless radiosity is applied, under the Global Illumination tab. This is in the Render Globals panel on the Render tab.

3. Set the value of Diffuse to roughly 60% to tell the glass surface to accept 60% of the light in the scene.

   The Diffuse value tells your surface what amount of light to pick up from the scene. For example, if you set this value to 0, your surface would be completely black. Although you want the glass to be black, you also want it to have some sheen and reflections. A 0 Diffuse value renders a black hole—nothing appears at all.

4. Set the value of Specularity to 90%.

   Specularity, in simple terms, is a shiny reflection of the light source. 0% is not shiny at all, whereas 100% is completely shiny.

   When you set Specularity, you almost always adjust the glossiness as well. Glossiness, which becomes available only when the Specularity setting is above 0%, is the value that sets the amount of the "hot spot" on your shiny (or not-so-shiny) surface. Think of glossiness as how much of a spread the hot spot has. The lower the value, the wider the spread. For example, **Figure 3.29** shows two spheres, one with a low Specularity setting of 5% and Glossiness set to 15%. The result resembles a dull surface, like plastic.

On the other hand, the sphere to the right has a Specularity setting of 75% and Glossiness of 40%. The result looks closer to a shiny glass surface with reflections turned on. A higher Glossiness setting gives the impression of polished metal, or glass in this case. There will be a lot of surfacing ahead in this book for you, such as glass, metal, human skin, and more.

5. Now, back to the surfacing your balls. Set the value of the Glossiness for the Ball_1 surface to 70%.

   This gives you a good, working glass surface for now.

6. Set the value of Reflection for the Ball_1 surface to 40%.

   Most glass and clear plastic surfaces generally reflect their surroundings. In this case, the balls are placed on a simple set composed of just a few polygons. Three basic spotlights illuminate the scene, along with one set light.

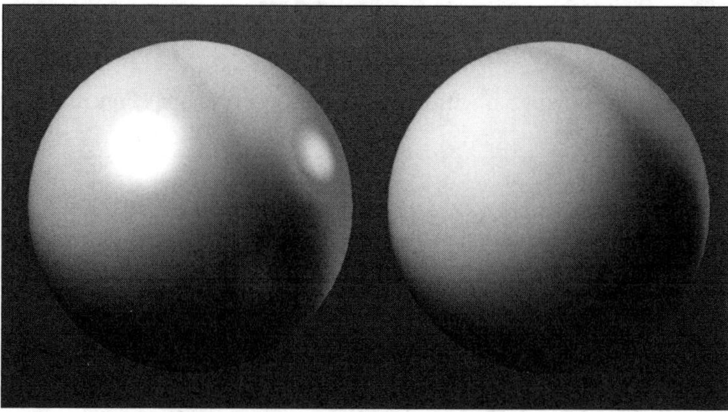

Figure 3.29 The sphere on the right has a low Specularity and a low Glossiness setting, which results in a surface that looks dull. The sphere on the left with a high Specularity and high Glossiness setting looks more like glass.

Note

It's a good idea when setting reflections to make the Reflection value and the Diffuse value add up to roughly 100%. The current surface has Diffuse at 60% and Reflection at 30% for a total of 90%. This is not law, but just a guideline. If your Diffuse setting is 100% and you add a reflection of 40% or more, you'll end up with an unnaturally bright surface.

7. To see the image underneath the glass ball surface, it needs to be transparent. Set Transparency to 90%. There's one more option—Smoothing. You use this setting to smooth the surface.

Note

A shader is an algorithm that affects the surface properties of an object. It can change color, reflection, smoothing, reflectivity, and more. Shaders also can add special effects like procedural brick textures or fractal noise. The Smoothing setting employs a *Phong shader*. Developed by Bui Tuong-Phong in 1975, this shader works well on surfaces that emulate plastics, metals, and glass. Later when we get to the Node Editor, you'll learn about LightWave v9's other cool shaders.

8. Because the ball_1 surface is round, the Smoothing option is necessary. With objects that are more round, this will take away any visible facets in the geometry. Turn Smoothing on and set the value to 30.

Note

Flatter surfaces are sometimes simply "too" smooth, and create odd renders. Reducing their smoothing thresholds can fix that.

9. Click the Environment tab within the Surface Editor panel (**Figure 3.30**).

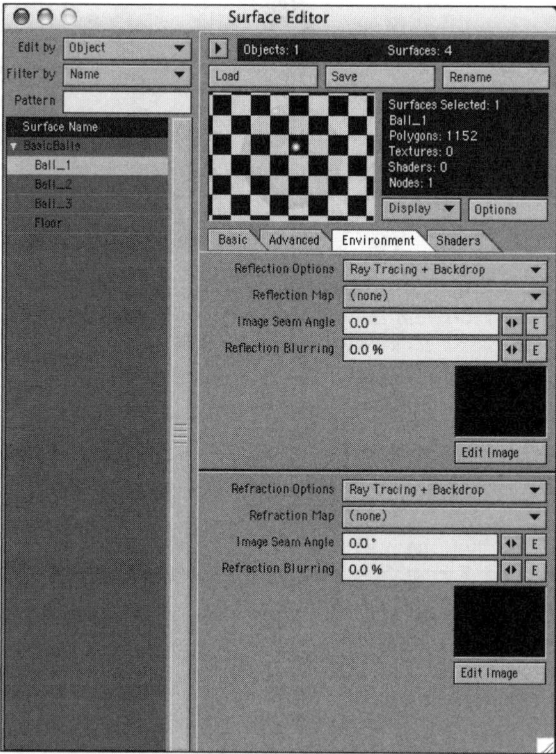

Figure 3.30 The Environment tab is where you set up reflection options in LightWave.

10. Make sure Reflection Options is set to Ray Tracing + Backdrop, if it's not already.

    This tells the surface to reflect what's around it (in this case, an essentially bare set). If other objects were in the scene, they would be reflected too.

    Because LightWave can calculate reflections, setting a reflecting image can often help create a more realistic surface. You'll do this for the metal ball surface (Ball_2). Glass, on the other hand, should reflect its surroundings, so Ray Tracing is used.

    For LightWave to be able to calculate and draw the reflections for the glass surface, you need to tell the render engine that you want it to calculate reflections.

11. In Layout, click the Render menu tab at the top. On the left side of the interface, click the Render Globals button to open the panel. Make sure Ray Traced Reflections is checked on the Render tab, as in **Figure 3.31**.

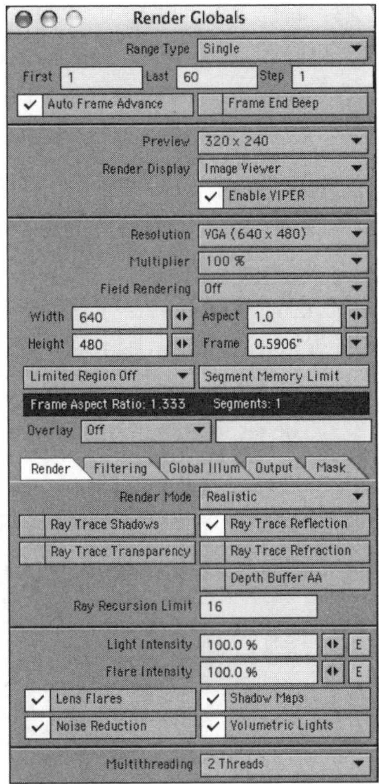

Figure 3.31 For Ray Trace Reflections to work for a surface, you must tell LightWave's renderer to calculate them.

12. After you have this turned on, press **F9** for a single frame render. While you're in the Render Options panel, make sure Render Display is set to Image Viewer to see a pop-up of your rendered image. **Figure 3.32** shows the render.

    What's that? It looks like a bubble? Not really glass? Figure 3.32 shows the render with the

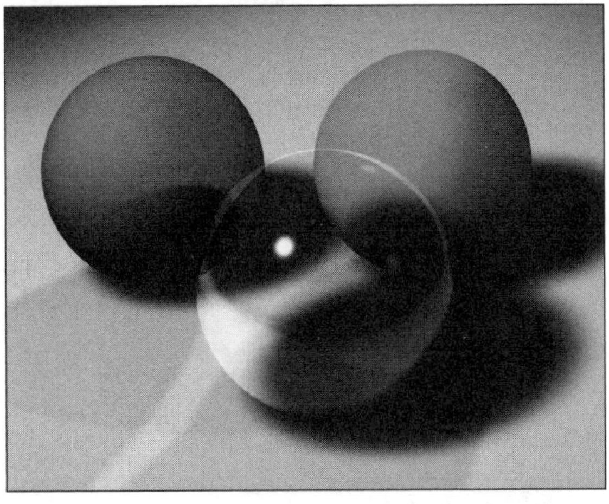

Figure 3.32 The Ball_1 surface is sort of looking like glass, but not quite. There's a problem with the surface!

surface changes to the Ball_1 surface, but for some reason, it's not quite right. If you look carefully, you can see right through the glass ball. You can see the hot spots from the specularity and glossiness, and even though you have a transparent surface set for the glass, it is still casting a shadow. There's one more thing to set to make this look more like glass.

13. Make sure the Ball_1 surface is still selected in the Surface Editor, and back on the Basic tab, set Refraction to 1.33. This tells the rays of light to bend, or distort, as they pass through the transparent surface. 1.33 is a general value often used for glass.
14. On the Render tab, back in the Render Globals panel, make sure that the Ray Trace Refraction option is selected. Press **F9** again to render the current frame. The result is shown in **Figure 3.33**.

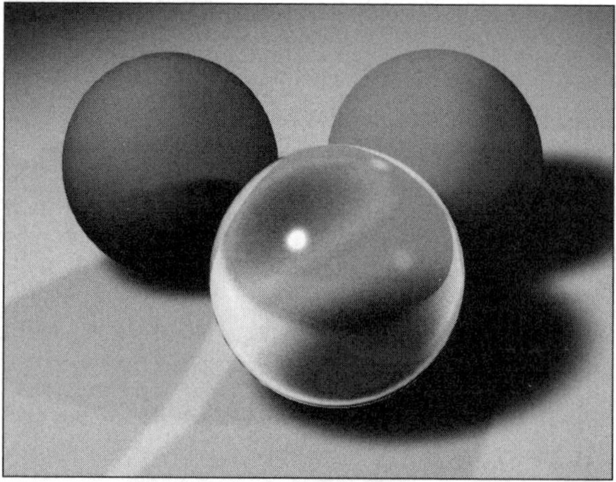

Figure 3.33 For glass to look like glass, light needs to refract. With ray traced refraction turned on in the Render Globals panel, and a refraction level of 1.33 set in the Surface Editor, the Ball_1 surface looks like a glass ball. Can you see your future?

15. Choose Save All Objects from the Save submenu in the File drop-down. This saves the surfaces you've just set. Then, choose Save Scene from the same Save submenu to save the lighting, ray trace settings, and so forth. Now it's time for the metal!

Creating Metallic Surfaces

With any object you create, even a few balls, you might think it would be difficult to match the real-world properties of metal. Believe it or not, this is easy to do within LightWave v9. The right amount of color, specularity, glossiness, and reflection helps create the visual effect. You've created the transparent glass surface, so how about something completely different? In this particular instance, a metal surface could work very well. This same metal can be applied to almost any metallic surfaces you create—from logos, to machines, to fasteners—with only minor variations. This section takes you through the steps required to create a metal surface.

Exercise 3.4 Creating a Metallic Surface

1. In the Surface Editor, select the Ball_2 surface. Set the color to a soft gray to simulate a silver metallic surface. Try setting all three RGB values to 180.
2. Set Diffuse to 70%, Specularity to 50%, and Glossiness to 40%.
3. A reflection is needed, so set Reflection to 25%.

   At this point, the surface doesn't look much different than when you loaded it other than a color change. Remember that other factors, such as surroundings and lighting, play a role in surfacing but you still need to apply the reflection environment. **Figure 3.34** shows the surface settings.

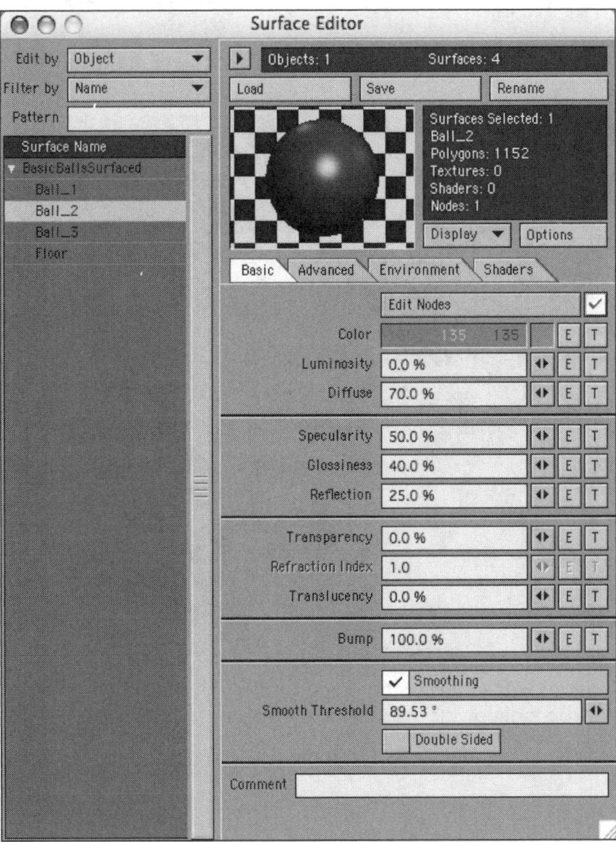

Figure 3.34 Metal surfaces begin with basic color properties and a low gloss setting.

4. With the Ball_2 surface still selected, click the Environment tab to the right of the Basic tab.
5. Set Reflection Options to Ray Tracing + Spherical Map, as in **Figure 3.35**. This tells the surface to reflect not only what's around it but an image as well.
6. For the Reflection Map option, click the drop-down and select Load Image, as in **Figure 3.36**. Load the foil image from this book's DVD.
7. Guess what? That's about it for this surface! Press **F9** to see how it looks. **Figure 3.37** shows the new surface applied to the backing.

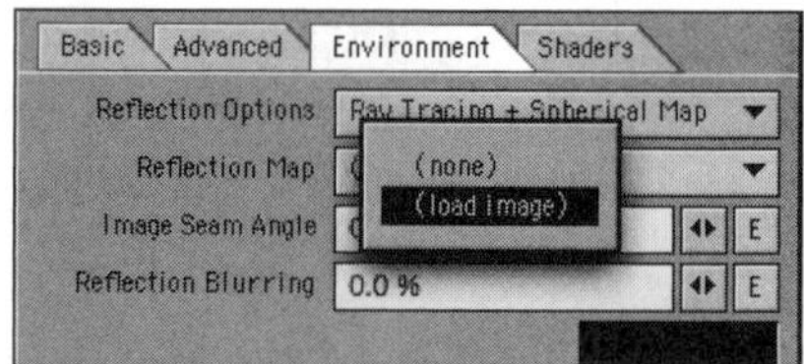

Figure 3.35 The Ray Tracing + Spherical Map setting is a great way to make realistic metallic surfaces.

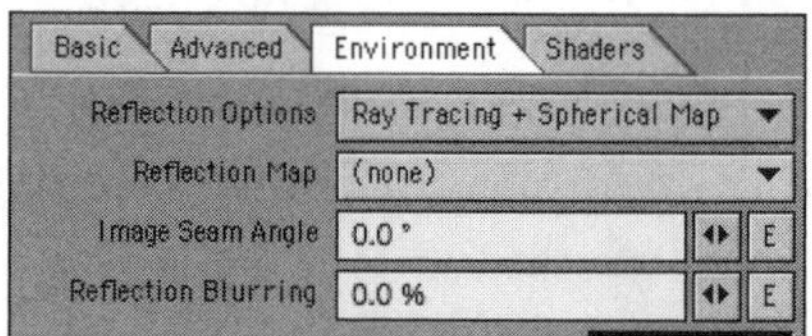

Figure 3.36 You can load an image directly from the Reflection Options in the Environment tab.

It's subtle, but effective. Now, you'll copy this surface to another surface.

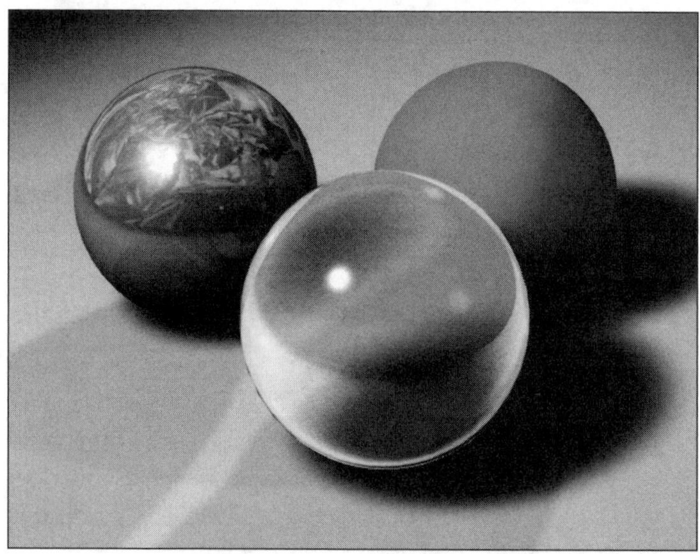

Figure 3.37 Adding ray-traced reflections and a reflection image to a gray surface helps sell a metallic look for the area under the glass.

8. Click back to the Basic tab, right-click on the Ball_2 surface (Mac people, Ctrl-click!), and select Copy, as in **Figure 3.38**.

   You can also open the Presets from the Window drop-down in Layout and then double-click the preview display window in the Surface Editor to save this preset surface.

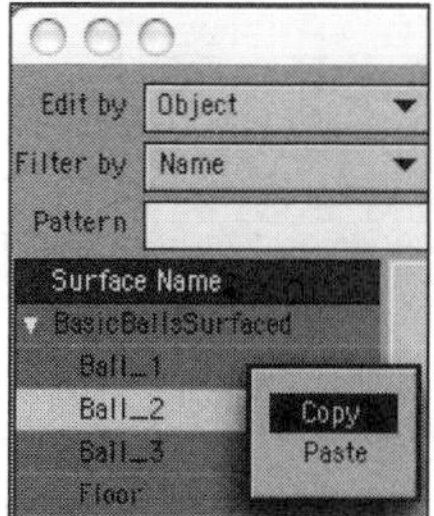

Figure 3.38
Right-clicking on a surface name in the surface list enables you to quickly copy all its settings.

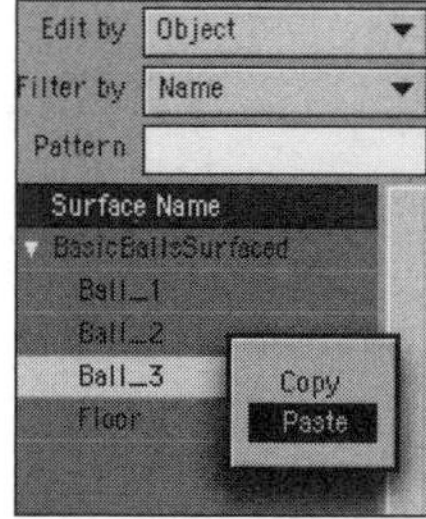

Figure 3.39
Right-clicking on a surface name in the surface list enables you to quickly paste what you've just copied.

9. As you might have guessed, you can now select another surface and paste what you've copied. Select the Ball_3 surface, right-click again (Mac people, you know what to do!), and paste the copied surface. **Figure 3.39** shows the operation.

10. Feel free to vary the color and reflection amount on the Ball_3 surface. By copying and pasting the surface from Ball_2, you've saved yourself a lot of work and helped keep the surface values consistent. Note that you do not have to right-click and copy the surfaces each time you want to paste them. Copy once, paste many! Just remember that if you accidentally copy something else, you need to go back and copy the desired surface again. **Figure 3.40** shows the render with the new surfaces applied, using a different color and different reflection image.

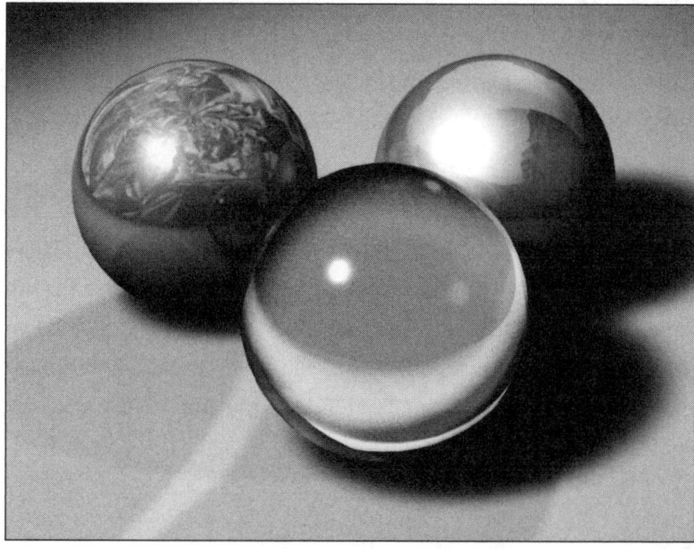

Figure 3.40 You can paste the metallic surface to other surfaces to quickly copy settings.

Note

While holding the Shift key on your keyboard, you can select the first surface in the Surface Name list, then select the last surface in the list and you'll select all of the surfaces. You can then change surface properties for all of them at the same time.

From this point, you can work with any other object surfaces you like, and apply similar metals, glass, or your own combination of both. You can even select all but the glass surface and change the basic gray color to a yellow-orange. Render again, and you've now made gold. All the other surface settings still apply.

A few final thoughts on surfacing with reflections: Many factors come into play, such as the glancing angle of the camera, light, and shadows. The angle of the camera in the previous steps could have been moved to reveal more of the reflection. You can also try changing the metal reflections to just a spherical map in the Environment tab, rather than using the Ray Tracing + Spherical Map setting. This tells the surface to reflect only the image.

Note

Remember that simply saving a LightWave scene file does not save your surfaces. You must save your object in addition to saving your scene if you want to keep the surfaces applied.

You'll often come across situations where you need to use the same surface settings on multiple surfaces, such as in the previous exercise. With so many variables being set within the Surface Editor, keeping track of identical surfaces could be a problem. Not to mention, you might want a quick reference to the changes you've made to the current surface. This is where the Preset Shelf comes in.

Working with the Preset Shelf

You may have noticed that the simple scene you've been working with is composed of more than just one surface. Two of the surfaces, Ball_2 and Ball_3, are the same because you copied and pasted the settings. Instead of redoing all the surface parameters, or constantly copying and pasting with the right mouse button as you did, you can use the Preset Shelf to save and apply the same surface and then simply make any necessary changes to the surface properties.

Note

Loading and saving surfaces works as well, yet the Preset Shelf shows you a small thumbnail of the surface. Nice!

From the Windows drop-down list in Layout, select Presets. You can also just press F8. The Preset Shelf defaults to a tall thin column (**Figure 3.41**) that appears when you access the Surface Editor, but it can be resized.

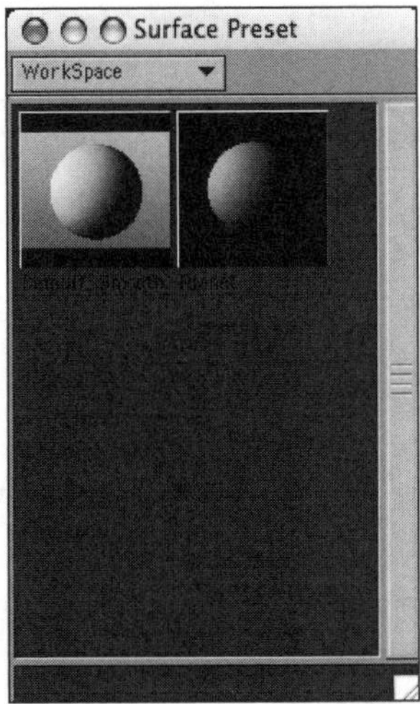

Figure 3.41 By default, the Preset Shelf opens as a tall window, but it can be resized to fit your screen.

If you don't care for the tall narrow look of the Preset Shelf, you can click and hold one of the corners of the panel and resize it to your liking. A good option is to stretch the shelf out across the interface from left to right and move it to the bottom of the screen. Because all of your Preset Shelf samples remain in the shelf, you also can open up the panel to fit your entire screen. The choice is yours.

Note

Using LightWave with a dual-monitor system is great when setting up surfaces. Simply set the Preset Shelf wide open on the additional monitor to maximize preset visibility and workflow real estate. If two monitors are beyond your needs, at least consider a bigger single screen. Monitors have become even cheaper, and it might be a good time to invest in a nice 24-inch-wide model—or go for broke and get the 30-inch-wide monitor from Apple or Dell. Go ahead, you know you want to. Dan said it's OK.

Exercise 3.5 Saving a Surface

If you set up a surface you'd like to keep, you can simply save it in the Preset Shelf. To do this, follow these steps:

1. Make sure the Preset Shelf is still open. Then in the Surface Editor, select the Ball_2 surface. Double-click on the display preview at the top of the Surface Editor.

   You'll see that surface sample appear on the Preset Shelf (**Figure 3.42**).

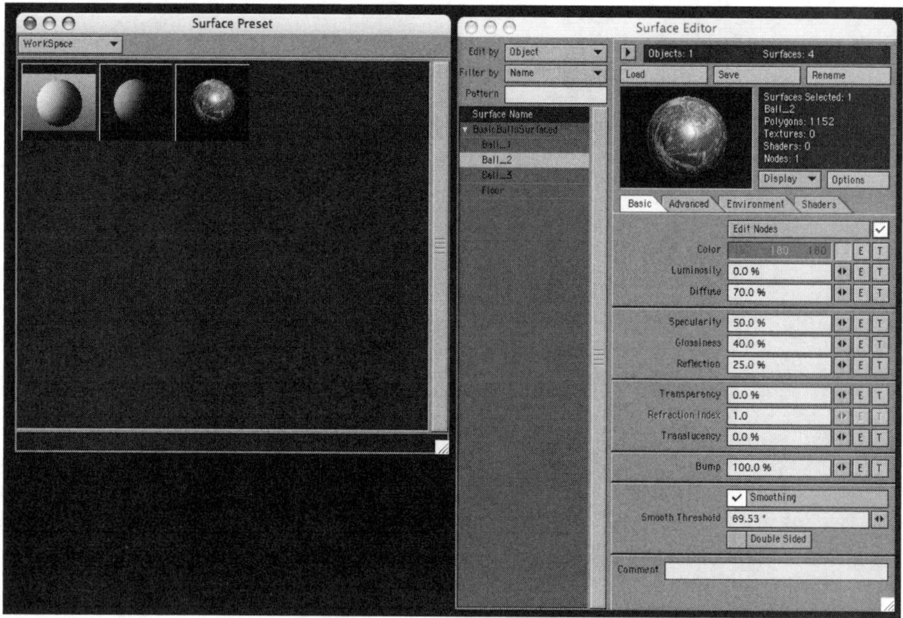

Figure 3.42 Double-clicking the display sample in the Surface Editor, shown on the right, instantly adds those surface settings to the Preset Shelf, shown on the left.

Note

Although double-clicking the sample display is one way to add a surface to the Preset Shelf, you can also right-click on the preview window and select Save Surface Preset. You can also just press the **s** key while in the Surface Editor. Finally, you can click Add Preset in the VIPER window.

2. Select the second surface you need to apply surfacing to, such as the Ball_3 surface, in the Surface Name list.
3. Go back to the Preset Shelf and double-click the sample you recently added.

A small window appears, asking you to load the current settings. This is asking if you want the settings from the Preset Shelf sample to be applied to the currently selected surface in the Surface Editor. In this case, you do.

4. Click Yes, and all the surface settings are applied from the preset to the Ball_3 surface. For any small changes, adjust as needed in the Surface Editor.

By using a preset to copy and paste a surface, you'll find it's much easier to change one simple parameter, such as reflection, than it is to reset all the surface and reflection properties again.

As you can see from the previous examples, it's not too hard to create simple, good-looking surfaces. The next step is to continue surfacing on your own, using the few simple parameters outlined in the previous pages. Color, diffuse, specularity, glossiness, and reflection form the base for nearly all the surfaces you create. After you have a handle on setting up the basics, read on to learn about the Node Editor. Now, there's a lot more to learn about surfacing, such as texture mapping, bump mapping, and using procedurals for computer-generated textures. You'll do this more throughout the projects in this book, but the information here should have you up and running with the basics of the Surface Editor.

Introduction of the Node Editor

New to LightWave v9 is the Node Editor. You could, if you chose, use the Node Editor in place of the Surface Editor 100% of the time. That said, the Node Editor isn't really meant to completely replace the Surface Editor. There are times when set up a quick surface with the Surface Editor as you've done with the exercises in this chapter is simpler and more practical than firing up the Node Editor. With that said, the Node Editor can help you take your textures and surfaces to the next level.

LightWave's surfacing has been a layer-based system up until now. This system is still in place, but with the Node Editor, the rules have changed. Node-based texturing is found in many high-end 3D applications, because it allows you to create custom shaders, mix and match various surface properties, and much more. Unlike a layer-based system, the node-based system is like a network. Everything can connect and interact, from a simple surface to advanced materials. This next section will get you up and running with the Node Editor. Later in the book, you'll create more advanced node-based surfaces. One last thing before the project: Although we're discussing the Node Editor here in the chapter about surfaces, you should know that the Node Editor also exists for volumetric lighting and deformations. Of course, you'll use these within the project chapters as well.

Note

While the Surface Editor is available in LightWave v9 Modeler, the Node Editor is not. You can only access the Node Editor in Layout—even more reason to perform all surfacing in Layout, not in Modeler.

1. In Layout, save any work you've done. Then, open the NodeBasic scene from the book's DVD in the "\Projects\Scenes\CH3\" directory. Press **F5** to open the Surface Editor. You'll see the Node_Basic surface listed in the Surface Name list. Select it, if it's not already selected, then click the Edit Nodes button, as shown in **Figure 3.43**.

Note

To apply nodes to a specific surface, always just select the surface in the Surface Name list. Be aware of this, as you might click the Edit Nodes without thinking and you will be applying node surfacing to the wrong surface.

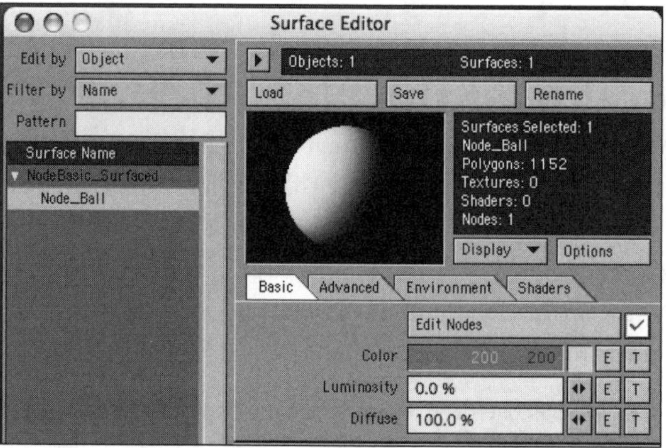

Figure 3.43 Select the surface you want to change and click Edit Nodes to open the Node Editor.

Note

If you can't seem to pull any connections off a node, there's a good chance you've sized down the view too much. In the top-right corner of the Node Editor are move and zoom controls just like in Layout or Modeler. Click, hold, and drag these two icons to adjust the view.

2. Next, when the Node Editor opens, position it as you like, and feel free to expand the size of the window but clicking and dragging the bottom-right corner. **Figure 3.44** shows the panel.

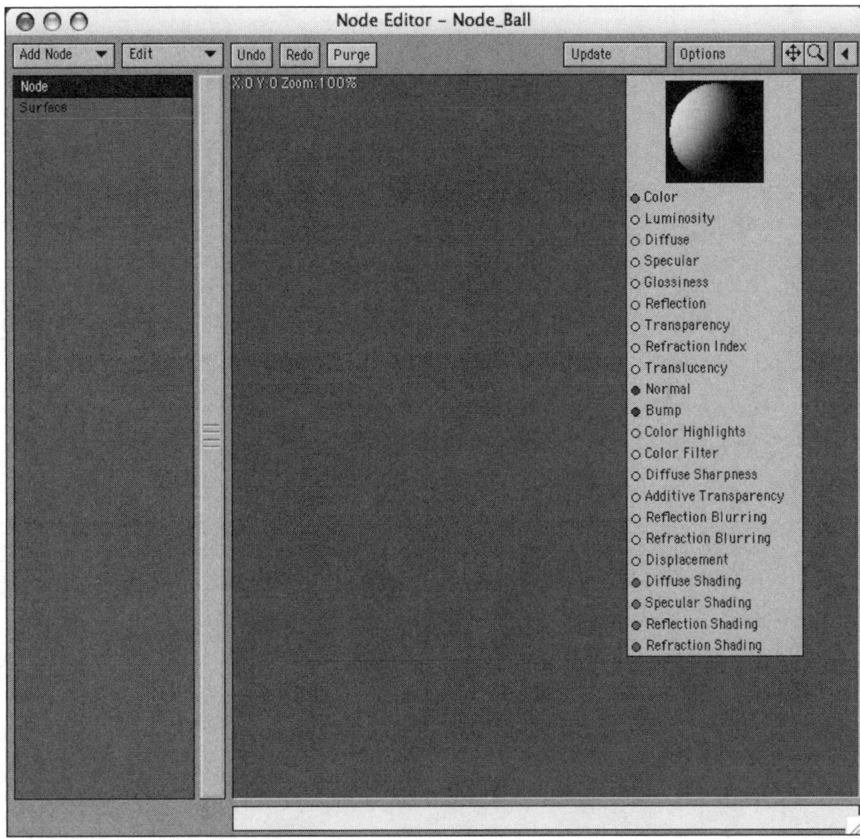

Figure 3.44 The Node Editor open and positioned.

3. The first lesson to learn is that there will always be a destination node. That's the tall column you see in Figure 3.44. This node looks slightly different if you're in the shading and texturing node (as you see here) or the lighting or displacement node editor. Regardless, there will always be the destination node. Click and move it around to fit it to view. You can quickly do this by pressing the **f** key on your keyboard (*f* for fit—get it?).

Note

A destination node is what drives your render. In a sense, it's the node, or part of the network, that outputs your other nodes.

4. At the top left of the Node Editor is the Add Node menu. Select this and you'll see a plethora of available nodes, from 2D and 3D textures, to gradients, and new and cool shaders. For now, select the 3D Textures, then Crumple, as in **Figure 3.45**.

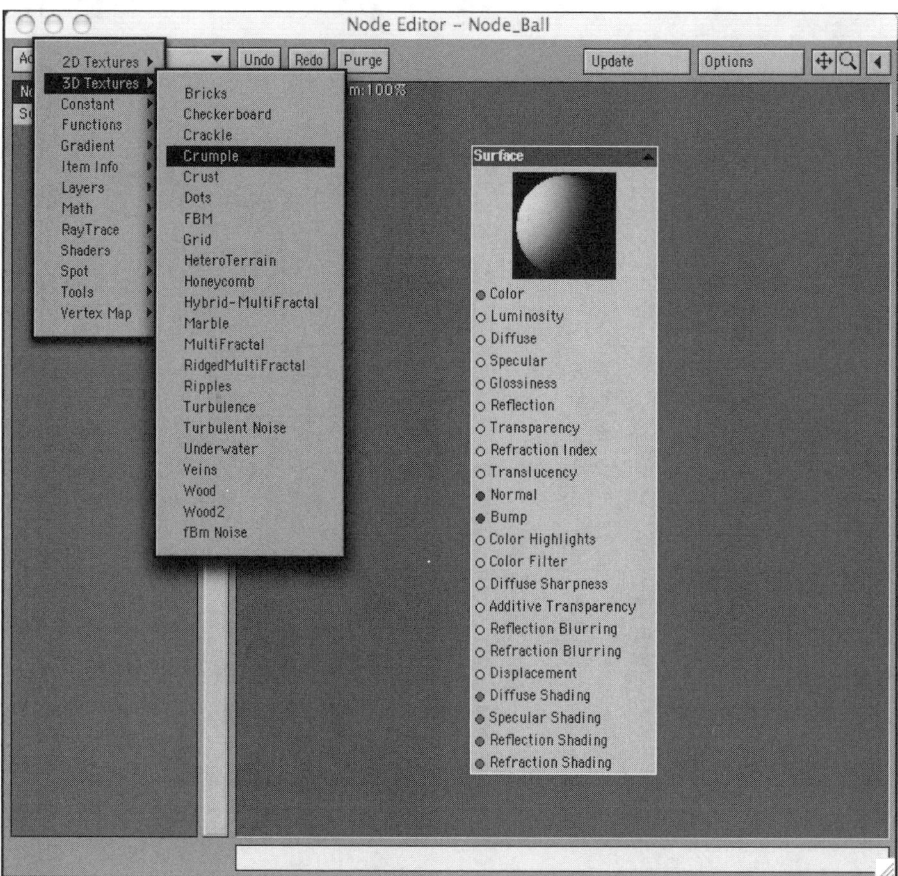

Figure 3.45 Adding a node is easy; simply select one from the Add Node menu. Here, a procedural crumple node is selected.

5. It's hard to wrap your brain around this new way of texturing—that's for sure. But don't worry, you'll get it. Just think of these nodes as ingredients that you can mix any way you want to create your final dish. Now, once the Crumple node has been added, it appears in the workspace area, as shown in **Figure 3.46**.

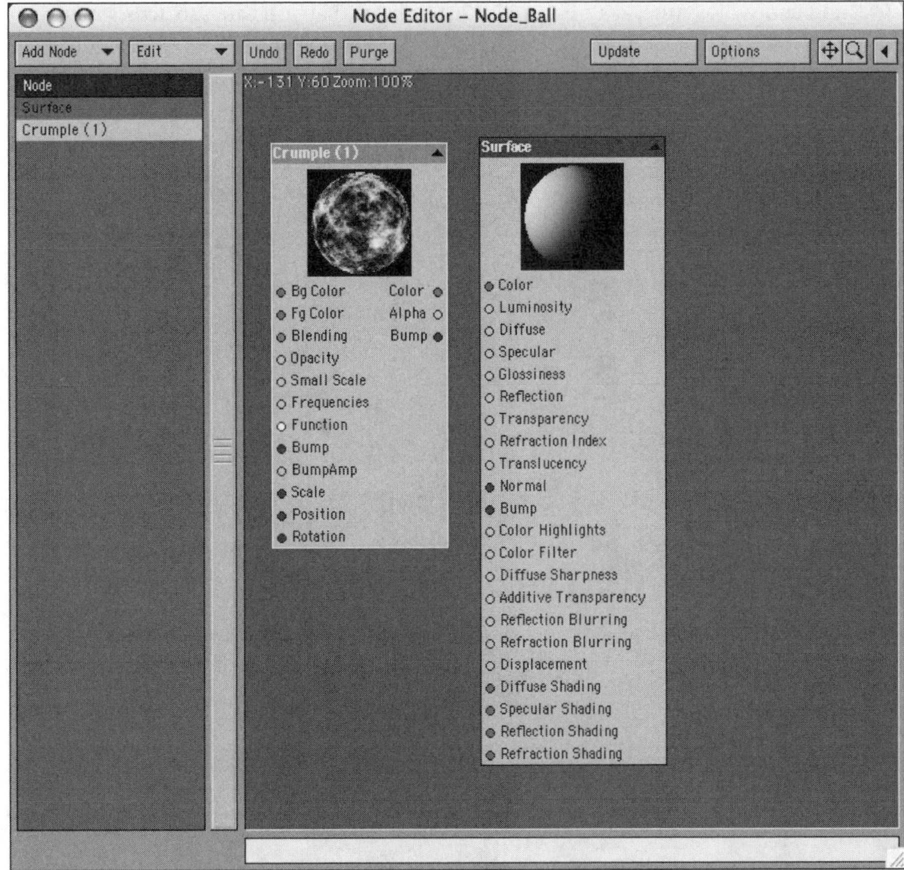

Figure 3.46 The Crumple node added to the workspace area in the Node Editor.

6. Taking a look at the preview thumbnail image at the top of the destination node (which reads Surface), it looks as if nothing has changed. This is correct. Nothing has changed. This is because even though you've added the node, you need to mix it in—that is, place it into the network. To begin getting organized, you can rename the default surface to something more specific. This is a good idea if you're creating larger scenes. Right-click on the Surface name in the Node list

and choose Rename, as in **Figure 3.47**. You'll see that you can also access many other commands with a right-click (Mac users, Cmd-click).

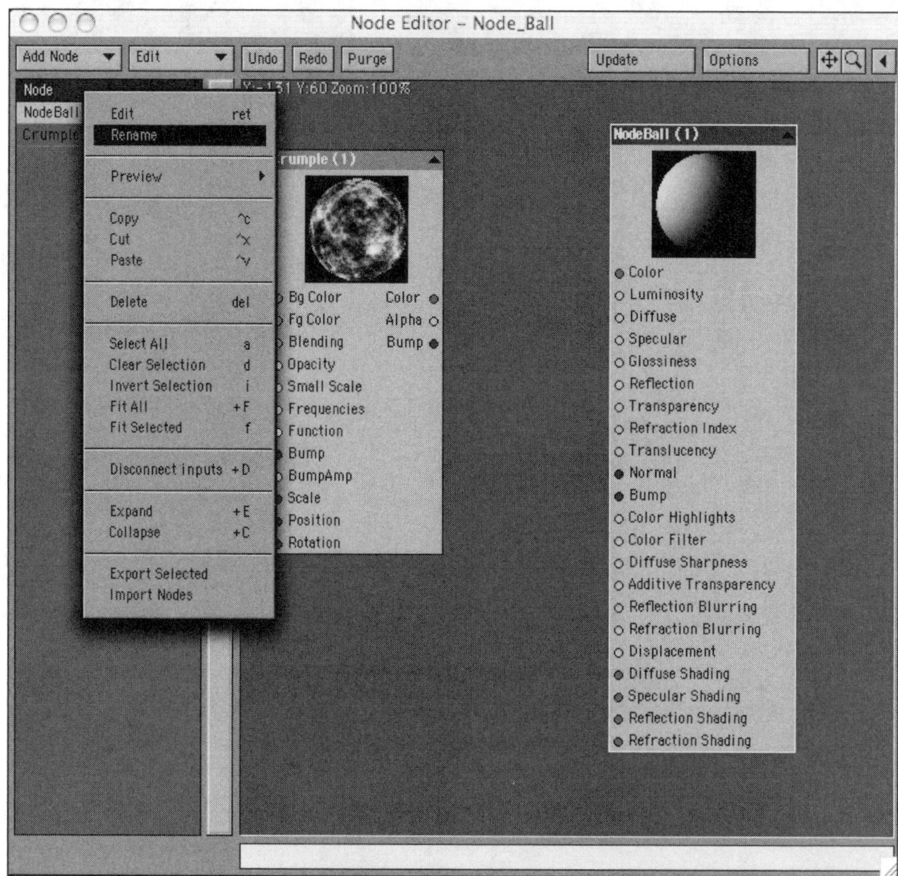

Figure 3.47 Right-click on the surface name in the Node list to rename it.

7. After renaming your surface, you'll see that the destination node now shows the same. Going back to the Crumple node, it needs to be connected to the destination node in some way. There are multiple ways to do this, and this is really the beauty of the Node Editor. For now, however, just click and drag on the red dot for Color from the Crumple node, to the red dot for Color in the Destination node. **Figure 3.48** shows the result.

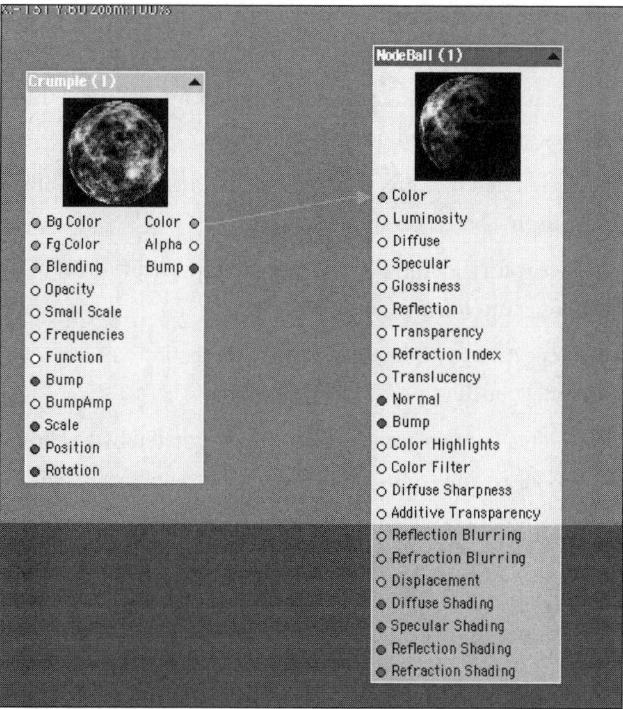

Figure 3.48 To connect a node, click and drag from one node to the next.

Guess what? You just used the Node Editor. It's that easy! Of course, you simply added one single procedural texture, but the process is the same no matter what you're creating. You add nodes and make the connections. Easy enough, isn't it? So what's the tough part? The tough part is understanding what connections to make and what all of the different nodes do. While we can't cover every single node in this book, we can show you how to use and, more importantly, understand these different node connections so you can experiment on your own. Chapter 11, "Node-Based Texturing," is entirely dedicated to the Node Editor in LightWave v9, so when you get there, you'll have good idea how what the node editor is from this chapter. And, you'll perform more complex projects.

Take a look at Figure 3.48, and you'll now see that the destination node preview shows the crumple surface applied. If you press **F9** to render a current frame, the crumple is on the ball. The red arrow you dragged from the Crumple node to the Destination node is a connection. There are five types of connections in the Node Editor. To identify each type of connection, NewTek has color-coded them. The red connection you just used is a color connector, and has inputs and outputs as you've seen. In most cases, you'll connect color to color as you've done here, even though the Crumple node is mostly gray. Here is a list of the connection types:

- Color—Receives input and outputs RGB color information. These connection types are designated by red dots on the nodes.
- Scalar—Designated by a green dot, a scalar connection is a value. You can have inputs or outputs based on single values.
- Integer—Great for blending, and designated by purple dots. In most cases, integers connect to other integers.
- Vector—Designated by blue dots, vector connections allow you to control different channels, such as position or rotation.
- Function—This is a two-way connection, designated by a yellow dot. Function connections allow you to transform values of the nodes in which they are connected. You should connect functions to functions.

Note

The NewTek manual, either printed or PDF, has a significant amount of information on each and every function of the Node Editor. In fact, the Node Editor feature of LightWave v9 is so deep, NewTek has dedicated almost an entire manual to it. For that reason, *Inside LightWave v9* is going to teach you the Node Editor through projects, rather than describing every button and node. Be sure to check out the "UsingNodes.mov" movie on the book's DVD in the "3D_Garage_Videos\Chapter_Videos\" directory for more information.

Before you move on to the next chapter to learn about LightWave v9 lighting, let's go a bit further in the Node Editor.

8. Back in the Node Editor, the crumple looks kind of dumpy just applied with a color connection. From the Add Node menu, select a Gradient, as in **Figure 3.49**.
9. A small node is added to the workspace. Now you need to connect this to the existing nodes. You need to build it into your network. Double-click on the Gradient node in the workspace. A panel opens showing you specific controls for the node.

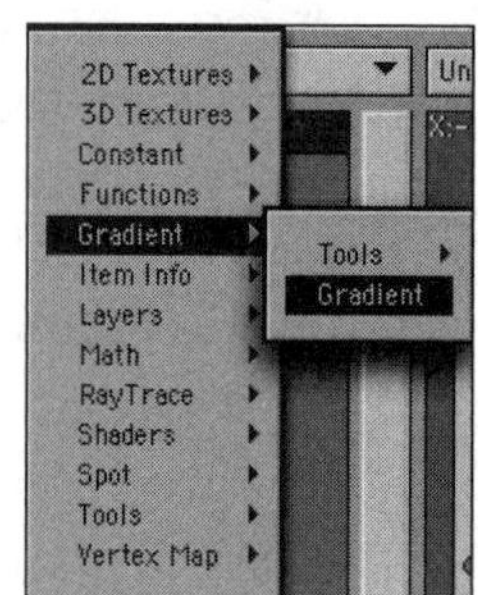

Figure 3.49
A Gradient node will help add color and interest to the Crumple node.

Note

You can keep the info panel open for all selected nodes (rather than double-clicking on one) by clicking the left-facing triangle in the upper-right corner of the Node Editor panel. This will open a numeric information panel that shows the info and preferences for any node when selected. Often, however, you don't always need specific control for various nodes, so it's closed by default. Certain node controls for things like a gradient can be opened by double-clicking the node itself.

10. In the Gradient node panel that opened, you'll see a tall black bar. A gradient allows you to vary settings based on different values. Click in the black bar, and a key is added. You'll see a small line, as in **Figure 3.50**.

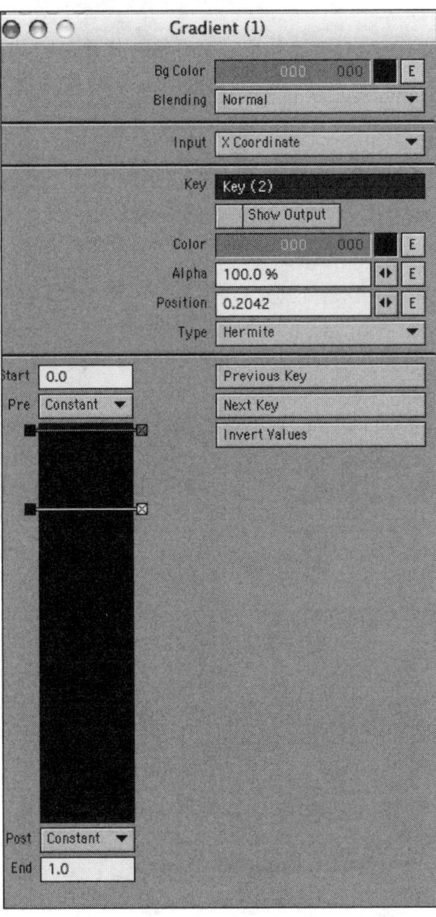

Figure 3.50 The gradient controls allow you to vary different values such as color. It begins by clicking in the gradient bar.

11. If you look carefully, you'll see that this key you've added is actually now selected, and highlighted with a soft blue. The default key is gray. With this new key still selected, change the color to red, but clicking and dragging the value where it says Color in the panel. **Figure 3.51** shows the area. Also, if you look at the Key listing in the panel, you can see that Key (2) is selected.

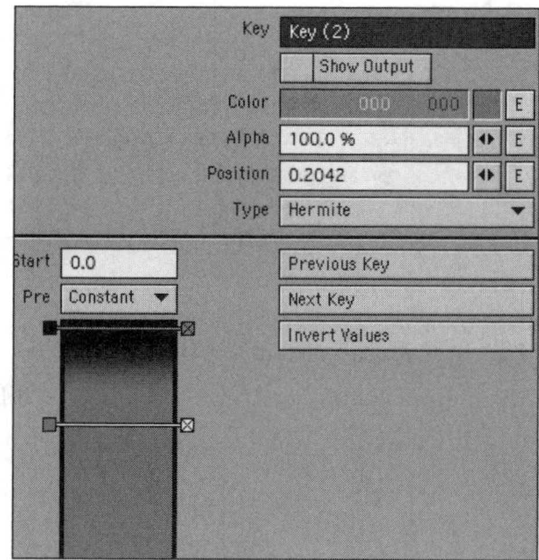

Figure 3.51 Drag the red value to the right to set a red color to the added gradient key.

12. Now add another key. Click in the gradient bar to add the key, then change the color to yellow by dragging the green value to the right. Remember, to change the RGB values, you can simply click and drag on the numeric value. Or you can click the color swatch to open a color palette. **Figure 3.52** shows the new key.

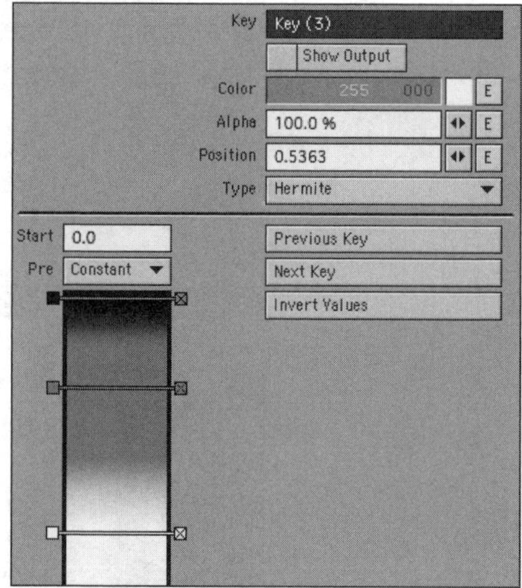

Figure 3.52 Add another key to the gradient bar, and make this one yellow.

13. Go ahead and make two more keys, making one blue and one white. **Figure 3.53** shows the final gradient. Note that you can click and drag on the keys to slide them closer together or farther apart to change how the gradient looks. Be careful, though; if you click off the key, most likely you'll end up creating an additional key. To remove keys, click the right side of the key itself—there's a small x. This will delete the key. You can add as many keys as you like.

14. Close the gradient panel. Back in the Node Editor workspace, you can see that your applied gradient shows in the node itself. Now all you need to do is connect it to the Crumple node. Try this: If you drag the color channel from the gradient node to the Luminosity input of the destination node, look what happens. The luminous values are changed for the destination surface. These are driven by the luminous output of the gradient. The yellow is brighter (has more luminance) than the red, and the destination node is updated accordingly, as in **Figure 3.54**.

15. Try something different now. First, to "unhook" a connection, just click on the arrow to remove it. Take the color output of the gradient and connect it to the opacity of the Crumple node. Just click on the red dot and drag, then drop it on the opacity.

Note

You don't have to move the nodes around in order to connect them. The system will pull the arrows to wherever you want, but it's not a bad idea to arrange the nodes in left-to-right fashion to help stay organized. Just click and drag the nodes around as you like, remembering to press the **f** key to fit them to view.

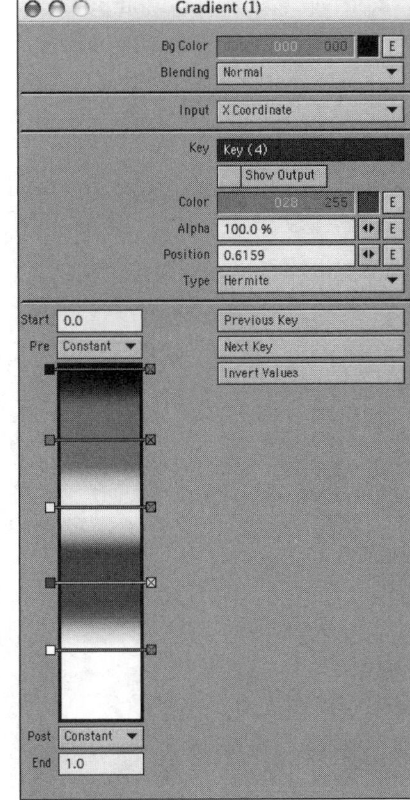

Figure 3.53 Add two more keys, one blue and one white.

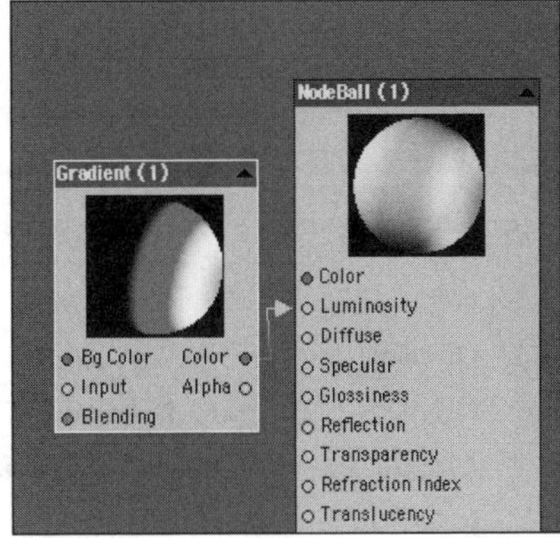

Figure 3.54 Taking the color output from the gradient node to the luminosity of the destination surface changes the values.

16. Then, take the color output from the Crumple node, and connect it to the luminosity of the destination node. The result is the crumple texture applied and then falling off based on the color values of the gradient. **Figure 3.55** shows the result.

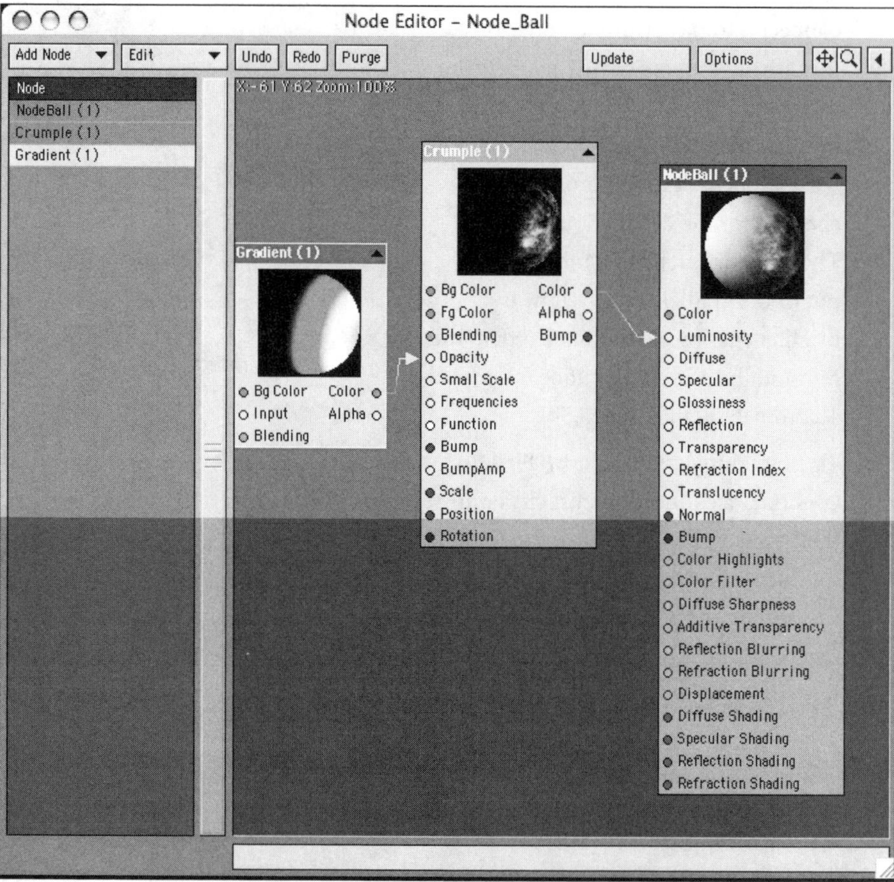

Figure 3.55 With the gradient's color connected to the crumple's opacity, and the opacity's color connected to the luminosity of the destination node, the surface is created.

17. Go back into the gradient controls. If you've closed the panel, double-click the Gradient node to open it again. Then, change the Input setting to Slope. By default, this value was set to X Coordinate, which is why the crumple was applied to the right side of the ball as you saw in Figure 3.55. **Figure 3.56** now shows the Gradient node applied based on the slope of the object. Note that this change fed through the network you've set up. Cool, eh?

Figure 3.56 Changing the gradient's input to slope also changes how the Crumple node is applied.

18. One more thing to try before you move on. Pull the color output of the gradient to the Fg Color input of the Crumple node. This puts the gradient RGB values into the foreground color of the crumple texture.

19. Next, take the crumple's color output and connect it to the color input of the destination node. **Figure 3.57** shows the result: a gradient blended with the crumple.

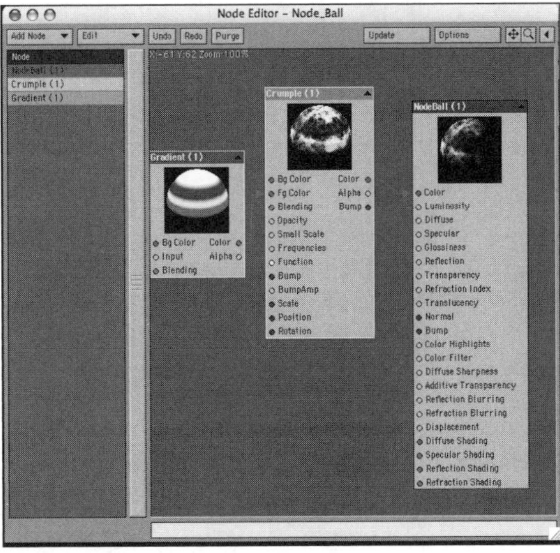

Figure 3.57 With the gradient color output driving the foreground color of the crumple node, the result is a blended surface.

Clearly, this is just the tip of the iceberg when it comes to using the Node Editor. As the book progresses, you'll use the Node Editor for more complex surface techniques, including lighting and deformations. And speaking of lighting, you'll learn all about that in the next chapter!

The Next Step

From this point on, you can experiment on your own. Add more layers, play with gradients, and adjust procedurals. As a matter of fact, add as many as you like. Your only limitations are time and system memory! Try adding some of the other Procedural surfaces, such as Smokey, Turbulence, or Crust. Keep adding these to your rusty metal surface to see what you can come up with. Now if you remember the copy and paste commands you used earlier with the Bump mapped marble tutorial, you can repeat those same steps. Try selecting Copy All Layers from the Color Texture and applying them as Bump and Specularity textures. The results are endless. In addition, try applying LightWave's powerful surface shaders.

This chapter gave you a broad overview of the main features within LightWave's Surface Editor, including the Texture Editor. There are countless surfaces in the world around us, and it's up to you to create them digitally. As the book progresses, you will use the information and instructions in this chapter to create even more complex and original surfaces such as glass, skin, metal, and more. The next chapter takes you deeper into the power of LightWave—read on to discover the cinematic tools available to you.

Chapter 4
Lighting

Light is everything. That's what they say, right? A picture is worth a thousand words? Ever heard that one? Well, no matter what the adage, working in 3D animation requires you to wear many hats. You're a draftsman, a 3D modeler, a producer, a painter, and even a gaffer. A gaffer is the person on a film set who takes care of the lighting. As a 3D animator, unless you're working in a big animation studio, you do your own lighting. And like many, you might consider lighting to be one of the less important aspects of your 3D animations, or perhaps it is an area you are just not comfortable working in. Lighting, which is crucial to your success as an animator, is not that hard to set up once you learn a few basic rules.

Lighting can be used for so much more than simply brightening a scene. Lighting can completely change the look of a shot. It can convey a mood, a feeling, or even a reaction. Lighting is vital in film, photography, and of course, 3D animation. Basic lighting can make your renders *hot* or *cold*; in other words, the color of the light you choose, where the lights are placed, and so on all play a role in the final image. Lighting can improve your animations. But you need to be aware of some basic real-world principles before you can put it all together.

Lighting has an evil twin: texturing. OK, maybe it's not evil, but understanding texturing and how it's affected by lighting is one of your main goals as a 3D artist. This is probably one of the areas animators struggle with the most, and an area that can often make or break your project. However, don't worry; LightWave makes it easy to apply complex surfaces and get instant feedback. The look of a texture can change significantly based on the lighting associated with it. So, the two go hand in hand.

The previous chapter introduced you to LightWave v9's surfacing capabilities and the new Node Editor. Take that knowledge and move through this chapter to learn how to light your models and scenes.

This chapter instructs you on the following:

- Understanding basic lighting principles
- Using different light sources
- Enabling Radiosity
- Lighting with gobos
- Creating soft shadows
- Interacting with materials

Working with Lights

Many LightWave animators come to this software after working in related traditional fields, such as television production, film production, or perhaps set design. If this describes you, you have a great asset for working with LightWave's lighting system. The lights in LightWave work in a way that is similar to lights in the real world, making it easier to understand. They do not exactly mimic lights in the real world, but with a few settings and adjustments, you can make any light appear realistic.

Five light types are available in LightWave Layout. Each has a specific purpose, but none is limited to that purpose:

- Distant lights. You can use a distant light for simulating bright sunlight, moonlight, or general lighting from a nonspecific source. Shadows from this light are hard. A distant light's position does not matter to your scene; only its rotation matters.
- Point lights. You can use a point light for creating sources of light that emit in all directions, such as a candle, lightbulb, or spark. Unlike a distant light, a point light's rotation does not matter in your scene; only its position matters. It, too, yields hard-edged shadows.
- Spotlights. The most commonly used lighting, spotlights can be used for directional lighting such as canister lighting, headlights on cars, studio simulation lighting, volumetric lighting, and more. Spotlight rotation and position play roles in your scene. A spotlight's shadows can be either hard or soft with shadow mapping.
- Linear lights. You can use linear lights as elongated light sources, such as fluorescent bulbs and neon tubes. Linear lights can have realistic shadows but consume additional rendering time.

- Area lights. The best choice for creating true shadows, area lights create a brighter, more diffuse light than distant lights and therefore result in greater realism. They do, however, take longer to render than spotlights, distant lights, or point lights.

Note

While you're working in LightWave's Modeler, you will not see a light source illuminating your shaded model in a Perspective viewport. Do not let that fool you because it has nothing to do with your final lighting setup. Lights are available only in Layout.

The environment in which your animation lives is crucial to the animation itself, which is why we dedicate a chapter to lighting and textures. You should consider color, intensity, and ambient light each time you set up a scene. Too often, tutorials overlook the power of light, but you know better! Using light, along with shadows, as elements in your animation can be as important as the models and motions you create. As you work through setting up lights in your 3D scenes, you should get used to setting one variable in particular: light intensity, also called brightness.

Note

Although we could dedicate this entire chapter and more to theory, design, and usage, we thought it better to demonstrate by doing. This chapter focuses on specifically using LightWave 3D's lighting system so you can achieve results immediately. For an excellent lighting reference book, check out *Digital Lighting & Rendering* by Jeremy Birn (New Riders 2000).

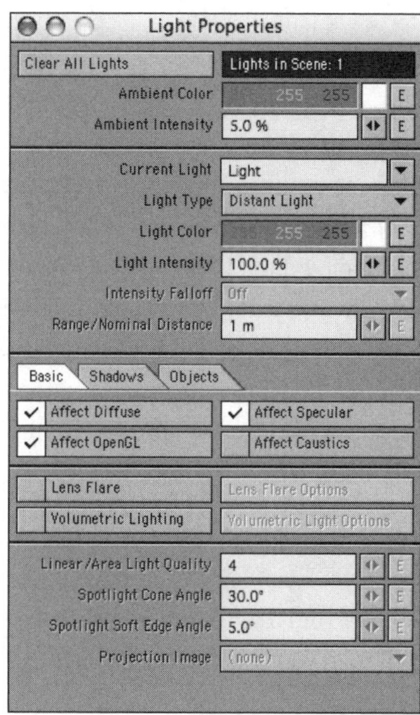

Figure 4.1 The Light Properties panel, as shown with a single default light.

As you work through lighting setups in this chapter and throughout this book, check out the types of lights LightWave has to offer. At the bottom of the LightWave Layout interface, you'll see the familiar item selection buttons—Objects, Bones, Lights, and Cameras. Click the Lights button, and then click the Properties button to the right. Conversely, you can always press **p** to open any item's properties. You'll see the LightWave Light Properties panel (**Figure 4.1**).

Looking closely at Figure 4.1, you can work your way down the panel, using the following explanations as your guide. At the very top of the panel, you can quickly clear all lights by clicking the Clear All Lights button. Be careful with this, as it clears *all* the lights in your scene, except for the single default distant light. If you've changed the default light, clicking this option resets it. Next to the Clear All Lights button, you'll see an information display called Lights in Scene.

Another interesting part of LightWave when it comes to lighting is the Global Illumination option. This is an important area of your 3D lighting setup. However, you won't find Global Illumination settings in the Lights panel but in the Render Globals panel. We'll cover these settings just after the basic lighting information, later in this chapter.

Note

The Current Light drop-down list near the top of the Light Properties panel contains the name of each light in your scene. The default single distant light is named, simply, Light. Select this entry in the list and you can quickly rename it. You can do this for any light you add. Lighting in 3D animation is an art all its own.

Light Color

The color of the light you use is important and useful in your images and animations because it can help set tone, mood, and feeling. No light is ever purely white, and it's up to you to change LightWave's default pure-white light color. The color selector works the same as the other color selectors in LightWave. You can also animate the RGB values with the Graph Editor. In LightWave, you can even animate colored lights. Clicking the E button takes you to the Graph Editor, allowing you to vary the light color over time. Very cool! You'll use this for all kinds of things, such as animating a rock concert where you need to have fast-moving lights shining on the stage. By animating the light color, you can change the colors over time at any speed you want.

Light Intensity

When you start LightWave Layout or choose Clear Scene, by default there is always one light in your LightWave scene. It has a light intensity of 100% and is a distant light. Although you can use this one light and its preset intensity as your main source of light for images and animations, it's best to adjust the light intensity to more appropriately match the light and the scene at hand.

Did you know that light intensities can range from values in the negative range to values in the thousands? You can set a light intensity to 9000% (or higher) if you want, just by typing in the value. The results might not be that desirable and perhaps even unstable, but you never know what your scene might call for. In general, if you want to create a bright sunny day, you can use a point light, which emits light in all directions, with a light intensity of 150% or so for bright light everywhere. On the other hand, if you want to light an evening scene, perhaps on a city street, you can use spotlights with light intensities set to around 60%. As you build scenes throughout this book, you'll be asked to set up different light types, with varying intensities. This will also help you get a feel for setting the right intensity.

Note

The mini-slider (the left and right arrows) next to the Light Intensity setting in the Light Properties panel allows you to click and drag values ranging from 0 to 100. However, by manually entering values, you can set higher or even negative values!

Negative lights, or "dark lights," can also be handy depending on the scene you're working on. Whereas lights with a positive light intensity can brighten a scene, negative lights can darken a scene. You might be asking why you would darken a scene with a negative light instead of just turning the lights down. For example, you might have to add a lot of light to make areas appear properly lit. Depending on the surfaces you've set, the extra light might make one area look perfect while making other areas too bright. This is where negative lights come into play. Adding a negative light (any light with a negative light intensity value) takes away light from a specific area.

Adding Lights

In most cases, you're going to use more than one single distant light in your 3D scenes. This section shows you how to add lights. Follow these simple steps to add lights to LightWave Layout to get a feel for how they work. And remember, unless you are working with Auto Key enabled, you'll need to create a keyframe to lock your lights into position after they're moved, just like objects.

Exercise 4.1 Adding Lights to Layout

1. Open Layout or select Clear Scene from the File drop-down menu.

   This sets Layout to its default of one distant light.

2. Make sure you are in Perspective view so that you have a full view of Layout. On the Items tab, under the Add category, select Lights, and then select Spotlight to add a spotlight to the scene. **Figure 4.2** shows the menus.

   You can choose to add any type of light you want.

3. Before the light is added to Layout, a Light Name panel appears (**Figure 4.3**).

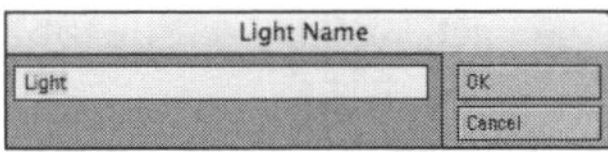

Figure 4.3 After a light is added, the Light Name panel appears, enabling you to set a specific name for your light.

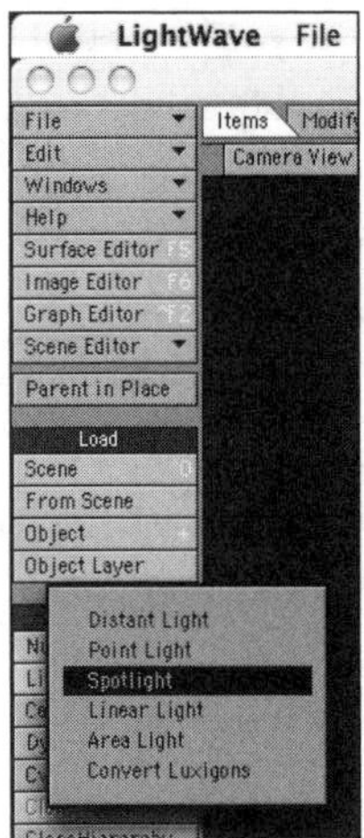

Figure 4.2 You can add lights directly in Layout under the Items tab.

4. Type in the name you want to give the new spotlight, such as the name of your favorite ex-boss.

Note

You don't have to change the name of a new light. Instead, you can accept LightWave's default light name by clicking OK when the Light Name panel appears. By default, LightWave names new lights Light (1), Light (2), Light (3), and so on.

Layout places the new light at your scene's origin point (the 0 coordinate shared by the X-, Y-, and Z-axes) (**Figure 4.4**).

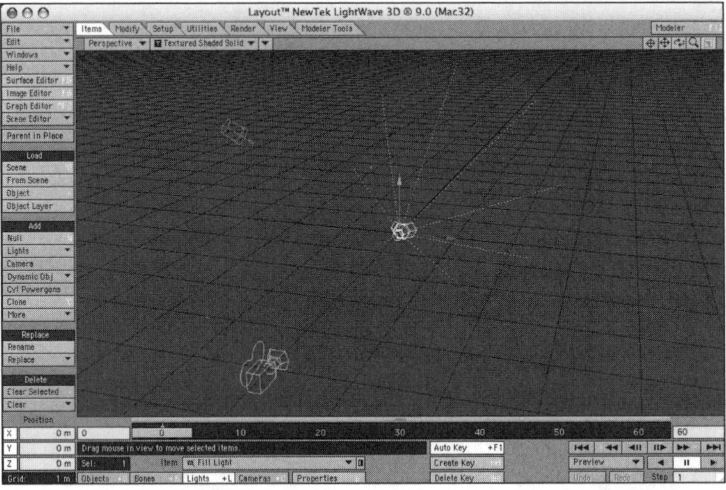

Figure 4.4 Layout places newly added lights at the origin point, aiming toward the back of the scene down the positive Z-axis.

Clone Lights

Besides adding lights, you can clone lights. Cloning a light creates an exact duplicate of a selected light. This includes the light's color, intensity, position, rotation, and so on. Any parameter you've set will be cloned. Cloning lights is just as easy as adding lights, but often good to do after you're sure of your existing light's settings. You don't want to clone a light 20 times, only to realize that you forgot to change the color! You'd need to make changes to 20 lights. However, should you have to make changes to many lights at once, you can quickly select the lights to change in the Scene Editor. **Figure 4.5** shows two lights in the Scene Editor selected at once.

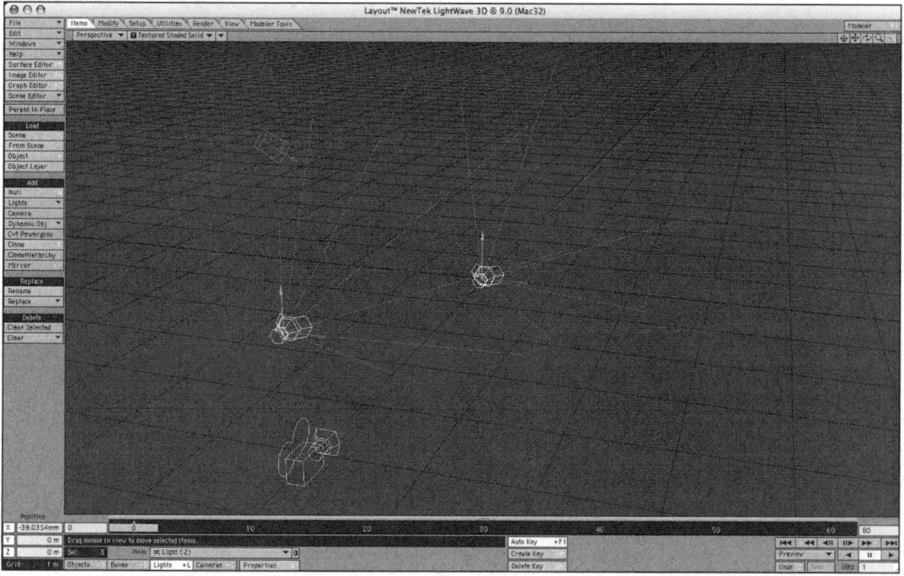

Figure 4.5 If you have one light, two, or twenty, you can use the Scene Editor to edit variables for those lights all at once.

Note

With LightWave 8, you can multiselect lights directly in Layout. Just hold down the Shift key and select them. Then, rotate, move, and so on.

To clone a light, first select the light to be cloned in Layout, and then select the Clone button under the Items tab in the Add category. Enter the number of clones (copies) of the light you want in the pop-up panel, and click OK or press Enter. Shazaam! The selected light is cloned. You know what else? This operation works the same for cloning objects or cameras. **Figure 4.6** shows the command.

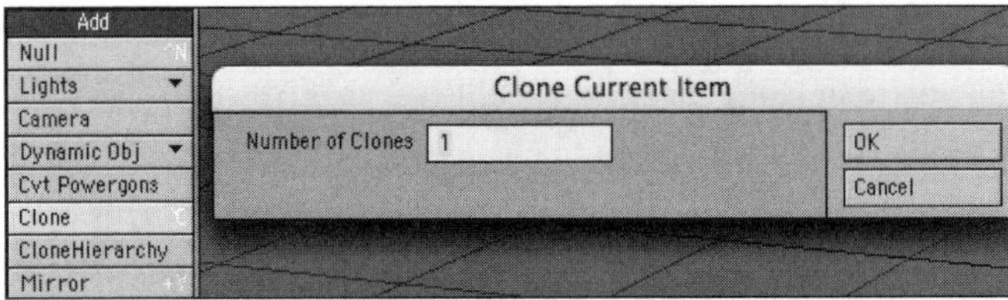

Figure 4.6 You can clone lights (or any other item) directly in Layout from the Items tab.

Mirror Lights

You know what's cool? Mirroring your light! Let's say you move the light to a specific position. Use the Mirror button in the Add category on the Items tab. Select a light (or other item in Layout) and click the Mirror button in the Item tab's Add tool category. Choose the axis to mirror across, and go! **Figure 4.7** shows the operation. You can also choose to mirror around an object's keyframes or at frame 0. Mirroring at frame 0 is important for more complex setups such as bone rigs for characters.

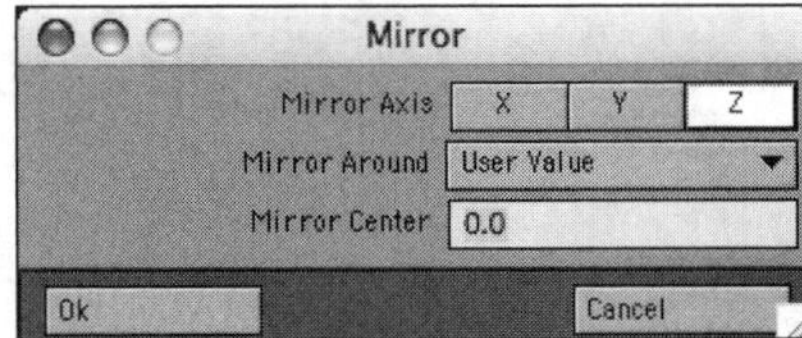

Figure 4.7 In addition to cloning lights, you can mirror them.

Ambient Light and Ambient Color

Did you know that the light around you is either direct or ambient? Direct light comes predominantly from a light source. Ambient light has no specific source or direction, such as the light underneath your desk or behind a door.

Back in the Light Properties panel, you can set the intensity of your ambient light. To open it, click the Lights button at the bottom of the interface and then press **p** or click the Properties button. The Ambient Controls are at the top of the panel. A typical Ambient Light setting is around 5%, which is LightWave's default value. In some cases, it is better to lower the value, sometimes to 0%, and use additional lights for more control over your scenes ambient. Don't rely on ambient light to brighten your scene. Instead, use more lights to make areas brighter. This will create a more dramatic look, with more depth in the final render.

You also can set the color of your ambient light so that the areas not hit by light still have some color to them. Let's say you have a single, blue light shining on an actor on a stage. Only the portions of the actor upon which the light falls directly will be lit. If you want to reveal more of the actor, or just lessen the severity of the boundary between light and shadow, you can apply an Ambient Intensity setting. Set the Ambient Color values to the same shade of blue as the light, and your shot will look accurate. Remember, ambient light hits all surfaces, not just those that are unlit by actual lights, which is why knowing about ambient intensity is important.

Lens Flares

The lens flare, often overused but needed, was introduced in LightWave v3. Lens flares are a popular addition to animated scenes, but too often when you add a light (such as a candlestick) to a scene, the light source emits but no generating source is visible. By adding a lens flare, you can create a small haze or glow around the candlelight. Other uses for lens flares are lights on a stage, sunlight, flashlights, and headlights on a car. Any time you have a light that is in view in a scene, you should add a lens flare so that the viewer understands the light has a source. Lens flares in LightWave can be viewed directly in Layout before rendering. You'll be setting up lens flares later in this chapter.

Volumetric Lights

You need to be aware of one more area when it comes to LightWave lighting before you start working through exercises. Volumetric lighting is a powerful and surprisingly fast render effect that can create beams of light. Have you ever seen how a light streaks when it shines through a window? The beam of light that emits from the light source can be replicated in LightWave with *volumetrics*. Volumetric settings add volume to a light source. Additionally, you can add textures to a volumetric light to create all sorts of interesting light beams.

Global Illumination Options

Have you ever stopped to look around you? Take your face out of this book or away from the computer for a moment, and just look around. Whether you're at your desk, in your living room, or outside, everything has global lighting properties. You can control these global properties—global light intensity, global lens flare intensity, ambient intensity, ambient color, radiosity, and caustics—on the Global Illumination tab of the Render Globals panel. To open it, click the Render tab at the top of the Layout interface, then click the Render Globals tool button. The Global Illumination settings are found in the third of five settings tabs in the bottom half of the panel (**Figure 4.8**).

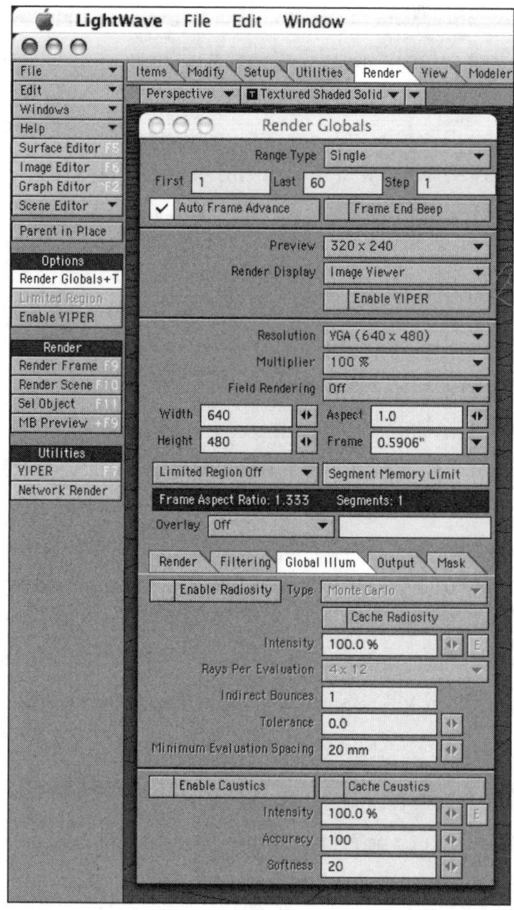

Figure 4.8 The Global Illumination control tab, found in the Render Globals panel, governs such properties as global light intensity, global lens flare intensity, radiosity, and caustics.

Global Light and Lens Flare Intensity

In the Global Illumination panel, click the Render tab at the bottom of the panel. At the bottom of the panel is a Light Intensity value, currently set at 100%. This is a Light Intensity setting but because it's in the Render Globals panel, it globally changes the intensity on all lights in your scene. This can be useful for scenes that have multiple lights that need to become brighter or dimmer over time.

Let's say you're animating a stage play or musical concert, for example. You have 29 spotlights shining on the stage, the players, and the actors. All their intensities are randomly and quickly changing to the beat of the music, and perhaps focusing on key performers. At the end of the song, you want all the lights to fade out equally. Instead of setting the light intensity 29 times for each light, which you could do through the Scene Editor, it is better to ramp down the Global Light Intensity setting. Similarly, if you have lens flares applied to these lights, you can globally change the Flare Intensity setting for lights, just below the Light Intensity setting.

Radiosity and Caustics

Also within the Global Illumination panel (within the Render Globals panel) are the Enable Radiosity and Enable Caustics settings. These two features in LightWave enable you to take your 3D creations even further by adding more real-world lighting properties.

Note

The radiosity and caustic features are not active by default. You need to activate them to see their effects on scene, but be warned: rendering times will increase.

Radiosity is a rendering solution that calculates the diffused reflections of lights in a scene. It is the rate at which light energy leaves a surface. This also includes the color within all surfaces. In simpler terms, radiosity is bounced light. A single light coming through a window, for example, can light up an entire room. The light hits the surfaces of the objects and bounces, lighting up the rest of the room, in turn creating a realistic image. Ambient light is often considered a poor man's radiosity. You can use it to brighten areas not directly lit by lights.

You'll use radiosity and learn more about its settings later in Chapter 15, "Advanced Cameras and Rendering".

Caustics are created when light is reflected off a surface or through a refracted surface. A good example is the random pattern often seen at the bottom of a swimming pool when bright sunlight shines through the water. The dapples of light that appear on floors or ceilings when light glints off a crystal vase or a gold-plated statue are another example.

Applying Lights in LightWave

You will encounter many types of lighting situations when creating your animation masterpiece. This next section steps you through a common lighting situation that you can use for character animation tests, product shots, or logo scenes.

Simulating Studio Lighting

One of the cool things about LightWave is that you don't have to be a numbers person to make things happen. You can see what's happening throughout the creation process from object construction to surfacing to lighting. Exercise 4.2 introduces you to basic three-point lighting often used in everyday video production. You can apply this lighting style to LightWave and create a photographer's backdrop (or *cyc*, short for *cyclorama*) to act as a set for your objects. Creating a set in LightWave is a good idea so that even simple render tests are not over a black background. By rendering objects on a set, you add more depth to your animation.

The goal of this project is to introduce you to a common lighting setup that can be useful in just about any type of render situation when simulating studio lighting. You'll use a premade scene from this book's DVD.

Exercise 4.2 Simulating Studio Lighting

1. In Layout, load the Teacup_NotLit.lws scene from this chapter's folder on the accompanying DVD (in the "Projects\Scenes\Ch4\" directory).

   This loads the multilayered object, which includes four layers—the floor, the teacup, the saucer, and a light box. The light box is a flat polygon that will be used to help light the subject. **Figure 4.9** shows the loaded scene.

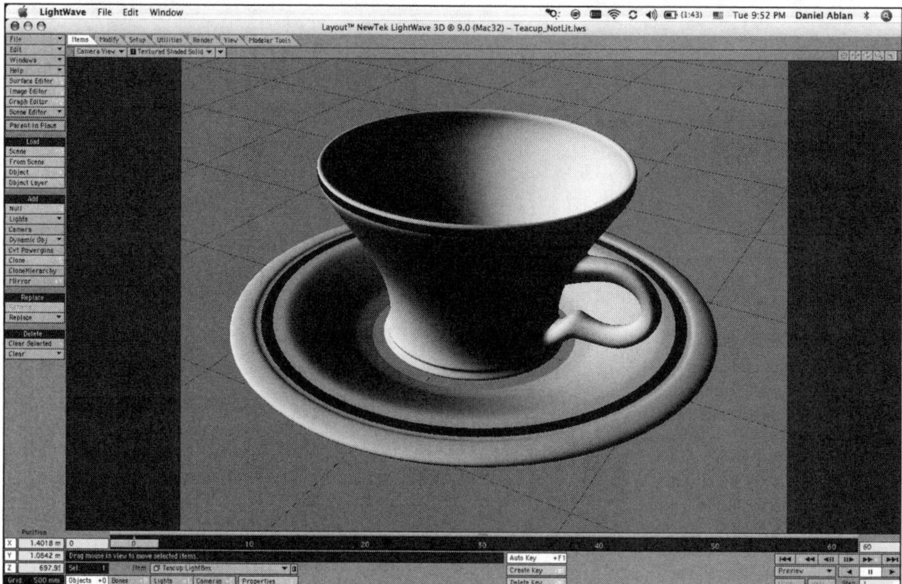

Figure 4.9 A preexisting scene with one multilayered object, perfect for testing some lighting configurations.

2. Click the Lights button at the bottom of the Layout interface (or press Shift+l) to select the only light currently in the scene, which is generically named Light. (If the scene contained more than one light, you'd also need to select the one you want to work with from the Item drop-down.) This is a distant light and is not the most effective lighting. To see how it lights the scene, press **F9** to render the current frame (**Figure 4.10**).

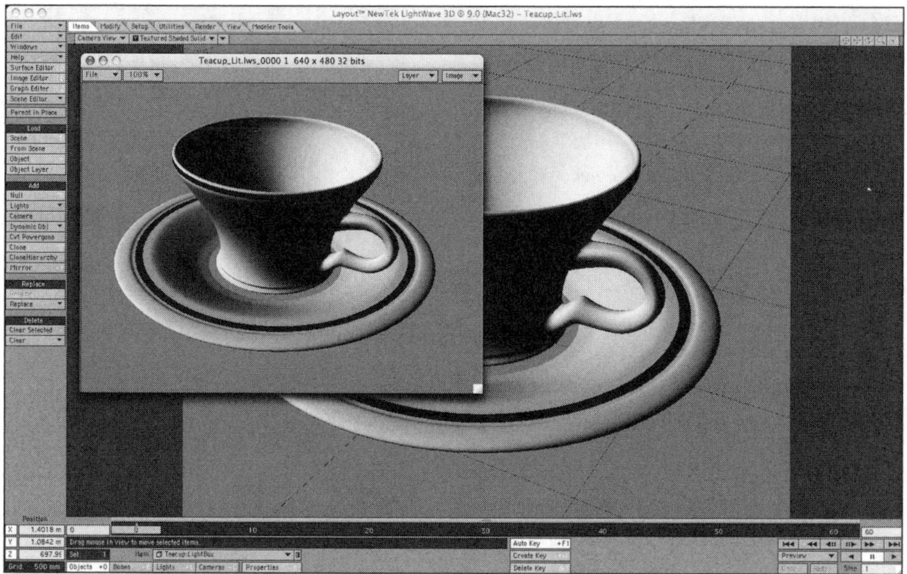

Figure 4.10 Pressing **F9** lets you preview a render of the current frame render. By default, the render isn't any different from what you see in Layout.

To see the render when you press F9, be sure that you have Image Viewer selected for Render Display selected with a chosen resolution (such as 320×240), or choose Render Frame from the Render drop-down. Go to the Render tab at the top of Layout. On the left, under the Options category choose Render Globals, and then apply the various options as shown in **Figure 4.11**. If your panels start to get in the way, feel free to move them aside as needed to free up screen real estate. It makes you want to go out and get that 30-inch display now, doesn't it?

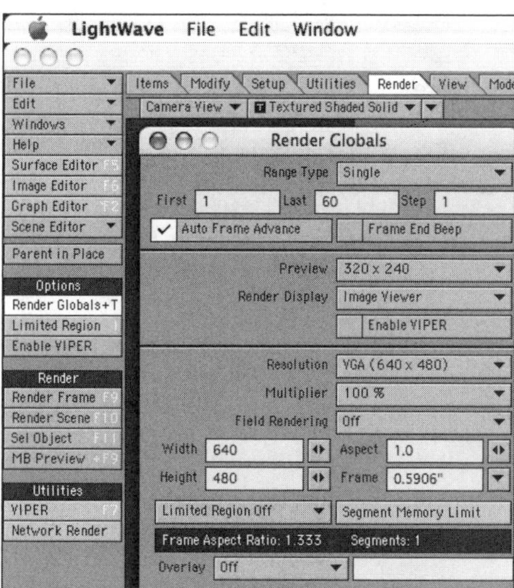

Figure 4.11 To see your render in progress, set Render Display to Image Viewer in the Render Globals panel.

3. With the default light still selected, press **p** to open the Light Properties panel. If the Render Globals properties panel is still open, press **p** twice; the first time closes the panel and the second opens Light Properties.
4. In the panel, change the Light Type setting to Spotlight.

   This spotlight will be the key light, or the main light, in the scene setup. You'll be creating a three-point lighting situation in this scene.
5. Change the Light Intensity to 90%. You can do this by either clicking or dragging the value slider in the Light Properties panel, or simply entering the value. **Figure 4.12** shows the panel with changes.

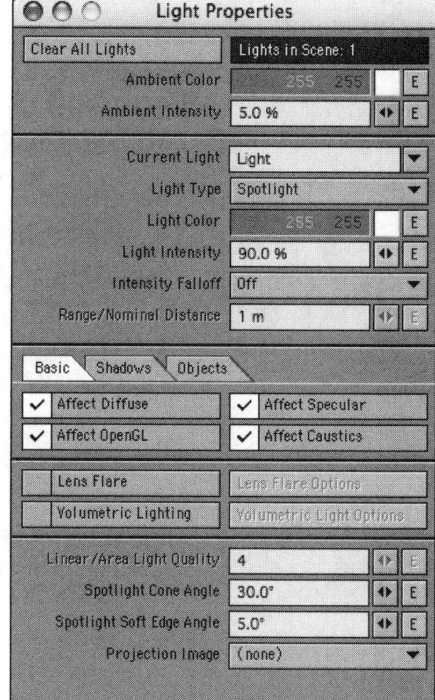

Figure 4.12 Change the default light to a spotlight for more accurate lighting, and set the Light Intensity to 90%.

Note

Three-point lighting is a common lighting setup used in most studios. It consists of a key light, which is the primary source of brightness; a fill light, which is less bright than the key and used opposite the key; and a backlight, sometimes referred to as a hair light, which is used to separate the subject from the background. You'll find a similarly set scene called Teacup_Lit.lws on the book's DVD.

6. Set the Light Color to off-white (R: 245, G: 245, B: 220). You can do this by clicking and dragging directly on the RGB values or by clicking the color swatch and using your computer's color picker to set the value.

   You've set the Light Color to off-white because light is never purely white. In a studio setting, the key light burns with a slight off-white tint. At the bottom of the lights panel, set the Spotlight Cone Angle to 40 degrees and the Spotlight Soft Edge Angle to 40 degrees. This creates a nice edge falloff for the key light (**Figure 4.13**). The cone angle determines how large the spread of the light will be, while the soft edge angle determines how soft the edge of the light cone will be.

7. Click the Shadows tab and set the Shadow Type option to Shadow Map, which creates softer shadows than ray-traced shadows. These are created from system memory, rather than processing power. The result is a soft, fast rendering shadow. Nice!

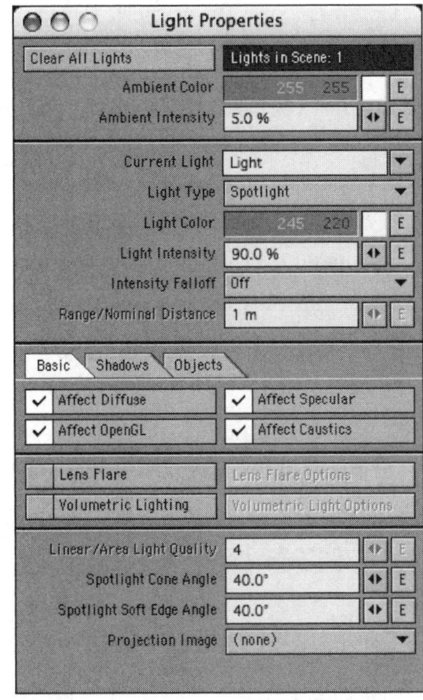

Figure 4.13 In the Light Properties panel, you can change the light color and the cone angle.

Note

You can use shadow maps only with spotlights.

8. Change the Shadow Map Size to 3000. This setting is the size of the pixels of the shadow map. Leave Shadow Fuzziness set to 1.0.

   The larger the Shadow Map Size setting, the more memory LightWave uses to calculate the shadow. Larger shadow map sizes produce cleaner shadows but increase render times. Choosing a value between 1000 and 2000 gives you a good size to work with, and you generally only need to boost Shadow Map Size to 3000 or more if you increase Shadow Fuzziness to 8 or so. Our Shadow Map Size setting of 3000 is a bit extravagant in terms of memory usage, but the result will be very clean shadows. That's not to say this is an unreasonable setting—just be prepared to have a lot of RAM if you have multiple spotlights with shadow map sizes this large. One or two lights are not a big deal.

Note

If you want to convert the Shadow Map Size to actual megabytes, square the size value, multiply by 4, and divide by 1,000. So, (2000 × 2000 × 4) ÷ 1000 = 16MB. That means a Shadow Map Size of 2000 will take an extra 16MB of memory for calculation.

9. Be sure the Fit Spotlight Cone box is checked. This tells LightWave to make the shadow map match the light's cone angle, which is what you'll most often do. Uncheck it to activate the Shadow Map Angle option, which lets you set a custom shadow map angle so that, for example, your light might shine over a large area of the scene but only casts shadows within a smaller region.

10. Press **5** on your numeric keypad to switch to Light view. Looking through the light to set it in position is the quickest and most accurate way to set up lights.
11. Press **t** to select Move from the Modify tab, and then right-click the light in the Layout viewport and drag the light about 2.025 m up the (vertical) Y-axis. The right mouse button will only affect the Y-axis. Pressing the left mouse button will move on the X- and Z-axis. Keep an eye on the information area at the bottom left of the Layout to see your movement increments. You may also choose to enter the value numerically. To do so, press **n** to enter the numeric value controls. Mac users with single-button mice, don't forget to Cmd-click to access right mouse button functions. Feel free to position the light while in Light view to focus it on your objects.
12. On the numeric keypad, press **1** for Back view or **3** for a Right (side) view to see the light's new position. You might need to use the various view tools in the upper-right corner to adjust the Front or Side view so you can see everything. **Figure 4.14** shows the Back view of the scene.

Note

When using a Back, Right, or Top view of your scene, you can press **a** to fit all elements to view.

Figure 4.14 The Front view of the teacup scene with the spotlight moved up.

13. Switch back to Light view (press **5**). To make sure your light is pointed toward the teacup, with the left mouse button move the light back away from the object so that it has a larger coverage area, as shown in **Figure 4.15**. Also, be sure to create a keyframe at frame 0 to lock the light into its new position.

    Setting the position of the spotlight from the Light view is quick and easy. Because of the way the object is shaded, you can see that the light is in front and to the upper left of the set. Often, a main key light like the one shown here works well from an upper side view, but you can place this light anywhere you like. But feel free to adjust as you like.

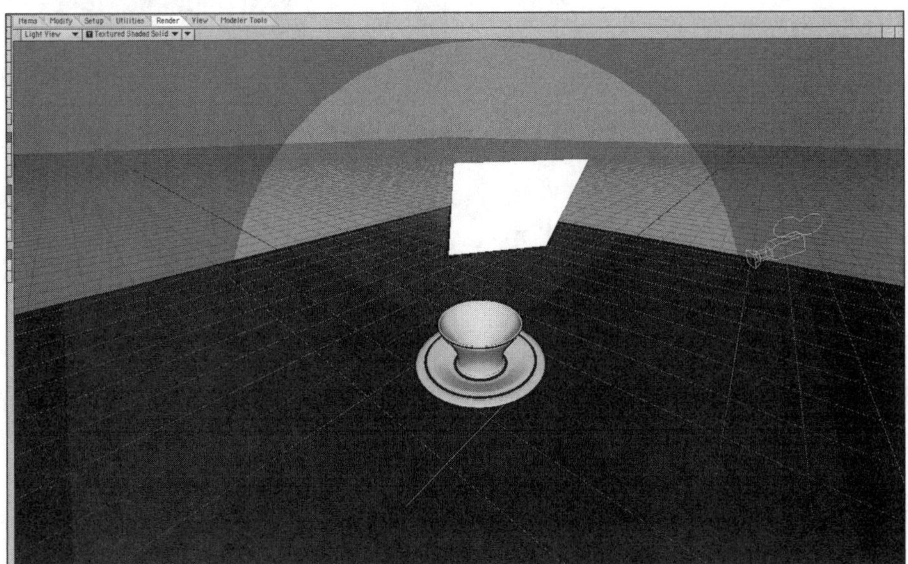

Figure 4.15 By adjusting a light from the Light view, you can easily and quickly place it into position.

14. Save your scene as **MyTeacup_Lit** or something similar.

    Before you add the other lights, you need to rename this light to keep your scene organized.

15. From the Light Properties panel, select the default light name (which is just Light) and rename it to **Key_Light**, as in **Figure 4.16**. When naming lights and objects in LightWave, you can use spaces. However, it's good practice to avoid them to make searches easier, for organization purposes, and to prevent any confusion. Try using underscores instead of spaces.

    You now need to add another light to create the fill light.

16. On the Items tab, click the Lights drop-down and choose Spotlight. After you add the light, LightWave asks you to name it. Name this light **Fill Light** (or Phil Light if your name is Phil).

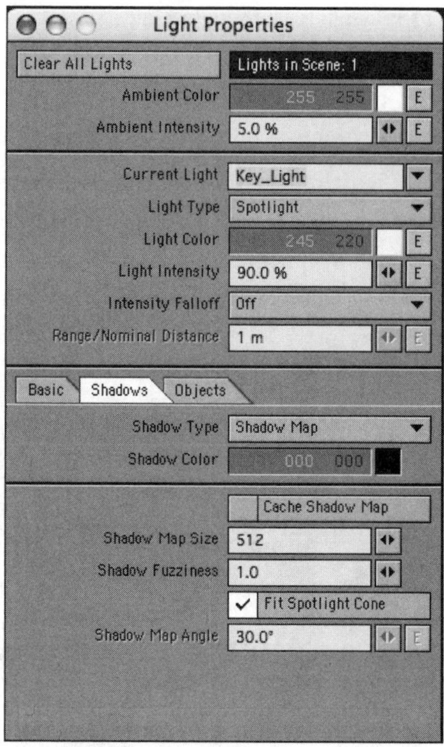

Figure 4.16 Rename a light from directly within the Light Properties panel.

17. In the Light Properties panel (select the light and press **p**), change the Light Intensity setting to 75%. Change the light color to a soft blue (R: 135, G: 170, B: 230).

    Adding a blue light as a fill light is often a nice touch when setting up lights, either in a studio or in outside situations. It helps create the feeling of distance while illuminating unobtrusively. It's also great for illumination at night.

18. Change Shadow Type to Shadow Map for this spotlight, as you did with Key Light; change Spotlight Cone Angle to 40; and change Spotlight Soft Edge Angle to 40. Do this from the Basic tab of the Lights Properties panel.

19. Move the fill light to the right of the teacup, which is towards the +X-axis. It might help to switch to a Perspective view to see more of your scene and the light position. You don't need to move this light too far from the teacup, but consider it in a position opposite of the key light. Press **y** for rotate and remember to rotate the light to encompass the entire teacup. Set the light lower to the floor in the scene. Create a keyframe at 0 to lock the light in place. **Figure 4.17** shows a view of the set from the fill light, and **Figure 4.18** shows a Perspective view of the entire scene so far.

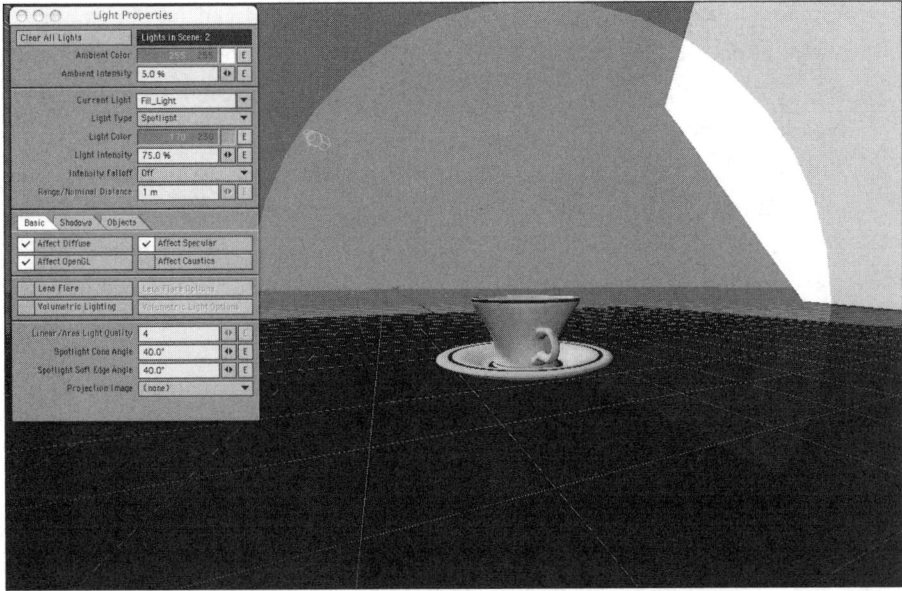

Figure 4.17 Rename a light from directly within the Light Properties panel.

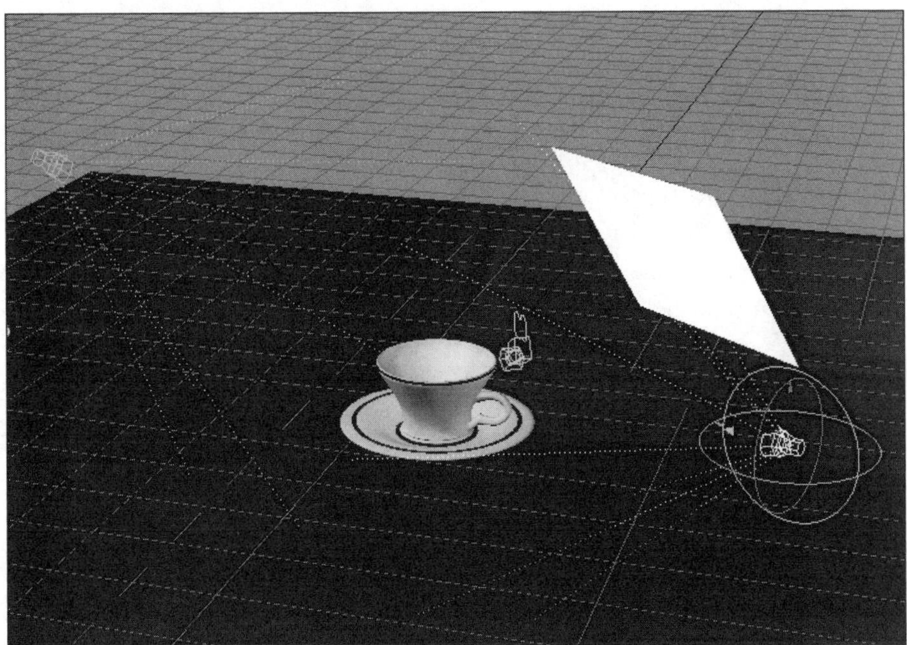

Figure 4.18 In this overview of the scene, you can see the key light to the left and the fill light to the right.

You need to add one more light to the scene to set up the backlight. This could also be a spotlight, but instead, let's use that big white polygon that's been hanging around behind the teacup. Now, a little clarification here before we continue. A typical three-point lighting setup means that you are using three lights. Duh! However, LightWave's Global Illumination features allow you to incorporate indirect lighting from the rest of the scene. With that, you can create a large, luminous polygon and use it as a light source. Cool, huh? But why would you do this, you ask? Good question! A large flat polygon that is bright white not only produces a soft subtle studio lighting effect in your scene but also creates a very nice reflection in your object. Dual purpose! Read on to set it up.

20. Based on the settings for Key Light and Fill Light, you could add another spotlight and set the values similar to the key light simply by cloning one of them. Instead, the white polygon is set above and to the rear of the teacup, out of camera range. When you position and size the large polygon, consider the size of the objects in your scene. If you're using this object as a reflection element (which you are), you should place the object in such a way that it reflects well in the teacup. To see how it looks, press **F9** to render the current frame to see how your scene is looking.

Note

You can quickly choose different lights in the Light Properties panel by clicking the small drop-down arrow to the right of the Current Light drop-down list.

21. After the render appears, you'll see a better lit scene than when you started (**Figure 4.19**). Note that Render Display is set to Image Viewer from the Render Options panel on the Render tab. You can load the Teacup_Lit scene from this book's DVD (in the "Projects\Scenes\Ch4\" directory) to see everything to this point.

Figure 4.19 A quick frame render shows how the lighting setup works.

Enhanced Studio Lighting

Now that you have some basic lighting set up, you need to create some drama and depth. You have a set and lights, but no textures, and thus no *life*. Exercise 4.3 shows you how to adjust your lighting situation using ambient light and textures to enhance the lighting environment.

Exercise 4.3 Enhanced Lighting Setups

1. Continue from the previous scene.
2. On the Render tab, open the Render Globals panel, then click the Global Illumination panel (labeled Global Illum). Turn on Enable Radiosity.

   Before you do anything else, press F9 to see the difference in the render. The dark areas behind the teacup are now brighter and softly lit (**Figure 4.20**).

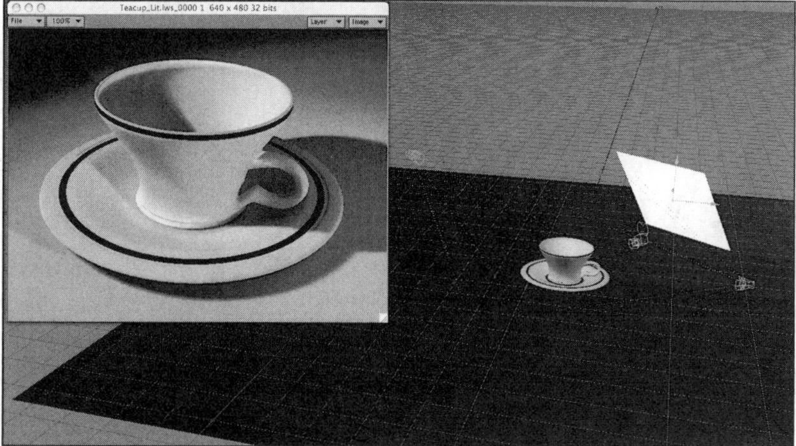

Figure 4.20 The large white polygon acts as a light source when Radiosity is applied to the render.

3. You can see that the bright white polygon acts as a light source when Radiosity is applied to the render. This feature calculates indirect illumination, and essentially is bouncing (or diffusing) the rays of light in the scene. Since the board is 100 percent luminous, this object acts like a reflector. If you've ever worked with a photographer or videographer, you might have noticed an assistant holding a big board or round, metallic-looking disc opposite of the key light on a subject. Figure 4.20, however, looks a bit noisy, doesn't it? Click the Noise Reduction option on the Render tab in the Render Globals panel.

4. Next, select the Global Illumination tab in the Render Globals panel, and set the Rays Per Evaluation setting to 9×27. This will take longer to calculate, but you'll eliminate the noisy render. Essentially, a higher Rays Per Evaluation creates a more accurate calculation of the rays bouncing around the scene. The result? A cleaner render. The drawback? Longer render times.
5. Finally, change the Intensity setting to 135% to make the radiosity effect stronger. Increasing this value increases the strength of the radiosity, which makes the indirect light stronger.
6. Save your scene by selecting Save from the File drop-down menu or pressing Ctrl+s. Press F9 to render the current frame. **Figure 4.21** shows the render.

Figure 4.21 With a more accurate Radiosity setting, the soft fill is more visible.

The results are subtle, but pleasing just the same. But there are a few more things you can set up with lighting to make the scene come to life. Next, you'll work with a few more lighting tricks, but then you'll make changes to the teacup and you'll see how important the light box is to the scene beyond its radiosity effects.

Using Projection Images on Lights

LightWave's Projection Image feature is a useful lighting tool that mimics real-world lighting situations in which cookies or gobos are used to throw light onto a set. A *gobo*, also referred to as a *cucoloris* or *cookie*, is a cutout shape that is placed in front of a light, sort of like a cookie cutter. Certain areas of the gobo hold back light, whereas other areas let light through. In Exercise 4.4, you use a gobo that creates the look of light coming through trees.

Although the previous exercise was basic in design, it is the core lighting situation for many of your LightWave scenes. Perhaps with a slight variation, this basic three-point lighting scheme can be used for product shots, animated plays, logos, and much more. Things like simple stage sets, equipment, figures, generic objects, or any element can benefit from this type of lighting design. Of course, you are not limited to using just three lights for these types of situations. You can start with the basic three, and then add or remove lights to highlight certain areas, brighten dark areas, or use additional lights as projection lights.

Figure 4.22 shows the gobo you'll use to create the effect. This image is nothing more than a photograph of tree branches. Using a simple image-editing program, it was converted to grayscale mode, its contrast was boosted, and the image was blurred. When this image is applied to a spotlight, the white areas allow light to shine through, whereas the black areas do not. The blurring helps create a soft, less harsh look where the light falls off.

Figure 4.22 A simple grayscale image can be used to cast light onto a set.

Tip

Gobo images can be created with a paint package such as Adobe Photoshop. Image dimensions should match your render resolution, and 24-bit color depth generally works best for most applications. However, if it's a smaller image that's not viewed close up in your 3D scene, you can save memory and use 8-bit images. Perhaps you just need to project a small logo onto a wall? A smaller image would serve your needs well. Video-resolution gobo images should have pixel dimensions of 720×486.

Exercise 4.4 Creating Gobo Lights

1. Add a new spotlight to the scene and name it **Gobo Light** or something similar. The idea is that you identify the lights properly as you set them up to stay organized. Select the new spotlight and press **5** on the keyboard to switch to Light view.
2. Move the gobo light up and to the upper-right or upper-left side of the scene, on the same side as the teacup object. Height doesn't matter too much; just be sure your projection will be able to hit the set. Point the light onto the floor, slightly behind the teacup, and be sure to create a keyframe for it at frame 0 to lock it in place.

   Remember, everything should have a keyframe at the first frame of your animation even if it is not moving. In this case, the first frame is 0.

Note

If you have Auto Key enabled at the bottom of Layout, this keyframe will be created for you automatically.

3. Make the new gobo light slightly off-white in color and set Light Intensity to anywhere from 60% to 90%. **Figure 4.23** shows the new light in place.

Note

While you can't tell LightWave to create off-white lights by default, you can change multiple lights to off-white (or any other color) at the same time. Select all of the lights you want to adjust, and change the color settings in the Lights Properties panel to affect all of the lights at once. In the same way, you can modify other light properties for all selected lights as well.

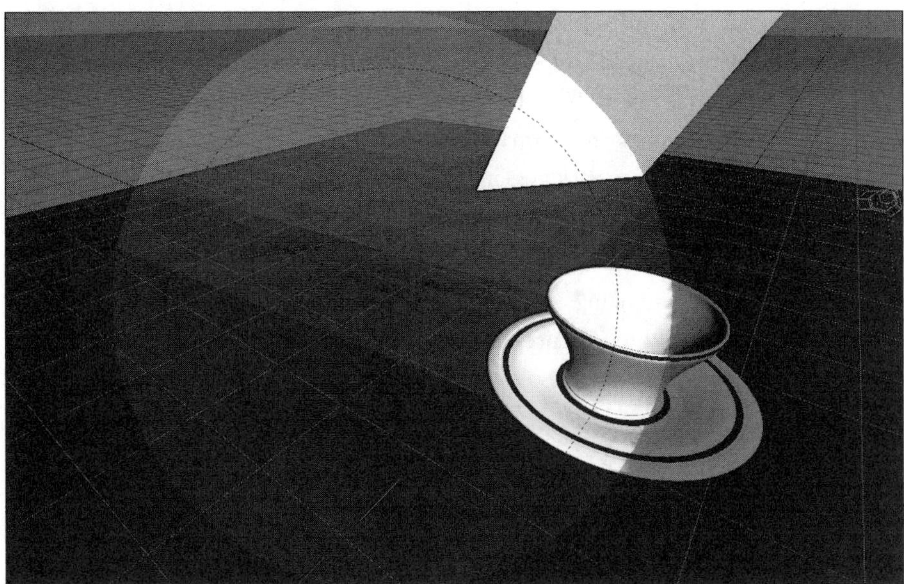

Figure 4.23 A new spotlight is added and focused on the set behind the teacup.

4. To project the image from the gobo light, select it, and press **p** to open the Light Properties panel. If the Light Properties panel is already open, you can select the light from within the panel by using the Current Light drop-down arrow. Make sure that Shadow Map is selected in the Shadows tab for this light as well, or the light will cast right through the teacup.

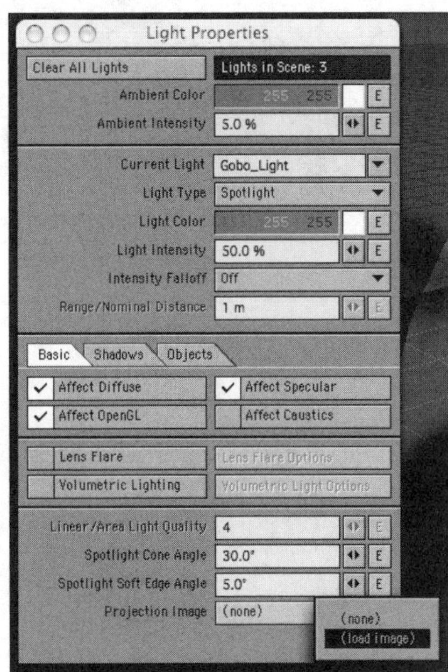

Figure 4.24 You can add a projection image to a spotlight, thus simulating a cool design projected on a set.

5. In the Light Properties panel for the gobo light, select the Projection Image drop-down list at the bottom and select (load image), as shown in **Figure 4.24**. Load the Tree_Gobo image from this book's DVD (in the "\Projects\Images\CH4\" directory). You can find it under the Images folder in the Projects directory for this chapter. LightWave v9 will show you the projected image when you're in Light view.

6. After the image has been loaded, press **F9** to render. You'll see what appears to be light through trees, across the set. The light is now projected through the grayscale image, which you can see from Light view (see **Figure 4.25**). You can take a closer look at the gobo image in the Image Editor. Note that your image might appear slightly different due to variances in light placements.
7. Press F9 to perform a single frame render to see how the gobo light looks projected on the back of the set. If you don't like it, move the light a little, press F9 again, and so on. Adjust to your liking. Moving the light further away works well for creating a streaked gobo image too. **Figure 4.26** shows the render with the gobo light added.

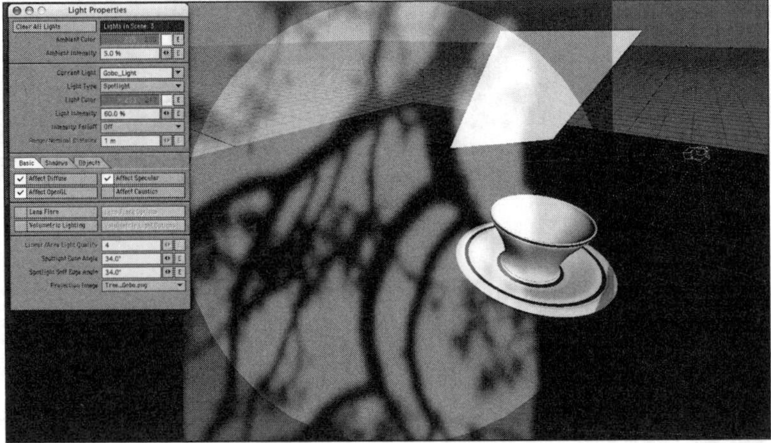

Figure 4.25 LightWave v9 allows you to see your projection images through Light view.

Figure 4.26 Just two lights in the scene, a light box, and a gobo on a spotlight give the set a different look.

You can load this final scene into Layout from this book's DVD and check the final settings if you want. The scene is called Teacup_Lit.lws (in the "Projects\Scenes\Ch4\" directory). Take a look at it and modify it for your own scenes if you like.

Adding gobos is easy. But it's probably a more powerful feature than you realize. Creating a simple pattern on a set is nice, but you can accomplish much more with gobos:

- Use a grayscale image of tree branches to simulate shadows from a tree.
- Use color images for added dimension. Darker areas will hold back more light, and lighter areas will shine more light. For example, you can create the effects of light through a stained-glass window.
- Use softer, blurry images for added effects.
- Use animation sequences as projection images.
- Use imported movie files! Create real projected movies in your animation by projecting an AVI or QuickTime movie onto a movie screen in 3D.
- Create windowpanes and project them onto your set to create the look of light coming through a window.

You also can apply volumetric effects for projection images. In Chapter 15, "Advanced Cameras and Rendering," you'll learn about volumetric lighting and the cool things you can create with this feature. Combine those techniques with these lighting techniques and you're ready to rock!

Using Area Lights

Distant lights and point lights produce hard-edged, ray-traced shadows. Ray-traced shadows take more time to calculate, which of course means more time to render. Spotlights also can produce ray-traced shadows, but with spotlights you have the option to use shadow maps, which take less time to render than ray-traced shadows. Softer than ray-traced shadows, shadow maps use more memory to render than ray-traced shadows. Ray-traced shadows use more processing power.

Area lights also can produce realistic ray-traced shadows, but to do so they require more rendering time. For example, say a person is standing outside in bright sunlight. The shadow that the person casts has sharp edges around the area by the subject's foot, where the shadow begins. As the shadow falls off and away from the subject, it becomes softer. Ray-traced shadows from distant lights, point lights, and spotlights cannot produce this effect—neither can shadow maps. Only area lights can produce these true shadows and create a softer overall appearance to animations.

Spotlights are the most common lights, and they are the most useful for your everyday animation needs. But on occasion, the added rendering time generated from area lights is worthwhile. An area light is represented in Layout by a flat square and emits light equally from all directions except for the edges, producing very realistic shadows.

Exercise 4.5 Working with Area Lights

1. Continuing from the scene you've been working on throughout this chapter, select Key_Light, and press **p** to open the Light Properties panel. Change Light Type from Spotlight to Area Light.
2. Change the Light Intensity setting to 60%. Keeping the default 100% Light Intensity setting would be too bright, and the image would appear washed out. Area lights are much "hotter" than spotlights and also give you more control.
3. Move the Light Properties panel aside and return to Layout.
4. If the new area light is not selected, select it and change your Layout view to Perspective to get an overall view of the scene. **Figure 4.27** shows the Perspective view. The area light appears as a box outline. This light is already positioned above and to the left of the teacup object. It's here because you originally set the key light in this position. All you've done now is change the type of light you're using. Everything else, such as position and rotation, has remained the same.

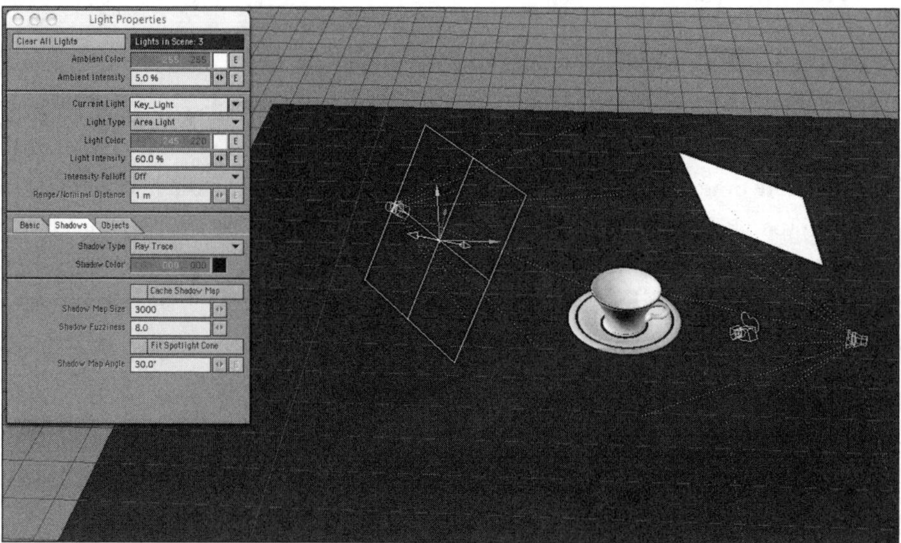

Figure 4.27 The single area light can create beautiful shadows, even on a simple object.

Note

To help set up lights in Layout, change the Maximum Render Level setting to Textured Shaded Solid. You can find this setting by clicking the drop-down arrow to the right of the viewport style buttons at the top of Layout. Make sure Max OpenGL Lights is set to at least 1 or above from the Display Options panel (press **d**). Also, always make sure that the Affect OpenGL option for the light in the Light Properties panel is turned on. This makes the light source's effect visible in Layout, and helps you line up the direction of the light source.

5. In Layout's Render tab, click Render Globals and then, on the Render Globals panel's Render tab, check Ray Trace Shadows to have LightWave calculate shadows for the area light, as shown in **Figure 4.28**.

Note

While you're in the Render Options panel, make sure you choose a Preview setting, such as 320×240. This enables you to see the render as it's being drawn. Also make sure that Render Display is set to Image Viewer to see a full-sized version of your render when it's complete. The full-sized version will be 640×480, as this is its resolution setting by default. You can also change this setting in the Render Globals panel. You'll learn more about different resolutions (and not of the New Year's kind) in Chapter 5, "3D Cameras."

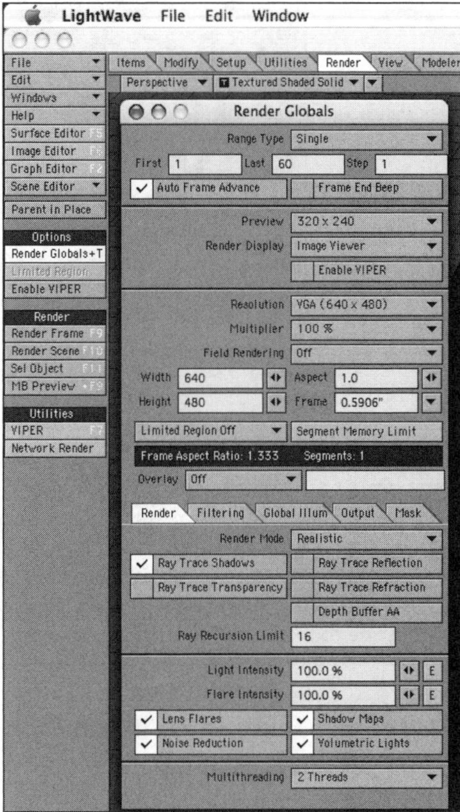

Figure 4.28 You tell LightWave to calculate Ray Trace Shadows while rendering from the Render Globals panel.

6. Press **F9** to render the current frame. You'll see that the shadow has a soft edge, as shown in **Figure 4.29**. But the light itself is a bit too hot, and the teacup is washed out in spots.

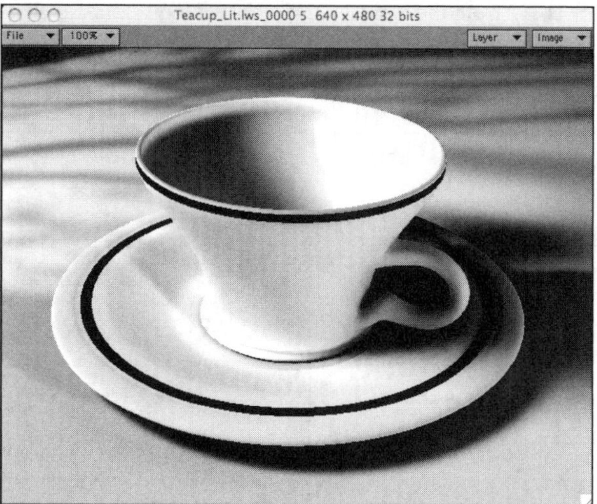

Figure 4.29 The default area light casts a sufficient shadow, but the light it casts might be a little hot.

Note

The cool thing about area lights is that you can size them. Because the area light here was originally a spotlight, its size has remained. If, however, you created a new area light, you would need to increase the size to soften the shadows. By increasing their size, you soften their shadows. Don't forget to keyframe any size changes. You can use the Size tool on the Modify tab. Try it out!

7. In Layout, select the area light, and then press **p** to open the properties panel. Change the Light Intensity setting to about 45%.
8. Press **F9** to perform another render. **Figure 4.30** shows the render with less intensity.

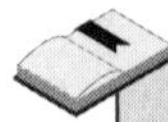

Note

If you increase the size of the area light, the shadow softens. However, it might appear grainy or jagged. If so, simply increase the Area Light Quality setting in the Light Properties panel. The default is 4—good for most renderings. Often setting a value of 5 works slightly better but takes more render time. Isn't that always the case? Note that 5 is your maximum value.

Figure 4.30 You can resize an area light for softer shadows, and by bringing the light intensity down, the light's effect is not as hot.

Sizing a light might seem odd, but it helps spread the amount of light and thereby the shadow as well. Notice in Figure 4.30 that the shadow is soft and very realistic. Area lights take a long time to render, but they produce the best results.

Here are a few more things to remember when using area lights:

- Quality settings can be adjusted. The default Area Light Quality setting of 4 results in 16 samples per area light. Values of 2 and 3 result in 4 and 9 samples per area light, respectively.
- Linear lights perform like area lights but emit light from a two-point polygonal shape, similar to a fluorescent tube.
- You can mix spotlights, distant lights, point lights, and linear lights with area lights for added effects.

The Material Connection

Earlier in the chapter we mentioned that textures play a key role in how your lighting affects your objects. This couldn't be more true for a scene such as the one you've been working on here. This next small project will take your teacup scene to the final render by enhancing the entire look with a few simple surface changes.

1. Continuing the project you've been working on, open the Surface Editor.
2. In the Surface Name list, expand the Teacup listing. Select the Cup surface, and set the color to ivory (about R: 253 G: 255, B: 246).

3. Set Specularity to 20%, Glossiness to 40% and Reflection to 90%.
4. Change the Diffuse value to about 70%. **Figure 4.31** shows the changes.

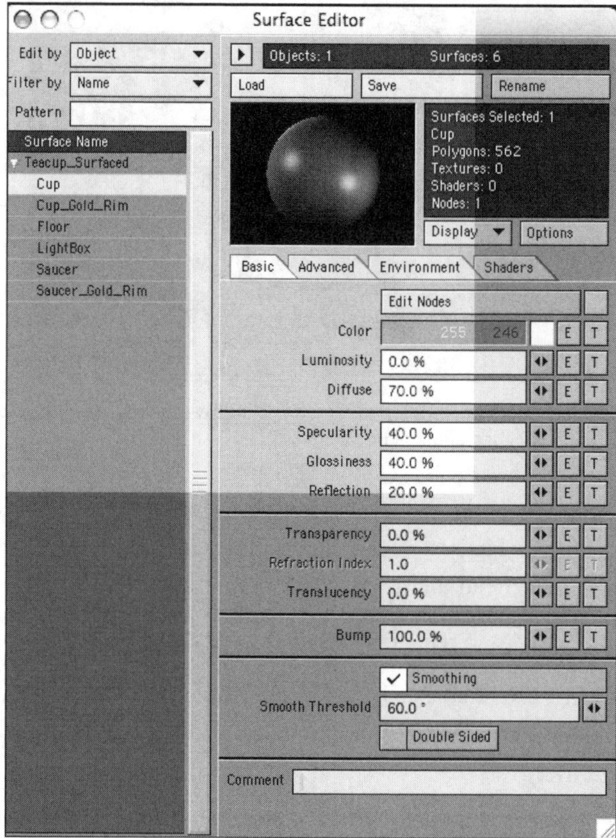

Figure 4.31 A few basic surface settings to the cup and you're on your way to making the final scene.

5. Next, select the Environment tab within the Surface Editor, and set Reflection Options to Ray Tracing and Backdrop. Most likely, this is on by default.
6. In the Surface Name list, right-click on the Cup surface entry and choose Copy.
7. Select the Saucer surface listing, right-click and choose Paste. Now both surfaces have the same properties, and you're still editing the surface attributes for both.
8. To make your teacup reflect its surroundings, you need to do three things. First, as you've done already, you give the surface a Reflection percentage greater than 0. You then tell the surface what to reflect, such as the environment. To have LightWave calculate the rays to reflect, open the Render Globals panel from

Layout's Render tab, and check the Ray Trace Reflection option, found in the panel's Render tab.

9. Save your scene, and also choose Save All Objects from the File menu to save the surface properties you've now applied. Press **F9** and view the rendered changes (**Figure 4.32**).

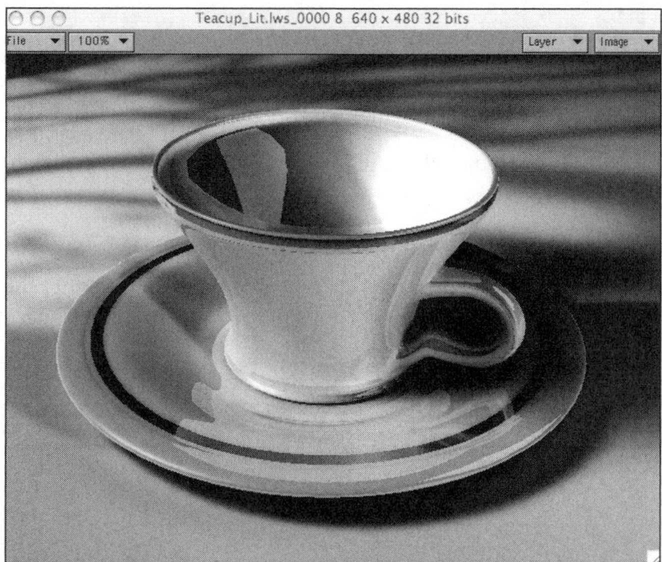

Figure 4.32 By adding a bit of reflection and shine to the cup and saucer and activating Ray Traced Reflections, you ensure that the lighting in the environment looks even better now that the cup interacts with it.

By changing the surface values to a medium specularity for a shinier surface and adding reflections, you've now blended the cup with the environment. Everything in your world interacts with its environment. Sure, not everything is shiny and reflective, but from a desk, to a chair, to a bug on the wall, whatever you see is the result of the object interacting with the light that surrounds it.

There are a few more things you can do to dress up the scene further. First, let's shine up the metallic trim on the cup and saucer.

10. Select the Cup_Gold_Rim surface in the Surface Name list. Holding down the Ctrl key, select the Saucer_Gold_Rim surface. In LightWave's Surface Editor, you can edit multiple surfaces at the same time.

11. With the two surfaces selected, set the color to a warm yellowish-orange to create gold (roughly R: 226, G: 181, B: 004).

12. Set Diffuse to 50% but leave the luminosity setting at 0, which is normal for most surfaces. Higher Luminosity is typically used for lightbulbs, flames, and other things that glow.
13. Change Specularity to 50% and Glossiness to 35%; too much higher and you'd make this object too shiny, like glass. If you decide to burnish the trim a little more, you can always increase these values later.
14. Set Reflection to 50%. This might seem high, but polished metal, even a trim on a cup, should be highly reflective. This setting is also good for things like stainless-steel faucets and chrome auto trim.
15. On the Environment tab, make sure that Ray Tracing and Backdrop are set for Reflection Options.
16. From the File menu in Layout, choose Save All Objects. This will save the surface settings you've applied. Then, save the scene and press **F9** to render the current frame (**Figure 4.33**).

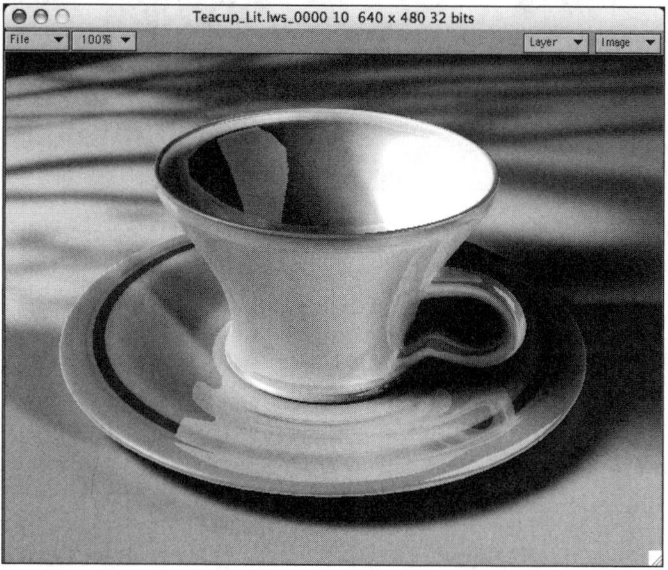

Figure 4.33 With a metallic gold trim added to the cup's surfaces, the shot is complete.

The reason the metallic surface works is because it's reflecting its environment. The Environment setting is currently black, which you can change by going to the Windows drop-down menu and choosing Background Options. But what happens with the highly reflective surface is that it reflects a black backdrop, which blends with the color of the surface. The reflection also picks up the cup and ground nearby, as well as the light box (the large flat polygon off camera). These added elements create the illusion of a metallic surface. Nice, isn't it? In the past, many artists would simply have the metallic surface reflect and image, but reflecting the environment is a bit more convincing.

From here, you can tweak, and perhaps add colored lighting as you like. Experiment with the information provided in this chapter and see what variations you can come up with. One dramatic thing you can do is bring the intensity of the key light down, and increase the Fill and Radiosity settings. Have the key light only as an accent so that the light is primarily lit from behind.

The Next Step

The information in this chapter can be applied to any type of scene you create in LightWave, from outdoor scenes, to sets, and even fantasy-type renders. It can be applied to any of the exercises and projects in this book. These basic lighting setups and core functions apply to all of your LightWave work in one way or another, either in simple or complex form. Use the information here to branch out on your own and create different lighting environments. Use lights to your advantage—remember, there are no wires or electric bills to worry about when creating virtual lighting situations. You don't need to worry about lightbulbs burning out either!

Experiment by adding more lights to your everyday scene or perhaps taking some away. Use negative lights, colored lights, dim lights, overly bright lights, and whatever else you can think of to make your models and animations look as good as they can. But what will make them stand out from the rest of the pack is your own creative input. Don't worry about rules too much. Learn the basics, understand how the tools work, and try it out! If you think you'd like more light on a particular area of the scene, add it. Don't ask people on Internet forums—just try it!

What adds even more interest to your scenes in the camera. LightWave v9's camera tools are quite powerful, so turn the page to understand this updated feature set.

Chapter 5

3D Cameras

Almost everyone has a camera, whether it's a webcam, a handy point-and-shoot, an old 35mm, a camera phone, or even a disposable from the grocery store. Chances are, you have experience taking pictures, and that will serve you well when considering one of the most overlooked features in 3D software—the camera. When filmmakers create motion pictures, they block out their shots, set up camera angles, and select the proper lenses before they shoot a frame of film. 3D animators, on the other hand, often take great pains to set up their models and lighting, and then treat the camera as an afterthought. Of course, you know better, and understand that the camera should be an integral part of the animation process, right? That's why you're reading this chapter: to learn all about the cameras in LightWave v9 so that you can plan your 3D camera shots.

The art of 3D animation involves more than creating models, applying textures, and setting keyframes. 3D animation is an art form all its own, and it's still in its infancy. Part of learning about this new and fascinating art form is understanding the digital camera. I don't mean the kind of digital camera you pick up at the local electronics store, but the kind inside the computer software—it's your digital eye.

This chapter introduces you to everyday camera techniques that you can apply to your LightWave animations. The camera and its settings, placement, and angle play a significant role in every LightWave animation you create. LightWave can set up more than one camera in your scenes—just like a television studio or movie set. (Cameras also can be animated—a topic we'll begin exploring in Chapter 6, "Principles in Motion.")

If you have any experience in photography or videography, the transition to "shooting" in LightWave will be smooth, and you'll find that LightWave v9 takes the camera to new levels you never thought possible. This chapter covers:

- Working with the 3D camera
- Exploring real-world camera settings
- Applying 3D cameras
- LightWave v9's new cameras

Focus on Cameras

At this point, you're probably familiar with LightWave's workflow. You should know that cameras are available in LightWave Layout, not in Modeler. As you work with Layout, you'll become familiar with the various Properties panels associated with objects and lights. The Camera Properties panel controls all the necessary camera settings, such as resolution, focal length, depth of field, masking, and more. However, you won't find render options in this panel. Those are located in the Render Globals panel, which you'll find by clicking Render Globals in Layout's Render tab. Some programs, such as Adobe After Effects, contain all camera, resolution, and output information in the same panel. LightWave uses the Render Globals panel as a single location for setting project resolutions, output options, render properties, and more.

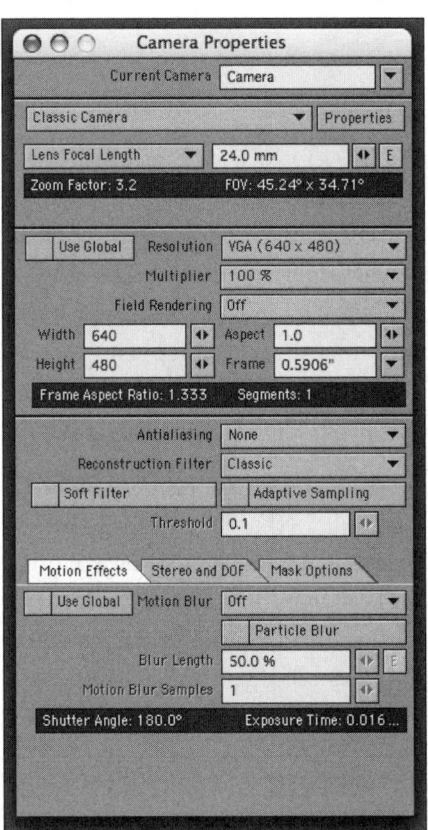

Figure 5.1 The LightWave v9 Camera Properties panel.

By now, having used several of Layout's Properties panels in earlier chapters, you can probably guess how to open the Camera Properties panel (**Figure 5.1**). Click the Cameras mode button at the bottom of the Layout interface, and then click the Properties button (or press **p**).

Near the top of the Camera Properties panel, you'll see an item labeled Resolution. **Figure 5.2** shows the various types of resolutions available to you. You'll learn about using these a bit later in this chapter.

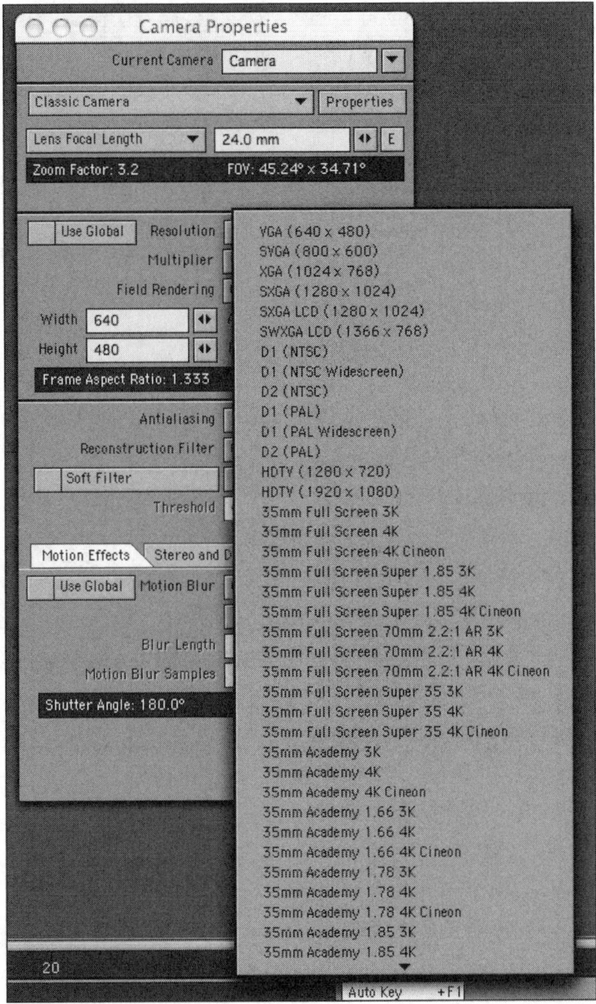

Figure 5.2 LightWave offers a wide range of camera resolutions and different types of cameras.

Setting Up a Camera

LightWave v9 has introduced a whole bunch of cameras. That's right, *cameras*, as in more than one! You were able to add multiple cameras in version 8, but the new LightWave v9 cameras offer even more options. This chapter introduces you to LightWave cameras and provides the groundwork for using them in different projects throughout the rest of book. **Figure 5.3** shows the available cameras in LightWave. The different camera names sound confusing, but soon you'll see how they all come together. You'll learn what each of LightWave v9's cameras are for and when to use them.

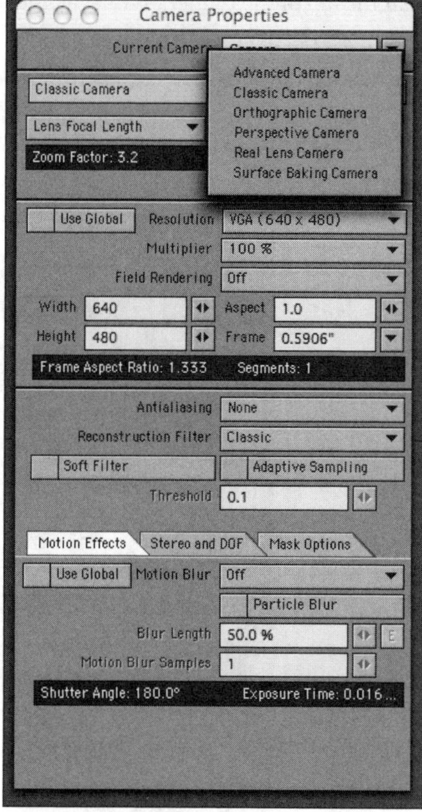

Figure 5.3 LightWave v9 has many different types of cameras, which you'll see in action throughout the book.

LightWave v9 cameras are not only easy to use but also easy to set up. Creative camera use can be useful for any type of scene, moving or still, and we've set up a number of projects along these lines for you to learn from. More specifically, you can use multiple cameras when you have a large scene that has action that needs to be covered from various angles, such as a stage play, virtual walkthrough, or an accident re-creation. Multiple cameras can help you save time setting up animations that need to be viewed from different angles. Using the Camera Selector plug-in from the Master Plug-ins, you can switch between specific cameras during rendering. Also, you can render passes from any camera in the scene. In Exercise 5.1, we'll begin exploring creative use of cameras in LightWave v9.

Exercise 5.1 Working with Cameras

1. From the File menu in Layout at the upper left of the interface, select Clear Scene. Of course, save any work you might have done first. If you're just starting LightWave, there's no need to clear the scene. LightWave remembers what you worked on last, but it does not load that project automatically.
2. Select the Items menu; under the Add category, click Camera. You now have two cameras in the scene: the default camera that's always in a blank scene and the camera you just added.

   When you click Add Camera, a small panel appears, asking you for a name. You can give the camera a new name or just click OK to use the catchy default name

"Camera," which appears with a number next to it, "Camera (2)," because the default camera is named Camera as well—and is now denoted as Camera (1). A third camera would be Camera (3), and so on.

If the default names get confusing, you can always rename any camera later.

3. Click OK to add a second camera to Layout.

   You'll set up each camera separately, so the first thing you must do is select the specific camera you want to work with. Adding, selecting, or deleting cameras is the same as selecting any other scene items, such as objects or lights.

4. Select the camera by first clicking the Cameras button at the bottom of the interface.

5. From the Current Item drop-down, choose which camera you want to use.

6. To rename a camera, select the Rename command from the Replace category under the Items tab.

   It really doesn't matter if you are working with one camera, two cameras, or ten—the settings are the same. Simply point and shoot!

   To get the most out of multiple cameras, set them up in a way that will be most beneficial to your animation. For example, suppose that you need to re-create a traffic accident and the client wants to see the accident from a bystander's viewpoint, an aerial viewpoint, and the driver's viewpoint. By adding three cameras to your scene and setting them in the desired positions, you can render the animation from any view. What's even cooler in LightWave v9 is that each camera can be of a different type. For example, you can set up a Classic camera (as you've done here) to render the majority of your animation. Then, set up a second camera as an orthographical camera to render just a side view of your scene. Set up a third camera as a Real Lens Camera, allowing you to specify a particular lens such as a Canon 24–70 f/2.8L, attached to a Canon 5D. Very specific, and very cool.

Setting Camera Resolution

After you've chosen the camera you want to work with, Resolution is commonly the first setting you apply in the Camera Properties panel. This setting determines the width and height at which images shot through the camera will be rendered. LightWave also will set the appropriate pixel aspect of your rendered images when a specific resolution is specified.

Note

Rendering is a generic term for creating or drawing an image. This is done in LightWave by pressing **F9** for single frames (Render Current Frame) and **F10** for multiple frames (Render Scene). Press **F11** to render the currently selected object only.

The resolution you choose in the Camera Properties panel determines the final output size of your images and animations. It's important to understand that you can set the output resolution setting in two locations in LightWave v9. You can set it in the Camera properties panel as you've seen here. But you can also enable the Use Global option in the Camera Properties panel, and your resolution can then be set in the Render Globals panel, found on the Render tab. For now, we'll use the standard Camera Properties panel for our examples.

Note

> You might find it confusing that you can set up camera resolution in two places in LightWave v9. You're not alone! It is confusing. The goal here in this section is to have you understand resolutions and settings. Where you set them is not as important right now. But you can get into the habit of setting up everything globally. Click the Use Global option in the Camera Properties panel, and then just use the Render Globals panel to set everything else.

The default resolution is VGA mode, which is 640 pixels wide by 480 pixels tall. This resolution is of a medium size, which is common for most computer work. You also can choose SVGA, which is 800 by 600 pixels, or XVGA, which is 1024 by 768 pixels. These are good resolutions to work with if your images or animations are being used in a computer environment, such as in QuickTime or AVI formats. You also have resolutions such as SWXGA, which is 1366×768, a popular resolution for many HD monitors. You'll find that LightWave v9 offers film resolutions presets as well, all found within the Resolution drop-down. The reason you'd use some of these higher resolutions is to match video or film, either imported and composited, or perhaps it's a resolution you're rendering to for later use.

Note

> *QuickTime* is Apple Computer's basic multimedia application and format, now common on both Macintosh and Windows computers. Rendering an animation to a QuickTime movie creates a playable computer file. AVI (Audio Video Interleaved), developed by Microsoft, is another type of compressed audio/video format. Each has varying levels of compression, so check your particular computer system for your ideal setting.

If you are creating animations that will end up on videotape, you'll want to use the D1 or D2 NTSC resolution settings (in the United States), or the D1 or D2 PAL resolution settings (in Europe).

Note

In 1953, the National Television Standards Committee (NTSC) developed the North American television broadcast standard. This standard is 60 half-frames, or fields, per second, with 525 lines of resolution. PAL stands for Phase Alternate Line. This standard, which most of Western Europe uses, is 625 lines of resolution at 50 fields per second.

Setting the Resolution Multiplier

A great time-saving feature in LightWave is the Resolution Multiplier (**Figure 5.4**). It lets you output an accurate version of the final render at a different size (usually smaller than the final version, to save time) without changing the actual pixel dimensions of the project. This is perfect for cranking out scaled-down versions of a render for testing or client-approval purposes, and it does a super job with enlargements as well . Multiplier values are limited to 25%, 50%, 100%, 200%, and 400%.

Figure 5.4 The Resolution Multiplier gives you an accurate view of your render at smaller or larger sizes.

Understanding the Pixel Aspect Ratio

You probably know that the images on your computer screen consist of tiny dots called *pixels*. You may even know that *pixel* is short for *picture element*, and that all pixels are rectangular. What you may not realize, however, is that all pixels are not created equal. What sets them apart is their shapes, which are described in terms of *aspect ratio*—the proportion of their width to their height. Images created for display on computer screens have square pixels, with an aspect ratio of 1.0. Images prepared for display on TV screens are another matter. Images generated for NTSC D1-standard TVs used in North America typically measure 720×486 pixels, and consist of pixels that are taller than they are wide, with aspect ratios between 0.86 and 0.90. Images created for PAL-standard TVs (used in Europe) measure 720×576 pixels, but consist of pixels wider than they are tall, with aspect ratios of 1.01 to 1.06.

In the course of most animations, LightWave sets appropriate camera and output pixel resolutions automatically, so you don't have to memorize all this. But it's wise to familiarize yourself with the effects of pixel aspect ratio settings, so you'll recognize what's happening in case problems arise.

For example, suppose you have a perfect square in your image. If you use an Aspect setting of 1.0, LightWave renders the square using the same number of pixels for its width and height. This looks good on your PC monitor, but if you show the image on an NTSC TV, it looks tall and goofy. This is because televisions have tall pixels and although the same number of pixels make up the square's height and width, because they are "tall" they make the box tall. If you use an Aspect setting of .9, LightWave compensates and the image looks correct. An NTSC television pixel aspect ratio might not always be exactly .9, but it won't be 1.0.

Field Rendering

Beneath the Resolution and Multiplier options in the Camera Properties panel you'll see the Field Rendering option. Like the Aspect setting, this setting is used when preparing animation for output to analog videotape. Activating field rendering tells LightWave to mimic the process analog video devices use to "draw" images on television screens: Each frame of video is divided into two *fields*, one consisting of the even-numbered horizontal rows of pixels and the other consisting of the odd-numbered rows. First, one field is drawn and then the other, completing the frame via a process called *interlacing*. (NTSC video draws screen images at a frequency of 30 frames per second, or 60 fields per second.) Standard 3D renderings are not interlaced, which generally means higher quality, but playing them back on interlaced devices can make motion look choppy, especially when objects are moving swiftly and close to the camera. Field rendering lets your animations synchronize better with an interlaced display, so motion looks crisp and clean. You can set LightWave to render the even or odd fields first.

Exercise 5.2 Working with Aspect Ratios

To give you an idea of how the different aspect ratios work, open LightWave v9 Layout and perform the following steps.

1. Clear the scene from the File drop-down menu. Then, select Camera View in the selection drop-down at the top of the Layout window (**Figure 5.5**).

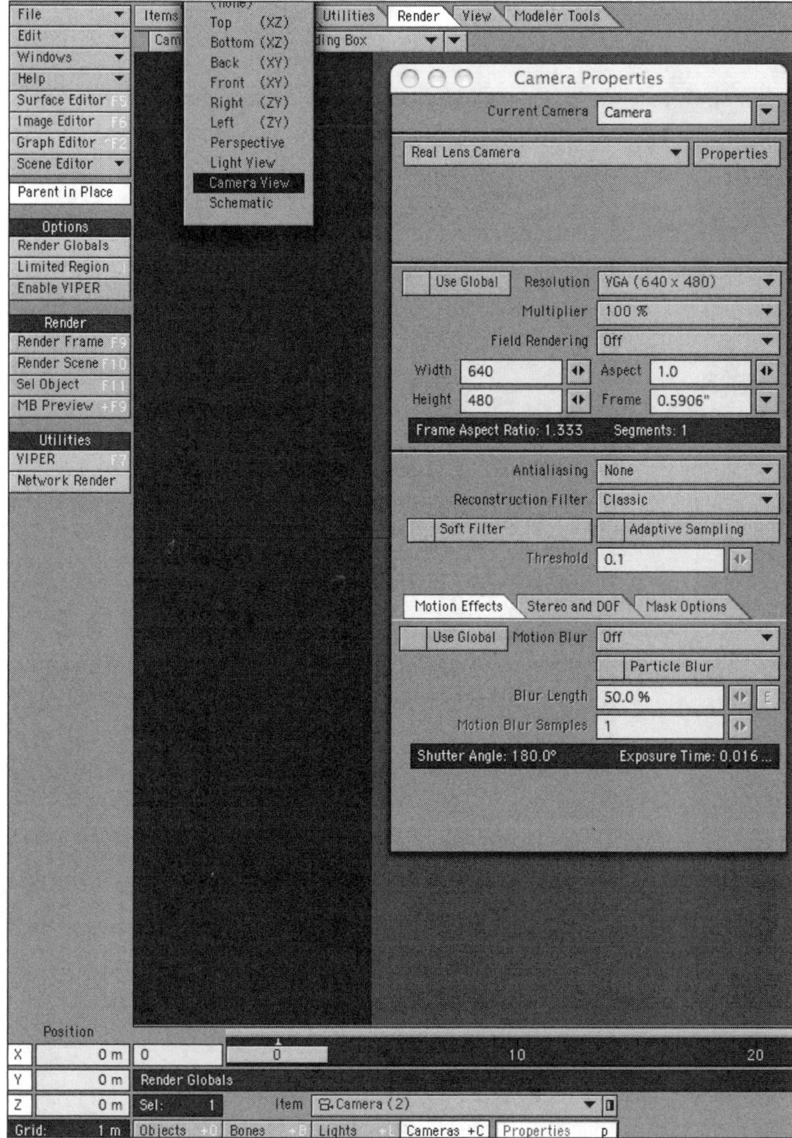

Figure 5.5 Resolution and the results of setting the pixel aspect ratios can be seen only through the Camera view in Layout.

Remember that, although resolution settings can be seen directly in Layout, you won't see the stretching due to an incorrect aspect in Layout. Rather, Layout merely shows you what portions of the scene will be in the rendered image. It is the projection of this image on the display device that causes the stretching, if any.

2. To make sure that Show Safe Areas is selected, press the **d** key to enter the Display Options tab within the Preferences panel.
3. Select Show Safe Areas under the Camera View tab at the bottom of the interface, as shown in **Figure 5.6**.

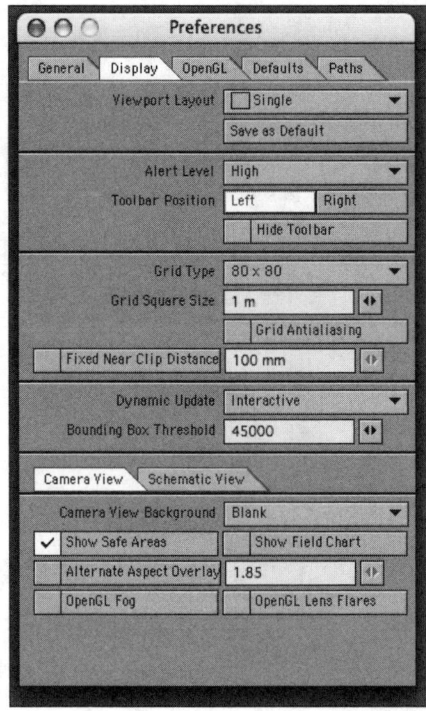

Figure 5.6 Selecting Show Safe Areas on the Display Options tab turns on a visible outline through the Camera view in Layout.

Note

Safe areas are important to use as shot references. The outer line represents the video-safe area—any animation elements outside this area will not be visible on a standard 4:3 ratio television monitor. The inner line represents the title-safe area; no text in your animations should travel beyond this bounding region. Video has something called overscan, and the area you're not seeing is within this region. Broadcast monitors allow you to view overscan, but standard 4:3 televisions do not. Keeping within these guidelines will help your relationship with video professionals as well.

4. Close the Display Options panel by pressing **d** again or **p** (for properties).

   Figure 5.7 shows the Camera view with the safe areas enabled, with a scene loaded. This safe area represents the title-safe and video-safe areas of your view. You should set up animations with this feature enabled to ensure that you know how your animation will appear when it is recorded onto videotape.

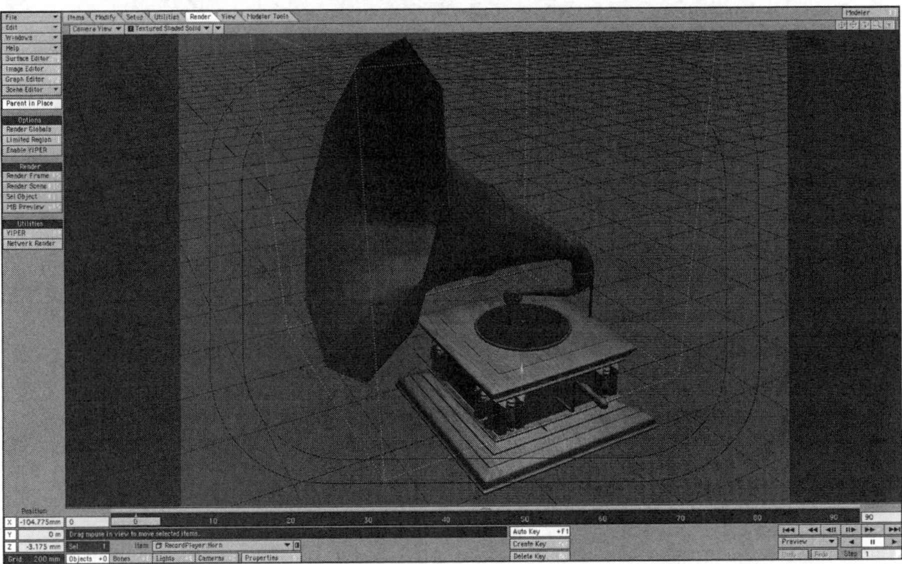

Figure 5.7 When Show Safe Areas is enabled, you'll see a television-style shape around your field of view through the camera.

Note

You can change the color of the safe area outlines by changing the overlay color selection on the Display Options tab (press **d**) of the Preferences panel. Doing this also changes the color of any overlays seen in the Camera view, such as field chart.

5. Select Camera from the bottom of Layout (or press Shift+c), and then choose the Properties panel (or press **p**). Move the Camera Properties panel over to the far right of the screen, revealing more of your Layout window.

6. Go to the Resolution drop-down list and select D1 (NTSC Widescreen), as shown in **Figure 5.8**.

   This resolution changes the width to 720 and the height to 486, with a pixel aspect ratio of 1.2.

Figure 5.8 You have a number of choices when it comes to resolution, such as LightWave's widescreen settings. Setting a resolution to D1 (NTSC Widescreen) changes the pixel aspect ratio to 1.2, making the safe area viewed through the Camera panel appear stretched.

7. Press **p** to close the Camera Properties panel if it's cluttering your workspace. Otherwise, feel free to leave it open.

Note

A quick way to hide any open panels is to press the Tab key. To unhide, press Tab again.

You can see in Figure 5.8 that the safe areas now appear stretched with the widescreen resolution option. You'll see the darkened areas on the left and right of the interface (through the Camera view) are minimal, compared to the first 640×480 resolution. These areas represent the scene that is outside of the frame, based on the resolution you've set.

8. Press **p** again to open the Camera Properties panel. Grab the mini slider button next to Pixel Aspect Ratio and drag it back and forth. **Figure 5.9** shows the slider button. You should see the safe area field of view changing in Layout.

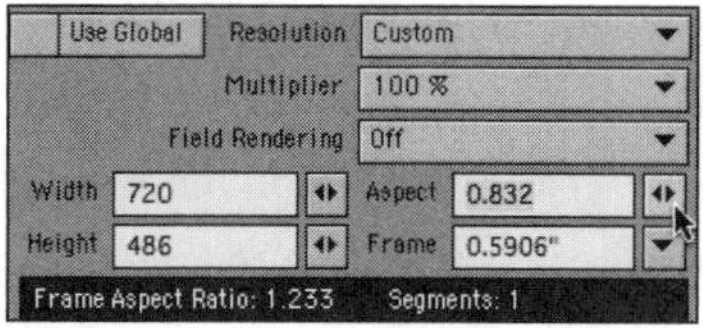

Figure 5.9 You can interactively control the pixel aspect ratio by clicking and dragging the small slider buttons.

As an animator, keep in mind that the pixel aspect ratio affects your renderings. Changing the resolution changes the size of the image, whereas changing the pixel aspect ratio changes the target pixel shape, which also can distort your final output if it is not set properly. Always remember what the target display device is, and set your resolution and aspect ratio accordingly. For example, if you are rendering an animation for computer video and accidentally set Resolution to D1 (standard for NTSC Widescreen broadcast video), your final animation will appear stretched when imported into an animation recorder or nonlinear editing suite. The computer will take the full image and squeeze it to fit the television-size frame your nonlinear editor or animation recorder uses. This happens because widescreen is the incorrect resolution for the standard video recorder. Resolution also determines the pixel aspect ratio, and D1 (NTSC Widescreen) applies the incorrect setting for converting widescreen to video.

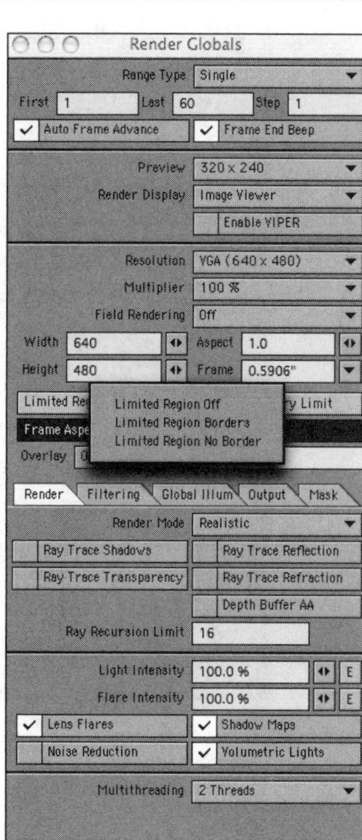

Figure 5.10 Limited Region lets you control the area of the screen to be rendered.

Setting Limited Region

Every now and then, there might be a situation in which the resolution settings are not the exact size you need for rendering. You sometimes might need to render just an area of an animation, saving valuable rendering time. For example, if you have an animation that has many objects, textures, reflections, and more, test-rendering the full image might take up too much of your time—especially if you want to see how one small area of the scene looks in the final render. Using the Limited Region setting helps you accomplish this. Activate it by choosing Render Globals in the Render tab and selecting the option, as shown in **Figure 5.10**.

You can have a limited region with or without borders. The borders setting may not have the effect you expect. For example, let's say your camera resolution is set to 1024×768, and you set a limited region render to just a small portion of the frame. With borders on, you'll see the full 1024×768 rendered frame, but only the limited region will display your 3D elements. LightWave will only render what's in that limited region, while presenting it full frame. With no borders, LightWave renders just your limited region.

You can easily turn on a limited region directly in Layout by pressing **l** (lowercase L). Also, you can simply select the option on the left side of the screen from within the Render tab. You see, we told you that there are many ways to do one thing in LightWave! Now, with Limited Region active, a yellow dotted line appears, encompassing the entire Layout area. From here, you can click the edge of the region and resize it to any desired shape. **Figure 5.11** shows a limited region for a small area of a scene. **Figure 5.12** shows how the image renders would look in the Render Display window with this Limited Region setting.

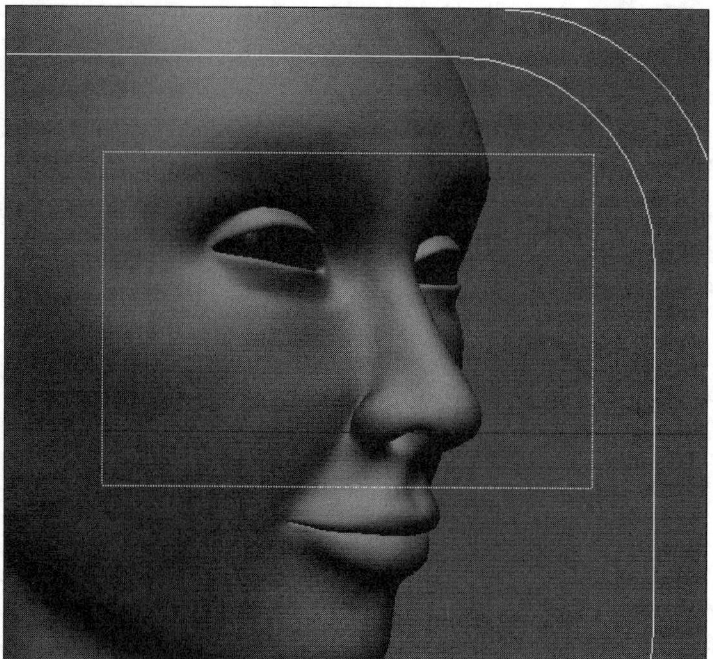

Figure 5.11 You can resize the limited region directly in Layout to render a selected area of the animation.

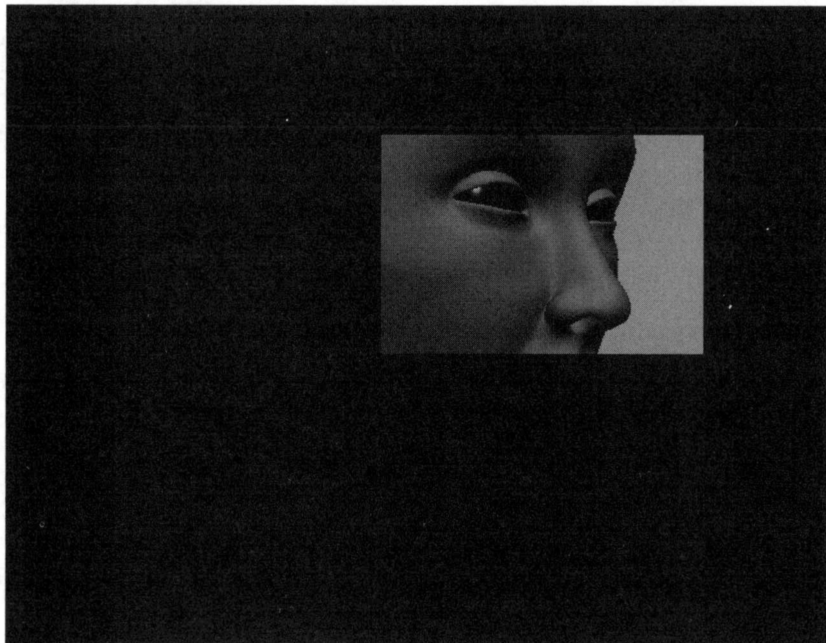

Figure 5.12 The Limited Region's rendered image is just the area assigned in Layout.

Limited Region settings are also useful for creating images for Web sites using LightWave. Perhaps you want to animate a small spinning globe or a rotating 3D head. Rendering in a standard resolution draws unwanted areas, creating images that are not only the correct size but also larger. Setting up a limited region can decrease file size and create renders in the exact size you need, such as a perfect square. Limited Region essentially renders a portion of what normally would be a larger image. Try using a Web GIF animation program and render out a series of small GIF files, set up with a limited region. The GIF animation program imports the sequence of images to create one playable file. Limited Region works differently from a custom resolution. You can specify a limited region as any size and for any area on the screen, whereas setting a custom resolution sets only the specific size for the center of the screen. Also, Limited Region enables you to render limited regions of very high-resolution images. A custom resolution would not work this way. To turn off Limited Region, just press **l** (lowercase L) while in Layout, or turn off the button from within the Render tab.

Note

If you render an image or animation with the borders setting, the image will appear with a border that represents the rest of the unrendered frame. Conversely, rendering with no borders displays only the limited region.

Segment Memory Limit

Head back over to the Render Globals panel (on Layout's Render tab) and, to the right of Limited Region, you'll see the setting Segment Memory Limit. Too often, you'll run out of RAM while you are creating animations. RAM, or the memory in your computer, is used quickly by many images, large objects, and hefty render settings. The Segment Memory Limit feature lets you tell Layout the maximum amount of memory to use for rendering. Lower values allow you to render a frame in segments, which means the frames might take a bit longer to load and execute. The trade-off is that you don't need as much memory.

For faster renders, you can increase the segment memory. Setting the segment memory to 60MB (or 60MB of RAM) often enables you to render higher resolutions in one segment. Although this setting is only an example, LightWave's Segment Memory setting is a maximum setting. This means you can set this value to the same amount of RAM in your system, and LightWave will only use what it needs, often eliminating the need for your system to use virtual memory or a scratch disk. The Segment Memory Limit setting defaults to 32.

Note

Remember that higher resolution settings require more system memory, so be careful when setting very high resolutions and high segment memory limits.

When you click the Segment Memory button, a small panel pops up, asking you to enter a value. You can enter a value as large as you want, provided you have the memory in your system. When you click OK, LightWave asks whether you want to make this value the default. Click Yes, and you won't have to change this value when you start creating another animation scene. **Figure 5.13** shows the Segment Memory selection in the Camera Properties panel.

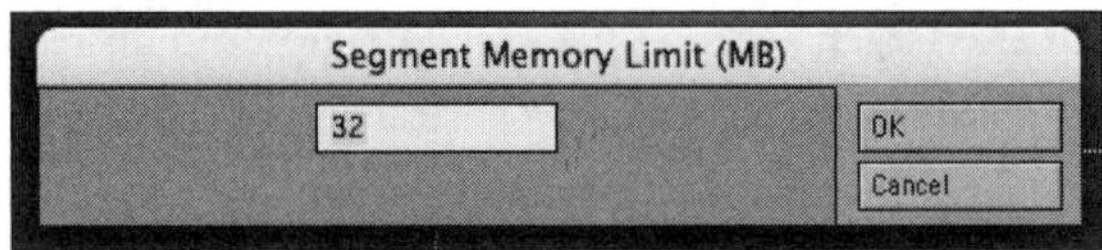

Figure 5.13 Setting a segment memory limit tells LightWave how much memory is available for rendering. Setting a higher value allows LightWave to render animation frames in one pass.

Rename and Select Current Camera

Because LightWave allows you to add more than one camera to your scene, you need a way to select them to adjust each item's properties. The Current Camera selection list is at the top of the Camera Properties panel. If you have not added any cameras to your scene, you will see only the item "Camera." As you can in the Light Properties panel, you can select and rename this camera (or any you've added) directly in the Camera panel. If you have added multiple cameras, they will be listed here (**Figure 5.14**). All cameras are available for selection in the Current Item selection list at the bottom of the Layout interface as well. No matter what type of camera you've chosen—a Classic Camera, Advanced Camera, or otherwise—they can all be selected here.

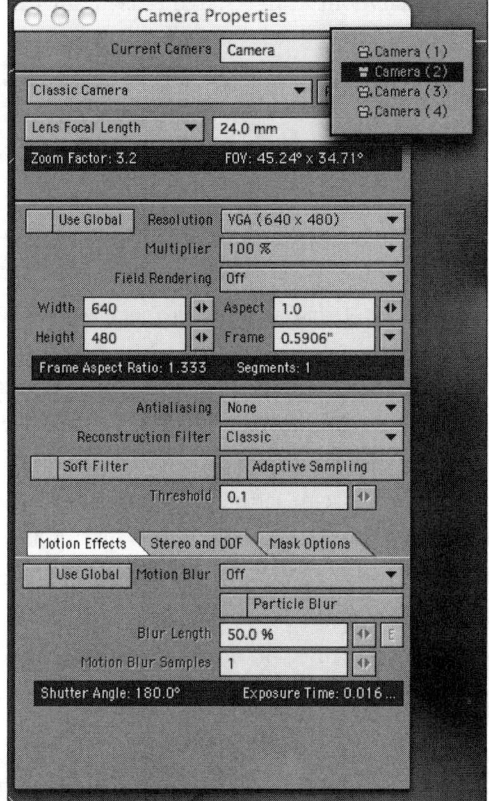

Figure 5.14 All of your scene's cameras can be selected within the Camera Properties panel, from the Current Camera selection list.

Lens Focal Length and Zoom Factor

Two interrelated settings, Zoom Factor and Lens Focal Length, are often misunderstood, and therefore overlooked, when it comes to working with cameras in LightWave. These attributes are different ways of expressing the same thing; change either one, and the other changes accordingly. Essentially, they define the range between the widest focus and tightest focus available through your camera's lens. Have you ever used a camera that allows you to switch from a standard lens to telephoto (for shooting at long distances) or macro (for magnifying small subjects)? Changing focal length or zoom factor in LightWave does much the the same thing, only in a virtual way thatgives you a practically infinitechoice of lenses. By animating changes to these settings, you can even "morph"one lens into another to vary your scenes.

The default zoom factor 3.2, is equivalent to a focal length of 24 mm, as shown in **Figure 5.15**.

Figure 5.15 LightWave's default zoom factor is 3.2, or the equivalent of a 24mm focal length.

The default, which is equivalent to a standard medium-wide video camera lens, is a good starting point for most animations , but to make something come alive in 3D, you'll want to "change lenses" in the course of your animation. **Figure 5.16** shows a scene with the default zoom factor setting. The image looks good, but the scene lacks depth. But take a look at **Figure 5.17**, in which the same shot has a zoom factor of 1.5, or a Lens Focal Length setting of 32mm. This creates a nice wide-angle view. Notice how wide the shot looks and how much depth is in the image. The camera is pushed in close to the dog—notice how the image looks more three-dimensional. This setting is only an example, and you should try different zoom factors on your own to see what works best for you.

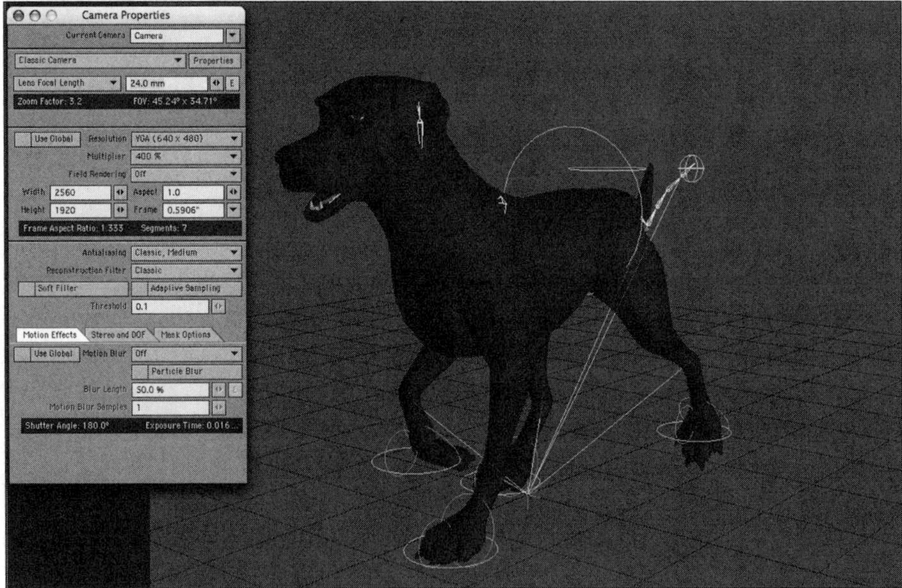

Figure 5.16 A scene set up with the default zoom factor of 3.2, or a Lens Focal Length of 24mm, looks fine but lacks depth.

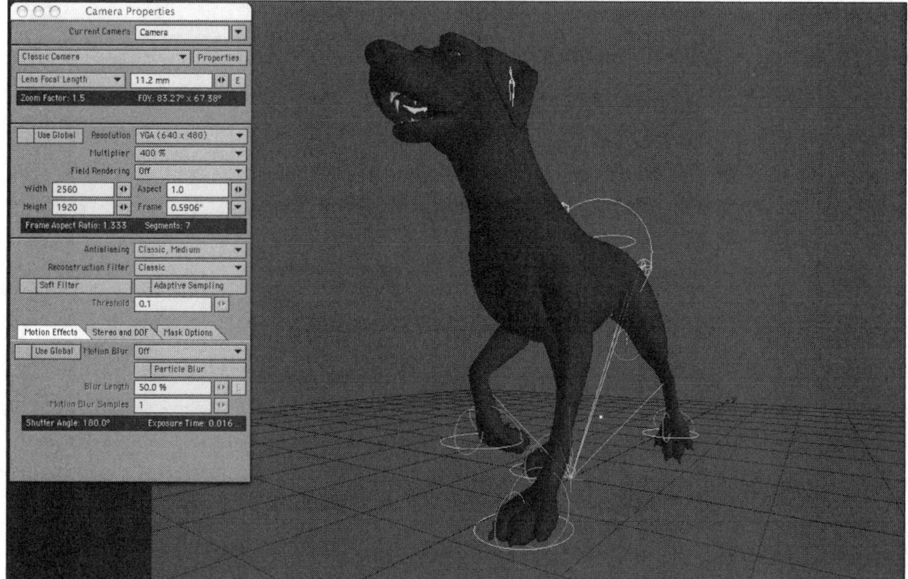

Figure 5.17 The same scene with a Lens Focal Length of 11.2mm gives the shot a lot more dimensionality and makes it much more interesting.

The cameras in LightWave are just as important as your objects. Don't overlook the possibilities of changing the zoom factor over time. Using LightWave's Graph Editor, you can animate the zoom factor with stunning results.

As mentioned, the zoom factor in LightWave directly relates to lens focal lengths—the focal length itself is measured in millimeters. The larger the focal length value, the longer the lens, and the tighter the focus (or the closer you'll be) on the subject. For example, a telephoto lens might be 180mm, and a wide-angle lens might be 12mm. Because focal lengths represent everyday camera settings, just like your 35mm camera, you may be more comfortable working with lens focal lengths instead of zoom factors. You can do this by selecting the desired option from the Zoom Factor drop-down list. Once chosen, you can see your setting in the Camera Properties panel. However, if you do have specific camera lenses you wish to match, you can use the Real Lens Camera, which we'll explore shortly.

Note

Each camera you add to Layout can have a different zoom factor. For example, in the Camera Properties panel, you can select one camera and set the zoom factor so that it renders like a telephoto lens. Then, you can select another camera in the Camera Properties panel and make it render like a wide-angle lens. Each camera in LightWave can be set differently.

Field of View (FOV)

In addition to zoom factor and lens focal length, you can set up a camera's field of view (FOV) using the Horizontal FOV or Vertical FOV settings. **Figure 5.18** shows the additional options in the Camera Properties panel.

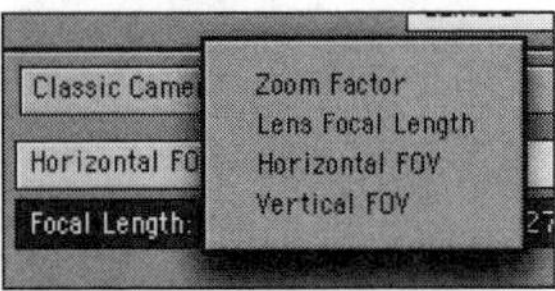

Figure 5.18 You have the option to choose Horizontal and Vertical Field of View (FOV).

Changing the values for zoom factor automatically adjusts the lens focal length, the horizontal FOV, and the vertical FOV. The horizontal and vertical fields of view give you precise control over the lens in LightWave. The two values listed next to FOV are the horizontal and vertical fields (horizontal is the first value). Working with FOV is useful when you are working in real-world situations and need to match camera focal lengths, especially when compositing.

Don't let all these settings confuse you, however. The Zoom Factor, Lens Focal Length, Horizontal FOV, and Vertical FOV settings all enable you to set the same thing. Simply use the one you're most familiar or most comfortable with—or choose whatever is called for to match a real-world camera. There is no inherent benefit in using one over the other.

Antialiasing

When you render an animation, it needs to look good, right? Certainly your model needs to be built correctly, but there are render settings you can apply to enhance the final output. The edges need to be clean and smooth, and no matter how much quality you put into your models, surfaces, lighting, and camera technique, you won't have a perfect render until you set the antialiasing. Antialiasing cures the jagged edges between foreground and background elements. It is a smoothing process that creates cleaner-looking animations. **Figure 5.19** shows a rendered image without antialiasing; **Figure 5.20** shows the same image with a low antialiasing setting applied.

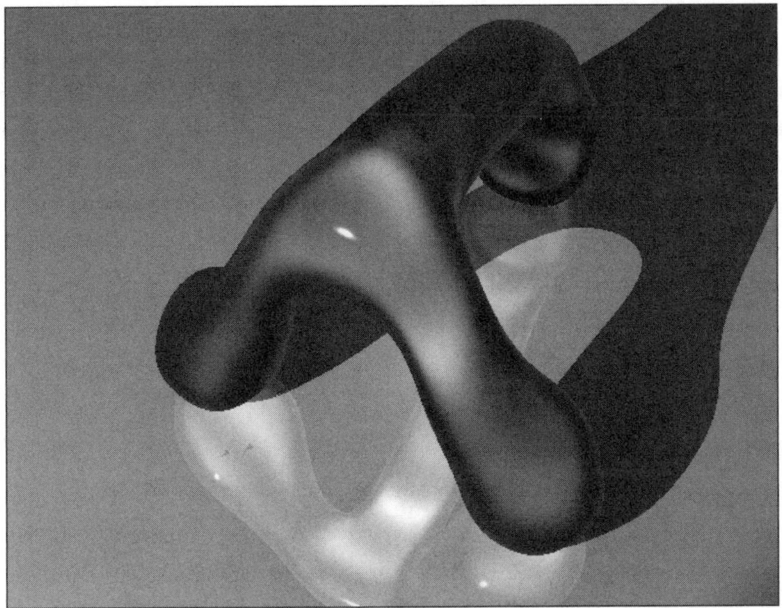

Figure 5.19 Without antialiasing, the rendered image can look jagged and unprofessional, especially when animated. Notice the edges of the model are jagged, or stair-stepped. This is not the result of a bad model but rather an un-antialiased render.

Figure 5.20 After antialiasing is applied, even at a low setting, the image looks cleaner and more polished. You'll see that the edges of the model are smooth, as is the shadow.

Antialiasing can really make a difference in your final renders. **Figure 5.21** shows the available Antialiasing settings, including different variations of PLD (Pixel Lattice Deformation). PLD can save you time, depending on the render. It uses data from the edges of your models and realigns them for the final image. The higher you set the PLD, the more calculations will be done. You'll use different antialias settings throughout the projects in this book to see how they differ.

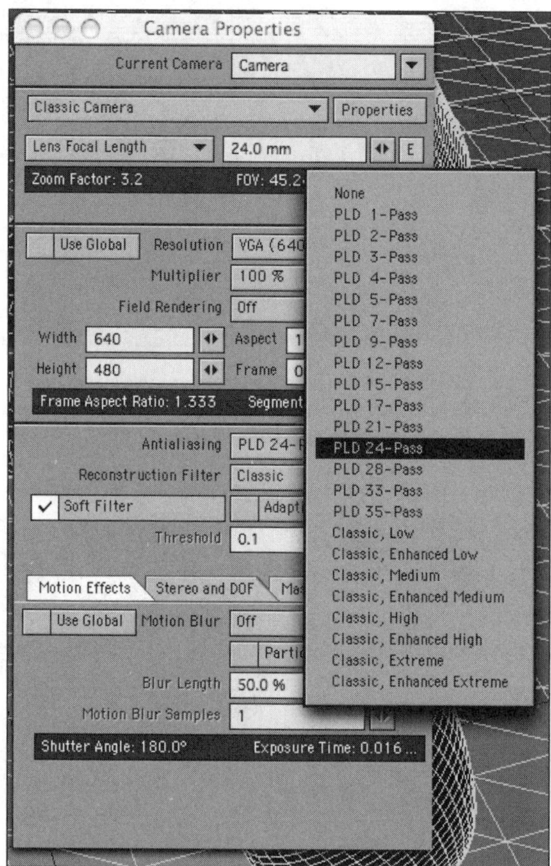

Figure 5.21 You can choose from a range of antialiasing settings, from none at all to Enhanced Extreme.

The higher the antialiasing setting, the more LightWave will clean and smooth your polygon edges. Of course, higher values mean added rendering time. Any of the Enhanced antialiasing settings smoothes your image at the subpixel level, which takes a bit more time to render, but it produces better results. In most cases, Medium to Enhanced Medium antialiasing yields great results. The Reconstruction Filter is one more way that LightWave v9 can produce top-notch renders by using sophisticated calculations to reconstruct the data for the final image.

Adaptive Sampling

Although you can set up an antialiasing routine for your renders, you still have to tell LightWave how it should be applied. Adaptive sampling is a flexible threshold that LightWave employs to evaluate the edges in your scene. Lower values evaluate more, enabling a more accurate antialiasing routine. Higher values evaluate less. A default setting of 0.1 is an average threshold value. Changing this to 0.01, for example, adds to your render times but helps to produce a cleaner render. A good way to work with adaptive sampling is to set a higher antialiasing setting, with a not-so-low threshold. For example, Enhanced Medium antialiasing, with a Threshold setting of 0.1, renders reasonably well (depending on your scene) and produces nice-looking images. For more details on adaptive sampling, refer to your LightWave manual.

Soft Filter

As an additional help to eliminate sharp, unwanted edges in a scene, you can turn on the Soft Filter option in the Camera Properties panel. As an alternative to setting higher antialiasing routines, you can set a lower antialiasing with Soft Filter applied. Soft Filter adds a small blur to your render, creating a "soft-focus" look that can make some renders appear too blurry. Its settings are either on or off. Sorry, no variable amounts!

Motion Effects

At the bottom of the Camera Properties panel are three tabs. Each tab offers even more control over your camera's settings. The first one, Motion Effects, is home to some common, everyday functions like motion blurs.

Note

You'll also see a check box for Use Global on the Motion Effects tab in the Camera properties panel. Enabling this option turns off the controls here and makes them accessible in the Render Globals panel.

Motion Blur

When antialiasing is applied (at a setting of least Low), the Motion Blur option becomes available. From time to time, you may need to create motions that mimic real-world properties, such as a speeding car or a fast-moving camera. To give things a more realistic look, you can apply motion blur to your scene. Motion blur in LightWave combines several semi-dissolved images on each frame to give the effect of blurred motion. Motion blur mimics real-world actions. Remember that the multiple rendering passes used with antialiasing are needed to compute the dissolved images, which is why antialiasing needs to be set to Low or higher. But you can quickly see what your motion blur will look like right in Layout (**Figure 5.22**) by clicking MB Preview on the Render tab or by pressing Shift+F9.

Figure 5.22 Motion blur is applied to a fast-moving object in a scene. Motion blur helps add the feeling of movement because in real-world cameras, the shutter speed is not fast enough to freeze the action.

Apply the motion blur effect any time you have something fast-moving in your scene. Even if it's only a slight motion blur, the added effect will help "sell" the look. If your animation is perfectly clean, perfectly smooth, and always in focus, it won't look realistic. It will look better with some inconsistencies, such as motion blur.

Motion blur also is important to actions like the flapping of a bee's wings, the spinning of an airplane's propellers, and so on. Many animated objects moving at high speed will require you to set the Motion Blur option. If you look at spinning propellers in the real world, all you see is a blur. To re-create that look in LightWave, turn on Motion Blur in the Camera Properties panel.

Classic Motion Blur

To activate LightWave's classic motion blur, antialiasing must be active. If it's not, LightWave v9 will turn it on automatically when you activate antialiasing. Antialiasing redraws the edges of the geometry in the scene, and blurs them accordingly.

PhotoReal

Another type of Motion Blur setting is PhotoReal. Basically, this motion blur can be more accurate, allowing you to specify the number of motion blur samples. More samples means cleaner blurs. But here's the cool part: with PhotoReal, you don't need to set antialiasing. Not that you'd want to render a scene without antialiasing, but to perform a render test to see your blurs in action, PhotoReal comes in handy.

Blur Length

Blur Length is the amount of motion blur you want to use. The default setting for this option is 50%, which produces nice results. Depending on the animation, you may want to set this value slightly higher—for example, to 60% or 65%—for more blurring. When you apply the Blur Length setting, corresponding Shutter Angle and Exposure Time values appear beneath the Blur Length window. Most of your motion-blurred animations should have a 50% Blur Length. This is because the blur length relates to the amount of time the theoretical film is actually exposed. Because of the physical mechanism, a film camera can't expose a frame for 1/24 of a second, even though film normally plays back at 24 frames per second. It turns out that this rotating shutter mechanism exposes the film for only 50% of the per-second rate; thus, a setting of 50% for Blur Length is perfect.

Particle Blur

The Particle Blur setting applies a special type of motion blur to particle systems—groups of similar small objects that behave in some ways like a single entity. Use it to blur animations of explosions, receding starfields, snow, rain, and the like. A Blur Length setting of 50% works well for Particle Blur.

Stereo and Depth of Field (DOF)

The second tab area at the bottom of the Camera Properties panel is named Stereo and DOF (**Figure 5.23**).

Stereoscopic Rendering

On the Stereo and DOF tab in the Camera Properties panel, you can turn on the Stereoscopic Rendering option, which lets you create 3D movies for viewing with special glasses, ViewMaster-style stereoscopic still images, and even *lintography*, the specialized printing process (used to produce 3D trading cards, for example), in which plastic is overlaid on a processed 2D image to give an illusion of depth. When this option is turned on, Layout renders left and right stereoscopic images for each frame in your project. To output red-and blue-tinted versions for viewing with classic 3D glasses, choose Windows > Image Processing and select Anaglyph Stereo: Compose from the Add Image Filter drop-down list. To output images for video-based virtual-reality glasses and headsets, choose Field Render from the same drop-down list instead and make sure the Field Rendering option is turned on in the Camera Properties panel. The Eye Separation value tells LightWave how far apart to render the left and right stereo images; the default mimics the average separation of adult human eyes.

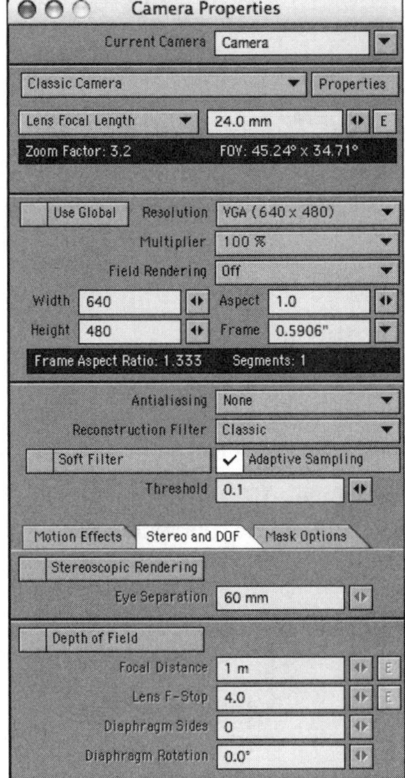

Figure 5.23 The Stereo and DOF tab offers stereoscopic rendering and depth of field functions to your cameras.

Depth of Field

Checking the Depth of Field option enables your LightWave camera to mimic an optical effect you've experienced yourself if you've ever looked through a camera lens. When you focus your camera on a subject, you'll notice that objects that are nearer or farther away than the subject appear less sharply focused than your subject. The range of distance in front of and behind the subject in which other objects stay in focus is called *depth of field* (DOF). High depth of field keeps objects in focus in front of and behind the subject and creates a sense of spaciousness; shallow depth of field "flattens" the scene, so that only the subject is in sharp focus.

You can only activate Depth of Field if the camera has antialiasing set to a medium or better level (PLD 7-pass or higher, or Classic-Medium or better). Checking the Depth of Field box then activates the Focal Distance and Lens F-Stop controls that you'll use to manage camera focus and adjust its depth of field.

Adjusting the depth of field is a fantastic way to add real depth to your animations. Without DOF, everything is in focus, as in **Figure 5.24**.

Figure 5.24 Without Depth of Field applied, everything in your scene is in focus.

Figure 5.25 shows the same image with DOF applied. Notice how the spheres become out of focus farther away from the camera.

Figure 5.25 With Depth of Field applied, the image is out of focus farther away from the set focal distance.

Focal Distance

When you apply DOF, you must also tell the camera where to focus by setting a *focal distance*. The default setting is 1m, and you can type any value into the Focal Distance field. Objects at the focal distance are in sharp focus in your frame, and those nearer or farther away will be out of focus to some degree, depending on how you use f-stop settings to control DOF (as discussed in the next section).

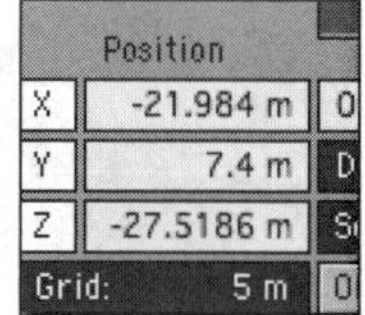

Figure 5.26 Using LightWave's grid measurement, you can easily determine where to set the focal distance from the camera to the objects in the scene.

Using LightWave's grid, which is the measurement system in Layout, you can easily determine the correct focal distance for a camera by counting the number of grid squares between the camera and the object you want in focus. Check the bottom of Layout's information window (**Figure 5.26**) to determine the grid size for the current view and multiply that by the number of squares to calculate the distance. (The default grid setting is 1m, but in larger scenes such as the one in Figures 5.25 and 5.26, LightWave may automatically scale the grid size up to 5m or higher.)

At a grid size of 5m, a focal distance of 15m would be appropriate for an object 3 grid squares away from the camera; objects nearer to and farther away from the camera will be out of focus.

F-Stop

Just as you would with a real-world camera, you adjust depth of field in a LightWave camera by adjusting its f-stop setting.

The human eye automatically adjusts to brighter or darker lighting situations. Under low light, the human eye's iris and pupil open to allow in the maximum amount of light. Bright sunlight, on the other hand, makes the human eye close to protect the eye.

By the same token, cameras also have an iris that allow in more or less light. Although the human eye smoothly opens and closes to control incoming light, cameras need to have this control set. This is done through f-stops.

F-stops are numerical values that represent the amount of varying degrees of light transmission. A smaller f-stop allows more light into the camera and reduces the depth of field, whereas higher values allow less light into the camera but increase the depth of field. Here are the common f-stop numbers used in the real world:

- **1.4**—Softest focus; allows a lot of light into the camera
- **2.0**
- **2.8**
- **4.0**
- **5.6**
- **8**
- **11**
- **16**
- **22**—Sharpest focus; allows little light into the camera

Note

One of the benefits of Depth of Field, beyond adding depth to your animations, is to steer the viewer's attention. By changing the focus from say, one animated element to a static element, you effectively are telling the viewer where to look.

Range Finder for DOF

Counting grid squares as I've described is adequate for setting camera focal distances, but it can gets tiresome. Here's a trick for creating an automatic range finder using a *null object*, a special type of object you can place in LightWave scenes for your own reference or guidance but that are never included in scene renders.

1. Click Null on the Items tab to create a new null object; rename it in the panel that appears (or just use default name **Null**), and click OK.
2. New objects are always selected by default, so press **p** to open this item's Object Properties and choose Range Finder from the Add Custom Object drop-down list (**Figure 5.27**).

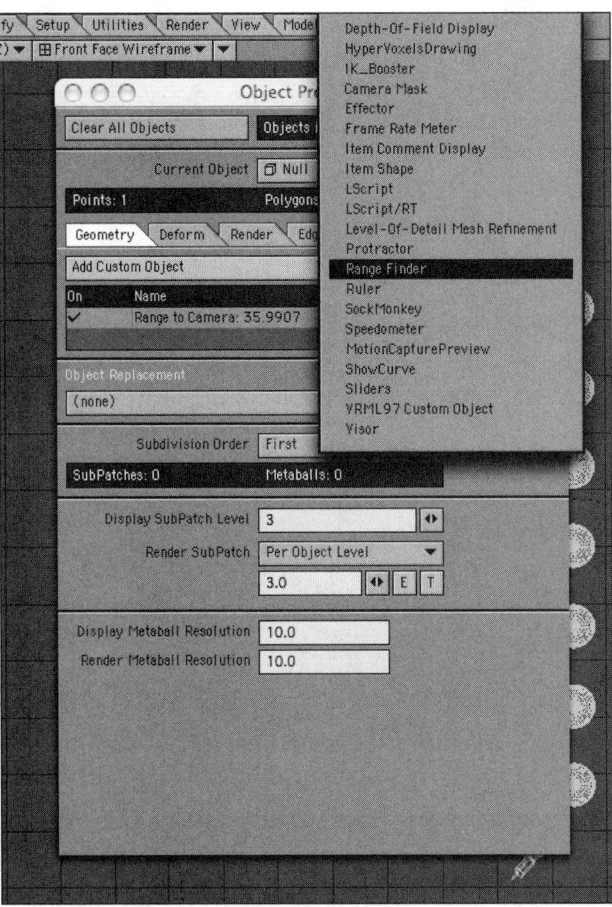

Figure 5.27 You can add a custom object to quickly measure distances in Layout from any item, such as the camera for setting DOF measurements.

3. Double-click Range to Camera in the Custom Object Name list, and in the numeric Range Finder pop-up that appears, leave Camera as the Item setting and check the Draw Link box (**Figure 5.28**).

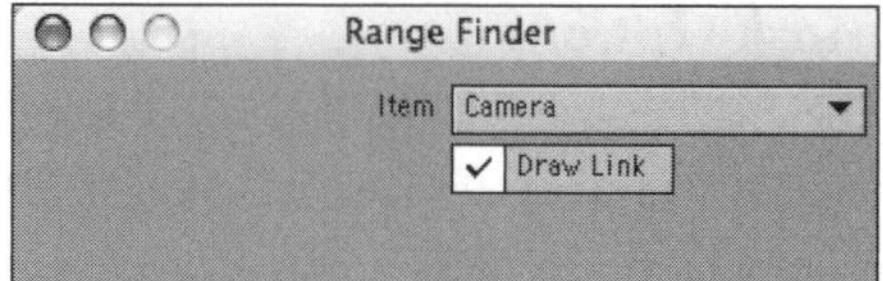

Figure 5.28 The Range Finder pop-up allows you to set the Camera as a link.

To use your range finder, select Null in the Current Object drop-down list. You'll see a small set of control handles and a value appear around the null object. With Auto Key enabled at the bottom of the interface, press **t** to select the Move tool, and drag Null slightly. You'll see a line between the camera's pivot point and the Range Finder null. Make sure that Auto Key is enabled, and move the null. Remember, everything in your scene needs a keyframe to stay in place, even if it's not animated. You'll see the measurement values change, as shown in **Figure 5.29**. This value is your distance from the camera that you can easily use to set the depth of field. If you're specifically trying to set the focus on an object, simply put the Range Finder null on the object, and take the measurement. This is a good way to calculate rack focuses for animating depth of field, as well. You can do this in LightWave easily by animating the focus values in the Graph Editor.

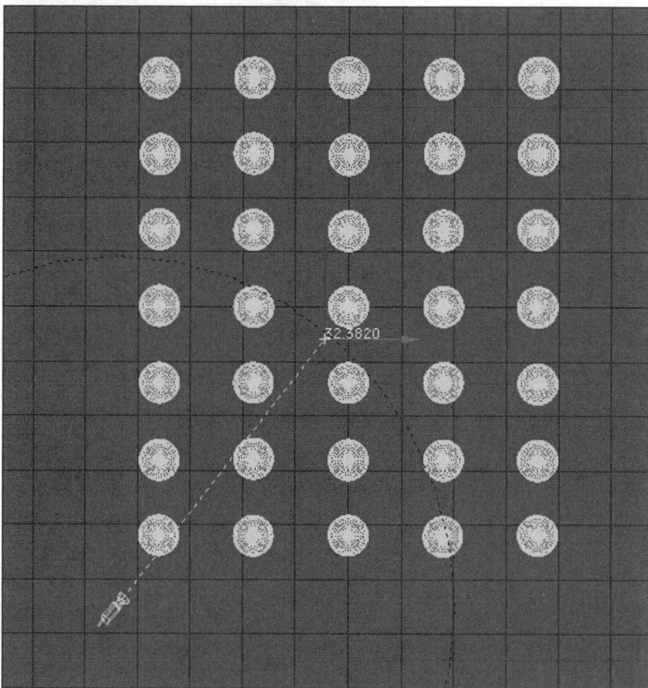

Figure 5.29 With the Range Finder custom object added, when Auto Key is on, you'll see a target line between the selected item (Camera) and the Range Finder. Couldn't be easier!

Mask Options

The final tab available in the Camera properties panel that allows you to enhance the LightWave camera is named Mask Options (**Figure 5.30**). Here, you can tell the camera in LightWave to render certain areas while excluding others. Areas that are excluded from the render, or *masked*, are denoted by a color. This option is great for setting up pseudo widescreen renders or a letterbox effect. You can set values for Left, Top, Width, and Height, as well as Mask Color. **Figure 5.31** shows a rendered image with Mask Options applied. You can use these options to create letterboxed images, simulating a 16:9 or widescreen look on a 4:3 television.

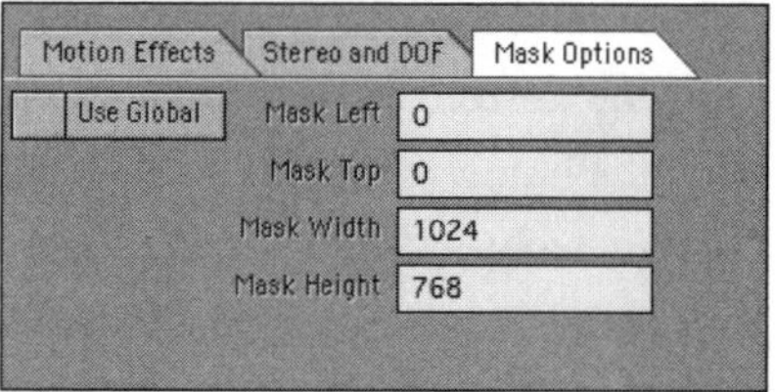

Figure 5.30 The Mask Options tab in the Camera Properties panel enables you to mask areas of your Camera view for rendering.

Figure 5.31 Mask options are great to use for rendering only portions of animations while setting a color for the unmasked area.

You can see that the control available to you for LightWave's cameras can be a significant element in the animations you create. Too often, the camera is ignored and left in place. This is a crime—remember the camera when you animate! Animate it as well as your objects.

Note

Remember that masking covers up your rendered image based on the parameters you set. It does not resize your image.

Camera Concepts

You want to incorporate the camera more into your animations but don't know where to begin? You may find yourself in situations where you don't know how to frame a shot or decide where to place the camera. This next section provides you with some basic instruction that you can use throughout any of your animations.

View in Thirds

To many animators, looking through a camera lens is like looking at a blank canvas. Where should you begin? How should you view a particular shot? Your first step in answering these questions is to get a book on basic photography and cinematography. References such as these can be invaluable to animators as well as a great source of ideas.

One of the first lessons such a book will teach you, and which you can apply when looking through your LightWave camera, is that images with subjects smack in the center are dull. Unbalanced compositions have a certain tension that makes them more engaging than those that are symmetrical.

So to make your shots, or compositions, more interesting, mentally slice the image in thirds, either vertically or horizontally. If there's a single subject to your composition, align it along one of the imaginary dividing lines, rather than in the center of the frame. If there are two subjects in the frame, let one dominate the larger two-thirds of the frame and place the other in the smaller portion, rather than giving them equal prominence. (If you're shooting two subjects of similar size, doing so may require you to get creative with your camera angle by placing one in the distance and the other in the foreground.) **Figure 5.32** shows a photograph of a room. It's a shot you can mimic in LightWave.

A shot framed in thirds takes into account not only the main focus but also the surrounding areas of the frame. If you visualize the image in thirds, as in **Figure 5.33**, you can

Figure 5.32 A photograph of a room might serve as a good reference for building 3D scenes, as well as framing shots.

Figure 5.33 When you visualize your shot in thirds, elements within the photo fall into place. Apply the same principle to cameras in LightWave.

see that areas of the scene fit into place. Visually look for three vertical and three horizontal areas when viewing your shots.

By framing your shot in thirds in the vertical and horizontal views through the camera, you have areas to fill with action. Remember, you need to visualize this grid when setting up camera shots in LightWave. There is not an option to do this. By visualizing, you can begin to think more about your shot and framing.

When thinking of thirds while setting up a shot, don't be too literal. Your objects don't need to line up exactly into each third area. Visualizing your camera shot in thirds is a way to help frame the entire field of view. Don't be afraid to try different camera angles and different perspectives. **Figure 5.34** shows the rule of thirds applied to a 3D scene in LightWave.

Figure 5.34 Visualizing a shot with the rule of thirds in LightWave can help you place objects and position your camera.

Camera Angles

After you get the hang of framing a scene, the next thing you should think about is the camera angle. Consider what you are trying to portray in the render. Do you want the subject to look small, or should it be ominous and looming? What you do with the camera in LightWave helps sell the mood of your animations to the viewer. As good as your models and textures might be, your shot needs to work as part of the equation as well. **Figure 5.35** shows a 3D building from a bird's-eye point of view. Shots like this are good for general views, fire safety, environment concerns, and so on.

Figure 5.35 Setting your camera to a bird's-eye point of view makes the shot unthreatening.

What if your goal is more than purely informational? Say you're preparing a "virtual unveiling" of a proposed building design, and you want to convey a sense of grandeur. **Figure 5.36** shows how a different camera angle changes the feel of a shot.

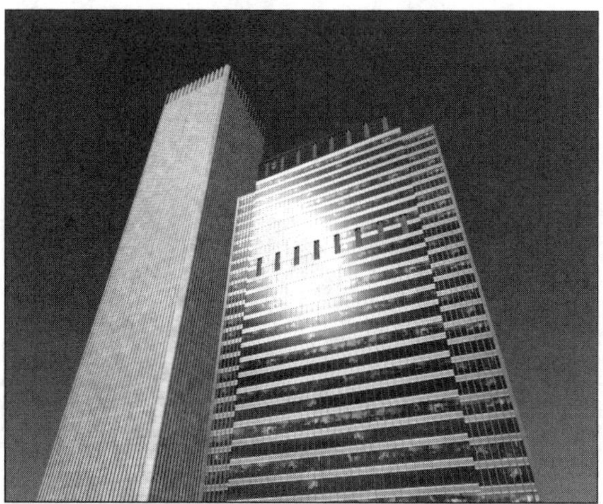

Figure 5.36 A wider camera angle, set low in front of the building, gives a grander look and feel to the shot.

Taking this a step further, you can also employ "dutch" camera angles, a cinematic technique that conveys a feeling of uneasiness or a creepy mood. You might shoot your building this way if you wanted to hint to your audience that trouble is brewing inside. **Figure 5.37** shows a shot similar to Figure 5.36 but with the camera rotated on its bank, or *dutched.*

Figure 5.37 Rotating the camera on its bank sets up a dutch angle that conveys the feeling of something being wrong, creepy, or uneasy.

Additional Camera Types

You'll use the techniques presented in this chapter throughout your LightWave career. However, LightWave v9 introduces some powerful cameras, allowing you to do things like make an object a camera, or create a camera based on the exact real-world camera and lens you specify. The next section introduces you to the different camera types, and you'll use variations throughout projects in this book.

Classic Camera

The Classic Camera has been demonstrated in this chapter. It's the default LightWave camera type, and is primarily used for most projects. You use the Classic Camera if you want to render any points or lines in your scene. **Figure 5.38** shows a shot rendered with a default Classic Camera.

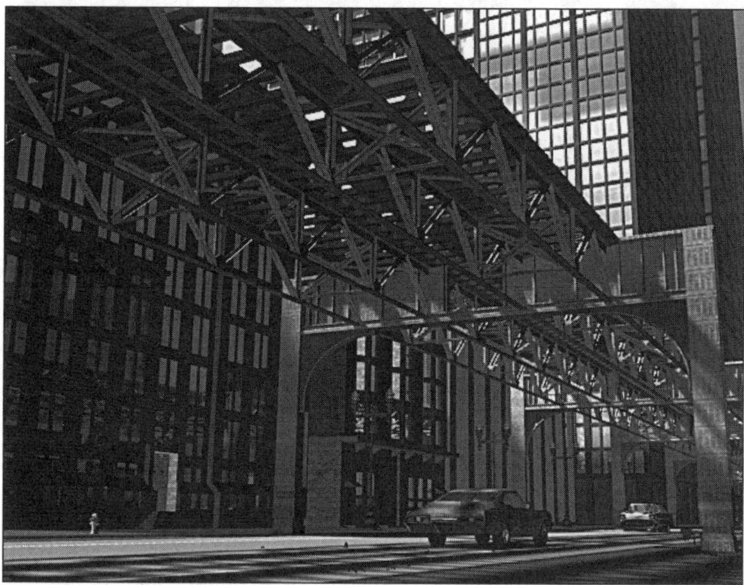

Figure 5.38 A 3D city shot, rendered with a Classic Camera and default settings such as a Zoom Factor setting of 3.2.

Advanced Camera

The Advanced Camera, new to LightWave v9, allows you to re-create lenses and real cameras normally not found in 3D applications.

For instance, the Advanced Camera option lets you define objects (mesh items) as cameras so you can obtain an entirely different look and gain more control than you could with a normal camera. For example, you can't really distort a camera, but with an object set up as a camera, that object can be bent, distorted, warped, and so forth, thereby distorting what your camera sees. Quite cool!

Figure 5.39 shows the same shot as Figure 5.38 but rendered using the Advanced Camera option to set up the car windshield as a camera. That's right, the windshield!

Figure 5.39 The Advanced Camera is a multipurpose camera, and one of the features is defining an object as a camera. Here, the windshield of the car shown in Figure 5.38 is now set up as a camera. What the car sees, you see.

The Advanced Camera option also lets you create spherical cameras. This allows you to render an entire scene in a spherical shape, sort of like a severe fish-eye lens. The advantage becomes clear when you're creating HDR (high-dynamic range) images. A HDR image is one that holds more data than a normal image. A normal image would be one that contains intensities up to 255 RGB. While an HDR image might look the same, the computer will understand it is higher intensity and can use it for lighting a scene.

Later in the book you'll see the Advanced Camera in action, and you'll learn how the various settings work.

Orthographic Camera

The Orthographic Camera is a little tricky to understand. When you render a scene, LightWave shoots out *rays*—these rays are used to calculate all sorts of things, such as shadows and reflections. You have more control over these rays in LightWave v9 than any time before, and the Orthographic Camera is just one way to work with different rays. With the Orthographic Camera, rather than rays bouncing all over the scene, their direction is the same. OK, so what does that really mean? It means that you can create a camera with a *forced perspective*. A forced perspective in computer graphics is more an optical illusion than anything else. In a sense, it's almost the opposite effect of a fish-eye lens, which widely distorts the image. The forced perspective flattens out the image, even when viewing 3D objects. A forced perspective makes your image appear flatter and closer than with a typical camera.

Perhaps you're a designer working in Autodesk AutoCAD or PTC ProENGINEER. You could use an Orthographic Camera for engineering or architectural type renders, or shots in which you need to see more of the model than can normally be seen in a single render from a standard camera (**Figure 5.40**). When a perspective created from a wider camera might take away from the object or scene you're rendering, an Orthographic Camera might do the trick. Before this camera was implemented in LightWave v9, artists would often pull the camera far away from the scene, and zoom in to create a similar look.

Figure 5.40 The Orthographic Camera allows you to view your work in a forced perspective.

Perspective Camera

The Perspective Camera renders like the Classic Camera, but with a few differences. The Perspective Camera renders the scene from top to bottom. In many cases, more complex scenes, such as **Figure 5.41**, render faster this way. However, the Perspective Camera will not render points and lines, which are used to generate smoke, fog and other *particle effects*, in which a system of tiny individual objects behaves like a single entity. If you're setting up particles, you'll want to render with a Classic Camera, not a Perspective Camera.

Figure 5.41 The Perspective Camera renders the frame to top down, unlike the Classic Camera. In many cases, a more complex scene will render faster.

Real Lens Camera

The Real Lens Camera option is great for real-world photographers and lets LightWave cameras mimic many popular still cameras. Emulations include pro-caliber SLR (single-lens reflex) camera-and-lens combinations, and even point-and-shoot models from Nikon, Canon, and Olympus. **Figure 5.42** shows the same city shot but rendered as if photographed using a Canon 5D camera with a 24–70 f2.8L lens.

Figure 5.42 The Real Lens Camera offers you the ability to set a number of presets for point-and-shoot and digital SLR cameras and lenses.

Surface Baking Camera

The Surface Baking Camera will come in very handy for game designers, architectural animators, and anyone who wants to speed up lengthy animations. The Surface Baking Camera allows you to "bake" your textures into one large image map. Say, for example, you have a complex scene with many image mapped textures, procedural textures, ray-traced shadows, radiosity for global illumination, and so on. That would all take a long time to render, especially if your scene is 30 seconds, 1 minute, or longer. By using the Surface Baking Camera, you render once, and all the calculations LightWave needs to perform are saved to an image map you specify. Then, you reload that image, and apply it to your entire scene. So, one image map contains all of the other image maps, procedurals, reflections, shadows, and so on. With that, you can turn off advanced ray-tracing features, complex lighting, and so forth, and LightWave can then crank through the frames for final render output in no time. The Surface Baking Camera looks at each pixel in your render as a UV coordinate. (You'll learn more about UVs a bit later in the book.) The UV will allow you to conveniently map a large image around complex shapes. The process can be time-consuming, but the camera is optimized to take full advantage of computers with two or more processors.

The Next Step

The cameras in LightWave are compelling storytelling tools—whether your story is a simulation of a car accident, a flying logo, or an animated epic. When you model, you create shapes and animate them. When you animate, your motions create a mood, and without the proper camera angles, your work will not be as powerful.

To understand this better, it may help to think about some of your favorite movie directors, and the way they use camera placement to aid their storytelling. Quentin Tarantino movies, for instance, often include a shot framed with the camera looking out from the inside of a car trunk. Imagine how different one of those scenes would feel if it were shot from a long side view instead, or from overhead, or from the perspective of another character. Or think of the famous opening scene of *Citizen Kane*, and how the intimacy of the dying word "Rosebud" might have changed if it were delivered in a wide shot of Kane's bedroom instead of a closeup on his whispering lips.

That said, don't worry about becoming the next Welles or Hitchcock. Experiment! Practice setting up different types of shots. Load some of the scenes from your LightWave directory that installed when you loaded the program. Study the camera angles used there and try creating your own. Use reference books from real-world situations, mimic the cinematography in movies, and most importantly, experiment. I hope this chapter got you thinking about the cameras in LightWave and the shots you can create and animate.

A large portion of what goes into a shot deals with lighting and environments. Be sure to use a generous combination of lighting, textures, motions, and, of course, cameras in your projects. Before you do that, you need to create some models! And hey, didn't you hear that LightWave was an animation program? Turn to the next chapter to learn how to keyframe and put items in motion. Then, you'll get into simple modeling and animation, branching out to more complex models and working your way up to dynamics and more.

Chapter 6

Principles in Motion

Here's how the American Heritage Dictionary defines *animation*: "The act, process, or result of imparting life, interest, spirit, motion, or activity." Motion. Activity. When you think about animation, you think about movement. Movement in animation is created with keyframes, and you might think that this should have been the first topic discussed in this book, given that LightWave is an animation program. However, knowing how to create an effect and understanding where to make the right adjustments saves you not only time but aggravation as well. Understanding timing is a constant in an animator's career, and it's also the focus of this chapter. As you know, 3D image creation isn't always about movement, and regardless of whether you're dealing with still or moving images, understanding the environment in which you are working is key to your success as an animator and 3D artist. There are so many facets to 3D animation—from modeling to texturing, lighting, and even scripting—that it's sometimes a real headache trying to figure out where to start.

LightWave v9 is uncluttered yet very functional. Many programs fill up the screen with useless icons—thankfully, LightWave names buttons clearly. This enables you to focus on your creative goals instead of having to figure out what a particular icon means. Going one step further, LightWave's powerful Graph Editor offers you complete control over a specific item's motion and timing. This item can be a camera, object, light, or any other type of parameter that can be enveloped or changed over time. As I mentioned in Chapter 2, "LightWave v9 Layout," you'll find those little E buttons throughout the LightWave interface. This chapter discusses what to do with those E's when you click on them.

The Graph Editor that opens when you click on an E button also gives you control over every channel of an item, such as the X position, heading rotation, dissolves, light color, and so on, all over a set duration. Each channel can be controlled through the use of expressions, modifiers, or even keyframes, all from within the Graph Editor. The Graph Editor is used to edit any type of parameter that can be enveloped, or as the nontechnical folk like to say, animated. In this chapter, you will learn about the following:

- Creating motion with keyframes
- Understanding motion splines
- Adjusting motions
- Working with the Graph Editor

Note

An *expression* is a LightWave function that lets you to set specific operations based on mathematical statements. For example, you can select an animated wheel object, and create an expression that tells Layout, "When the wheel rotates a full 360 degrees, turn on a light and rotate another object." Expressions are very powerful and one of LightWave's most advanced features.

Creating Motions with Keyframes

You might think that the title of this section is redundant. Creating motions with keyframes? Duh! How else would you do it? Well, actually there are many ways in LightWave v9 to create motions without keyframes: procedural motions, expressions, and of course dynamics. Dynamics enable you to move one item and have it affect another item. Or, you can just add gravity to an object and watch it move.

So why even use keyframes? Timing, my friend. Timing. To create an animation that's really "in the pocket," you need to master the art of timing. That's right, the *art* of timing. It is an art, and you've either got it or you don't. Not to sound harsh, but timing is everything—in life, in comedy, and in animation. In 3D animation, you control timing with keyframes. The more often you work with keyframes, the more quickly you will get a feel for animation timing.

Keyframing is the act of setting or marking an animatable attribute in time. For example, when you want a ball to move from point A to point B over two seconds, you need to set a keyframe at point A to tell LightWave to "start here" at point A in time, and another keyframe, two seconds later in the timeline at point B, to say "end here." The way it moves from that point is up to you, but each stop, detour, or change in orientation it makes along the way will be controlled by additional keyframes. Wobbles? Keyframes. Bounces? Keyframes. Get the idea?

Keyframing goes beyond just animating position and rotation. In LightWave, "animatable attributes" encompasses properties such as light intensity, color, and a host of surface characteristics. Essentially, if a Layout characteristic has a numeric value, you can animate changes to that value over time. And the way you control those changes is with—say it with me—keyframes. As you'll see later in the chapter, animating surface attributes also often combines keyframes with another powerful Layout tool, the Graph Editor.

Because the Layout interface was covered in previous chapters, as well as navigating the timeline, this chapter focuses on putting you to work. You'll start by setting up some basic keyframes. From there, you'll use multiple objects and then learn how to set targets and parents and adjust the motions in a variety of ways.

Automatic Keyframing

The Auto Key button at the bottom of the Layout interface is turned on by default. We discussed this briefly in Chapter 2, but the following is a hands-on tutorial to further explain when and why to use this feature. Auto Key adjusts the values of existing keyframes automatically. For the Auto Key feature to automatically create keys, you need to make sure the Auto Key Create option is enabled in the General Options tab (press **o**). Set this to Modified Channels so that any commands such as Move, Rotate, Size, or Stretch are remembered for selected items at the current frame. Exercise 6.1 explains this feature further.

Exercise 6.1 Using the Auto Key Feature

For this exercise, you won't even need to load a scene or any objects. The Auto Key feature in LightWave makes creating animations pretty easy. But what's more is that almost everything in LightWave can be animated! For that reason, this quick project will have you animate the two default items in Layout, the camera and light.

1. Open LightWave, and if you're already working on something, save it. Then from the File drop-down menu, select Clear Scene. You'll see a perspective view with the default camera and light visible, as in **Figure 6.1**.

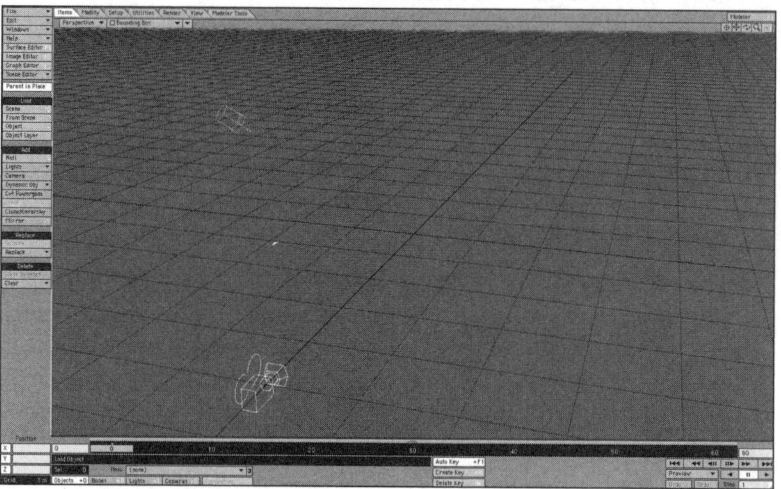

Figure 6.1 A simple scene with two default items, a camera and a light, ready to be put in motion.

2. Select the camera in one of two ways: by clicking directly on it, or by choosing the Cameras button at the bottom of the interface.
3. When selected, the camera will highlight yellow, and you'll see a dotted projection extend out from the camera, as shown in **Figure 6.2**. This area is what the camera sees.

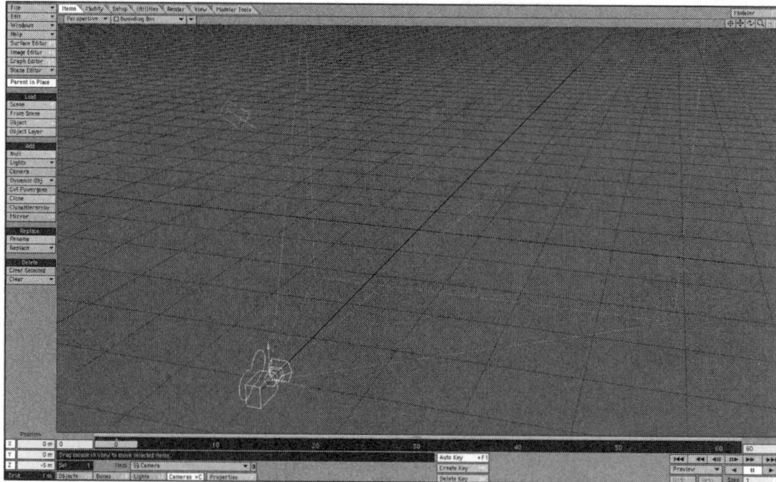

Figure 6.2 When you select a camera, Layout highlights it in yellow and extends dotted from its "lens" to indicate its field of view.

Note

> The virtual cameras shown in Layout scenes are merely representational. Their focal points are at their pivot points, where their positioning handles appear when they're selected, not at their drawn "lenses."

4. Make sure your timeline is set to frame 0, which will be the start of your simple animation.

   To understand how Auto Key works, we'll compare creation of a simple camera animation with Auto Key on and off.

5. If it's activated, click the Auto Key button at the bottom center of the Layout interface to turn it off. (The button is white when Auto Key is on and blue when it's off.)

Note

> In the Layout window, you'll notice that there is always a key at frame 0 by default. Thus, an object is locked in place even without Auto Key. Auto Key merely lets you make an adjustment at frame 0 (or any other existing keyframe) without having to re-create the key.

6. Press **t** to activate the Move tool. This tool is also found on the Modify tab.

7. With the Move tool active, click and drag on the green handle that appears for the selected camera. Drag it up slightly from its current position, about 600mm or so, as shown in **Figure 6.3**.

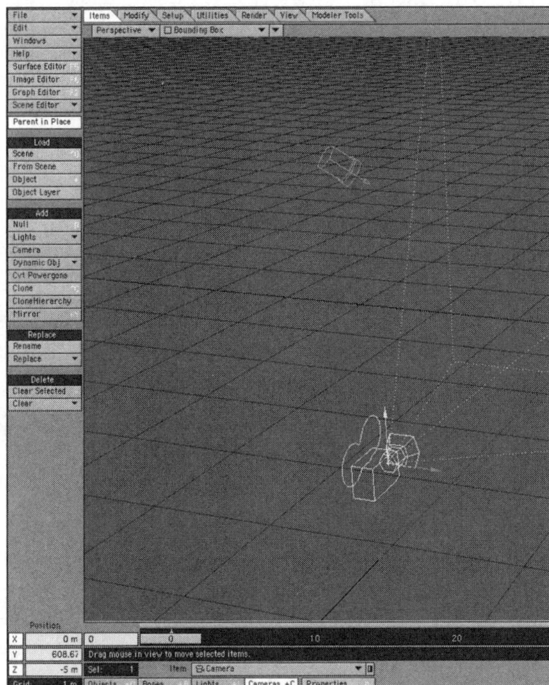

Figure 6.3 Using the Move tool, drag the camera up a bit on the Y-axis.

Note

If you can't see the object to grab it, you can switch to the Back view by pressing the number 1 on the keyboard. Mac users, remember to use the Apple key for right mouse button commands.

8. Click and drag the timeline slider forward to another frame.

   The camera seems to jump back to its original position. Move the slider back to frame 0, and the camera is back in its original keyframed position. Unless you set a keyframe (or reset an existing one) after you change an object's position, orientation, or other attributes, the adjustments aren't captured and LightWave "forgets" them.

9. Click the Auto Key button to activate it (the button will turn white) and repeat steps 6 and 7.

10. Drag the slider to frame 60, the last frame of your animation. (LightWave's default length for new animations is 60 frames.)

    This time, the camera stays where you put it. Auto Key automatically reset the keyframe in frame 0 to capture your camera move.

11. With the timeline slider at frame 60, click and drag the blue handle for the camera and move it to the back of Layout, as shown in **Figure 6.4**. Auto Key automatically creates a new keyframe this time, capturing the new position information.

    So now your animation has two keyframes: one at frame 0, indicating the camera's starting position, and another at frame 60, reflecting its end position. Let's see how the camera gets from the first keyframed position to the other.

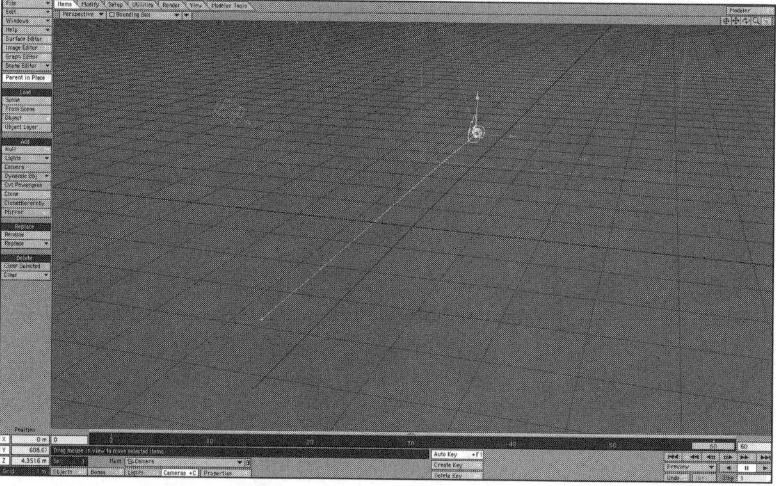

Figure 6.4 With the timeline slider at frame 60, and the camera moved to a new position.

12. Drag the timeline slider back and forth and you'll see the camera move through the scene. LightWave automatically fills in the motions needed to move objects between keyframes. Congratulations, you just made an animation!

    This is a very basic example, but the principles are the same for even the most complex of objects. Pick a point in time, position the item, and you're building an animation.

13. Now, press **y** to select the Rotate tool. At frame 60, click and drag the red ring to rotate the camera 180 degrees so that it's facing in toward the scene (**Figure 6.5**).

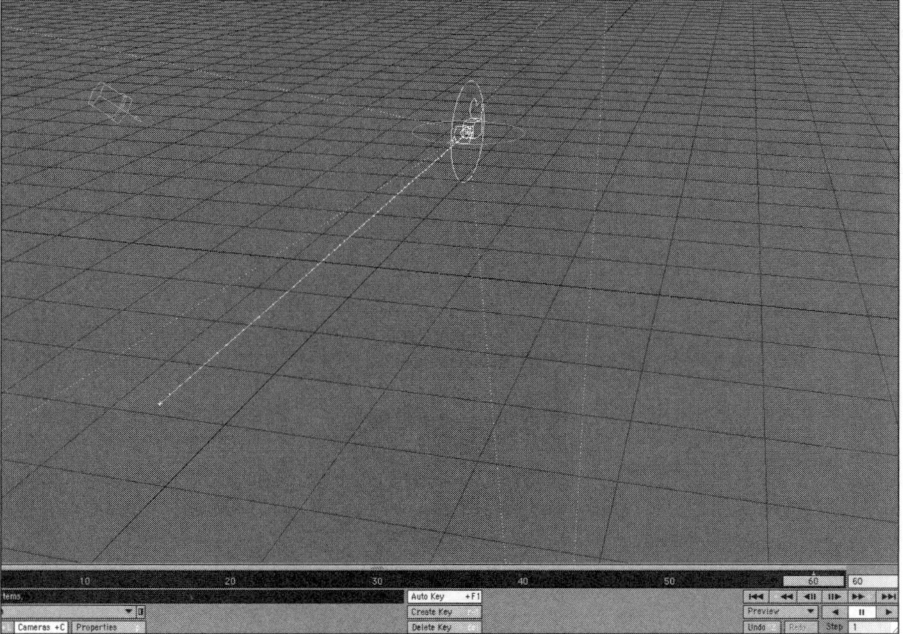

Figure 6.5 With the timeline slider at frame 60, rotate the camera so it faces the scene.

14. Click the rewind button at the bottom right of the interface, and then the play button (the right-facing triangle). The camera will now move from frame 0 to 60, across the scene down the Z-axis, rotating as it goes.

    To recap, at frame 0, Auto Key captured the camera's position along the *X*-, *Y*-, and *Z*-axes and its *H*-, *P*-, and *B*- (Heading, Pitch, and Bank) rotation coordinates. At frame 60, the position and rotation change you made were also recorded in a new keyframe, and LightWave interpolated the movements in between the two keyframes. Welcome to animation!

15. To help you visualize movement within your project as you work in individual frames, LightWave can display a motion path that shows the route an object will take between keyframes. To see your camera's motion path, press **o** to open the LightWave Preferences panel and check Show Motion Paths on its OpenGL tab.
16. Drag the timeline to about frame 30, deactivate the Auto Key button at the bottom of the interface, and then move the camera to a new position.
17. Once the camera is in a new position, click the rewind button and then the play button to see the animation. Notice a change? Of course not. With the Auto Key feature off, the position change for the camera was not recorded. You'll also see that its motion path didn't change.
18. Slide the timeline back to frame 30. Turn Auto Key back on. Now move the camera again to a new position, and this time rotate it a little as well. Feel free to change the camera position on the Y-axis too.
19. You'll see that the motion path has now changed (**Figure 6.6**). Click the rewind and play buttons to watch the motion along the new path. Now the camera moves between three keyframes: 0, 30, and 60. Each keyframe stores object position and rotation information in time. The keyframes tell the camera to "be here" or "stay here" at a specific point in time.

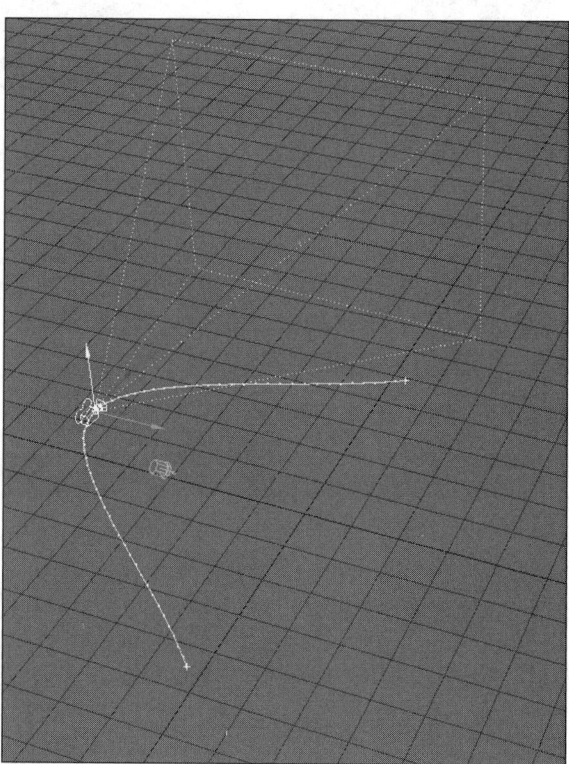

Figure 6.6 When Auto Key is active and Show Motion Paths is turned on, manual adjustments to camera position are reflected in its motion path.

Note

> Using the Auto Key feature also requires that the Auto Key Create option be set to Modified Channels. You can find this by pressing **o** to open Layout's Preferences panel.

A word of caution about Auto Key. It can be quite helpful in setting up animations, but it can also be hazardous when you're working on crowded scenes that require precise object placement. Accidentally nudge the wrong object with Auto Key on, and you can lose hours of painstaking adjustments. For those situations, you'll want to become adept at manual keyframing.

Manual Keyframing

Auto Key appeals to our natural sense of the world. When you move something, it should stay where you put it. But there are times when Auto Key doesn't provide enough control. In many ways, it's like using a point-and-shoot camera. Everything is automatic and easy, but sometimes the automatic methods, which work more than 90 percent of the time, won't let you do what you need to do. Just as a great photograph may demand manual camera control, LightWave setups with nuanced model motion and interaction require manual keyframing. Manual keyframing is vital to superb timing in your animations, and while you can't develop that overnight, a few practice animations can get you started.

A good way to work is to turn off the Auto Key Create option in the General Options tab (press **o**) and work only with Auto Key enabled. While it's not necessary to do, the Auto Key adjusts existing keyframes without the need to create them again after any changes are made. If there are no keyframes already created, either manually or with the Auto Key Create option previously enabled, no keyframes will be created automatically. This way, if you accidentally move the timeline, you won't create unwanted keyframes, destroying a precisely placed item.

So, here's how you can think of it: If there are already keyframes for a Layout item, working with Auto Key on at the bottom of Layout will automatically record and keep any changes made to that item, at that frame. If Auto Key Create is off in the options panel, changes made to an item that does not yet have a keyframe will not be recorded. To make things a bit clearer, watch the video called AutoKey.mov on the book's DVD (in the "\3D_Garage_Videos\Chapter_Videos\CH6_AutoKey.mov" directory).

Exercise 6.2 Manual Keyframing with Auto Key

Before you begin, there are a few things you should know here: When there's a blank scene and you load a single object into it, that object should automatically be selected. If you click to select the item and it's not selecting, be sure you have Left Button Item Select turned on in the General tab of the Preferences panel (press **o**), as in **Figure 6.7**. If the control handles do not appear in the center of the object, make sure that the Show Handles option is turned on in the OpenGL tab within the Display Options tab (press **d**).

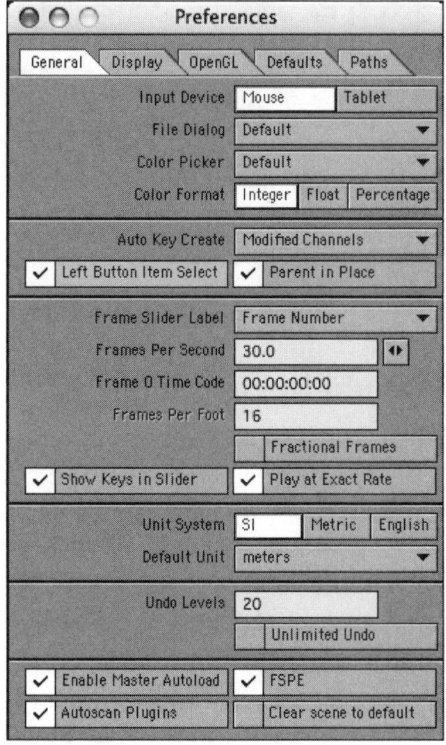

Figure 6.7 The Left Button Item Select feature is found on the General tab of the Preferences panel. Press **o** to open the panel.

By default, Layout assigns new scenes a duration of 60 frames, or 2 seconds. If your animation runs longer than that (most do), just increase the last frame number in the timeline. Be sure to add extra frames after your last keyframe, to give viewers time to register the actions that occur at that last keyframe. You also can change the default animation length in the Preferences panel (press **o**) by changing the default frame number on the Defaults tab. You'll need to quit and restart Layout to keep these settings. With that said, on with the exercise!

Manual keyframing is more deliberate than using Auto Key alone. But what confuses many new animators is deciding when to use Auto Key or manual keyframing in their animations. But you don't have to worry about that! This exercise will instruct you on deliberately setting keyframes while still keeping the Auto Key feature active.

1. A scene has been created for you to begin keyframing. Here, the cup will fall, bounce slightly, and land on the saucer. Load the scene by going to the File drop-down list and selecting File, then Load Scene. Choose the TeacupStatic scene from the book's DVD (in the "\Projects\Scenes\CH6\" directory). Alternatively, you can

load a scene by clicking the Scene button under the Load category of the Items tab. **Figure 6.8** shows the scene loaded into Layout.

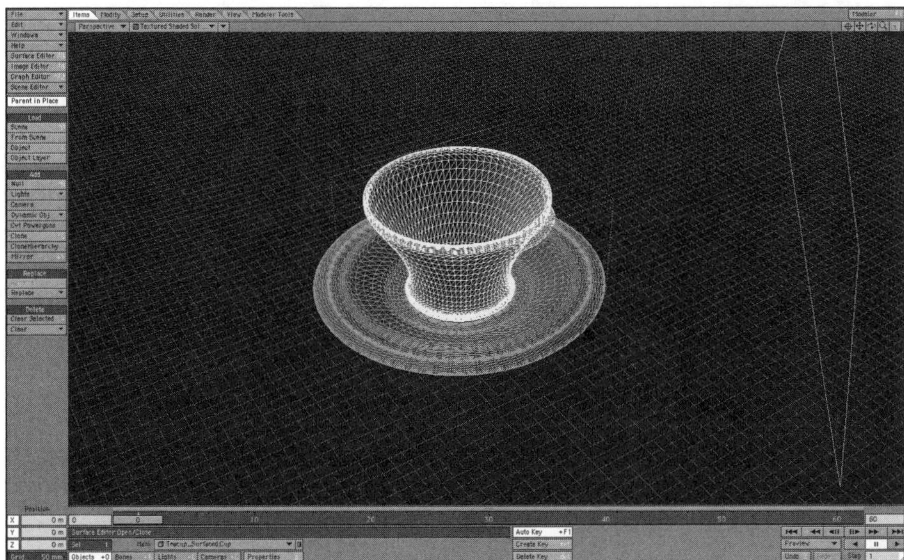

Figure 6.8 A simple scene with a few objects, ready to be put in motion.

2. With the teacup scene loaded, be sure the frame slider at the bottom of the Layout interface is at 0, be sure Auto Key is enabled, and activate Auto Key Create on the General Options tab within the Preferences panel (press **o**) to have keyframes created automatically.

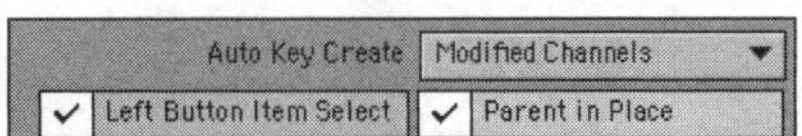

Figure 6.9 Be sure to set the Auto Key Create option to Modified Channels on the General Options tab.

3. Select Modified Channels from the selection area of the Auto Key Create command, as in **Figure 6.9**. In Modified Channels mode, new keyframes are created only for those channels that have been changed, whereas setting Auto Key Create to All Motion Channels creates a new keyframe for everything in your scene anytime you make a change to your selected item. While this feature might seem useless, it is just another option for you in LightWave. It's not something you'll use often, but at times you might need it. Suppose you're creating an animation of characters dancing on a stage and all items need to follow specific timing; creating keyframes with All Motion Channels enabled will save you time.

It's often convenient when animating to assemble all the objects or characters in a scene exactly as you want them to end up, then work backward to specify how they got there. Let's do that with our teacup and saucer. We want them to be arranged as they are in the current scene at the end of our animation, so we'll place the current scene in the final frame and then keyframe backward.

4. Select the teacup object itself. It will highlight yellow. You can do this by clicking the Objects button at the bottom of Layout, then choosing the Teacup_Surfaced: Cup listing from the Item drop-down list. This animation is 200 frames long, so create a keyframe for the teacup at frame 200, the last frame. Since it's already in its "final" position, you can simply lock it in place now. Click the Create Key button beneath the timeline. It will have a 0 for the Create Key At entry because your timeline is at frame 0. Enter **200** in the requester, and make sure that Selected Items is chosen and that all of the channels are clicked, as in **Figure 6.10**.

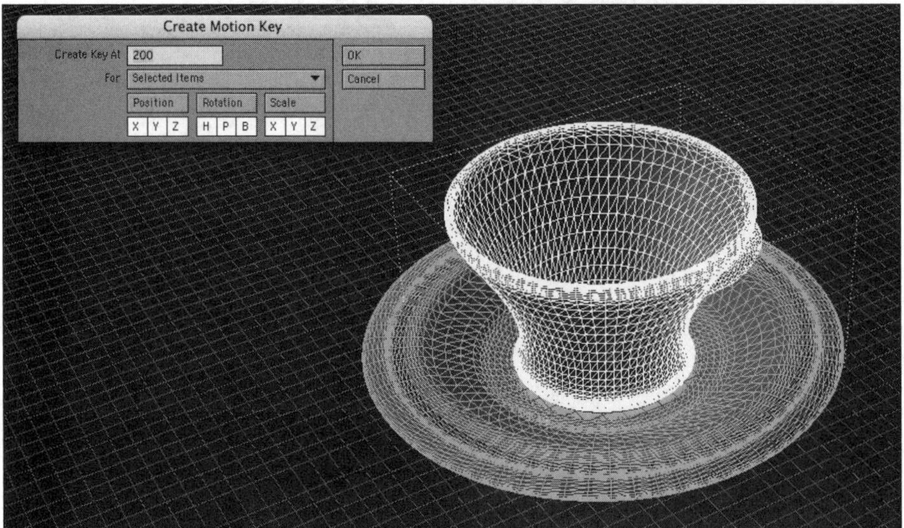

Figure 6.10 Create a keyframe at 200 for the cup.

5. Click OK to close the Create Motion Key panel. With the timeline at 0, and with the cup selected, press **t** to select the Move tool (or click the Move tool on the Modify tab). Move the cup up in the scene, about 1.5m, by clicking and dragging on its green (*Y*-axis) handle. You can see the amount of movement in the numeric display at the bottom-left corner of Layout (**Figure 6.11**).

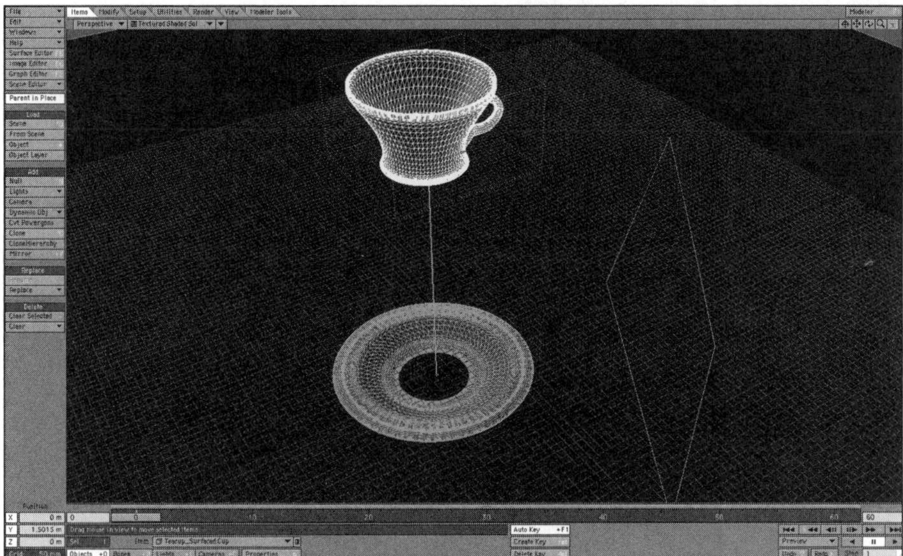

Figure 6.11 Move the teacup up and away from the saucer.

6. Now you should see a small white line tracing from the saucer to the cup. This is a motion path. Because you created a keyframe at 200, you haven't moved the cup at frame 0, and AutoKey with AutoKey Create is on, a keyframe has automatically been created for you at 0, in the cup's new position. If you were to drag the timeline or click the play preview button at the bottom right of the interface, the cup would slowly fall down into its original position.

Note

If you don't see a motion path, you need to make it visible. Press **o** to open the Preferences panel and check Show Motion Paths on its OpenGL tab.

7. Click and drag the timeline slider forward to frame 200. The cup should be resting on the saucer at this point, in its original position. This is also where you want the cup to land when it first falls down. You can copy the current keyframe value by clicking the Create Key button (or press Enter) and then enter **10** in the Create Key At value (it will read 200 because this is the current frame your timeline slider

is on). After you enter 10, click OK. You've now copied a keyframe. **Figure 6.12** shows the keyframe.

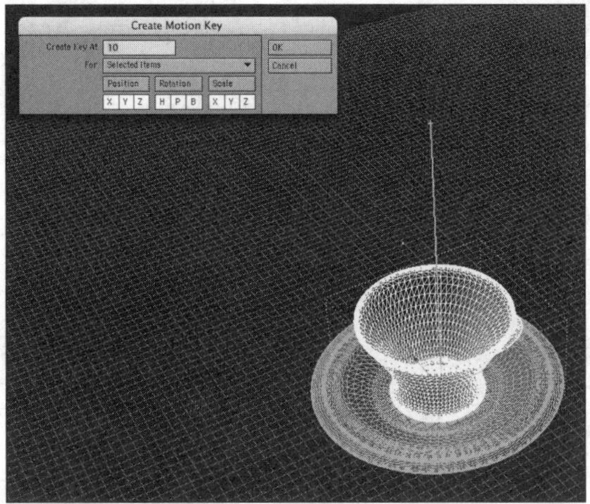

Figure 6.12 Make a keyframe at frame 10, with the cup in the same position as in frame 200.

8. With the teacup still selected, make sure your timeline is on frame 10. Then, press **y** to activate the Rotate tool (also on the Modify tab). When the tool is active, you'll see rings around the selected object. Click and drag on the blue ring to rotate the cup on the Bank channel about 30 degrees. The degree amount of the rotation is visible in the bottom-left corner of the interface. **Figure 6.13** shows the example.

Figure 6.13 Using the Rotate tool, rotate the cup at frame 10 on its Bank channel.

Note

A quick way to jump to any frame in Layout is to press **f** to call up the Go To Frame command. When it appears, just enter the desired frame number and press Enter (or Return on a Mac). Note that you do not need to highlight and delete the value in the Go To Frame requester. The old value will be highlighted when the requester appears, so you can just type the new frame number to replace it.

9. Drag the timeline slider to frame 20. Now use the Move tool by selecting it from the Modify tab (or by pressing **t**), move the object up a bit, and give it different rotation. Remember that you can press **y** to jump to the rotation tool. **Figure 6.14** shows the change.

Note

Because the Move and Rotate commands are used so often, Layout provides many ways to get to them. In addition to clicking their tool buttons on the Modify tab and pressing **t** for Move and **y** for rotate, you can press the spacebar to cycle through the Move, Rotate, Size, and Stretch tools. Additionally, if your computer mouse has a scroll wheel, you can use it to toggle between Move and Rotate.

Figure 6.14 Using the Move and Rotate tools, reposition the cup at frame 20.

10. Click the rewind button at the bottom right of the interface, just above the Preview menu. Then, click the Play button, which is the right-facing arrow, also at the bottom right of the interface.

    When you play the animation, you'll see your cup fall and quickly bounce. It's sort of OK, but it drifts through the saucer. What's up with that? Didn't you keyframe it at frame 10 to land on the saucer? You did, but because LightWave's motions are actually spline curves, there's a fluidity between keyframes. This interpolation is your friend in most animations, but often you need to control it. We'll set up a few more keyframes first, to finish the animation, then you'll see how to control the "drifting" you see before and after set keyframes.

11. Press **f** to call up the Go To Frame command. Enter **200** to jump to the cup's final resting position, and then copy its keyframe information to frame 30, using the method described in step 7 earlier.

Click the play button. You should see the teacup move and rotate between keyframes 0 and 30. You can shuttle through the animation by grabbing the timeline slider and dragging.

Note

You do not need to move the timeline slider to set keyframes throughout an animation if you are manually setting keyframes. However, moving it helps keep you organized and aware of the current animation frame.

Pretty good start, but there are still a few problems with the motion, right? The cup doesn't really bounce or land realistically; it sort of floats and drifts a bit before it comes to a rest. Because LightWave creates motion curves between keyframes, you need to control the curves for each keyframe. You can do this with the Graph Editor. However, there is a quicker way to change this motion right in Layout. We'll use that option first and then use the Graph Editor, so you can see both methods.

Before we tweak our teacup animation further, note that you can delete keyframes as easily as you create them. Press Delete with the frame slider on a keyframe, and you'll call up the Delete Motion Key dialog box, with the current frame already selected in the Delete Key At field (**Figure 6.15**).

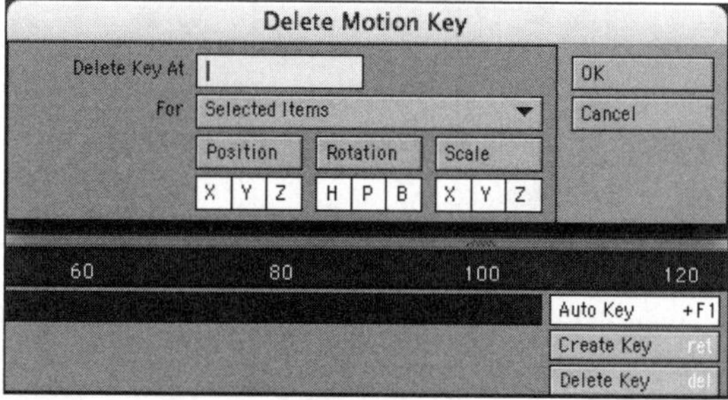

Figure 6.15 Deleting keyframes works the same way as creating them. Select an item to adjust, go to a specific point in time, and click the Delete Key button at the bottom of Layout.

As with creating keyframes, the timeline slider does not need to be on the specific keyframe to delete a key. Enter the number of the key you want to delete when the Delete Motion Key dialog box opens. Again, use your numeric keypad to save time! And remember, just as you can create keyframes for specific channels, you can delete them as well.

The tutorials in this motion chapter are really basic, and probably the simplest things to do in this book, but it's important for you to get the hang of keyframing. You told the cup to be at a certain position at frame 0, the beginning of the animation. Then, you moved the object to its resting position at the end of the animation at frame 200. You then told LightWave to copy that position of the cup at frame 10, and then again at frame 30. You also changed its position and rotation at frame 20. It will then sit there until frame 200, unless you make another keyframe change. LightWave interpolates the frames between 0 and 200, even if there is no movement from 30 to 200. Sort of like magic, you made an animation. Automagically, the motion curve that the computer created is the in-betweening that traditional animators would have to draw by hand. (*Automagically* is a technical term.)

Control Curves with the Move TCB Tool

Now, let's move on to correcting the "drift" in our teacup animation. We'll start by using Layout's Move TCB tool, and later in this chapter we'll look at an alternate approach that uses the Graph Editor. The Move TCB tool, found on Layout's Modify tab, is perfect for quickly controlling the motion curve created from multiple keyframes.

Exercise 6.3 Working with the Move TCB Tool

1. If you don't have your teacup scene still in Layout with the multiple keyframes you created, load the TeacupMotion.lws scene from this book's DVD (in the "\Projects\Scenes\CH6\" directory).

   Click the Play button again to review the animation. The teacup droops down too low, into the saucer object, on frame 10. Due to the motion curve, the teacup slides between the curves. Not desirable, but fixable.

2. Press **f** to call up the Go To Frame window and type **0** (zero), or drag the slider to the beginning of the timeline.

3. On the Modify tab, select the Move TCB tool (see **Figure 6.16**). Alternatively, you can press Ctrl+g to activate the tool.

4. Note the info area on the bottom left of the Layout screen. You'll see that this area now lists values for T, C, and B—shorthand for Tension, Continuity, and Bias. I'll explain these terms in greater detail a little later, but for now let's see how some tension adjustments can correct our teacup animation. Clicking and dragging in the current frame will increase or decrease the tension for the current frame, which is 0.

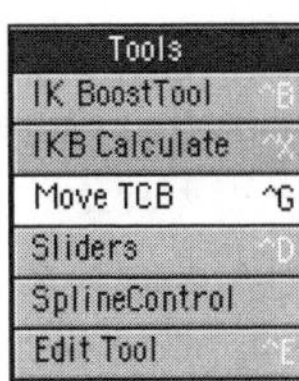

Figure 6.16 The Move TCB tool can be found on the Modify tab in Layout.

5. Click and drag to the right until the tension reads 1.0, as in **Figure 6.17**.

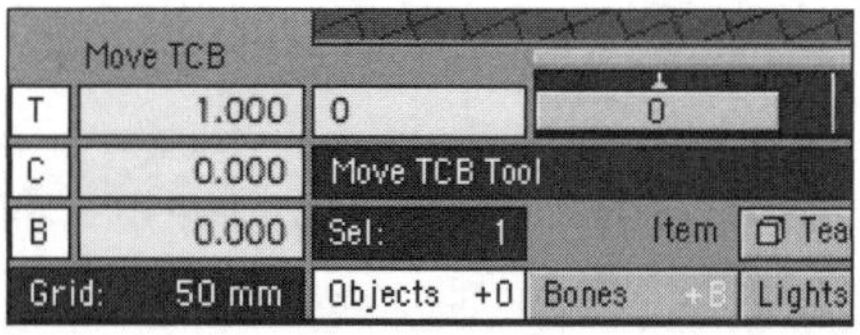

Figure 6.17 A Tension value of 1, as reflected in the Move TCB tool's info area.

6. Go to frame 10 and this time, set a tension of -1.0 by clicking in the Layout window and dragging to the left.
7. Now set a 1.0 tension for frames 30 and 200. This will help control the motion at these keyframes. Leave frame 20 alone. You want the cup to come up to this keyframe and drop back down. Setting a tension value here would make it pause it mid-air.

   Play back the animation, and you'll see that the teacup starts out slower and hits the saucer with more force. It bounces up at frame 20, and comes to rest at frame 30, then holds firm through frame 200. The ease in/ease out at frames 0 and 30 are set with a positive tension value. The negative tension value helps to force the motion for the teacup at frame 10. But notice that frame 10 still slopes down into the saucer. While the motion of the fall and bounce are better, the motion still needs a bit of adjustment. The reason is that settings for each keyframe in a motion curve affect all the other keyframes. You set keyframes before and after frame 10, and the motion settings before and after the frame affect frame 10's settings. Fortunately, this is easy to adjust.

Figure 6.18 A slight keyframe adjustment fixes the motion curve.

8. Go to frame 10, and select the teacup. Simply move it up on the *Y*-axis enough so that it rests on the saucer, as in **Figure 6.18**.

You can add frames to a resting position by simply creating another keyframe. For example, if you wanted the teacup to stay in place only until frame 150, you would create an additional keyframe in the same position. Just think about your timeline process and what you're trying to accomplish. Be specific in what you want your object to do, and you'll have an easier time creating motions.

Now, there are a few things to know about TCB and how to set the values:

- T, C, and B values can range from -1.0 to 1.0.
- Tension is used to ease in or ease out of a keyframe. You would set a tension of 1.0 to make an item slow down as it reaches its keyframed position. On the flipside, you'd use a tension of -1.0 to make an object speed up as it reaches its specified position—perhaps for things like a ball bouncing. As we've seen, to set tension using the Move TCB tool, just click and drag in an item's desired keyframe.
- Continuity is used to smooth or punctuate changes in motion. A positive continuity setting tells an object to "glide" smoothly as it passes through a keyframe. A negative continuity setting briefly "freezes" an item in its keyframed position before its motion continues, and is useful for exaggerated or robotic character movements. To set continuity using the Move TCB tool, hold the Ctrl key and click and drag in an item's desired keyframe.
- Bias is used for setting up anticipation. You can set a positive bias to create slack after a keyframe. Let's say your fire truck is speeding around a corner. Add bias to that keyframe, and it will slide around that corner. A negative bias creates slack before a keyframe. You could use this for, say, a racecar before it goes into a sharp turn. To set bias using the Move TCB tool, right-click and drag with the right mouse button in Layout for an item's desired keyframe to change Bias.

Keyframe Rules for Thought

There are a few more things you should know about keyframing in LightWave v9. A common misunderstanding with keyframes is that the more of them you have, the more control you will have in a scene. Not so! You see, when you create keyframes in LightWave, you're creating curves. Perhaps you've worked in an illustration program like Adobe Illustrator—you'll know that a smooth curve can be made with as little as three points. But if you were to add more points, or in this case, more keyframes, it is that much harder to control timing and fluidity in your motions.

A good rule of thumb to use when setting keyframes is to start by setting your object's first and last keyframes, and then setting any that fall in between. For example, say you want an object to move down a path and around an obstacle. The movement needs to be smooth, and trying to guess the timing might be tough to do. Set the beginning keyframe and then the ending keyframe to create the initial motion path. If you drag the timeline slider, the object moves between the two keyframes. If you move the timeline slider to the point where the object would move around the obstacle, you'll have the exact frame to set your next key. By creating the keyframe at this point, you've adjusted the motion path evenly.

In later chapters, you'll have many more opportunities to work with advanced keyframe techniques.

Navigating the Graph Editor

You've now worked through a series of basic keyframing steps. The process of creating keyframes for our simple exercise is the same as the one used for large-scale animation projects. The only difference is that big projects have a lot more keyframes. Overall, the increase in complexity results from the fact that there simply are more items to control in larger scenes. To help manage scenes that contain multiple keyframes, LightWave provides the Graph Editor.

You can access the Graph Editor by clicking the Graph Editor button at the top left of the screen in any Layout tab, or you can press Ctrl+F2 to call up the panel (**Figure 6.19**).

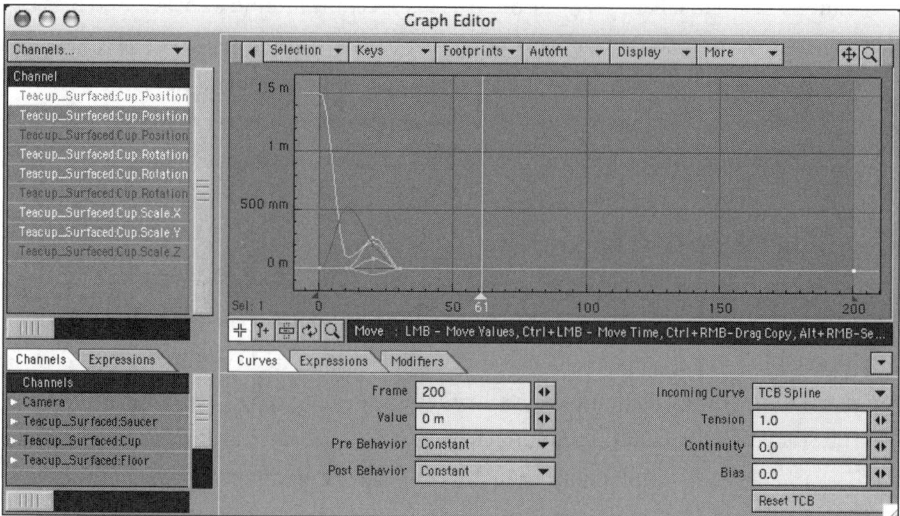

Figure 6.19 Opening the Graph Editor from the top left of the Layout interface gives you specific controls over your item's motions.

Note

A reminder that all those small buttons marked E in Layout's control panels also summon the Graph Editor. You'll find the buttons next to the controls for attributes, such as Surface Color, that can be changed over time in the Graph Editor. Why E? A long time ago, in a galaxy far, far away (Topeka), LightWave was born with a tool called Envelope. (Technically, animating a motion channel is "enveloping" its values.) Envelope evolved into the Graph Editor but retained its ancestral initial. Here, you can animate just about any value or channel in LightWave. If you feel that the next version of LightWave should have "A" for animate rather than "E" for a nonexistent Envelope panel, email our friends at NewTek.

When you open the Graph Editor, you'll notice four general areas:

- The Curve Bin is the top-left quadrant (**Figure 6.20**) of the panel (you won't see the name "Curve Bin"). This is the area of the Graph Editor where you place and select the specific channels (the curves) you want to edit.
- The Curve Window zone is in the largest area, the top-right quadrant (**Figure 6.21**). This is the area where you edit curves. Here, you can adjust attribute values, edit keyframes, and more.

Figure 6.20 The Curve Bin zone of the Graph Editor is the area where you've put channels you want to edit.

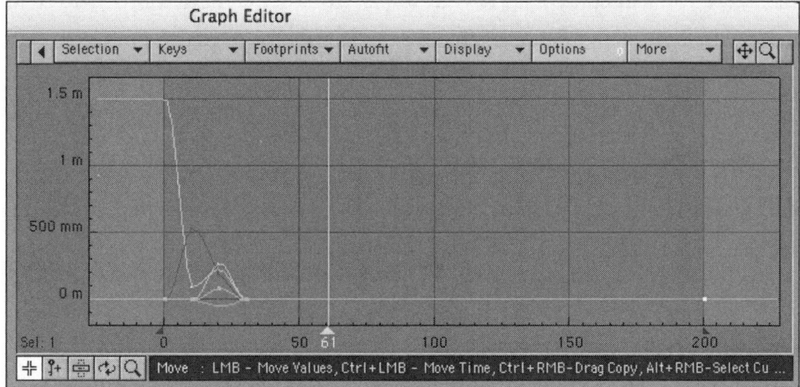

Figure 6.21 The Curve Window is the large main area of the Graph Editor, where all curve editing takes place.

- The Curve Controls zone is in the bottom-right quadrant (**Figure 6.22**). Here you can set frames, values, behaviors for keys, and modifiers, apply expression plug-ins and spline controls, and so on.

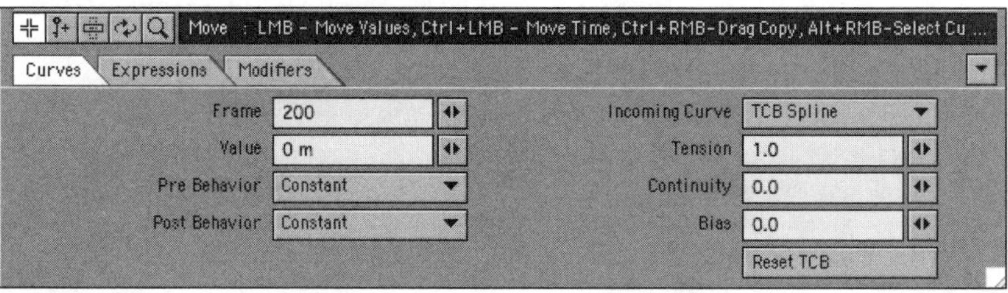

Figure 6.22 The Curve Controls zone at the bottom-right quadrant of the Graph Editor is where you set specific controls such as expressions, modifiers, spline controls, and more.

- The Scene zone is in the bottom-left quadrant and shows the elements of your current scene (**Figure 6.23**). Lights, cameras, and objects are listed here, and you can select any or all of their channels and drag them into the Curve Bin to begin editing. This area also shows you any expressions that might be applied.

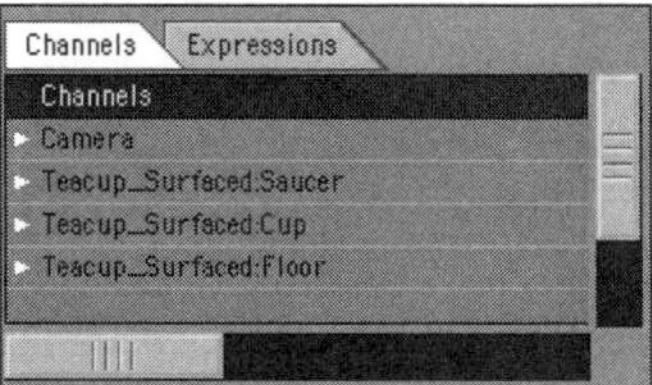

Figure 6.23 The Scene zone in the bottom-left corner of the Graph Editor shows a list of items in your currently loaded scene.

You will work with each zone to adjust, modify, or create various motions, timing, and values for LightWave elements. Here you can control all Layout items, from the camera to lights to objects—including color, light intensities, morph envelopes, and more. You may be asking yourself where you should begin with the Graph Editor and wondering what it really does. Good questions! The Graph Editor is a complex part of Layout, one that is best explained through examples.

The exercise in the following section illustrates how to navigate through the Graph Editor interface.

Working with Channels

When you begin creating an animation, you will often need specific control over one keyframe or a group of keyframes. The Graph Editor gives you this control, but you first must understand how to set up the channels with which you want to work. This exercise introduces you to working with the Position and Rotation channels for a light and a camera.

Exercise 6.4 The Position and Rotation Channels

1. In Layout, save any work you've been doing and select Clear Scene from the File drop-down menu. Then, select the default Camera.
2. Click the Graph Editor button on the toolbar (or press Ctrl+F2) to enter the Graph Editor.

   You don't need to load anything into Layout as you follow along here.

   Look at **Figure 6.24**, and you'll see that the attributes in the Scene list (lower-left quadrant) relate to the items in Layout, such as the Camera. In the top-left quadrant, you'll see all of the Camera's channels already loaded. If you've got an item selected when you open Graph Editor, all that item's channels will automatically load into the panel. Click the small white triangle next to the Camera entry in the Channels tab to expand and display see all the appropriate motion channels for the camera.

Note

> You can maximize the Graph Editor window by clicking the standard system maximize button next to the X in the top corner of the panel window. You can also reorder items in the Curve Bin by clicking and dragging them. Neither action affects your scene.

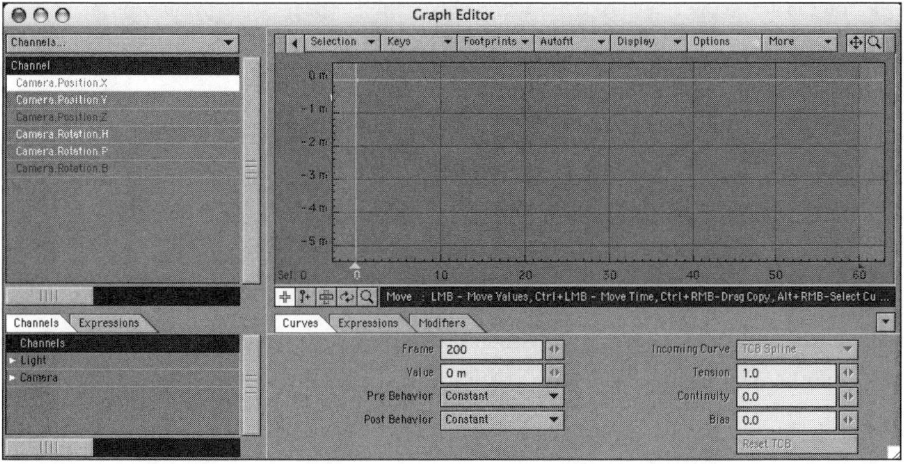

Figure 6.24 The Scene list in the lower left of the Graph Editor shows the items in your scene. Clicking the small white triangle next to an item expands to show all its channels. The selected Camera in Layout has all of its motion channels loaded in the Curve Bin.

3. Double-click the Light label in the Scene list area, just above the Camera listing. This is in the lower-left corner of the Graph Editor interface.

Double-clicking the Camera item adds all its channels to the Curve area, overriding any channels already in the bin. Doing this now makes those channels available for editing. If you were to hold the Shift key while double-clicking, you'd add to the current list of channels in the Curve Bin.

You can also just click and drag a specific motion channel from the Scene list to the Curve area. This is great if you just want to add a selected channel or two. If you hold the Shift key, select a channel, and then select another channel, all channels in between will be selected. You can then drag those channels to the Curve area. And, as in many areas within LightWave, such as the Surface Editor, holding the Ctrl key while selecting enables you to select noncontiguous channels.

4. Go back to the Scene list area at the bottom left of the Graph Editor and expand the Camera's channels if you haven't already by clicking the small white arrow to the left of the Camera label. **Figure 6.25** shows the expansion.

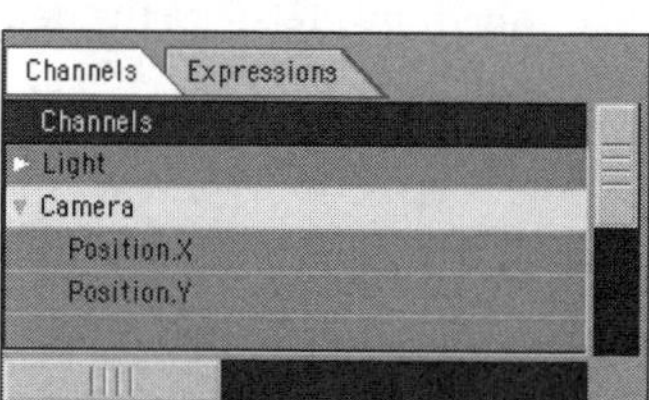

Figure 6.25 When you expand an item's channels, you can use the scrollbar on the right of the Scene Display quadrant to access them; you can also resize the display area.

Note

You can resize the individual quadrants in the Graph Editor by placing your mouse cursor on the borders between areas and then clicking and dragging them.

5. Double-click any of the Camera's channels in the bottom-left zone.

   The channel is now added to the Curve Bin and replaces any other channels stored there. (You can add more channels to the Curve Bin without replacing the active channels by holding Shift when you double-click a channel.)

6. To add the Position.X and Rotation.H channels to the Curve Bin, hold down the Ctrl key and click their name listings. Then drag them up to the Curve Bin. This is another way of adding channels without replacing them.

Note

If you have noncontiguous channels (channels not in order) to select, use the Ctrl key rather than the Shift key to make your selections in the Scene list.

Now that you know how channels are added to the Curve Bin, you can modify or edit them in many different ways.

Working with the Graph Editor

Editing curves is one of the primary functions of the Graph Editor. To help understand the flow of editing curves, think of your workflow from bottom left, to top left, to top right, to bottom right.

Editing Curves

Layout generates editable curves any time you specify a change in a setting's value over time, to control object position and rotation, or any animatable property of a light, object, camera, or surface. No matter what the property or attribute is, you work your way through the Graph Editor the same way, and the Curve Window is where you control its curves.

Figure 6.26 shows the Graph Editor in full frame with the same teacup scene from earlier in this chapter loaded (TeacupMotionFixed.lws). Use your own version of the scene, or load it from Projects/Scenes/CH6/.

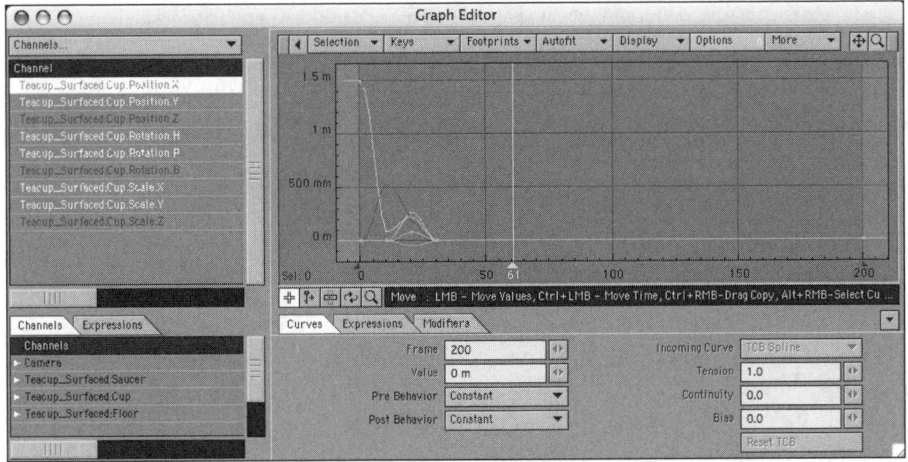

Figure 6.26 With a scene loaded into Layout and the train car object selected, opening the Graph Editor reveals all motion channels already in place for the selected teacup object in the Curve Bin.

In Figure 6.26, the first channel (Position.X) in the Curve Bin is selected by default. In the Curve Window, the channel that represents the object's X position is highlighted. On your computer, you'll notice that each position channel has a specific color in the Curve Bin: X is red, Y is green, and Z is blue. The same color represents the corresponding curve in the main Curve Window. If you move the mouse pointer over one of the small colored dots (which represent keyframes) on an active curve (in this case, the item's motion path), numeric information appears (**Figure 6.27**).

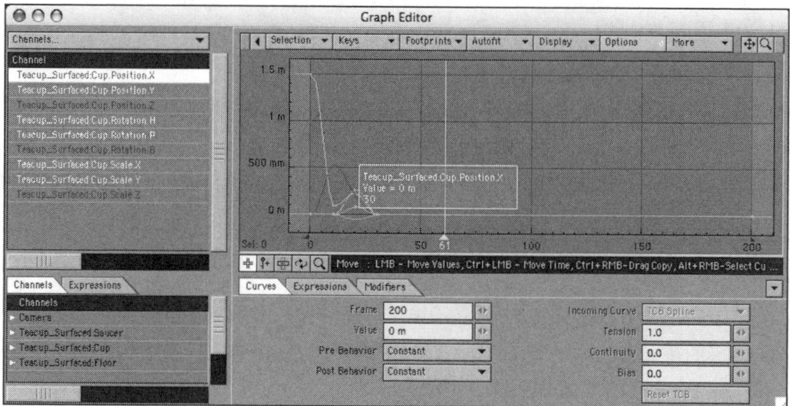

Figure 6.27 Moving the mouse pointer over a keyframe instantly displays the keyframe number, the value, and which channel (such as Position.X) you're working with.

If you like, and have the screen real estate, feel free to resize the Layout window, as well as the Graph Editor to keep both panels fully visible all the time. To resize the Graph Editor, you can do the following:

1. Drag the lower-right corner of the Graph Editor window. Make sure that the window is not maximized.
2. Click and drag the Layout window from the top of the panel, and move it to the upper-left portion of your screen.
3. Open the Graph Editor and resize it as well. Move it beneath the Layout window.

Additionally, you can keep the Surface Editor and Preset Shelf (found under the Window drop-down) open while you're working in Layout if you like, perhaps also using the Dope Sheet. This is beneficial because you can make a change, see the result in Layout, and continue working. You do not have to continually open and close panels—simply leave them open. Either a large monitor or a dual-monitor setup is helpful for screen real estate when setting up configurations like this.

Adjusting Timing in the Graph Editor

The Graph Editor enables you to do many things, such as create, delete, or adjust keyframes for specific channels. You can also modify various entities within LightWave, such as surface color and light intensities. One of the more common uses for the Graph Editor is adjusting the timing of elements in your LightWave scenes. The Graph Editor has many uses, which you will inevitably take advantage of at some time during your career as an animator.

Exercise 6.5 Working with the Graph Editor

1. Load the Capsules scene into Layout from the Projects\Scenes\CH6\ directory on this book's DVD.

   This loads a simple scene with two spinning capsules. Each has a rotation and position change throughout the animation.

2. The Capsule_1 object should already be chosen because the scene was saved with it selected. Open the Graph Editor.

   You'll see that all the object's channels are automatically loaded into the Curve Bin. However, in this tutorial, you are adjusting only the object's timing on the X-axis; therefore, the remaining channels are not needed. For safety, not to accidentally change a curve you don't want to, isolate the specific curve to edit in the Curve Bin.

3. In the Scene window, expand the Capsule_1 listing in the Scene Bin, and double-click the Rotation.P channel. All existing channels in the Curve Bin will be replaced by the Rotation.P channel (**Figure 6.28**).

Note

As you work through scenes with the Graph Editor open, the channels will not automatically update in the Curve Bin. You can choose Get Layout Selected from the Selection drop-down (Shift+G) to update the Graph Editor.

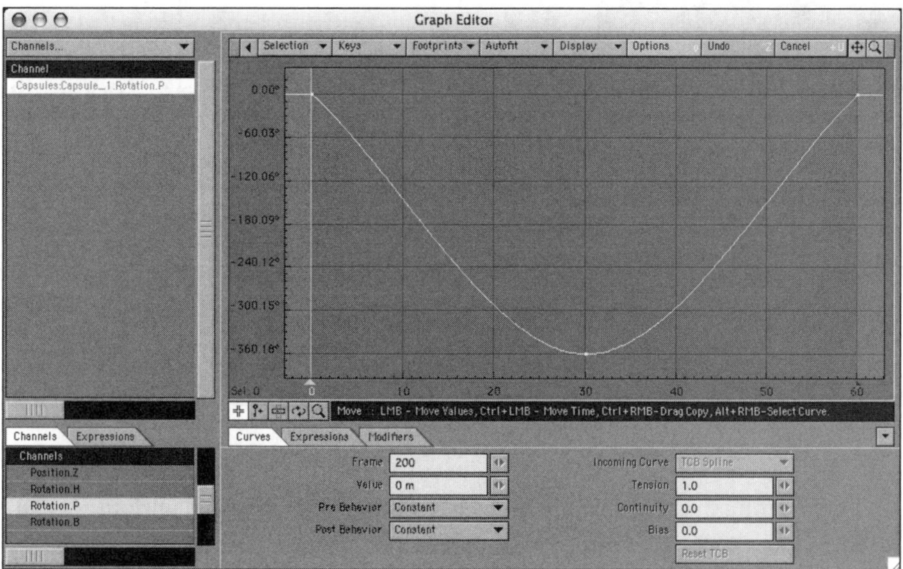

Figure 6.28 Double-clicking the Rotation.P channel in the Scene Bin adds the motion channel to the Curve Bin.

The Rotation.P channel already existed in the Curve Bin before you double-clicked to add it by itself. You can, however, select all of the channels you're not interested in using and remove them. You can right-click the selections and choose Remove from Bin (**Figure 6.29**). You also can choose Remove Channel from Bin (**Figure 6.30**) or Clear Unselected Channels (**Figure 6.31**) from the Selection drop-down at the top of the Graph Editor panel.

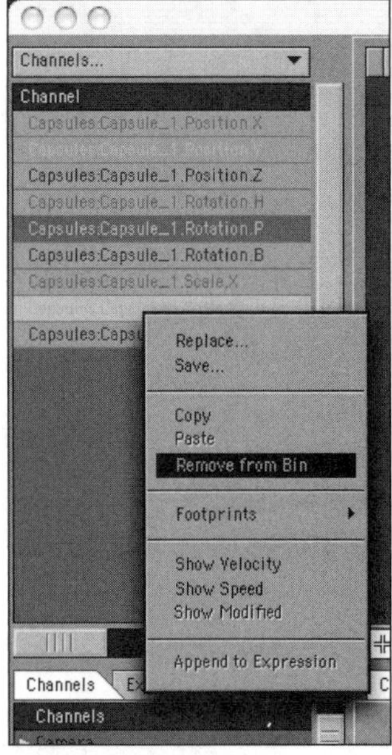

Figure 6.29 To remove selected channels, you can right-click the selections and choose Remove from Bin.

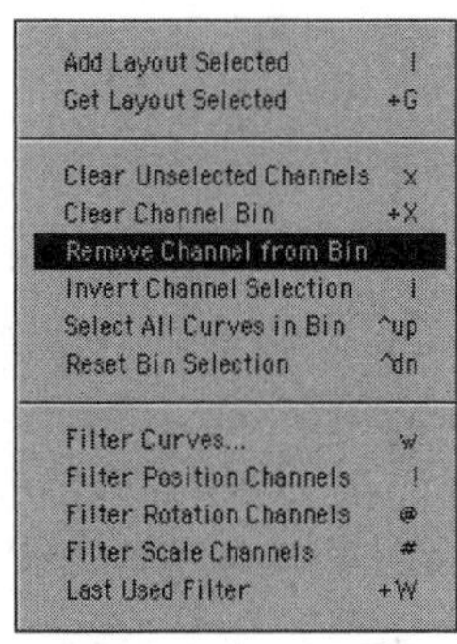

Figure 6.30 Choosing Remove Channel from Bin from the Selection drop-down list removes selected channels from the Curve Bin.

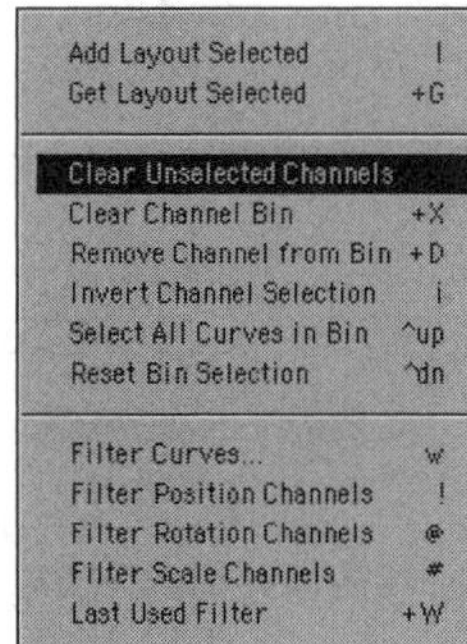

Figure 6.31 The Selection drop-down list at the top of the Graph Editor gives you access to a number of controls, including the ability to clear unselected channels from the Curve Bin.

Note

If you take a close look at the functions available in the Selection drop-down, you'll see that you can do much more than simply remove channels. You can clear the Channel Bin, reverse selections, select all curves, and more. Experiment with these options to get a feel for their uses.

You don't *have* to remove channels you don't plan to edit from the Channel Bin, but clearing channels you don't need helps keep the Channel Bin uncluttered and organized. It also prevents you from accidentally editing the wrong curve.

4. Back in the Curve Bin, the single Rotation.P channel should be selected since it's the only channel there. You'll see it highlighted in the Curve Window.

   This represents the motion of the P (pitch) channel for the object. The tall vertical line is the current frame.

5. Move your mouse over the first small dot (the first keyframe) on the curve for Rotation.P to see the information for that keyframe (**Figure 6.32**).

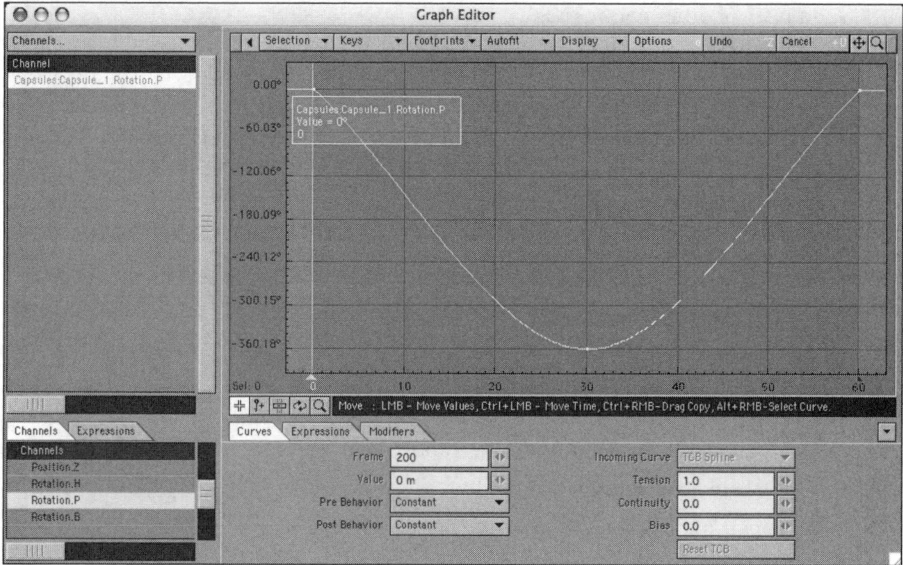

Figure 6.32 Move your mouse cursor over the first dot, which represents the first keyframe for the pitch (P) rotation motion channel.

The information tells you what curve it is, which in this case is Rotation.P for the Capsule_1 object. It also tells you the frame number of the keyframe and the value of the relevant setting at that frame. In this case, the setting value is the object's rotation at frame 0, which reads –0 degrees. This means the object is not rotated at frame 0. As the object rotates in successive frames, its rotation value is reflected in the Curve Window.

It can be hard to identify that first keyframe in the curve. To simplify this, we'll use the Graph Editor's Custom Point Color function.

6. While still in the Graph Editor, press **d** to call up the Graph Editor Options panel with its Display tab open. Click Custom Point Color at the bottom of the list, and

the color selector will become active, as in **Figure 6.33**. The default color, white, is fine, so simply click OK to close the panel. Your keyframes in the Curve Window will now be easier to identify.

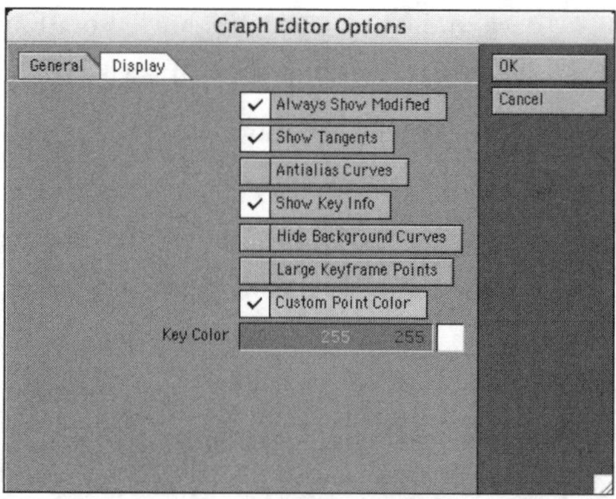

Figure 6.33 Setting the Custom Point Color in the Graph Editor Options panel helps make a curve's keyframes more visible.

A number of other commands within the Options panel can help you when working with the Graph Editor. You can also access these commands and others easily by clicking the

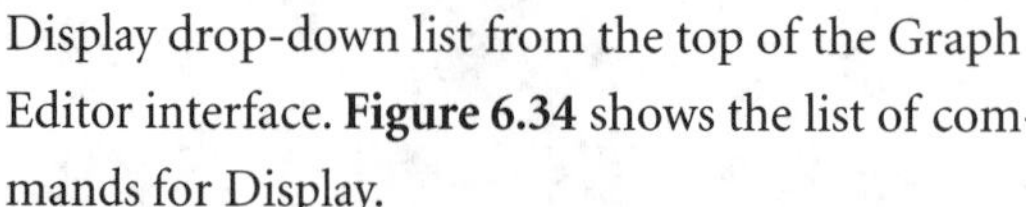

Display drop-down list from the top of the Graph Editor interface. **Figure 6.34** shows the list of commands for Display.

7. In the Curve Window, click the first keyframe to select it. Be sure that the Move edit mode button is selected. It is the first button located above the Curves tab, beneath the Curve Window, as shown in **Figure 6.35**. You can directly click the key to select it, or use the right mouse button to draw a region of selection. This second method is good for selecting multiple keyframes.

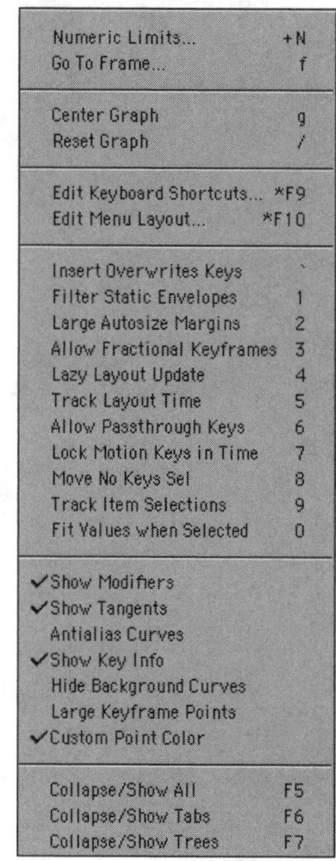

Figure 6.34 The Display drop-down list at the top of the Graph Editor interface gives you controls for working in the Graph Editor Options panel.

Figure 6.35 The Move edit button in the Graph Editor resides just below the Curve Window, along with Add, Stretch, Roll, and Zoom. Selecting a specific tool displays the appropriate keyboard legend. Here, the Move tool is selected, enabling you to move selected keyframes in the Curve Window.

With the Custom Point Color active, you'll see the keyframe highlight slightly, and the values throughout the Curves tab will appear at the bottom of the screen, as shown in **Figure 6.36**.

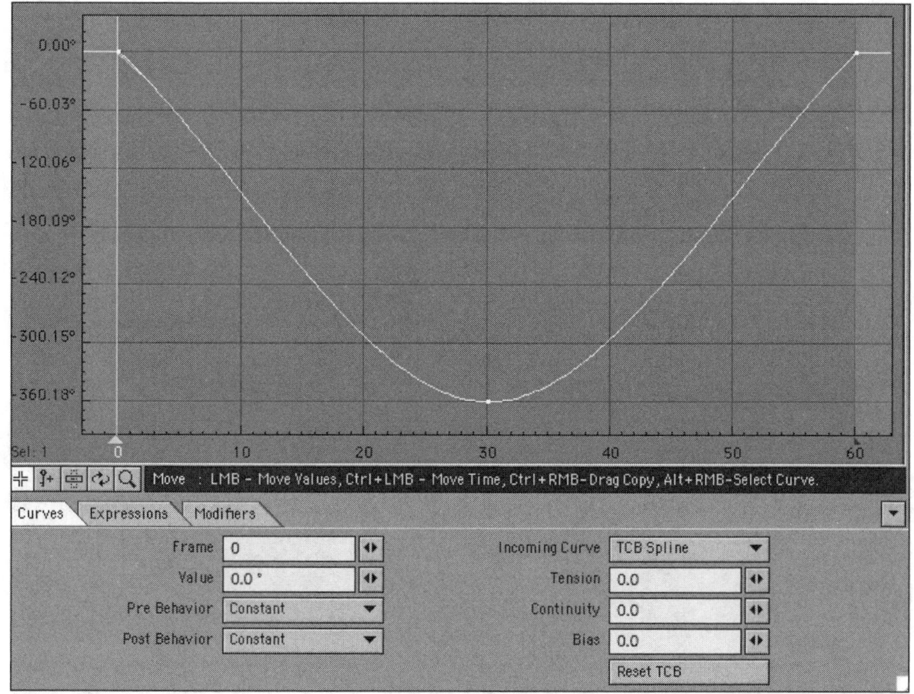

Figure 6.36 When a keyframe is selected, the commands in the Curves tab area become available. Here, a right-click and drag lasso-selects the key.

Note

Beware of clicking around too quickly in LightWave. It happens to the best of us! Doing so in the Graph Editor can really screw up your keyframes, because it's easy to click-select a keyframe, then accidentally click-drag slightly to change its value. Instead of clicking in the window to make a selection, right-click to make a lasso selection. Not only will you be sure you're getting the correct keyframe (they are pretty tiny), you also won't accidentally change it, because the lasso tool can't change settings values.

The middle of the Graph Editor interface offers five small tool icons for you to choose from: Move, Add, Stretch, Roll, and Zoom (see Figure 6.35). When you select one, information is displayed to its right, explaining its function and keyboard shortcut.

The Move tool can be used to select and move single or multiple keyframes in the Curve Window.

8. Select the Move tool and click and drag the first keyframe in the Curve Window.

   Notice that you can move only its value. Doing this changes the position of the object in Layout.

9. Move the keyframe down to set the value around -90 degrees.

   Let's say we do not want the Capsule_1 object to rotate until frame 10, rather than starting its motion right at frame 0. This kind of delayed movement is easy to do in the Graph Editor.

10. Make sure that the Move tool is selected. While holding down the Ctrl key, click and move the 0 keyframe to the right. You'll see the frame number appear over the keyframe (**Figure 6.37**).

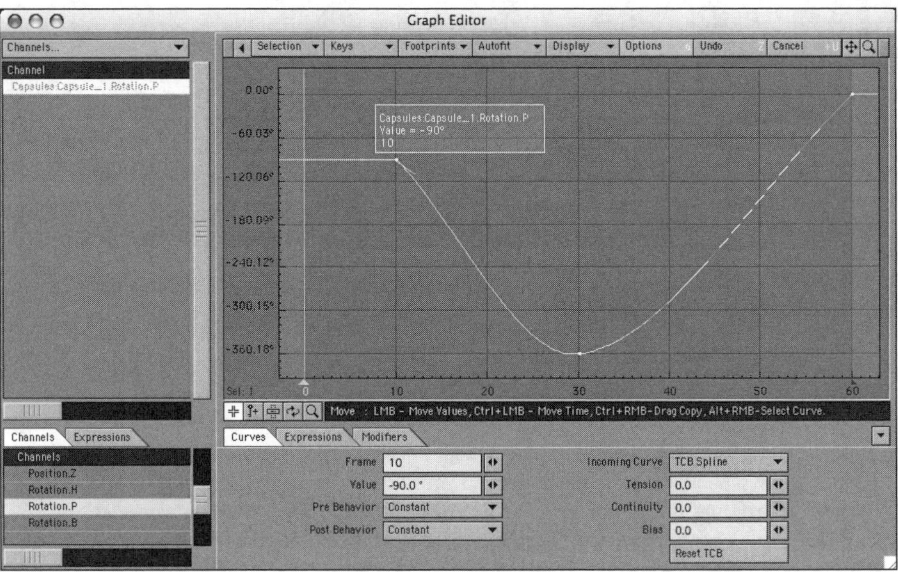

Figure 6.37 Holding the Ctrl key and moving selected keyframes adjusts timing. You didn't realize it was this easy, did you?

Note

If you don't care to hold down the Ctrl key and use the mouse, you can type in a keyframe number instead. At the bottom of the screen in the Curves tab, you can enter the selected keyframe by clicking in the Frame field and typing its frame number. You also can set values by typing in the Value field.

11. Adjust the value and keyframes of selected objects and return to Layout to see the effects. You can adjust values by dragging the keyframes in the Curve Window or by entering them numerically in the Curves tab area.

    Additionally, you have a number of key controls available from the Keys drop-down list at the top of the Graph Editor panel. **Figure 6.38** shows the Move Keys selection, which enables you to numerically set offset values. You will soon get the hang of editing in the Graph Editor.

Take a look at your animation. Click the play button to see how the values you've edited in the Graph Editor have changed the object's motion. Feel free to play around with various movements of keys from different channels in the Graph Editor to see the results.

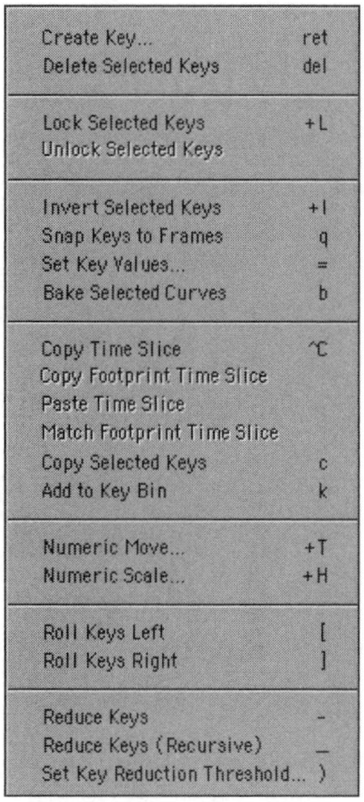

Figure 6.38 The Move Keys selection enables you to set a specific numeric value to move a key.

There's much more to the Graph Editor than this. One really good option to try out is the Lock Selected Keys from the Keys menu. This is really handy if you don't want to accidentally move a perfectly set keyframe. The first part of this chapter guided you through basic navigation and editing of channels and keyframes. Up next, you'll learn about moving groups of keyframes, adjusting their curves, and add modifiers to them.

Copy Time Slice

Going beyond just basic keyframes, you can control your animations with the Copy Time Slice command. Let's say you'd like to copy an object's position at a point where there is no keyframe. What do you do? You could do it manually, by writing down the Move and Rotation values for that frame and entering them in a new keyframe. A much easier way, though, is to use Copy Time Slice in the Graph Editor.

Exercise 6.6 Using the Copy Time Slice Feature

1. Select the curve you want to edit, such as the Position.Z channel, using the previous exercise files. You can double-click this channel in the Scene Bin to quickly add it to the Curve Bin. Drag the timeline bar to the desired frame of motion,

such as frame 15 (in the main Curve Window), as shown in **Figure 6.39**. To drag the timeline slider, grab it from the bottom.

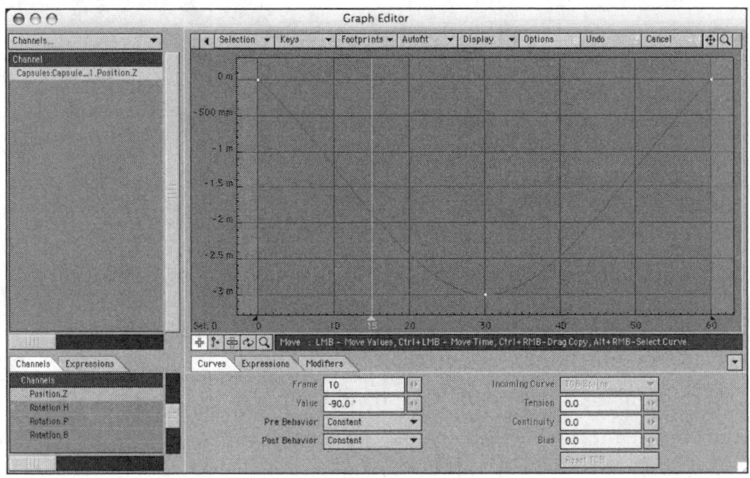

Figure 6.39 Use the timeline slider in the Graph Editor to move through your item's motion.

2. From the Keys drop-down list, select Copy Time Slice (**Figure 6.40**).
3. Drag the timeline slider to frame 40 where there is no keyframe.
4. From the Keys drop-down list, select Paste Time Slice, and a new keyframe will be created with the values from the previous position.

Note

You can also use the keyboard shortcuts for Copy Time Slice: Ctrl+c for copy, and Ctrl+v for paste. This is the same for Macintosh and PC systems.

Copy Time Slice is an extremely handy function of the Graph Editor. If you set two keyframes in Layout for an item—at frames 0 and 90, for example—LightWave will interpret the motion for the frames in between those two keys. We talked about "in-betweening" earlier. Using Copy Time Slice enables you to copy the settings LightWave has calculated for any interpolated frame and copy them to any other frame or keyframe on that curve.

Figure 6.40 The Copy Time Slice command, accessed from the Keys drop-down list, captures the channel values for whichever frame is selected with the timeline slider.

Multicurve Editing

But wait! There's more! You can also use multicurve editing when you want to edit multiple curves simultaneously or use curves of different items as references. By selecting the desired curves in the Curve Bin (as demonstrated earlier in this chapter), you can edit them together as one in the Curve Window. You easily can drag and drop curves from the Scene Display window (in the bottom-left zone of the Graph Editor) into the Curve Bin. For example, you might combine the Position.X of an object with the Rotation.Y of a light, and add in the Scale.Z of a camera. You can use any channel you want.

Note

Here's a really quick way to instantly select all curves in the Curve Bin. Hold the Ctrl key and press the up arrow on your keyboard. Deselect all by holding the Ctrl key and pressing the down arrow.

Foreground and Background Curves

When you add selected curves to the Curve Bin, you can see them in the Curve Window and view them as either foreground or background curves. Curves that are selected in the Curve Bin will become editable foreground curves in the Curve Window; conversely, the curves unselected won't be editable background curves.

Working with foreground and background curves has its benefits. You can interactively cut and paste keyframes from one curve to another. You also can replace an entire curve with another, or lock areas of curves together. By having multiple curves selected when you create keys, the curves can be identical at those selected areas during an animation. Additionally, you have the capability to compare one curve to another, such as a light intensity to the H rotation of a camera. If you remember how Chapter 1, "LightWave v9 Modeler," talked about using layers both for reference and as a tool, the same can be said for foreground and background curves in the Graph Editor. This next tutorial demonstrates some of these features.

Exercise 6.7 Working with Foreground and Background Curves

1. Clear Layout (you can press Shift+n) and open the Graph Editor. You might need to click into the Layout window to activate the Shift+n command to Clear Scene. If the Graph Editor was already open, it will automatically be cleared with the Clear Scene command.
2. Move Camera Position.X and Light Position.Y to the Curve Bin. Do this by expanding the item in the Scene Display (bottom left) and then dragging the desired motion channel up into the Curve Bin.

3. When loaded, hold down the Shift key and select both channels in the Curve Bin.

   You'll see both curves highlight in the Curve Window. Right now there are only straight lines because the channels have no motions applied.

Note

Remember that you can click and drag on the bar between the Curve Bin and the Scene Display windows in the Graph Editor to quickly resize the two windows.

4. Select the Add Keys button beneath the Curve Window (**Figure 6.41**).

Figure 6.41 You can choose to add a key from the Graph Editor window, and you can also use the Move, Stretch, Roll, and Zoom commands.

5. Click once in the top area of the Curve Window and once near the bottom right, similar to **Figure 6.42**. You'll see the two curves adjust to the keys you just created.

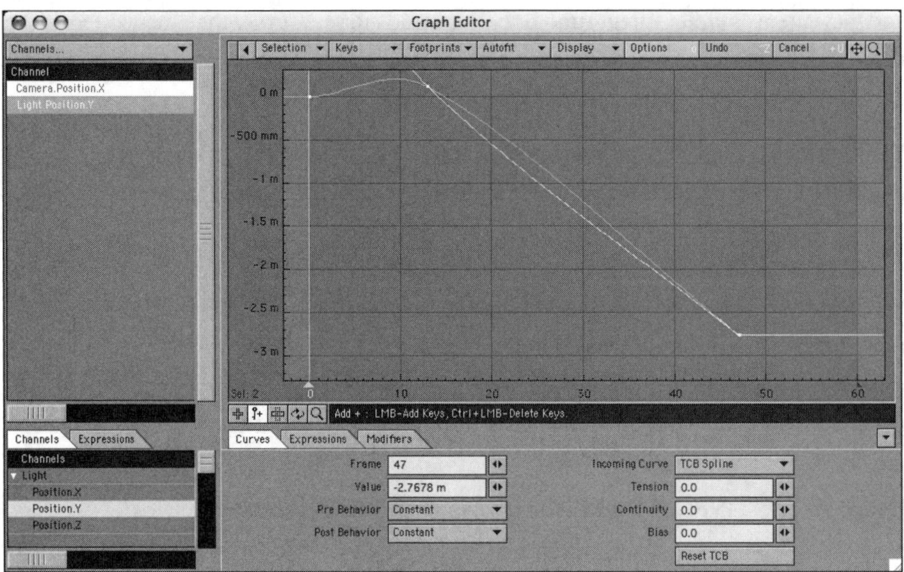

Figure 6.42 You can create keyframes for the selected motion channels directly in the Curve Window.

Note

At times, your curve may be out of view in the Curve Window. As in Modeler and certain views in Layout, just press **a** to "fit all."

Navigating the Curve Window

When you select multiple curves, you can edit them together, create keyframes together, and so on. However, you also can adjust one of these curves based on the background curve: Simply select only the curve you want to adjust in the Curve Bin. The remaining curves in the Curve Bin appear slightly darkened in the background of the Curve Window. From there, you can select the Move tool and click and drag a keyframe to change its value. Here are a few quick steps to remember when working in the Graph Editor:

- Select the Move keyframe button (in the center of the Graph Editor) and click and drag to adjust the selected key(s).
- Select the Move keyframe button and click and hold the Ctrl key to adjust the selected key's position in time—for example, to move a keyframe from frame 5 to 15.
- Hold the Alt key and click in the Curve Window to adjust the entire Curve Window view.
- Press **.** (period) to zoom in in the Curve Window; press **,** (comma) to zoom out.
- Press **a** to fit all contents of the Curve Window into view. For example, after you're done working in a zoomed view of the Curve Window, press **a** to instantly fit all editable keyframes into the window.
- Pressing Shift+g to import curves into the Graph Editor. There's no need to close the Graph Editor, select your next item in Layout, and then reopen the Graph Editor to add a particular curve. Instead, just move the Graph Editor aside, select an item in Layout, return to Graph Editor, and press Shift+g to update with the new selection.
- Choose Numeric Limits from the Display drop-down list at the top of the Graph Editor window (or press Shift+n) to set minimum and maximum frames for the Curve Window (**Figure 6.43**).

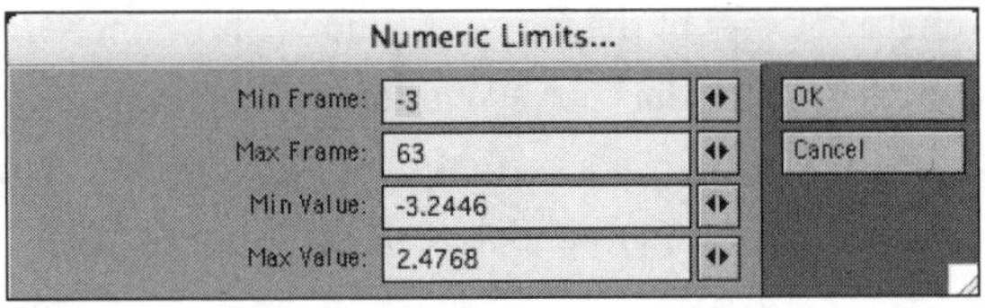

Numeric Limits...

Min Frame:	-3	OK
Max Frame:	63	Cancel
Min Value:	-3.2446	
Max Value:	2.4768	

Figure 6.43 Use Numeric Limits to control the frame and value settings in the Curve Window.

- Hold Ctrl+Alt while moving the mouse left and right, or up and down, drags and zooms the Curve Window. You also can set a minimum and maximum value. Alt-drag options are similar to their use in Layout's Perspective viewport.

Exploring Additional Commands in the Graph Editor

In addition to the commands you'll use most often as you animate your scenes, you should know about the Graph Editor commands that can help you increase the speed of your workflow. As you've learned in other areas of LightWave, right-clicking in certain areas gives you access to additional tools that enable more control. The same goes for the Graph Editor.

Key Pop-Up Menus

You can access additional controls by right-clicking in both the Curve Bin (**Figure 6.44**) and the Curve Edit window (**Figure 6.45**). (The right-click pop-up appears in the Curve Edit window only if your mouse cursor is positioned directly over a key.) All these controls are available in one location as well: the Keys drop-down list at the top of the Graph Editor interface.

Figure 6.44
Right-clicking a selected channel opens the key pop-up menu for additional control.

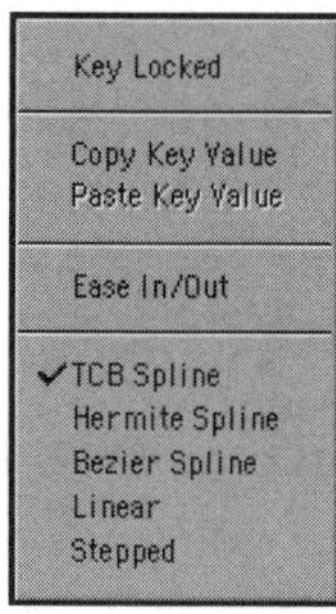

Figure 6.45
Right-clicking a selected keyframe opens the key pop-up menu for control in the Curve Edit window.

Selecting a specific channel and right-clicking it in the Curve Bin gives you controls to perform a number of tasks. You can replace a channel with a preexisting one. You can also save a specific channel's properties, which is useful when you want to save and reuse motions like a flickering light or a rotating globe. Instead of setting up new keyframes, you can save the channel motion and reload it later.

You also can copy and paste a specific channel's motion if you want to create a duplicate. Other controls include Show Velocity, which you can use to display a visual representation of the selected channel's velocity in the Curve Window; Show Speed, to make the speed of the selected channel visible in the Curve Window; and Remove from List, to delete a channel from the Curve Bin. Velocity is a vector quantity, and is the rate at which an object changes positions. Speed, on the other hand, is scalar and is how fast an object is moving.

Footprints

A handy feature of the Graph Editor is its ability to create *footprints* for a selected channel. To help you keep track of your adjustments to a keyframe or curve, a footprint cues you visually to remind you how the item looked before you began adjusting it. A footprint also lets you retrace your steps, or *backtrack*, if you choose to undo an adjustment. Follow this next tutorial to learn more about footprints.

Exercise 6.8 Creating Footprints

1. Open Layout, clear the scene, and open the Graph Editor.
2. Select the light in the Scene window of the Graph Editor and drag it to the Curve Bin.

   All the motion channels for the light are added to the bin, as shown in **Figure 6.46**.

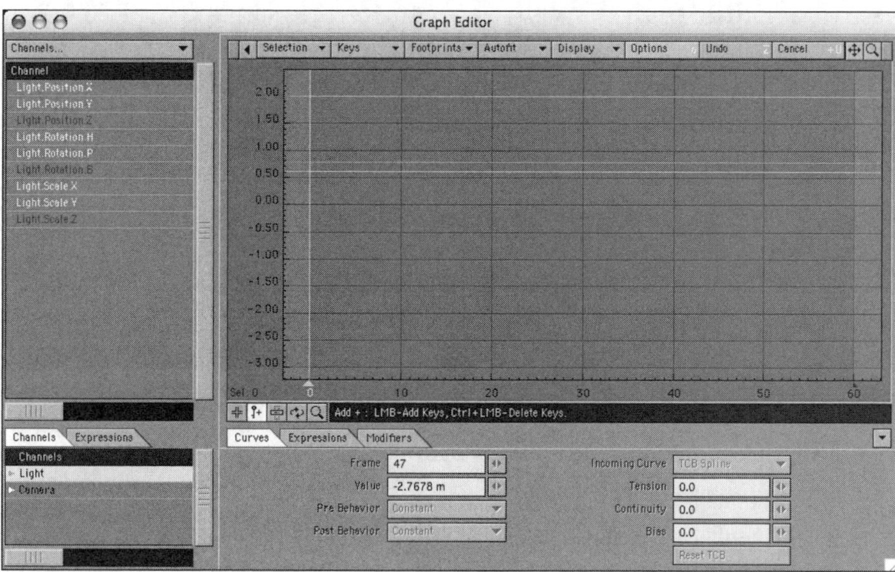

Figure 6.46 Selecting just the light from the Scene Display area and dragging it to the Curve Bin adds all its motion channels.

3. Select the light Rotation.P, which is the Pitch rotation for the light. Of course, any selected channel will do for this exercise.

   When a channel is selected, you'll see it highlighted in the Curve Window.

4. Select the Add Keys command, the second small icon beneath the Curve Window, and then click throughout the Curve Window to create some keyframes for the selected channel. **Figure 6.47** shows the channel with a few keys added.

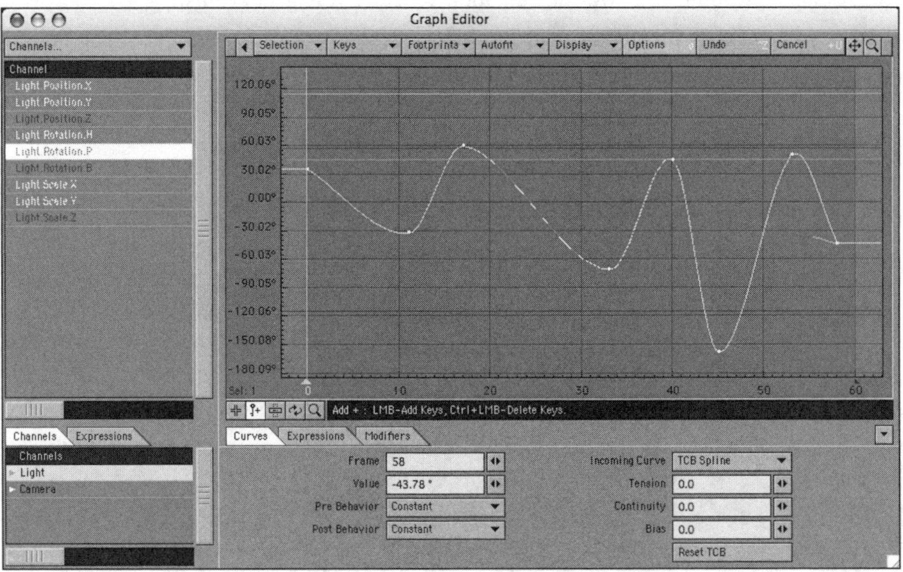

Figure 6.47 A few keyframes are added to the light's Rotation.P channel in the Curve Window.

5. Go back to the Curve Bin, and with the Rotation.P channel still selected, right-click it to open the pop-up menu.

6. Choose the Footprints selection and then select Leave Footprints. You also can do this through the Footprints drop-down list at the top of the Graph Editor, as shown in **Figure 6.48**.

   It won't look like much has happened in the Curve Window, but wait.

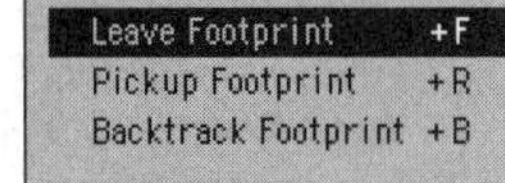

Figure 6.48 Right-click a selected channel to select the Footprints option, or select the Footprints drop-down list at the top of the Graph Editor.

Note

You also can hold the Shift key and double-click in the Curve Window to select all keys. Move mode must be selected to do this. Clicking once in the blank area of the Curve Window deselects keyframes.

7. Right-click and drag to select all your keyframes in the Curve Window, as shown in **Figure 6.49**.

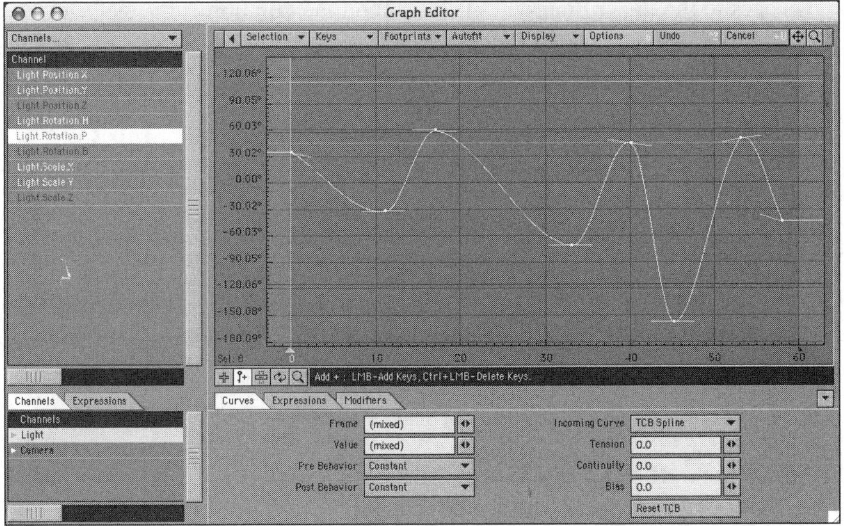

Figure 6.49 Right-clicking and dragging in the Curve Window lets you select multiple keyframes. Mac users, don't forget to hold the Command key while clicking the mouse button to perform a right mouse button function in LightWave.

8. With all the keyframes selected, select the Move tool (press **t**) and click and drag in the Curve Window to move the entire motion curve up, as shown in **Figure 6.50**.

   You'll see a faint line beneath the curve you just moved. This is the footprint that tells you where your curve was.

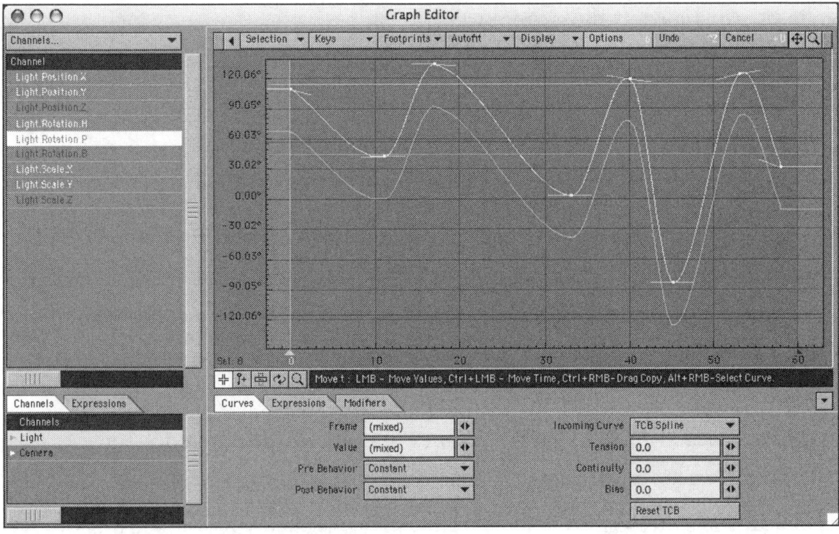

Figure 6.50 When the Footprints option is enabled, moving one or more keyframes reveals the footprint.

9. Go back to the Curve Bin, right-click again on the Rotation.P channel, and choose Pick Up Footprint or Backtrack, or choose one of these commands from the Footprints drop-down list. (Note the keyboard shortcut for each command on its respective button.)

   Picking up the footprint removes it from the Curve Window. Selecting Backtrack resets any channel adjustment to the footprint position.

Footprints provide a simple way for you to keep track of what you're doing and where you've been while working in the Graph Editor. It is easy to make too many changes and lose your place when adjusting various channels. The Footprint option helps you organize your steps by enabling you to retrace your steps if you need to.

Using the Curves Tab

At the bottom of the Graph Editor interface is the Curves tab. (This area is unavailable until a keyframe is selected.) Here, you can set the value of a selected keyframe and adjust its pre- and post-behaviors. For example, suppose that you have created a spinning globe that takes 200 frames to make a full 360-degree revolution. Your total scene length is 600 frames, and the globe needs to rotate throughout the animation. Instead of setting additional keyframes for the globe, you can set the post-behavior to repeat. After the globe completes its 200 frames of motion, the Graph Editor's post-behavior takes over. You can also set pre-behaviors. A pre-behavior is what happens before the first keyframe. You can set either pre- or post-behaviors to the following settings:

- Reset, which reverts the current value to 0.
- Constant, which holds a values equal to the first key's value in a pre-behavior, the or last key's value in a post-behavior.
- Repeat, which replays the motion from the first keyframe to the last for the duration of the scene.
- Oscillate, which repeats a channel behavior from the first keyframe to the last, then reverses it from the last keyframe to the first, for the duration of the scene. For example, if you change a spotlight's heading rotation between frame 0 and frame 30, an Oscillate post-behavior will swing it back to its original position in frames 31-60, then repeat the whole back-and-forth process until your scene ends.
- Offset Repeat, which is similar to Repeat but offsets the difference between the first and last keyframe values.
- Linear, which keeps the curve angle linearly consistent with the starting or ending angle.

The Curves tab also is home to Spline controls. Earlier in the keyframing section of this chapter, we discussed how to use the Move TCB tool in Layout to adjust Tension, Continuity, and Bias (TCB). Remember, LightWave's motion paths (the channels that you're editing in the Graph Editor) are curves. Using TCB is one way to work with these curves, but LightWave offers more control than simple TCB splines.

Spline Controls

When an item or its elements are put into motion in LightWave, it instantly has a curve. The Graph Editor gives you control over the individual channels of an item's motion as you've seen throughout this chapter. You can adjust the keyframes of the curve that is created with various types of splines. **Figure 6.51** shows the Incoming Curve types. An incoming curve is the type of curve that precedes a keyframe. This is an important setting because not only should you be able to control a curve and motion, but you should also be able to control what happens before and after a curve. Perhaps you want to have an object drift a bit before it goes into full motion, or maybe you want to have an item hold in place before it moves. Setting the Incoming Curve type offers you more flexibility in how an item behaves for a selected key.

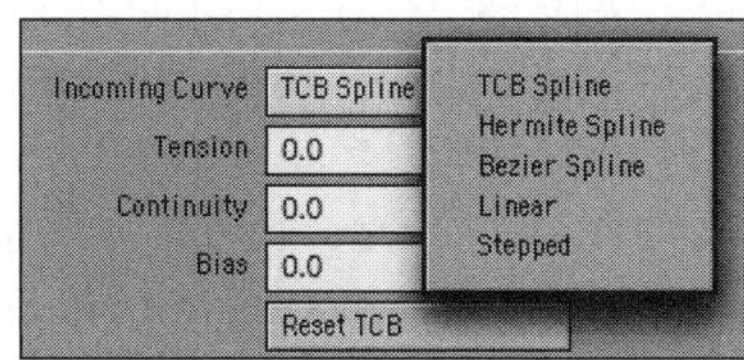

Figure 6.51 LightWave has numerous curve types from which to choose.

TCB Splines

To add a little more information about the TCB splines, they are easy to set and are useful for creating realistic motions. As mentioned earlier during the keyframing section, the values for each spline range from 1.0 to –1.0.

A tension value of 1.0 is often the most commonly used TCB spline because it enables an item to ease in or out of a keyframe. For example, a 3D-animated car needs to accelerate. Setting it in motion without a custom tension setting (at the default T value of 0) causes the car to jump from sitting still to moving at a constant rate, without having to speed up. Try it if you like; it's very unnatural.

TCB Shortcuts

LightWave enables you to quickly and easily control Tension, Continuity, and Bias controls in the Graph Editor. You don't even need to click! Simply move your mouse over a particular keyframe. Press **F1** and drag the mouse to the left to set a negative Tension, or drag to the right to set a positive Tension. Do the same for Continuity with **F2** and Bias with **F3**. Cool stuff.

TCB splines are not the only spline controls you have when it comes to controlling keyframes. This version of the software employs Hermite and Bezier spline curves as well.

Hermite and Bezier Splines

Although TCB splines are often used for common, everyday animated elements, such as flying logos or animated cars, Hermite and Bezier splines offer a wider range of control.

Both Hermite and Bezier splines can help you control your curve. It's up to you to experiment and try both when working with the control of an item's motion. Knowing when to apply curve controls such as these is important. As you work through the tutorials in this book, the necessary controls are used so that you can see the direct effect. Keep an eye out for their use. You might find, however, that the majority of animations you create work best with simple TCB-adjusted curves.

Hermite splines have tangent control handles that allow you to control the shape of a curve. **Figure 6.52** shows a sequence of three keyframes with Hermite splines added to the middle keyframe. Its handles are adjusted.

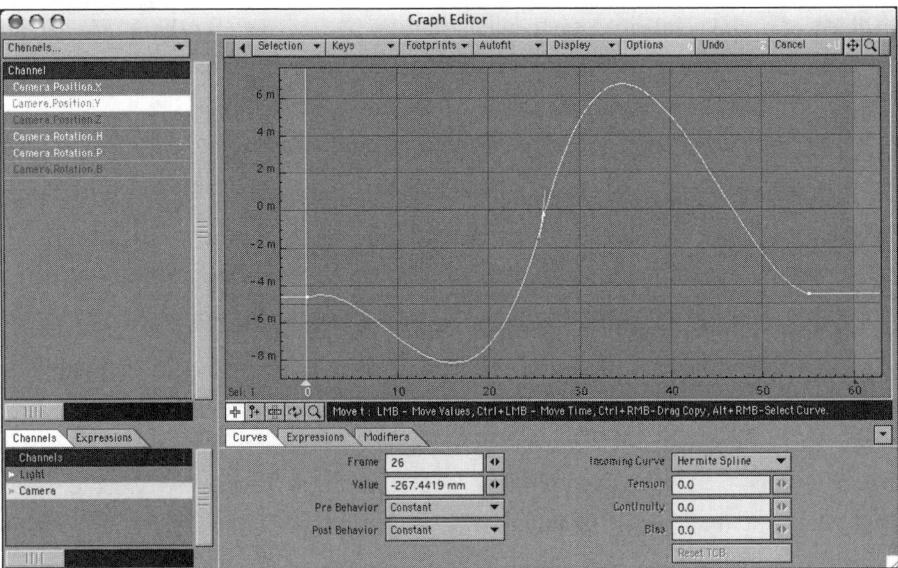

Figure 6.52 Hermite splines are added to the middle keyframe. These splines offer more control than regular TCB splines.

Figure 6.52 shows three keyframes—one low, one high, and one low again—in a sort of bell shape. However, the middle keyframe has a Hermite spline applied and the left handle of it has been pulled down quite a bit. The figure shows how an adjustment to one keyframe can have a drastic effect on the shape of a curve. You can do this by clicking and dragging on the small purple handles that appear on a selected keyframe after the spline is added.

If you apply a Bezier curve, you acquire a different type of control than for a Hermite spline. A Bezier spline is a variant of a Hermite spline and also shapes the curve. **Figure 6.53** shows the same bell curve of three keyframes with one handle of the Bezier curve pulled down drastically.

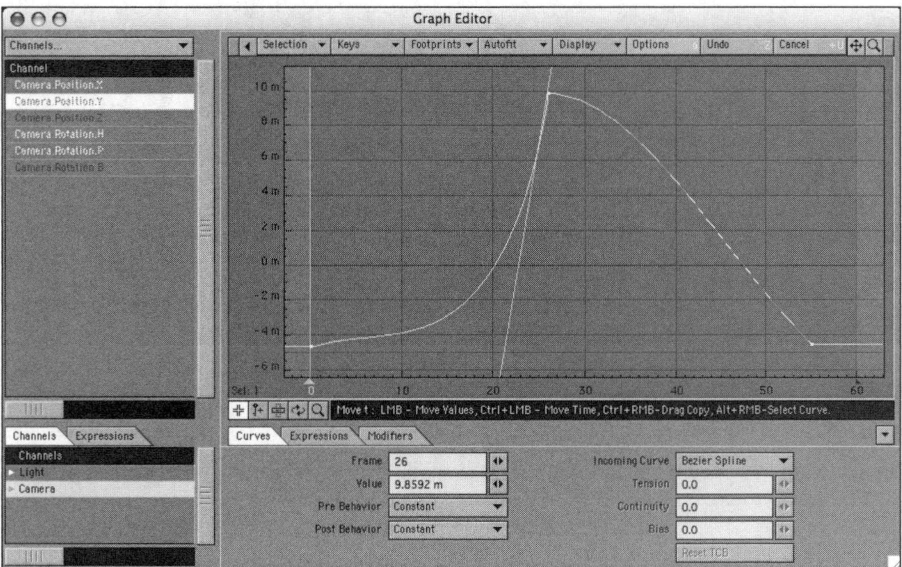

Figure 6.53 Bezier splines, although a variant of Hermite splines, work when the next key is also set to Bezier.

Stepped Transitions

Using a stepped transition for an incoming curve simply keeps a curve's value constant and abruptly jumps to the next keyframe. **Figure 6.54** (on the following page) shows the same three keyframes seen in Figure 6.53, but with a stepped transition applied.

Stepped curves are usable when you want to make drastic value changes between keyframes for situations such as lightning, interference, or blinking lights. You might also find that applying stepped transitions works well for pose-to-pose character animation at times.

Whether you create motions in the Graph Editor or simply adjust preexisting ones, you should understand the amount of control the Graph Editor gives you. The Graph Editor in LightWave v9 even enables you to mix and match spline types for individual channels. Follow along with this next exercise to make and adjust curves in the Graph Editor.

Although you have many options for curve control in LightWave's Graph Editor, using the Tension, Continuity, and Bias (TCB) controls can provide the most natural motion for your animations.

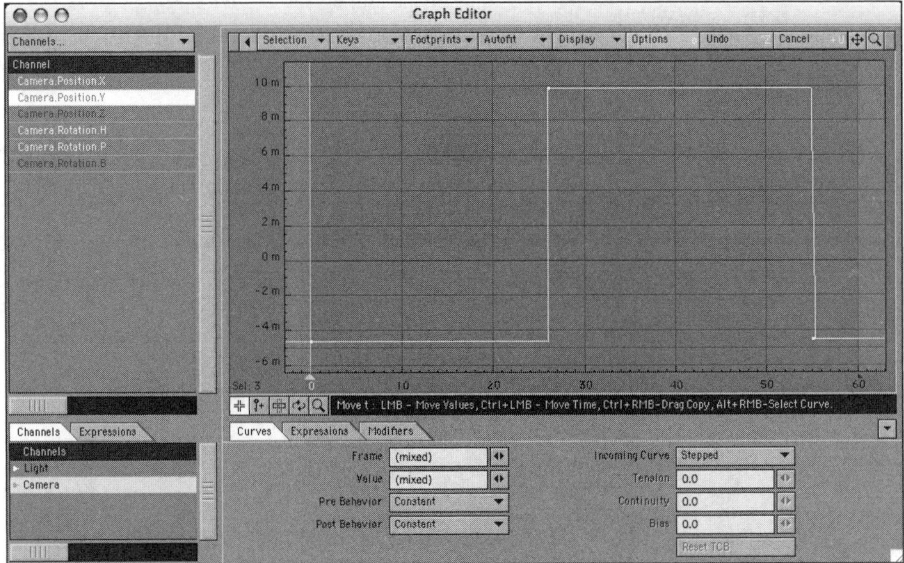

Figure 6.54 Stepped transitions for curves abruptly change your motion from one keyframe to the next.

Press **o** in the Graph Editor to opens the General Options tab of the Graph Editor Options panel. Here, you can set Default Incoming Curve values as well as other default parameters (**Figure 6.55**).

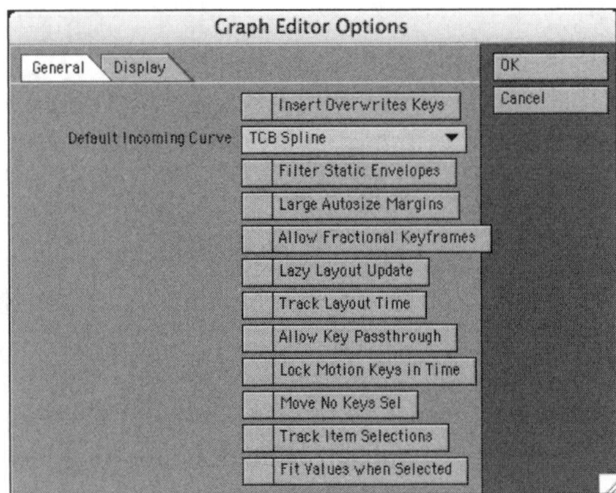

Figure 6.55 You can define the Default Incoming Curve in the General Options tab of the Graph Editor Options panel. Press **o** to access this panel.

Note

By default, the Graph Editor opens with your currently selected Layout item's channels already entered into the Channel Bin. You can leave the Graph Editor open while you work, but if you want to have additional item channels to edit, you need to manually bring them into the Channel Bin. However, if you press Shift+g, the Graph Editor is updated with the currently selected item in Layout. What's more, you can turn on Track Item Selections from the General Options panel of the Graph Editor.

Exercise 6.9 Creating and Adjusting Curves

Start by saving anything you've been working on in Layout and then clear the scene. These next few steps provide the information to create curves and adjust them so that certain areas match perfectly. These techniques can be used with any of your projects.

1. Open the Graph Editor, and in the Scene Display, double-click the Position.Z channel for the camera.

   The Camera's Z position is now added to the Curve Bin, and your Graph Editor interface should look like **Figure 6.56**.

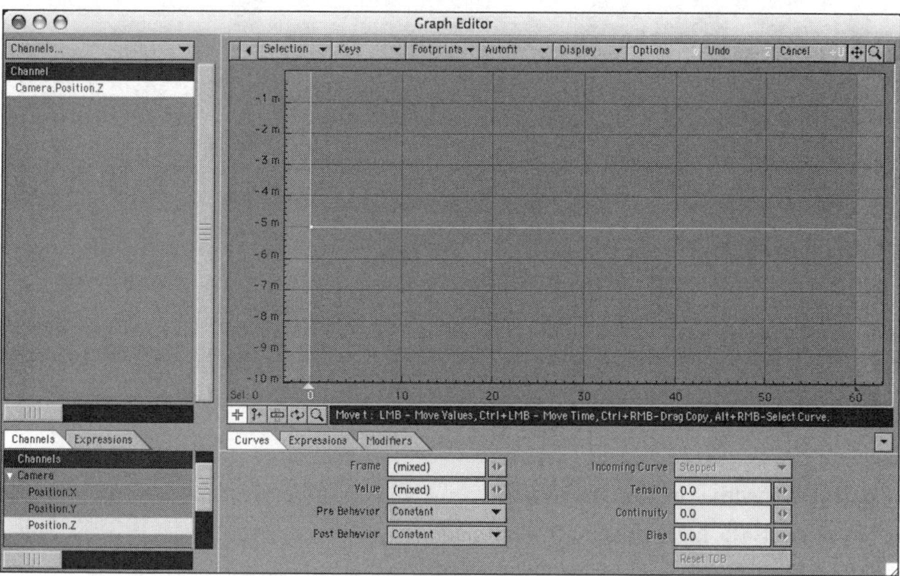

Figure 6.56 Double-clicking the camera's Z position channel adds it to the Curve Bin.

2. Expand the channels for the light in the Scene Display by clicking the small white triangle.
3. Hold down the Shift key and double-click the light's Position.Z channel to add it to the Curve Bin. If you don't hold the Shift key while double-clicking, the new selection overrides anything already added to the Curve Bin.
4. In the Curve Bin, hold down the Shift key and select both the Camera Position.Z and Light Position.Z channels. Or, hold Ctrl and press the up arrow on your keyboard.
5. Select Add mode, and in the Curve Window, create three keyframes to the right of the first keyframe at zero. **Figure 6.57** shows the Graph Editor with the additional keyframes.

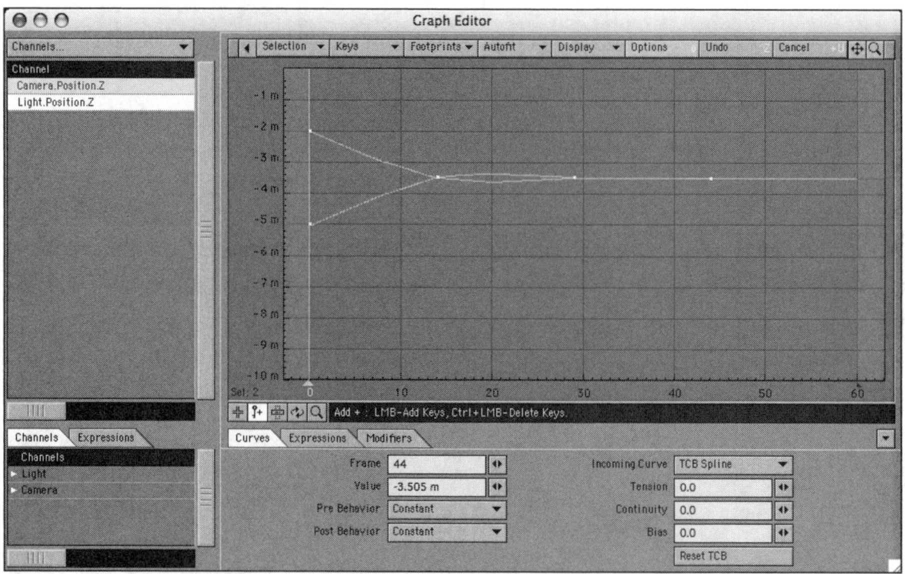

Figure 6.57 With multiple curves selected, you can create identical keyframes for both channels at once.

6. Select just the Camera Position.Z channel in the Curve Bin. This automatically deselects the Light Position.Z channel.
7. Select Move mode and move up the last keyframe.

   You'll see the Light Position.Z channel in the background. You've created similar motions on the Z-axis for both the camera and light, but toward the end of the motion, the value has changed. **Figure 6.58** shows the adjusted channel.

Note

When modifying identical channels on one keyframe, you need to compensate surrounding keyframes slightly. Because of the spline curves, one keyframe affects another.

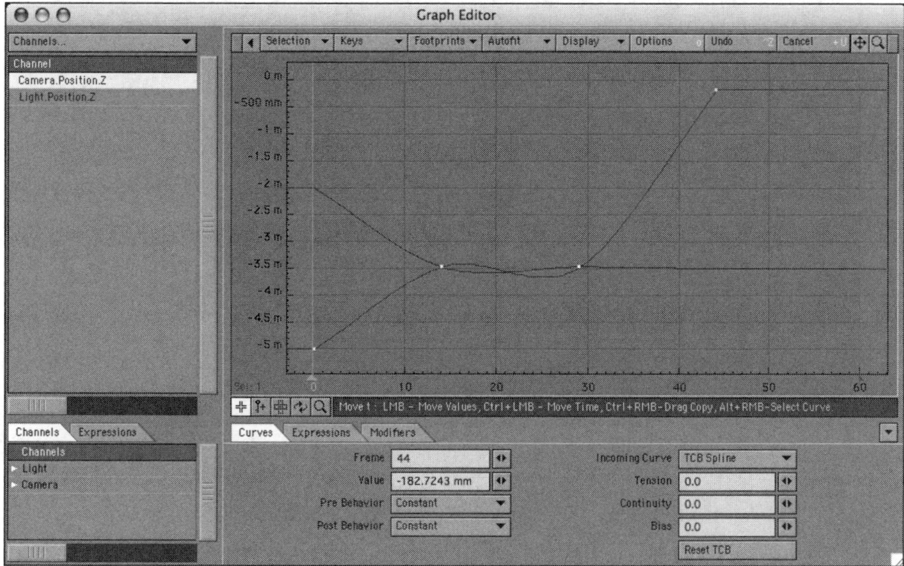

Figure 6.58 One keyframe in a pair of matching channels is adjusted.

A more realistic example of matching curves is a formation of flying jets. Each jet flies in unison, swooping, looping, and twisting in perfect sync. After the formation, one or two jets might need to fly off from the pack. Using the preceding example, you can easily select the appropriate channel and adjust the value at the desired keyframe.

It's easy to see where you would move the jet in Layout, but in the Graph Editor, translating the visual motion to a value might take a little more work. Don't worry; this next exercise helps you adjust values in the Graph Editor.

Exercise 6.10 Adjusting Values

1. Select Clear Scene from the File drop-down menu, or press Shift+n.
2. In the Graph Editor, click the small white triangle to expand the Camera channels in the Scene Display window.
3. Double-click the Camera Position.Y channel.

   Because only one channel is in the Curve Bin, it is automatically selected.

4. In the Curve Window, click on the curve to create a few keyframes, as in **Figure 6.59**.

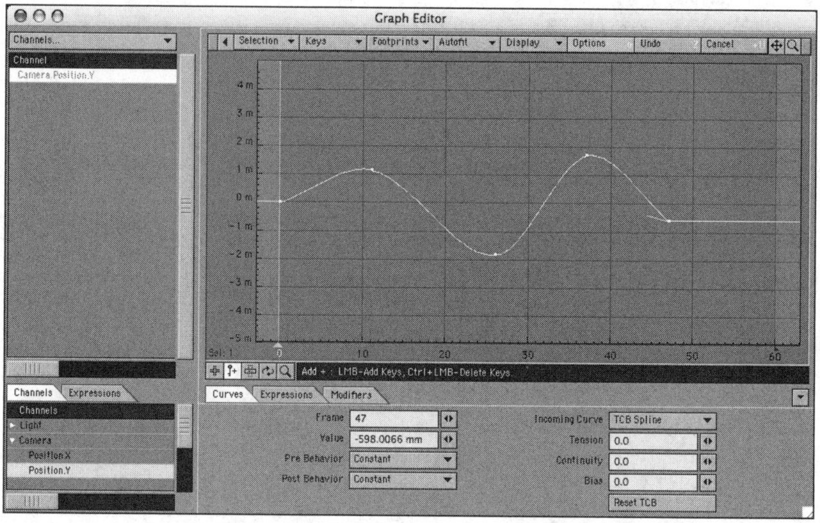

Figure 6.59 One channel is added to the Curve Bin, and additional keyframes are created in the Curve Window.

5. With Move mode selected, hold the Shift key and double-click in the Curve Window to select all keyframes, as shown in **Figure 6.60**. When the keyframes are selected, you'll see small lines extending out from each. These are control handles for the particular incoming curve setting.

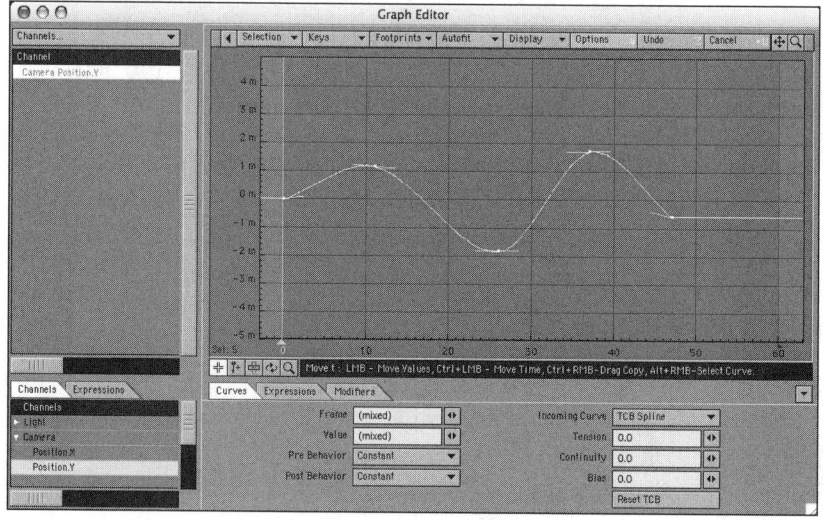

Figure 6.60 Hold the Shift key and double-click in the Curve Window to select all keyframes. Also, you can use the right mouse button to draw a bounding box to select multiple keyframes in the Curve Window.

Take a look at the Frame and Value areas under the Curves tab. Instead of values, they are highlighted with "[mixed]" (**Figure 6.61**). This means that the currently selected keyframes have different values.

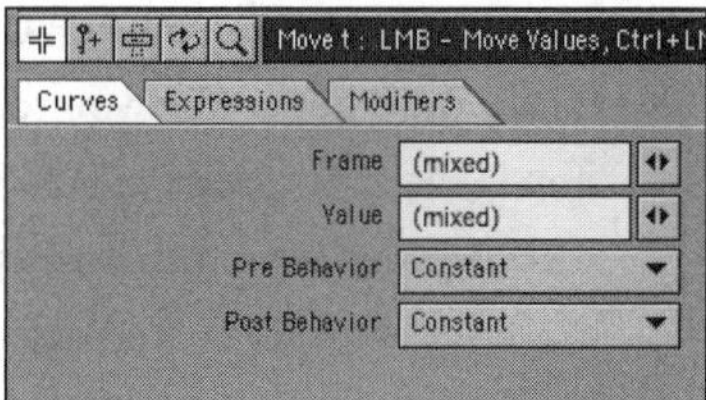

Figure 6.61 Because multiple keyframes are selected, the word [mixed] represents different Frame and Value areas.

6. Type **10** in the Value field and press Enter.

   All selected keyframes now jump to the same value, and perhaps even out of sight. Press **a** to make the curves fit back into view.

   Setting the same value for multiple keyframes is useful when you need to adjust many keyframe values, of course. Instead of selecting a keyframe and adjusting individual values, you can change values in one step as long as multiple keyframes are selected.

Editing Color Channels

Everything discussed in this chapter with respect to object position and rotation also applies to settings such as light intensity, objects dissolves, and much more. Let's look at LightWave Graph Editor's ability to animate color channels, which is really cool for animating such things as stage lighting or a gradually changing sunset.

Exercise 6.11 Animating Color Channels

1. Close the Graph Editor, clear the LightWave scene, and then select the scene's default light. You can do this by first selecting the Lights button at the bottom of the LightWave Layout interface.
2. Press **p** to enter the light's Properties panel. You can also get to the properties by clicking the Properties button at the bottom of Layout.

   You will see a series of small buttons labeled E. As mentioned earlier, these let you access envelopes, meaning their accompanying values can be animated—changed automatically over time, in the course of an animation. Anywhere you see them throughout LightWave, they will guide you right back to the Graph Editor. However, when you access the Graph Editor in this manner, you have control over only the specific area from which you have selected an envelope, such as Light Color.

   It's important to note that entering the Graph Editor by using the E buttons tells LightWave that you want to perform a specific function. For example, if you click the E button next to Light Color, you are telling LightWave that you want to animate the Light Color, and the Graph Editor opens accordingly. Entering the Graph

Editor on its own from the Layout interface would not enable you to animate the Light Color initially. After you have entered the Graph Editor using any E button, the value you enter remains there until you clear it. Therefore, you need to enter the Graph Editor from particular E buttons only once.

3. Click the E button next to Light Color, as shown in **Figure 6.62**.

   After you've clicked the E button, the Graph Editor panel will open. It looks essentially the same as when you used it earlier this chapter, but now there's a strip of color along its bottom edge. LightWave enables you to use the Graph Editor's capabilities on color channels as well as motion channels. **Figure 6.63** shows the Graph Editor with the color channel.

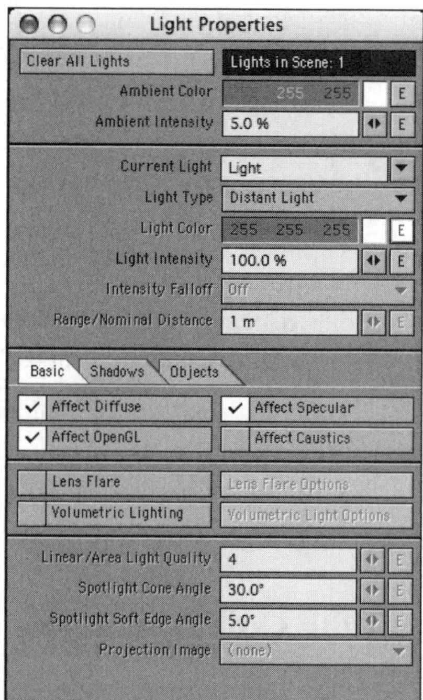

Figure 6.62 The E (Envelope) button guides you to the Graph Editor for specific control over Light Color.

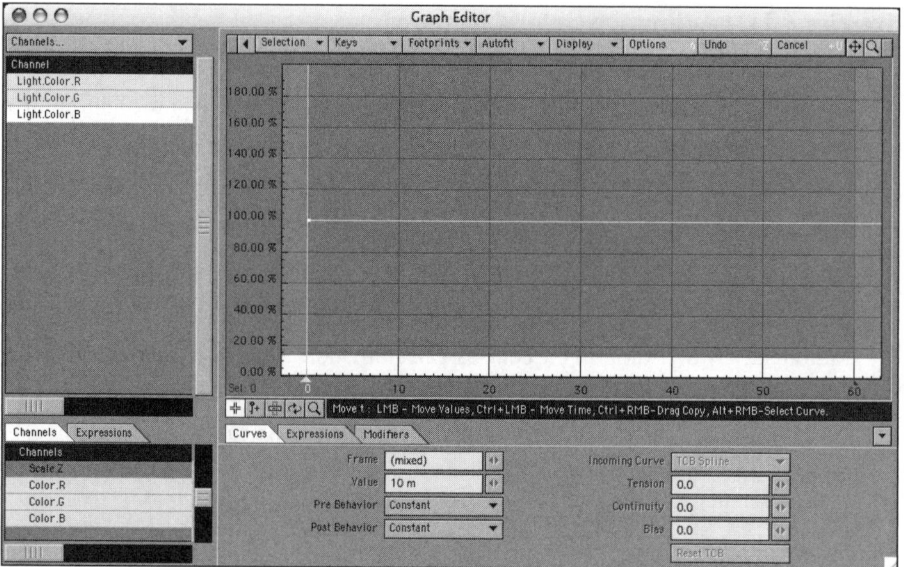

Figure 6.63 By clicking the E button for Light Color, the RGB values are now added to the Curve Bin, and available for animation.

In Figure 6.63, the Curve Bin doesn't show position, rotation, or scale channels, but rather color channels.

4. Select a color channel, such as Light.Color.G, for the green color value. You can also select all color channels at once if you like. By default, though, they should all be selected as soon as you click the E button.

5. Create a few keyframes in the Curve Window as you've done previously in this chapter. Then, right-click one of the keyframe points, and then choose Open Color Picker.

   Using system's standard color picker to choose a new color for the keyframe. **Figure 6.64** shows what just one color channel looks like after it's been adjusted.

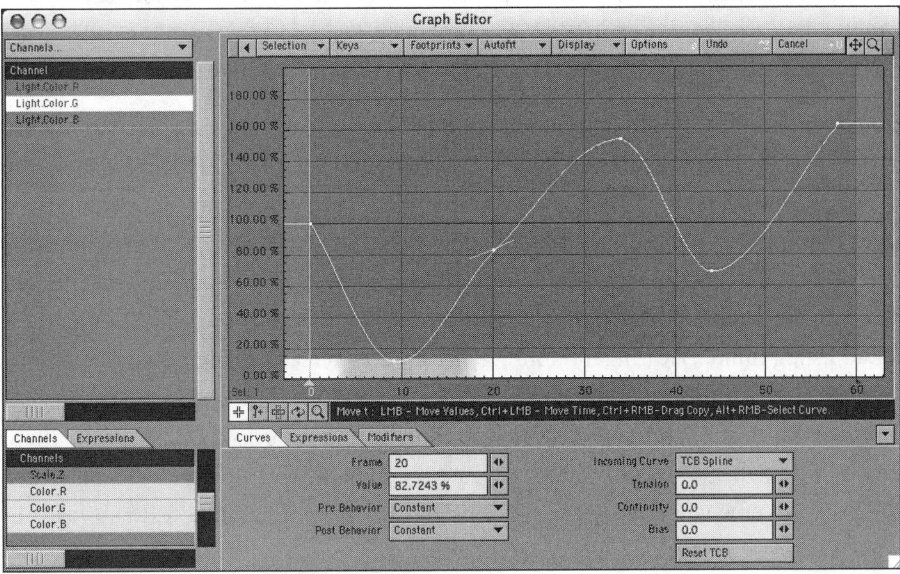

Figure 6.64 Scaling the value for a particular RGB color channel changes the color channel for a set keyframe.

6. You can change the value of a key as well. From the Curves tab at the bottom of the Graph Editor, adjust the value and watch how the curve changes.

   You'll see the color you've selected appear as a gradual change in the Curve Window.

7. Set colors for the other keyframes and adjust their values accordingly to set precise timing. Experiment with these values to see the different types of results you can achieve.

   You can cycle colors like this for lights, backgrounds, textures, just about anything! And all this goes back to one thing—timing! Cycling lights is cool, but if you master the timing and keyframing aspects of animation, you can make your lights *dance*!

The Next Step

So there you have it—keyframing, timing, splines, curves, motions, and the Graph Editor in Layout. While the Graph Editor is a home base for your animations and envelopes, it's not always necessary for putting objects in motion. When you want more control, or need to animate color values, intensities, and more, the Graph Editor is the way to do it.

Before long, you will be setting up motions without even thinking about it. At times, you'll be able to create full animations without using the Graph Editor; other times, you'll keep it open while you work. Try using the Selection drop-down list above the Curve Window to access more control over your keyframes. LightWave's panels are nonmodal, which means that you don't have to be in a certain "mode" to keep them open. Additionally, you can shrink the size of Layout and configure your computer screen to show Layout, the Graph Editor, and even the Surface Editor all at once. Remember that you can collapse the left side and lower portion of the Graph Editor to reveal just the Curve Window, too.

Don't let motions, keyframing, and the Graph Editor overwhelm you. A good way to work is to use traditional keyframing methods directly in Layout so that you can see what you're doing, and then use the Graph Editor for tweaking and adjustments. As with much of LightWave, you have multiple ways to achieve the same result. Refer to this chapter any time you need to control your keyframes with splines or specific modifiers or when you need specific control over individual channels. You'll find yourself using the Graph Editor for adjusting timing, clearing motions, saving motions, creating object dissolves, or animating color channels more often than you think. Practice creating, cutting, and adjusting keyframes and channels in the Graph Editor. Just remember one thing—save often! Save in increments so you can always take a step back! Now, when you're confident of your ability (you know you already are), read on to get started animating text and logos in LightWave v9.

Chapter 7

Text and Logo Creation

Animated text is the bread and butter of many 3D animators, and it's also a good way to get started creating some of the most basic 3D models there are—animated letterforms. Although this basic 3D creation does not take an enormous amount of modeling skill, it will help you feel more comfortable with LightWave, and it'll provide you with skills you can put to work right away for your clients. (Seeing their name, company slogan, or logo in glorious 3D never fails to impress.)

The primary focus of this chapter is modeling; however, it's important to see a result, and therefore, you'll also create a full animation for the text. It will be a simple animation, but with some complex motion added for good measure.

With the advent of increased computing power and increased software capabilities, television stations, postproduction houses, and even corporations do most 3D art and animation in-house. Years ago, 3D was highly specialized, and very costly. Today we see it everywhere and it's more accessible than ever. Regardless, logo creations and animated text are still the meat and potatoes of 3D. Although you might wince at the mention of the term, flying-logo animations pay the bills in many animation studios, and for independent animators around the globe.

Nevertheless, flying-logo animation is a generalized term. Even though the term is easily misconstrued as entry-level or nonprofessional work, you can rest assured that many companies and independent animators still make a very good living creating these types of animations. And not every job is for broadcast television; a significant market exists for logos in corporate and industrial video environments. This chapter focuses on modeling text in LightWave Modeler that can be animated into broadcast-style animations for television and corporate video. This chapter takes you full-speed ahead into a complete broadcast-style animation that goes beyond the typical chrome flying logo you might be familiar with. LightWave has a powerful rendering engine and excellent texture tools that will make your job easier, especially when creating logos. **Figure 7.1** shows a still from the finished logo that you will create.

Figure 7.1 The final logo you'll create in this chapter.

A typical "flying logo" is not so typical these days; with more than 200 channels of programming, you need to stay ahead of the curve. In this chapter, you'll learn how to model text and elements to create animations of text elements—all in LightWave v9. This chapter instructs you on techniques you can use for broadcast quality work. You'll put things in constant motion, not just move one text object from point A to point B. This chapter gives you the knowledge to create stunning professional graphics and animations—and it will also get you excited about doing it! You'll learn about the following:

- Working with Modeler's Fonts tools
- Modeling text
- Setting up a text-based scene
- Importing background animations
- Creating smooth, continuous motions
- Creating 3D text from EPS files

Modeling 3D Text

Take a look at any television news or entertainment show and you'll see that they have one thing in common—text graphics and animations. Such graphics and animations are bold, colorful, and downright cool to look at. Creating graphics and animations for video can be fun and lucrative. Networks and TV stations in major markets pay well for animation packages for their news shows and for titles and "bumpers"—those short animations that appear when shows go into and out of commercial breaks. Animation packages must represent the feeling and style the broadcaster is trying to convey for the station—serious and strong, classy and cute, sharp and hip, and so on. Animated titles and logos are also used widely in corporate and industrial videos, professional wedding videos, and even home videos.

LightWave is powerful enough to even make simple logos look cool. You'll see in this chapter how simple models put together with proper surfacing and lighting can create a cool and unique 3D look. You'll take it a step further using top lighting techniques and slick reflections.

Often, text and logo animation jobs are done in multiple passes and composited together in programs like Adobe's After Effects, eyeon's Digital Fusion, or Apple's Motion. But because those tools are not always available, this chapter will show you how you can model text, import moving backgrounds, and then animate text using nothing but LightWave (and your growing modeling and animation skills).

Working with Backdrops in Modeler

For this project, you'll start by working with text in Modeler. One thing you should remember when working through these tutorials is that text modeling is not just for titles and logos. You can use text to create shapes or various animation elements, such as using a 0 (zero) for a doughnut shape, or the letter I for an I-beam in a construction scene. Text shapes in 3D are just additional three-dimensional shapes. Think in those terms and you'll have an easier time making the most of the toolset. Follow along to begin creating and surfacing text in Modeler.

Exercise 7.1 Setting Up Backdrop Images in Modeler

1. Open Modeler.

   Start by first creating the background elements. Your client has a design that is initially created flat for a print piece. You've been hired to make it in 3D, and you'll use LightWave to bring this flat (and fairly dull) design to life.

2. Press **d** to open the Display Options panel. Click its Backdrop tab, and then click the viewport button labeled BottL, which stands for bottom left (**Figure 7.2**).

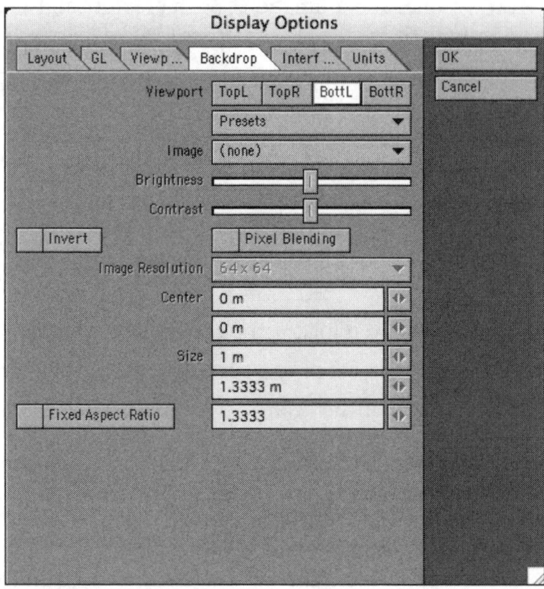

Figure 7.2 Begin creating your titling package by using the Display Options panel to load a background image.

3. For the Image selection in the panel, click Load Image and load the CurvyA.png from the Chapter 7 folder on this book's DVD (in the "Projects\Images\CH7\" directory).

   Here, you can import various images as background references to build from. This image is a curvy letter A that your client uses behind their main title font. You of course, have every font under the sun, except for this one. Why? Because the client's in-house print team has decided to come up with its own custom letter A. So, you'll need to build this letter from the flat image.

Note

You can load any image that LightWave accepts, which includes common formats such as JPEG, TIF, TGA, PNG, and even PSD (Adobe Photoshop's native file format). If you can't seem to load an image, there's a chance that your input-output plug-ins are not properly loaded. You can load them by going to the Utilities tab, selecting Edit Plug-ins, and then choosing Scan Directory. Point the scan to your installed LightWave plug-ins folder and click OK.

After the image is loaded, you'll see it appear in the bottom-left viewport, as shown in **Figure 7.3**. Telling LightWave to use the BottL for the viewport meant that the loaded image is placed in that particular view.

Figure 7.3 Loading a background image instantly shows it in the bottom-left viewport.

As you can see, the image is a bit larger than the viewport. Creating in 3D is relative, and building a tiny logo or a large logo makes no difference when it comes to rendering. However, you'll have an easier time flying a camera through the logo's elements if you make it a bit larger than this default size. You'll also notice some serious jagged edges around the image.

4. In the Backdrop tab of the Display Options panel, change the Size to 5m from the current 1m.
5. Change the Image Resolution to 2048. This will allow you to see the image clear and sharp in the background.

Note

Changing the Image Resolution in the Display Options panel has nothing to do with the actual resolution of the image or your 3D model. This is a display option only. LightWave v9 allows display resolutions up to 4,096 pixels.

6. Bring the Brightness and Contrast down so that the backdrop image is not overpowering. When you create 3D models, your points and polygons might be hard (or impossible) to see if the backdrop image is excessively bright. So dim the backdrop until you can just see it as a reference. Click OK and then press **a** to fit the image into view. **Figure 7.4** shows the results of the last three steps.

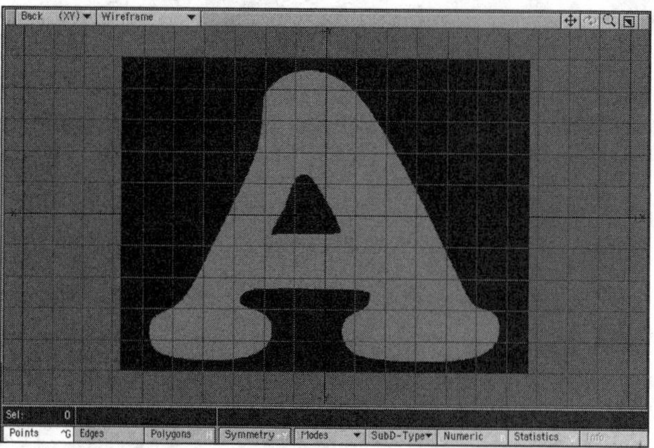

Figure 7.4 Increase the size and resolution of the background image while decreasing the brightness and contrast gets the background image ready for modeling.

7. Just in case you want to use this backdrop later, go ahead and save it. Click Presets in the Display Options panel's Backdrop tab. Choose Save Current Backdrop (**Figure 7.5**) and give it a name such as **CurvyA_bkd**. Then, when you want to use this again, just click Presets and Load Backdrop.

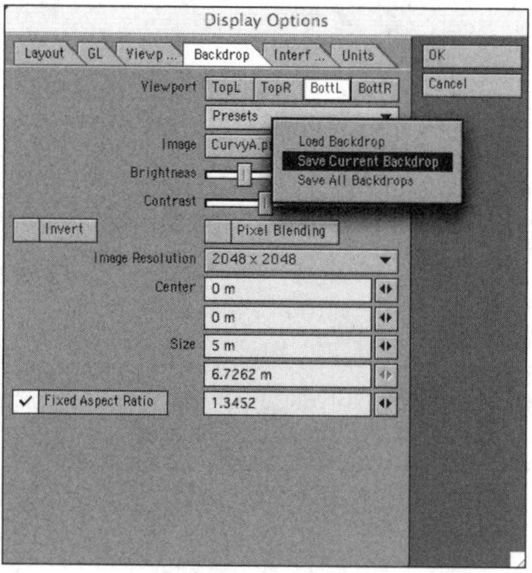

Figure 7.5 Save your backdrop to keep your settings for future use.

You're now ready to begin creating the background blocks that your camera will fly through. Read on to create these elements.

Building Over Images

Using 2D images in your 3D modeling process is not only a good idea but also a smart way to create accurate models. The following technique is something you might find yourself using often in Modeler. You can use it for characters, automobiles, and, in this case, a logo. That's right, logos. It seems that designers like to create cool print design elements, which often are a nightmare for animators. However, by placing an image in the background as you've done in the previous steps, it's quick and easy to build 3D elements right over the image.

Exercise 7.2 Using Backdrop Images for Modeling

1. With the same backdrop image (the CurvyA_bkd) loaded into the bottom-left view, select the Pen tool from the Create tab. Then, click the Maximize Viewport button (**Figure 7.6**) at the upper-right corner of the viewport at bottom left. This expands your view to full screen. You'll click it again later to return to a Quad view.

Figure 7.6 Use the Maximize Viewport button to make the bottom-left view full screen.

2. Press . (period) a few times to zoom into the view. Or click, hold, and drag on the Zoom tool at the top right of the viewport.
3. With the Pen tool, click with the left mouse button to create points, evenly spaced, about 60 in all. Click the points around the curvy A, as shown in **Figure 7.7** (on the following page).

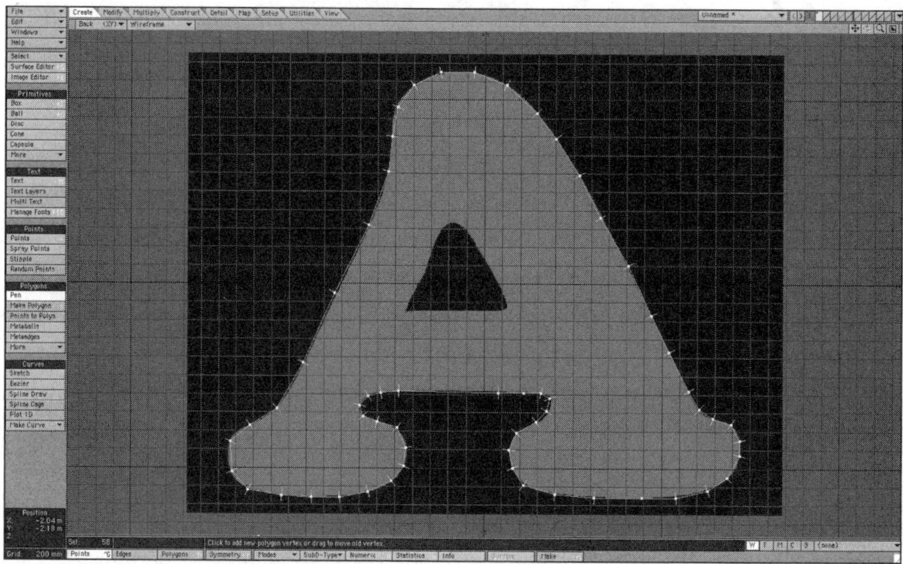

Figure 7.7 Use the Pen tool to click around the outline of the A; each click creates a point in a polygon.

4. The Pen tool instantly creates polygons by connecting points in succession as you click them. Click the Pen tool button again to deactivate the tool, and then click the button in the top-right corner of the viewport to return to Quad view. You should see a shape in the Perspective view similar to **Figure 7.8**.

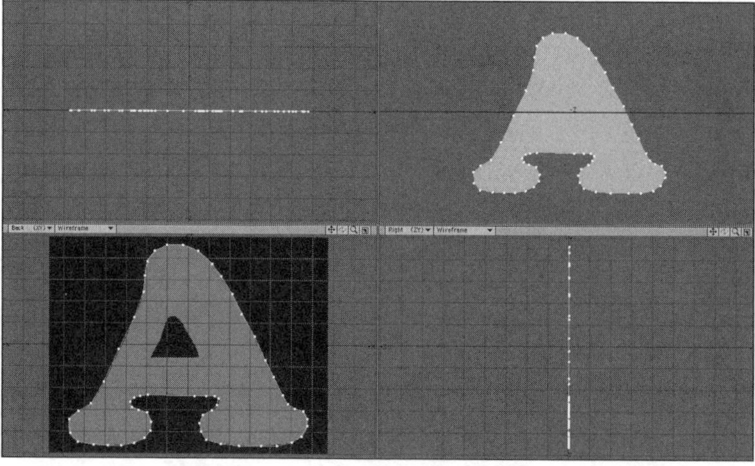

Figure 7.8 Going back to Quad view shows the polygon you've created with the Pen tool.

Note

If you don't see your model in Perspective view, its visible, editable surface, or *surface normal*, is probably facing away from you, toward the negative Z-axis. Press **f** to flip the normal forward.

5. You have the first part of the logo block built, so save it! Press Ctrl+s to Save As, and save it as CurvyA. Each version you create from this point will be saved in increments as 001, 002, 003, and so on, using Shift+s.

Note

A cool feature in LightWave v9 is the ability to save in increments. After you save an object or scene for the first time, each time you press Shift+s afterward, you'll save an incremental, numbered version of your project. For safety's sake, get in the habit of using Shift+s to make incremental saves. That way, even if you make a mistake in an editing session, you'll have the previous version as a backup.

6. Start working in a new layer. To do this, click an empty layer button in the top right of the interface. How do you know if it's an empty layer? A layer that has geometry in it will have a small black dot. So, pick a layer without the dot. In a new layer, also using the Pen tool, evenly create about 12 points around the center space of the A, as shown in **Figure 7.9**.

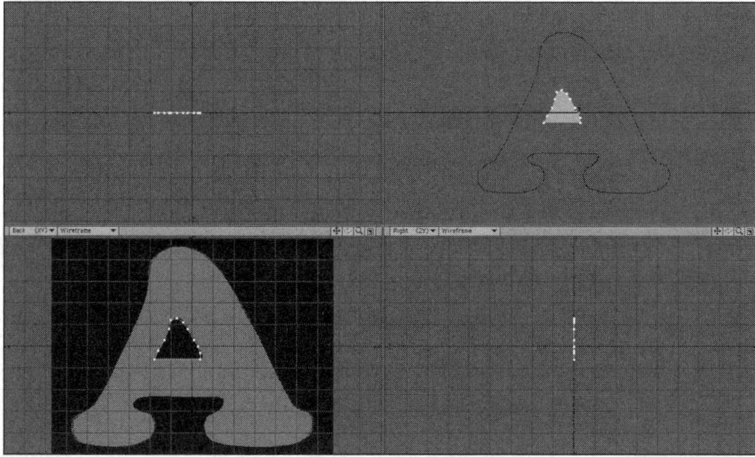

Figure 7.9 In a new layer, use the Pen tool to outline the center space in the letter A.

7. Save your work by pressing Shift+s. This will save your object as a new version with an incremental save.

8. You may have noticed that the object you created with the Pen tool looks kind of chunky. No worries, we'll make it smooth and curvy soon. For now, make sure that the larger A is in the foreground layer and that the center space of the A is in a background layer, as shown in **Figure 7.10**. To place a layer in the background, simply click beneath the slash on the layer button.

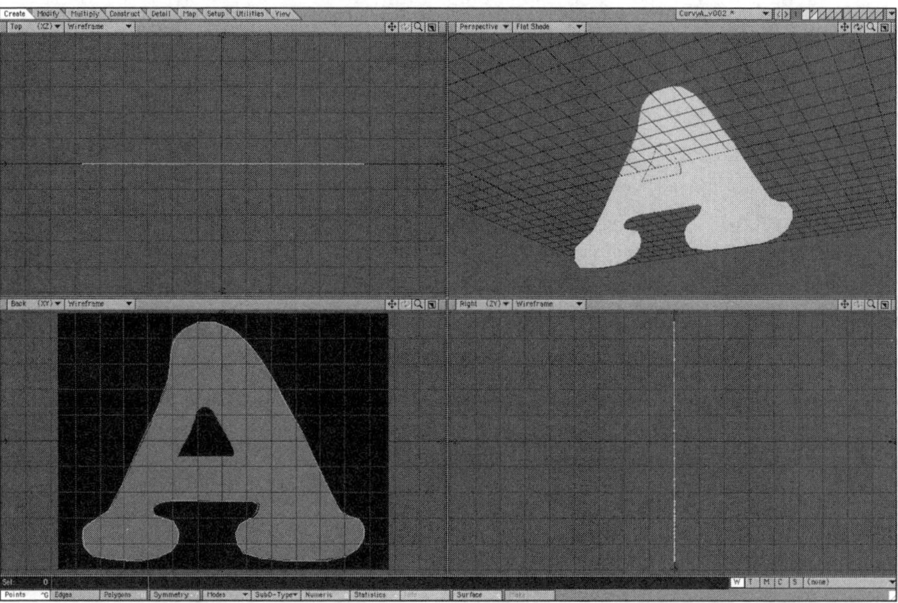

Figure 7.10 Place the larger part of the CurvyA object is in a foreground layer and the center of the object in a background layer.

9. In the Construct tab, click the Drill tool (found in the Combine tool category), or press Shift+r to activate the tool and open the Template Drill panel.

   The Drill tool allows you to "drill" a flat (2D) shape in one layer through one or more objects or shapes in different layer(s). (The Solid Drill tool works similarly but uses a 3D object as the "drill.")

10. In the Template Drill panel, click the Operation button marked Tunnel; then click the Axis button labeled Z (**Figure 7.11**). Click OK, and in a moment, you'll see a nice hole in the center of the letter outline (**Figure 7.12**).

    You built these objects using the Back view, which faces down the Z-axis; choosing Z aligns the drill operation along that axis. The Tunnel operation works as its name implies, using the background shape to bore a tunnel through the foreground shape. If you choose the Drill function, it performs just like the Template Drill, except that it's used for objects that have more than two sides—that is, objects that have more dimension.

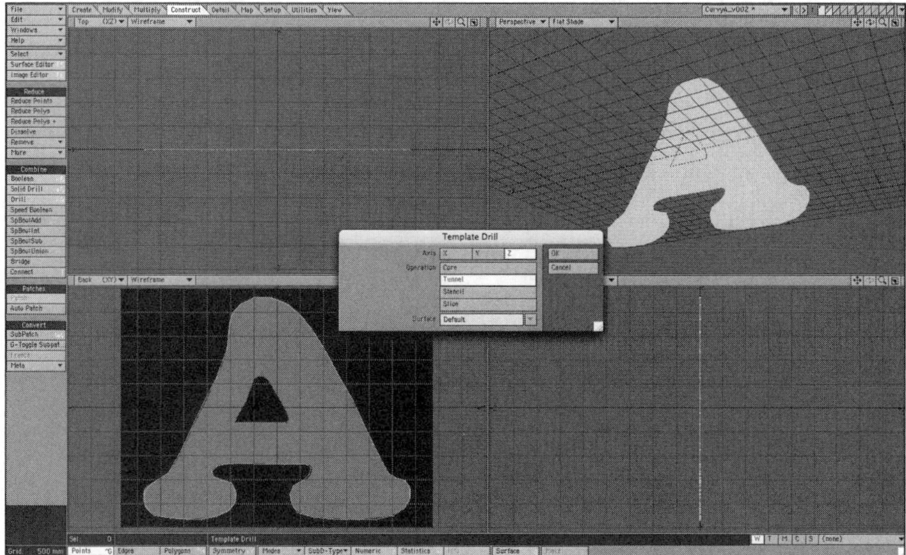

Figure 7.11 Use the Drill tool's Template Drill panel to create a hole in the CurvyA letter.

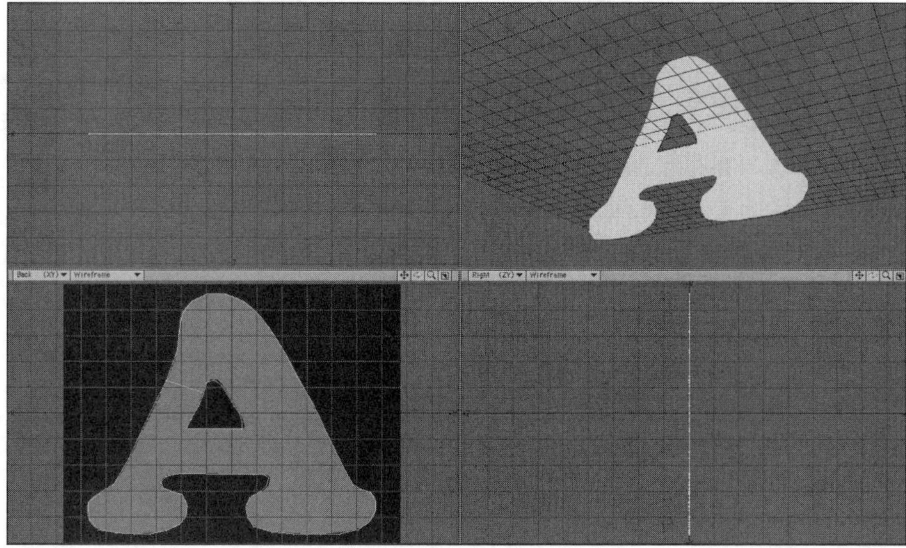

Figure 7.12 Using a Tunnel operation takes the background layer and cuts it through the foreground layer.

11. In the Top viewport, click and drag to the back to extrude the objects.
12. Now we need to clean up the points and smooth them out a bit. The points might be a little hard to see with the background image active. So, select two points on the outer edge, in order. Then, from the Select drop-down menu at the top left of the interface, choose Select Loop. This will select all the continuing points.
13. Press Ctrl+t to activate the Drag tool, and then click and drag on points to smooth them out, as shown in **Figure 7.13**.

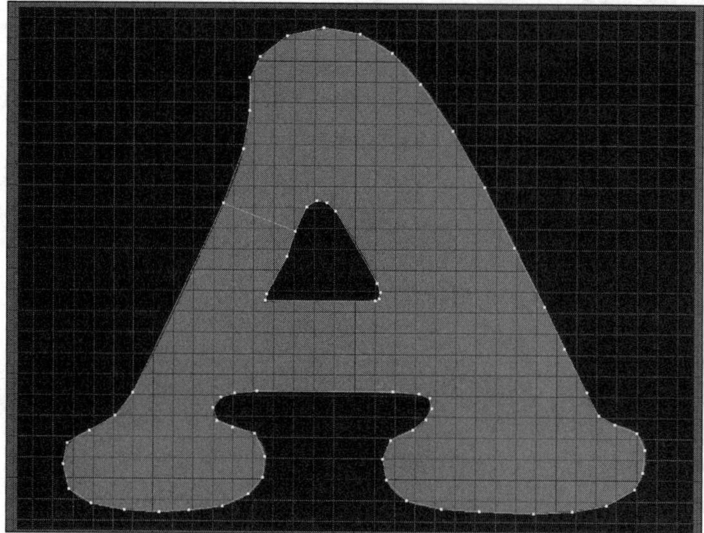

Figure 7.13 Using the Drag tool, you can fine-tune the position of the object's points.

Note

If you feel like your model needs a few more points in certain areas, you can first select the polygon (in Polygons mode) and then choose Add Points from the Subdivide category on the Multiply tab. Then, click with the tool on the edge where you'd like to add a point.

14. After you've positioned the points, save your work. Press the spacebar to deactivate the Drag tool, then press / to deselect the points.
15. Collapse the full-frame front view by clicking the small icon in the upper right of the viewport, returning your view to a Quad view.
16. Press **d** to open the Display Options panel, and in the Backdrop tab, click the BottL Viewport button. Choose "none" in the Image drop-down list to remove the background image.

Note

You easily turn the backdrop image on and off. Press **d** to open Display Options and on the Backdrop tab of the Display Options panel that opens, click the BottL viewport. Change the Image to None to remove it from the background of the viewports. The image is still loaded in Modeler, but it is not displayed. You may find that you will turn the background image on and off a few times while you are modeling, for visual reference. The backdrop image is not part of the model, but it's still loaded in Modeler whether it's visible or not. You can delete it for good from Modeler through the Image Editor.

This model is complete. This curvy A, looming large and semitransparent, will appear in the background of our final scene. You'll call this object up later in Layout.

A few more things to know about using background images:

Pen isn't the only tool you can use to trace background images. Try the Sketch, Bezier, and Spline Draw tools; you can even use a background image as a reference when creating full 3D primitives or other objects. You're using the Pen tool in this project because it creates polygons as soon as the points are laid down. If you'd used the Bezier tool, you'd have been creating curves, which would have required an extra step to "freeze" the curves into polygonal faces. Remember, polygons are necessary to apply a surface and render. The Bezier or Spline Draw options will create a smoother edge, and are very useful for more detailed objects. Be sure to view the SplineDraw video on the book's DVD to learn how to use this tool over backdrop images.

Note

If you would like to completely remove the image from Modeler, open the Image Editor, found on the top left of the Modeler interface. Select the image in the panel and press Delete on your keyboard.

Exercise 7.3 Creating Text in Modeler

When you create text in LightWave Modeler, you don't always have to use a backdrop image.

1. From the File menu, choose Close All Objects. This clears all geometry from LightWave Modeler. Then, press **a** to fit and reset the views.

2. On the Create tab, click the Manage Fonts button (in the Text tool category) or press **F10** to open the Manage Fonts dialog box (**Figure 7.14**).

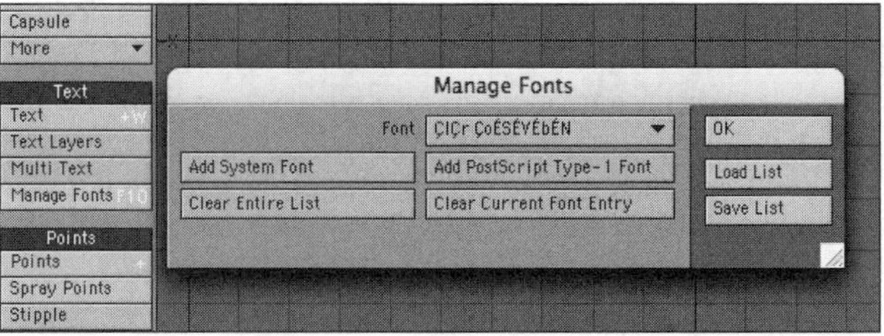

Figure 7.14 The Manage Fonts dialog box, accessible from Modeler's Create tab.

3. Depending on the fonts on your system, the first font listing that appears might look sort of messed up, like the one you see in Figure 7.14. Certain system fonts won't display properly in Modeler, but the majority of your installed fonts should work in LightWave. Click the Font drop-down list in the Manage Fonts dialog box. You'll see a list of your installed fonts, as shown in **Figure 7.15**.

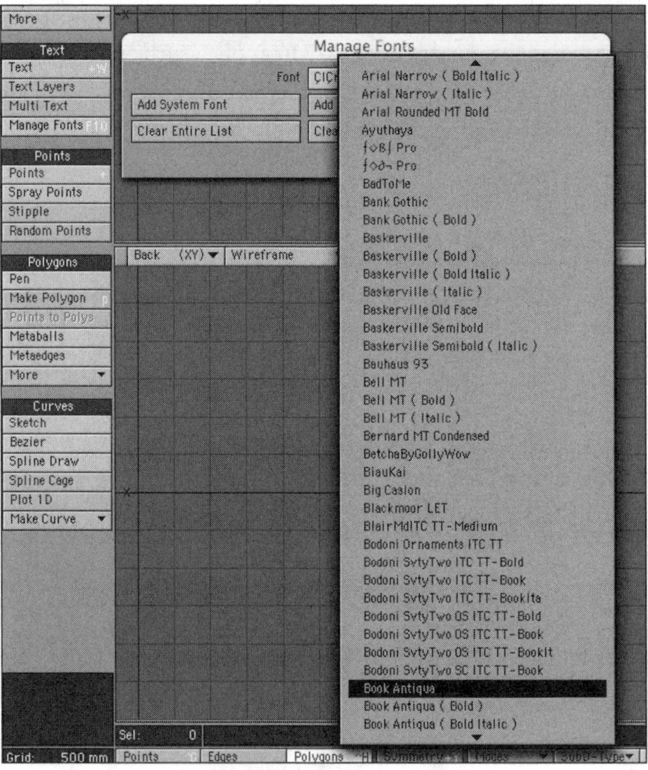

Figure 7.15 The Font drop-down list in the Manage Fonts dialog box lists your installed fonts.

4. Pick an ordinary font, such as Book Antiqua. Any font will do, so if you don't have this font, pick another, such as Arial. After you've chosen a font, click OK.

   You can use the Manage Fonts tool to embed fonts in your model. Its buttons let you add system fonts as well as PostScript fonts, and lets you clear all embedded fonts. Embed any number of fonts, and they become part of your model, available for use whenever you need them.

5. Now, click the Text button, and then click in the Back viewport. You'll see a cursor appear. Your keyboard is now a typewriter, and LightWave will not respond to keyboard equivalents. Type **ABN**, the call letters for the Ablan Broadcast Network (**Figure 7.16**).

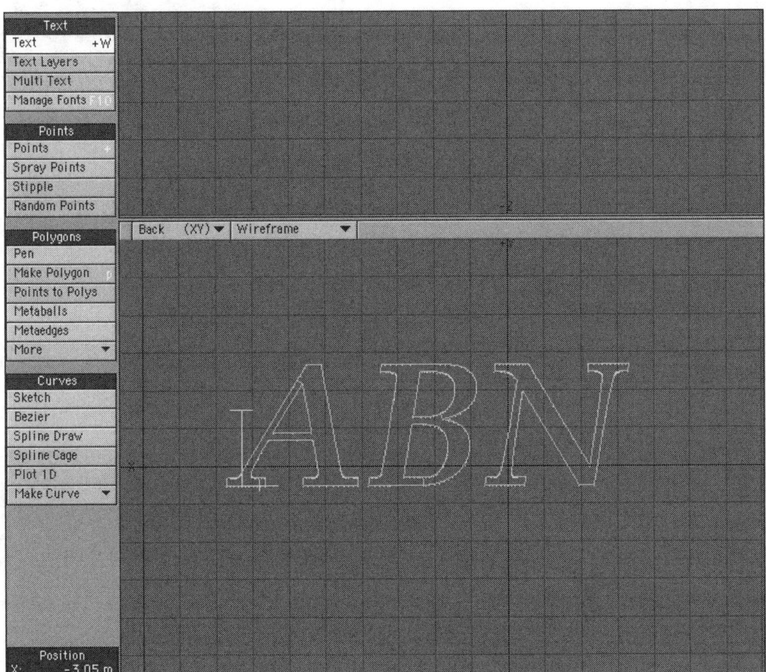

Figure 7.16 With the Text tool, you can add type to Modeler projects.

With the Text tool active, you can interactively adjust your font. You must do this before you turn off the tool, however. When you turn off the tool, the text object will become polygons, just like a box, ball, or anything else you might create. You can then size, adjust, and change the shape as you like; however, turning the text tool back on does not allow you to edit this text but rather creates new text. With the light blue text cursor still active, you can click and drag on the top of the cursor to size the fonts. And you can click and drag on the bottom vertical slash to adjust spacing between letters. Click and drag the bottom-right corner of the cursor to position your text.

6. Before you turn off the Text tool, try one more thing. Click the Numeric button at the bottom of the interface. Here's what's cool about the fonts in LightWave v9—in past versions, you had to load fonts into the system. With this version, you don't. As you read earlier, you can add specific fonts if you like, but by default, all of your fonts are readily available. In the Numeric window, click the Font list. **Figure 7.17** shows the panel.

   The Manage Fonts tool tells LightWave to list only the fonts you want to use for a particular project or modeling session. Without using the Manage Fonts tool, LightWave will list all the fonts installed on your system.

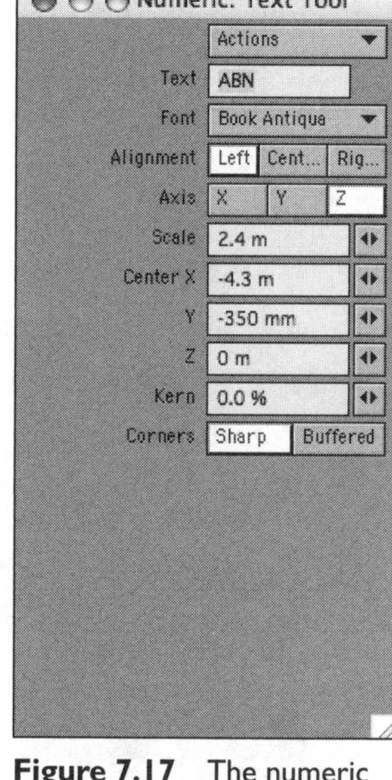

Figure 7.17 The numeric panel for the Text tool allows you to change your fonts as well as set sizing options.

7. If you like, you can change what text you're typing right in the Numeric window as well. For now, set the Scale to 4m, and set the Center X, Y, and Z values all to 0.

8. Close the Numeric panel, then click the Text tool to turn it off. Press **a** to fit the type you just created into the viewport. **Figure 7.18** shows your soon-to-be-3D text.

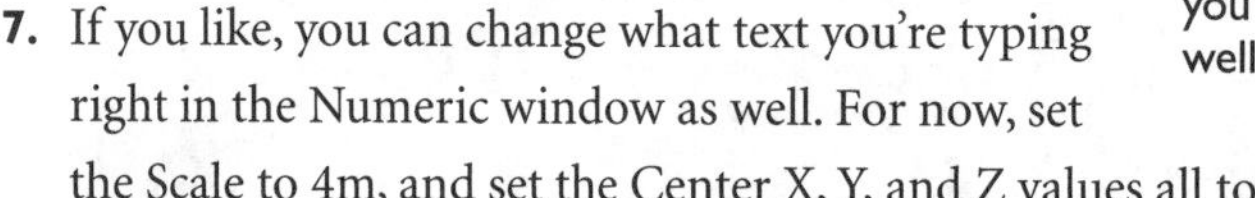

Figure 7.18 Once your text is sized, close the Text tool and press **a** to fit your logo to view.

9. Press Ctrl+s to Save As, and save your font at ABN_Flat. It's a good idea to always save a flat version of type-based objects, in case you want to use them as an element in your animation, or perhaps need to rebuild the full logo. Press Ctrl+s again and save the fonts as ABN_3D. Now your flat version is saved and safe. Your newly saved version will be made into a 3D logo with a few more modeling tools.
10. Press **F2** to center the text. This will move it to the the 0 coordinate shared by the X-, Y-, and Z-axes. On the Multiply tab, click the Extrude tool under the Extend category.
11. In the Top or Right view, click and drag to extrude the text about 2m on the Z-axis, as shown in **Figure 7.19**.

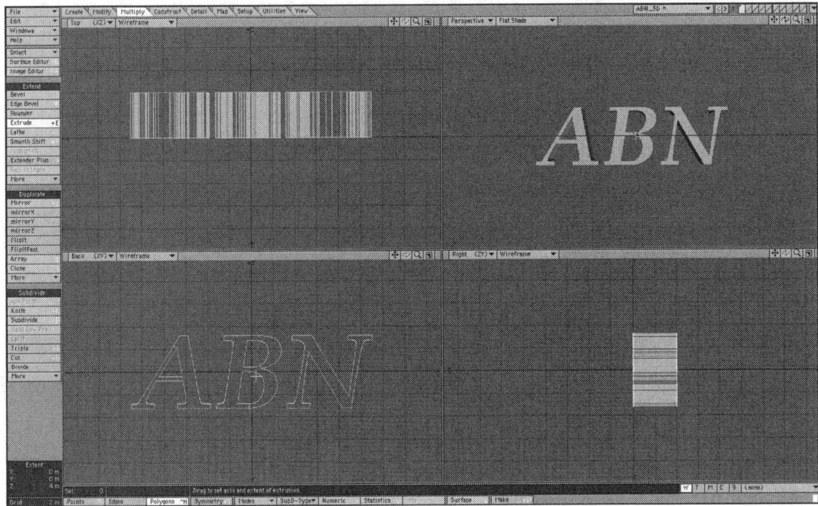

Figure 7.19 To create depth for your text, use the Extrude tool.

12. Press the spacebar to turn off the Extrude tool. Press **s** to save.

You now have 3D text! Congratulations! OK, it's not that great-looking—but it will be! You need surfaces, and more importantly, bevels!

Exercise 7.4 Surfacing and Beveling Text in Modeler

LightWave v9 Modeler offers you a lot of control. You can build just about anything your brain can conjure. But when it comes to 3D text, you really have no reference. If you build a lamp, or a house, or even a dog, you can use the real thing for comparison, but huge flying letterforms are scarce, so how do you determine what they should look like? As a start, take a look at what major networks are doing with 3D text. You'll see a lot of letters with slick, gleaming surfaces and beveled edges—and that's what we'll be using in our logo.

1. The process of applying bevels to type is easy, but there are a few things to do first. You see, to get the most out of your 3D text in the final animation, you'll want to apply separate surfaces to the faces and sides of the text, and to the bevel you'll soon create. To begin, press / (slash) to deselect all and then press **q** or click the Surface button at the bottom of the interface to open the Change Surface dialog box.

Note

The Surface button at the bottom of the Modeler interface and the Surface Editor button at the top left of the interface do very different things. The Surface button at the bottom of the interface creates surfaces for your objects. The Surface Editor button at the top left of the interface changes your surface settings. Be sure to click the right button based on your task.

2. You use the Change Surface dialog box to create surfaces. Enter **ABN_Sides** in the Name field.

   Despite its name, the Change Surface dialog box is used to *create* surfaces—identify them and assign colors to them. In case that's not confusing enough, if you try to use it to change the color existing surface, you'll see an error message that says *Control Is Disabled*. The reason for this is that when you create, or identify a surface and assign it a color, there's no going back—at least within the Change Surface dialog box. To change the surface's color settings, you must use the Surface Editor. So again, Change Surface is not really about changing surfaces; it's about creating them. However, if you assign a color in the Change Surface dialog box, that color will be attached to the selected geometry and show up in Layout when you render. You can, of course, change this value later in the Surface Editor.

3. After you've entered the name ABN_Sides, turn off Make Default. Then click OK. Leaving Make Default on would mean that any new geometry you created in Modeler would be named ABN_Sides. It's good practice to have any nonsurfaced geometry assigned the generic name, *default*, so you can easily spot polygon regions that don't have assigned surfaces. Don't worry about setting a color just yet. Click OK to close the panel.

   You just applied a surface name to your entire object. If no specific geometry is selected, actions you take in Modeler, including changing a surface, apply to your entire object. So why did we use "_Sides" in a name applied to all surfaces of every letter? Because it happens to be easier to select and rename the flat faces of the letters than it is to select all their side surfaces separately. If we select and rename the faces, everything left over will be assigned the correct "_Sides" surface name.

Clever, huh? (In fact, before we name the letter surfaces, we're going to use the same trick again to add and name a surface bevel.)

4. Click the Polygons selection-mode button at the bottom of Modeler, or press the spacebar a few times to cycle to it. Then, select just the faces of the letters. You can do this quickly in the Perspective view by holding the Shift key and clicking on each face (**Figure 7.20**).

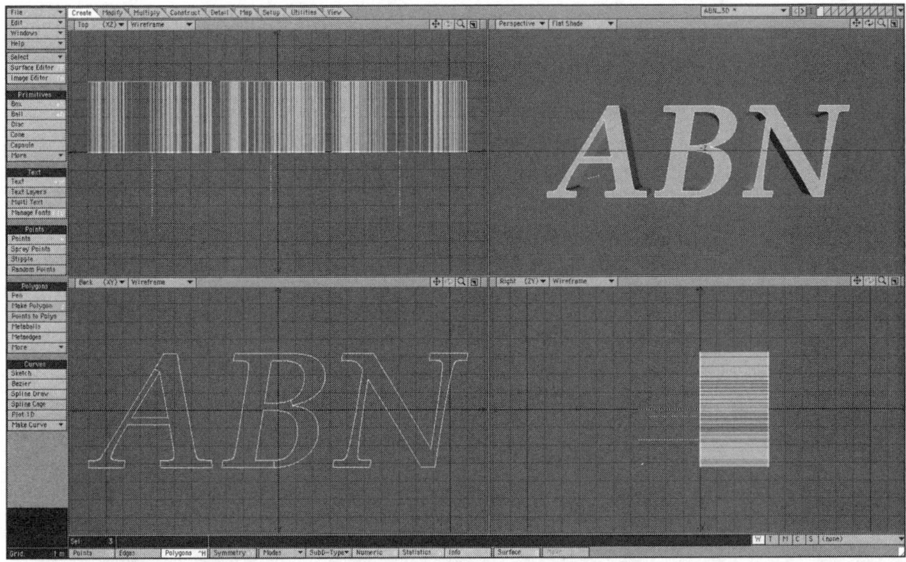

Figure 7.20 Select just the faces of the letters.

5. With the three letter-face polygons selected, click the Surface tool again (or press **q**), and type **ABN_Bevel** in the Name field. Change the color slightly, perhaps to a light blue, to distinguish it from other parts of the object that are assigned surface names. You will change any colors assigned here in Layout; colors assigned in Modeler help you tell named surfaces apart. Click OK to close the Change Surface dialog box.

   You're probably wondering why you named the letter faces "ABN_Bevel," right? Good question. The Bevel tool adds new polygons to the current selection, and if a surface name has been assigned to that selection, it applies that name to the new geometry. So we're temporarily naming the surface polygons "_Bevel" to apply that name to the new bevel geometry. When we're done beveling, we'll click those easy-to-select letter-face polygons one more time and finally give them their proper name.

6. With the faces still selected, press **b** to call up the Bevel tool.
7. Click and drag in any viewport to bevel the selection. Click and drag up to set the Shift, and click and drag left or right to change the Inset. You can also press the **n** key to open the Numeric panel. You'll want to bevel your text to about 200mm for the Shift, and 100mm for the Inset (**Figure 7.21**). Think of the Shift property as pushing and pulling the selected geometry. Inset then, is more like increasing or decreasing the size of the selected geometry.

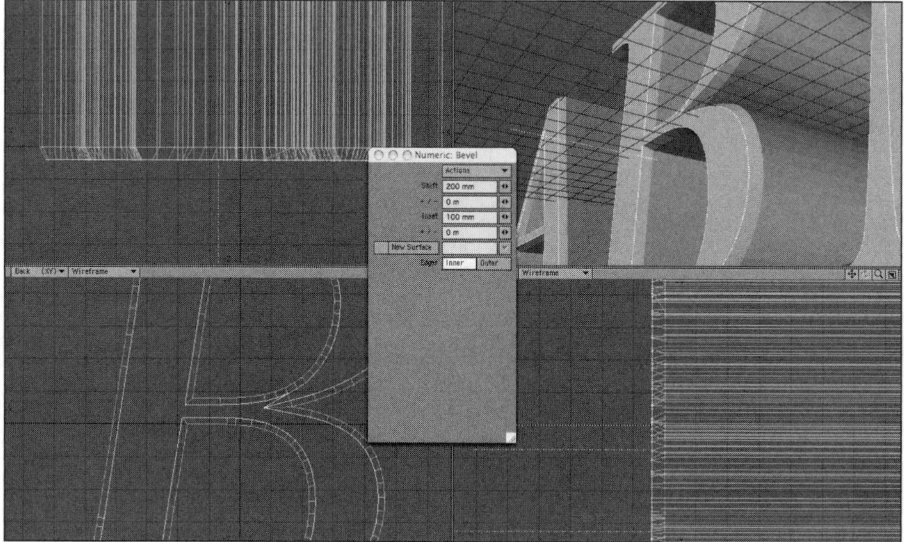

Figure 7.21 Bevel the selected faces of the letters.

Note

Beveling can be awkward unless you pay close attention to your mouse movements. Concentrate first on forward-backward motion, which controls the bevel's *shift*, then focus on just left-right motion, which controls *inset*. When you randomly click and drag, it's difficult to bevel accurately. Also, be sure not to bevel so much that the polygons cross over each other. You want only a slight bevel for added depth.

8. If you look closely at the Perspective view (see Figure 7.21), you'll see that the letter-face polygons are still selected, and the new bevel geometry is not; so press **q** again to open the Change Surface dialog box and change the surface name for the selection to **ABN_Face**. Set a varying color to make sure that your surface name takes effect. This is not always necessary, and is merely an organizational step. You don't need to assign a color when you create a surface name. And, even if you

have two surfaces that will have the same surface and texture later on, such as the sides and bevel of the text, it's still a good idea to give each its own surface name. The reason for this is not only flexibility in surfacing but also for smoothing. Certain surfaces will be smoother than others, even with the same color and reflections applied. **Figure 7.22** shows the beveled and surfaced text.

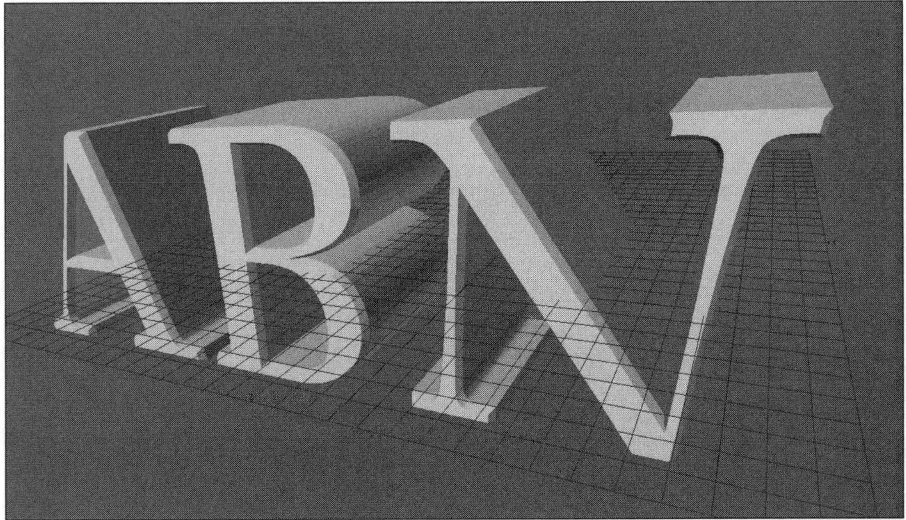

Figure 7.22 With the newly beveled selection surfaced, you now have surfaces applied to the face, bevel, and sides of the text.

9. Press the spacebar to turn off the Bevel tool. Then press / to deselect all geometry. Press Shift+s to save your work.

Duplication in Modeler

This next section will quickly show you how to finish the logo by adding a series of identical abstract design elements. You'll draw this "swoosh" element using spline curves, then duplicate it a few times and arrange the copies so they can all be animated independently.

Exercise 7.5 Creating Duplicate Elements

1. Back in Modeler, make sure the logo you've created, extruded, and surfaced is loaded. Go to a new blank layer and make the existing model a background layer. Assuming your object lives in Layer 1, you can add a new layer by just pressing **2** on the keyboard (at the top of the keyboard, not the number pad).

2. Place the text object in a background layer by clicking beneath the slash in its layer button (**Figure 7.23**).

3. In the Back view, you'll draw a design element. Select Spline Draw from the Create tab. Click at the bottom-left corner of the A, then click three or four more times in an arc up toward the top right of the logo. Click again a bit downward and back to the left to "turn" the curve, then make three or four more clicks to arc back to your starting point (**Figure 7.24**). You'll make about 10 points to create the curve.

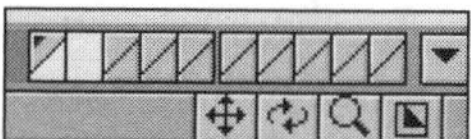

Figure 7.23 A new blank layer is selected while the original text object is set to a background layer.

4. Open the numeric panel from the bottom of the interface and check Closed Curve (see the panel in Figure 7.24).

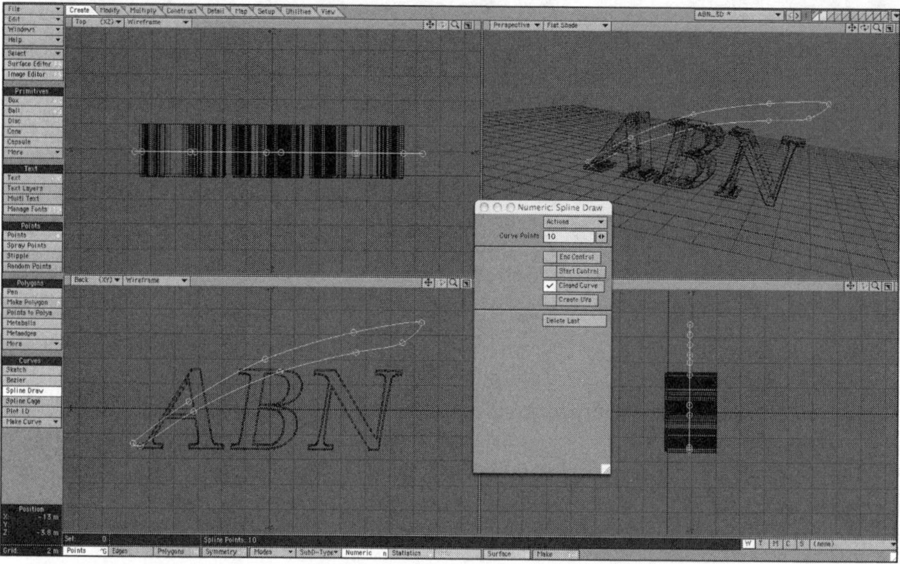

Figure 7.24 Using the Spline Draw tool with a closed curve, you can make a cool design element for the logo.

5. This spline you've created is a curve. It's very useful for creating smooth lines and shapes. Once the shape is to your liking in a nice arc, turn off the Spline Draw tool. This is different from the Pen tool in that it creates smooth flowing curves versus straight, hard-edged polygons.

6. You can use the Drag tool (Ctrl+t) to select and move points on the curve to its refine shape. When you're happy with the shape, press Ctrl+d to "freeze" the

curve, or turn it into a polygon so it can be rendered. When you do this, you'll see a polygon in the Perspective window, as in **Figure 7.25**.

Once a curve is converted to a polygon, it can be assigned a named surface, and that's what we'll do next with this swoosh object.

Figure 7.25 Once the curve from the Spline Draw is created, you can freeze the curve to turn it into polygons.

7. Press **q** to call up the Change Surface dialog box, and enter the name **ABN_Swoosh**. Feel free to add a little color to the surface, and then click OK to close the panel.
8. Save your work as an incremental save by pressing Shift+s.

   There are many ways to duplicate objects in Modeler, including use of the Clone, Array, and Mirror tools. But sometimes it's easiest to just copy and paste, as we'll see now.
9. Check the bottom of the Modeler interface to make sure Polygons selection mode is active (the Polygons button should be white). Then, click the new ABN_Swoosh object to select it.
10. Press Ctrl+c to copy the object, and then press Ctrl+v to paste. It may appear that nothing happened, but you've just duplicated the object and pasted the copy on top of the original. But because you had it selected first, the original, not the copy, is still the active selection.

11. Make sure your Action Center is set to Mouse in the Modes drop-down list at the bottom of the interface. Then, press **y** to activate the Rotate tool (also found on the Modify tab). Click and drag on the bottom-left corner of the swoosh object and you'll see the duplicate fan out, as in **Figure 7.26**.

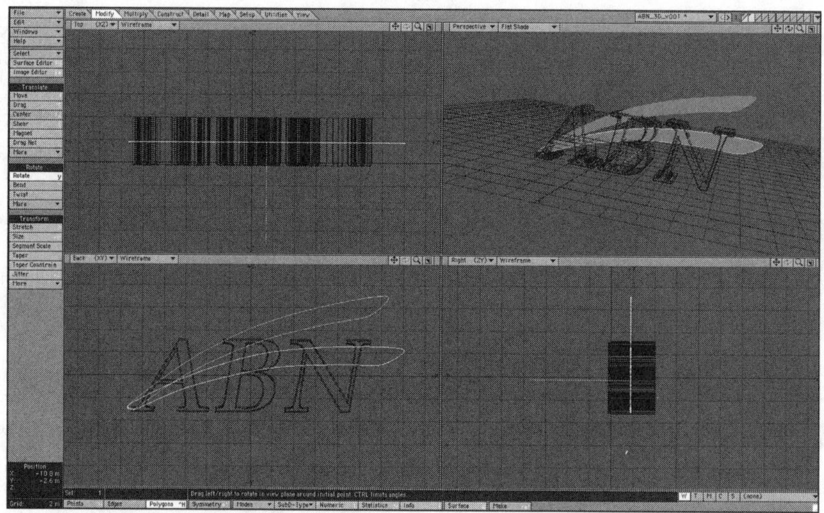

Figure 7.26 Using a copy of the original object, a simple rotation makes the copy visible.

12. Repeat the last two steps to make one more copy of the swoosh, being sure to rotate it down so there are three objects. **Figure 7.27** shows the result.

Figure 7.27 Another copy of the swoosh object, rotated, creates the final design elements.

13. Press **s** to save your work.

Note

Be sure to check out the "duplication" video on the book's DVD to learn about the other cool LightWave duplication techniques, such as the Clone to Layer tool.

Now you have your individual elements created. You cloned each in the same layer. They will be animated as one object. But if you wanted to animate them separately later in Layout, you'd need to get each of them into their own layer.

14. Select the second swoosh. Press Ctrl+x to cut it from the second layer. Press **3** on your keyboard (not the number keypad) or just click to Layer 3. Then, press Ctrl+v to paste it down. You just moved an object from layer to another!
15. With the third swoosh object back in Layer 2, cut and paste it to Layer 4. You now have Layer 1 as the ABN object, and Layers 2, 3, and 4 as the swoosh objects. Press Ctrl+s to save your work.

If you were not going to animate them, you could leave them all on the same layer. However, another thing you need to do to animate each layer properly is set their individual pivots.

Pivot Points in Modeler

Each layer in Modeler has its own X-Y-Z coordinate system, and when you create (or add) an object to a new layer, the object is centered by default on the layer's origin point (coordinates 0, 0, 0). Modeler also uses that origin point as the object's default *pivot point*, around which it will spin when rotated. This is fine for many things, but for precise animation, it can cause problems. This section shows you how to change objects' pivot points.

Exercise 7.6 Setting New Pivot Points in Modeler

1. Start by selecting layer 1 of your ABN logo from the previous exercises. This model's center is probably pretty close to the origin point. It was at this position, the default pivot point, when you pressed **F2** earlier to center it. But since you've extruded and beveled it, the pivot is now at the face of the object. The pivot did not change—the object did.

   The default pivot point for this object will not cause too many issues when animating in Layout; however, it could be a little more precise. Because this object is just three letters, press **F2** again to perfectly center the ABN logo at the origin.

   The Swoosh objects, on the other hand, have precise placement and pressing **F2** would change where they live in 3D space.

2. Go to Layer 2, the first swoosh object. Click the View tab, and on the left under the Layers category, select the Pivot command.
3. When you activate the Pivot command, crosshairs appear in the viewports. Move the pivot to the bottom-left corner of the object (**Figure 7.28**). Be careful to pay attention to all views and move it on the Z-axis as well as the X-axis and Y-axis.

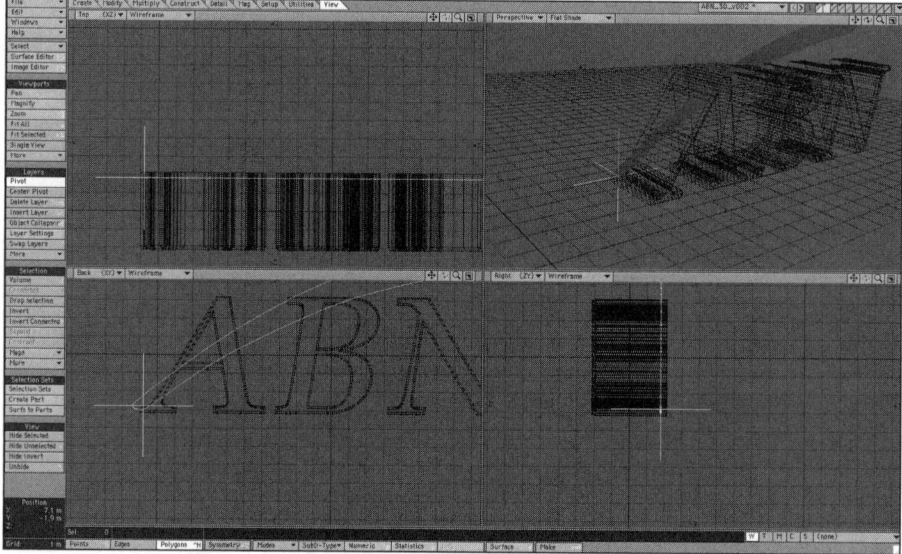

Figure 7.28 Manually move the pivot for Layer 2's object.

4. With the Pivot tool still active, click over to Layer 2. You can quickly move the pivot for this object. Again, center it out.
5. Set the pivots for the rest of the layers in the same position and save the object. You do not have to turn off the Pivot tool to change layers. Just change to the new layer, adjust the new pivot, and away you go.
6. Save your work!

You've now created all the base animation elements for the logo treatment. The next steps are to build the main logo and the subtext that you'll animate as individual letters.

Importing EPS Files

LightWave also offers you the ability to import Adobe Illustrator files or EPS files. This is extremely handy for more complicated graphics designed out-of-house—that is, you'll often be hired to animate a logo you haven't designed. When you import a logo as an EPS file, Modeler automatically recognizes its outlines as spline curves you can scale, "freeze," and surface. No tracing of a background image is required. This not only saves tons of time, it also allows you to create a more accurate 3D version of the original piece. To better explain how this feature works, there's a cool tutorial video on the book's DVD showing how to use this feature of LightWave v9 Modeler.

Animating Text

Now that you have your three objects in Layout (see Figure 7.25), you can begin setting things up. First, you'll set the placement, and then the lighting. After that's in place, you'll enhance the surfaces and set up camera moves. Are you ready?

Exercise 7.7 Text Setup in Layout

1. Make sure you've saved your work in Modeler, and then select Send Objects to Layout from the drop-down list marked with a arrow at the top right of the Modeler interface (**Figure 7.29**).

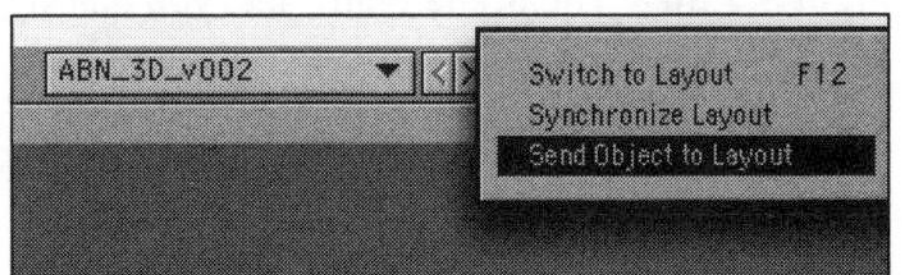

Figure 7.29 Send the new ABN_Logo to Layout for animation.

2. When you select Send Objects to Layout, LightWave should automatically launch Layout (if it isn't running already) and make it the active program, with your objects loaded into a new scene. If it doesn't, from this same drop-down menu, you can also select Switch to Layout, or press **F12**.
3. Once the objects are loaded into Layout, select the ABN logo. Move it forward on the Z-axis in front of everything else. Create a keyframe at 0 to lock it in place.

Note

Be sure the Auto Key option is turned off for this project.

4. Add a null object to the scene from the Items tab. Name this null **ABN_Master** or something similar.
5. From the Scene Editor menu at the top left of the interface, select Open. In the Scene Editor, select all four layers of the ABN object. You can do this by clicking the first layer name, then Shift-clicking the name of the last layer. Drag the

selected layer names under the null object's name, until the selected names are indented, indicating that those layers are parented to the null (**Figure 7.30**).

Figure 7.30 The Scene Editor lets you quickly parent all objects to another object, such as a null.

6. Press Ctrl+s, the shortcut for the Save As command. Name your scene **ABN_Logo** or something similar and click OK to save the work you've done. From now on, you can press Shift+s to save incremental scenes.
7. Click Object in the Items tab's Load tool category and load the Curvy_A object you created earlier in the chapter.
8. Select the Curvy_A object and increase its size by pressing Shift+a. Size it up and then move it back behind the swoosh objects.
9. Rotate the Perspective view around and make sure that none of the objects are touching. **Figure 7.31** shows the objects.

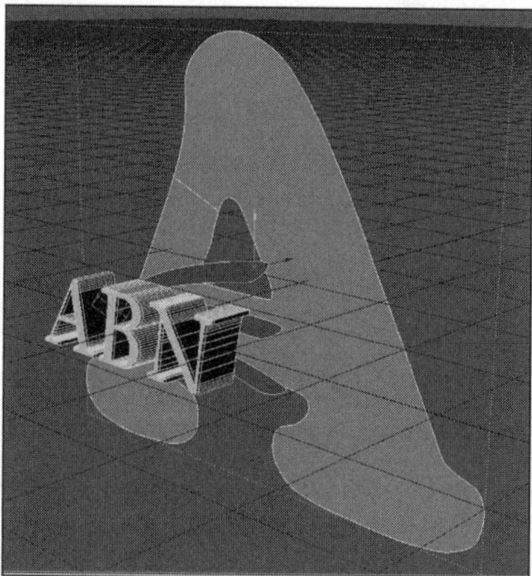

Figure 7.31 Position the objects with the large Curvy_A behind the swoosh objects and the ABN_Logo.

10. Save the scene and press **6** on your keyboard to jump to Camera view.
11. In the Camera view, push the camera in to fit the logos to frame (**Figure 7.32**). After the camera is in place, create a keyframe to lock it in place.

Figure 7.32 The camera is moved in to view the full ABN_Logo.

A master null object like the one you've just created makes it easy to move a multiple objects together as a group. Each object can still be animated separately, and that's what you'll do next.

Lighting, Motion, and Backgrounds

Until now, you've seen the basic setup before lighting. What you do next is totally up to you. Many people put everything in motion first, then light, then render. Others light first, then animate. Here, we'll do a little of everything!

Lighting is important in any scene, even a relatively simple logo animation. This section shows you how to set up lighting for your scene and how to animate the text you've built—including the pivot points you changed for the swoosh objects. From there, you'll create a cool moving background that provides an interesting environment for your scene.

Exercise 7.8 Lighting Text

Lighting for logos is really no different than other lighting we've already tried. What often works well is three-point lighting with spotlights.

1. You have a default distant light in your scene already. Select it, and press **p** to open the Light Properties panel. Change the Light Type to Spotlight, as in **Figure 7.33.**

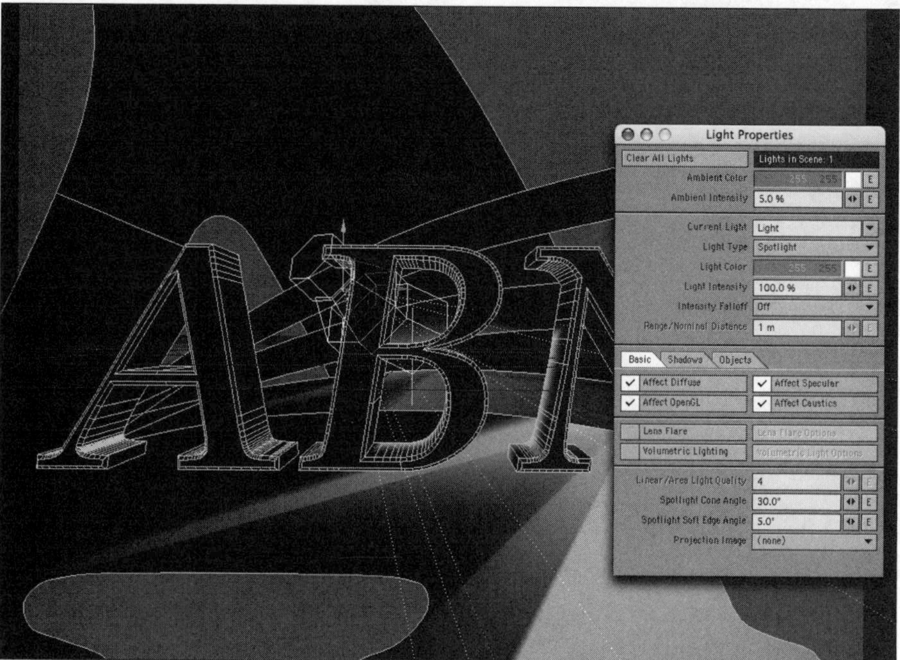

Figure 7.33 Change the default distant light to a spotlight.

2. Set the Light Color to an off-white, somewhere around R: 255, G: 250, B: 245.
3. Change the Spotlight Cone Angle to 40 degrees, and set the Spotlight Soft Edge Angle to 40 degrees as well. This will help make the light have a softer edge. On the Shadows tab within the Lights Properties panel, change the Shadow Type to Shadow Map. Then, close the panel.
4. Press **5** on your keyboard to switch to Light View. Press **t** to select the Move tool, and move the light up and away from the logo, as shown in **Figure 7.34**. Using the Light view, you can easily position your light to see that it encompasses your scene.

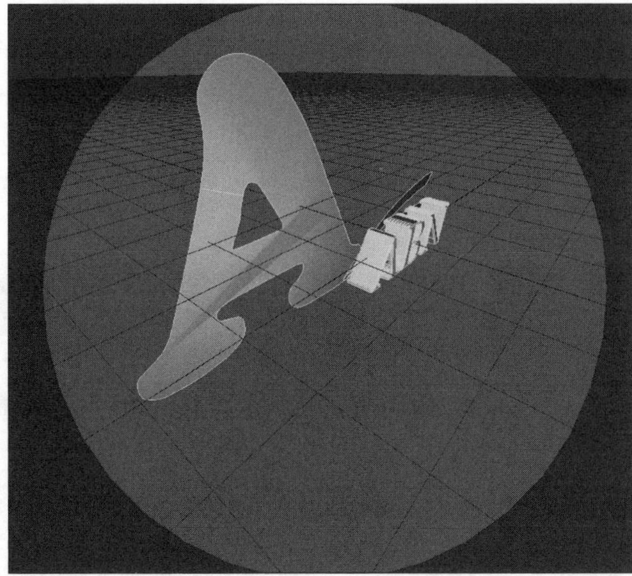

Figure 7.34 Position the light to encompass the entire logo scene.

5. Press Create Key at the bottom of the interface to keep the light in its new position at frame 0.
6. Press **F9** to test-render the scene. **Figure 7.35** shows the not-so-nice-looking logo. But wait, there's more!

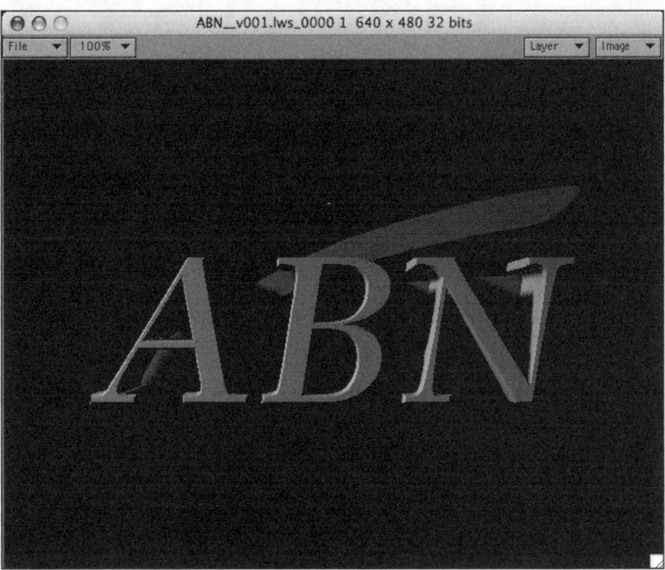

Figure 7.35 After the first light has been set, the render leaves a lot to be desired.

7. With the light selected, press Ctrl+c to clone the light. In the Clone dialog box that appears, just create one clone for now. Click OK, then press **t** for the Move tool and move the light to the right side of the logo. Remember to right-click to move up and down on the Y-axis. (Mac users, use Command-click!)
8. Press **y** to rotate the light. **Figure 7.36** shows the view from the second light. Be sure to create a keyframe for the light position.

Figure 7.36 Position the cloned light at the opposite side of the logo.

9. Press **p** to open the Light Properties panel, and set the second light's color to a medium-blue color, roughly R: 103, G: 128, B: 255.

10. Press **F9** again to render the scene and see how it looks. Probably a bit better, but still pretty dark inside those letters! Clone this second light, and move it to the back of the logo. Raise it up to shine down on the logo and elements, and change the color to a bright orange in the Lights Properties panel. **Figure 7.37** shows the light position. Remember to create a keyframe for the light in this new position.

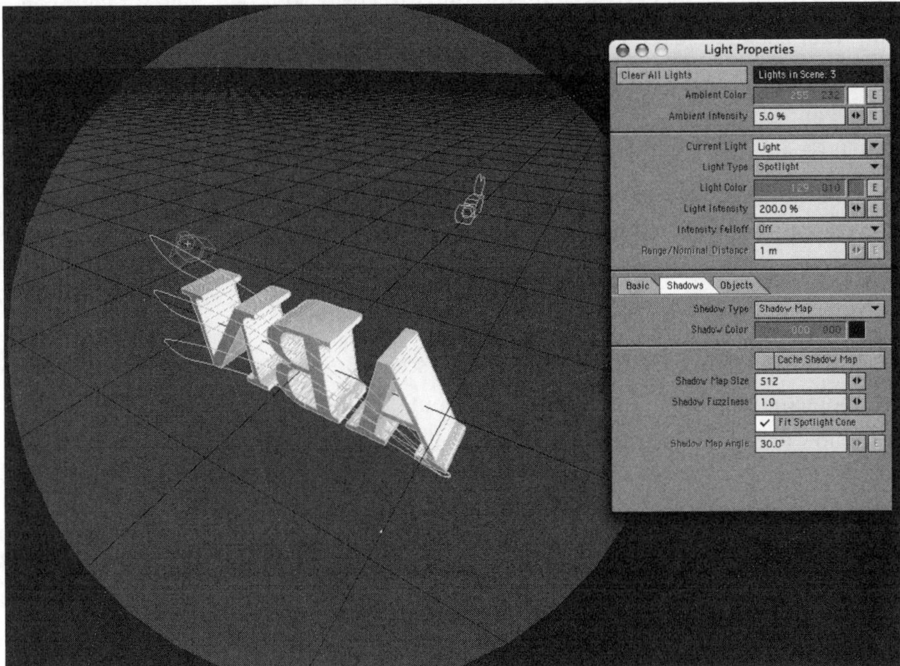

Figure 7.37 The new light position, in back of the logo.

11. Now if you press **F9**, your logo will pop off the background a bit more. Still, you need a bit more. Two things can help: surfaces and a background.

This project showed you a great working three-point light setup. But what's more is that you can use additional lights for added interest. And what will really make this project stand out is the surfacing and background.

We have so much more to cover with LightWave v9, and it's time to move on. But there is a lot more to this project, and I don't want to leave you high and dry. Pop open the book's DVD and view the QuickTime movies showing you how to surface the text and then animate it. From there, you'll see firsthand how that big large Curvy_A object will be used with the background.

The Next Step

This chapter took you through some of the most basic LightWave operations. But the tools used, the process in which you used them are always the same no matter how complex your project might be. The next step, after you watch the videos on the book's DVD, is to move on to Chapter 8 and learn about modeling still-life objects. As for this logo project, it's up to you to use these steps and procedures to create your own logo for your company, your client, or just for fun. In this chapter you've learned how to build over background images, use the text-creation tools, copy and paste into layers, set up lighting in Layout, and set up parent-child relationships between objects. The videos for this chapter will extend your learning even further. And remember that as you model and texture, you also have to tweak. Tweak, tweak, tweak! There's always more you can do with a scene, so take some time and do it. Later in Chapter 11, "Node-Based Texturing," you'll learn how to harness LightWave v9's new texturing engine and apply what you learn to your animated text scene. This too will open new doors of tweakness!

Any little change you make to your models and scenes are what give your animations that extra something. Take your modeling and layout skills a step further in the next chapter. Learn how to model, texture, and render a cool, still-life object.

Chapter 8

Modeling Still-Life Objects

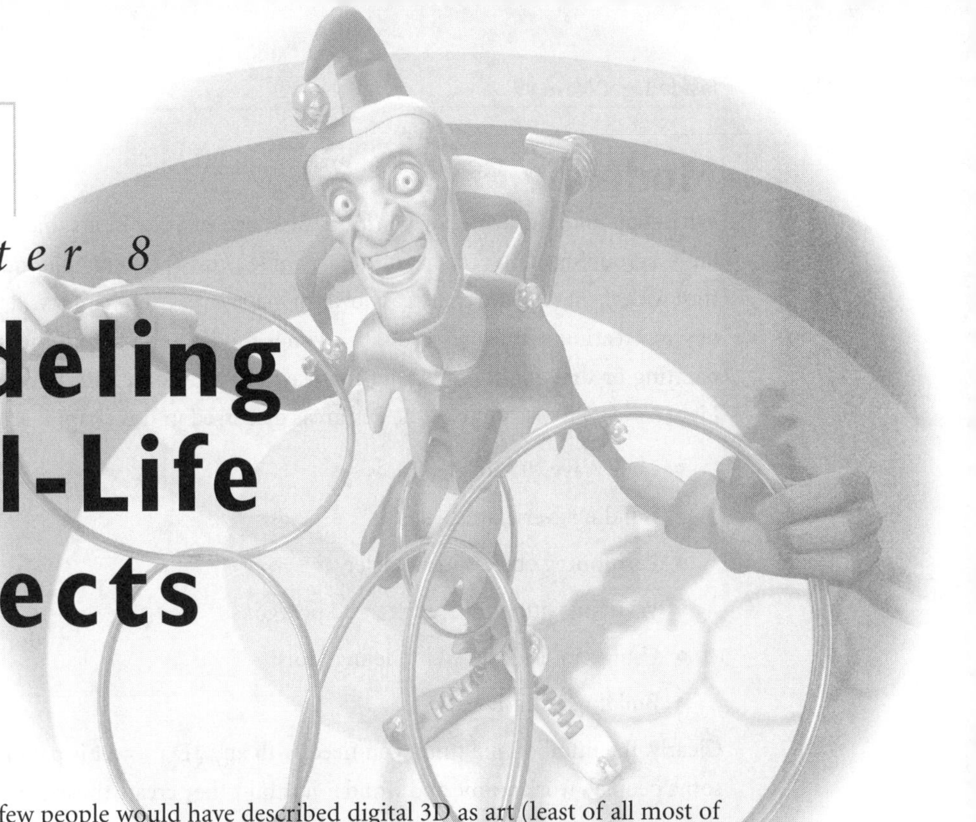

In its early years, few people would have described digital 3D as art (least of all most of its creators). Modelers and animators did some design work, of course, but they were mainly technicians. The time and money required to create 3D models, and the highly specialized (and limited) tools available to do the job, limited 3D's uses to diagramming, engineering, and occasional Hollywood special effects. Today it's different. Computing power, software advancements, and the ever-growing world of 3D content make truly artistic creation possible, and open the doors for you to go beyond your job as a 3D expert to create 3D scenes simply for the joy of creating. This chapter explores some of LightWave's potential as an artistic tool.

Modeling Fruit

When you take a drawing or painting class, one of your first subjects is typically a still life—a grouping of objects that usually includes fruit or flowers, plus other items that contrast with them in texture, such as bowls or glassware. This chapter will take you on a journey in creating a still-life scene, but you'll model and surface the objects, instead of painting or drawing them. Along the way, you'll become even more familiar with the LightWave v9 tools. Some of the key areas discussed in this chapter are:

- LightWave v9 Modeler Tools
- Building everyday objects
- Positioning objects in Modeler
- Working with points, edges, and polygons
- Using more advanced modeling tools
- Building a still-life set

Clearly, the number one thing you need with any 3D project is patience. You might see some people's work online and wonder just how they create those 3D images. Here's how they do it: They work at it! There is no magic "make art" button in 3D. But by knowing the tools, and understanding your goal, you too can create anything you want. This chapter will help you do just that by breaking down the elements, and stepping you through them, one piece at a time. If you're ready, get a snack, a drink, and start creating.

Begin with Bananas

Talk to anyone has taken an art class and they will most likely tell you that there's always fruit. Not to eat, but to re-create, through drawing or painting. That's what this chapter is going to have you do, but in 3D. You'll start with the leader of the fruit pack, the banana.

Exercise 8.1 One Banana, Two Banana, Three Banana, Four

If a catchy little tune popped into your head when you read this project's title, you're definitely showing your age. Yes, we're talking about Fleegle, Bingo, Drooper, and Snork—the Banana Splits gang from the '70s television show. What does this have to do with modeling a 3D banana? Nothing! But it was a great way to get the exercise going. Now, on to the project:

1. Open LightWave v9 Modeler. This project begins by modeling the fruit that will be placed in your soon-to-be-modeled fruit bowl. You'll start with a banana. Click the Create tab and select the Box tool.

2. Press **n** to open the Numeric panel, and create a box with the following dimensions (**Figure 8.1**):

Width	2.1m	
Height	1.75m	
Depth	6.95m	
Center	X	0m
	Y	0m
	Z	0m
Axis	Y	
Radius	0m	
Radius Segments	1	
Segments	X	3
	Y	3
	Z	9

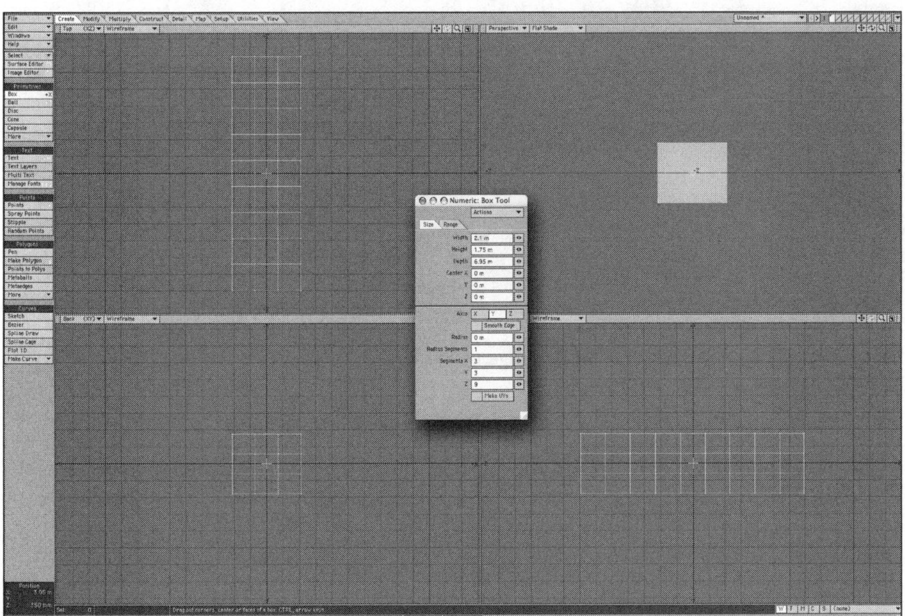

Figure 8.1 Create a box with multiple segments to begin creating a banana.

3. Once you've entered the settings, close the Numeric panel, or move it aside, then press the spacebar to quickly turn off the Box tool. Remember, you can turn off tools by pressing the spacebar. Conversely, choosing another tool automatically turns off the current tool.

4. Save your work.
5. Press the spacebar again, until the Edges selection mode button is highlighted at the bottom of the interface.
6. In the Back view, at the bottom left, using your right mouse button (the Cmd key and mouse on the Mac) lasso, select the top-right corner of the box. This will select the edge running along the top corner, down the Z-axis, as shown in **Figure 8.2**.

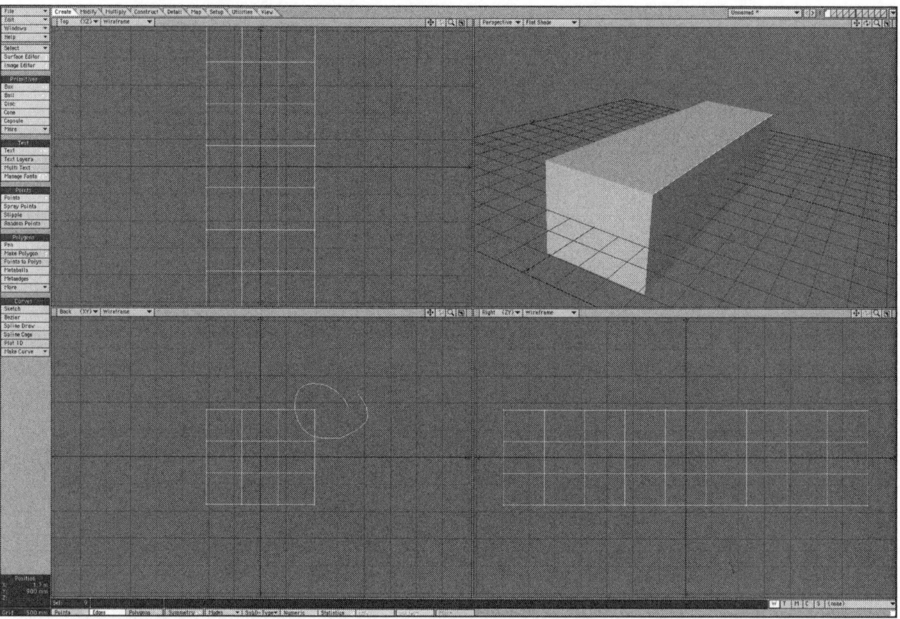

Figure 8.2 Lasso-select the top right edge of the box.

7. Now select the three other edges. To do this, hold the Shift key to add the selection, then right-click around each corner from the Back view. **Figure 8.3** shows the four selected edges.

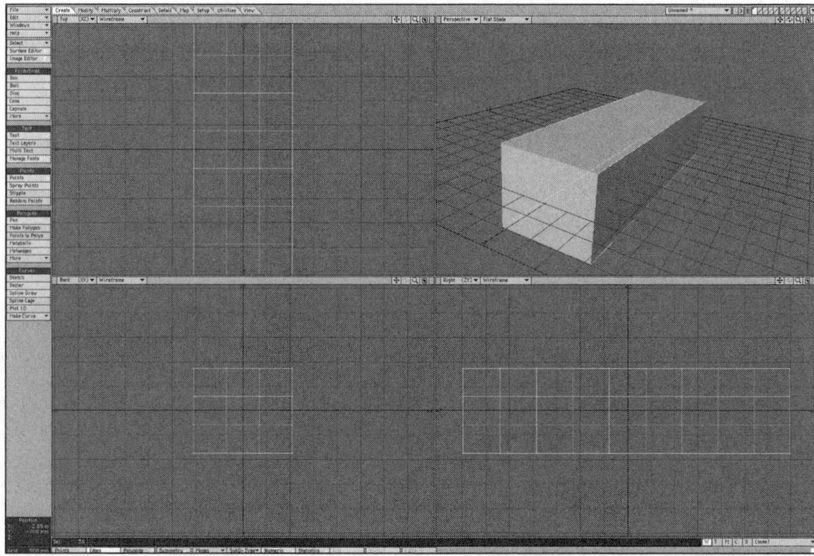

Figure 8.3 Select the remaining three edges. Now, all four edges of the box should be selected.

8. Now you'll bevel the selected edges. You can't use the usual bevel command when it comes to edges. For this, you'll use the Edge Bevel tool. On the Multiply tab, select Edge Bevel under the Extend category. You can also just press Ctrl+b. As soon as you do, you'll see the edges expand, as in **Figure 8.4**.

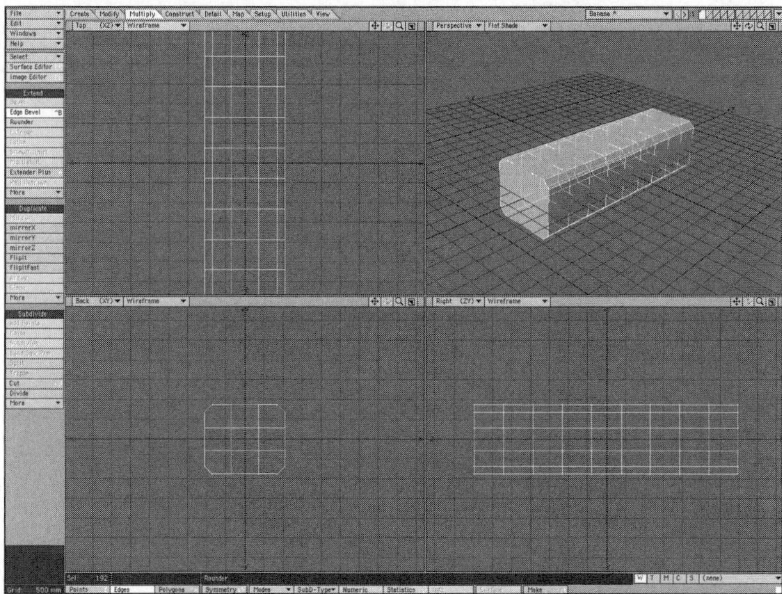

Figure 8.4 As soon as you activate Edge Bevel, your model begins to change.

9. Notice that with Edge Bevel active, yellow highlights appear around the edges. This is normal; it also means that the tool is active. Click and drag in one of the views and you'll see the amount of the bevel change. You can select the Numeric button at the bottom of the interface to see the specific values. Set the Edge Bevel to 300mm, as in **Figure 8.5**.

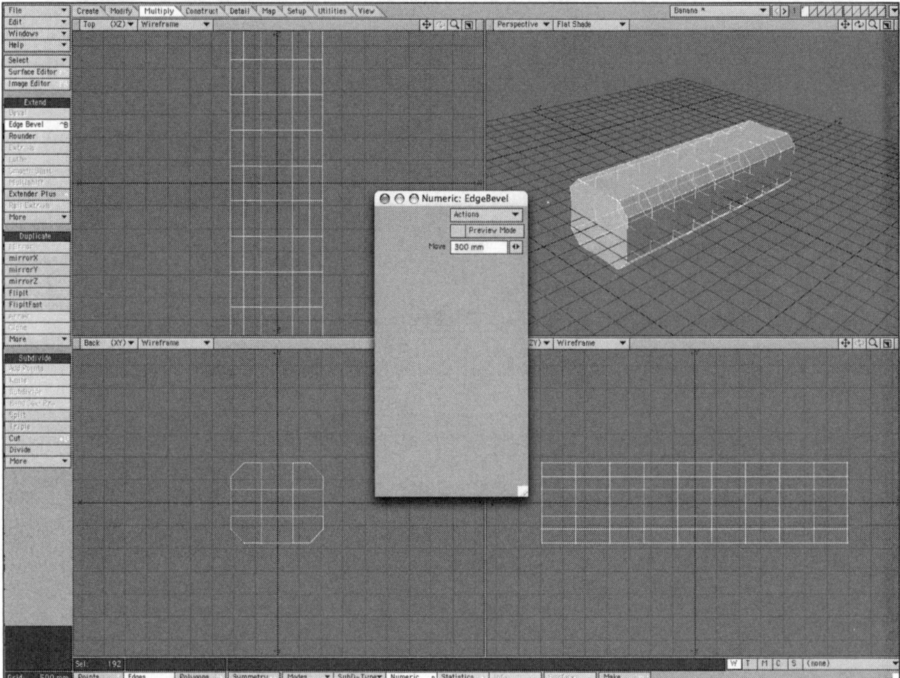

Figure 8.5 Set the Edge Bevel to 300mm.

Note

The requester for Edge Bevel shows an option to enable Preview Mode. Doing so allows you to preview the edge bevel, and is shown with blue outlines in the viewports. The bevel is not actually applied but only previewed.

10. Close the Numeric panel and turn off the edge bevel. You'll notice that the edges are still selected. That's good, because you can tell Modeler to convert this selection from edges to polygons. From the Select drop-down menu at the top left of the interface, choose Sel Switch, which switches your selection from edges to polygons, as shown in **Figure 8.6**.

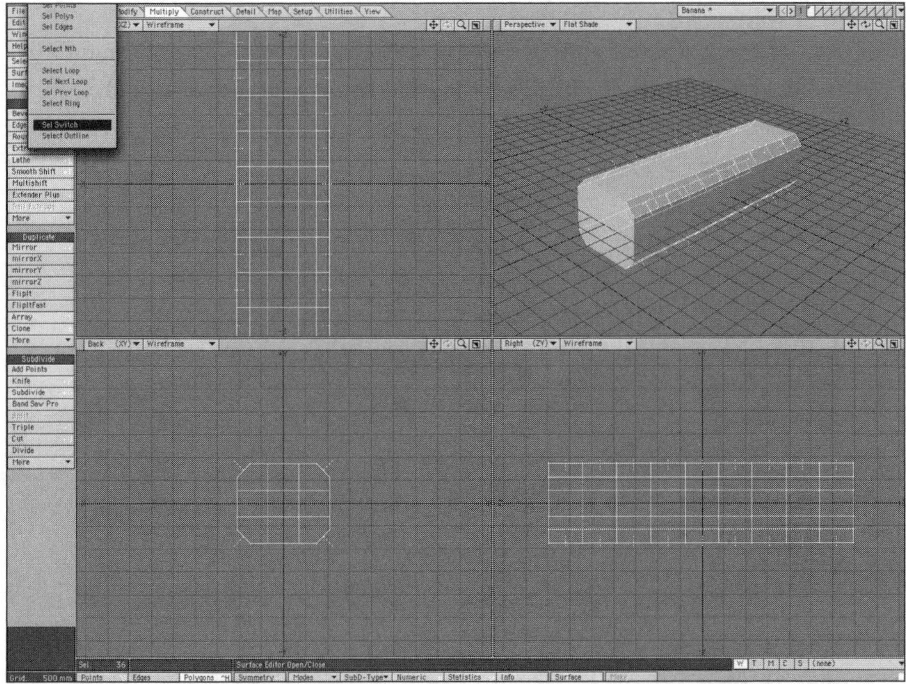

Figure 8.6 You can use Sel Switch to convert from one selection to another.

Note

How does Modeler know to switch the current selection to polygons? Good question! If you had edges selected, the next option is Polygons. If you had Polygons selected, the next option is Points. If you had Points selected, the next option is Edges. Just as you press the spacebar multiple times to toggle between the three selection models, the Sel Switch tool works in a similar fashion.

11. With the newly created polygons now selected, click the Multishift tool on the Multiply tab under the Extend category. Then, open the Numeric panel from the bottom of the interface. Basically, you want to bevel these polygons running down the corners of the soon-to-be banana. But LightWave's bevel tool will separate the multiple polygons. Instead, Multishift can be used to bevel groups of polygons.

12. In the requester for Multishift, make sure Group Polygons is checked on. Then, click and drag in a viewport to bevel the selected polygons. Moving the mouse left and right will change the Inset amount, while moving the mouse up and down changes the Shift amount. Set the values to 118mm for the Inset, and 142mm for the Shift. **Figure 8.7** shows the values.

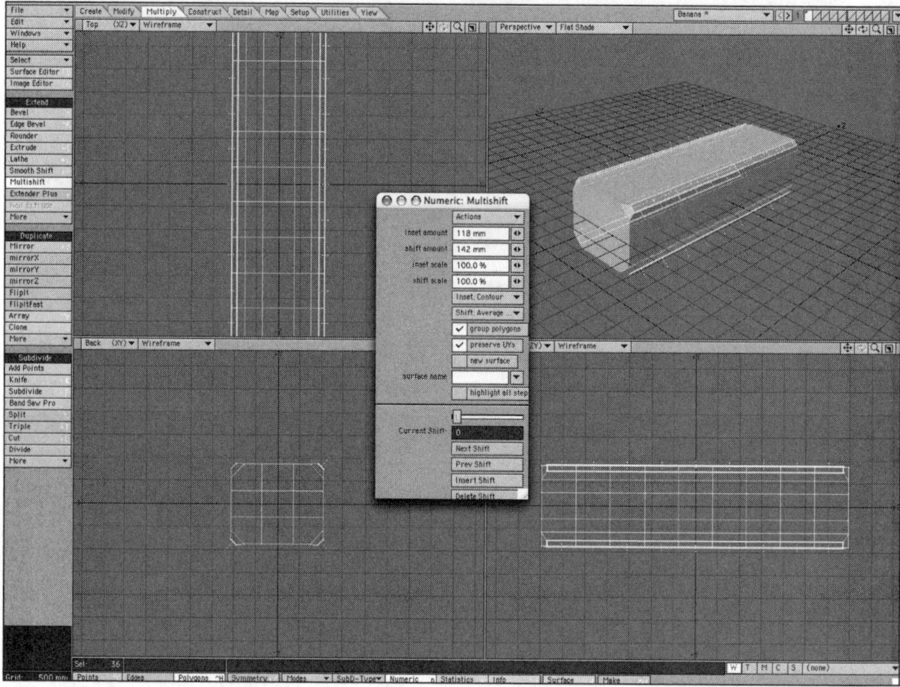

Figure 8.7 Using Multishift, you can bevel large groups of selected polygons.

13. Turn off the Multishift tool and close the Numeric panel.

14. Save your work. Feel free to use and save incrementally by pressing Shift+s.

15. In the Back view, select the center row of polygons for each side of the elongated box. You might find that some of the end polygons become selected as well, and that's normal. After you select the desired polygons, hold the Ctrl key and click on the polygons you want to deselect. **Figure 8.8** shows the selection.

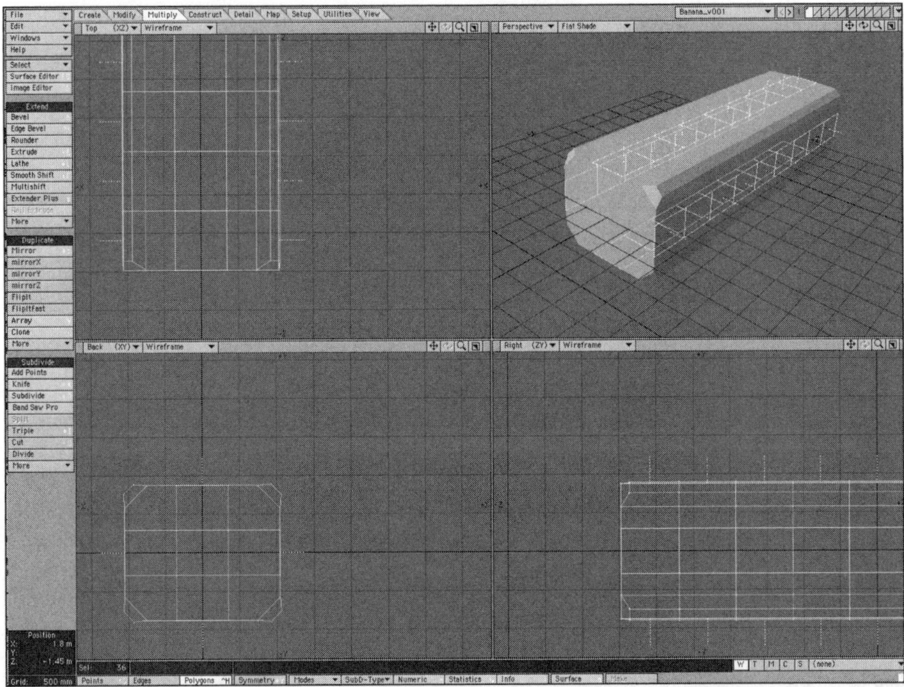

Figure 8.8 Select the center row of polygons for each side of the box.

16. At the bottom of the Modeler interface is the Modes menu. Click this and choose Action Center: Selection. This tells Modeler to apply tools based on the selection, not the Mouse position, as it was by default.

17. Then, press Shift+h to activate the Size tool. Click and drag in the Back view to expand the size of the selection about 15%. As you click and drag, pay attention to the lower-left corner of the interface. The Numeric panel will show your Size value as you use the tool. The default is 100%, so you'll want to click and drag to size the selection to 115%. **Figure 8.9** shows the result.

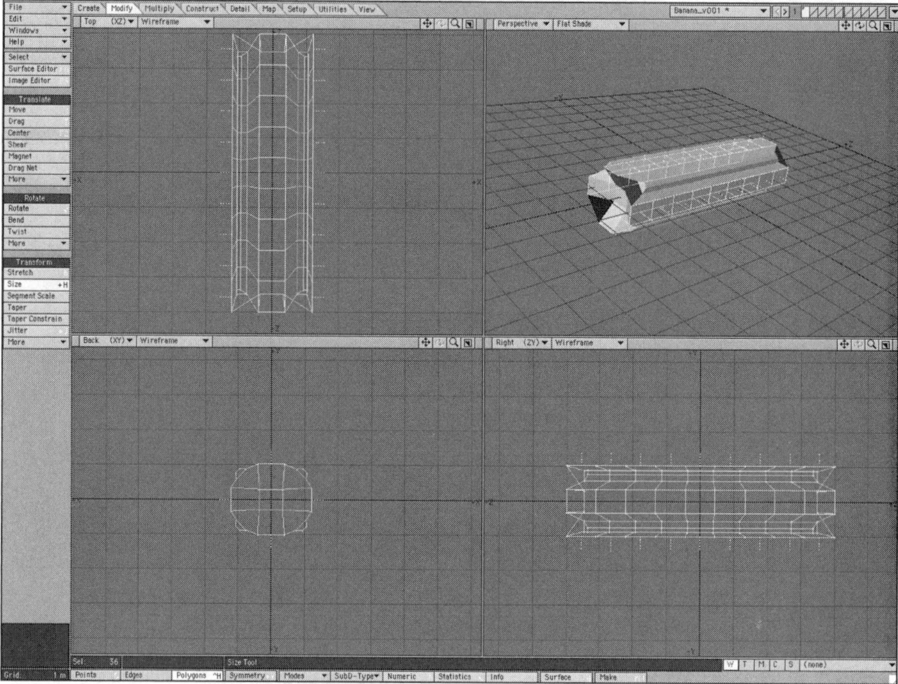

Figure 8.9 Increase the size of the selection by 15%.

18. Turn off the Size tool by clicking on it or pressing the spacebar. If you look at Figure 8.9, you might notice that the ends of the object are a bit gnarly. Let's fix that. First, deselect the currently selected polygons by pressing the / key on your keyboard. You can also click into a blank portion of the menu in Modeler.
19. Change to Points selection mode at the bottom of the interface to tell Modeler you want to work with points (also known in the 3D industry as vertices).

20. In the Right view, using your right mouse button (Cmd-click on the Mac) and lasso-select the endpoints of the box on the negative Z-axis. You should have 28 points selected, as shown in **Figure 8.10**.

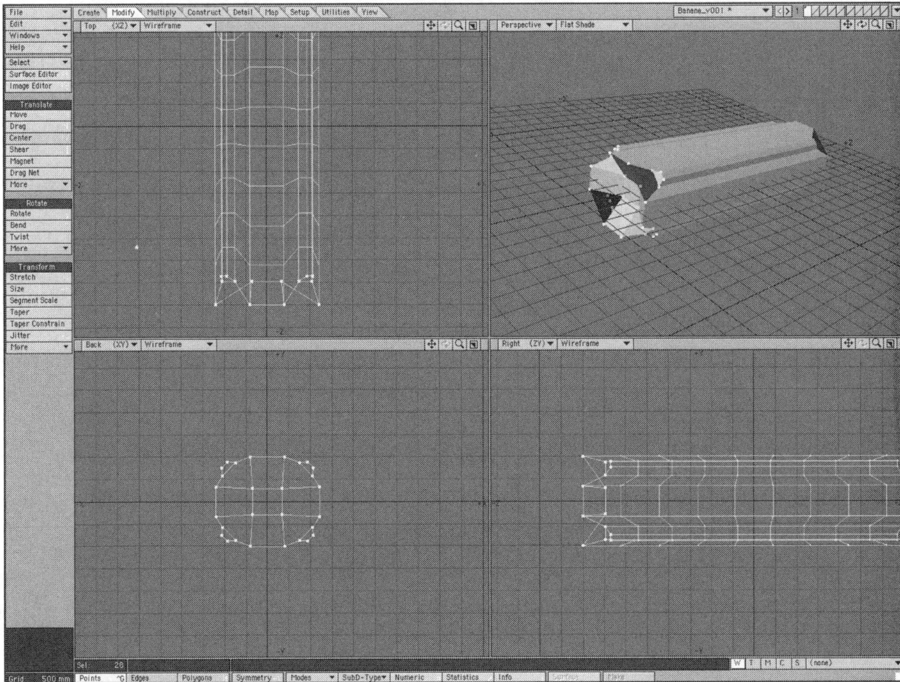

Figure 8.10 Lasso-select the endpoints on the negative Z-axis.

21. Now, position your mouse just to the front of the selection, and take a look at the info area at the bottom-left corner of the interface. As you move the mouse, you'll see the numeric position. Note the Z-axis position at about -4.25m. Then, press **v** to access the Set Value dialog box.

22. Choose Z for the axis, and enter the value you noted from your mouse position, -4.25m. Click OK and the selected points will jump to that value on that axis, as shown in **Figure 8.11**.

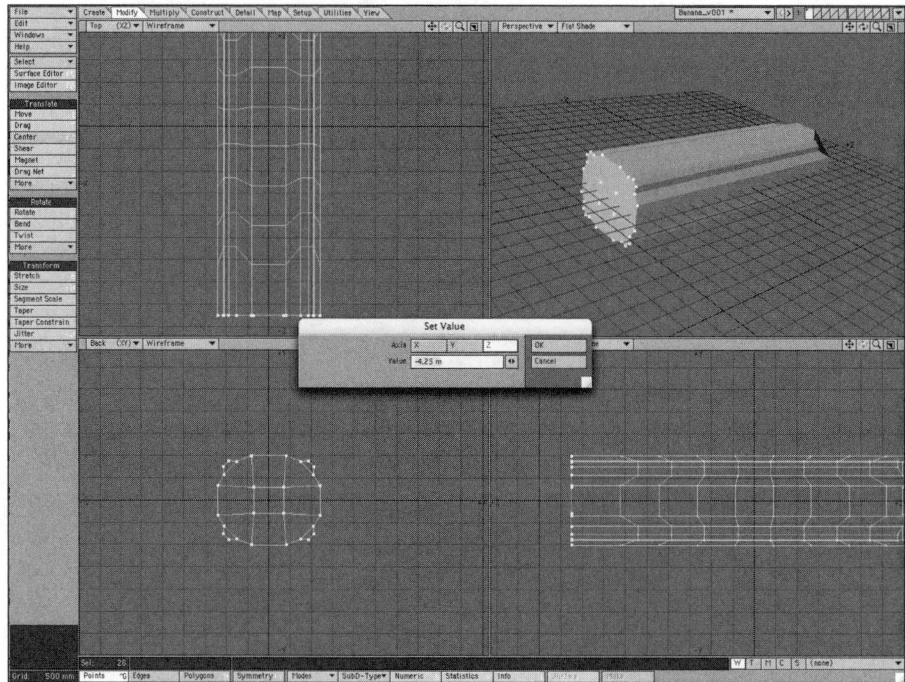

Figure 8.11 Using the Set Value dialog box, you can quickly adjust all points to one position.

23. With the newly positioned points still selected, activate the Move tool (press **t**) and then move them back toward the model a bit, about 500mm.
24. Now you'll bevel the polygons on this end. You adjusted the points using Set Value to flatten out the polygons. This will make your life easier when trying to bevel. But you want to bevel polygons, not points, so rather than deselecting points and reselecting polygons, use the Sel Switch command as you did earlier. From the Select drop-down menu at the top left of the interface, choose Sel Switch. The selected points now change to selected edges. Run the command again, and the selected edges become selected polygons.
25. Press Shift+a to fit the selection to view.
26. When you bevel polygons, there are times when the geometry crosses over itself, creating unwanted results. So, before you bevel, adjust a few points. Press Ctrl+t

to activate the Drag tool. Then, click and drag the points that make up the ends of the edge bevels you created earlier. Do this in the Back view.

It's important to understand that first rule of modeling here—if nothing is selected, whatever you do applies to everything. So if you were to drag points in the Back view, the points would change all the way down the elongated box. But since just the polygons are selected from step 24, the point adjustment from the Drag tool in the Back view only affects the selection. The result is that you're only editing the end of the object.

27. Drag the points in to flatten out the edge bevels, as shown in **Figure 8.12**.

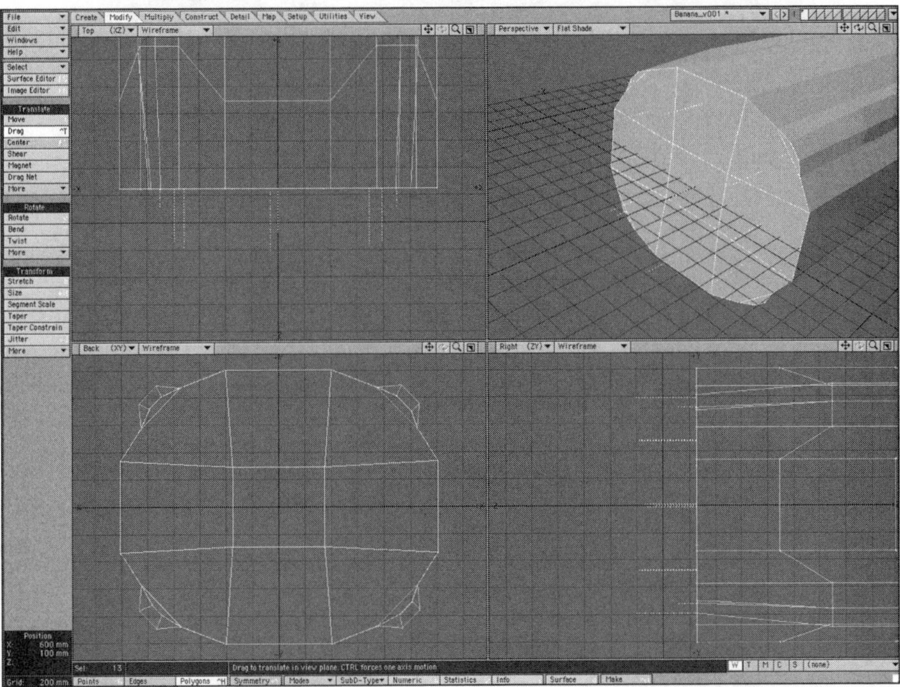

Figure 8.12 Using the Drag tool on selected polygons, you can click and drag the points of the edge bevels to flatten them out.

28. Once you've adjusted the edge bevels, select the Multishift tool on the Multiply tab. Click and drag on the selected polygons to 225mm for the Inset and 535mm for the Shift. You can use the Numeric panel as you did earlier for specific value entry. **Figure 8.13** (on the following page) shows the change.

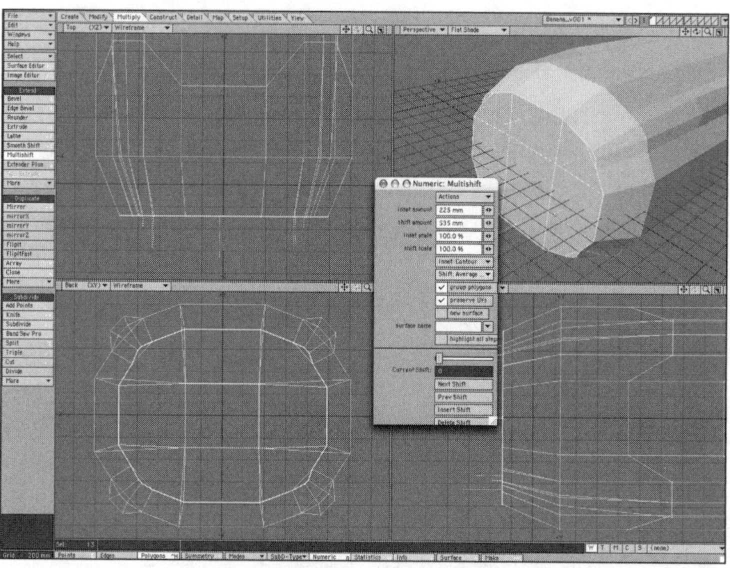

Figure 8.13 Using Multishift, bevel the end polygons to create one end of the banana.

29. Right-click one time to reset the Multishift tool, effectively adding to the existing geometry with a new bevel. Multishift the selection without allowing the corners to cross, about 344mm for the Inset and 920mm for the Shift. **Figure 8.14** shows the operation.

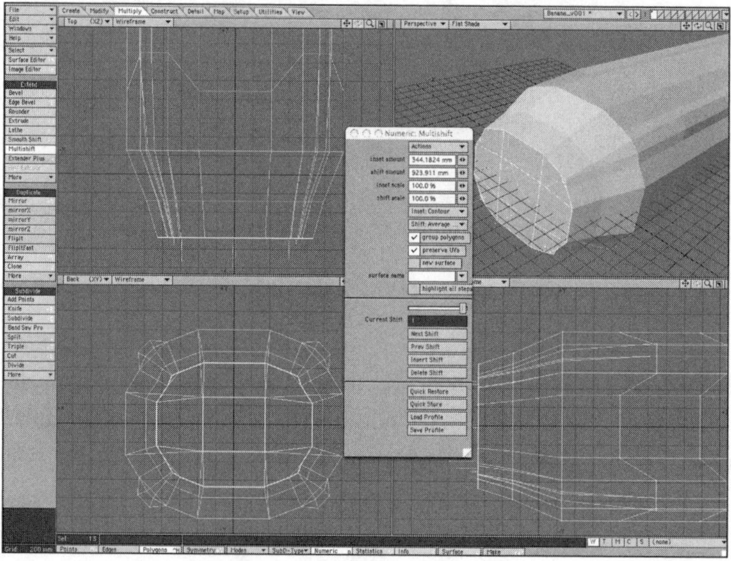

Figure 8.14 Perform one more Multishift to multiply the selection, but be careful not to cross the corners.

30. Press Shift+h to select the Size tool. This will automatically turn off the Multishift tool. Reduce the selection size down to about 80%, as in **Figure 8.15**.

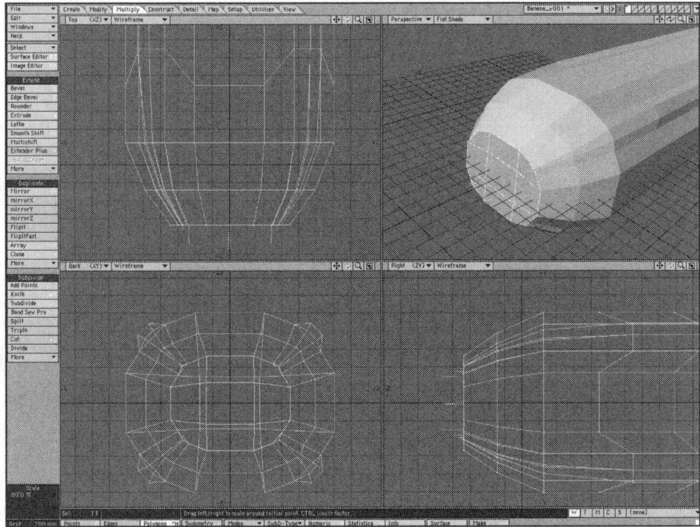

Figure 8.15 Now that you have additional geometry for the end of object, you can scale it down. This will help avoid edges and points from crossing over each other as they would with the Multishift tool.

31. Deselect the ends of the edge polygons, leaving just the nine polygons that make up the center, as shown in **Figure 8.16**. If it's easier, deselect all polygons, then select just the center nine polygons.

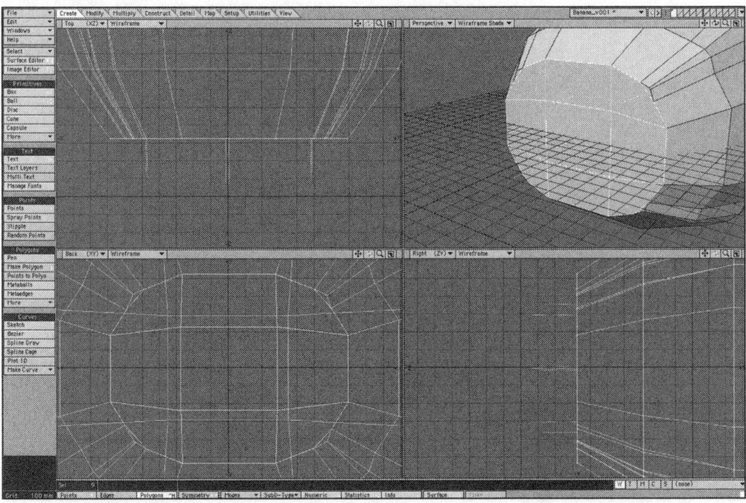

Figure 8.16 Deselect the small edge polygons in the corners, leaving just nine polygons selected.

32. You need to use Multishift again, but if you kept the edge polygons selected, you would start to see some serious errors. So, with just the nine polygons selected at the end of the object, turn on Multishift, and set the Inset to 240mm with a 305mm Shift. **Figure 8.17** shows the result.

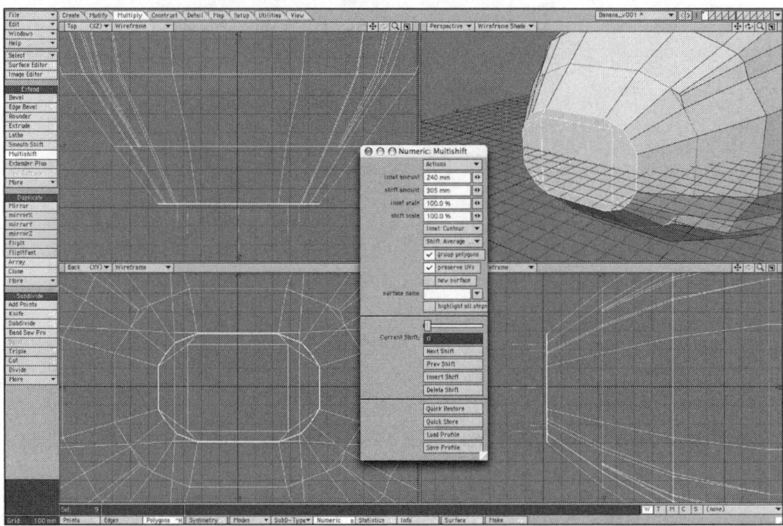

Figure 8.17 Using Multishift, extend the end polygons just a bit further.

33. Turn Multishift off, then turn it on again to extend the selection just one more time. But this time, only apply a Shift value of 240mm (**Figure 8.18**).

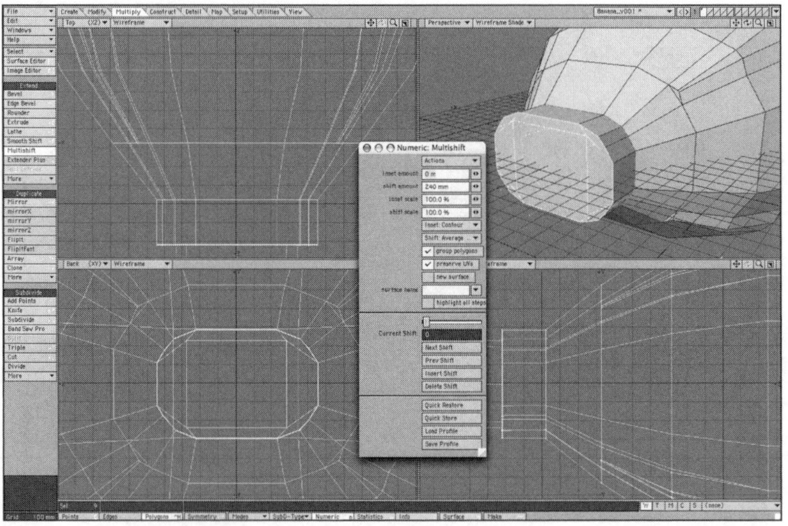

Figure 8.18 Multishift the selection again, but only for a Shift value, not an Inset.

34. Close the Numeric panel and turn off the Multishift tool. Then, deselect the polygons.
35. Save your work!
36. Select the four points that make up the very center of the newly created polygons, and size them down, as in **Figure 8.19**. This helps even out the mesh at the end, and will allow you to add additional Multishift operations if you want.

    You're probably wondering at this point how it's all coming together, so before you move on to add more details, how about taking a look at the overall progress?

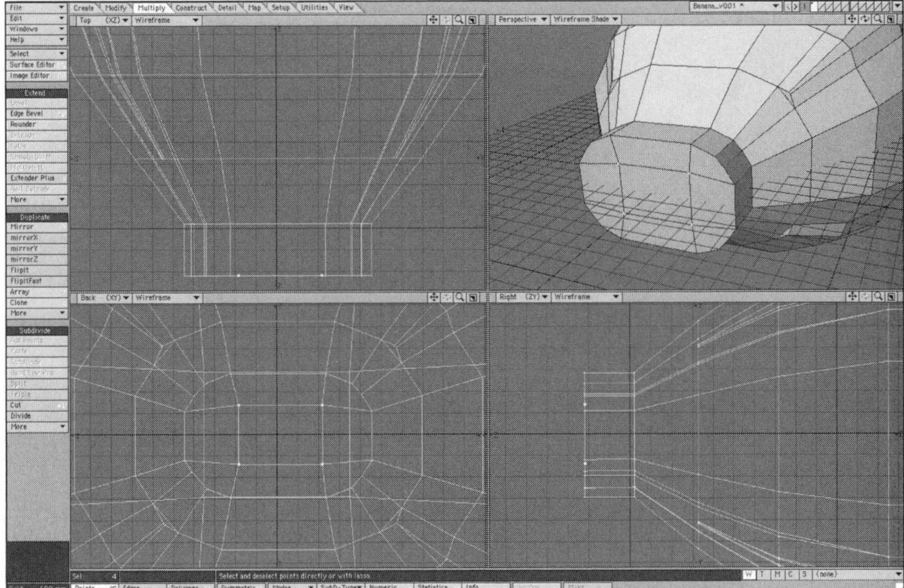

Figure 8.19 Scale down the center points on the end of the geometry.

37. Make sure any points or polygons are deselected. Then, press **a** to fit all objects to view.
38. Press the Tab key. What? You got an error? That's OK—don't worry. Click OK to close the error warning and press Tab again to turn off the attempted Subpatch. Close the second error box.

    You see, the beveling of edges earlier in the chapter changed the subpatch mesh so that some of its polygons have more than four sides. Earlier versions of LightWave balked at that, but LightWave v9 can handle larger polygons using Catmull-Clark subdivisions.

39. From the bottom of the interface, you'll see the SubD-Type drop-down menu. Change this to Catmull-Clark.

    Catmull-Clark subdivisions are sometimes referred to as *n-gons*. Essentially, by using this method of subdivision, your objects do not need to conform to just three or four vertices like the old Subpatch method. The original Subpatch method still works well, and modeling with quads in mind (polygons with four vertices) is always the best way to approach a model. However, at times you need to go beyond convention, and this is where Catmull-Clark subdivisions come in handy.

40. With the SubD-Type set to Catmull-Clark, press the Tab key. Ah, no error message! **Figure 8.20** shows the banana starting to take shape.

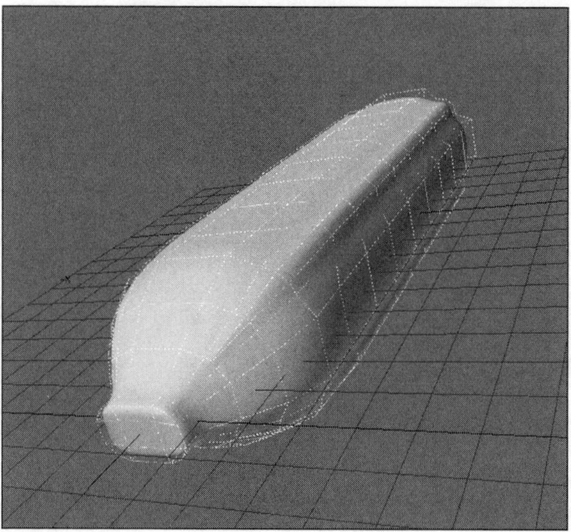

Figure 8.20 Using Catmull-Clark subdivisions, the original box is starting to look like a banana. Sort of.

41. Make a few more detail changes and you're almost there. First, press the Tab key to turn off the SubD mode. It's sometimes better to work with subdivision mode disabled for speed and visual ease. It can be confusing to see the subdivision cage when trying to adjust edges.
42. Make an incremental save by pressing Shift+s.
43. Now, how about tightening up the shape of the end polygon? Make sure Polygons selection mode is set at the bottom of the interface, and Ctrl+click the nine polygons that make up the end of the banana (Cmd-click on the Mac).
44. Press Shift+] (the right bracket key) to expand the selection, as in **Figure 8.21**.

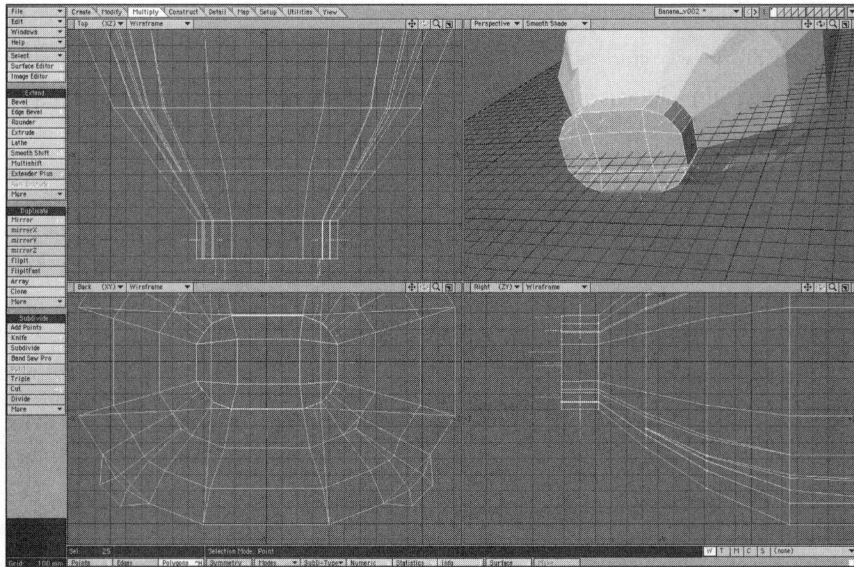

Figure 8.21 Select the end polygons of the banana.

45. Press **h** to select the Stretch tool from the Modify tab.
46. Stretch the selection to about 65% along the X-axis and 93% along the Y-axis, as in **Figure 8.22**.

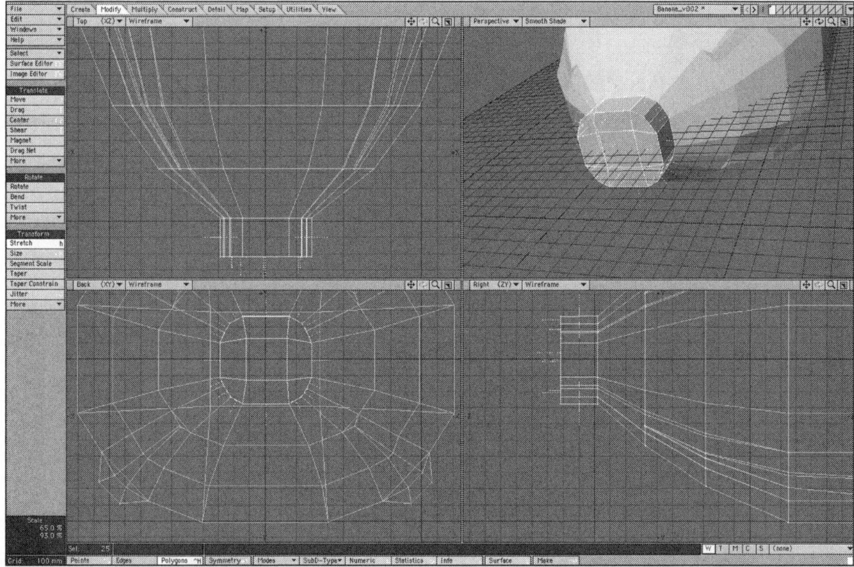

Figure 8.22 Scale the end of the banana so that it's more a square than a rectangle.

47. Turn off the Stretch tool (or press the spacebar), then deselect the polygons (press /).

48. In the Top view window, click on any edge of the banana tip's base. Then, from the Select drop-down menu at the top left of the interface, choose Select Loop. The entire edge loop will be selected (**Figure 8.23**).

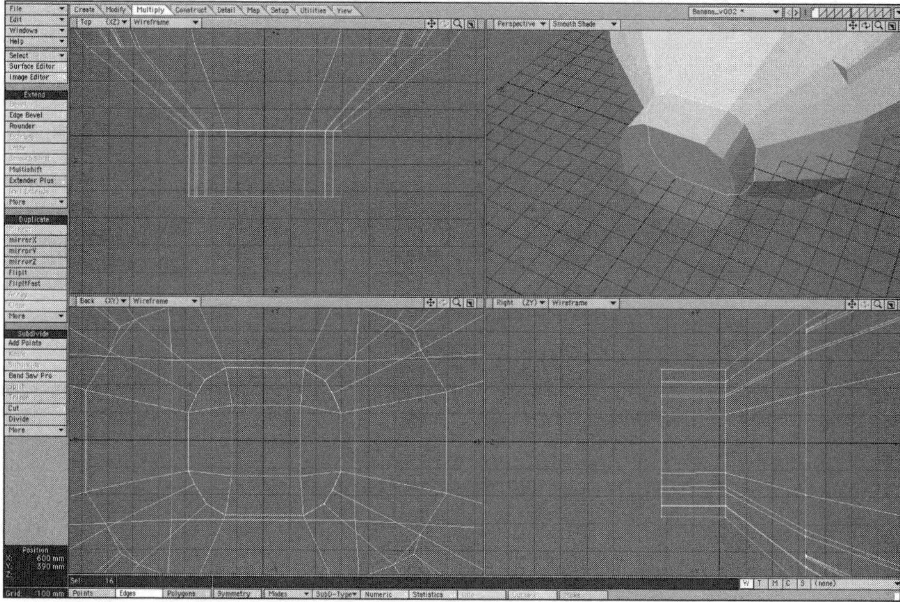

Figure 8.23 The Select Edge Loop option lets you quickly select an entire edge.

49. With the edge selected, press Ctrl+b to activate the Edge Bevel tool. Click and drag to bevel the selected edge about 20mm or so (**Figure 8.24**).

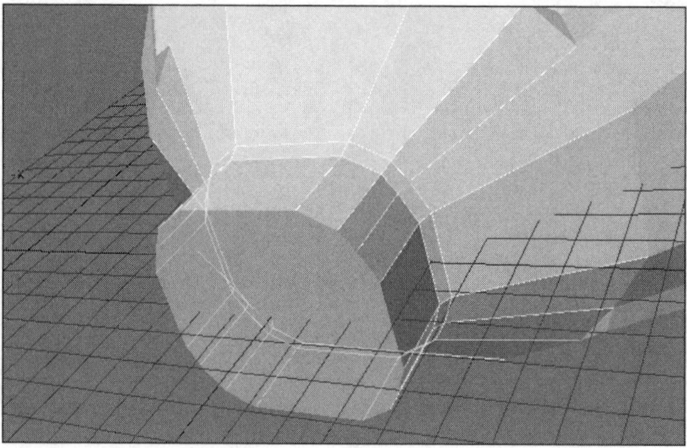

Figure 8.24 Bevel the edge to add detail at the neck of the banana.

50. Select the outer edge of the banana tip, and bevel it as well (**Figure 8.25**).

Figure 8.25 Bevel the outer edge of the banana tip.

51. Using the right mouse button, lasso-select the points of the end of the banana, and extend them about 180mm on the negative Z-axis, as shown in **Figure 8.26**.

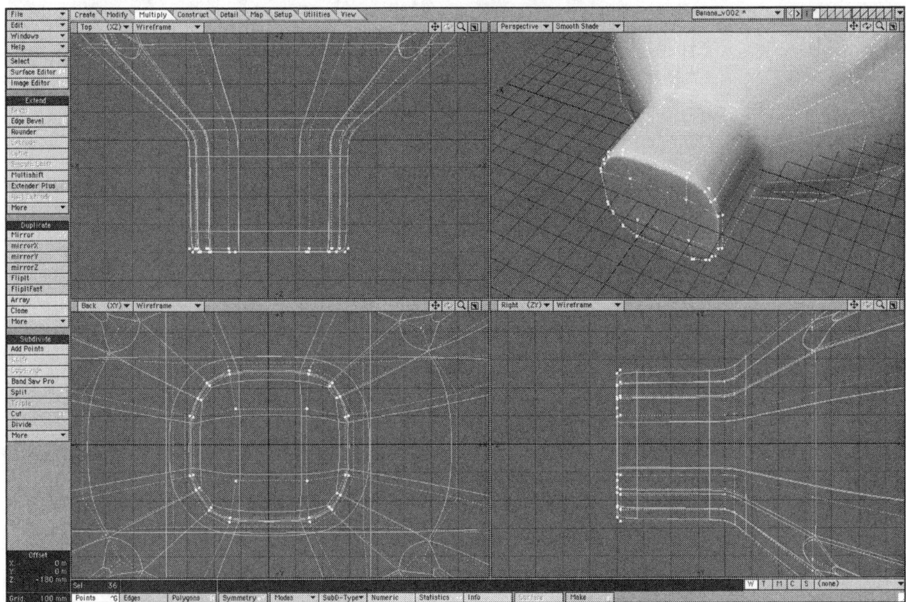

Figure 8.26 Select the points around the end of the banana and move them out on the negative Z-axis.

52. With the points still selected, change the Action Center to Mouse, using the Modes drop-down list at the bottom of the interface. Then, press **y** to select the Rotate tool. Click and drag slightly in the Top view, directly on the edge of the selected points, to rotate the selection in a clockwise direction, about 15 degrees. By setting Action Center to Mouse, you're telling Modeler to make adjustments based on your mouse position. Therefore, a Rotate command will pivot around where you click and drag. **Figure 8.27** shows the rotation.

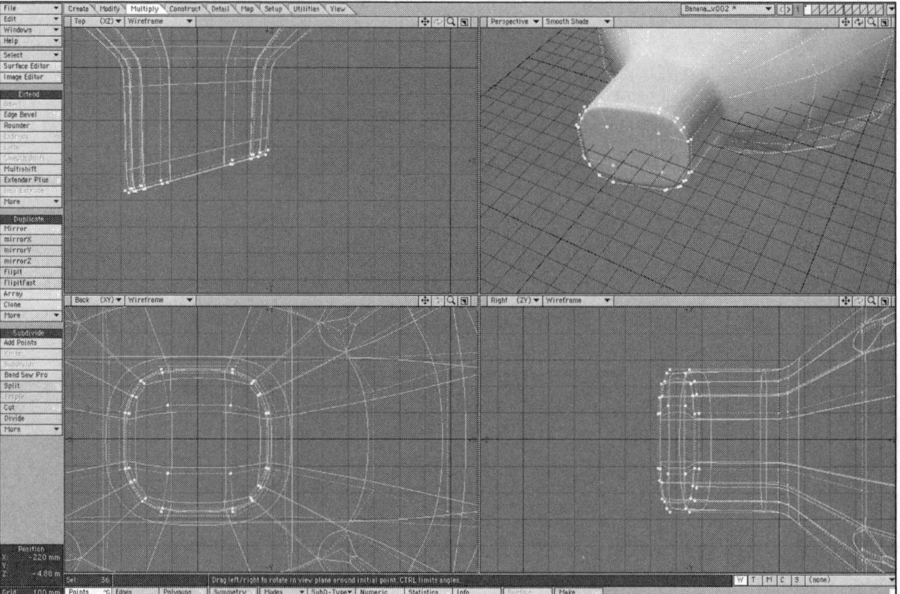

Figure 8.27 Rotate the endpoints about 15 degrees.

53. At this point, you can use all of the tools and procedures we've already covered in this project to adjust the model as you like. Feel free to use the Drag tool to adjust the ends, bevel additional edges, and sort of "mess up" the model a bit so it's not so perfect. On your own, repeat the Multishift, Drag, and Size operations on the other end of the banana. The only difference is that there wouldn't be as much of a stem as there is on the end you've already been working on. **Figure 8.28** shows one way in which bevels and other adjustments can be applied to the opposite end of the banana.

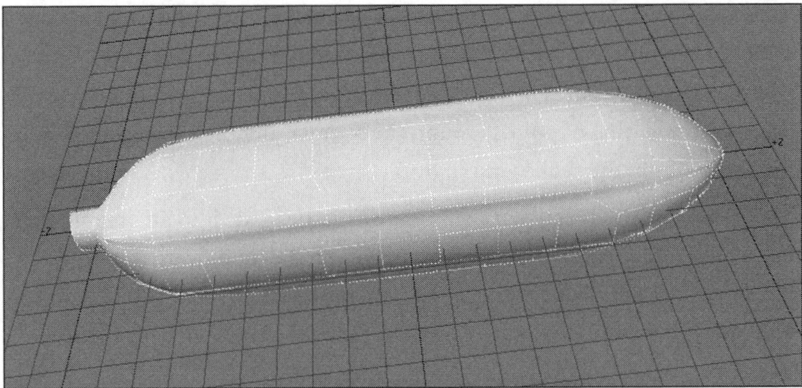

Figure 8.28 Use the Drag, Multishift, and Size tools to create the base of the banana on the opposite end of the model.

54. OK, now all you need to do is bend it. On the Modify tab, select Bend, then in the Back view, click in the center of the object and drag to the right. Bend the object as you like.

55. One last thing to get you in a banana state of mind: Press **q** and apply a surface name of **Banana** to your model. Also, give it a bit of a yellow color. You can always change this later. Save your banana. **Figure 8.29** shows the result.

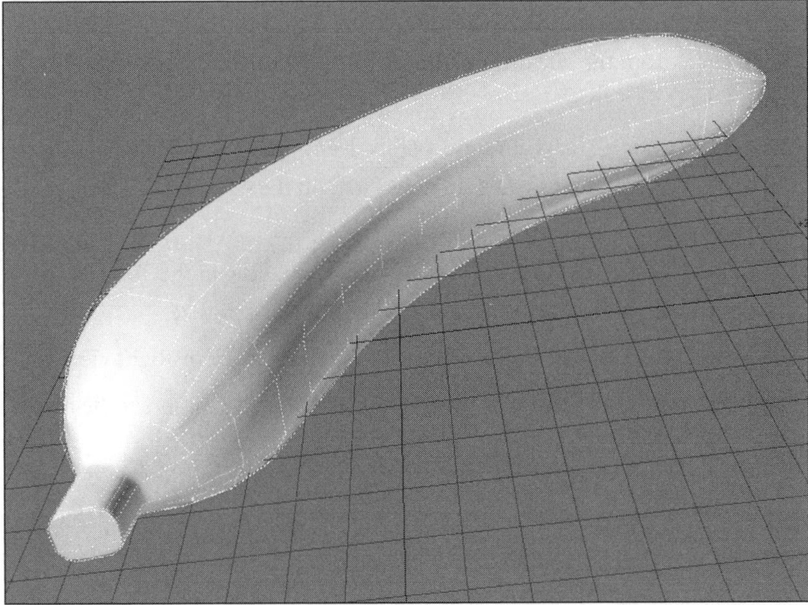

Figure 8.29 Bend the banana as you like and add a surface to it.

At this point, you can adjust the mode as you like. Perhaps the banana made here is too fat. No problem. Undo the bend, then using the Size tool in the Back view, adjust the banana. Then, bend again. You can also use the right mouse button to lasso-select any ring of points around the banana, and then size them to add imperfections in the shape, and so on.

This project showed you how a simple box can be made into an organic shape. LightWave v9's edge tools, multiply tools, and basic modification tools allow you to easily create any shape you like. Add to that Catmull-Clark subdivisions and you can work without having to keep your model to three or four vertices.

This is just the first part of the still-life project, but also the longest. The next project will have you model some additional fruit such as a pear and grapes. From there, you'll build a bowl and a set for the objects.

Orange You Glad You Got This Book?

Wow, these project titles are lame, but it's just so easy to make stupid jokes. Why should modeling fruit be so serious? Anyway, this next project will show you how to model an orange. Sure, it's just a ball, but there are a few small details you'll add to help "sell" it.

Exercise 8.2 Model an Orange with the Multishift and Magnet Tools

1. In Modeler, be sure your banana from the previous project is saved. Don't eat it! Then, from the File drop-down menu at the top of the interface, select New Object.
2. Creating an orange is easy, and most of its detail will come from surfacing. But there are a few things you'll do now. First, on the Create tab, select the Ball command.
3. Holding the Ctrl key to constrain all axes, click and drag in the Top view to draw out a ball on the Y-axis. This should be about 3m in size.
4. Still holding the Ctrl key, click and drag in either the Back or Right view.
5. Press the spacebar to commit to the new object. **Figure 8.30** shows the model.

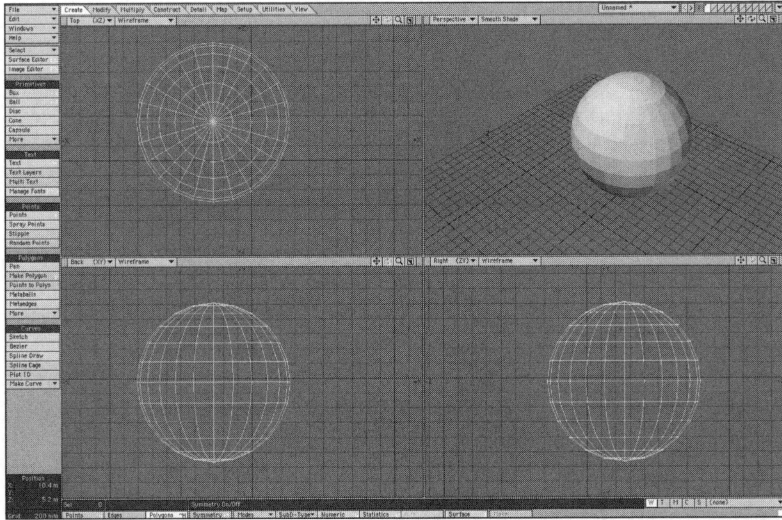

Figure 8.30 Create a ball with a radius of 3m on every axis.

6. Press **F2** to center the object at the origin. Press **a** to bring the model to view.
7. Taking a look at the top of the ball, you can see how the geometry all comes together. It's not that smooth and useful in many situations, but for an orange, these "poles" at the top of the ball can help create the detail. You want to select five areas of edges at the top of the ball. Starting from the center point, and making sure you're in Edge selection mode, click to select the edges, as shown in **Figure 8.31**.

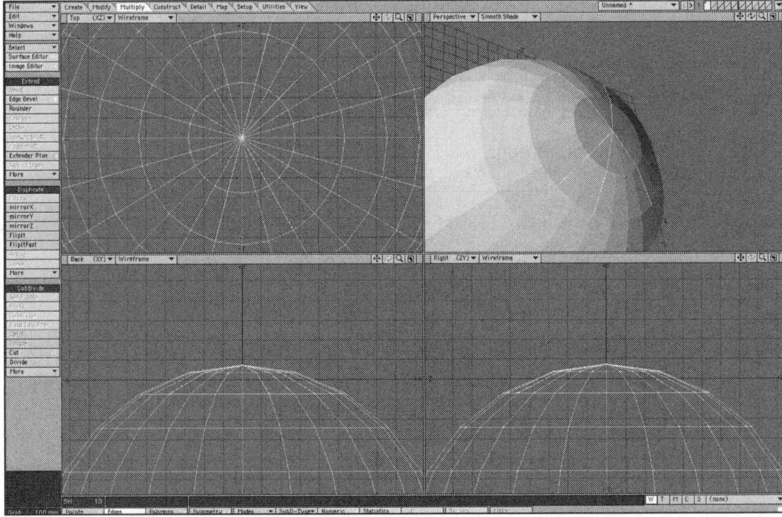

Figure 8.31 Select two edges from the center point at the top of the ball. Do this five times.

Note

When selecting the edges at the top of the ball, be careful not to select the edges at the bottom of the ball. This will happen if you use a wireframe view to select. Instead, select the edges in a shaded view, such as the Perspective view. Pressing Shift+a to fit the selection to view will also help you see if you have more selected than you should.

8. The selected edges do not need to be even and, in fact, shouldn't be. These edges will become the area where the stem will be. With the selected edges, press Ctrl+b for Edge Bevel, and bevel them about 20mm, as shown in **Figure 8.32**.

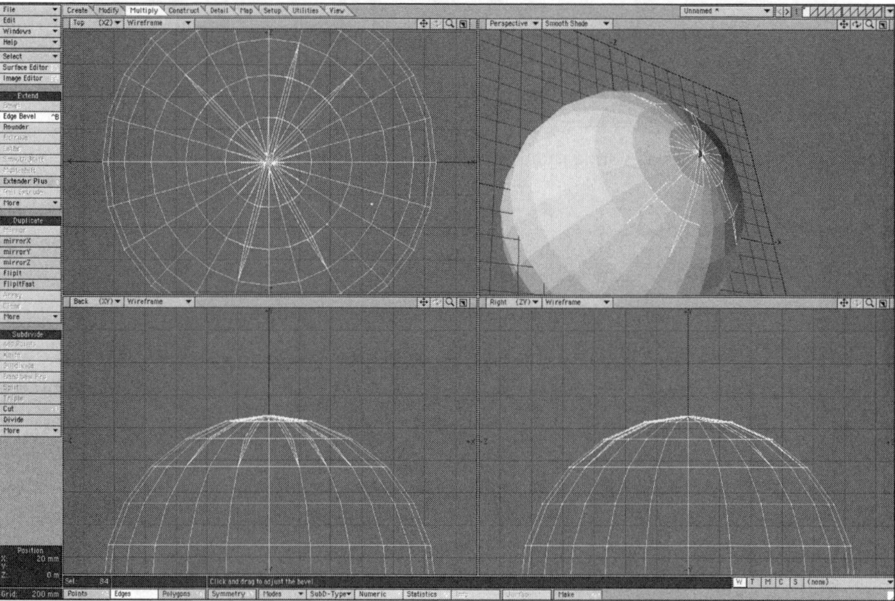

Figure 8.32 Bevel the selected edges.

9. Turn off the Edge Bevel, the choose Sel Switch from the Select drop-down menu. This changes the selected edges to selected polygons. Be sure to deselect any wanted selections. You might have a few extra outside of the initial edge areas.

10. Using the Multishift tool from the Multiply tab, click and drag to bevel the selected polygons just a bit. Bevel them about 5.8mm for the Inset, and 4mm for the Shift. **Figure 8.33** shows the operation.

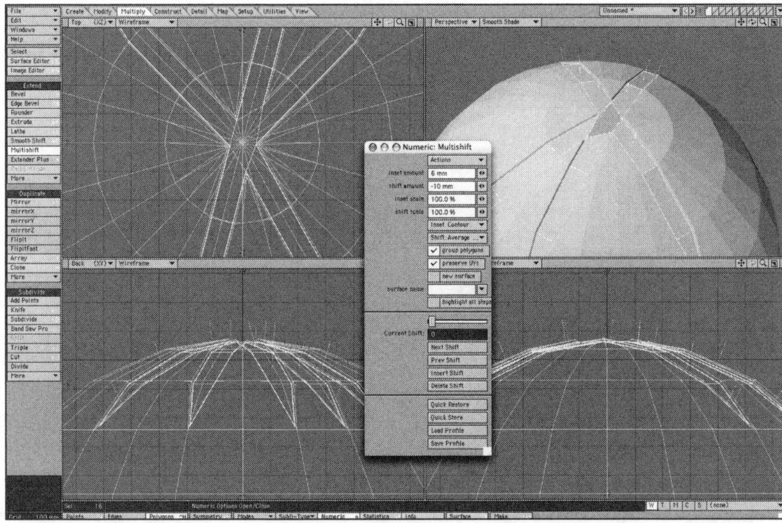

Figure 8.33 Bevel the selected polygons with the Multishift tool.

11. Turn off the Multishift tool. The polygons will still be selected, and you'll adjust them next.
12. Save your orange!
13. Click the Modify tab and select the Magnet tool. This will give you the effect of the Drag tool, but with a falloff.
14. Right-click (Cmd-click on the Mac) in the Top view and drag. You'll see a blue outline appear (**Figure 8.34**). This determines the amount of influence the magnet tool will have.

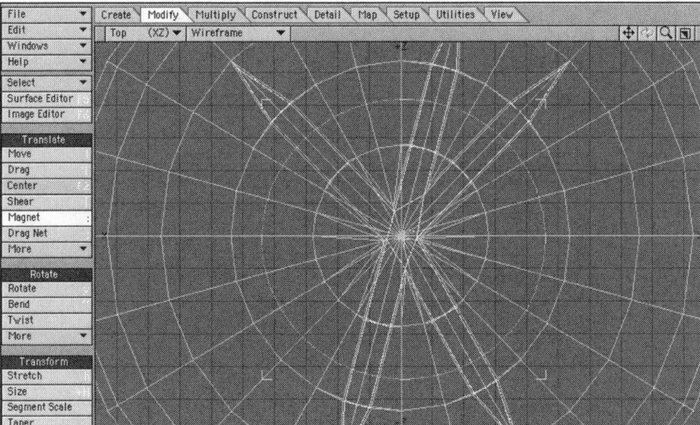

Figure 8.34 Using the right mouse button with the Magnet tool, you tell Modeler how much influence the tool has.

15. Click and drag down on the selected polygons in the Back view. Remember, this is a drag tool with a falloff, so what you'll see is the polygons being moved, but only within the circumference area you specified with the right mouse button. **Figure 8.35** shows the operation.

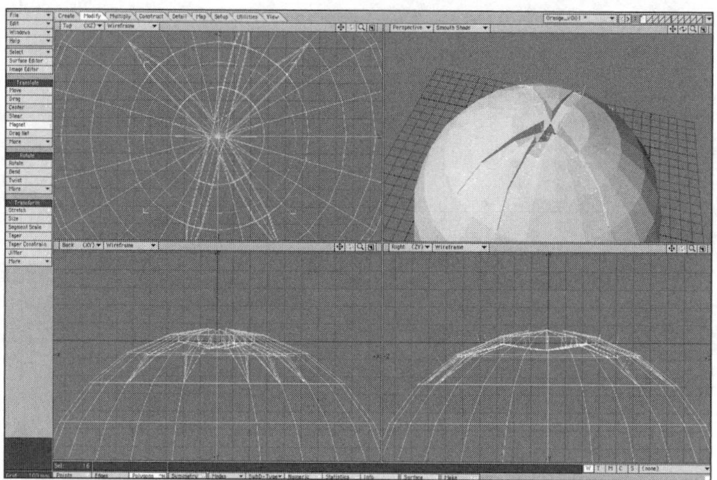

Figure 8.35 Use the Magnet tool to bring just the center of the selected polygons down into the orange.

16. Turn off the Magnet tool (press /) and then deselect the polygons. Save the object. Then, press the Tab key to turn on subdivision surface mode. You should still be using Catmull-Clark subdivisions (**Figure 8.36**).

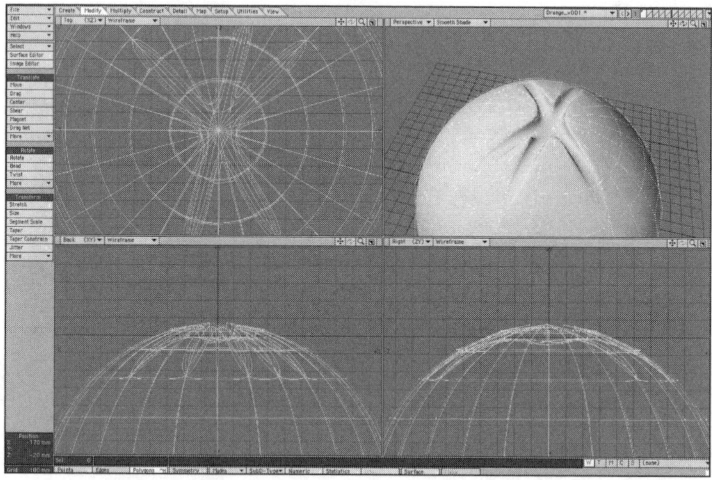

Figure 8.36 With Catmull-Clark subdivisions applied, the bevels at the top of the orange start to shape up.

17. Press Ctrl+t to turn on the Drag tool. Now, take some time and click and drag on the points around the top of the orange to smooth out the beveled areas. Just shape it, and clean it up so that the bevels are more separations in the skin rather than sharp cuts (**Figure 8.37**).

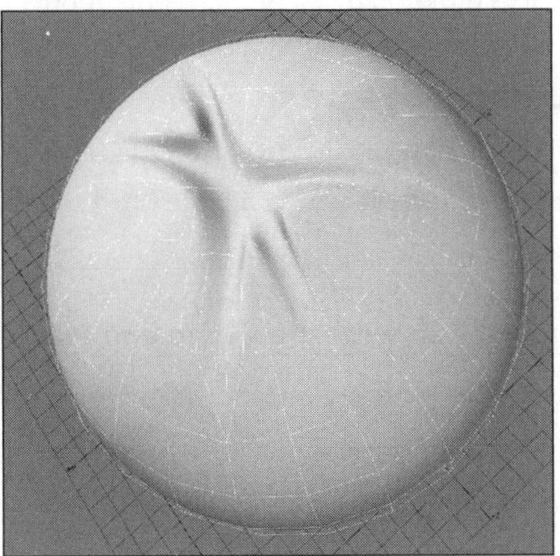

Figure 8.37 Use the Drag tool to adjust the shape of the orange.

18. Save your model when you're done tweaking. Then, the rest of the orange is simply too round. You need to shape it slightly. Use the Magnet tool again, but this time, set the range of influence (with the right mouse button) to encompass most of the orange. Then, with the left mouse, click to effectively push parts of the orange to shape it. **Figure 8.38** shows the effect.

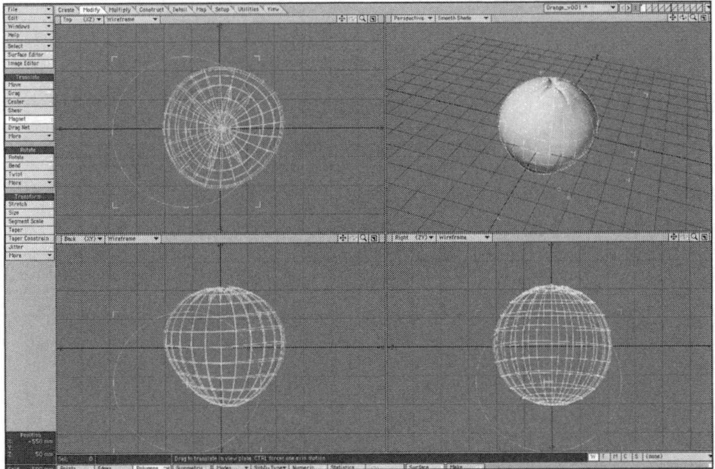

Figure 8.38 Use the Magnet tool to shape the orange, or basically deform it a bit so it's not so perfectly round.

19. Press **q** to call up the Change Surface dialog box and create a surface name of **Orange** for the object and give it a little color. Save your work.

Much of the orange's surface will really come from texturing, which you'll do later in Chapter 11, "Node-Based Texturing." But the initial shape is also important, as you've seen here in this project. Now, let's move on to using a few more modeling tools to create grapes.

Create a Cluster of Grapes

This next project will show you how to create a cluster of grapes in LightWave v9 Modeler. Later, you'll call up this object and place it in a large bowl that you'll model, along with the banana and orange.

Exercise 8.3 Bunches of Fun with the Clone and Magic Bevel Tools

1. Save anything you've been working on, and from the File drop-down menu, select New Object.

   You might have noticed that you're not building with layers in these projects. You could if you wanted to—create the banana in one layer, the orange in another, and the grapes in a third layer. But instead, you're building entirely new objects. This is good because these objects can be used to build your 3D library, as they are saved as individual objects. It also helps save any confusion as to what you're working on, and for this project, you'll use multiple layers to help the modeling process. Having multiple objects in different layers might make your life difficult with the upcoming steps.

2. On the Create tab, select the Ball tool. Create a ball the same size as you did in the previous project (when you created the orange). Press **F2** to center the ball. **Figure 8.39** shows the ball.

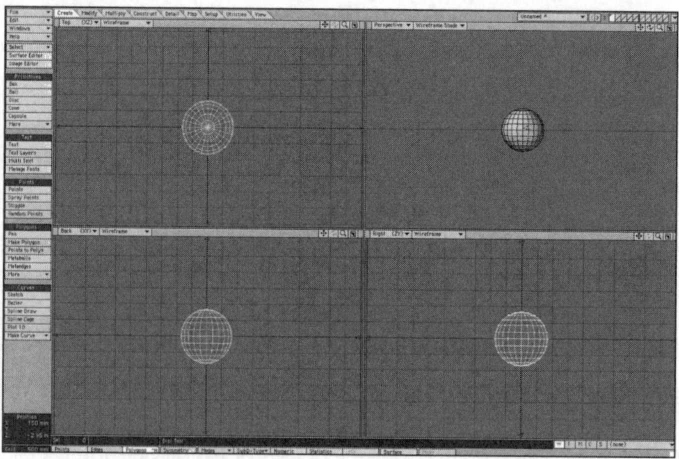

Figure 8.39 Begin creating grapes by making a simple ball.

3. Press **h** to activate the Stretch tool, then click in the Back view and drag up slightly to elongate the ball. **Figure 8.40** shows the result.

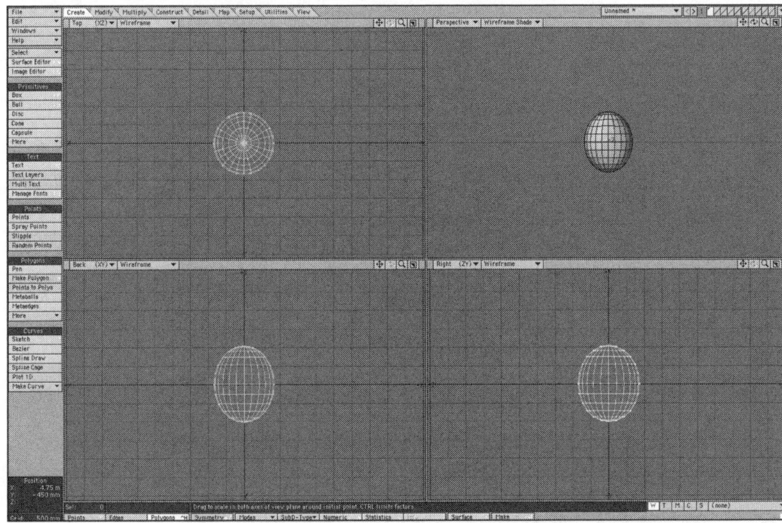

Figure 8.40 Use the Stretch tool to elongate the ball.

4. Click a new layer at the top right of the interface. Place the ball as a background layer by clicking beneath the slash mark in the first layer.
5. On the Create tab, click the Random Points tool in the Points category. In the panel that appears, enter **35** for points, then check on Sphere and Falloff, as shown in **Figure 8.41**.

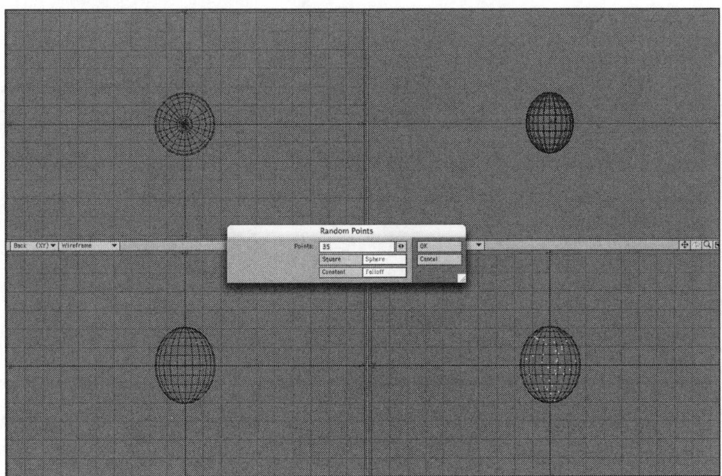

Figure 8.41 Use the Random Points tool to create a clump of points.

6. You'll see a group of points created in the views. The points might be hard to see, and there's a way you can adjust that in Modeler. Press **d** to call up the Display Options panel. Click the Interface tab, and check Simple Wireframe Points. Set the Point Size to 3.5, as shown in **Figure 8.42**.

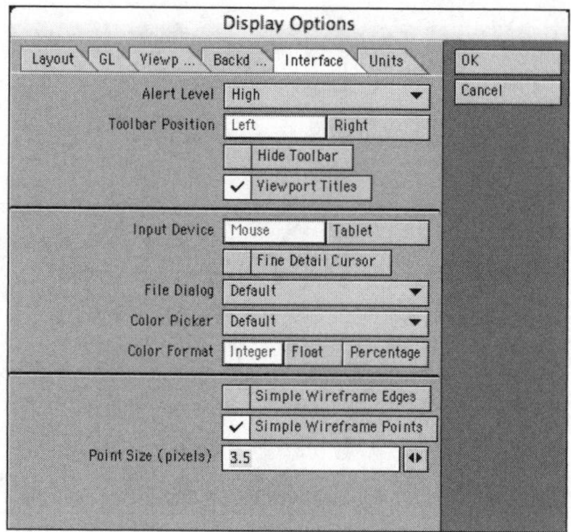

Figure 8.42 Increase the visual appearance of points in the Display Options panel.

7. Click OK to close the Display Options panel. With these points now created, press ' (the apostrophe key) to reverse layers. This puts Layer 1 in the foreground and Layer 2 in the background.
8. On the Multiply tab, click the More drop-down menu in the Duplicate category. Select Point Clone Plus. A large panel appears (**Figure 8.43**).
9. Enter a few settings:

   For Random Rotation:

   Min H **20**

   Min B **30**

   For Random Size:

   Min **0.75**

   Max **1.0**
10. Leave all other settings at their defaults. Basically, the Point Clone Plus tool will generate duplicates of the foreground layer (the ball) based on the position of the points in the background layer. The values you've just set are simply adding some randomness to the duplicated objects. Click OK to close the Point Clone Plus tool and see what happens (**Figure 8.44**).

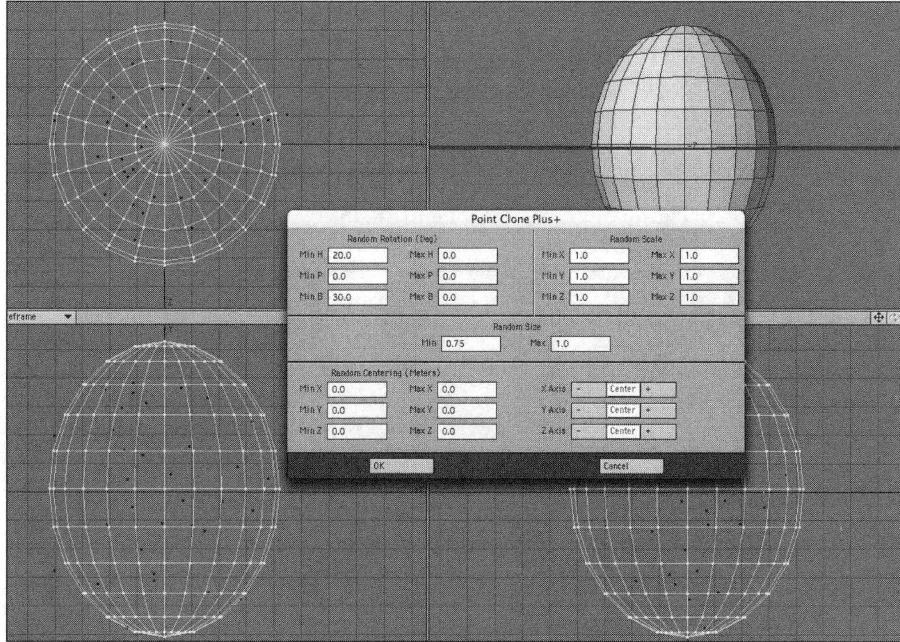

Figure 8.43 Once the Point Clone Plus tool is set up, you'll be able to duplicate your foreground object based on the point positions in the background layer.

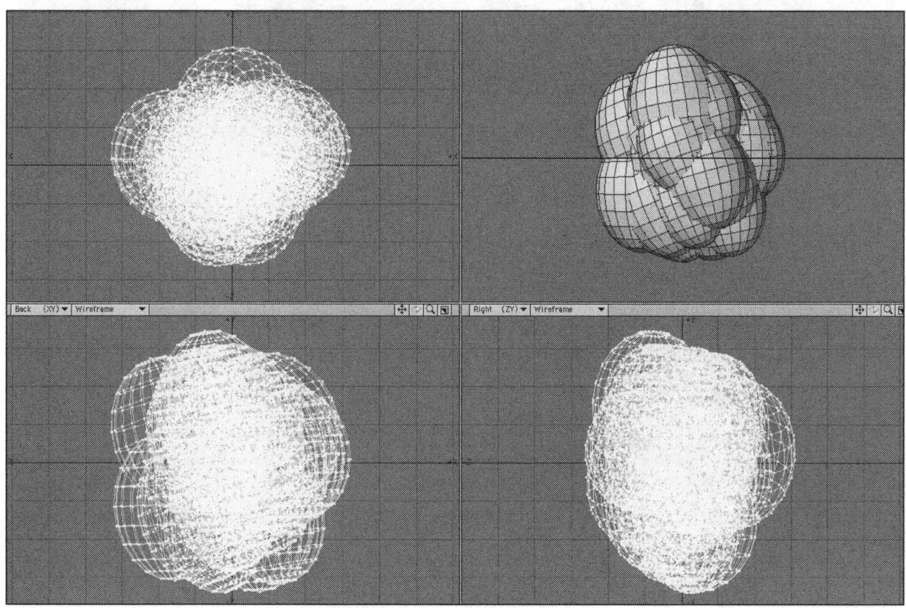

Figure 8.44 The Point Clone Plus tool creates 35 duplicates of the ball (grape), each with randomness throughout.

11. Wow! Those are some fat grapes! Why did this happen? The size of the initial ball was too large based on the position of the points. Click Ctrl+z (Cmd-z on the Mac) to undo the Point Clone Plus operation.
12. Press Shift+h for the Size tool, and size down your grape about 30%. Then, rerun the Point Clone Plus tool. The settings you've entered will still be there. Click OK, and you'll see a clump of grapes, as in **Figure 8.45**.

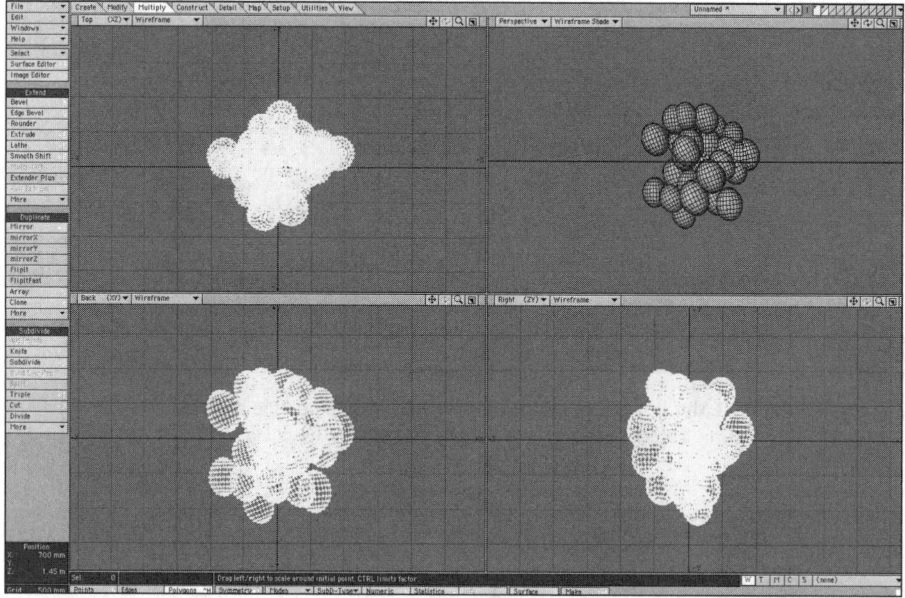

Figure 8.45 Using Point Clone Plus along with a ball has created a clump of grapes.

13. A few grapes might be overlapping other grapes, and some might be floating too far out from the rest. You can easily move these with a few steps. Making sure you're in Polygons selection mode, click once on a grape. Then, press the right bracket key, the shortcut for the Select Connected command. Every polygon connected to that selection (the rest of the individual grape) is now selected. Press **t** and move the grape.
14. Feel free to resize, rotate, and adjust the grapes as needed. You don't need to be too precise because these grapes will end up in a bowl, but if you plan to use them later for something more close-up, try to align them more accurately so that none are overlapping. If you feel you need an additional grape or two, select one, press Ctrl+c to copy, move the selected grape, and then press Ctrl+v to paste.

15. To deselect, press the / (slash) key.
16. Continue adjusting the grape positions as you like, and remember to save your work.
17. Press **q** to open the Change Surface dialog box. Create a surface name **Grapes**, and give it a bit of color. Perhaps you prefer red grapes over green seedless? Click OK to close the panel and save your object.
18. To create a stem for added impact, go to a new layer, leaving the grapes in a background layer. This process can get tedious to make a branch extend from each grape. However, it's easy to create the initial look, starting with a box.
19. Create a small box just above the clump of grapes in the new layer, as shown in **Figure 8.46**.

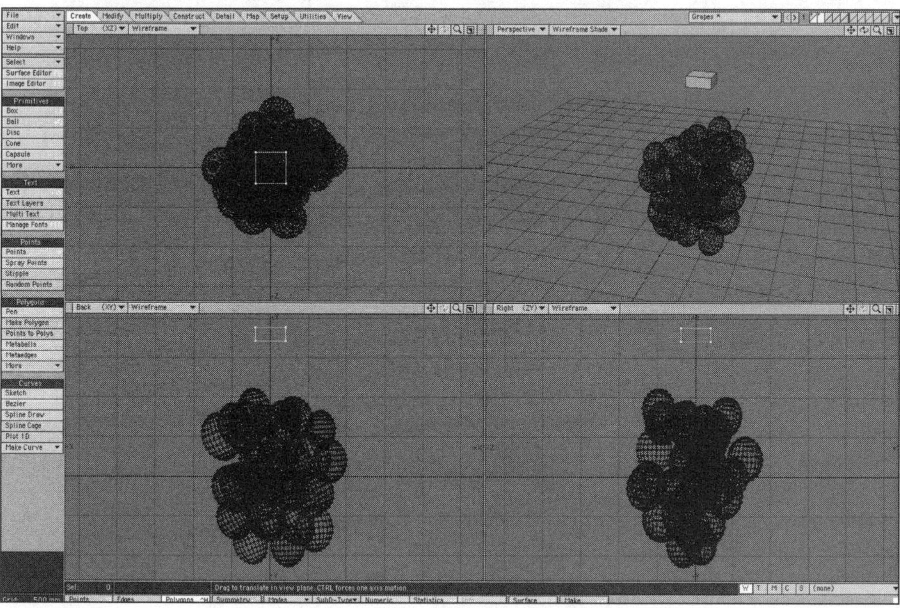

Figure 8.46 To begin creating the stem for the grapes, build a small box above the grapes in a new layer.

20. Select just the bottom polygon of the box, as shown in **Figure 8.47**.

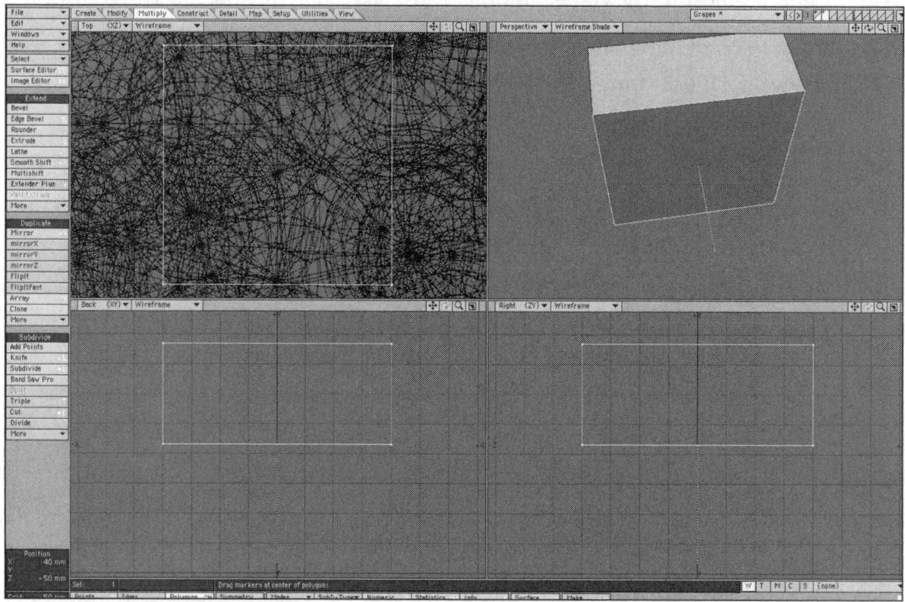

Figure 8.47 Select just the bottom single polygon of the box.

21. Click the Multiply tab, then click the More drop-down menu in the Extend category and select Magic Bevel, as shown in **Figure 8.48**.

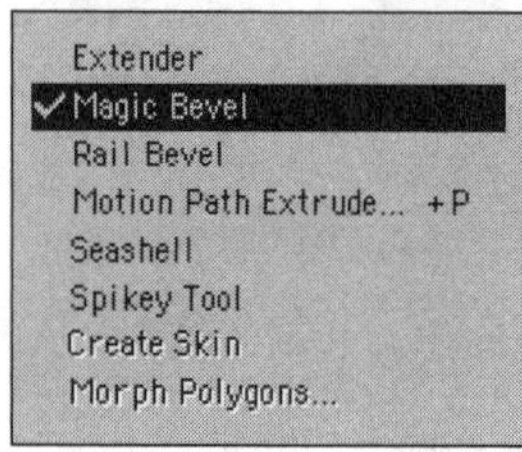

Figure 8.48 Choose the Magic Bevel tool from the Multiply tab's Extend category.

22. When you turn on the Magic Bevel tool, you'll see small circles appear around the box (**Figure 8.49**).

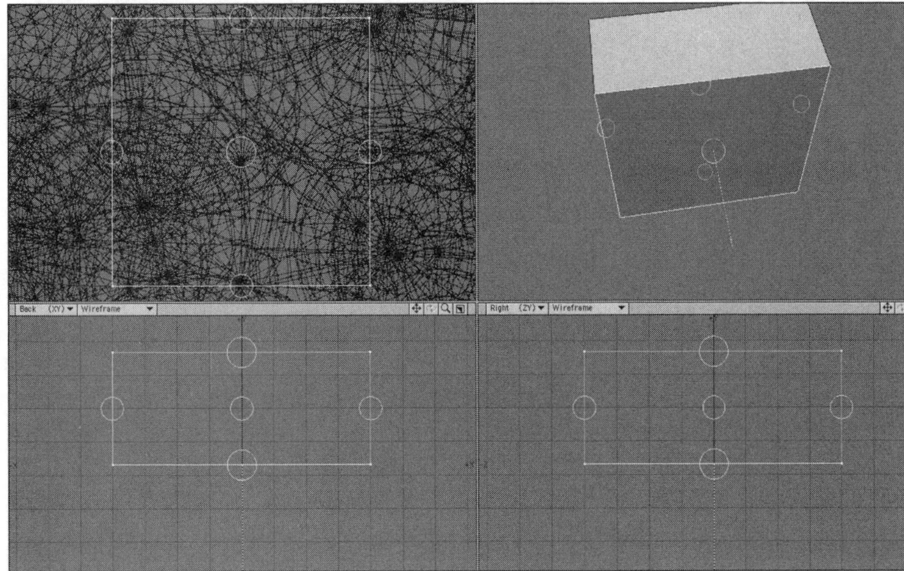

Figure 8.49 Magic Bevel begins with small circles on each polygon.

23. Click and drag the circle at the bottom of the box, and drag downward into the grapes. You can do this in the Back or Right view. Feel free to move the mouse slightly to create a curvature. **Figure 8.50** shows the result.

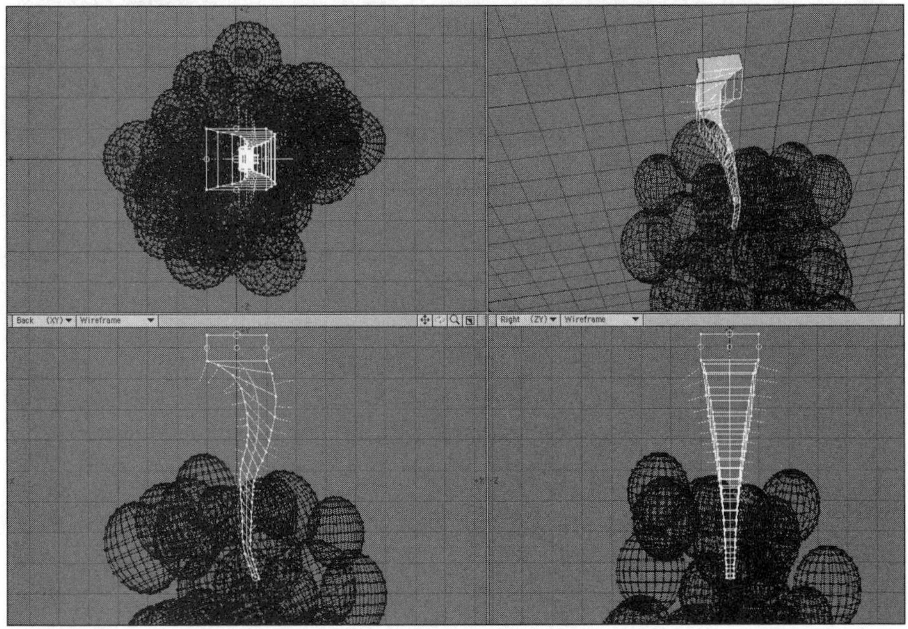

Figure 8.50 Click and drag the bottom circle to instantly create a multiple-beveled object.

24. Press the spacebar to turn off the Magic Bevel tool. Then, click its button to turn it on again. You'll now see circles for the Magic Bevel on each of the newly created polygons (**Figure 8.51**).

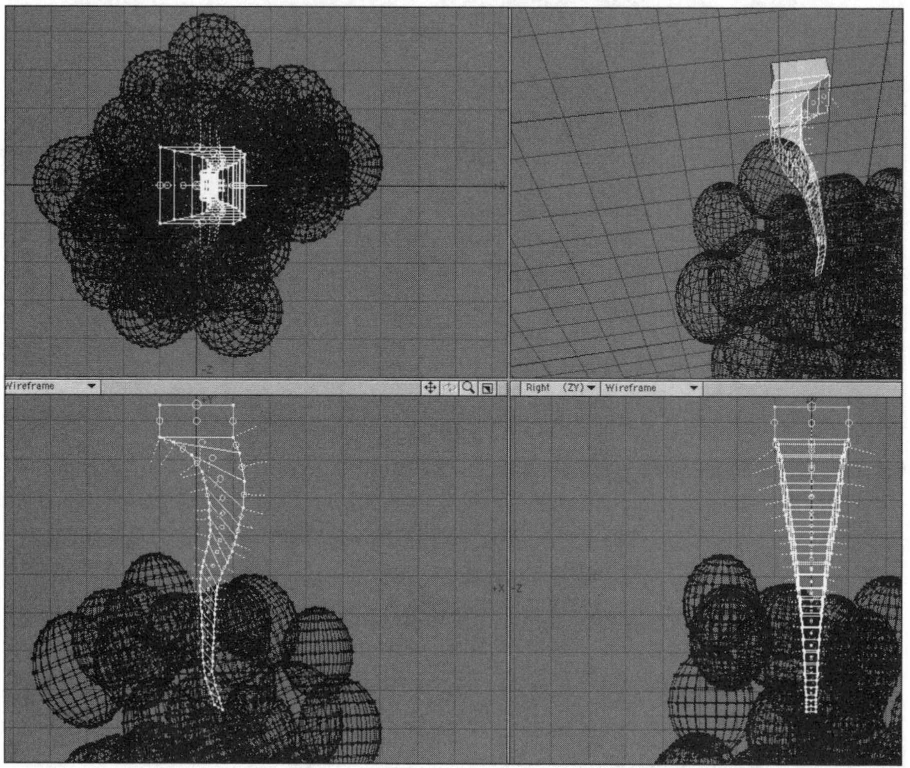

Figure 8.51 Turning Magic Bevel off and then on again resets the tool so you can apply it to newly created geometry.

25. In the Back view, click and drag downward from the middle of the stem, creating another branch, like the one shown in **Figure 8.52**.

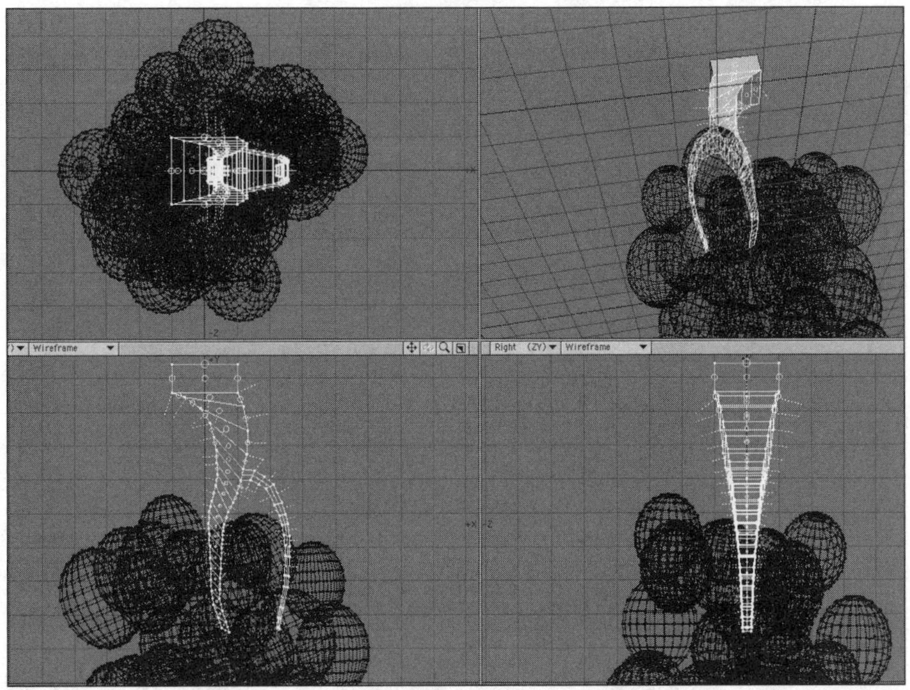

Figure 8.52 Create another branch from the middle of the original stem.

26. In the Right view, create another stem.

27. From here, you can apply new Magic Bevels to the stems you've created. If you open the Numeric panel, you can adjust their scale. Changing the value to 100% prevents the bevel from tapering as it extends when you click and drag. You can also choose to spin the bevels as they are created.

28. After you've created a few branches, press the spacebar to turn off the Magic Bevel tool. Then, press / to deselect.

29. Make sure Subpatch is selected in the SubD-Type drop-down list at the bottom of the Modeler interface, and then press the Tab key. You'll see the beveled box become smooth (**Figure 8.53**).

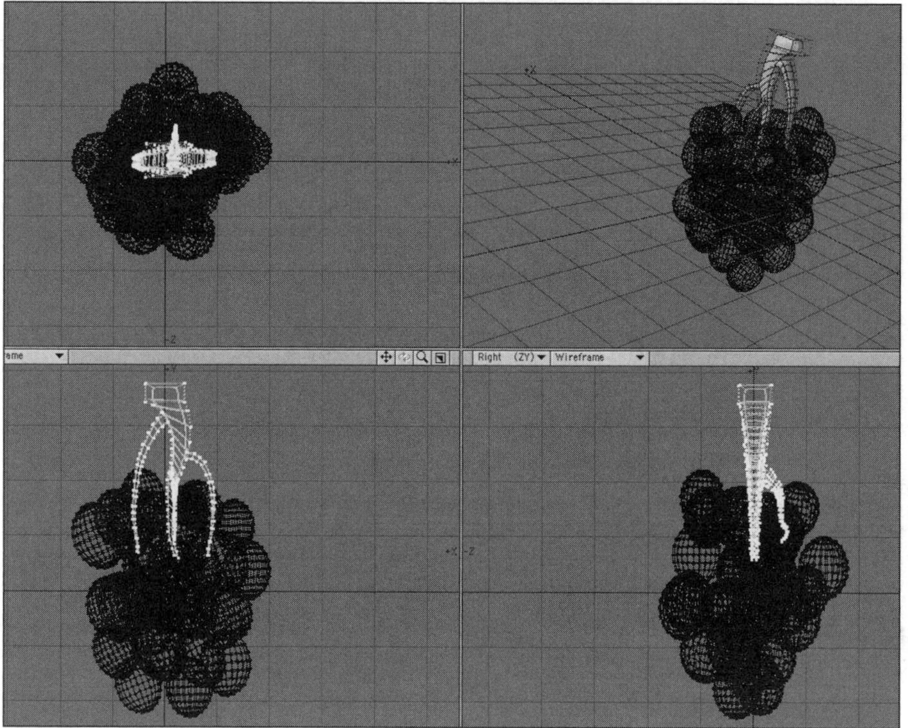

Figure 8.53 Apply subdivision surfaces to the stem by pressing the Tab key.

Note

You can also apply subdivision surfaces to the grapes to smooth them out.

30. You can adjust points as you like, and even bevel a single polygon on the stem before you apply a Magic Bevel, to help determine the shape. When you've finished shaping the stem, assign it a surface using the Change Surface dialog box (press **q**).
31. Press Ctrl+x (Cmd-x on the Mac) to cut the stem from the current layer. Switch to the grape layer, then press Ctrl+v (Cmd-v on the Mac) to paste it. Save your object.

The stem is not attached to the grapes, but you can connect it up if you like. Use the Magic Bevel tool to drag a stem bevel right to each grape, or move the grapes around to touch the stem, but keep in mind that the stem is not going to be seen too closely in the final shot, since the grapes will be sitting in a bowl. And hey, speaking of bowls, let's make one!

Building a Fruit Bowl

Building a fruit bowl doesn't sound very exciting, does it? This next project, while not glamorous or too complex, is nevertheless important for your still-life scene. Furthermore, you can use the lathing technique it demonstrates to build plates, glasses, and other similar vessels.

Exercise 8.4 Sculpting with Splines and the Lathe Tool

1. From the File menu in Modeler, select New Object.
2. Press the comma key three times to zoom the Modeler view. This changes the overall grid to 2m. You can see the grid size in the bottom-left corner of the interface.
3. On the Create tab, click and select the Spline Draw tool in the Curves tools category.
4. In the Back viewport, click on the origin to create a point, and then click a few grids to the right along the X-axis, then again slightly above that, and so on, until you have an arc of 9 or 10 points that provides a cross section of the bowl's outer profile, from its center on the Y-axis to its outer rim to the right (**Figure 8.54**).

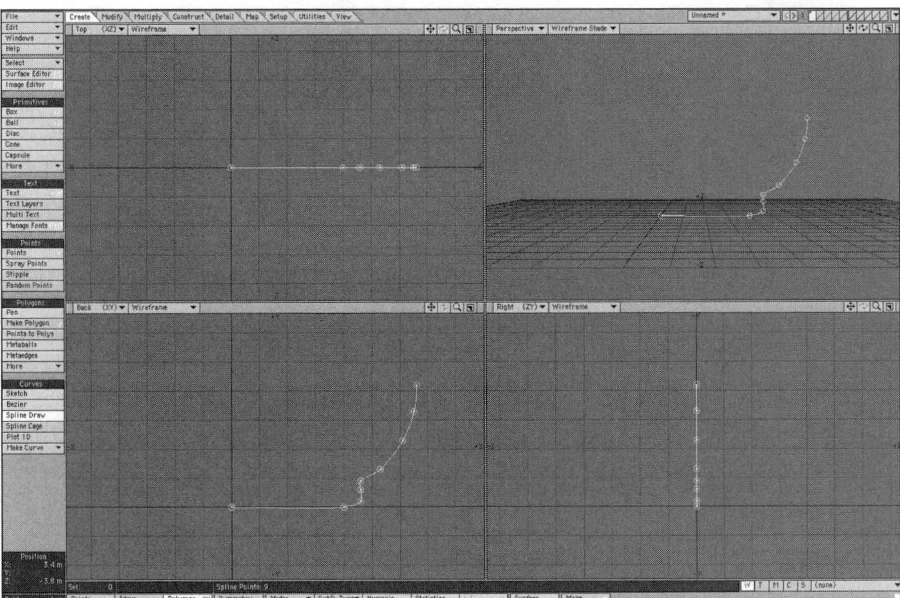

Figure 8.54 Using the Spline Draw tool, you can begin creating a curve to model a bowl.

5. Click a little to the left of your last point to create a lip for your bowl, then click a new series of points, more or less parallel to the first set, to shape the bowl's inner-surface profile, ending back at the Y-axis (**Figure 8.55**).

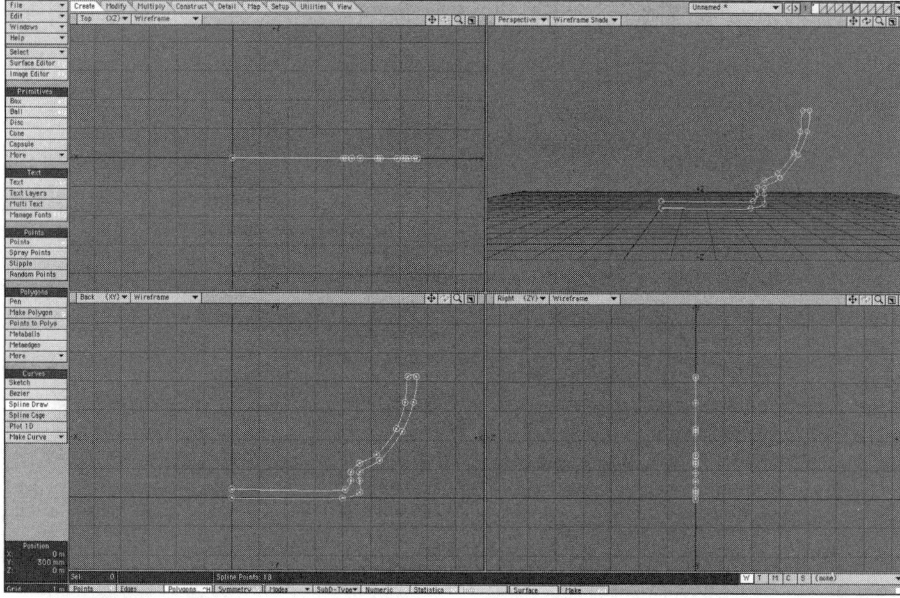

Figure 8.55 Continue creating points to finish building the cross section of the bowl.

6. Before you commit to this curve, you can click and drag on any point you've created to adjust it. Be careful to precisely click on any point you want to adjust. Clicking *near* a point will add a new one and continue your curve.

Note

If you find that it's difficult to create a point close to another point, just click a bit farther away, then drag the point in closer to the desired position.

7. When you've got the points along the curve positioned as you like, press the spacebar to turn off the Spline Draw tool.
8. Switch to Points selection mode, and select the two endpoints on the Y-axis.

9. Press **v** to open the Set Value dialog box. Choose X for the Axis, and set the value to 0m. Click OK, and the selected points will be positioned exactly at the origin. This is important for the upcoming steps.
10. Deselect the two points.
11. From the Multiply tab, select the Lathe tool from the Extend category.
12. Press **n** to open the Numeric panel, and you'll quickly see the tool activate. The default axis for the lathe is the Y-axis, so that's good! You'll also see that End Angle is set to 360 degrees; that's also good, because we want to apply the lathed shape through a full circular sweep. (If you'd wanted to make a "half-bowl" [or Hollywood Bowl] shape instead of our fruit bowl, you could have set End Angle to 180 degrees.) The only default setting you need to change is Sides, from 24 to about 48. This will help smooth out the object, as shown in **Figure 8.56**.

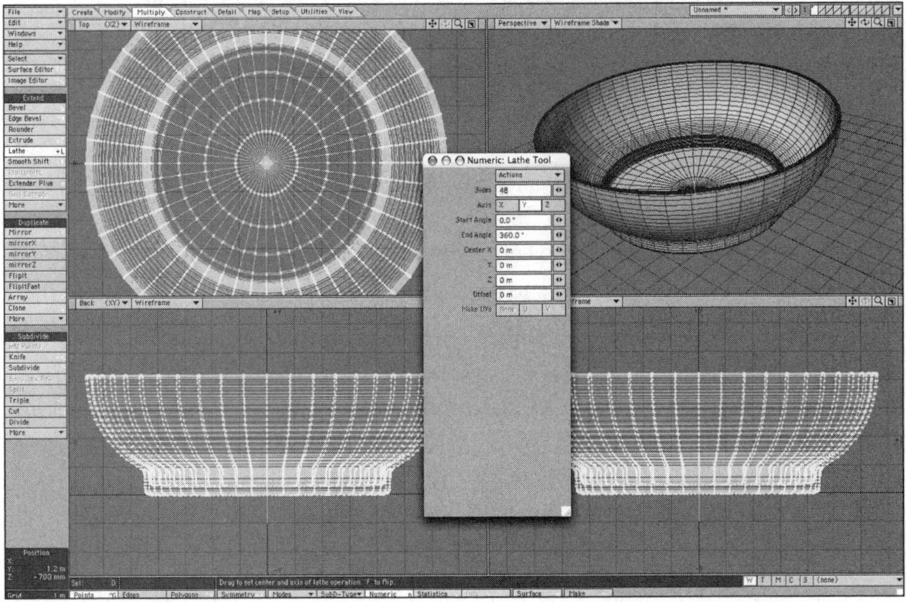

Figure 8.56 Changing the Sides value to 48 adds more detail to the lathed curve.

13. Press the spacebar to turn off the Lathe tool. Use the Change Surfaces panel (press **q**) to give it the surface name **Bowl** (how original!) and then save the object. **Figure 8.57** shows the final bowl.

Figure 8.57 The final fruit bowl, before it's filled up with tasty treats.

14. Save your bowl (press **s**).

    Now that you've seen how the Lathe tool works, can you see why was it important to use the Set Value dialog box to set those two endpoints? We lathed around the Y-axis, and setting the X-values of the endpoints to 0 ensured that they'd lie on that axis, at the bowl's exact center. Positive X-values for the endpoints would have created a hole in the bowl, and negative X-values would have caused the center of the bowl to overlap itself, complicating the model needlessly. Neither error would really be noticeable once fruit is placed in the bowl, but you should learn to build items like this the right way.

Perhaps you want to make a bottle or a glass? Use this exact process for a clean, smooth model. You can also use a Spline Curve with the Lathe tool to create very tight but smooth corners—sort of the same effect as beveling an edge, but with less work.

Now, let's fill up the bowl.

Exercise 8.5 Filling a Fruit Bowl

You could use Modeler to arrange your still life by loading each piece of fruit and the bowl and pasting them each into separate object layers, but you'll have more flexibility if you simply load each object into a scene in Layout and position them there.

1. Open LightWave Layout and click the Items tab. From the Load category, select Object. When the Load Object dialog box appears, you can select all of the objects you created in this chapter: the banana, the orange, the grapes, and the bowl. Click OK to load them. **Figure 8.58** shows the objects loaded from the Perspective view.

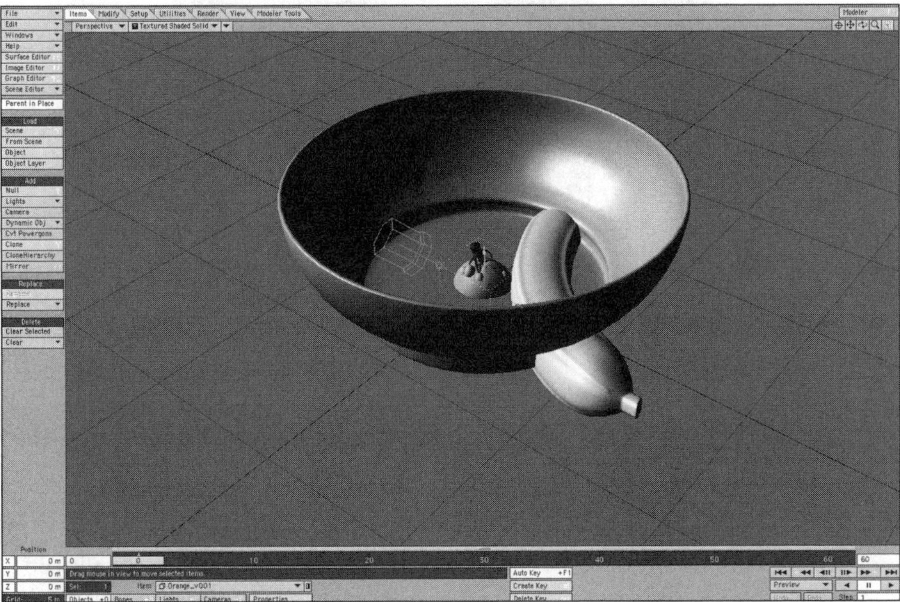

Figure 8.58 The four objects you created in this chapter are loaded into LightWave Layout.

2. The objects aren't quite in the bowl, are they? That's OK—you can easily position them now. First, select the Orange object. Press Shift+h to size the object. Scale it up to about 1.8. You can click and drag to size it, and watch the values in the lower-left corner of the interface.
3. Note that your Auto Key should be on and the timeline slider at frame 0. Once the orange is up to size, press **t** to select the Move tool. Move the orange up on the Y-axis until it rests on the bottom of the bowl. You can then move it off to one side of the bowl.
4. With the orange still selected, press Ctrl+c to activate the Clone tool. When the Clone dialog box appears, enter **5** to make five copies of the orange.

5. You can use the up arrow on your keyboard to select each orange copy. Then, move each one to fill the bowl, as in **Figure 8.59**. Don't be afraid to rotate them for a more random look, and place one on top of another.

Figure 8.59 Clone the orange and position the copies in the bowl using the Move and Rotate tools.

6. Save your scene by pressing Shift+s. Name the scene **FruitBowlSetup** or something similar.
7. Now take your banana and position it on top of the orange. Remember that when you select the Move and Rotate tools, you can use the handles to specifically control position on a desired axis. **Figure 8.60** shows the banana in place.

Note

When using the Move tool, dragging with the right mouse button constrains movements to the Y-axis. With the Rotate tool, dragging with the right mouse button constrains to the Bank channel.

Figure 8.60 The banana you modeled is positioned on top of the oranges.

8. Clone the banana (Ctrl+c) one time and position the copy on top of the existing one, with a slight offset as in **Figure 8.61**.

Figure 8.61 A second banana suddenly becomes top banana.

9. Finally, select the grapes, and position them with the other fruit, resting on the oranges and the side of the bowl. Feel free to resize, rotate, and reposition the grapes until you like the way they look. **Figure 8.62** shows the bowl of fruit.

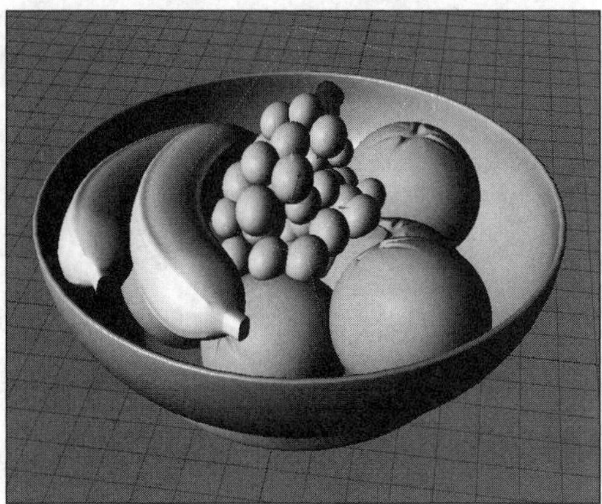

Figure 8.62 The bowl is now full of fruit in LightWave Layout.

10. Save your scene and hop back into LightWave Modeler. You can press **F12** to get there.

You can see that working in Layout to position, size, and clone the objects is a bit easier than doing so in Modeler. You can quickly clone, position, and rotate in real time. Perhaps more to the point, Layout is where you'll render the final scene. There's one more thing to do: create a set for the fruit bowl.

Building a Set for the Still Life

When creating a still-life scene, you need more than just a bowl of fruit. You can't just have a bowl of fruit floating in 3D space. Instead, you can use a cloth. Yes, LightWave can create cloth, and in this exercise, you'll model it. Later, in Chapter 14, "Dynamics in Motion," you'll learn how to create physically based cloth that can be animated. In this project, you're not animating the cloth, but it'll be fun to model it.

Exercise 8.6 Modeling a Tablecloth

1. In LightWave Modeler, create a new object.
2. Create a box in the Back viewport, specifying **5m** for the width and **8m** for the height. For the segments, enter **8** for the X, **11** for the Y, and **1** for the Z, as shown in **Figure 8.63**.

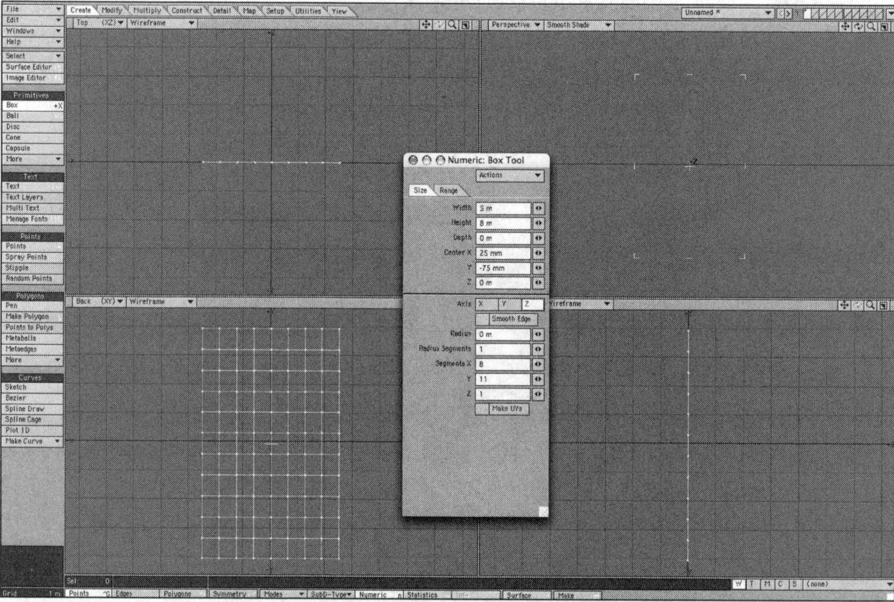

Figure 8.63 Create a tall, flat box with multiple segments to begin making your cloth.

3. Turn off the Box tool. If you can't see your object in the Perspective view, make sure the polygons are facing toward the negative Z-axis. You can press **f** to flip them.
4. Press the Tab key to activate subdivision surfaces for the object.
5. Make sure you're in Polygons selection mode, and using the right mouse button, lasso-select around the top two-thirds of the polygons, as shown in **Figure 8.64**.

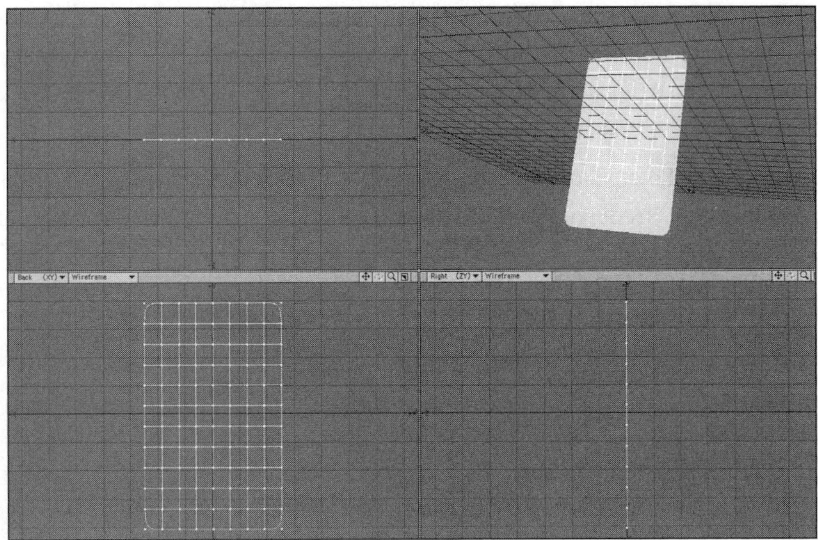

Figure 8.64 Lasso-select the top two-thirds of the box.

6. On the Modify tab, select the Rotate tool. Make sure your Action Center is set to Mouse from the Modes drop-down menu at the bottom of the interface. Then, in the Right view, click and drag at the very bottom of the selection, and bend the selected polygons back on the Z-axis. **Figure 8.65** shows the example.

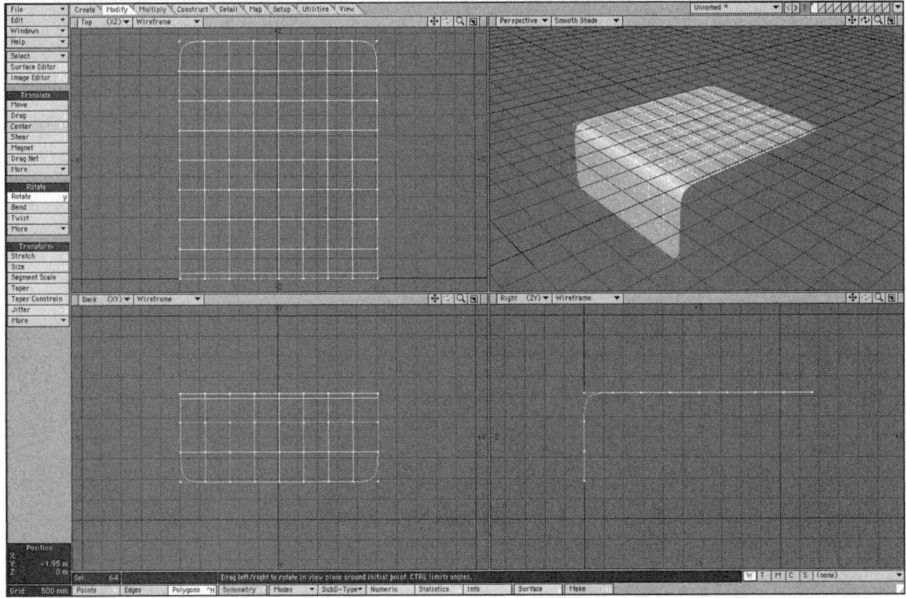

Figure 8.65 Using the Rotate tool, the tall box is bent backward to create a smooth fold.

7. The reason you're rotating the selection rather than bending is that you want to create a tabletop look. The Rotate tool, in combination with the subdivisional surface, makes a tight, smooth edge. Now, turn off the Rotate tool, and then deselect the middle third set of polygons, so that only the top third remains selected.
8. Activate the Rotate tool again (press **y**) and then click on the base of the selection to rotate the selection upward. Don't rotate a full 90 degrees; give it just a bit of a pitch (**Figure 8.66**).

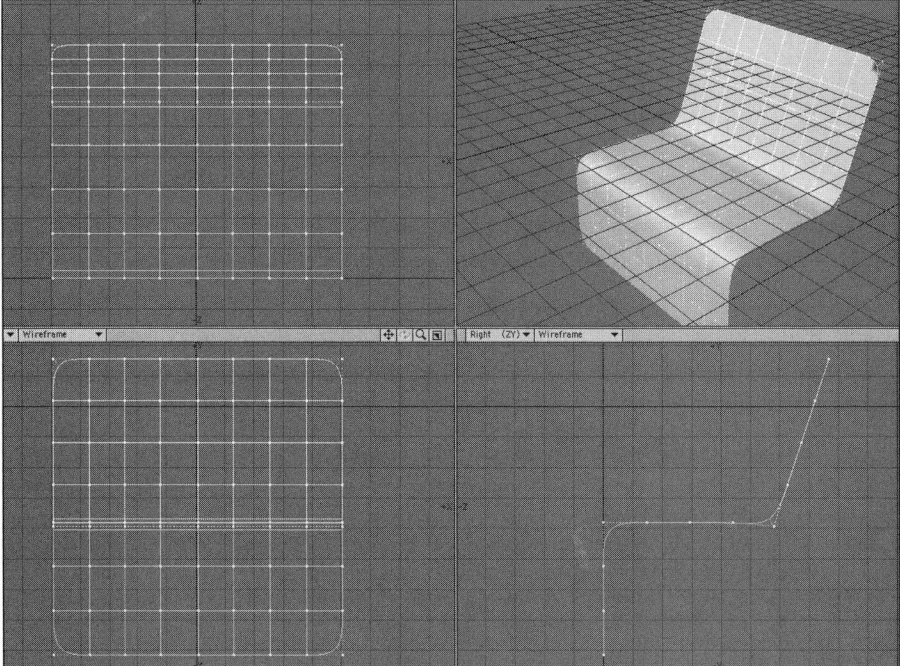

Figure 8.66 Rotate the top third of the object upward to create the back of the tabletop set.

9. Deselect the polygons, apply a surface name to the object using the Change Surfaces dialog box (press **q**), and then save it as **ClothSet** or something similar.

10. Select the second row of polygons from the top, as shown in **Figure 8.67**.

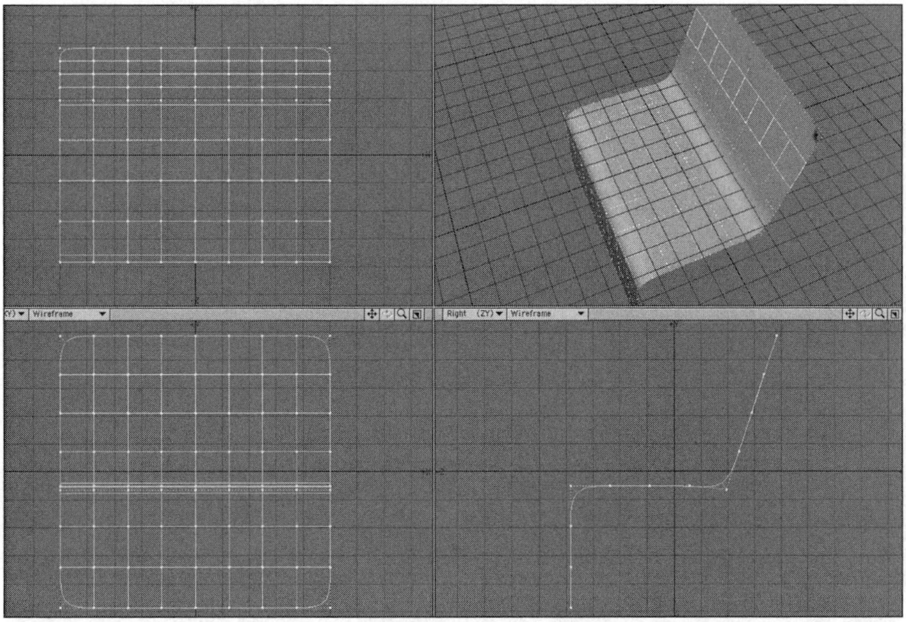

Figure 8.67 Select the second row of polygons from the top of the set.

11. On the Multiply tab, select QuickCut 1 from the More drop-down list under the Subdivide category. The selected polygon will be split in two, and the new points will automatically be selected.
12. With the points selected, press **t** to activate the Move tool, and then move the selected points forward along the Z-axis just a bit, to create a bump in the cloth.

13. Press **y** and, in the Back view window, rotate the selection slightly (**Figure 8.68**).

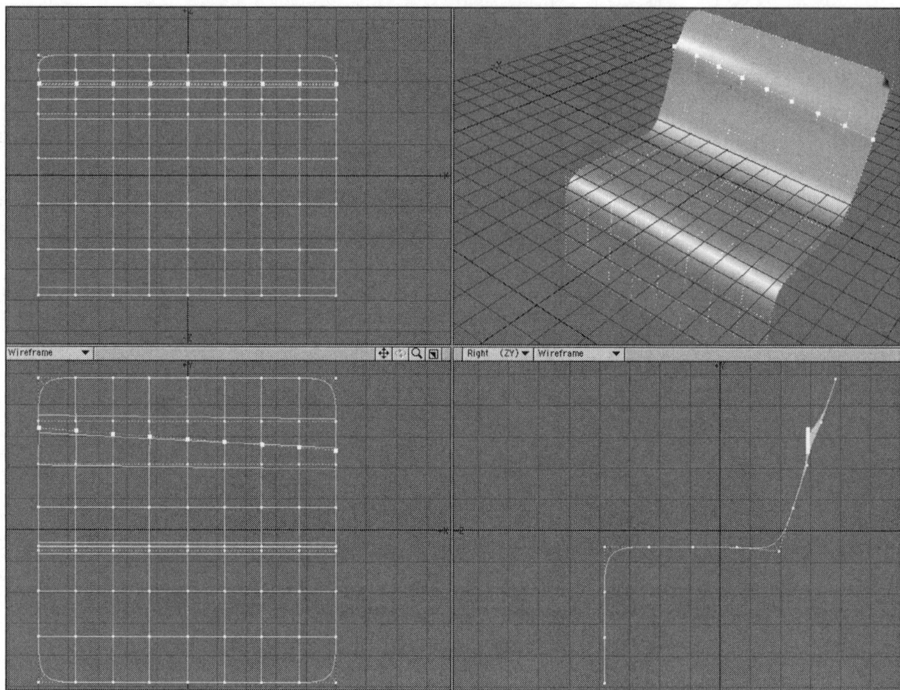

Figure 8.68 Move and rotate the split row of points to create a bump in the cloth.

14. Click the Polygons selection-mode button and Ctrl-click each polygon in the row beneath the row of points you just adjusted to select the entire row.
15. Run the Quick Cut 1 command again, and with the newly created points, move them back toward the first bump, creating another ripple (**Figure 8.69**).

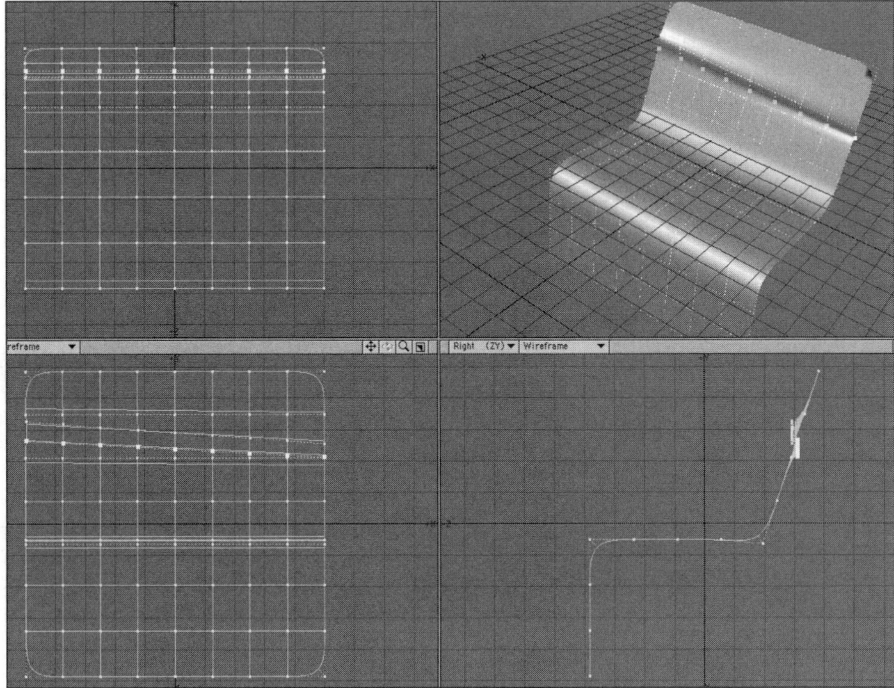

Figure 8.69 After another Quick Cut operation, move the second row of points to help fold the cloth a bit more.

16. Save your model.

From here, you can continue bending, quick cutting, and adjusting points to create folds in the cloth. You can use the Drag tool (Ctrl+t) to click and drag any points for added adjustments. What makes this work is that you're adjusting the points of the model in a subdivision surface mode. That helps smooth out all the geometry, thus making a smooth cloth. When you've finished, save the object and send it to Layout. You can send it to Layout by using the command in the top-right corner of the Modeler interface (click that small triangle to access the Send to Layout command). You can also just load it in Layout as you did with the fruit.

17. In Layout, position the set underneath the bowl of fruit. If you need to size the set, be sure to make sure Auto Key is enabled so that your changes are captured.

18. Be sure to check your cloth set position not only from the Perspective view but from a Right or Left view as well. **Figure 8.70** shows the setup from the Perspective view.

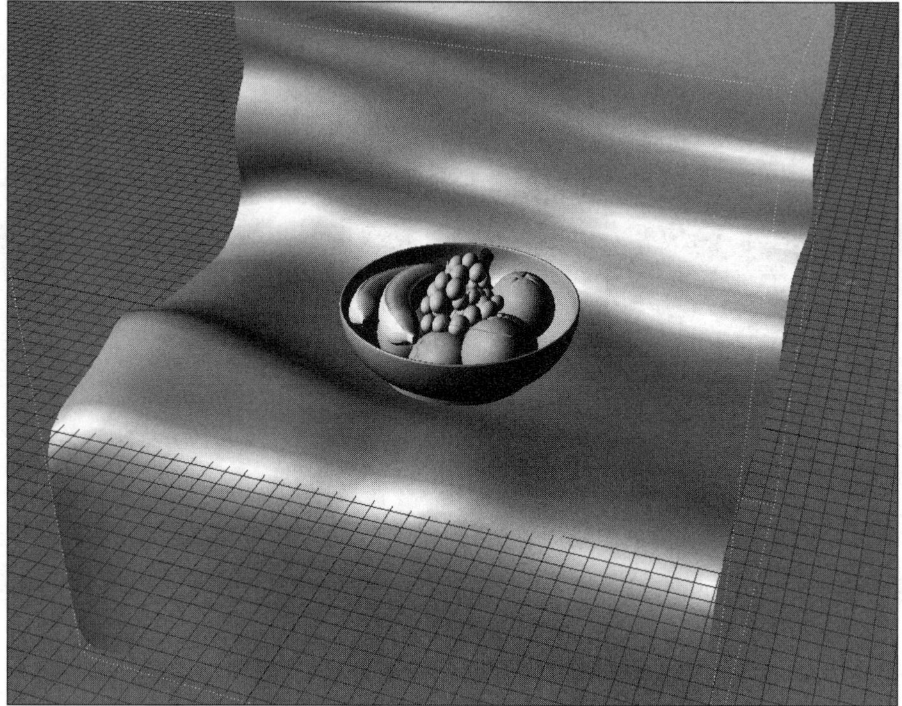

Figure 8.70 The modeled cloth is positioned and sized to fit under the bowl of fruit, in Layout.

19. Save your scene.

There you have it! Still life! Well, it's not complete yet. LightWave offers you control to model just about anything you want. There are many ways to build objects, and this chapter gave you a very good overview of the toolset and how it can be used to create smooth organic shapes. You can take the exercises here even further by modeling more fruit, such as a pear or an apple. How about taking the lesson of the bowl, and creating a wine bottle to add to the scene?

The Next Step

What's really going to make this shot stand out is the texturing, lighting, and rendering. You'll be doing all of this soon, but before you move on to these key Layout features, stay in modeling mode and learn how to create more detailed objects in the next chapter.

Chapter 9

Gadget Modeling

If you're like most modern computer users, you love gadgets. OK, maybe you're not a gadget lover, and keeping up with technology simply drives you bananas! Yes, that's two chapters now in which have mentioned bananas. But this chapter is not about bananas—or any other kind of fruit. It's about gadgets—gadgets that make your life simpler or even more complicated. And while you don't necessarily need to fall into a debate about the pros and cons of gadgets and the society in which you live, you should know how to model them in 3D. Why is this, you ask? Good question! Gadget modeling is about modeling everyday objects. It's about noticing details and creating realistic-looking models that can be used for television commercials, props in other 3D scenes, or even for resale on Web sites such as TurboSquid.com. In this chapter, you'll learn about

- LightWave v9 modeling for hard surfaces
- Creating small details for added realism
- Working with edges
- Creating models with curves
- Preparation for rendering

Types of Gadgets

Visit Wikipedia.org, and you'll find *gadget* defined as a specific and useful device for a practical purpose or function. And even if you'd pick a few choice words other than "useful" and "practical" to describe them, there are gadgets in your life—whether it's one of those newfangled cell phones or the latest Bluetooth earpiece; a vintage Atari game system or a PlayStation 3, or maybe just a calculator, a TV remote control, or an everyday telephone? Even if you miraculously lack any of these gizmos, you're using a computer to create LightWave models and animations, so a keyboard and mouse are close at hand. For purposes of this chapter, all these items can be considered gadgets, and the lessons you'll learn in this chapter can be used to model any one of them in LightWave v9. The benefits of this chapter are that you'll learn common modeling characteristics, such as uniformity, smooth surfaces, edge control, buttons, and geometric shapes.

Studying the Details

Before you attempt to model anything in LightWave v9, it's helpful to study a real-world version of the object. There are times when you'll model something completely original that has no reference (the flagship of an alien fleet) or when only photo references will do (the Chrysler Building). But this isn't one of those times, so seize the opportunity to study your subject up close. **Figure 9.1** shows the black Apple iPod you'll model in this chapter.

Figure 9.1 The practical and useful gadget you'll model in this chapter.

Take a close look at the photo. Really look at it. How does the light fall upon its surface? Are the markings inset or beveled? It's these details that will make your model come to life. (That goes for any model, not just this one.) The lessons you'll learn in this chapter will help you identify and create those details.

Exercise 9.1 Building an iPod, Part I

There are a couple of ways you can approach this model, and determining which is best really depends on you. You can begin with just a box, then bevel the edges to round them out. Or you can use a background image and build over it. For this project, we'll choose the latter approach because we want to be very accurate. The elements of an iPod are fairly easy to model, and it'd be easy to freehand something recognizable as an iPod, but for it to be truly convincing, our model's proportions have to be just right. Make an edge even a bit too large, or the video screen a hair too small, and the realism is lost.

1. Start up LightWave v9 Modeler and, from the Create tab, select the Disc tool.
2. Press **n** on your keyboard to open the Numeric panel, or just click the Numeric button at the bottom of the interface.

Note

You can keep the Numeric panel open all the time while you work in Modeler. As you change tools, the panel will update accordingly.

3. Press **d** to open Modeler's Display Options panel and then click its Backdrop tab.
4. In the Viewport drop-down, select BottL for the bottom-left view. For the image, choose the iPod_Face.jpg from the Chapter 9 folder of the book's DVD (in the "\Projects\Images\CH9\" directory).
5. Set the Image Resolution to 1024×1024. You can leave all other settings alone. Click OK to close the panel.
6. You should see an image of an iPod's front panel in your bottom-left viewport, as shown in **Figure 9.2**.

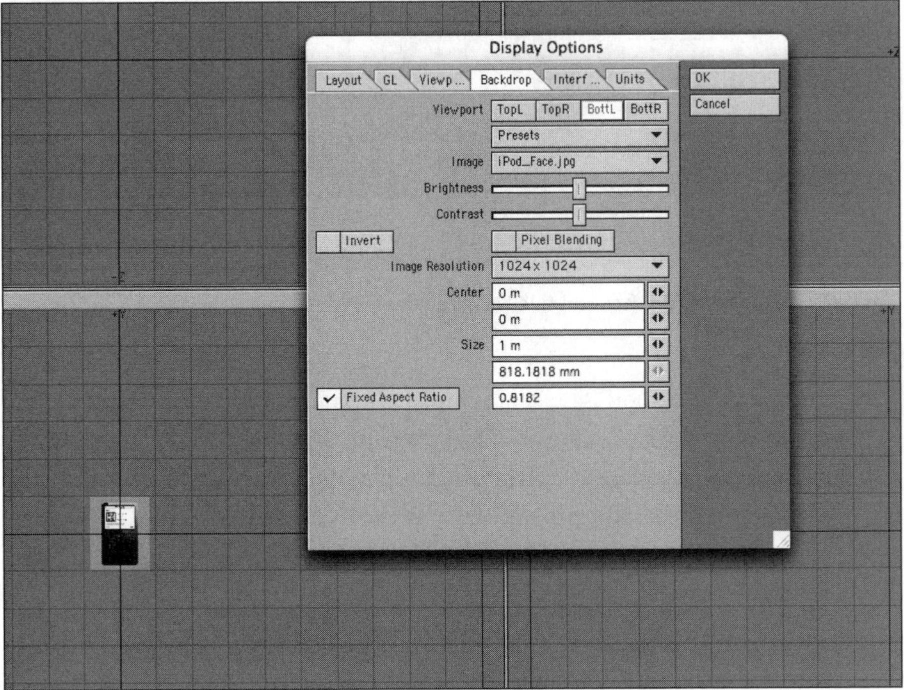

Figure 9.2 To begin the project, load an image of an iPod in your bottom-left view.

7. Click, hold, and drag the zoom control in the top-right corner of the bottom Back viewport to enlarge the backdrop image.

   You can see that the image resolution is somewhat low, but for a gadget like this, that's not too important. This is because you only need this backdrop image for an initial shape. If you were modeling a more complex object, such as a cell phone or remote control, you might want to use a higher resolution image.

8. Head on back to the Display Options panel (press **d**) and click its Backdrop tab again.

9. Click BottR for the bottom-right view. For the image, select iPod_Side.jpg from the book's DVD (in the "\Projects\Images\CH9\" directory). Set the Image Resolution again to 1024×1024, and then click OK to close the panel. **Figure 9.3** shows Modeler with the two backdrop images loaded.

   The backdrop images line up on the Y-axis, and they align perfectly because they were created at the same scale and resolution in Adobe Photoshop. That's always the best approach with reference images, but if you ever need to align differently scaled backdrop images, you can adjust their sizes in the Display Options panel.

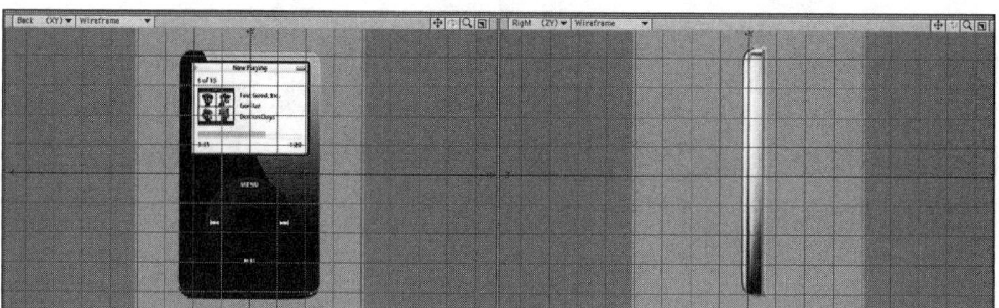

Figure 9.3 You now have face and side backdrop images as references in your Modeler viewports.

10. Now, the Side viewport is looking at the left side of the iPod. If you consider the orientation of the face of the iPod, and where the 3D camera will be in Layout, you'll see that the image is facing toward the positive Z-axis in the Right view. The iPod front-panel backdrop in the Back viewport is facing the negative Z-axis, so, you need to make an adjustment. Change the Right view to a Left view, and your reference image will flip over (**Figure 9.4**).

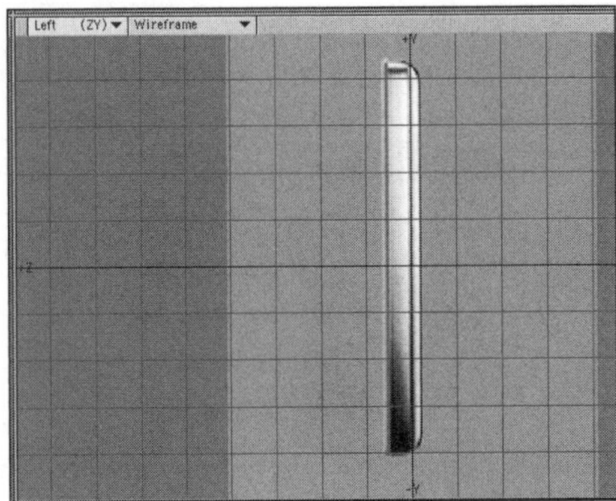

Figure 9.4 Changing the bottom-right viewport Right to Left view correctly orients the backdrop image.

11. If you want, you can save the backdrops for use later. To do so, in the Display Options panel's Backdrop tab, choose Save All Presets from the Presets drop-down.
12. To begin creating the base model, click the Create tab and select the Disc tool.

    You'll use the Disc tool, which creates perfect circles, to make the iPod's rounded corners—by making a circle of the right size and trimming away the portion that falls inside the straight sides of the iPod case, you'll form a box with rounded corners.
13. Place your mouse over the top-left corner of the backdrop image, and press **g** to center the view on your cursor position. This is a quick way to move about a viewport. From there, press the period key two or three times to zoom into the view (**Figure 9.5**).

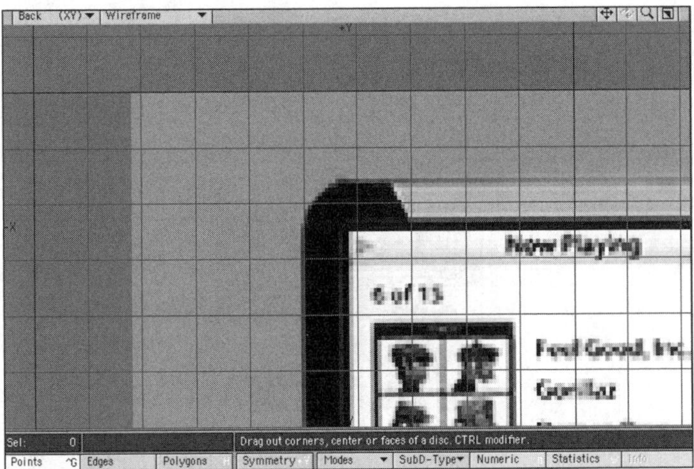

Figure 9.5 Zoom in close to the top-left corner of the backdrop image.

14. With the Disc tool selected, hold the Ctrl key to constrain the axis, and draw out a disc with a radius that matches the corner arc, as in **Figure 9.6**.

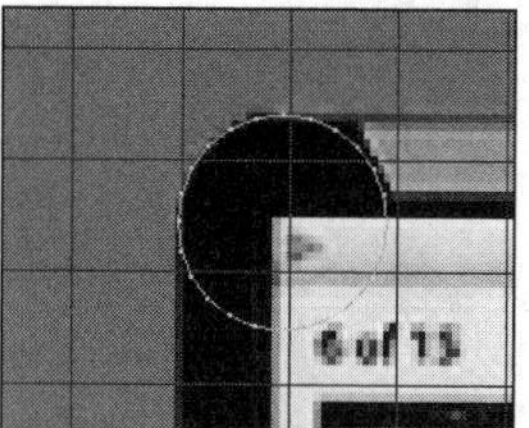

Figure 9.6 Create a disc that matches the curvature of the rounded corner of the iPod reference image.

Note

To position the disc against the reference image as you build it, keep the Ctrl key pressed and click and drag directly in the center of the disc object. Then, still holding the Ctrl key, you can size the disc by dragging any of its corner control points. If you have trouble getting the position precise, turn off the Snap feature in Modeler: Press **d** to open the Display Options panel and then set Grid Snap to none in its Units tab and click OK to close the panel.

15. If you find that the backdrop image is too bright and makes it hard to see your disc object, press **d** to open Display Options. Select BottL viewport in its Backdrop tab, and then reduce the Brightness and Contrast values to help see your geometry better. Click OK to close the panel when finished. You can do the same for the Left view.

16. In the Back view, zoom out to see more of the background image. Then, with your disc positioned over the left corner of the iPod reference image, press **k** to "kill" the polygons. Removing the polygons leaves behind just points, as shown in **Figure 9.7**.

Figure 9.7 Pressing **k** removes polygons. It "kills" them, leaving just the points (vertices).

17. Press Shift+v to activate the Mirror tool. If the Numeric panel isn't still open, press **n** to access it, and note the Mirror tool's settings. By default, it creates mirror-image duplicates of selected geometry, "reflected" across the X-axis. Since your image has left-right symmetry and it's perfectly centered, the default mirror settings need no further adjustment; the ring of points you created on the top-left corner of the iPod image has been duplicated and reflected perfectly on the top-right corner (**Figure 9.8**).

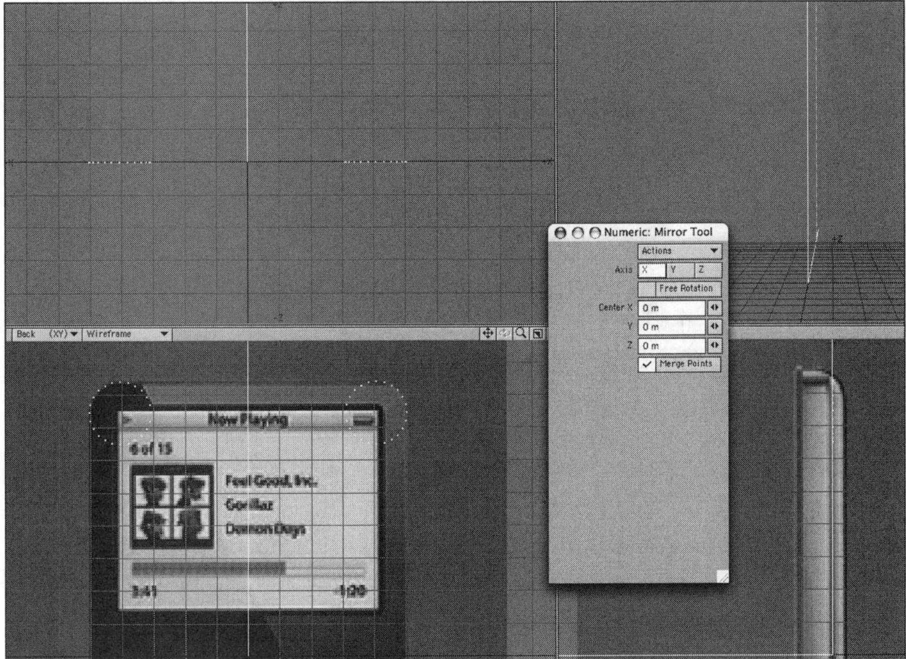

Figure 9.8 The default mirror settings make it easy to copy the points from the left side of the view to the right.

18. Close the Numeric panel, and then press the spacebar to turn off the Mirror tool.

19. Now to edit the points a bit before you move further. Make sure you're in Points selection mode at the bottom of the interface. Then, select the points of each disc that make up just the inside of the iPod. If your disc were a clockface, these would

be the along the edge from 3 through 12 for the disc on the right, and from 12 to 9 for the disc on the left, as shown in **Figure 9.9**.

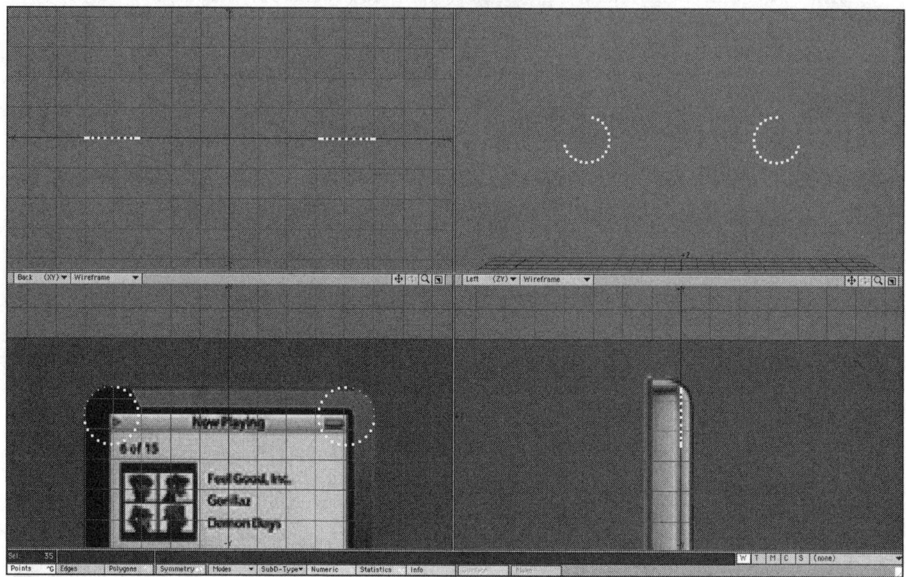

Figure 9.9 Select the points not associated with an outside edge of the iPod reference image, then delete.

20. With the points selected as shown in Figure 9.6, delete them. Yes, you could have done this before you did your initial mirror operation, but by keeping the full ring of discs while you mirrored, you are able to see the mirrored copy a bit better, should there have been a need for alignment.

    You've just used a *primitive object*, the disc, to lay down points. Rather than trying to arrange individual points evenly, it's often easier to take them from a primitive object. This technique originated with Ron Thorton, a LightWave pioneer and a friend of the *Inside LightWave* series.

21. Save your work as this point, just in case.
22. Now, zoom out your view just a bit more to see the entire backdrop image. Then, select the Mirror tool again. You can get the tool from the Multiply tab, or press Shift+v.
23. Press **n** to open the Numeric panel (if it isn't open already) and change the Axis setting to Y. The two sets of points will be mirrored to the bottom of the iPod image. Again, because the image was perfectly centered at the origin, mirroring the points is a snap! **Figure 9.10** shows the result.

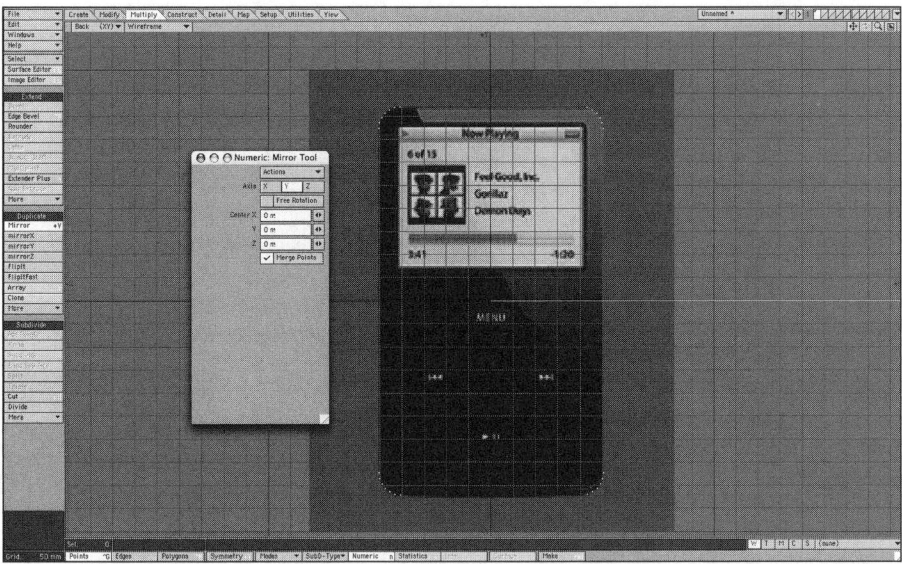

Figure 9.10 The top-bottom symmetry of the iPod shape, and the fact that the model is centered at the origin, makes mirroring across the Y-axis a perfect modeling technique.

24. Close the Numeric panel and press the spacebar to turn off the Mirror tool. Or just click the Mirror tool to turn it off.

25. Make sure you're still in Points selection mode and, starting in the top-left corner and working your way clockwise around the outline of the reference image, Shift-click each point in the model, in order. It's very important to select the points sequentially; you're going to play "connect-the-dots" to create a polygon, and polygon segments will be drawn between each selected point in succession.

    If you accidentally select a point out of sequence, release the mouse button and Shift key, and then click the point again to deselect it. Now you can go back to Shift-clicking the points in order. **Figure 9.11** shows the model with all points selected.

Figure 9.11 Select all of the points, in order.

26. With all of the points selected, press **p**. You've just created a polygon (**Figure 9.12**).

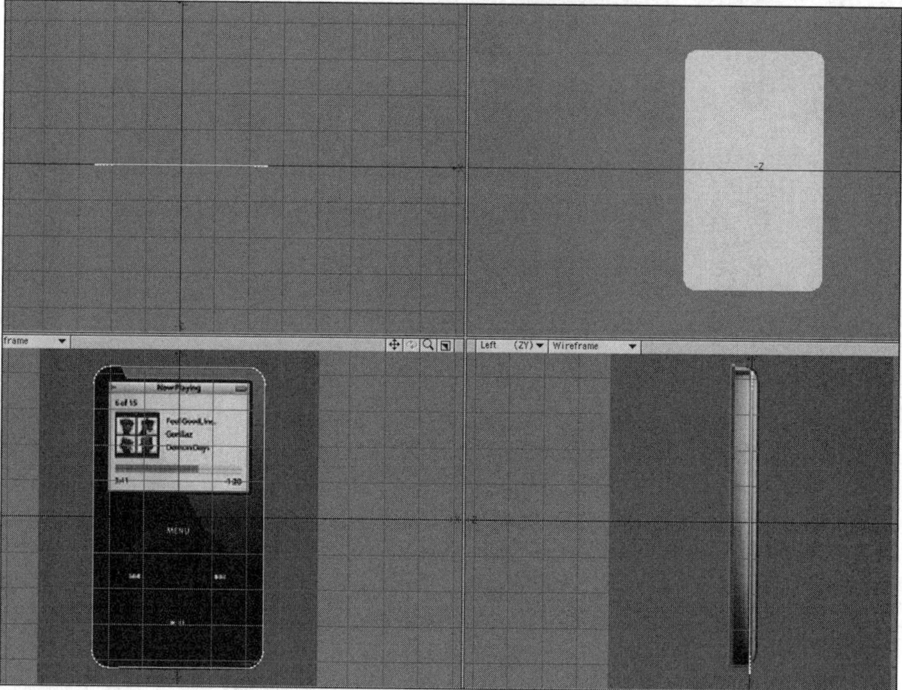

Figure 9.12 After you select all of the points, in order, press **p** to create a polygon.

27. Save your work. It's not a bad idea to create an incremental save by pressing Shift+s.

    Now that you have a base polygon to work with, you can start creating the rest of the iPod quite easily. First, you need to align this polygon before any other adjustments are made.

28. If you take a look at **Figure 9.13**, you'll see that the flat polygon is not lined up with the actual face of the model, based on the background images. Sure, the Back view lines up, but for the Left view, you need to make an adjustment.

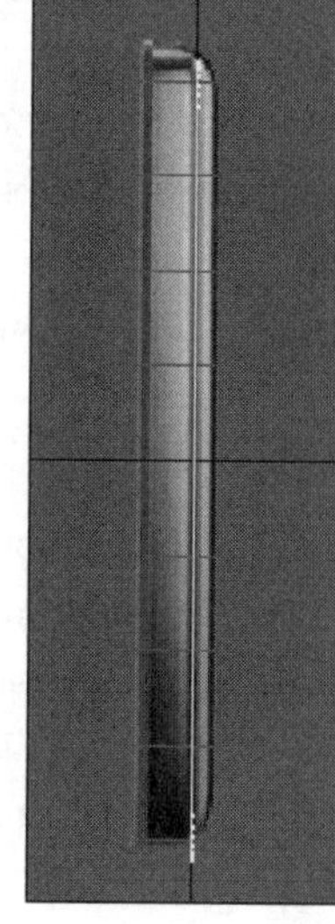

Figure 9.13 By creating the polygon over the face of the object in the Back view, it's perfectly lined up. But, the side, or Left view, is a bit off.

29. Press **t** to select the Move tool. Making sure nothing is selected so that you move the entire object, click and drag in the Left view, and line up the polygon to the face of the iPod, based on the background image. **Figure 9.14** shows the example.

30. Save your work.

    It might seem that the process up to this point was a bit tedious, but it's really not. This process of using a backdrop image and creating a base shape can be applied to all kinds of models, from gadgets, to furniture, to characters. From this point, you'll begin creating depth, and then you'll add in the details.

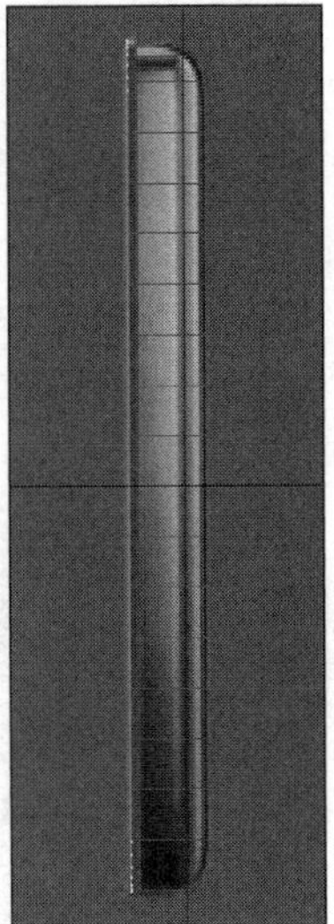

Figure 9.14
Use the Move tool to reposition the polygon so it lines up with the face of the object.

Adding Depth

OK, on to part II of this project. This exercise will show you how to create depth in your model and keep the front edge of the iPod squared-off and sharp, while the back edge is smooth and more round.

Exercise 9.2 Building an iPod, Part II

1. Enter Polygons selection mode, either by pressing the spacebar until you rotate into that mode or by clicking the Polygons button at the bottom of the interface.

2. Click the single polygon you've created to select it, and then press **f** to flip the polygon so its back surface is facing you.

   You're going to bevel toward the back of the model, adding new polygons to the existing one as you go; the new polygons' surfaces will face the same way as the one you're beveling. If you started beveling with the polygon facing you, the iPod surface would be facing inward, and your iPod would effectively be inside-out.

3. Press **b** to activate the Bevel tool, and then click and drag in the Left view to bevel the selected polygon to create the back of the model. Bevel the selected polygon back about 10mm, as shown in **Figure 9.15** (on the following page).

   When you bevel, it may feel tricky. But remember, move the mouse up and down first to set the Shift value, then left and right to set the Inset value. Concentrate on these two moves and you'll have an easier time beveling. It might take you a few tries to get this right, so don't worry. Just Ctrl+z to undo and try it again.

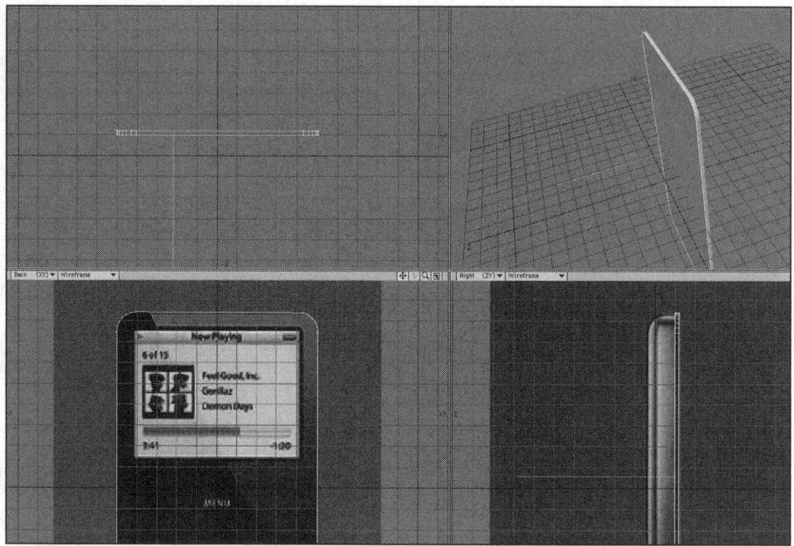

Figure 9.15 Bevel the flat polygon just with a Shift value to begin.

4. Right-click once to reset the bevel. You won't see anything happen, but what you've done is effectively turn the bevel off, then on again. This tells the Bevel tool to use the new polygon created in the last bevel operation as the starting point for a new bevel. Click and drag to inset a bevel that matches the backdrop image, as shown in **Figure 9.16**.

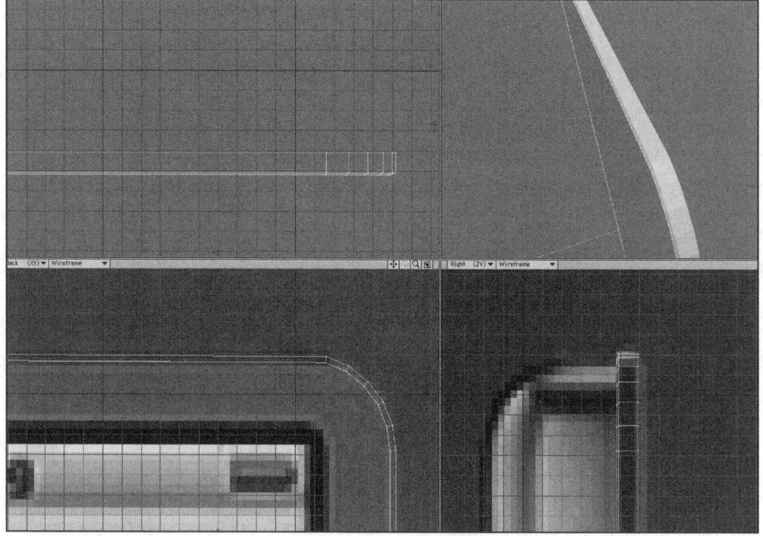

Figure 9.16 Bevel again to inset the selected polygon.

5. Right-click to reset the Bevel tool again, and then click and drag to adjust the Shift value and bevel further toward the back of the model, as shown in **Figure 9.17**.

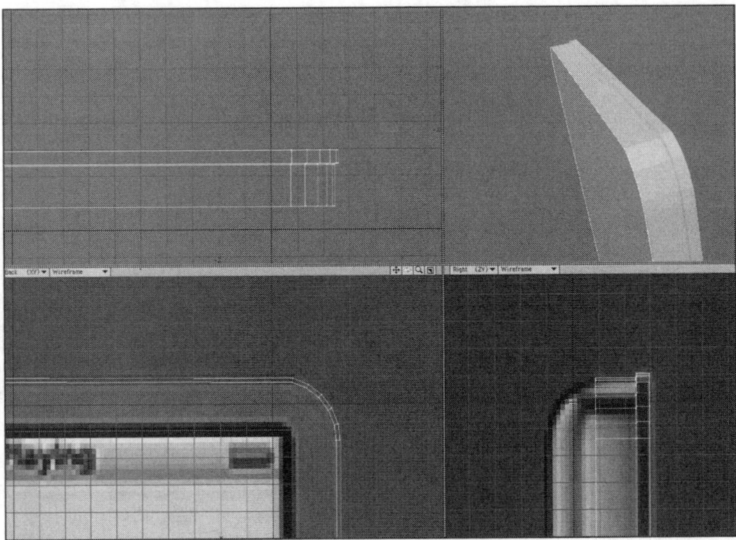

Figure 9.17 Bevel again, shifting the selection out toward the back of the model.

6. Now for a few more precise bevels. Right-click to reset the bevel, then shift and inset together, about 4mm or so, as shown in **Figure 9.18**.

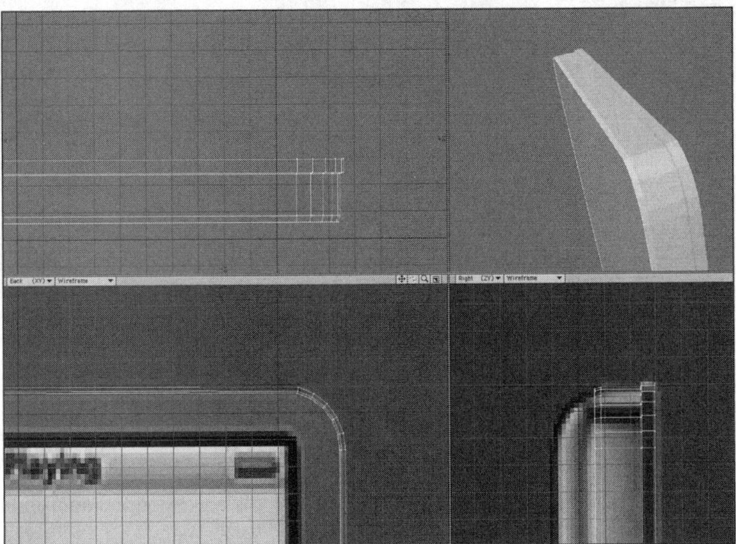

Figure 9.18 Bevel again, shifting and insetting, about 4mm or so to follow the slope of the back of the iPod image in the backdrop.

Note

If you find that you're having trouble beveling in small amounts, press **d** to open the Display Options panel, and then set Grid Snap to none in its Units tab.

7. Now bevel five more times, repeating the previous operations: Right-click to reset, then click and drag to inset and shift. Follow the outline of the backdrop image and bevel each new polygon to follow the iPod curvature (**Figure 9.19**).

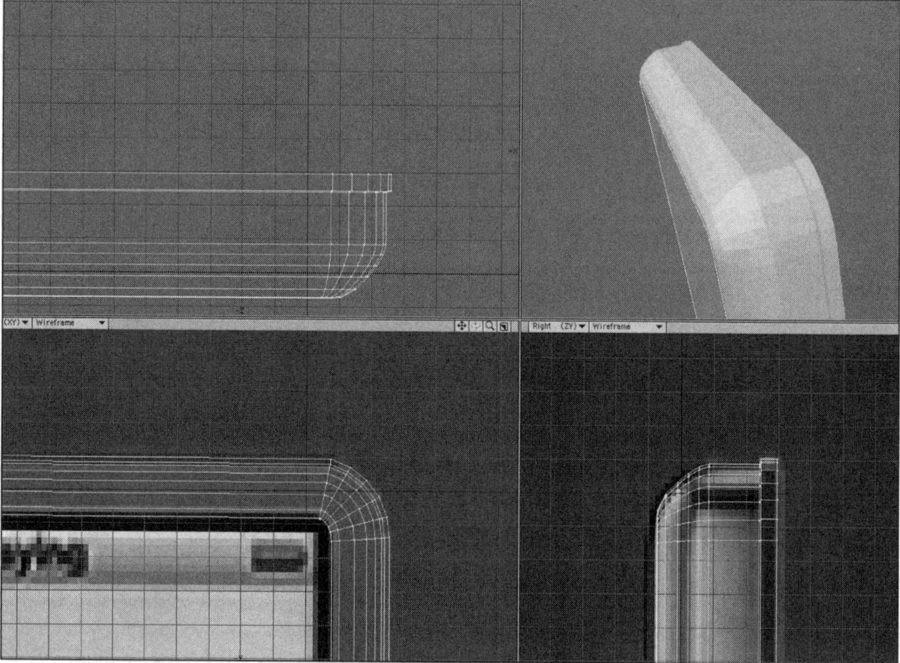

Figure 9.19 Bevel five more times to follow the contour of the backdrop image.

8. When your beveling is done, press the spacebar to turn off the Bevel tool, then press / (slash) to deselect all polygons. Save your model!
9. If you rotate the Perspective view to see the model, you'll see its face is flipped (**Figure 9.20**).

   Remember that earlier, you flipped this first initial polygon. You did this so the new beveled polygons would face outward. That worked well, but now there's no polygon for the front of the object! No worries; this is easy to fix, and you'll see how to create more detail.

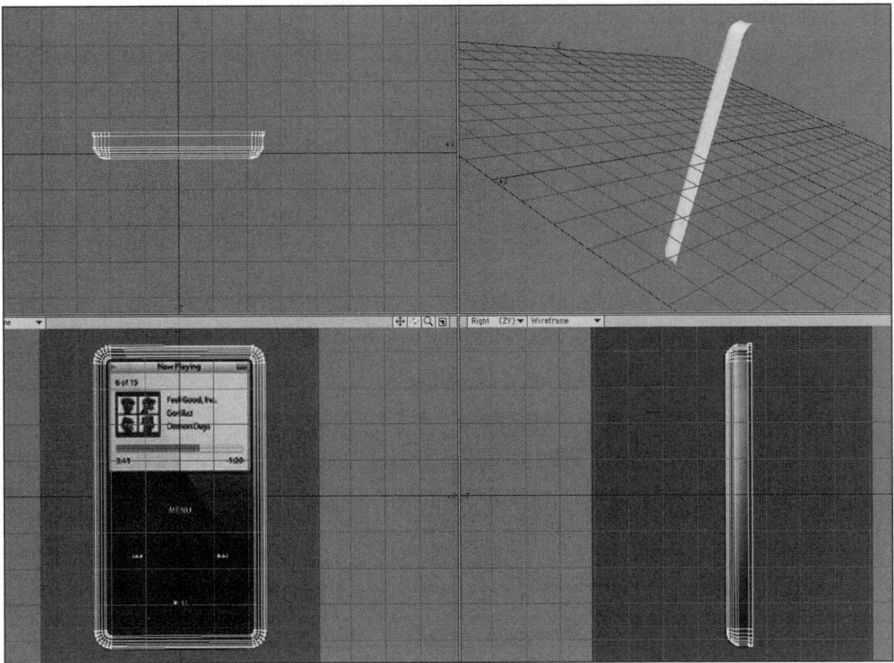

Figure 9.20 Take a look at the face of the object and you might notice the polygon is flipped.

10. Switch to Edges selection mode at the bottom of the LightWave v9 interface. Carefully select one edge of iPod object's front-panel polygon. You can make the selection in the Perspective view; changing the view style to Wireframe Shade may make things easier to see. Confirm that only one edge is selected by viewing the *Sel* info in the bottom-left corner of the interface. **Figure 9.21** shows the selection.

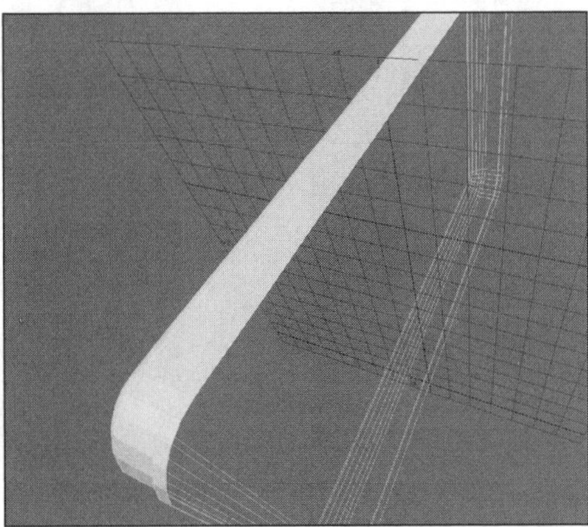

Figure 9.21 Select just the one edge of the area that makes up the face of the object.

11. Once the edge is selected, go to the Select drop-down at the top left of the interface and choose Select Loop. The entire edge around the face will become selected (**Figure 9.22**).

12. With the entire edge loop selected, switch to the Multiply tab, and then click the Extender Plus button (**Figure 9.23**).

    When you click the Extender Plus button, nothing obvious happens. That's normal; don't click the button again in exasperation. The Extender Plus tool will generate a new edge from the selection. But it won't move it or give you any sort of indication that it has done so.

13. Set the Action Center to Selection in the Modes drop-down at the bottom of the interface.

14. Press Shift+h to activate the Size tool, and then click and drag in the Perspective viewport to scale down the selection. You'll see a duplicate of the iPod-face object, with its surface facing inward (**Figure 9.24**).

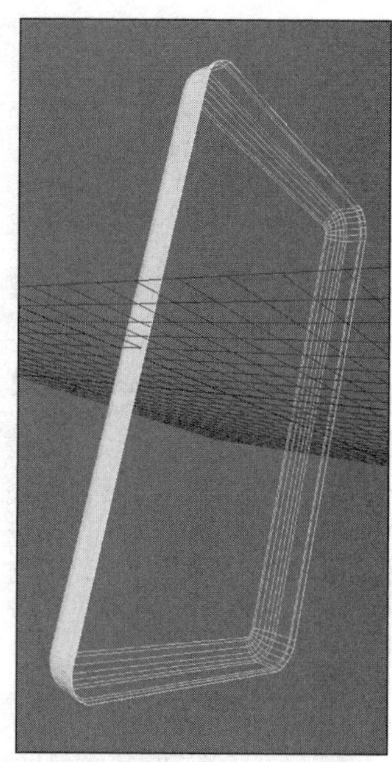

Figure 9.22 The entire edge of the iPod object's face area, selected via the Select Loop feature.

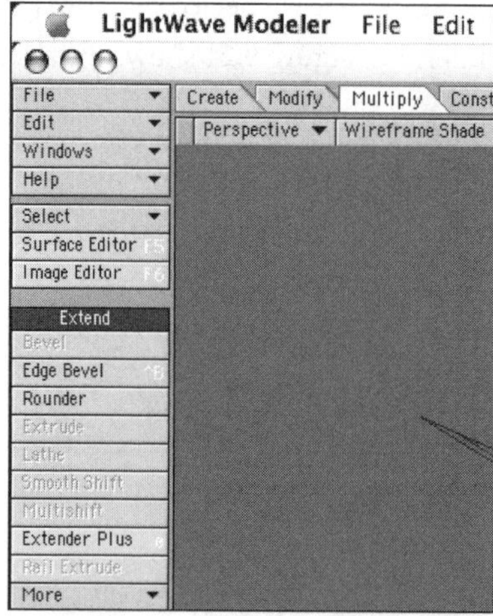

Figure 9.23 The Extender Plus tool generates new edges from a selection.

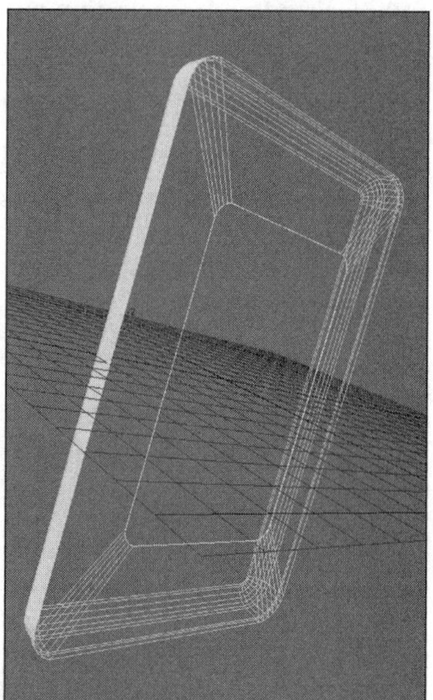

Figure 9.24 After you create a duplicate edge with the Extender Plus command, scale down the new geometry with the Size tool.

15. Without changing the selection, switch to Polygons selection mode at the bottom of the interface.
16. In the Perspective view, drag your mouse over the newly created polygons to select them. There should be about 26 polygons (**Figure 9.25**).

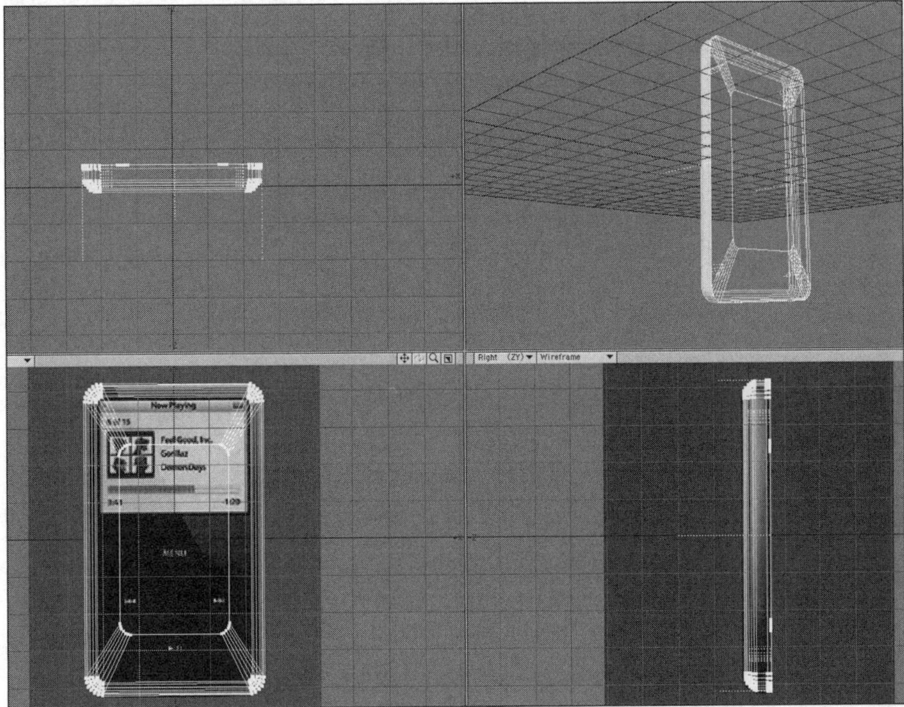

Figure 9.25 Select the newly created polygons from within the Perspective view.

17. Press **f** to flip the polygons.
18. Once they're flipped, press **/** (slash) to deselect the polygons, and then, switch back to Edges in the Selection Mode drop-down.

    Note that your edge loop is still selected: LightWave lets you keep separate selections at the same time—one in each of the Points, Edges, and Polygons selection modes. If you leave geometry selected in one selection mode (Edges, in this case) when you switch to another (such as Polygons), the first selection is "remembered" when you revert back to its mode.

Note

LightWave's ability to store multiple selections comes in handy for working on different bits of geometry at the same time, but unless you need to "remember" selections between modes, it's a good idea to get in the habit of deselecting geometry before switching selection modes. Here's why: If you make a selection in one mode and then switch into a mode *that has no prior selection to "remember,"* your initial selection will be retained in the new selection mode. The vertices of a selection made in Polygons mode are selected as points when you switch to Points selection mode, for example—but only if there were no points previously selected in that mode.

19. The edge loop you created and scaled down will become the LCD screen of the iPod. Ah-ha! Tricky! You first want to continue sizing down the edge, to something like **Figure 9.26**. The reason for this is to tighten the corners of the selection. Once the corners are sharpened this way, we can scale back up to the actual size of the LCD display.

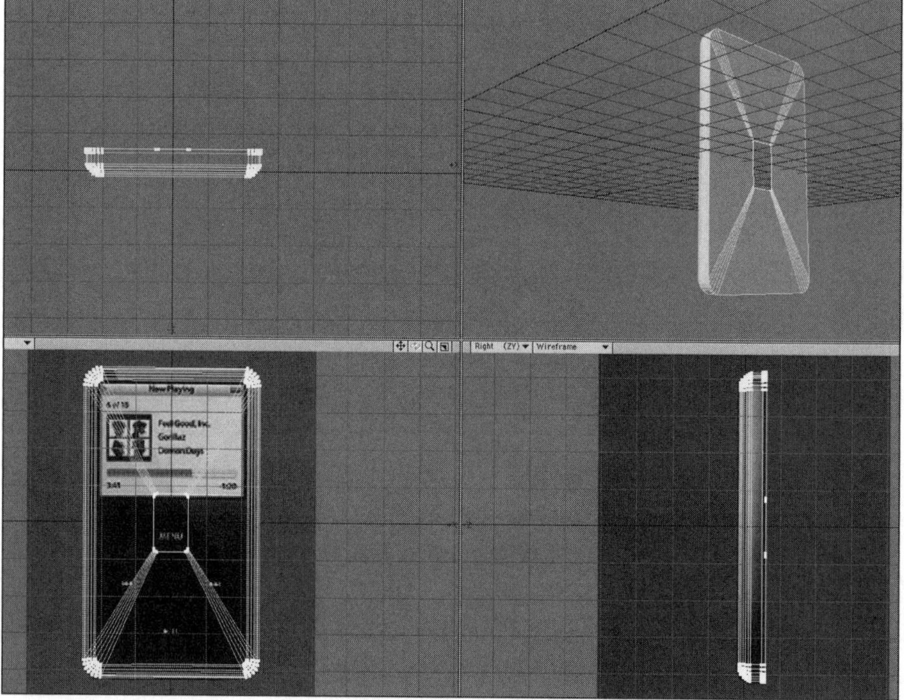

Figure 9.26 Scale down the selected edge toward the center of the iPod model.

20. Press **t** to activate the Move tool, and then reposition the selection, using the Back view. Use the Backdrop image as a guide, and line up the top-left corner of the selection with the top-left corner of the LCD screen in the backdrop image (**Figure 9.27**).

21. Press Shift+a to fit the selected edge to view. Switch to Points selection mode, and then right-click and drag to lasso the points that make up the right side of the edge loop, as shown in **Figure 9.28**. Note that if the edge points are already selected (or you grab any extras), you can click or lasso selected points to deselect them.

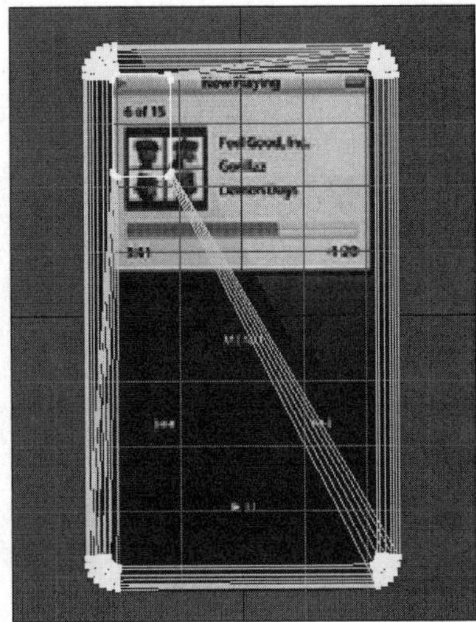

Figure 9.27 Move the selected edge loop up to the top-left corner of the model, based on the background image.

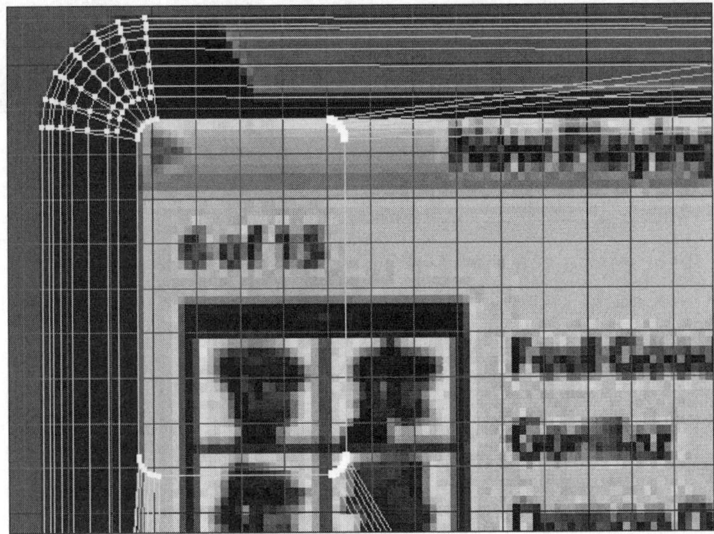

Figure 9.28 Select the points that make up the right side of the edge loop.

22. With the points on the right side selected, press **t** to activate the Move tool and then drag the points over to the top side of the backdrop image's LCD panel. You can hold the Ctrl key to constrain your movement to keep the top edge straight.

23. Press / to deselect all points, and then lasso just the points along the bottom of the edge loop. Using the Move tool with the Ctrl key pressed, drag the selection down to align it with the bottom of the backdrop image's LCD panel (**Figure 9.29**).

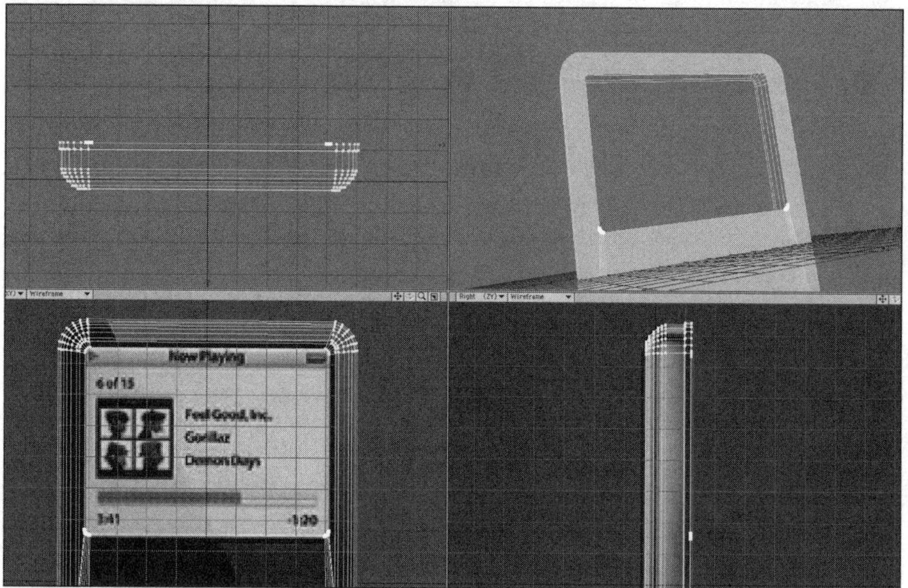

Figure 9.29 Move the bottom edge points down to finish shaping the LCD panel.

24. Save your model.

    You might wonder how this iPod will ever play video at this point—it's hollow! That's OK because you won't be seeing the inside. But you will need to fill the hole to create the LCD display.

25. Jump back to Edges selection mode, and as long as you didn't deselect it, the edge loop will be still be selected. Click Extender Plus (in the Multiply tab), as you did earlier. This will extend the selected edge.

26. Press **t** to access the Move tool, and in the Top or Left view window, drag the selected edge about 10mm toward the back of the iPod model. You're creating a recess in the front panel (**Figure 9.30**).

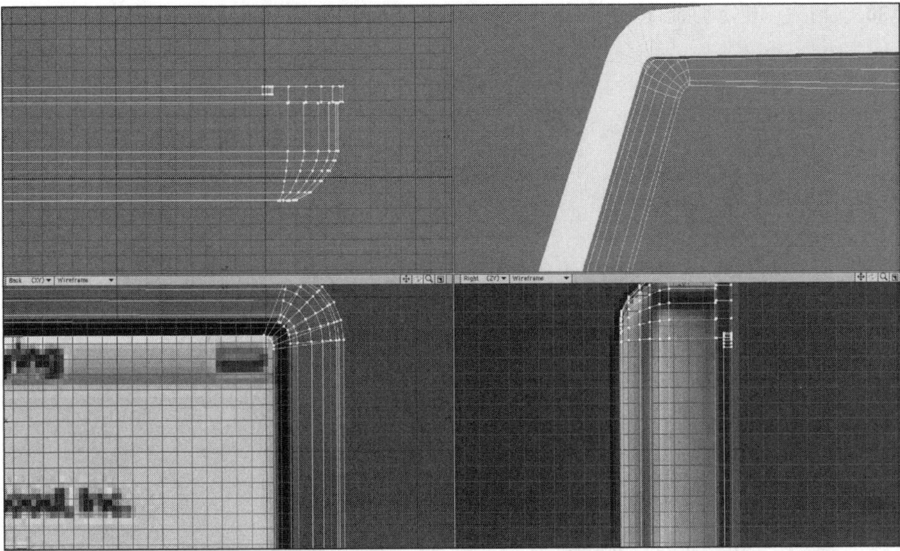

Figure 9.30 Once the edge is multiplied, drag it "inside" the iPod object.

27. Now, switch to Points selection mode, and the corners of the selected edge will be selected. With these points selected, press Ctrl+c to copy them. Go to a new layer and press Ctrl+v to paste.
28. Press **d** to open the Display Options panel, and from the Backdrop tab, remove the backdrop reference images. This will help you see the points better in the viewports.
29. Close the Display Options panel, and in the Back view, select the points in order, from right to left. The reason for this is that the polygon will face forward once created. If you can't see the points, press **a. Figure 9.31** shows the selected points.

Figure 9.31 Select the points from right to left, in order.

30. Once you've selected the points, press **p** to create a polygon. **Figure 9.32** shows the result.

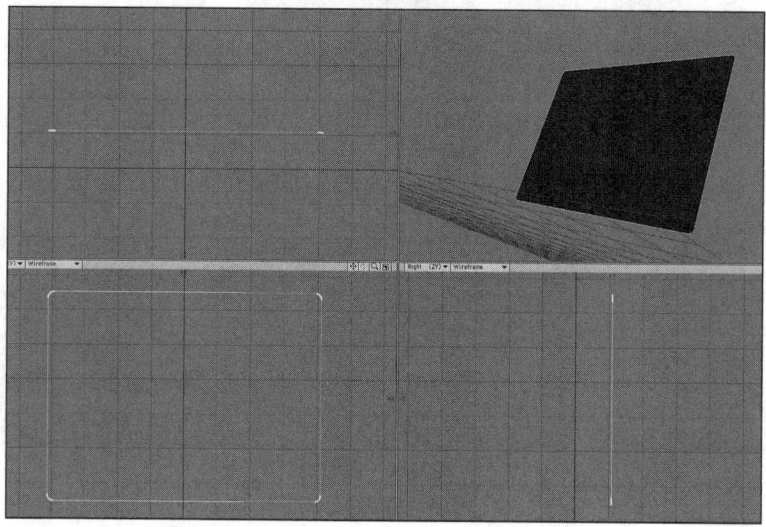

Figure 9.32 Once the points are selected, press **p** to create a polygon.

31. Switch to Polygons selection mode at the bottom of the interface, and press Ctrl+x to cut the newly created polygon.
32. Go back to the first layer with your iPod object, and press Ctrl+v to paste the polygon. **Figure 9.33** shows the polygon in place.

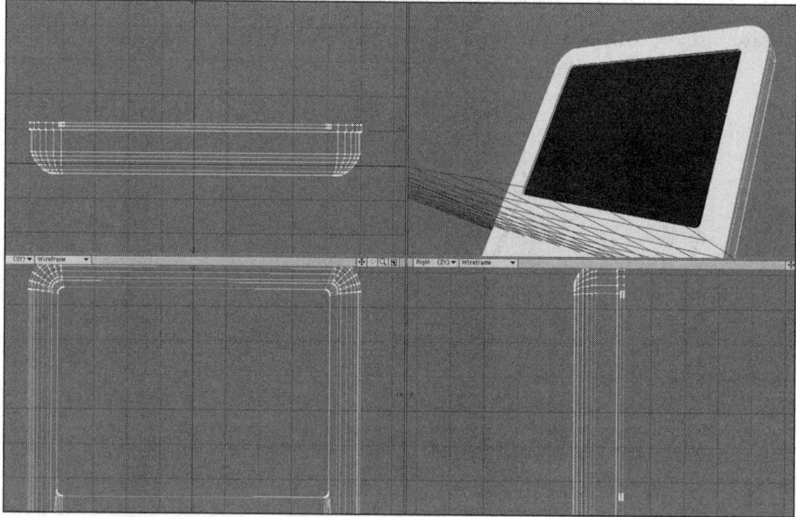

Figure 9.33 The pasted polygon will serve as the iPod model's display screen.

Because you cut and pasted the polygon, it's not actually attached to the large model—it's just sitting in place. Sometimes that's good; sometimes that's bad. In this case, you want to make sure the new polygon is attached.

Modeler's Merge tool is perfect for this job because it's used to fuse multiple points with the same coordinates into single points. When you copied the points, used them to create a polygon, and then pasted that polygon back to the original object, you made the duplicate points occupy the exact same space as the originals. The Merge tool will combine the duplicate sets of points into one.

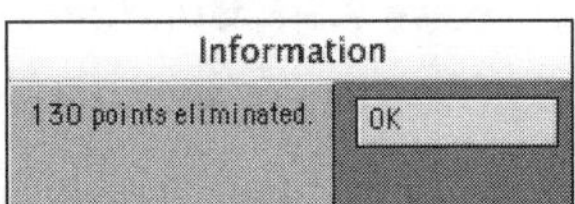

Figure 9.34 Using the Merge command, you can quickly remove the extra points that are keeping the newly created polygon as a separate object.

33. Press **m** for Merge. In the dialog box that appears (**Figure 9.34**), leave the Range set to Automatic and click OK. This fuses each pair of identically positioned points into one and "seals up" the iPod model (**Figure 9.35**).

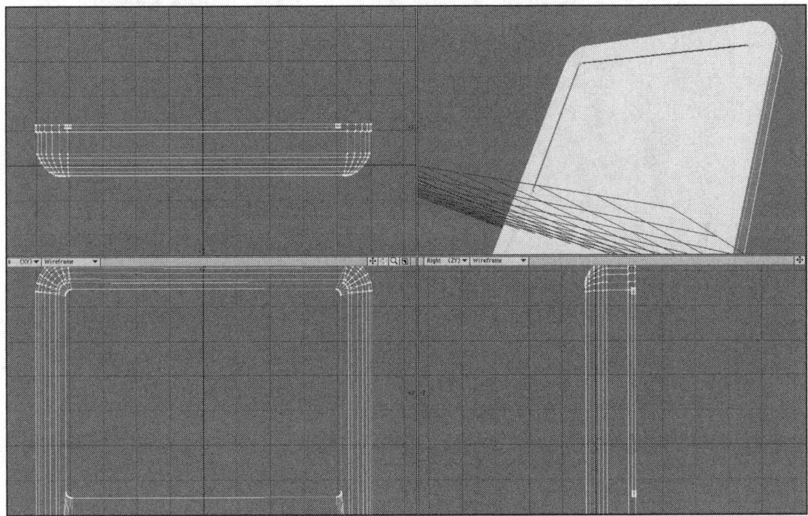

Figure 9.35 After the merge, the base iPod is ready for final details.

34. Save your model. It's not a bad idea at this point to save an incremental version by pressing Shift+s.

What you've done so far might have been a bit tedious, but the results are worth it. The model is simple and clean and will render quick and look good. But what will make the model look even better are the smaller details in the edges. Read on to create additional details.

Details, Details

Too often, people getting into 3D think that you need a ton of polygons to build a great-looking model. This is not often the case, and in fact, less is usually more. This next project will help you build the details by beveling and then creating a copy of the LCD panel to serve as its protective glass covering.

Exercise 9.3 Building an iPod, Part III

1. Working with the model you've built this far, make sure you're in Edges selection mode, then click on the outer edge of the LCD panel.
2. From the Select drop-down at the top left of the Modeler interface, choose Select Loop to select the entire edge loop, as shown in **Figure 9.36**.

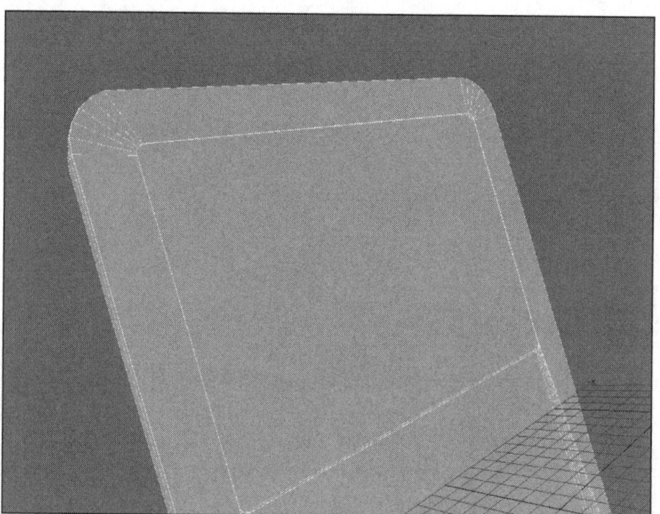

Figure 9.36 Select the outer edge loop of the LCD panel.

3. With the edge selected, press Ctrl+b to activate the Edge Bevel tool. You can also press **n**) to open the Numeric panel, which allows you to see your tool settings. Bevel the edge about 1mm or so, as shown in **Figure 9.37**.

Figure 9.37 Perform an Edge Bevel on the LCD panel.

4. Press the spacebar to turn off the Edge Bevel tool, and then press / to deselect the edge.
5. Next, click an inside edge of the LCD panel object and again choose Select Loop from the Select drop-down menu. **Figure 9.38** shows the selection.

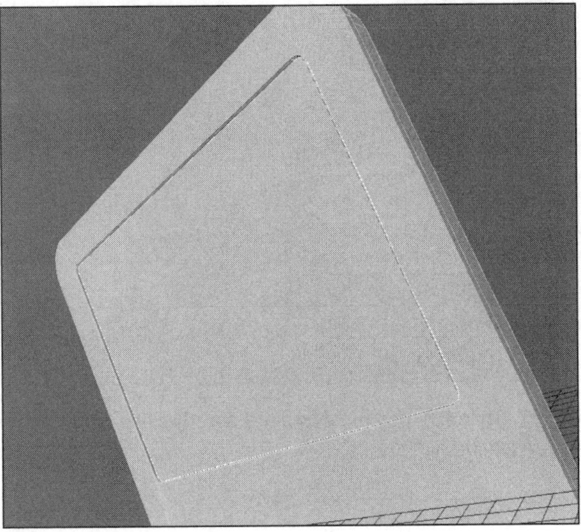

Figure 9.38 Select the inside edge loop for the LCD panel.

Note

Occasionally, the nature of connections between polygons prevents Select Loop from selecting an entire edge loop; if this happens, just Shift-click the omitted segments to select them manually.

6. We could use Edge Bevel again here, but let's try another tool that will also do the job. On the Multiply tab, click Rounder (in the Extend tool category). Press **n** to open the Numeric panel.
7. In the Numeric panel, choose Edges for Round Only. Leave the Rounding Polygons selection set to 1. This value allows you to add multiple polygons when the tool is applied. Finally, from the Preset Insets, choose the top value, 0.001000, which equals a 1mm inset. **Figure 9.39** shows the operation.

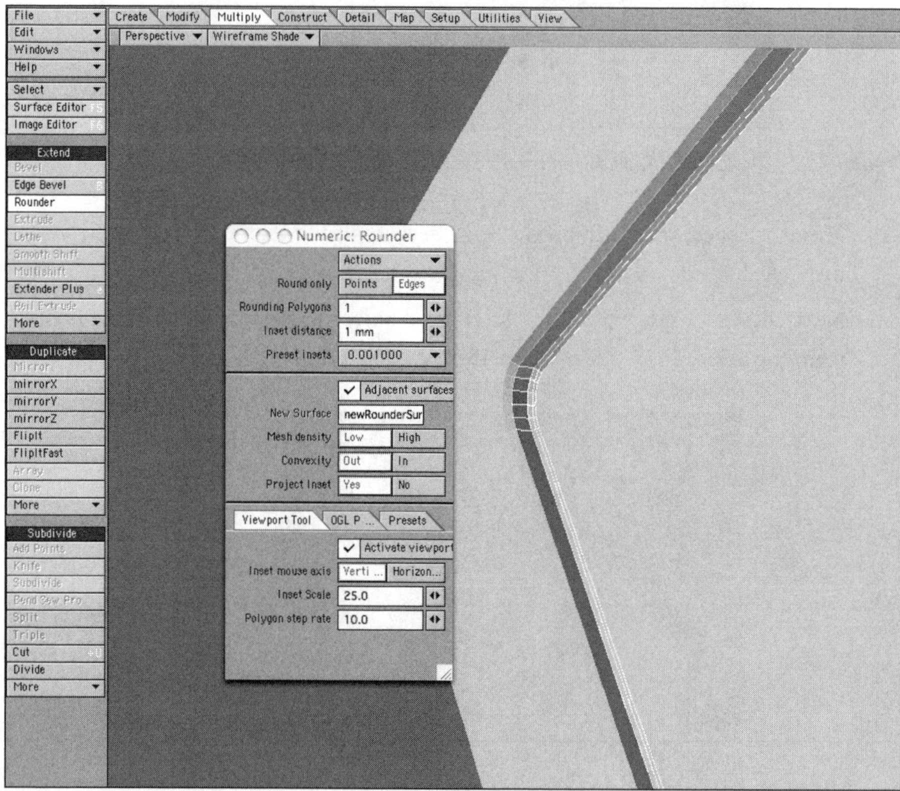

Figure 9.39 Using the Rounder tool, you can easily add that fine detail on the inside edges of the LCD panel.

8. Save your work.

   Figure 9.40 shows the model so far, and you can see how the edges now have just that extra bit of detail for added realism. These added edges will catch the light when rendered, later in Layout.

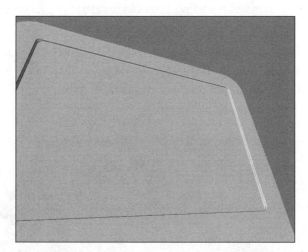

Figure 9.40 The iPod model is coming along nicely and starts to look better with beveled edges.

9. On your own, go ahead and bevel the outer edges of the iPod object, using either the Edge Bevel or Rounder. Figure **9.41** shows the model with added edge bevels.

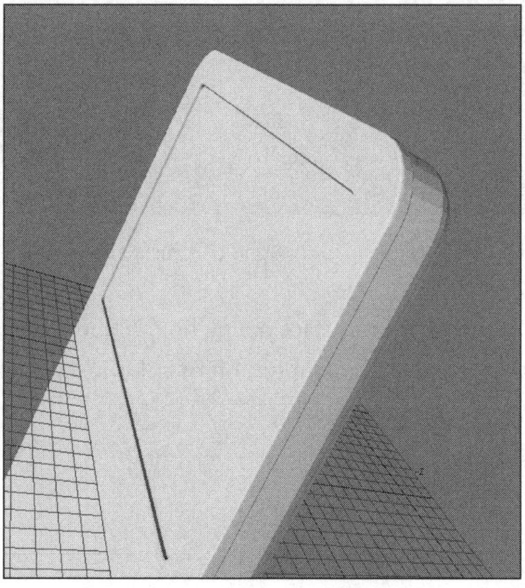

Figure 9.41 Using the same techniques described in previous steps, bevel the edges on the outside edge of the model.

10. When you're done, save your model.

    Working with edges in LightWave v9 is the best way to create added details without extra geometry that can weigh down your model. It also offers you more control than simply beveling polygons. There's still a bit more to do until this model is ready for lighting and rendering. You need to create the glass cover, and then build in the charger and earpiece ports.

11. In the Perspective view, click the center of the LCD-panel polygon to select it, as in **Figure 9.42**. Because the Perspective view is generally set to a Shaded view, you can click directly on the polygon you want to select. When working with wireframe views, you can't select as easily.

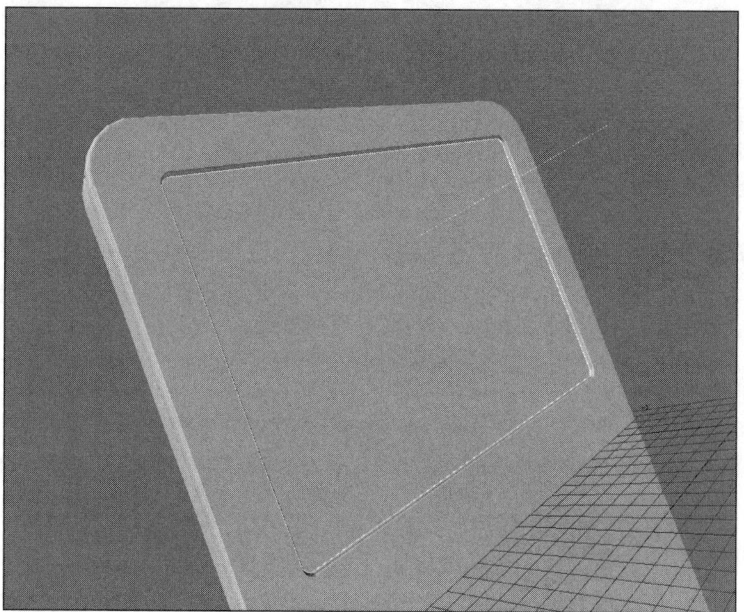

Figure 9.42 Select the LCD polygon from within the Perspective view.

12. Press **q** to call up the Change Surface dialog box. Name the selected polygon **LCD Panel** or something similar, and apply a bit of color just to help you remember it has been assigned a unique surface.

13. Switch to Points selection mode.

14. Shift-click each of the points around the outer edge of the LCD-panel object, working your way around in order until all the points are selected (**Figure 9.43**).

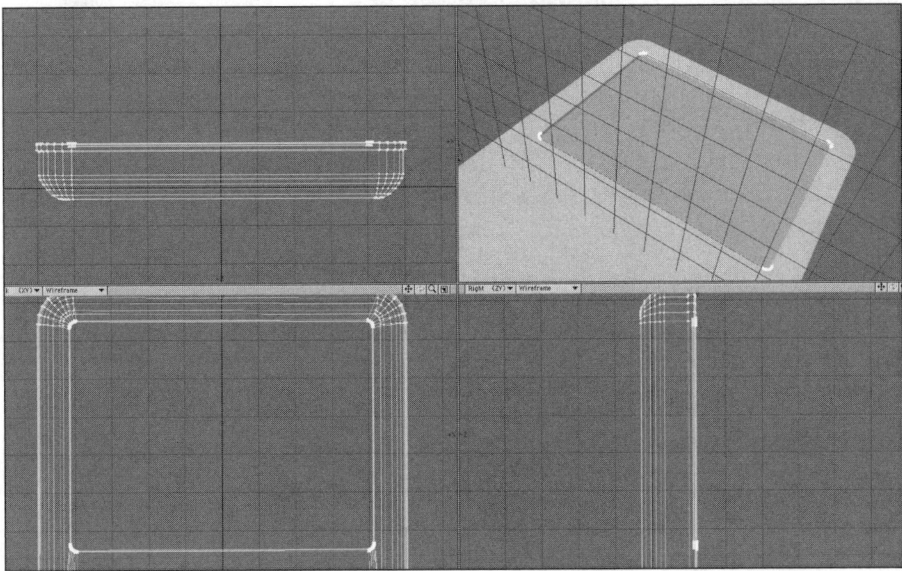

Figure 9.43 Select the outer-edge points of the LCD panel, in order.

15. Once the points are selected, press **p** to make a polygon.
16. Switch to Polygons selection mode at the bottom of the interface. Your new polygon should be selected. If it is facing inward, press **f** to flip it. (You can tell which way the surface normal for the polygon is facing because you'll see a dotted line extending out of it when it is selected.)

    Selecting the points and creating a polygon the way you just did seamlessly integrates the new polygon with the existing geometry, but it designates the new geometry as a separate editable surface. This will make to make the new polygon transparent, so it will reveal the LCD panel beneath it.
17. With the newly created polygon still selected, press **q** to open the Change Surface dialog box. Name the new polygon **Glass** or something similar. **Figure 9.44** (on the following page) shows the model.

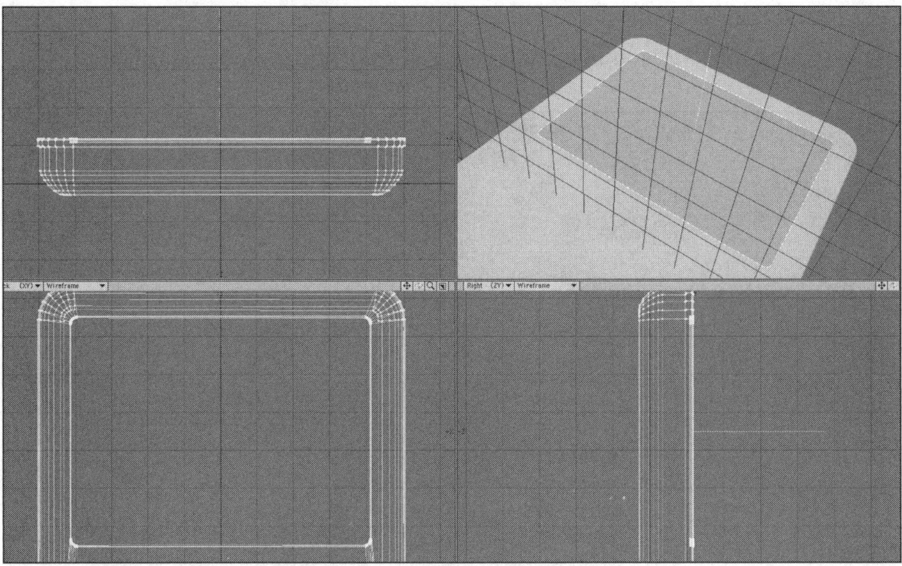

Figure 9.44 Create a surface for the newly created polygon called Glass.

18. Save your work.
19. Select the polygons that make up the rest of the face of the model. These are everything on the face other than the glass polygon you just created. **Figure 9.45** shows the selection.
20. Create a surface for the selected polygons. Name them **iPod_Face** or something similar. Color it black. **Figure 9.46** shows the surface.
21. Now you'll select the other polygons to apply surfaces to them. Here's a quick and easy way to do it: Press **w** to open the Statistics panel.

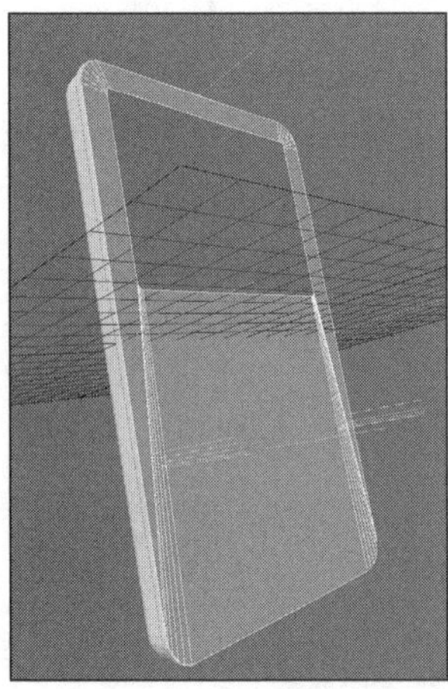

Figure 9.45 Select the polygons that make up the face of the iPod object.

Figure 9.46 Apply a surface to the face of the iPod.

22. Making sure you're in Polygons selection mode, and within the Statistics panel, click the Surf (surface) listing. Here, you can see what and how many polygons have surfaces. You can see the LCD Panel surface, the Glass surface, and so on. Select Default. These are the polygons without any surfaces. **Figure 9.47** shows the choices.

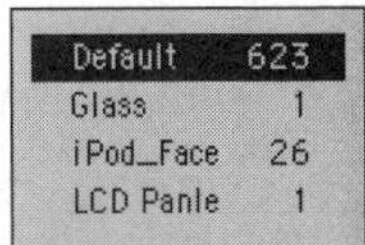

Figure 9.47 Using the Statistics panel, you can see what surfaces area applied to different polygons.

23. If you select the Default listing in the Statistics panel, you can click the tiny plus sign to the left, as shown in **Figure 9.48**. Doing so selects all of the default polygons—those that have yet to be assigned surface names. By the same token, clicking the minus mark deselects.

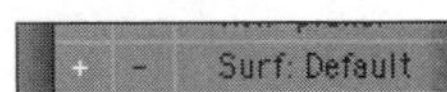

Figure 9.48 Click the tiny plus sign to select all of the default polygons.

24. Clicking the plus sign selects the default polygons, which make up the iPod's back and side surfaces. In a moment, you'll assign separate surfaces to the back and the sides, but for now, press **q** to open the Change Surface dialog and then type **iPod_Sides** in as the surface name and assign it the color black (**Figure 9.49**).

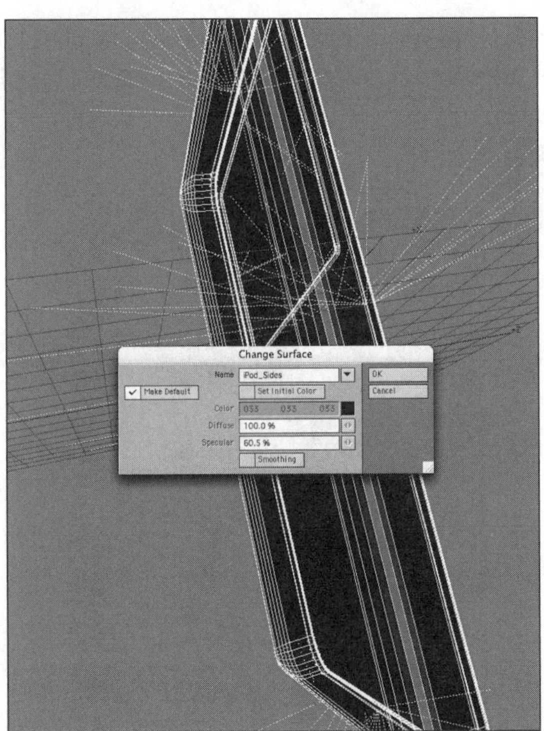

Figure 9.49 Designate the surface of the default polygons as iPod_Sides.

25. Save your model. Press / to deselect all polygons and then select only the single polygon on the very back of the unit (**Figure 9.50**).

Figure 9.50 Select the polygon that makes up the back of the iPod model.

26. With this single polygon selected, hold the Shift key and press] (the right bracket key, two over from the **p** key on your keyboard) to expand the selection. Do this a few times, until your selection "grows" to include the iPod model's back panel (**Figure 9.51**).

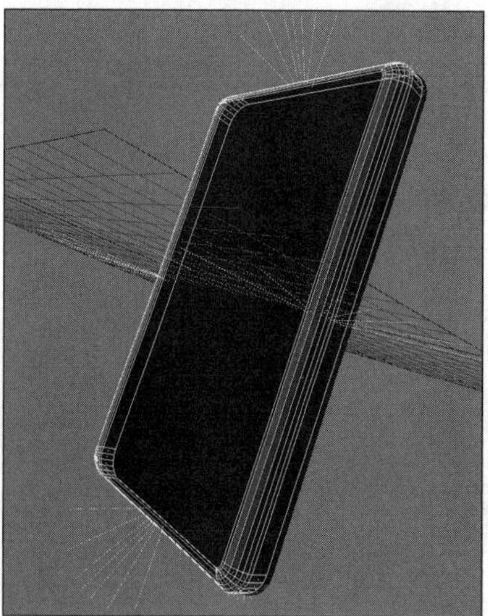

Figure 9.51 Grow the selection by pressing Shift+] (the right bracket key).

27. Expand the selection up to the beveled edge just behind the face. Then, press **q** to open the Change Surface dialog box. Set this surface as **iPod_Back** and set the color to a bright gray. Click on Smoothing as well. **Figure 9.52** shows the iPod with its new surfaces.

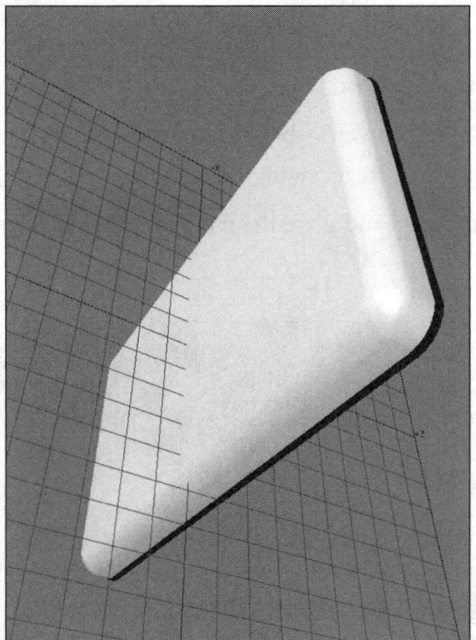

Figure 9.52 After the merge. The base iPod is ready for final details.

28. Save your model!

    So now you have most of the base model. It has surfaces set up and ready for you to apply textures, add reflections, shading, and so on. But there's still the issue of the connectors. The next project will take you further with a few more modeling steps.

Drilling the Connectors

You've seen that detailing the edges makes a big difference in the appearance of the model, as well as some basic surface colors. But the final details for the model will be in the connectors at the top and bottom—one for the earplugs, and one for the charger—in addition to markings and the main dial.

Exercise 9.4 Building an iPod, Part IV

1. Continue with the model you've been creating. But at this point, if you haven't already, press Shift+s to create an incremental save.
2. Go to a new blank layer, and place the iPod object in a background layer, as shown in **Figure 9.53**.

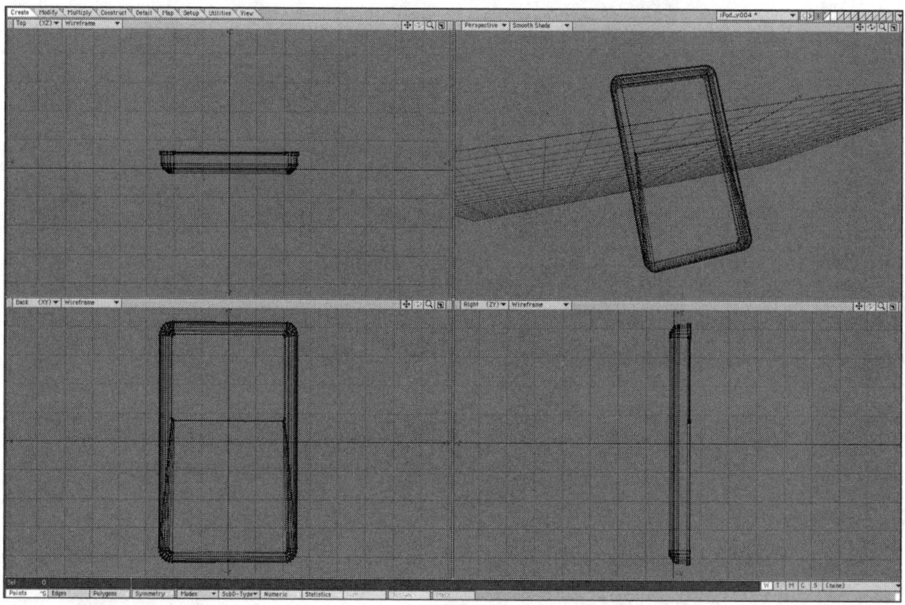

Figure 9.53 Place the iPod in a background layer, and select a new blank layer as the foreground.

3. Select the Disc tool on the Create tab. Holding the Ctrl key, draw out a disc in the Top view, as shown in **Figure 9.54**. Place it toward the left side of the iPod in the view.

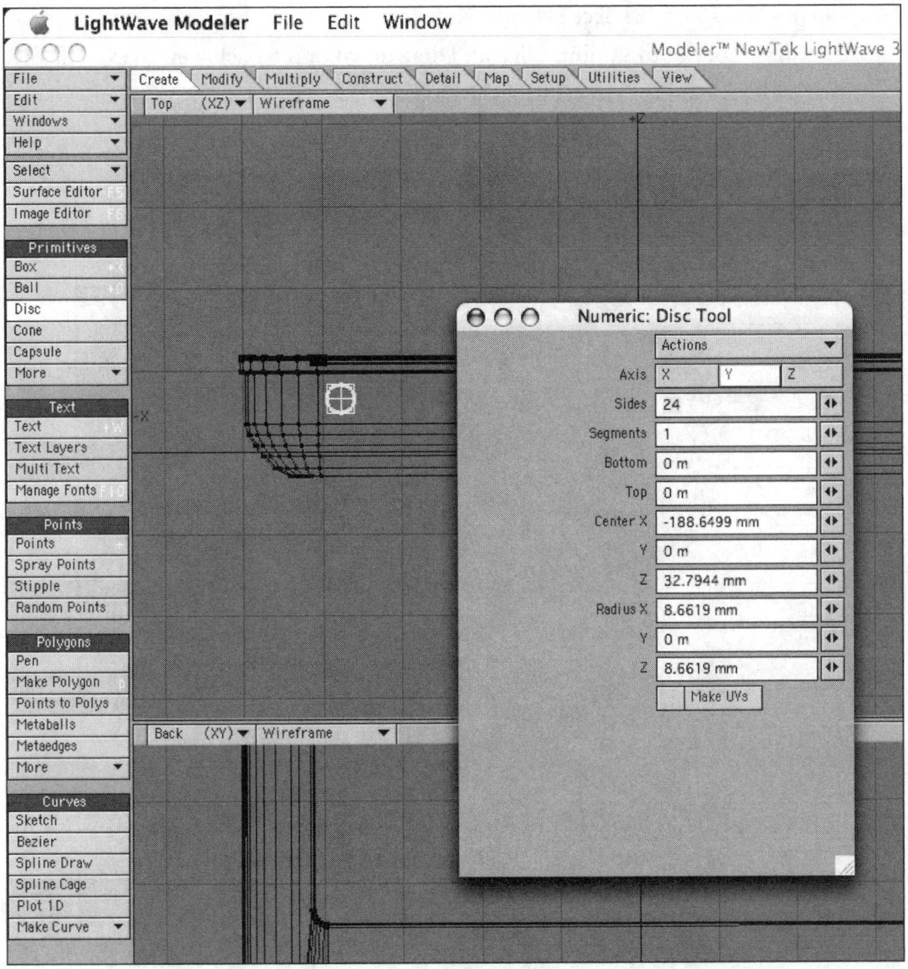

Figure 9.54 Create a disc in the Top view to begin making the earplug port of the iPod.

4. If you look in the other views, you might notice that the disc is located at the center of the object. This is because you only concentrated on modeling it in the Top view, which is fine. Now, you can press **t** and move the disc up toward the top of the model, in the Back view. **Figure 9.55** shows the example. If you hold the Ctrl key, you can constrain movements.

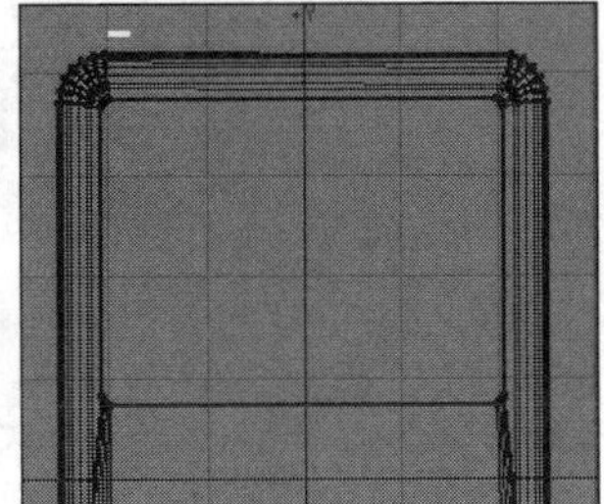

Figure 9.55 Move the flat disc up to the top of the model.

5. On the Multiply tab, select Extrude. Note that you should be working in Polygons selection mode at this point. Click and drag down in the Back view to extrude the disc a bit so that it intersects with the iPod, as shown in **Figure 9.56**. Again, you can hold the Ctrl key to constrain the operation.

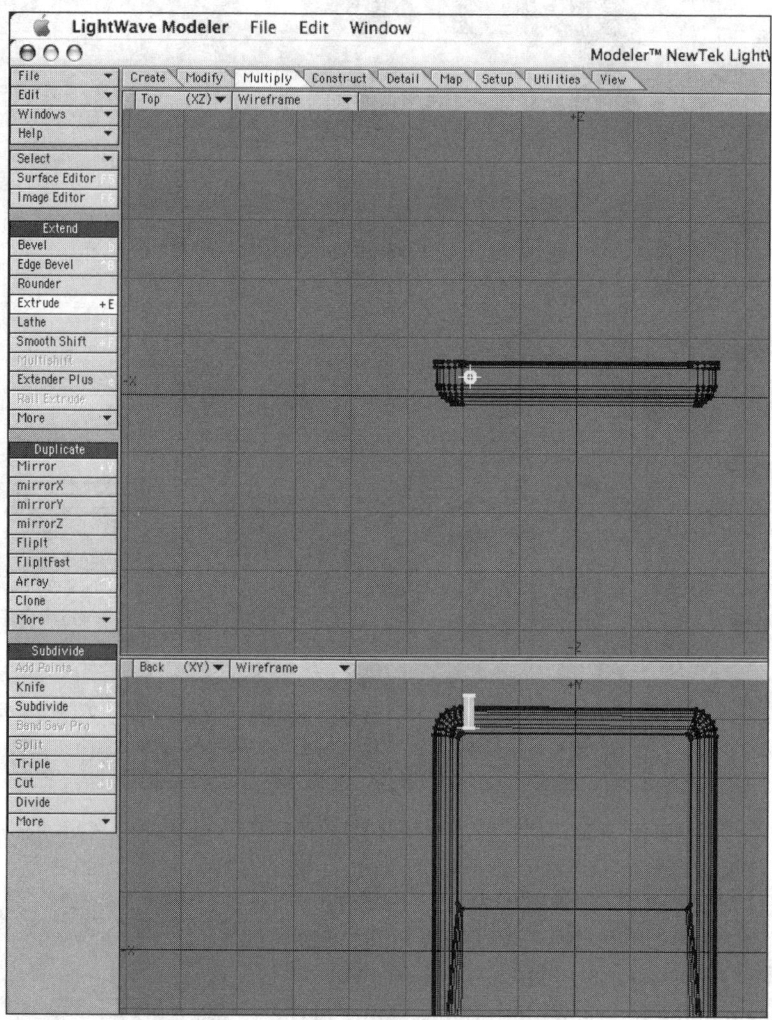

Figure 9.56 Extrude the disc so that it intersects with the iPod.

6. Press the spacebar to turn off the Extrude tool. Then, press Shift+a to fit the selection to view.

7. Next, after a quick save, press **q** to open the Change Surface dialog box. Give the earplug object a surface name, and color it a bright yellow (**Figure 9.57**). You'll see why in a moment. Click OK to close the Change Surface dialog box.

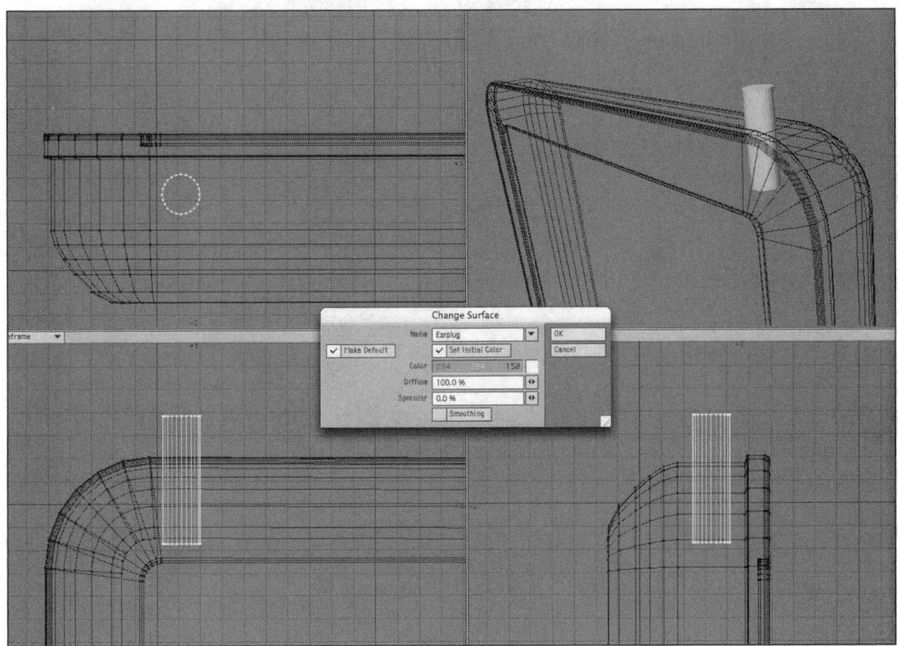

Figure 9.57 Create a surface for the earplug.

8. Press ' (the apostrophe key, two keys to the right of the **l** on your keyboard) to make the current layer (containing the earplug object) a background layer and brings the iPod layer to the foreground.

   The earplug object must occupy a background layer for the next step to work. You're going to use it to cut a hole in the iPod.

9. Press Shift+b on your keyboard to activate the Boolean CSG tool, which is also found in the Construct tab (**Figure 9.58**).

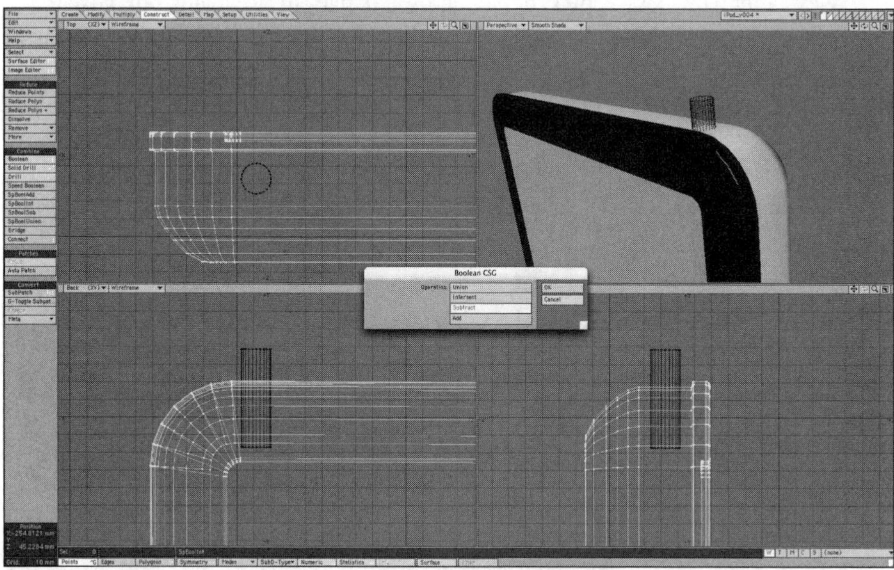

Figure 9.58 The Boolean CSG tool is used to intersect and subtract objects from one another.

10. Select Subtract, then click OK to subtract the contents of the background layer from the object in the foreground layer (**Figure 9.59**).

    If you take a close look at the iPod model after the Boolean operation, you'll see two things: The iPod now has a hole in it, and the hole is colored yellow. If you apply a surface to a Boolean "cutting" object, that surface's name and characteristics are assigned to the surface of the hole or cavity it creates. It makes life a lot easier as you won't have to try to select and surface polygons inside the tiny earplug hole!

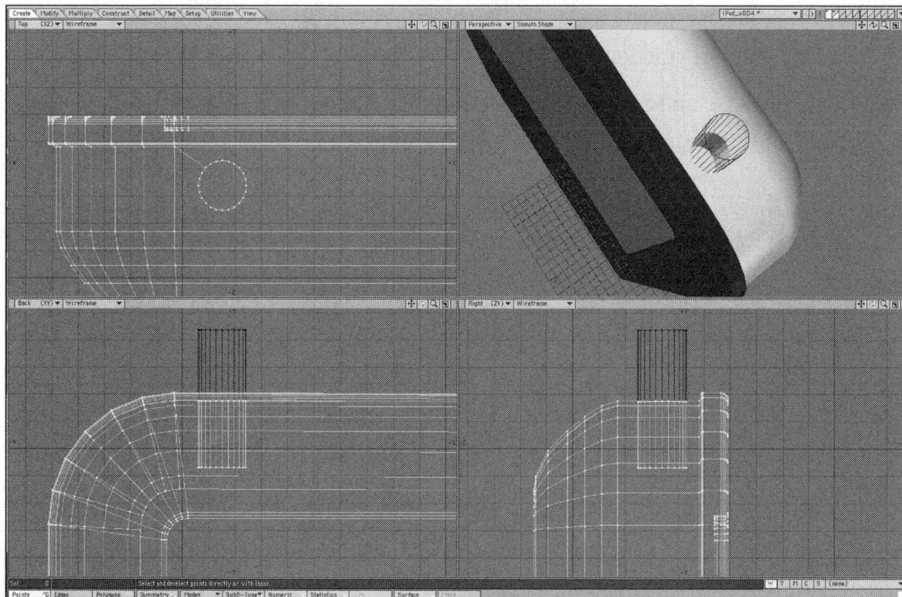

Figure 9.59 The background earplug object is used to cut a hole in the foreground iPod layer.

11. Press the apostrophe key to reverse layers, and press Shift+h for the size tool. Increase the size of the original earplug disc by about to about 15%, as shown in **Figure 9.60**.

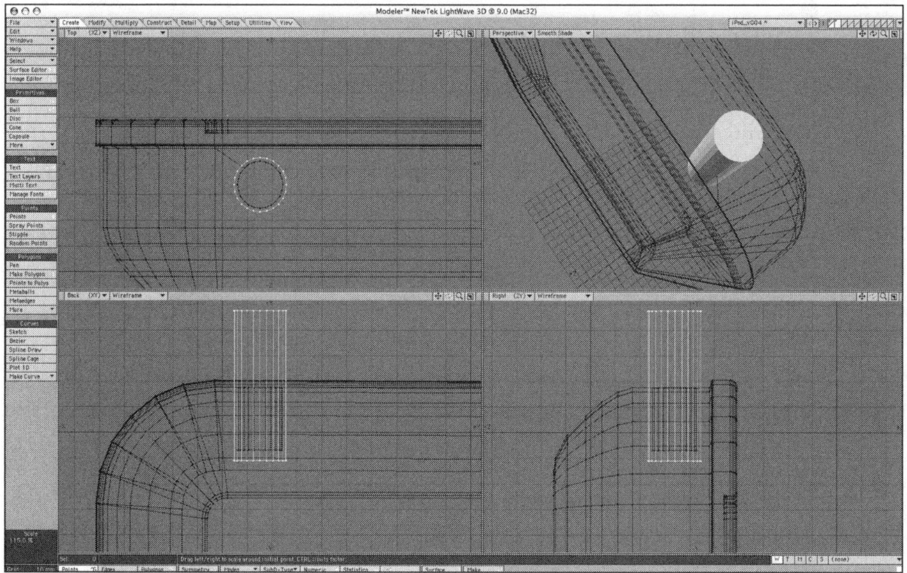

Figure 9.60 Increase the size of the earplug disc by about 15%.

12. Press **q** and change the surface to **Earplug_Trim** or something similar. Set the color to an off-white or gray.
13. Move the disc up so that it intersects with the background layer (the iPod object) just below the surface edge, as shown in **Figure 9.61**.

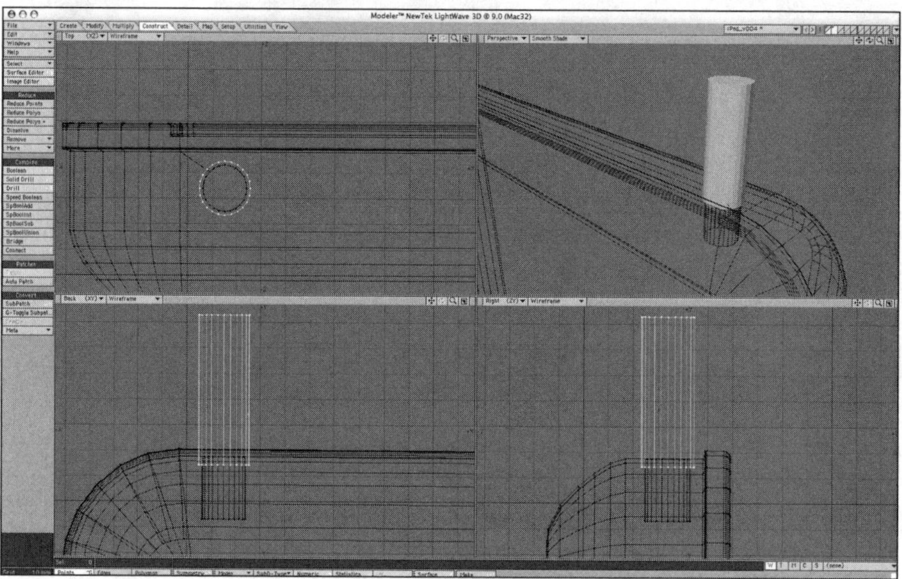

Figure 9.61 Recolor and position the newly resized disc.

14. Then, press ' (the apostrophe key) again to reverse layers.
15. On the Construct tab, select the Solid Drill command, or press Shift+c.
16. In the Solid Drill dialog box, choose Stencil. For the Surface listing, make sure the surface name you created, Earplug_Trim, is selected. Then, click OK to perform the operation.

    In a moment, the outer edge of the earplug hole will have a colored ring, as shown in **Figure 9.62**.

Note

The Solid Drill command with a Stencil allows you to effectively create a 3D branding iron for your models. You can create a letter, for example, and stencil it into another object. The only caveat is that you must intersect the objects in two layers. The branding iron, or cutting tool, must be located in a background layer.

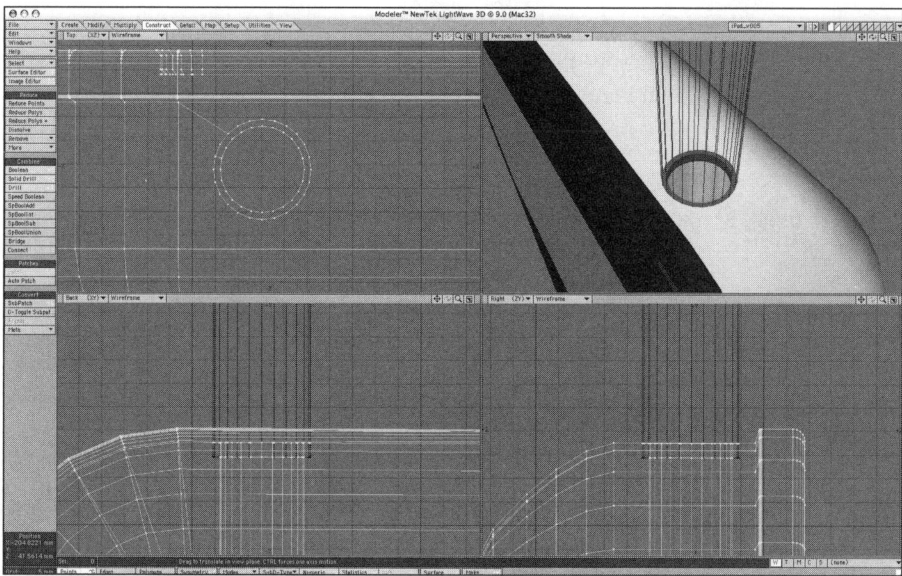

Figure 9.62 The Solid Drill command with a Stencil allows you to create a surface in a unique shape on the model.

17. Save your object. Then, press ' (the apostrophe key) to reverse layers. Then, delete the disc tool, as you'll no longer need it. You can press Delete (on your keyboard) or Ctrl+x to cut it.

Note

Pressing Ctrl+x to cut an object works similar to a delete, except that it keeps the item in memory. Since the current object is so minor, there's no issue with keeping it in memory, no matter what system you're working on.

18. You can go back to the iPod layer and view your model in the Perspective view to see how it's coming along. Be sure to save your work.

19. Perform an incremental save to save a new version of the object. Go to a new layer (you can press the apostrophe key to reverse layers again) and in the top view, create a rectangle, as in **Figure 9.63**.

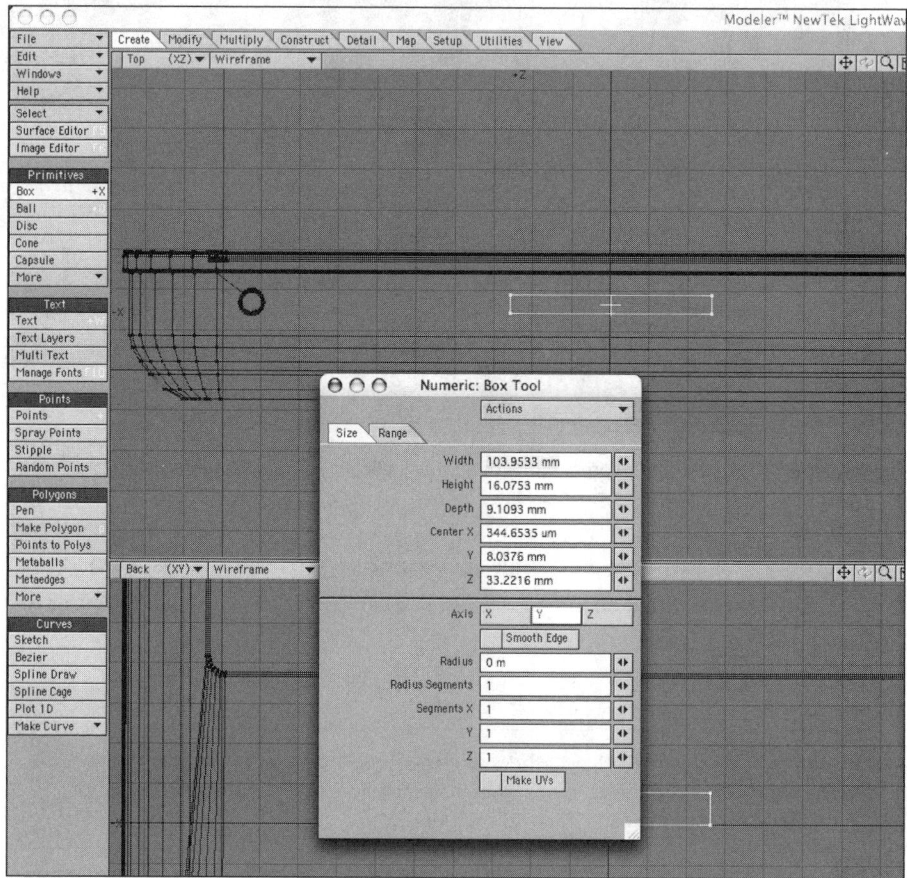

Figure 9.63 Create a rectangle, which will serve as the recess for the iPod Dock connector.

20. Move the box to the bottom of the model, making sure it's centered and slightly intersected with the iPod in a background layer, as shown in **Figure 9.64**. You're doing the same thing here as you did with the earplug.

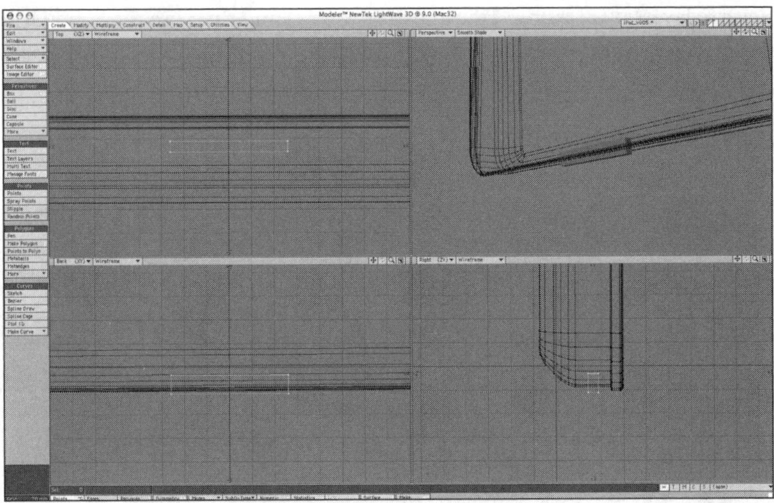

Figure 9.64 Create a box that intersects the bottom of the iPod.

21. With the box in position, reverse layers and add a surface to the box, calling it **iPod_connector** or something similar.
22. Then, Boolean-subtract the box from the iPod (press Shift+b to access the tool).
23. Reverse layers, then size up the box, just as you did with the disc earlier. Give it a new surface name, **Connector_trim**, and then change its position to only slightly intersect the iPod, as in **Figure 9.65**.

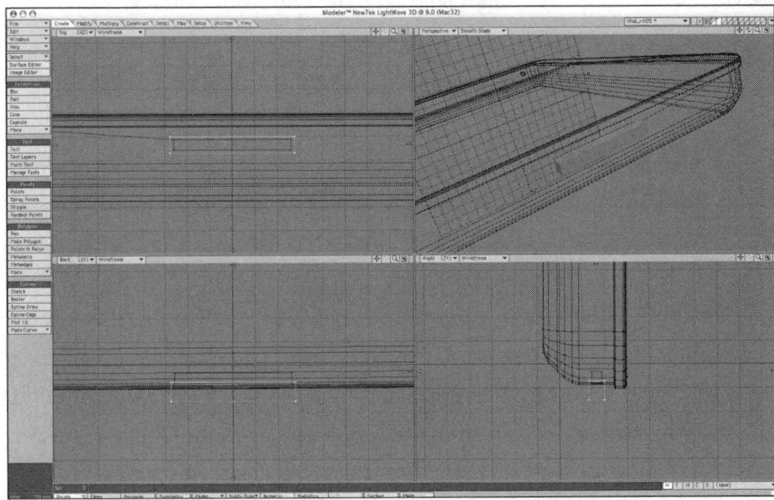

Figure 9.65 Increase the size of the box, and then give it a new surface name to create the trim of the connector panel.

24. Reverse layers by pressing ' (the apostrophe key) and then use the Solid Drill command to stencil the box into the iPod. Make sure you choose the new Connector_trim surface for the stencil. Press Shift+c for the Solid Drill tool. **Figure 9.66** shows the operation.

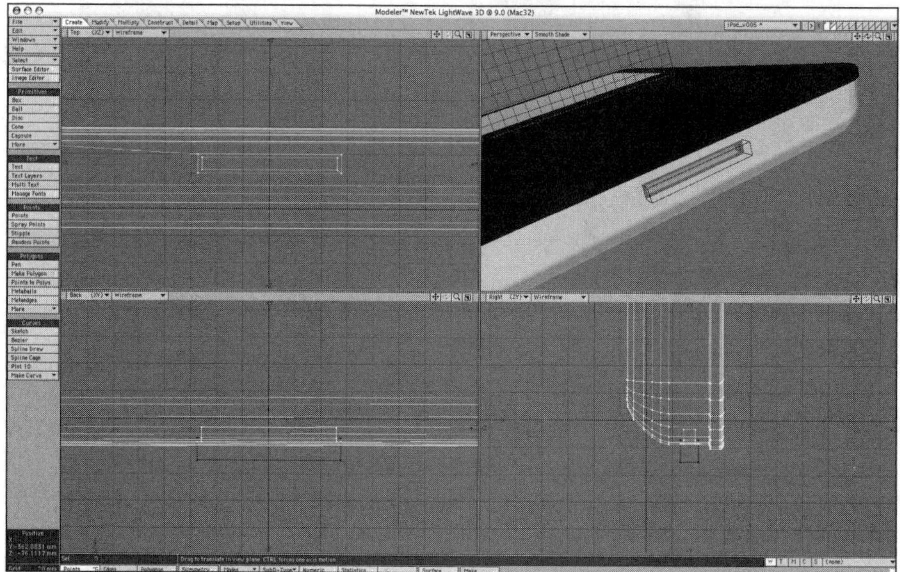

Figure 9.66 Stencil the box into the iPod to create the trim of the connector plate.

25. Delete the box from the second layer, and then save your model.

You've completed your iPod model! Congrats!

The Next Step

This chapter has guided you through building an everyday gadget, an Apple iPod. Sure, you might want to use these techniques to build a Microsoft Zune. The choice is yours. But no matter what you create, all of the procedures here can be used to build the model. It's simple, effective, and efficient—and that should always be your goal no matter what you model. But hold on; you're not getting off that easy! There's a lot more to this project than just what's here. You need to build a cord, then surface, light, and render this unit. You'll find these projects in video form on the book's DVD, in the Chapter 9 folder. You'll also see how to use the tools presented in this chapter to create the dial and controls. The surface and rendering will be there, too, showing you how to place an image on the LCD screen under the glass and add a realistic environment. Now, move on to the next chapter to learn about character modeling!

Chapter 10
Character Modeling

Character modeling is an art form like no other. Unless you've been living under a rock the past few years, there's no way you could have missed the slew of movies fraught with animated 3D characters. Characters in these movies range from talking automobiles, to goofy animals, to comedic rodents. There's a trend to create simple yet charismatic 3D creatures these days, and why should you not be in on the fun? This chapter will show you how to create a fun little character with a lot of personality. You'll learn how simple shapes can be used quite effectively to develop a character while making it easy to animate at the same time.

Types of Characters

Character modeling can be considered a broad term. You see, characters today can be anything from dancing telephones, to walking credit cards, talking cows, or a computer-generated humans. In previous *Inside LightWave* books, we covered modeling human heads, a cool giraffe, and even a crusty old man's head. With *Inside LightWave v9*, we'll take a different approach and show how to create a character that's cute and simple, but very expressive. And what better character than a penguin?

There are many techniques for modeling characters, and one of the most popular is the box modeling technique. The basic concept of box modeling is to start with a basic box primitive and, using subpatches or subdivision surfaces, transform it into a high-polygon object while retaining the ease of manipulating a low-polygon object. Another technique for building characters is called point-by-point, wherein you create points, connect them to form polygons, adjust their shape, and then *multiply*, or add polygons, as needed to add detail. Another is the splines method, in which you use curves to create a basic outline of your model, then patch it together—a method that is often time-consuming.

For the model you'll create in this chapter, you'll work with several primitive shapes—connecting, multiplying, and adjusting them to build your final model. While there's so much talk about which method to use to build a character, this chapter isn't going to have you worry about a set method—rather, you'll concentrate on your model, its shape, and its form. After all, it's this final character that will be used in your renders, and the person watching doesn't care whether it was built with a box, a point, or a curve. What is important is polygonal flow and the shape of the polygons that make up the model using subpatch techniques.

Standard polygonal surfaces often need many polygons to approximate a smooth surface. Even so, a smooth surface made up of polygons will eventually reveal its inherently sharp-edged nature if it's examined closely enough. Although you can create such polygon-heavy objects, they are often difficult to manipulate and manage from the perspective of memory consumption and editing. In this chapter, you'll model a fun but useful penguin. The techniques shown here can be used for any type of character you want to build, and even ones with more than two legs! You'll learn about the following:

- Creating and blending shapes from primitives
- Working with subdivisions
- Using the multiplication tools
- Adding detail and controlling flow

Building with Primitives

Get yourself comfortable and ready to learn one of the most valuable modeling techniques for creating organic objects quickly and with ease. **Figure 10.1** shows the character you'll create in this chapter.

The goal in this chapter is to create a penguin character using just a handful of tools. You will take a ball primitive and turn it into a full-grown organic penguin model. These tools are used almost every time when creating characters or other organic models. You'll then make the primitive shape smooth through the use of subdivisional surfaces, commonly known in LightWave as subpatches.

Figure 10.1 A fun character made with box modeling methods.

The idea behind subpatching is to repeatedly refine the control mesh until you achieve a smooth surface, called the limit surface. And as you've seen earlier in the book, LightWave v9 offers a new type of subdivision, Catmull-Clark. You'll work primarily with subpatches in this chapter for efficiency.

Organic modeling is very different from modeling a car or a building. In this project, you will be asked to manipulate the object using your own ideas of what looks right to you, but with a good bit of guidance. You'll begin with specific shapes, then use your talent to freeform-model the details. The Numeric panel won't come into play that often, and you will be asked to judge the placement of points and polygons by eye in some cases. That's what makes organic modeling so much fun—the freedom to explore and design as you go. Modeler's interface layout will be the default setup. **Figure 10.2** shows Modeler at startup.

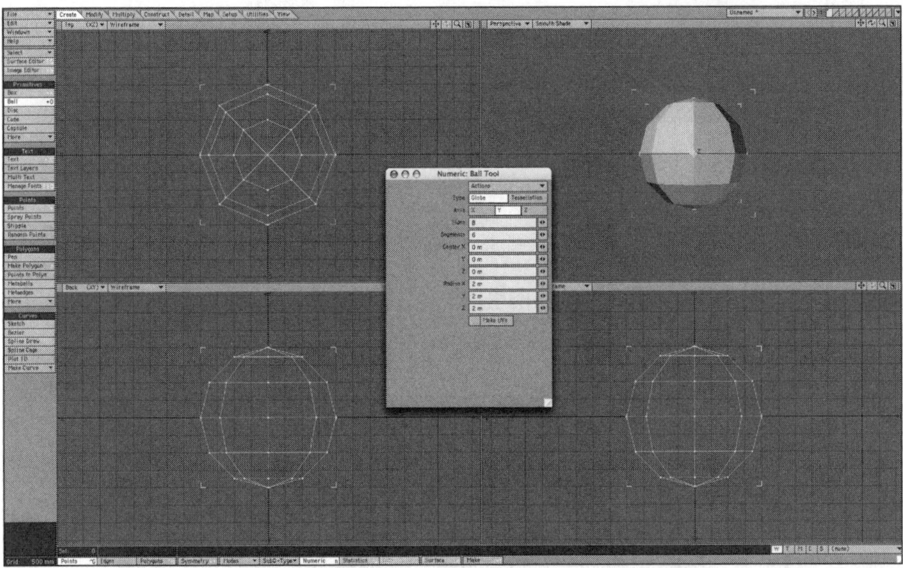

Figure 10.2 LightWave v9 Modeler, set to a Quad view by default, ready for some character making!

Exercise 10.1 Using Geometric Shapes to Build the Penguin Body

Each project you encounter is different. That also means that your approach to modeling changes based on the task at hand. You might hear 3D artists claim that box modeling is the only method to use and that you must start with the eyes. Others swear by spline curves and start with the head, working their way down to the details. But locking into any one technique for everything is like eating the same meal every day: It gets boring, and it's not the right thing to do. For a cute penguin, two characteristics stand out: the body and the eyes. The eyes for this project will go in last, as you need a body and head reference before you can build them. So for this project, you'll start by modeling the penguin's body.

1. Start LightWave Modeler, and click the Ball tool button on the Create tab.
2. Select the Numeric button at the bottom of the Modeler interface, or press **n**.
3. Now, in the Numeric panel, choose Activate from the Actions drop-down menu at the top of the panel. This begins the ball primitive.
4. Next, enter the following:

Type	Globe	
Axis	Y	
Sides	8	
Segments	6	
Center	X	0m
	Y	0m
	Z	0m
Radius	X	2m
	Y	2m
	Z	2m

5. Press the spacebar to turn off the Ball tool and confirm your settings. Close the Numeric panel. **Figure 10.3** shows the result.

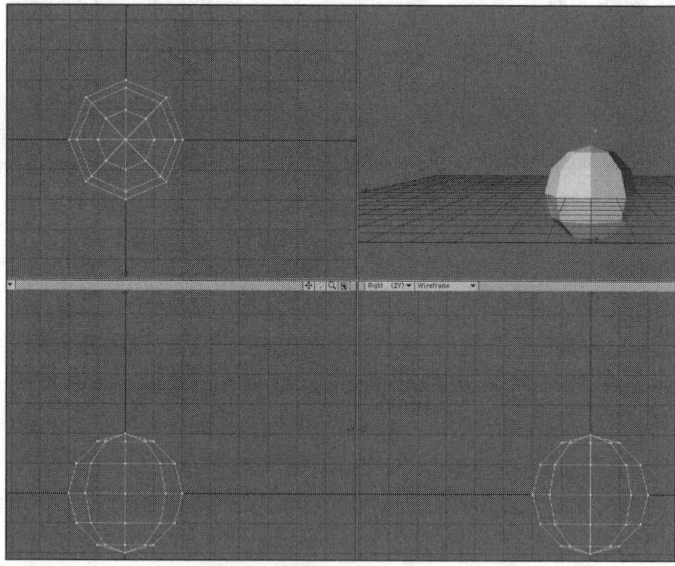

Figure 10.3 Begin creating the character with a very simple ball primitive.

You might be thinking, why such a low-quality ball? The answer is that you want to be able to manipulate the geometry to shape the character. Too much geometry can lead to control and flow problems. Also, you'll be converting this object to subpatches very soon.

Note

As you're moving around the views and selecting points, remember to zoom in or out as needed, using the period and comma keys on your keyboard. You can also use the viewport controls at the top right of each viewport—just click, hold, and drag.

6. Press Ctrl+c to copy the ball.
7. Press **t** to activate the Move tool, and then move the ball up along the Y-axis about 4.5m.
8. Once the ball is moved, press Ctrl+v to paste the model you've copied (**Figure 10.4**).

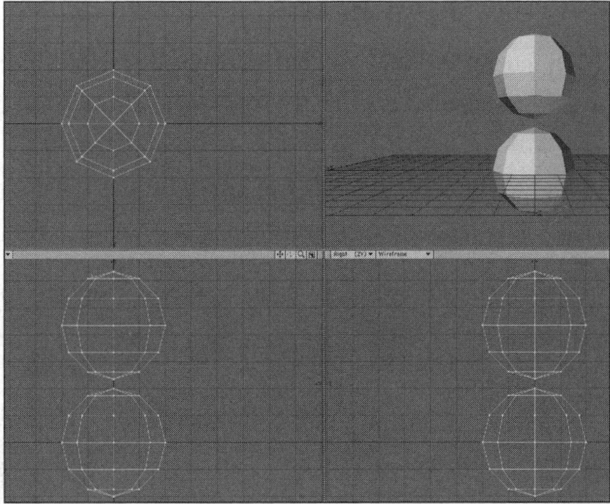

Figure 10.4 Copy the ball, and then move it up 4.5m on the Y-axis and paste the copy.

9. Make sure you're in Polygons selection mode and select the top ball in either of two ways. Click once on the model to select any polygon, and then press] (the right-bracket key, two keys to the right of the **p** key on your keyboard) to select all contiguous polygons, or right-click and drag to lasso the object.
10. Once the object is selected, press Shift+h to select the Size tool (it's also found in the Modify tab). Reduce the ball size down to 70%, as shown in **Figure 10.5** on the next page. You can see the value of the size operation in the info area at the bottom-left corner of the interface.

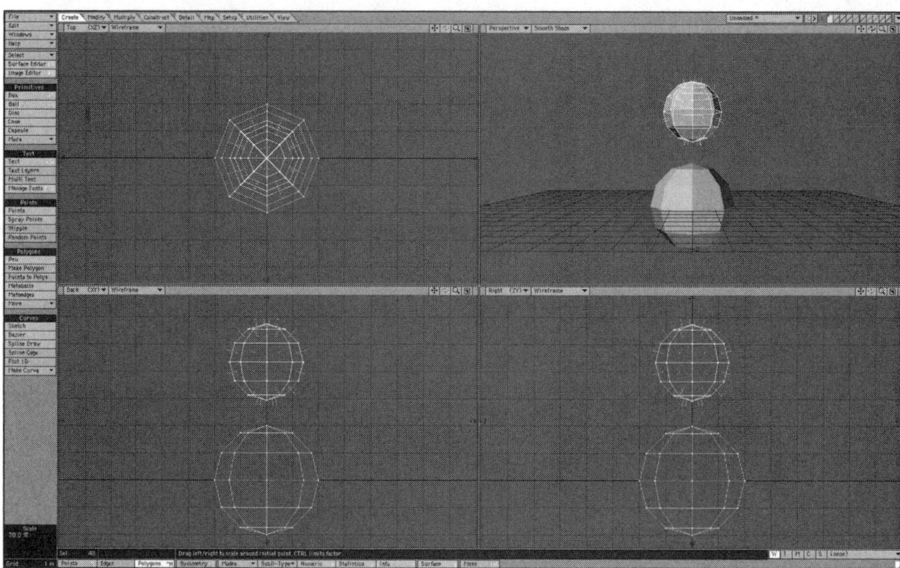

Figure 10.5 Reduce the size of the copied ball.

11. You're probably wondering how you'll combine these two balls to make a penguin. You might have figured out that the smaller ball will become the head, but it needs to blend with the body. Begin by deselecting all of the top ball's polygons.
12. Now select the polygons that make up the bottom of the top ball and the top of the bottom ball. There should be eight polygons on each, as shown in **Figure 10.6**.

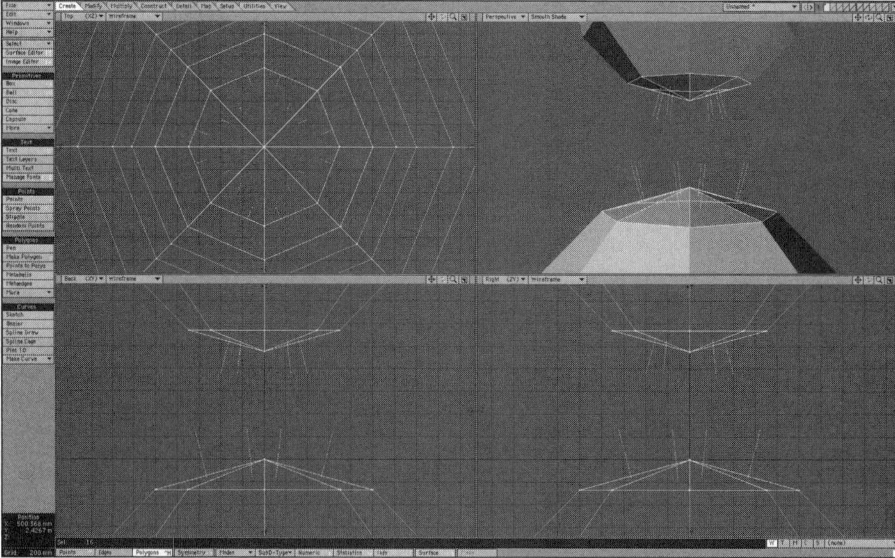

Figure 10.6 Select the polygons at the top and bottom of the two balls.

13. Click the Construct tab and locate the Bridge tool, as shown in **Figure 10.7**.

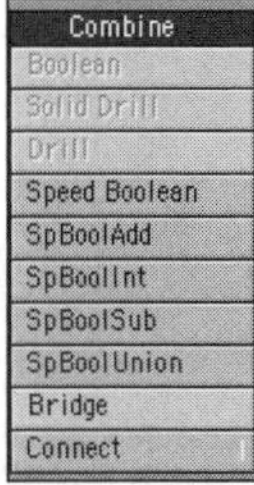

Figure 10.7 The Bridge tool is located in the Construct tab's Combine tool category.

14. Click the Bridge tool button one time, and the selected polygons will connect, as shown in **Figure 10.8**.

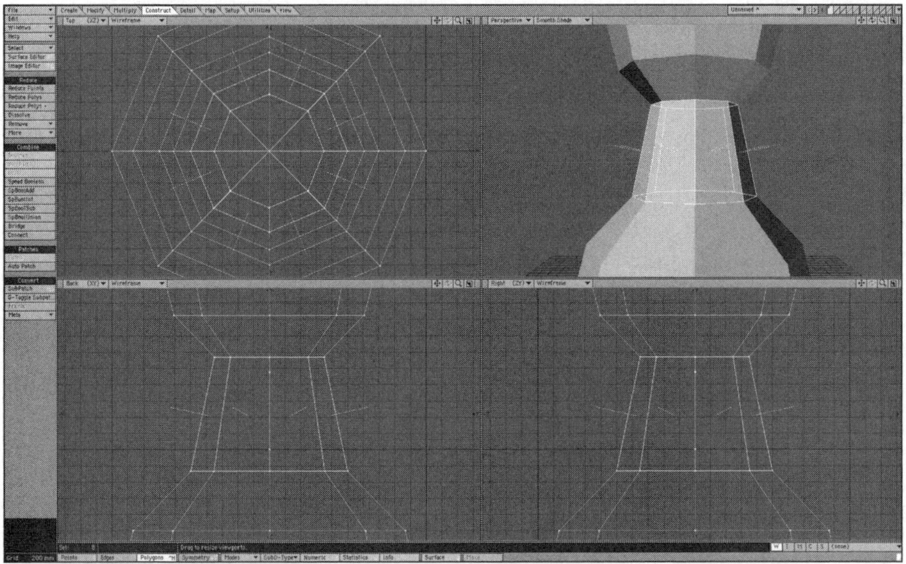

Figure 10.8 After you run the Bridge tool, the selected polygons are joined together.

15. The Bridge tool is a great way to weld together selected polygons, but it leaves behind a few unwanted points. Press **w** to open the Statistics panel.

16. Press the spacebar to jump to Point Statistics and, at the top of the panel, you'll see a listing for 0 Polygons (**Figure 10.9**). This represents the points associated with 0 (zero) polygons.

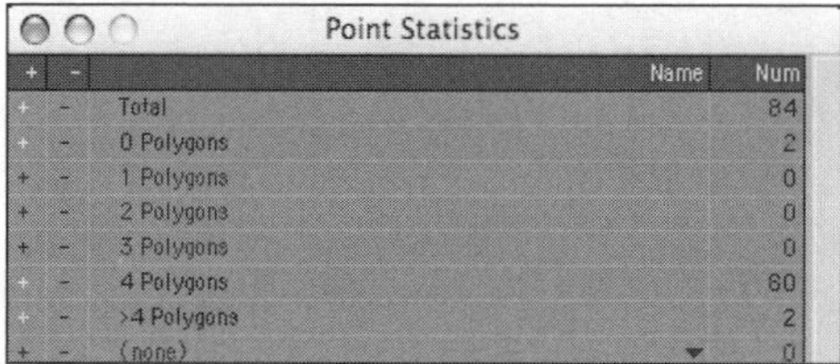

Figure 10.9 The Point Statistics panel allows you to see which points in your model are associated with which polygons.

17. Click the plus sign to the left of the 0 Polygons listing. This will select all points that are not associated with polygons, a total of 2.

18. Close the Statistics panel, and you'll see the two selected points in the viewports. Press Delete on your keyboard to remove them.

19. Save your model.

The points not associated with any polygons would not have affected anything in the final render. However, it's always better to work efficiently and remove unwanted points, even if they're not posing a problem. There might be a situation in your modeling process where you'll extend points or bevel, and if so, these unwanted points could get in the way.

20. Right-click and drag to lasso the points in the top ball (**Figure 10.10**).

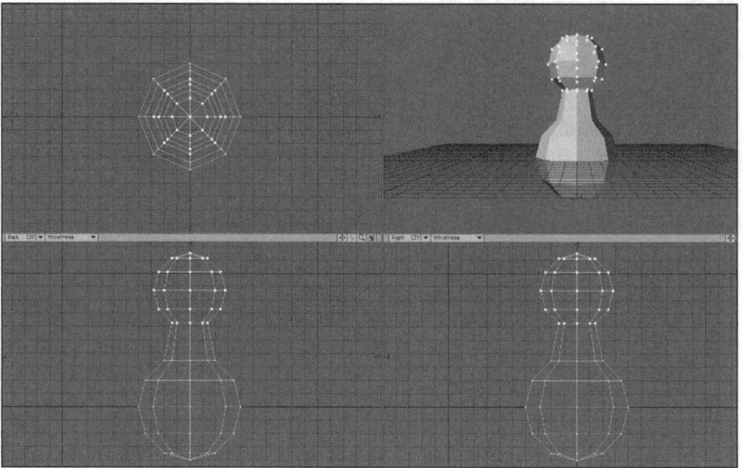

Figure 10.10 Lasso-select the points in the top ball.

21. With the points selected, press **t** and move the selection down toward the larger ball. You can hold the Ctrl key as you move to constrain the movement in the up-down direction. **Figure 10.11** shows the position change.

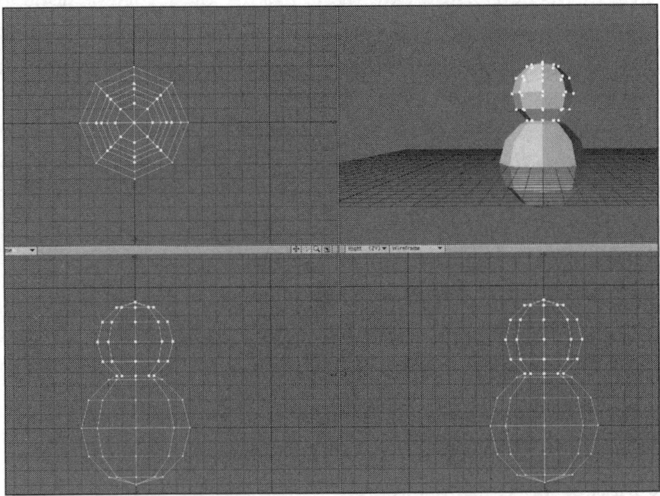

Figure 10.11 Move the selected points down closer to the bottom ball.

22. Turn off the Move tool by clicking it or pressing the spacebar. Then, deselect the points by pressing / or by clicking a blank area within the menus.
23. Press the Tab key to activate subpatch mode. **Figure 10.12** shows the two ball objects, now blended together and smooth.

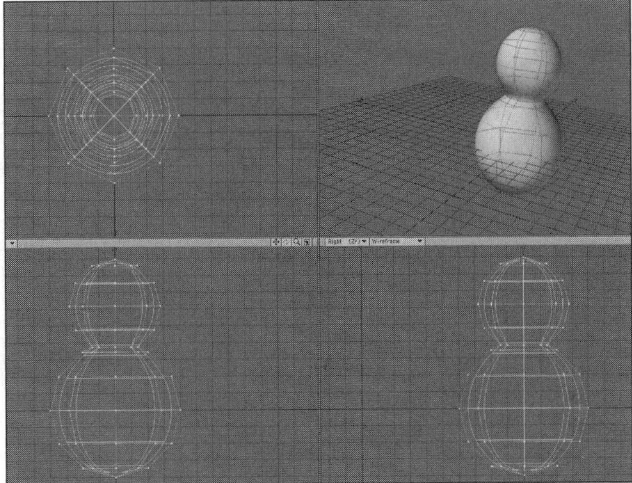

Figure 10.12 When subpatch mode is active, the primitive shapes are much smoother.

24. Save your model.

You can see that working with very simple primitive shapes is easy—obviously since there is less geometry to work with. However, it's not hard to create smooth-flowing characters once subpatch mode is active. You can toggle the use of subpatch mode as you build, which is one of the great features of LightWave. You're not forced to just apply it and leave it, but you can toggle it on and off. It's often easier to work with subpatches off, but the choice is yours.

But you're not nearly finished yet. Read on to start building the penguin's flippers, feet, and eyes.

Exercise 10.2 Giving the Penguin Flippers

It's important to remember that the techniques in this chapter can be applied to just about any character you create. For example, you could build a giraffe's legs, or a cat's paws, using methods like these. Taking things a step further (pun intended), you could build a troll, elf, or other human-type form. This next section will show you how to create the penguin's flippers using tools in the Multiply tab.

1. Continuing with the model you've been working on, press Shift+s to create an incremental save of your model. This will keep the original model safe, and your upcoming changes will be applied to a new copy.
2. Press **F2** to center the object at the origin. Then, press Shift+y to activate the Symmetry tool. You can also click the Symmetry button at the bottom of the interface to turn it on. This will allow you to work on one side of the model and have the other side mirror your work.
3. Click to Polygons selection mode at the bottom of the Modeler interface, and then select the polygons on the top-right side of the body, as shown in **Figure 10.13**. Selecting the right side with the Symmetry tool active will automatically select the left side as well.

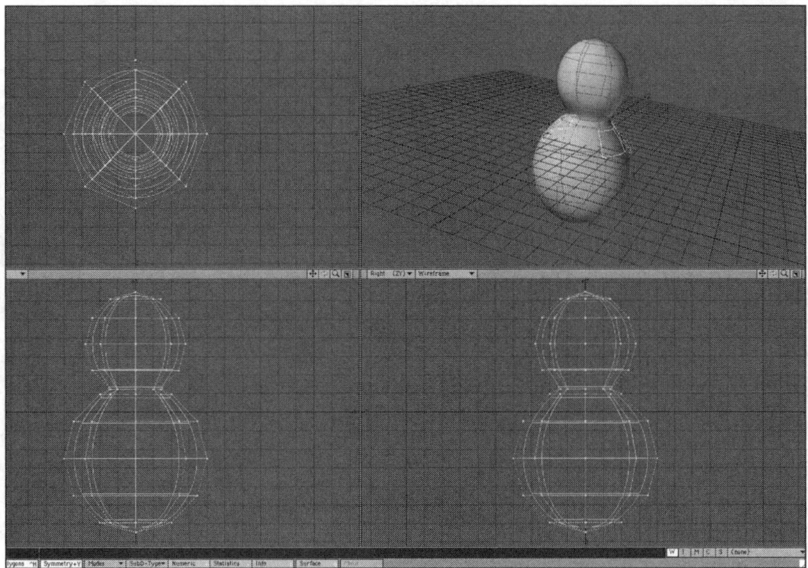

Figure 10.13 Select two polygons at the top right of the body.

4. Press Shift+a to fit the selection to view. Because Symmetry is on, the right side polygons will come to view, even though you see both left and right sides selected.

Note

Remember, when working with Symmetry, a "reflected" duplicate of everything you create on the right (positive) side of the X-axis is created on the left (negative) side of the X-axis. It's important to only use Symmetry deliberately as its accidental use can cause problems during normal Modeler operations.

5. Press **n** to open the Numeric panel.
6. On the Multiply tab, select the Multishift tool from the Extend category.
7. In the Numeric panel, make sure Group Polygons is checked and enter the following settings:

Inset Amount	**200mm**
Shift Amount	**60mm**
Inset Scale	**100%**
Shift Scale	**100%**
Inset	Contour
Shift	Average Point Normal
Group Polygons	On
Preserve UVs	On

Leave all other settings at their defaults. **Figure 10.14** shows the settings.

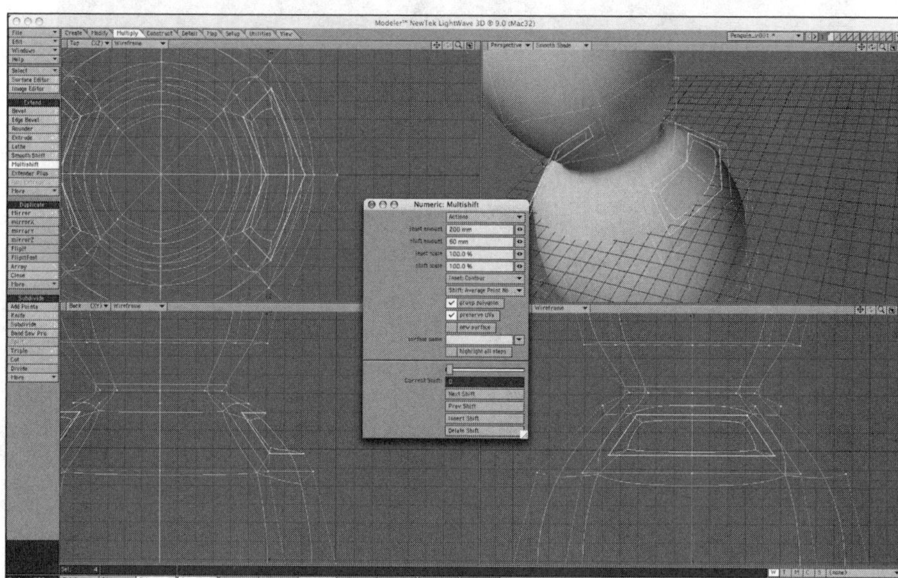

Figure 10.14 Use the Multishift command to begin creating the penguin's flippers.

You'll use Modeler's Multishift tool to shape the flippers because it allows you to bevel groups of polygons all at once. (The Bevel tool, by contrast, works on just one polygon at a time.)

8. Close the Numeric panel, then press the spacebar to turn off the Multishift tool. You're now on your way to building the penguin's flippers. Keeping the two polygons selected (the selection remaining after the previous Multishift operation), turn the Multishift tool on again.
9. This time, set the Inset and Shift for the Multishift tools to **30 mm** to add a slight bevel to the selection, similar to **Figure 10.15**. You can also apply Multishift manually by clicking and dragging in the viewports; move your mouse up and down to set the bevel's Shift value and move it left and right to set the Inset value. Be careful, however, because a manual Multishift adjustment might disrupt the perfectly symmetrical model; entering the numeric values will not.

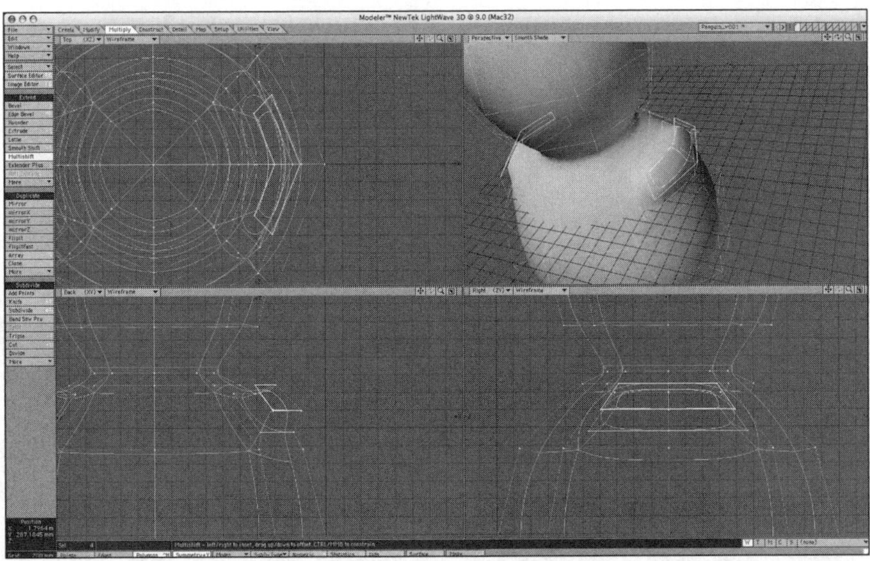

Figure 10.15 Apply another Multishift operation to continue creating the flippers.

10. With the polygons still selected, turn off the Multishift tool and make sure Action Center is set to Mouse in the Modes drop-down menu at the bottom of the interface. Press **y** to activate the Rotate tool.
11. Place your mouse toward the inside of the flipper at the body, then click and drag slightly to rotate the selected polygons downward, as shown in **Figure 10.16**.

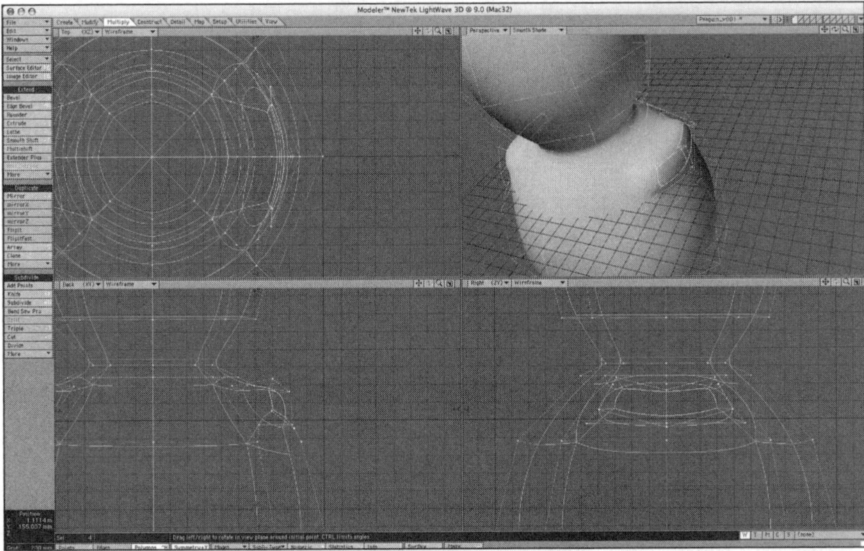

Figure 10.16 Rotate the selected polygons downward before you use the Multishift tool again.

12. Multishift the selection one more time, as shown in **Figure 10.17**.

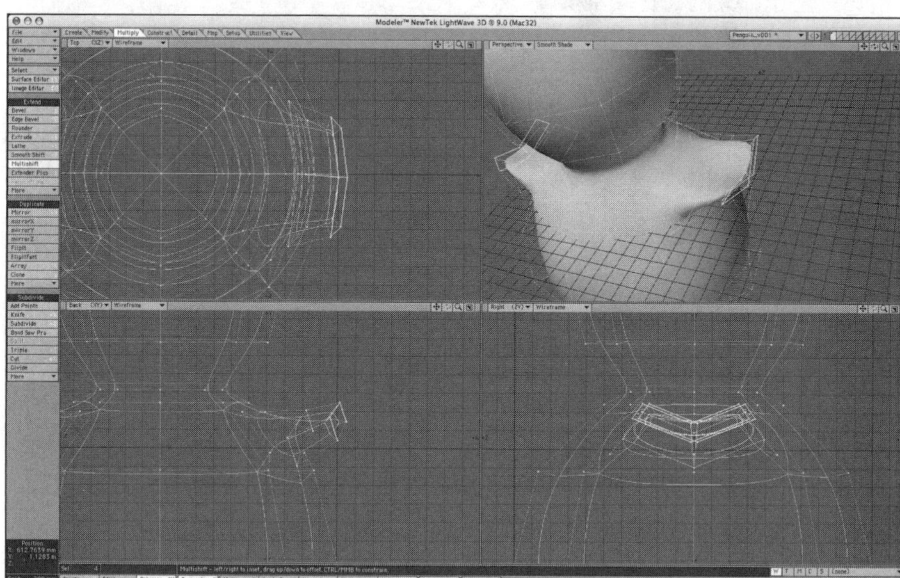

Figure 10.17 Multishift again to create additional geometry.

13. Press the spacebar to turn off the Multishift tool. Deselect all polygons (press /). Save your work by pressing **s**.
14. Next, press the Ctrl+t to activate the Drag tool.

    With the Drag tool, you can easily click and drag a point to shape the geometry. And because your model is in subpatch mode, made up of simple polygons, you'll be able to easily control its shape.

Note

You don't need to turn off one tool before you use another. Simply pressing the button or keyboard shortcut for a new tool automatically deactivates whatever tool you're using. However, because it's important that you're aware of your process, the instructions here are explicit about deactivating tools and activating new ones.

15. Make the Perspective viewport full screen. You can do this by placing your mouse in the view and pressing **0** on your numeric keypad. Or, click the small triangle icon in the top right of the viewport.
16. Change the viewport style to Wireframe Shade, as shown in **Figure 10.18**. This will help you see the points to drag.

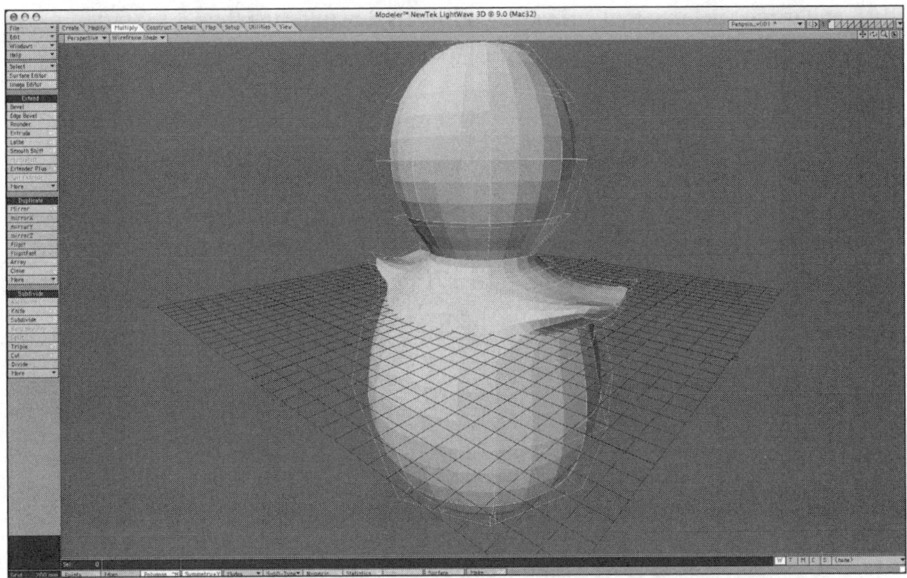

Figure 10.18 Make the Perspective view full frame, and change the viewport style to Wireframe Shade.

17. Click, hold, and drag on the point in the top center of the flipper. Drag it up on the Y-axis to round out the top of the flipper. **Figure 10.19** shows the operation.

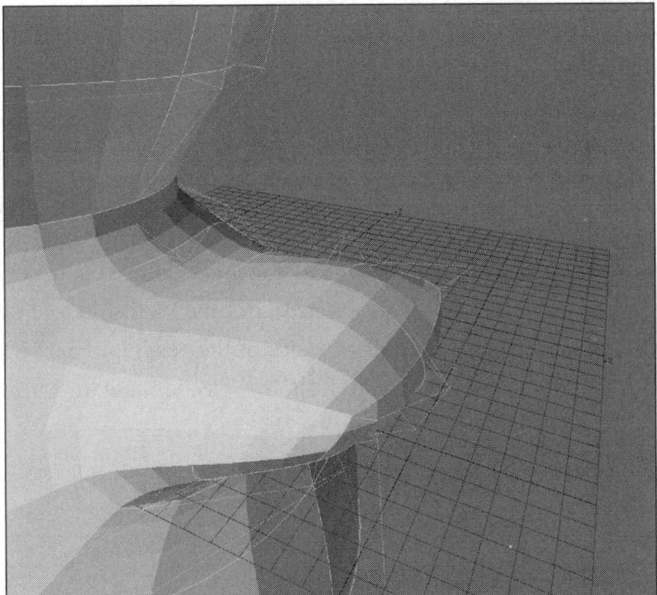

Figure 10.19 Click and drag on the point at the top of the flipper to round out the top.

18. Still using the Drag tool, bring the endpoints down for the flipper to start a curvature. Bring the bottom center points up into the flipper a bit to help the shape. **Figure 10.20** shows the example.

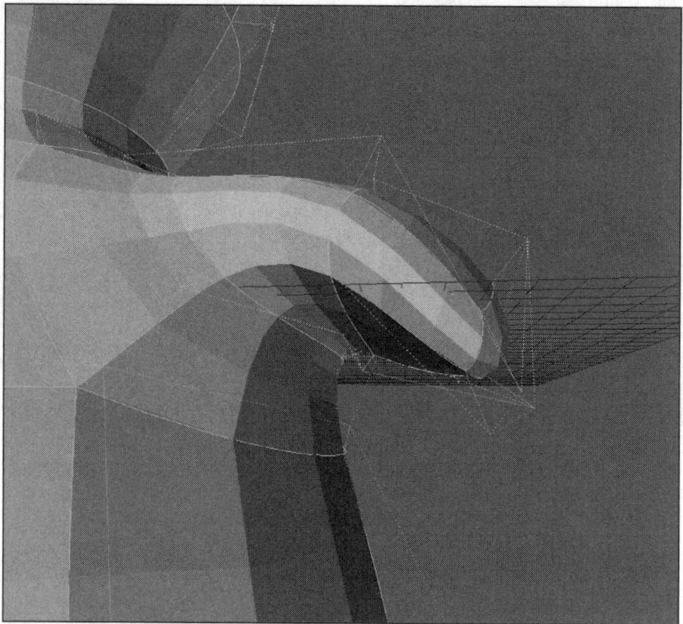

Figure 10.20 Continue shaping the flipper by dragging points downward.

Note

If you find that it's hard to grab specific points, press the Tab key to toggle off Subpatch mode, and then press Tab again to turn it back on.

19. After you've shaped the flipper using the Drag tool, you need to make it a bit longer. With the two end polygons selected, click the Multishift tool twice more to extend the selection down toward the side of the penguin. After you've applied Multishift to generate more polygons from the selection, use the Move and Rotate tools to adjust the flipper, as in **Figure 10.21**.

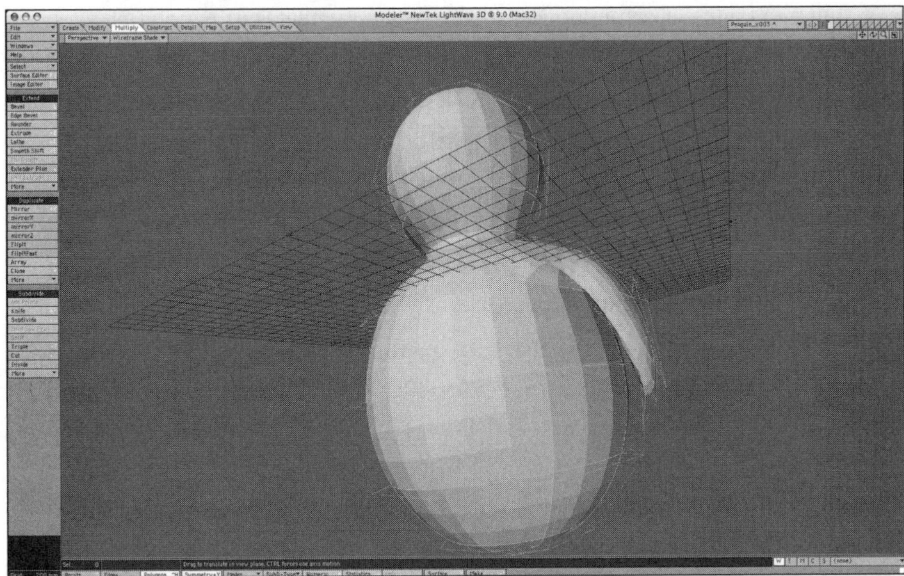

Figure 10.21 Use Multishift to multiply the two end polygons, then use Move and Rotate to pull them down toward the side of the penguin.

20. From here, use the Drag tool (Ctrl+t) to shape the flipper, and narrow it at the ends. When you like the shape of the flipper, save your work.

You can see that with just a few extra polygons beveled off the main body, you can create additional elements on your model. The same technique can be used for legs, arms, or even tentacles. Now that the flippers are shaping up, you'll shape and blend the head and body spheres for a more continuous look.

Exercise 10.3 Shaping the Penguin Body

Now that the flippers have been created, it'll be easier to shape the body and head of the penguin. Could you have done this earlier when you built the body? Sure, but it will help the overall proportion of the model by first creating the limbs, then fine-tuning details such as the eyes. Some artists prefer to build the eyes first, then the body, so it comes down to what you prefer and also the type of character you're building. For the penguin, the eyes can be detailed in after the body. This next exercise will help you shape the penguin and build better flow from the body to the head.

1. Save your work as a new increment by pressing Shift+s.
2. Jump back to a Quad view by clicking the small triangle in the top of the Perspective viewport, or by pressing **0** on your numeric keypad.

3. Jump to Points selection mode, and also make sure that your Action Center is set to Selection from the Modes drop-down menu at the bottom of the interface.
4. Most importantly, turn off the Symmetry tool. You're going to be working on the entire model's points, and using Symmetry will have a negative effect on your task. It will do this because your actions will be normal on the positive X-axis, but mirrored (or opposite) on the negative X-axis.
5. Press the Tab key to turn off Subpatch mode for now, if it's on. It will be a little easier for you to see your point selections.
6. Select the two rows of points that make up the shoulder area and neck. Select with the right mouse button in the Back view. **Figure 10.22** shows the selection.

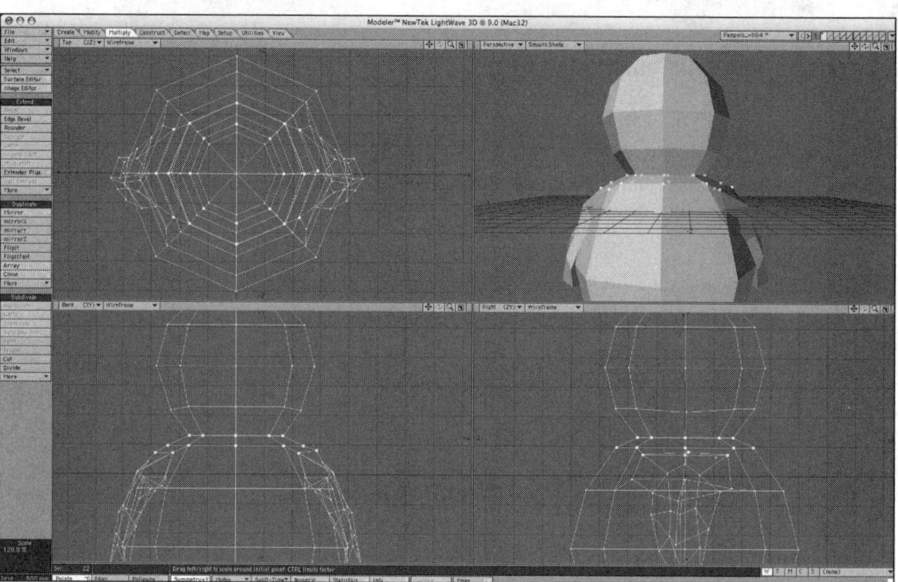

Figure 10.22 Select the two rows of points in the Back view and scale them up 20%.

7. Press Shift+h for the Size tool, and increase the size of the selection by about 20%, as shown in Figure 10.22.
8. Deselect the row of points around the shoulder area, leaving just the points around the neck selected. Increase the size of the selection by about 70%, as shown in **Figure 10.23**.

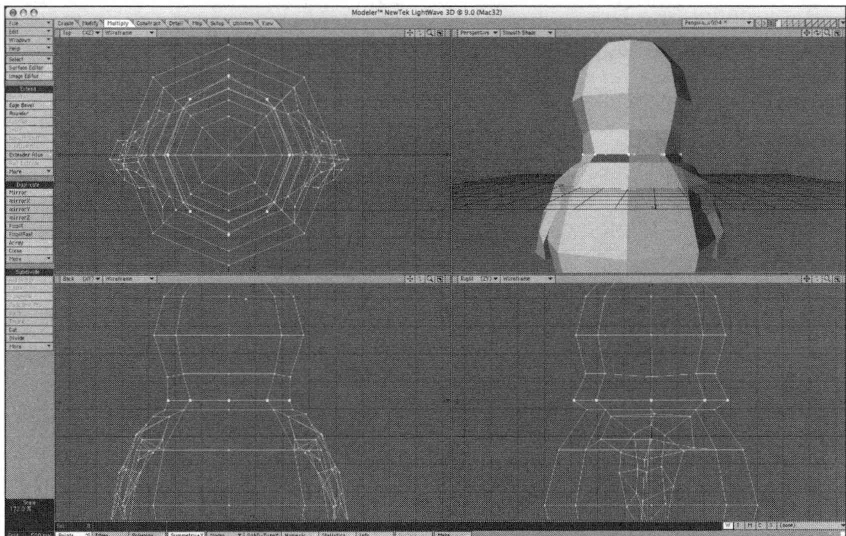

Figure 10.23 Deselect the row of points around the shoulder area, leaving just the points around the neck, then increase the size of the selection.

9. You might notice that in the Right view, the points now extend too far on the Z-axis on the front and back. Press **h** to open the Stretch tool, and in the Right view, click and drag to stretch the points in, making sure they are aligned with the points beneath them, as shown in **Figure 10.24**.

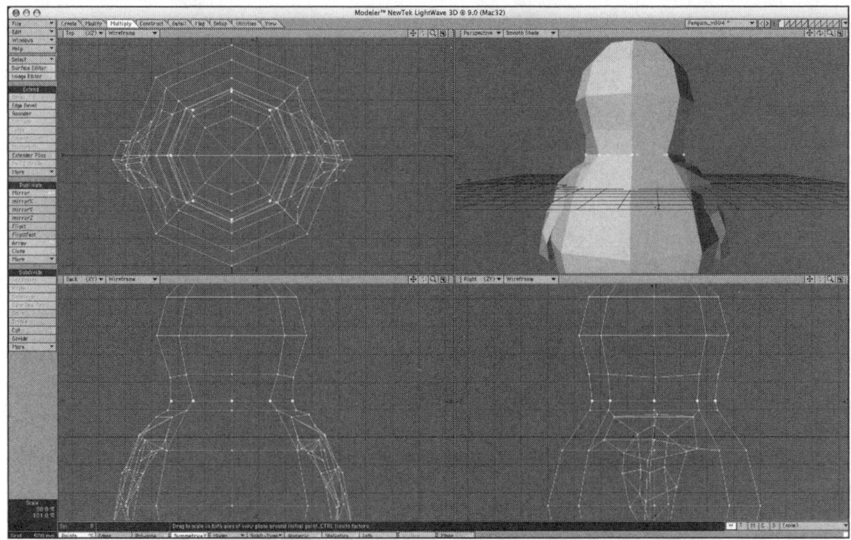

Figure 10.24 For the points that extend too far in the positive and negative Z-axes, stretch them in to flow with the rest of the model.

10. Turn off the Stretch tool. Deselect all points, and then press the Tab key to see the model with subpatches applied. **Figure 10.25** shows the penguin, now with a head that is not quite as separate from the body.

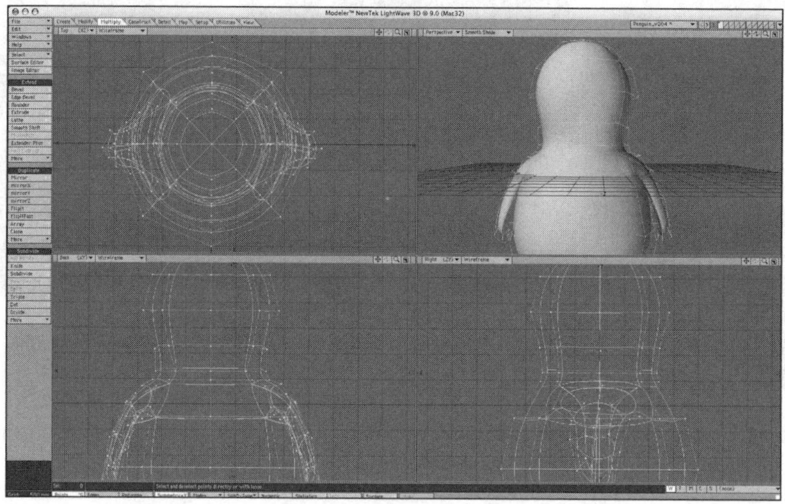

Figure 10.25 The head now blends better with the body when subpatches are applied.

11. The neck is a good size—not too small, and not too large. However, you're not building a perfect penguin here but rather a caricature of a penguin. So, select the points around the top half of the head for some additional shaping, as shown in **Figure 10.26**.

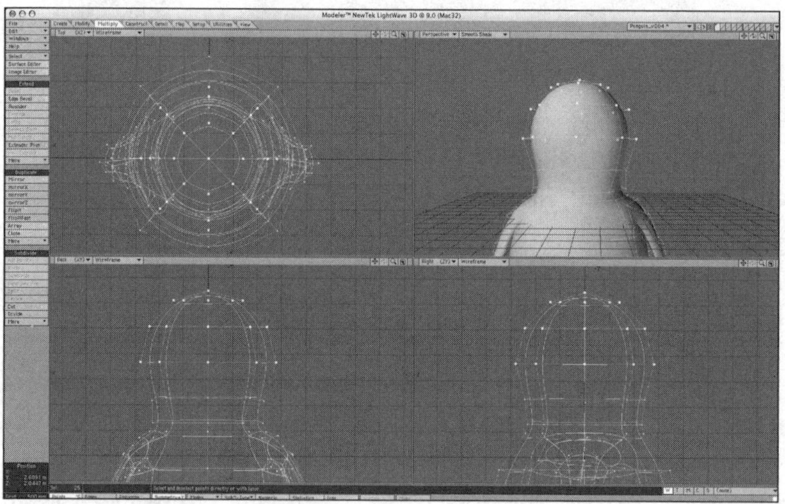

Figure 10.26 Select the points that make up the top half of the penguin head.

12. With the points selected, press Shift+h for the Size tool, also found on the Modify tab. Reduce the size of the selection to about 80%, as shown in **Figure 10.27**. Remember that you can view the Size amount in the lower-left corner info panel. You want to scale the selection down enough so that the edges are almost straight, coming up the side of the head from the body.

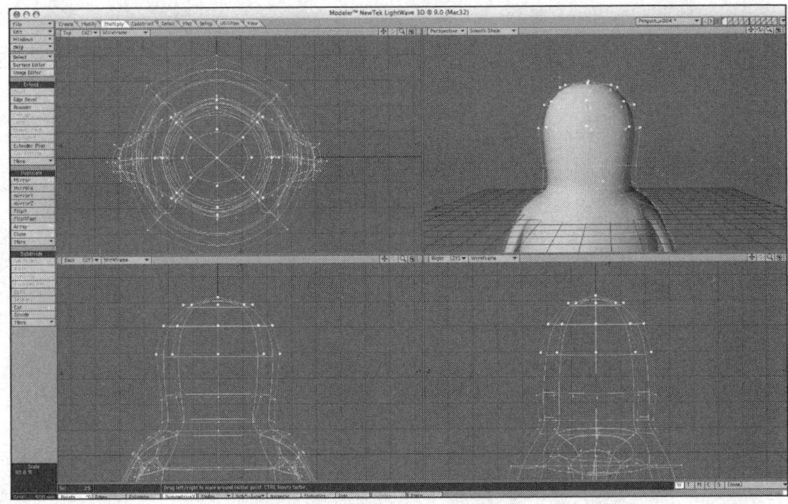

Figure 10.27 Reduce the size of the selection to about 80%.

13. Press **t** and, holding the Ctrl key, move the selected points down toward the body to even out the mesh (**Figure 10.28**).

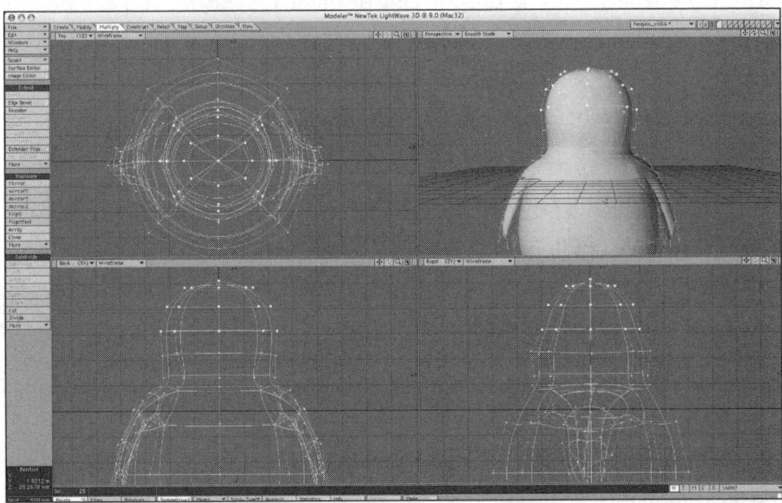

Figure 10.28 Move the selected points down toward the body to balance out the head and body.

14. Now take some time on your own and adjust any points as you see fit. Take the bottom two rows of points on the body and stretch them together a bit. **Figure 10.29** shows the shape. You can use the Drag tool, lasso-select an entire row of points and stretch them, and so on.

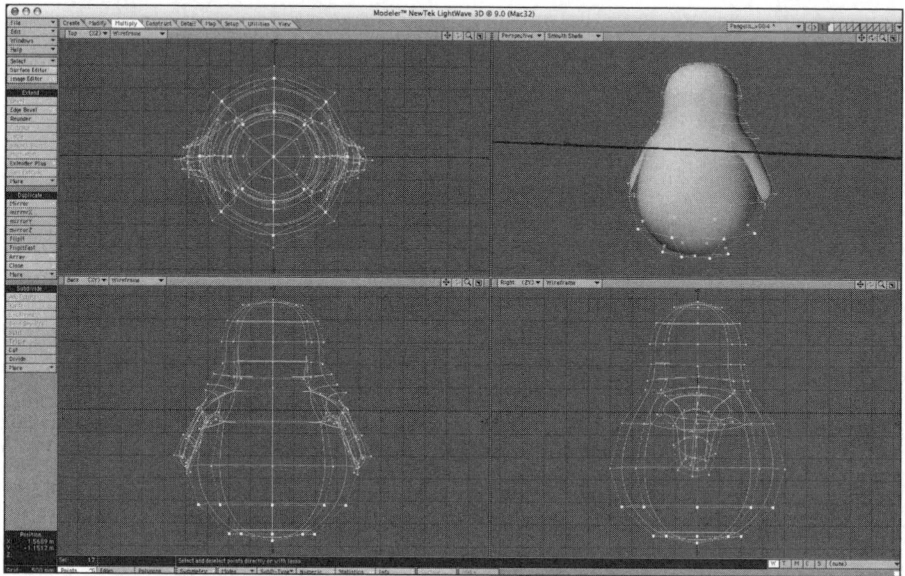

Figure 10.29 Squash the penguin a bit to pull the shape up at the base.

15. Save your work!

Adjusting the model is not so hard, is it? One of the main reasons you can make simple adjustments here and see results is because you're working with subpatches on simple geometry. It's a powerful combination. But wait, there's more! You need to add some feet and eyes to this little guy before you get to surfacing.

Exercise 10.4 Building the Penguin's Feet

The relative importance of body features such as feet varies from character to character. With hoofed animals, for example, feet are relatively nondescript and don't require too much detail. Penguin feet are another story, however. Along with their eyes (which you'll build shortly), penguin feet are major defining characteristics—critical to their look and their motion. So make your penguin some happy feet.

1. Turn Symmetry back on by pressing Shift+y.
2. Rotate around to the bottom of the model in the Perspective view, and select the two polygons, centered on the right (positive) X-axis, as shown in **Figure 10.30**.

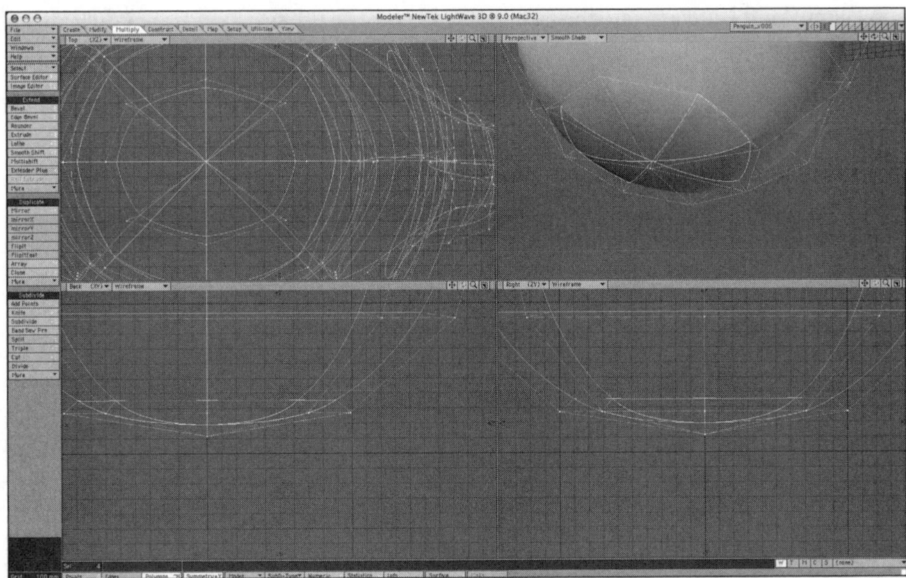

Figure 10.30 With the Symmetry tool active, select the bottom two polygons to begin creating the feet.

3. Press **e** to activate Extender Plus. Press it only one time.
4. Then, press **t** to activate the Move tool. Click and drag down, just a slight amount, as shown in **Figure 10.31**.

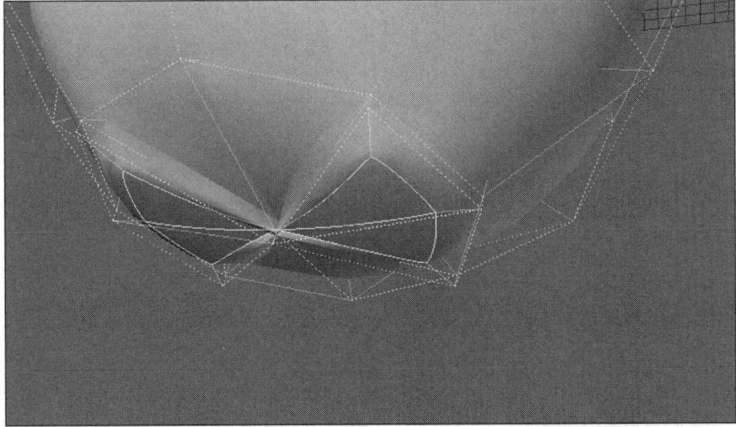

Figure 10.31 Use Extender Plus to multiply the selection, and then use the Move tool to bring the polygons down a bit from the body.

5. Now press **e** again for Extender Plus. This *multiplies*, or generates additional polygons, from the selection.

6. Press Shift+h to activate the Size tool, and increase the selection size by 30% or so. When the polygons start to expand into the penguin-body sphere, press **t** and pull them away from the sphere, as in **Figure 10.32**.

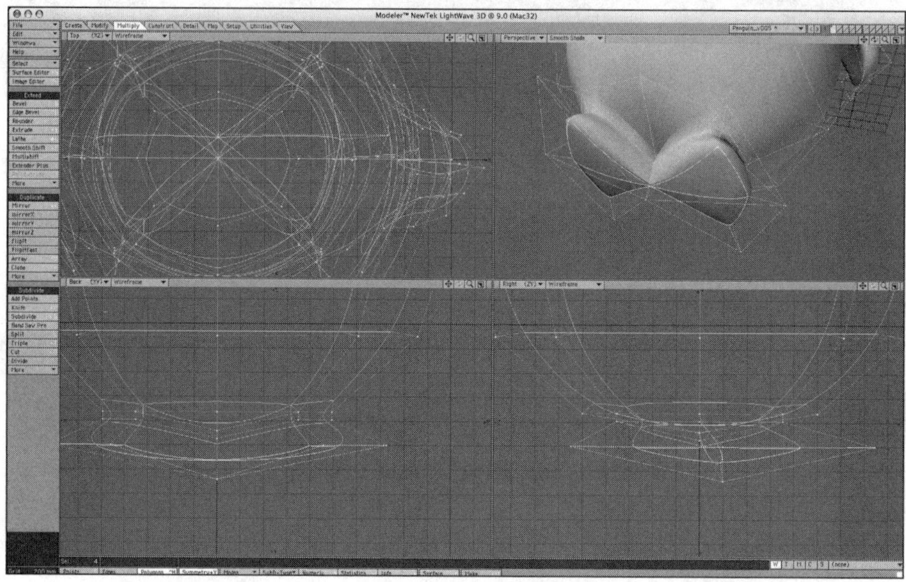

Figure 10.32 Use the Move tool to pull the expanded feet downward, away from the penguin's body.

7. Press **s** to save your work.
8. Use the Drag tool (Ctrl+t) to shape the feet to round out the corners (**Figure 10.33**).

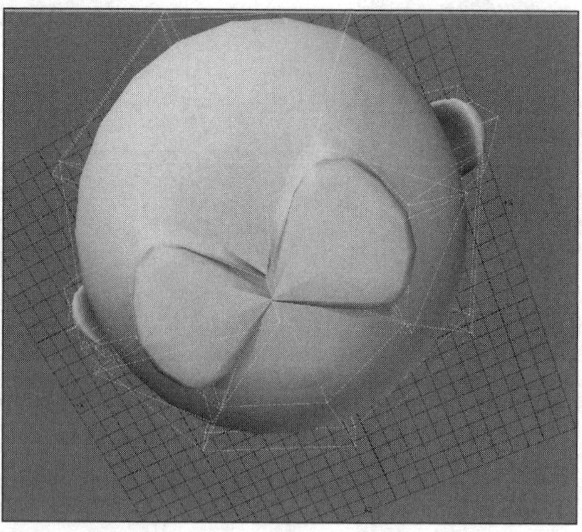

Figure 10.33 Shape the feet so that they're more oval in shape.

9. As you start creating the feet, you can see that even with subpatches active, the geometry is a bit sharp. Press **o** to open the General Options panel and then set the Subpatch Divisions value to 4, as shown in **Figure 10.34**.

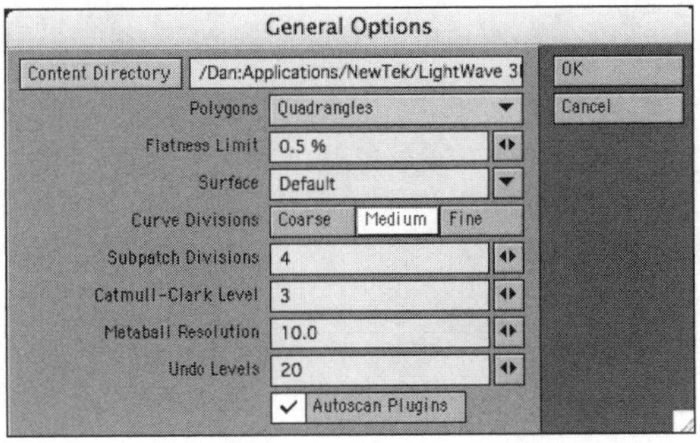

General Options
Content Directory /Dan:Applications/NewTek/LightWave 3
OK
Cancel
Polygons Quadrangles
Flatness Limit 0.5 %
Surface Default
Curve Divisions Coarse Medium Fine
Subpatch Divisions 4
Catmull-Clark Level 3
Metaball Resolution 10.0
Undo Levels 20
Autoscan Plugins

Figure 10.34 Increase the Subpatch Divisions setting to create even a smoother mesh.

10. Select the two front polygons on the feet. Remember, Symmetry is still active, so selecting these polygons on the right side of the character will automatically select their counterparts on the left. Then, press **e** to multiply the selection with the Extender Plus tool.

11. Once the selection is extended, activate the Move tool (press **t**) and move the polygons forward on the Z-axis. You can move them in the top of right views, or rotate the Perspective view around to control axis movement (**Figure 10.35**).

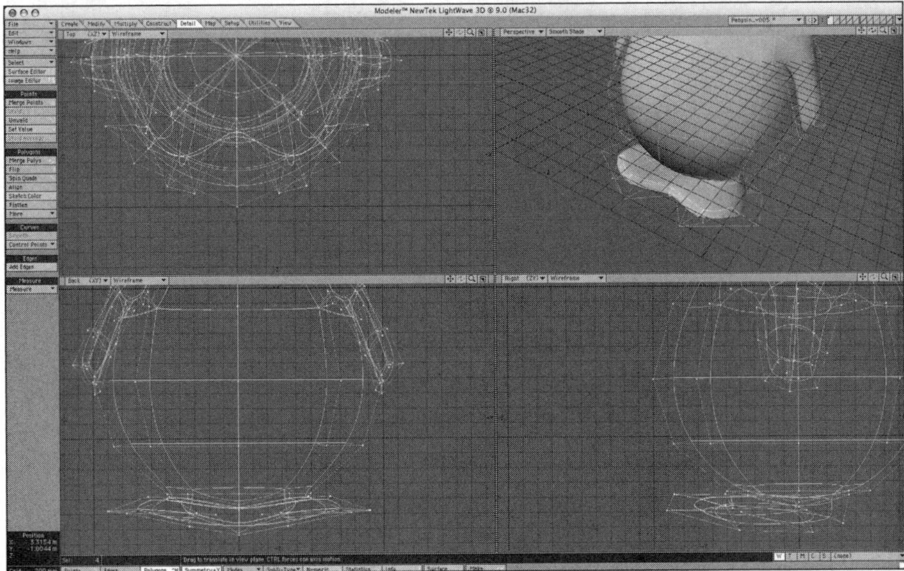

Figure 10.35 Pull the newly created polygons forward to extend the feet.

12. Use the Drag tool (Ctrl+t) to round out the tops of the feet. Grab points on the top and side to shape, as shown in **Figure 10.36**.

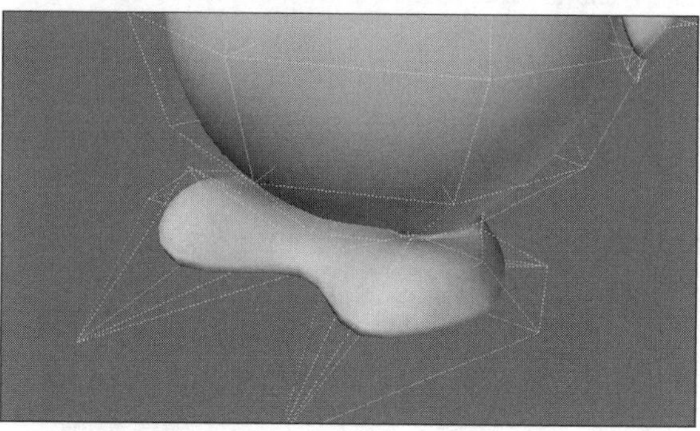

Figure 10.36 Shape the feet by rounding them out.

13. Now the feet are connected at the center. This is because you were using the Symmetry tool with polygons that were already connected. To separate them, you'll need to turn off the Symmetry tool first. Then, select the two front polygons of the right foot, as shown in **Figure 10.37**.

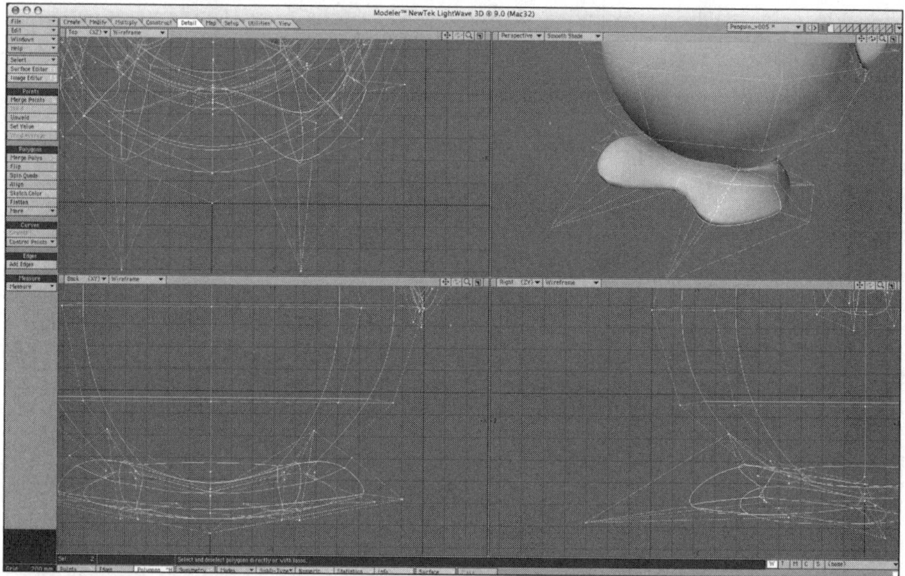

Figure 10.37 With the Symmetry tool turned off, select just the two front polygons of the right foot.

14. Press **e** to run Extender Plus on the selected polygons, then use Move (press **t**) and Drag (Ctrl+t) to shape. **Figure 10.38** shows the result.

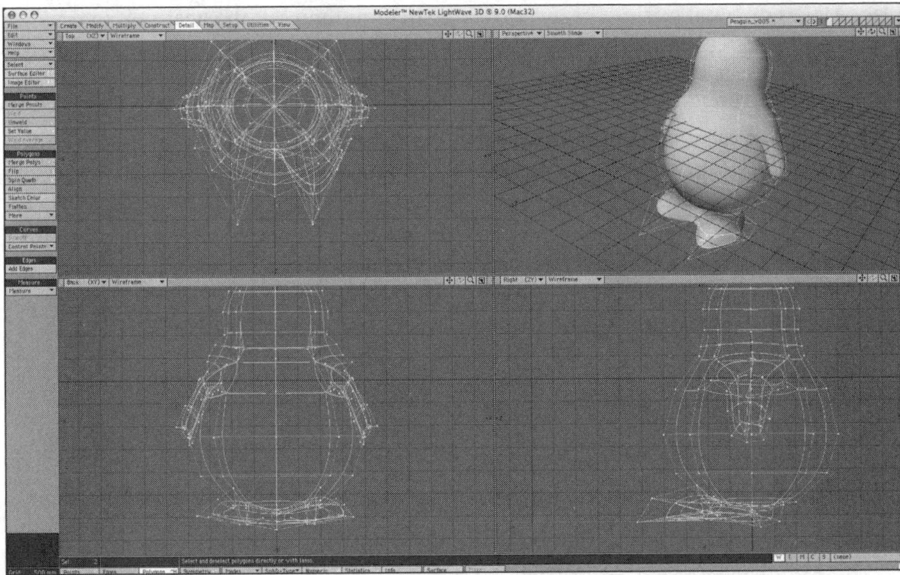

Figure 10.38 Multiply the selected polygons and pull them forward, and then shape with the Move and Drag tools.

15. Deselect the polygons, and repeat the last two steps on the left foot. It's OK if the feet are not identical—in fact, it's good to have a slight variation as no animal or human is perfectly identical on both sides. **Figure 10.39** shows the feet.

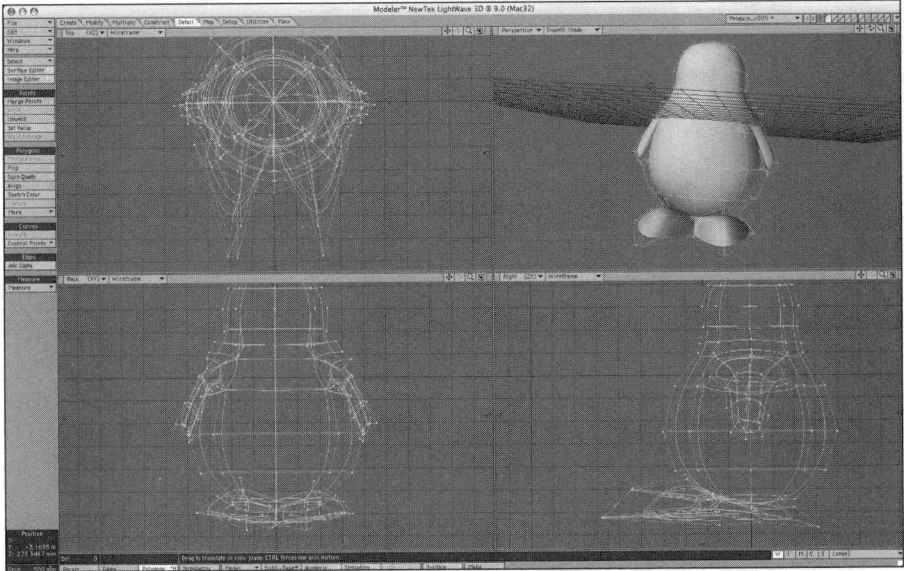

Figure 10.39 Repeating the process for the left foot results in two penguin feet.

16. Make any tweaks using the Drag tool, perhaps pulling out the heel a bit in the Right view, and then save your work.
17. One last thing you can do to the feet area is to drag the belly down for the penguin. First, turn on Symmetry (Shift+y) and then select the polygon on the right front side of the body, at the lower belly, as shown in **Figure 10.40**.

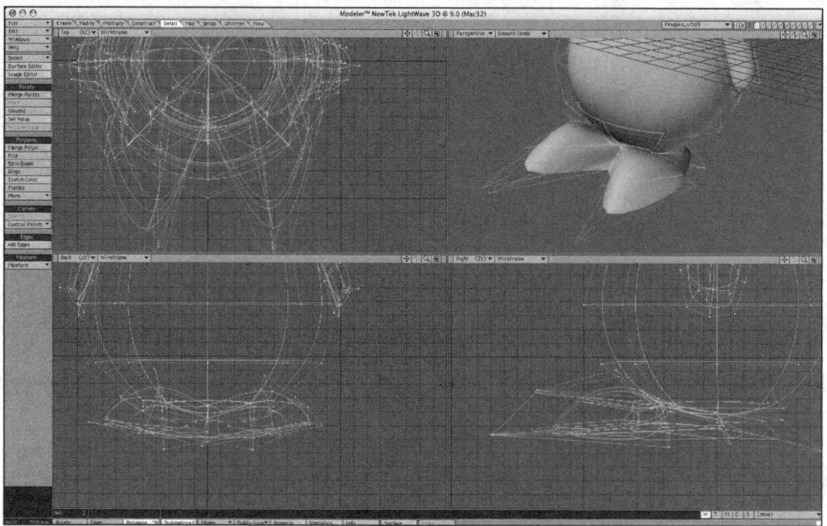

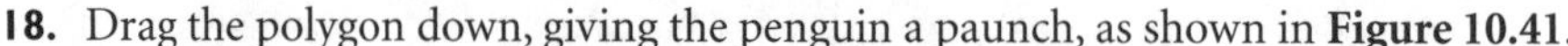

Figure 10.40 Select the bottom belly polygon on the right side of the body, with Symmetry active.

18. Drag the polygon down, giving the penguin a paunch, as shown in **Figure 10.41**.

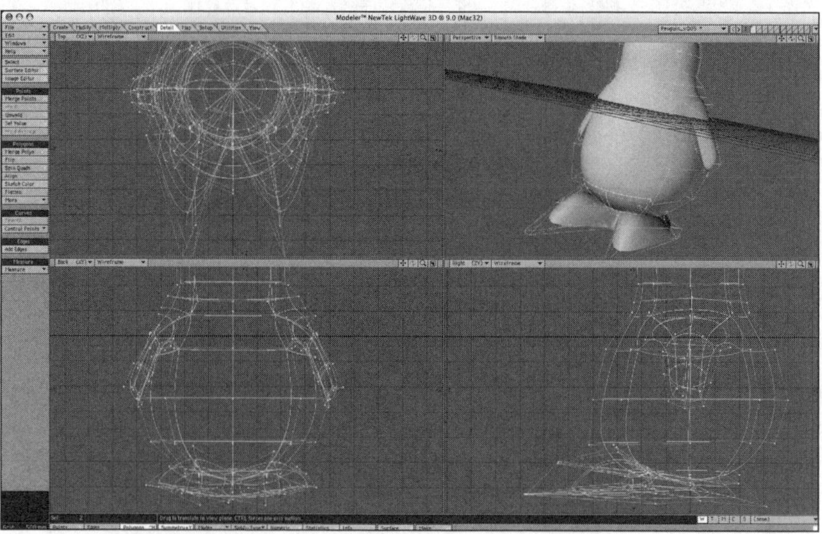

Figure 10.41 Pull the selected polygon down to extend the belly.

19. Save your work.

Again, using simple multiplication tools, along with move, rotate, and drag, you can build your character with little effort. Sure, the tweaking takes time, and if you ask any professional 3D artist, they might even tell you that a good majority of their creation time is in the "tweaking" process—the fine-tuning.

Exercise 10.5 Building the Penguin's Eyes

They say you should save the best for last. Are the eyes the best part of this model? That's hard to say, but we can say the eyes are the most important part of the model, as they can be the most expressive, making your character appear happy, sad, or angry. The eyes evoke emotion, and they are going to be a large part of this character.

1. Continuing from your saved project, press Shift+s to save an incremental version of your penguin character.
2. Turn Symmetry off for this next part; you'll model each eye separately to give the penguin an expressive look. But first, you'll create an eye socket. Select the three polygons at the base of the head, on the right side, as shown in **Figure 10.42**.

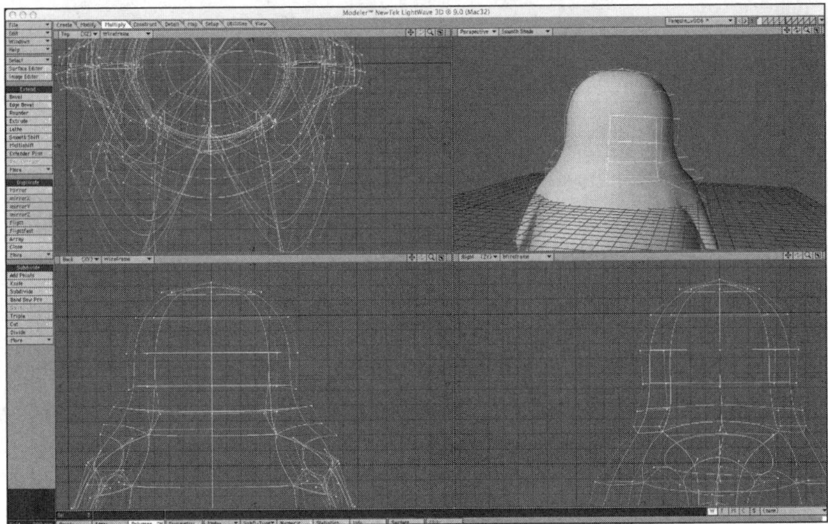

Figure 10.42 Start to create the eye socket by selecting three polygons at the base of the head.

3. Select the Multishift tool on the Multiply tab, then click and drag to inset and shift the polygons. Don't worry about how deep to inset the geometry—the idea is that you're creating a small cavity for the eye to rest in, about 300mm. **Figure 10.43** on the next page shows the effect.

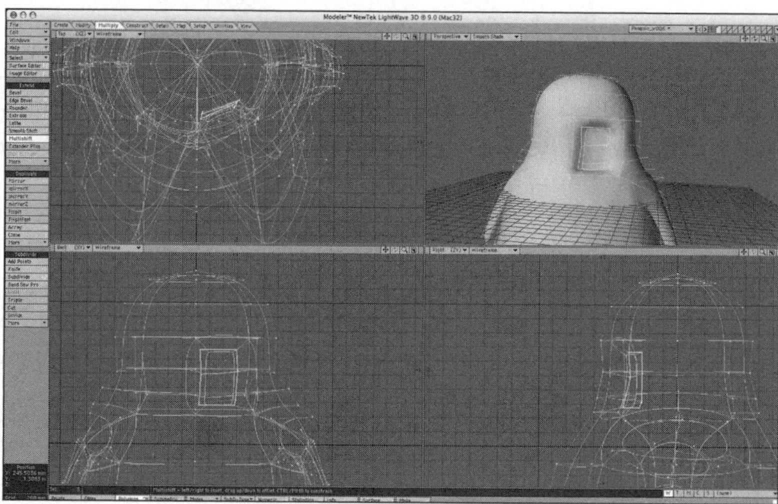

Figure 10.43 Use Multishift to bevel in the multiple polygons to create the eye socket.

Note

You should have the Numeric panel's Group Polygons option checked when using the Multishift tool.

4. Select the Drag tool (Ctrl+t) and pull the sides of the eye-socket polygons outward to round out the eye socket, as shown in **Figure 10.44**. Just click and drag on the points, and use the shaded Perspective view as your guide.

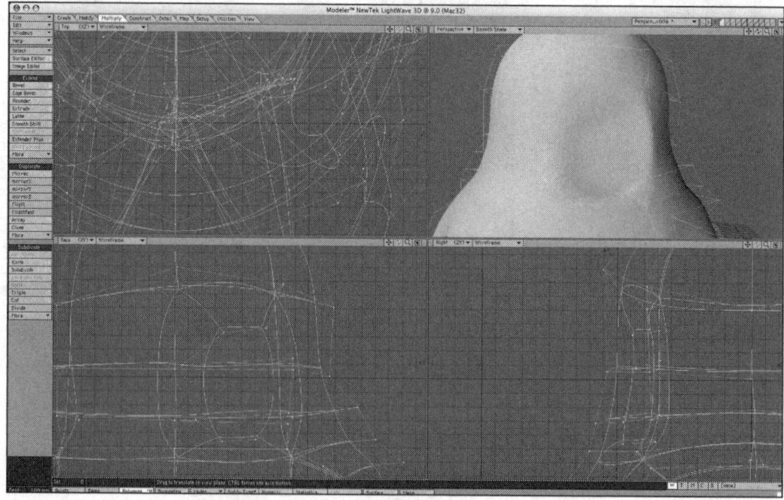

Figure 10.44 Round out the eye socket using the Drag tool.

5. Now, repeat the previous two steps for the other side of the penguin's head. Make the left eye socket a bit larger than the right, as shown in **Figure 10.45**, but round it out the same way you did the right socket. When you've finished, save your work.

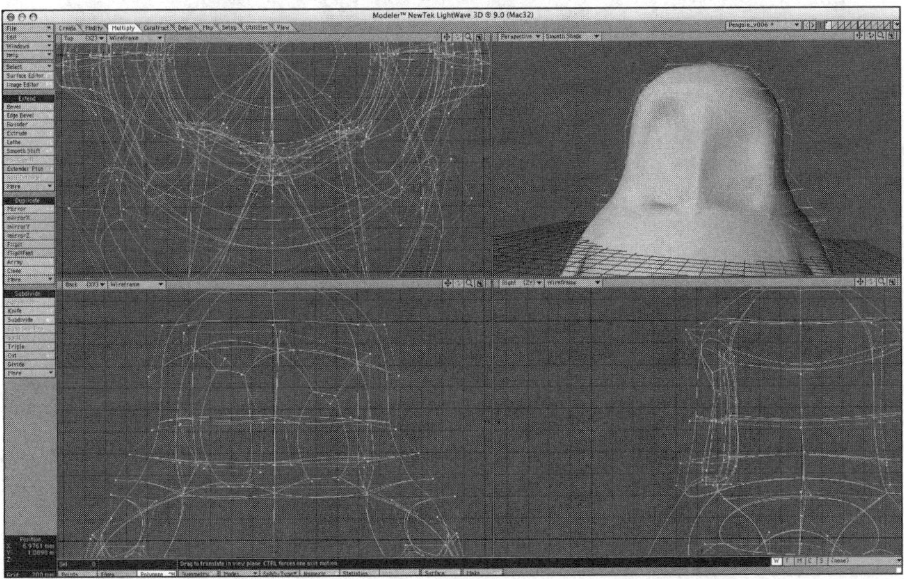

Figure 10.45 Create the left eye socket with the Multishift and Drag tools, but make it larger than the right eye socket.

Note

When selecting polygons, be careful that you don't accidentally grab polygons on the back of the penguin's head. Always pay attention to your selections, and look at the Sel: info at the bottom of the interface to see your selection amount. If you're trying to select three polygons, and the Sel: indicator says "6," you know you've selected too many. A good trick is to press Shift+a after you make a selection. This maximizes the selection within the window, and usually reveals any polygons you may have selected accidentally.

6. Save your model once the left eye socket is created, then go to a new layer, placing the penguin on a background layer.
7. In the new layer, create a ball on the Z-axis to fit the eye socket. **Figure 10.46** on the next page shows the screen.

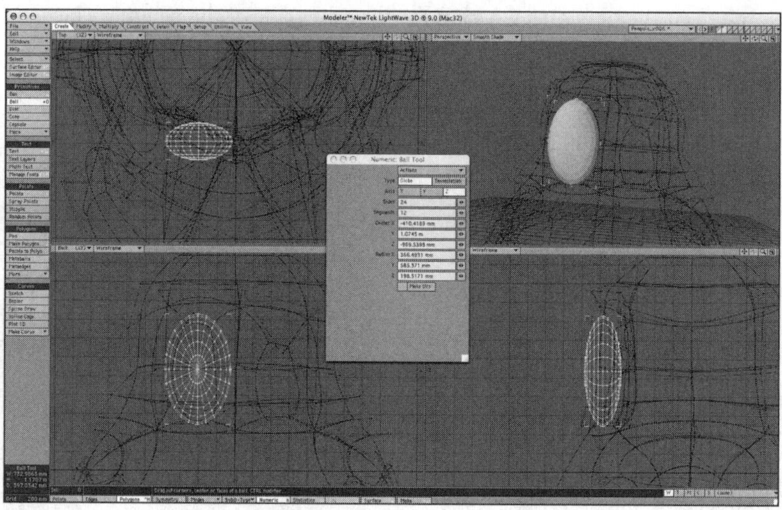

Figure 10.46 Create a ball to build the eye.

8. Rotate the ball slightly and move it to fit into the eye socket.
9. Press Shift+v to activate the Mirror tool, then open the Numeric panel by pressing **n** to mirror the ball across the X-axis to create the right eye. You'll see the eyeball instantly mirrored across the X-axis (the default "reflection" axis for Mirror operations). Close the Numeric panel, and then press the spacebar to turn off the Mirror tool.
10. Select the mirrored eyeball, then press **h** for the Stretch command and squash the eyeball down (stretch on the Y-axis) a bit. **Figure 10.47** shows the two eyes.

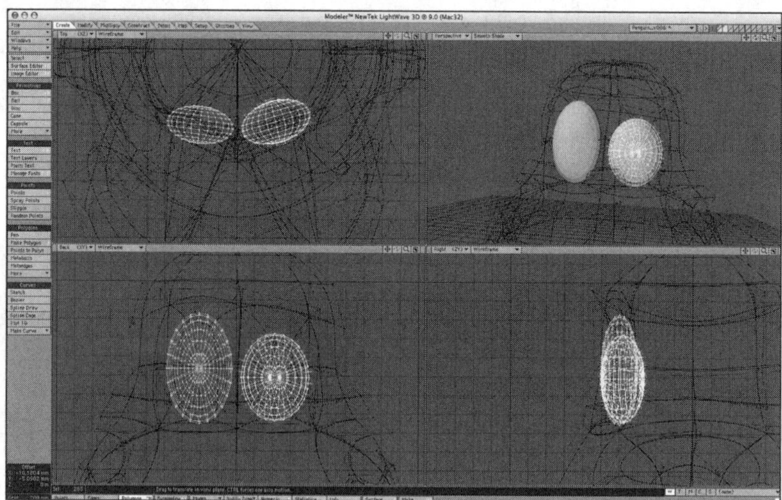

Figure 10.47 Mirror the eyeball using the default numeric values and squash it down.

11. Hold the Shift key and click the thumbnail for Layer 1 to display the shaded penguin model along with the eyes. **Figure 10.48** shows the character so far.

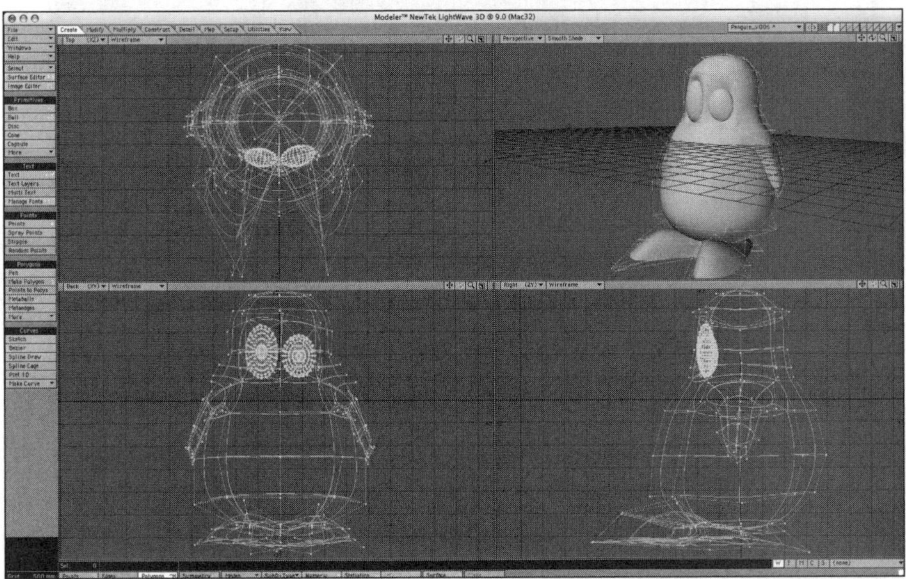

Figure 10.48 Hold the Shift key to select both the eye and penguin layers to see them full-shaded in the Perspective view.

12. Click back into the second layer where the eyeballs are. Select just one of them, and then press Ctrl+x to cut it. Click the thumbnail for a new blank layer, and then press Ctrl+v to paste.

    Placing each eye in its own layer will let you animate them individually.

13. Save your work.

14. The eyes need a little more work before you surface them. Eyelids can help with their range of expression. Start with the left side of the penguin in Layer 1. Choose three polygons that make up the top half of the eye socket, as shown in **Figure 10.49** on the next page.

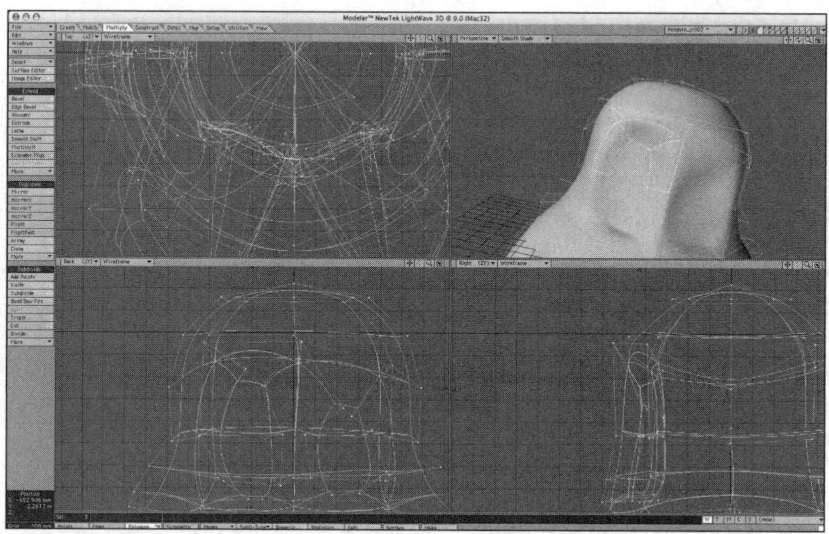

Figure 10.49 Select three polygons that make up the top part of the left eye socket.

15. Using the Multishift tool (found on the Multiply tab), click and drag to pull the selected polygons up and away from the penguin's head, similar to **Figure 10.50**.

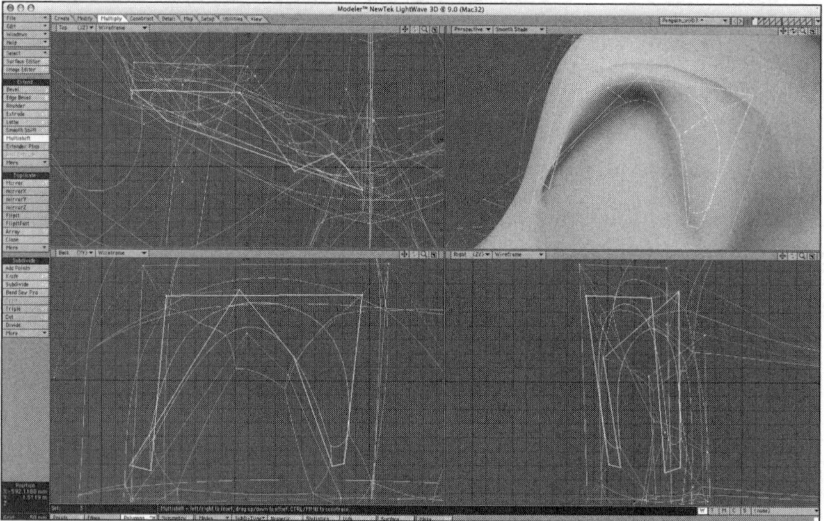

Figure 10.50 Use Multishift to bevel in the multiple polygons to create the eyelid.

16. Use the Drag tool (Ctrl+t) to shape the eyelid and blend it smoothly with the head. Hold the Shift key and click the thumbnail for the layer containing the left eye to see how the eyelid looks with the eye. Feel free to drag points to shape the eyelid as you see fit. **Figure 10.51** shows the example.

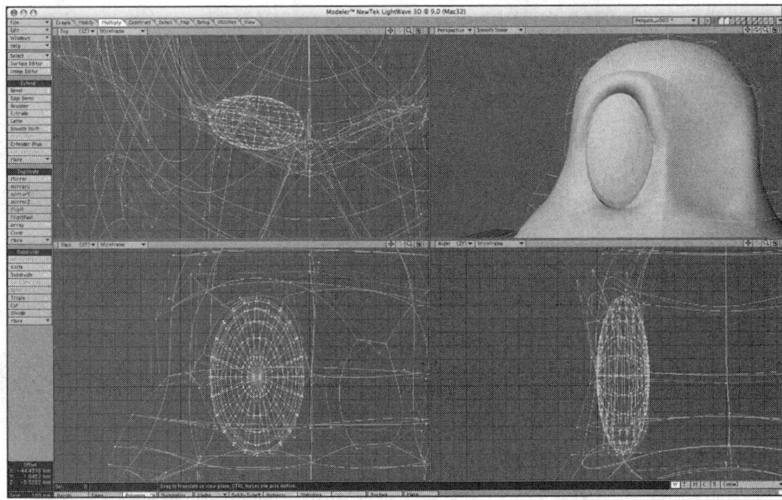

Figure 10.51 Using the Drag tool to smooth out the polygons, you can blend the eyelid with the head.

17. Go ahead and repeat the previous steps to create the eyelid for the right side of the penguin. Start by selecting a few polygons, use the Multishift tool, and then use the Drag tool to shape. **Figure 10.52** shows the two eyes with eyelids.

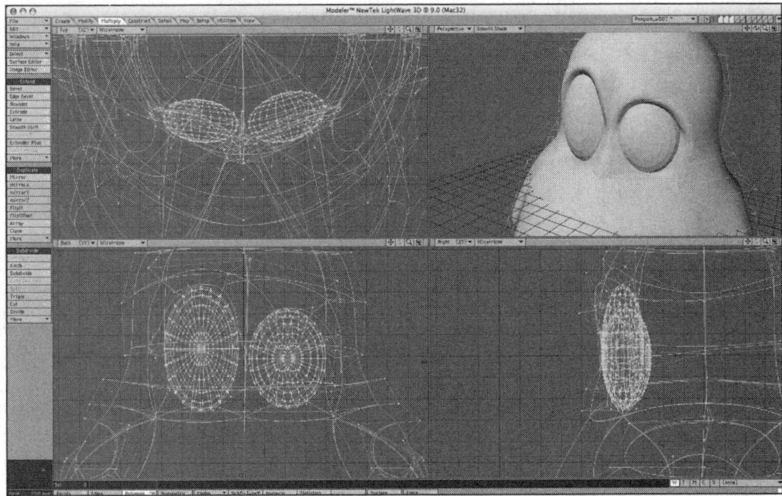

Figure 10.52 Create the second eyelid, tweak to taste, and save your work.

18. Save your work!

Just a little more to go, and the surfacing will begin. You'll soon start to see the character taking on a personality.

19. Select the four polygons that lie directly between the bottom halves of the eyes, as shown in **Figure 10.53**.

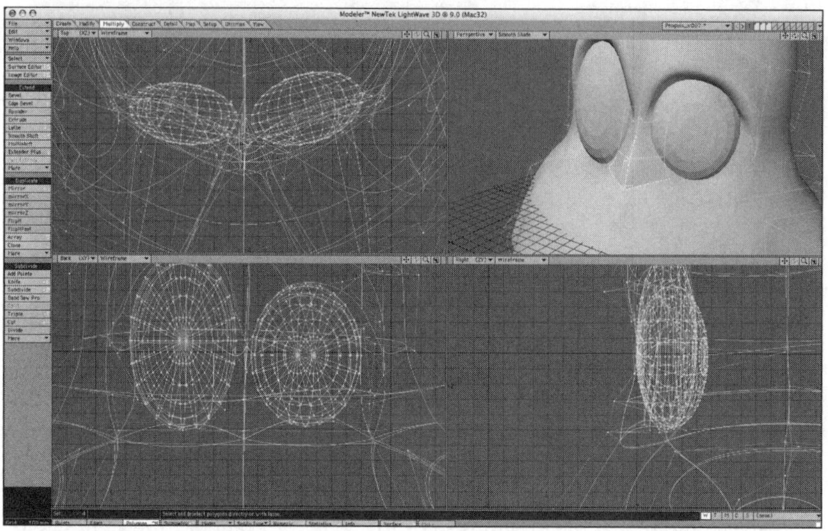

Figure 10.53 Select these four polygons to begin creating the beak.

20. Using Multishift again, click and drag to pull out a beak for the penguin. It is a bird, after all! Overdoing it with Multishift might make the beak look a bit like a botched nose job, so only bevel out the polygons a small amount. **Figure 10.54** shows the operation.

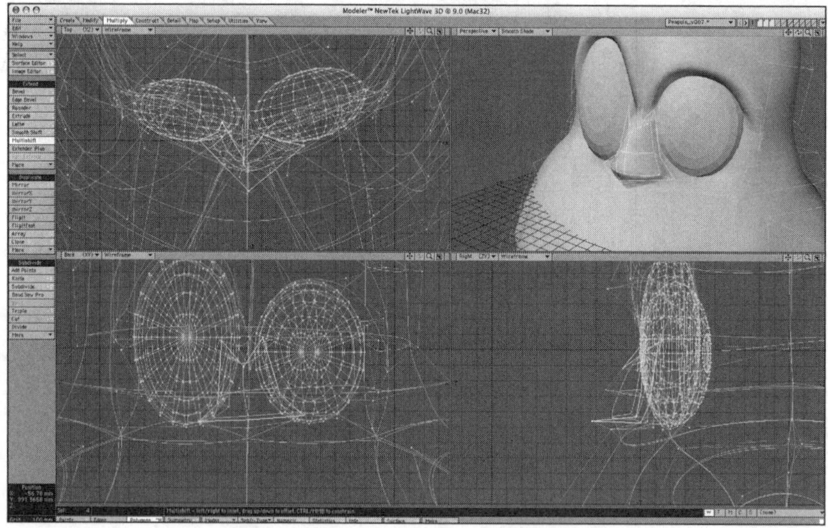

Figure 10.54 Use Multishift to bevel out the beak.

21. Now use the Drag tool (Ctrl+t) to shape the beak, making it triangular in shape, with more height and a flat bottom. **Figure 10.55** shows the operation.

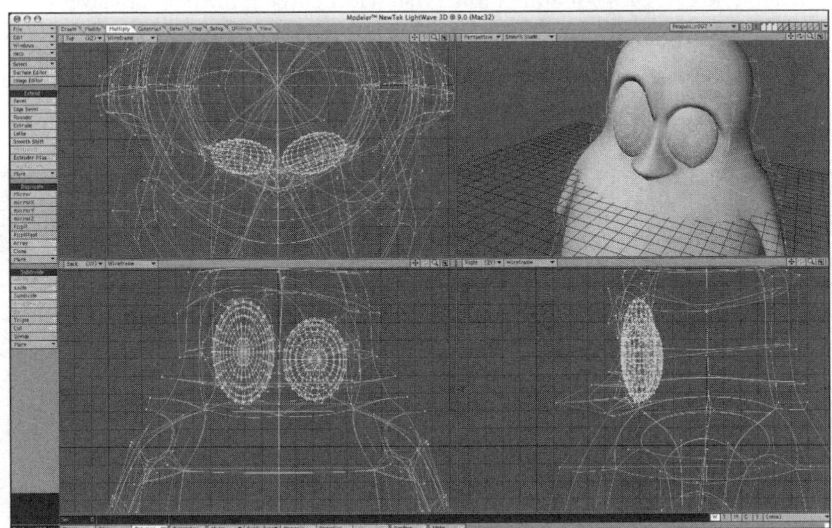

Figure 10.55 Use the Drag tool to shape the beak.

22. Save your work. From here, it's a matter of tweaking (there's that word again) the shape and overall flow of the character. To increase the model's quality a little, open the General Options panel (press **o**) and set the Subpatch Divisions option to 5. Note that you will control this later in Layout for both display and rendering.

    You might want to play with the shape of the eyelids, which also serve as eyebrows. Bringing the center down, you'll create more of a mean-looking character. Bringing them up and drooping the sides, you'll create a sweeter-looking character. But what's really cool is to animate these with morphs. To do that, you first need to create selection sets so that at any point, you can easily go back and make adjustments.

    To further enhance your learning, this chapter is continuing through the use of a QuickTime video, found on this book's DVD (3D_Garage_Videos\Chapter_Videos\CH10_SelectionMorph.mov). You'll learn how to create selection sets and morphs, and how to animate this little guy! Be sure to check that out.

23. You'll see how to surface the penguin in the videos on the book's DVD; however, it's good to see the model as complete as possible now, before you add other details and get ready for animation. First, select Layer 1, the penguin layer. Press **q** to open the Change Surface dialog box. Name the surface **Penguin_Body**; choose black as the surface color; and type in a Specularity setting of **80%**. Click OK to close the panel. **Figure 10.56** shows the results.

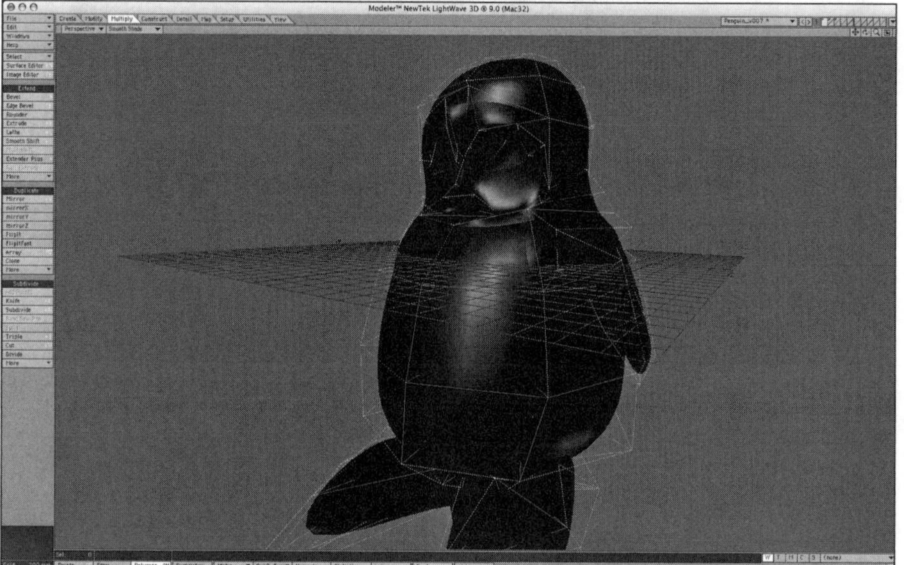

Figure 10.56 Set the entire penguin color to black.

24. The entire object won't be black; the nose, the feet, and the belly remain to be assigned separate surfaces and colors. But since the majority of the character is black, you can set this surface first. Select the polygons that make up the beak of the penguin.
25. Press **q** and set the color to an orangey-yellow and name these polygons **Penguin_Beak**.
26. Next, select the feet of the penguin in Polygons mode, change their surface name to **Penguin_Feet**, and color them yellow. **Figure 10.57** shows the changes.

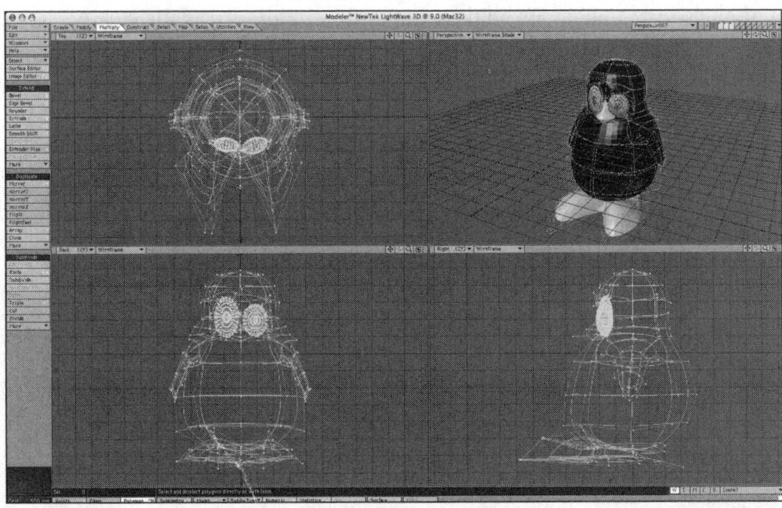

Figure 10.57 Change the surface of the penguin's feet to a yellowish color.

27. Save your model!
28. Now, jump to one of the eye layers, change the surface name to **Penguin_Eye_White**, and, as you might have guessed, set the color to white.
29. Then, carefully select the polygons that make up the front of the eye, as shown in **Figure 10.58**. This is the reason you created the ball on the Z-axis, so that the polygons face forward and allow you to apply multiple surfaces.

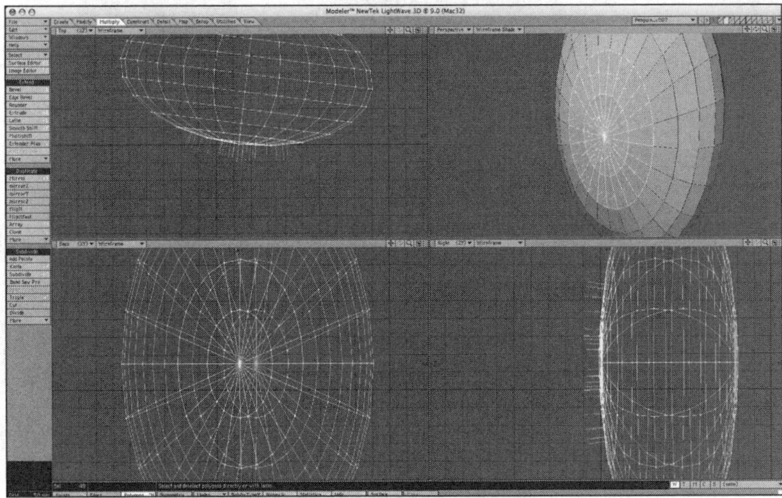

Figure 10.58 Select the polygons on the front of the eye that will make up the iris.

30. With the selected polygons on the front of the eye, press **q** again, change the surface name to **Penguin_Eye_Iris**, and color it blue. **Figure 10.59** shows the adjustment.

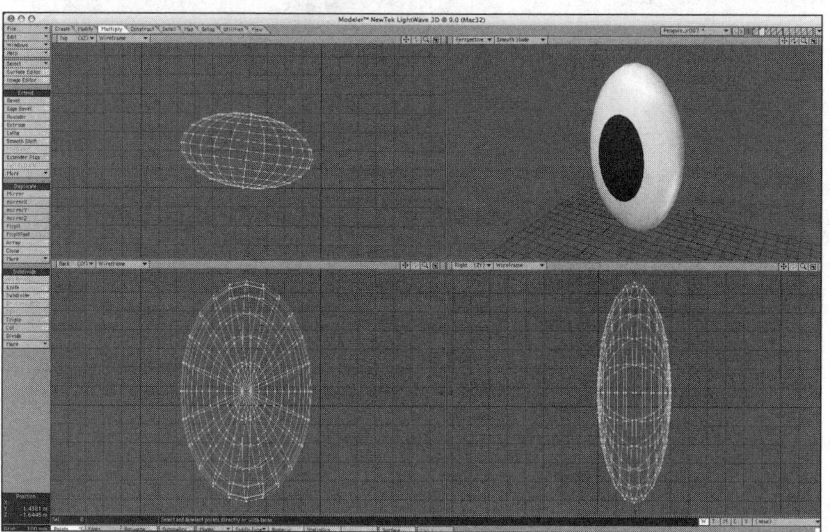

Figure 10.59 Set the selected polygons to a new surface name and color them blue.

31. Press the spacebar to deselect the polygons, then select just the inner ring of polygons inside the blue area, as shown in **Figure 10.60**.

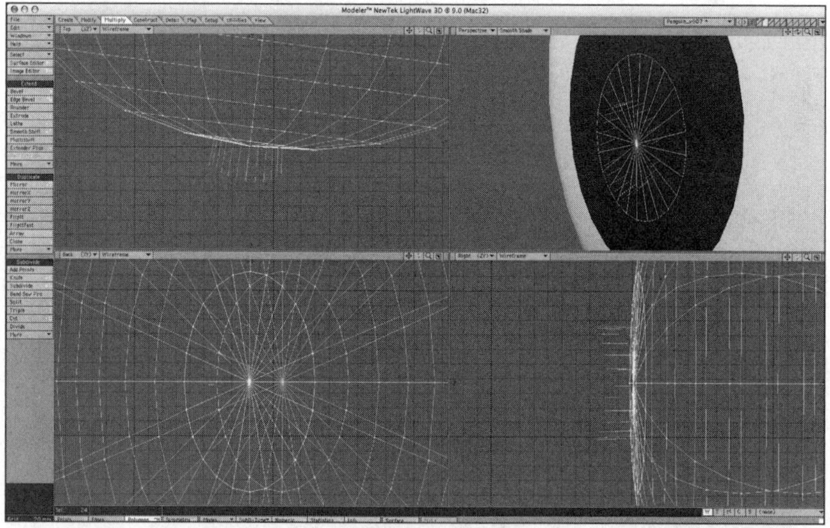

Figure 10.60 Select the polygons on the front inside of the eye to surface the pupil.

32. Set the surface name of the selected polygons to **Penguin_Eye_Pupil**, and color the surface black. **Figure 10.61** shows the eye.

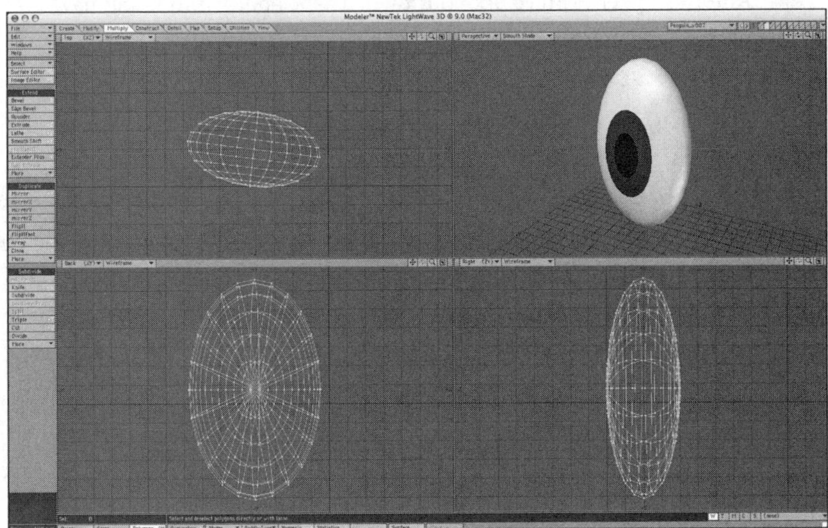

Figure 10.61 Change the surface name and color the last part of the eye to create a pupil.

33. Repeat the previous steps to surface the other eye in Layer 3. **Figure 10.62** shows all three layers together—the penguin and the two eyes. You can use the same surface settings, so it's only a matter of selecting the desired polygons, pressing **q**, and applying the surface.

Figure 10.62 Adding surfaces to the penguin and the eyes starts to give the character more charm.

34. Save your work. You did it!

While it's taken a little bit of work, you have successfully modeled your own character in LightWave. And most likely, you've put your own artistic ability into it and have created something much better than what was described here.

The Next Step

Use the techniques presented here to build whatever you want—the process is the same throughout. It's a matter of generating the basic shape and then molding it into the shape you desire. You add details with multiplication tools, transition tools, and rotation. This chapter has given you a good overview of not only the modeling process but also the most common tools used to accomplish a task. But it's not over yet! On the book's DVD are QuickTime videos that take you to the next level with the character. You'll learn how to surface the belly and then add added surface details. From there, you'll set up a bone structure and animate the character. Chapter 12, "Bones and Rigging," will use this character as a project for learning LightWave's deformation tools, commonly known as bones.

But before you get there, how about continuing the surfacing process with some added information on LightWave v9's new, cool, node-based texturing tools. Read on to understand this complex area of the program.

Chapter 11
Node-Based Texturing

LightWave 3D has always had a powerful texture editor. In recent years, the team at NewTek has even brought this power and ease of surfacing to LightWave Modeler. With LightWave v9, you have another option for creating surfaces that can take you far beyond what the original Surface Editor is capable of. This new addition to LightWave is called the Node Editor. You'll find it in LightWave Layout's Surface Editor panel; just click the Node Editor button to activate it.

The Node Editor does not replace the Surface Editor, and in many cases, you won't always need to use this feature. The Node Editor is an addition to the existing Surface Editor, but there's more to the Node Editor than just surfacing. You can also use nodes for displacements, a technique you'll see later in this chapter. This is one reason why you did not learn about the Node Editor earlier in the book when we discussed surface textures in Chapter 3.

This chapter will describe what a node actually is and how it's used in LightWave v9, and then I'll show you how to use it. You'll then go further and use nodes for displacements. Specifically, you'll learn about:

- What nodes do and when to use them
- Setting up basic node surfaces
- Setting up complex node surfaces
- Using nodes for displacements

It's important to remember that the Node Editor is not always needed for surfacing and texturing objects. Certainly, you could use it exclusively and avoid the classic Surface Editor entirely, or choose to use only the Surface Editor. But no matter which surfacing tool you prefer, you should learn something about both. That's because, if you use LightWave with any regularity, you'll eventually come up against a project in which you can achieve better results using your "nonpreferred" surfacing tool. When you're working on simple, solid-colored objects, or ordinary image-mapped polygons, the Surface Editor is the better choice, even if you're a Node Editor expert. Conversely, if you've created a killer-looking dinosaur model, the Surface Editor won't let you create the same level of kick-Jurassic details you'll want for the scale, claw, and teeth surfaces; the Node Editor is the tool for that job.

Before getting into any projects, keep in mind that the Node Editor is very powerful, and it comes equipped with far too many different nodes to cover in a single chapter. We could fill up this entire book trying to cover just the Node Editor alone. But the NewTek manual, in both hard-copy and electronic PDF form, offers extensive coverage of every node. Please refer to that for specific technical explanations of the various nodes. This chapter will supplement the descriptions in the manual by showing you how to use the Node Editor to set up various surface types.

Edit Nodes

You access the Node Editor through the Surface Editor panel's Edit Nodes button. **Figure 11.1** shows the Surface Editor with an object loaded and the Edit Nodes button toward the top of the panel.

When you click the Edit Nodes button, a blank panel opens up (**Figure 11.2**) and you're left wondering, "Where do I begin?" Before we answer that question, it will help you immensely to understand what a node is and what nodes do.

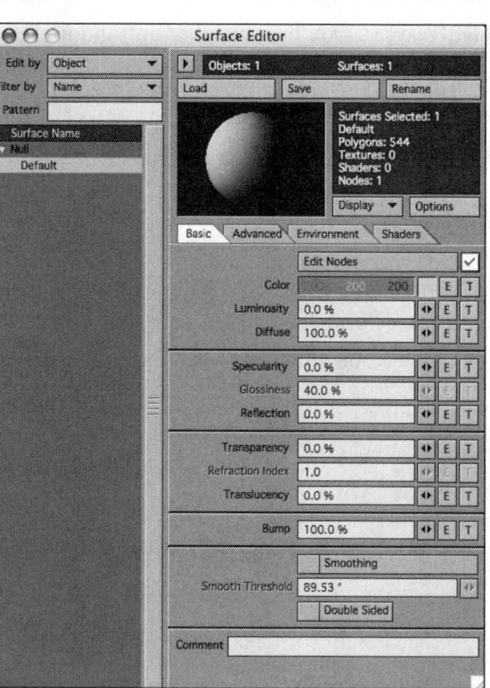

Figure 11.1 Access the Node Editor through the Surface Editor panel.

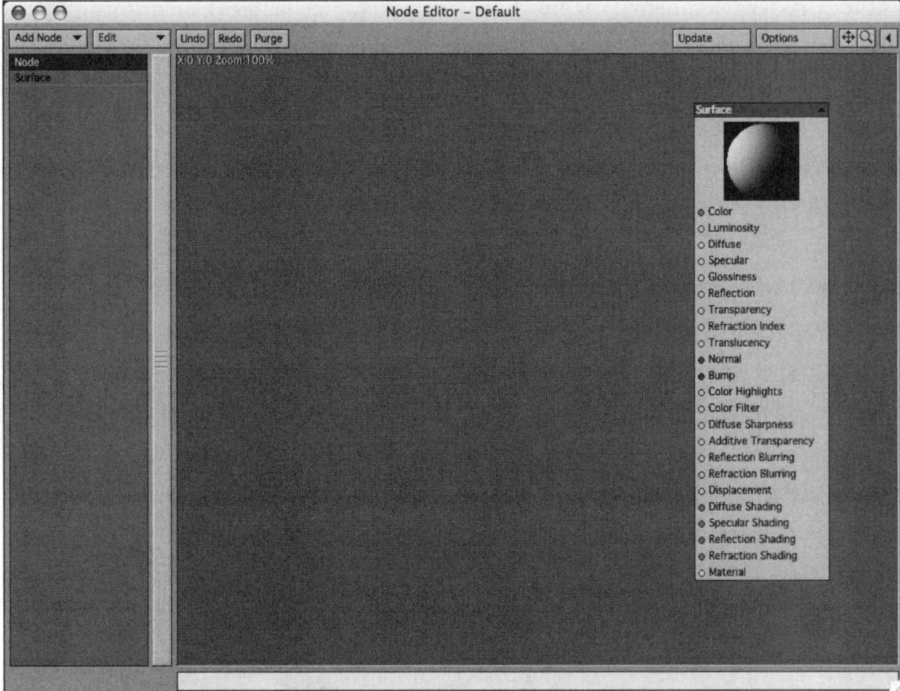

Figure 11.2 When you open the Node Editor, you're probably wondering just where to begin.

What in the World Is a Node?

A LightWave Surface node is similar to a node on a computer network—one of a series of linked devices that share information and contribute to collaborative work. Imagine, for instance, an office network. Tom might be busy at node 1, creating 3D graphics for an upcoming TV show; Nancy might be at node 2, creating the show's end credits; and at node 3, Robert might be editing video for the program—and eagerly awaiting the graphics that Tom and Nancy are creating. Each person in the network—each node—plays a part in the final production.

Getting back to LightWave, the final production our imaginary team is creating is analogous to the *destination node* in a LightWave surface-node array. The destination node links to one or more surfaces in a LightWave model and controls its surface attributes. But instead of specifying those attributes based on a handful of settings and shader attributes, the destination node generates surface characteristics based on inputs from other specialized nodes—comparable to Tom, Nancy, and their colleagues—each contributing its own specific surface-attribute information. LightWave nodes can contribute textures, images, mathematical functions for generating patterns or distortion, and much, much more. A given destination node may only require input from a few nodes, but it's possible to pool the input of dozens or even hundreds of them at a time to create extremely sophisticated surfaces. Starting with Exercise 11.1, you'll see how connecting nodes lets you create a web of textures, shaders, materials, and other attributes to create amazing surfaces.

Exercise 11.1 Building a Basic Node System

1. Open LightWave Layout. If it's already open, save your work and then clear the scene from the File menu.
2. On the Items tab, select Null from the Add category, as shown in **Figure 11.3**.

Figure 11.3 Add a null object from the Items tab.

3. Give your null a name if you like, then click OK to close the panel.
4. Next, click the Modeler Tools tab. Click the Geometry drop-down (in the Create tool category) and choose Toroid, as shown in **Figure 11.4**.

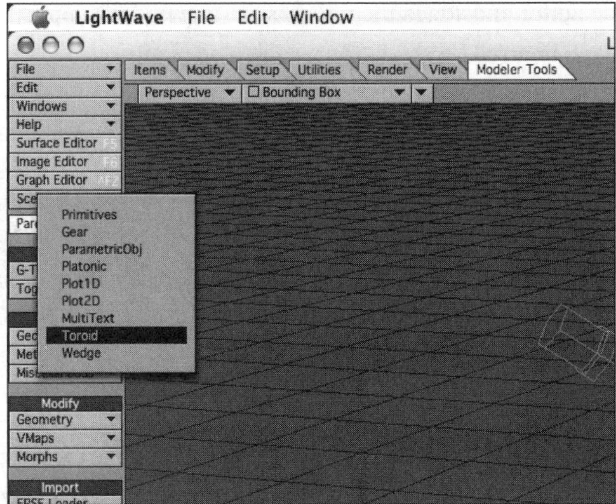

Figure 11.4 Add a toroid from the Modeler Tools tab.

5. In the Torus panel that appears, click OK to use the default settings.

   You've just used Layout's Modeler tools, which allow you to quickly add simply geometry to Layout without the need to fire up LightWave Modeler. This is useful for creating stand-in objects for animation tests, simple shading tests, and any other application where a primitive shape might come in handy. To add a new shape with the Modeler tools, your scene must contain a null object, and it must be selected when you apply tools from Layout's Modeler tab.

6. Open the Surface Editor from the top left of the interface. You'll see the object name (currently *null*) and one surface labeled *default*. The default surface is the torus. You can click the Rename button at the top of the interface if you like, but the name is not important at this point.

7. Now that you have an object with at least one surface, you're ready for some nodes! Click the Edit Nodes button at the top of the Surface Editor, as shown in **Figure 11.5**.

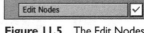

Figure 11.5 The Edit Nodes button is located at the top of the Surface Editor panel.

8. When you open the Node Editor by clicking the Edit Nodes button, you might find the panel a bit small. Grab the bottom-right corner and resize it to your liking. When you're satisfied, take a look at the panel and you'll see a node already in place. Yes, that column of information is a node—or at least the LightWave representation of a node. This is the default surface node for output. You'll add nodes

in the Node Editor and attach them to this existing node to apply them to your object surface. **Figure 11.6** shows the resized Node Editor.

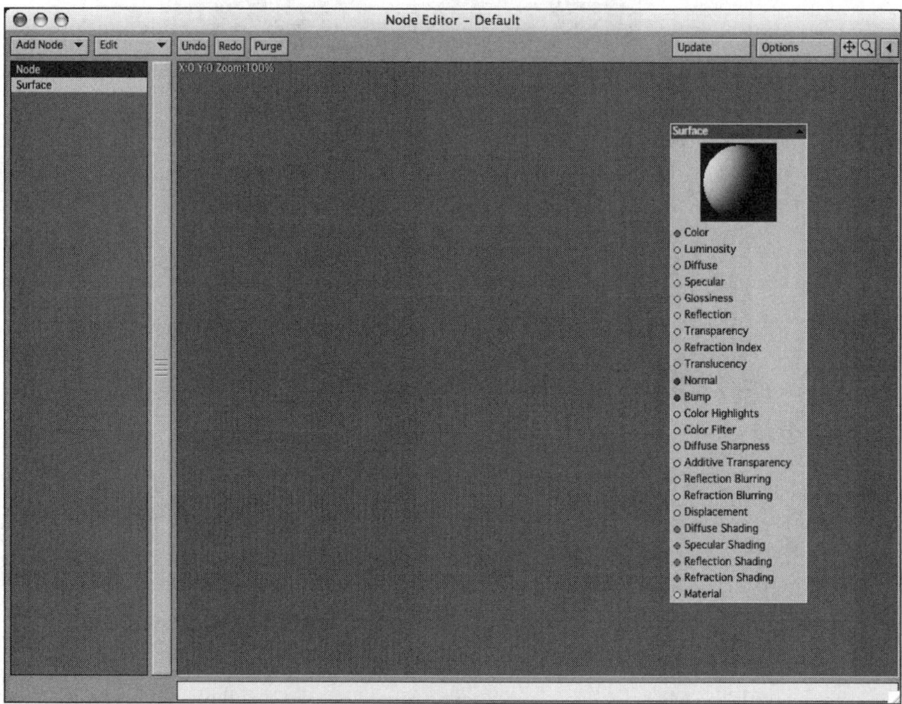

Figure 11.6 Feel free to resize the Node Editor and get ready to build a surface.

9. At the top of the Node Editor panel is the Add Node drop-down menu. Click it and you'll see a list of available nodes, including gradients, shaders, and more (**Figure 11.7**).

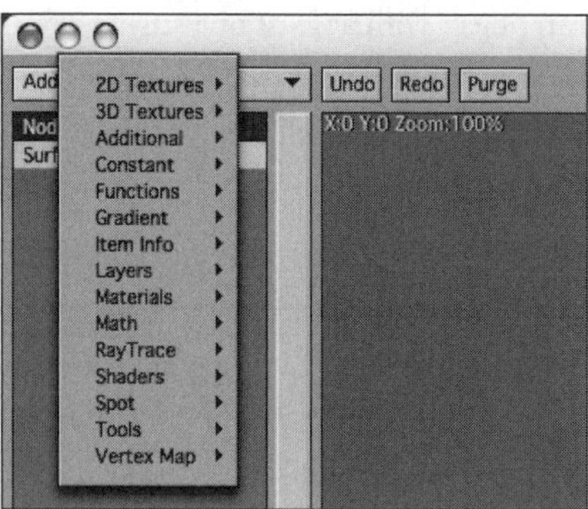

Figure 11.7 LightWave v9 ships with a plethora of nodes for you to assemble.

10. From the Add Node drop-down menu, select 2D Textures, and then choose Turbulence2D. You'll see a node appear in the editor window, as in **Figure 11.8**.

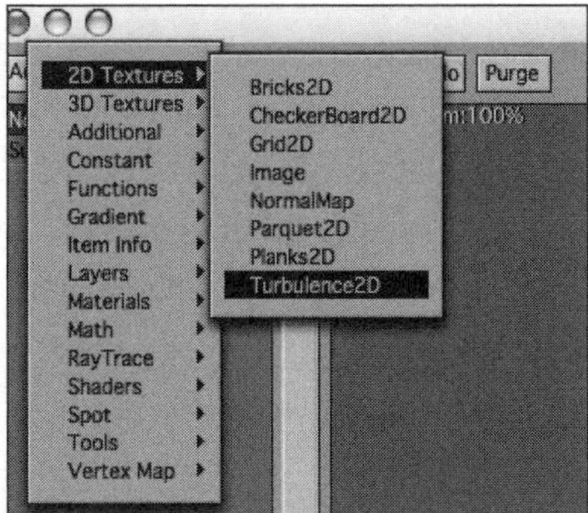

Figure 11.8 Add a Turbulence2D node to begin creating your surface.

11. Adding a node in itself does nothing. You need to connect it (in other words, *network* it) to the base surface node that feeds the LightWave render engine. Before you do that, change the node settings a bit. Double-click the sample sphere at the top of the Node Editor. This will open the settings for that node, as shown in **Figure 11.9**.

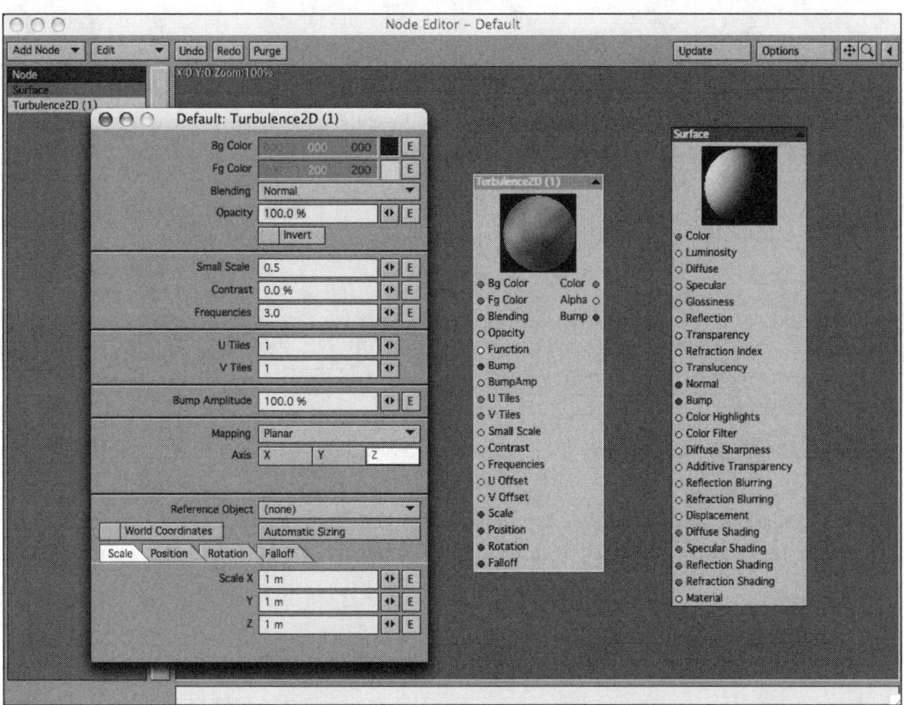

Figure 11.9 Double-click the sample sphere to open the properties for the node.

12. In the Properties panel, set Bg Color to a dark blue and Fg Color to a bright yellow. You see, the Turbulence2D node applies a two-color computer generated noise. What you've just set is the background and foreground colors.

13. Like LightWave's traditional Surface Editor, you can blend each node in a variety of ways, such as Multiply, Darken, Lighten, and so on. For this node, leave Blending set to Normal. Many of the other values are merely controls for size and position of the computer-generated texture. As you adjust these values, you can see the change in the sample sphere within the node. Change the U Tiles and V Tiles both to 3. This will repeat the texture and give a stronger appearance, as shown in **Figure 11.10**.

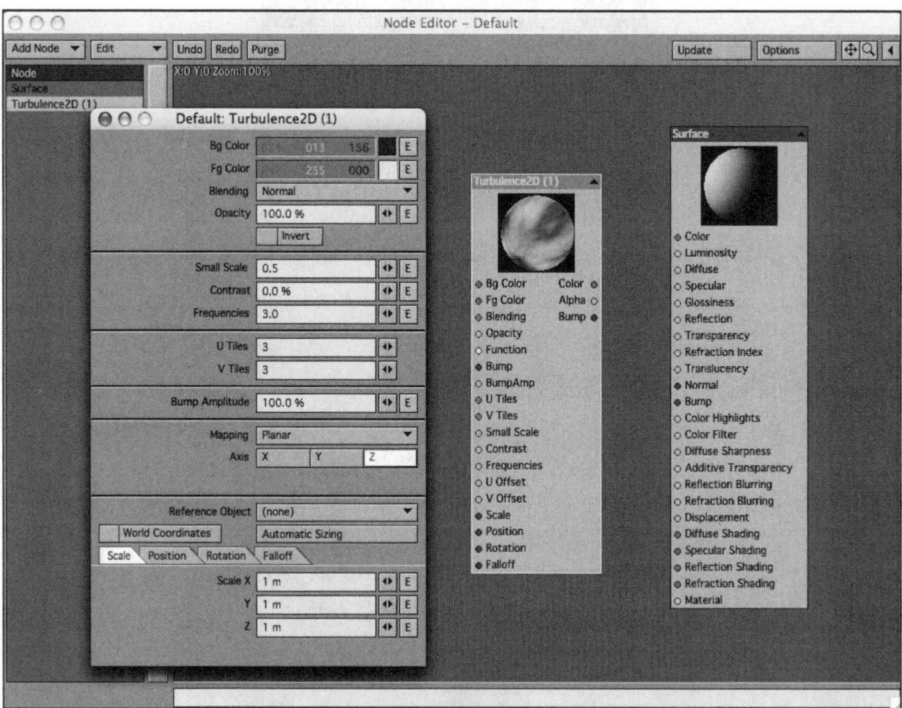

Figure 11.10 Adjust the U and V Tiles to add more noise to the node.

14. Go ahead and close the Properties panel for the Turbulence2D node. Now, if you take a look at your Surface Editor's sample sphere, as well as the base node sample sphere, they are both still gray. The Turbulence 2D properties you just set won't appear in the sample surface until you hook your nodes together and thus make them part of the network. So, click the Color listing's red dot on the right side of the Turbulence node and drag it to the Color dot on the base node (**Figure 11.11**).

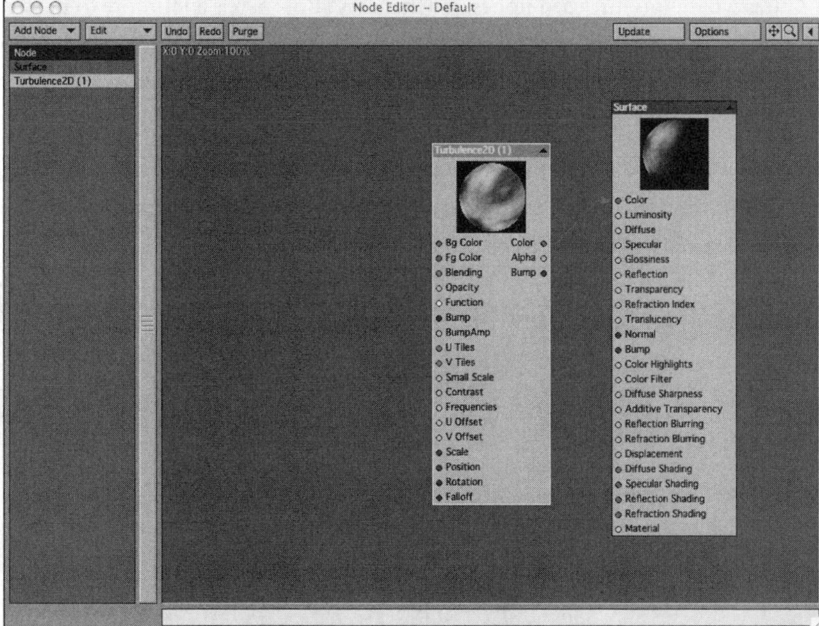

Figure 11.11 To connect your Turbulence2D node's color settings to the base node so that they will be applied during the render, drag the red Color-listing dot from the Turbulence 2D node to onto the base node's Color dot.

15. You can now see that the two color settings and UV size you set in the properties for the Turbulence2D node are visible in both the base node and main surface editor (**Figure 11.12**).

Figure 11.12 Once the node is part of the network and hooked into the base node, its settings are reflected in the surface.

Guess what? You just used nodes. It's that easy! But there's a lot more to it, as you probably have guessed. For example, what do all of those other controls do? Where do you connect them? Read on to learn a bit more and enhance the surface of the simple geometric torus with nodes.

16. Grab the blue dot next to Bump in the Turbulence2D node and drag it to the Bump listing in the base node. Watch your surface sample change. You now have bumps on your surface as well as color (**Figure 11.13**).

Figure 11.13 Drag the Bump on the Turbulence2D node to the Bump on the base surface node.

17. We'll get into what the colored dots mean and how the other values play a role in a little bit. But first, let's add another node. From the Add Node drop-down menu, select Shaders, then Reflection, then Reflections, as shown in **Figure 11.14**.

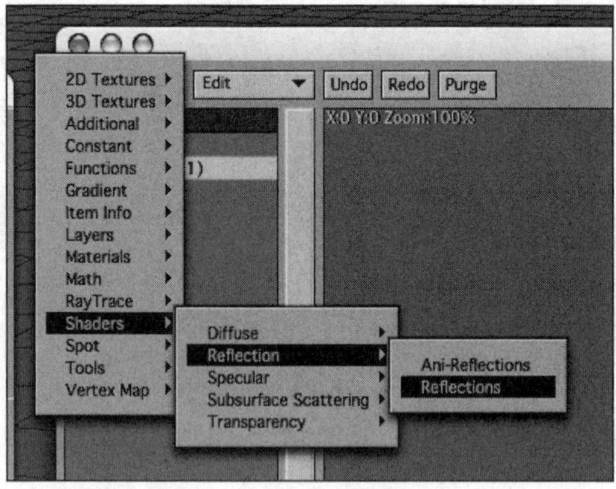

Figure 11.14 Add a reflection shader to your surface.

You'll see that the Reflection node panel you've just added is a good bit smaller than the Turbulence2D node. It has fewer settings options, but it works pretty much the same as Turbulence2D—and all other nodes. Add it from the Add Node menu, and then hook it into your surfacing network. Because you opened the Node Editor for a single selected surface, everything you're doing here is being applied to that surface (the torus's exterior) via the destination node.

18. You can double-click the Reflection node to get to its properties as you did with the turbulence node, but there's another option as well. At the top right of the Node Editor, you'll see a left-facing triangle. Click it, and your Node Editor panel will expand to display any selected node's properties automatically (**Figure 11.15**).

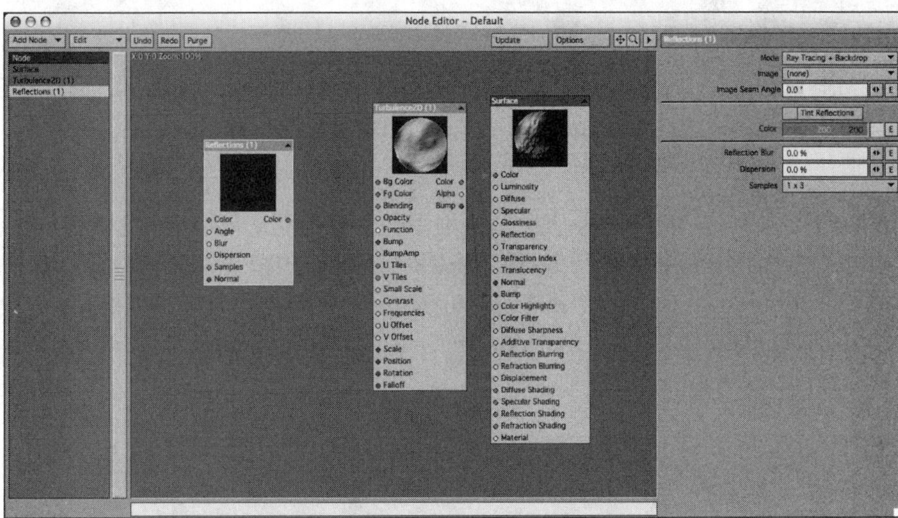

Figure 11.15 Expand the Node Editor to always display a selected node's properties.

19. Now, with the Reflection node selected, set Mode to Spherical Map.

20. Choose Foil.jpg as the image, which you can find on this book's DVD in the Projects\Images\CH11 directory.

21. Click Tint Reflections and set the color to a pale blue.

    You can also set a blur to the reflections, change the dispersion, and even increase the samples. You can leave all other values at their defaults. Feel free to adjust them and watch the sample sphere within the node to see the effects.

    So you've set up a reflection, but how does it hook into the other two nodes?

22. Click and drag the red dot for Color from the Reflection node, and drop it onto the red dot marked Reflection Shading on the base node. **Figure 11.16** on the next page shows the example.

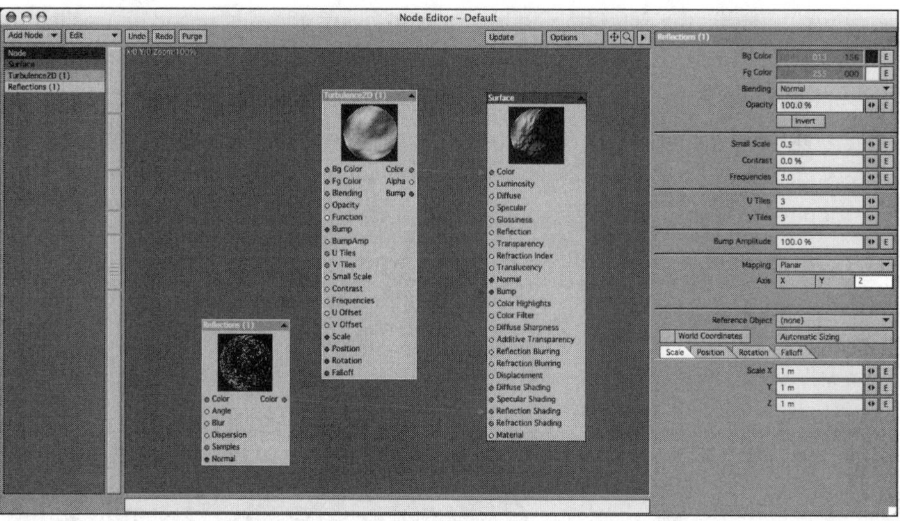

Figure 11.16 Drag the red dot for Color from the Reflection node to the red dot marked Reflection Shading on the base node.

23. If you take a look at your surface sample in the base node, it doesn't look like much has changed, does it? So make one more adjustment: Link the green Alpha output from the Turbulence2D node to the green Reflection input on the base node (**Figure 11.17**). The Alpha channel is a portion of the surface (or image) that holds transparency data.

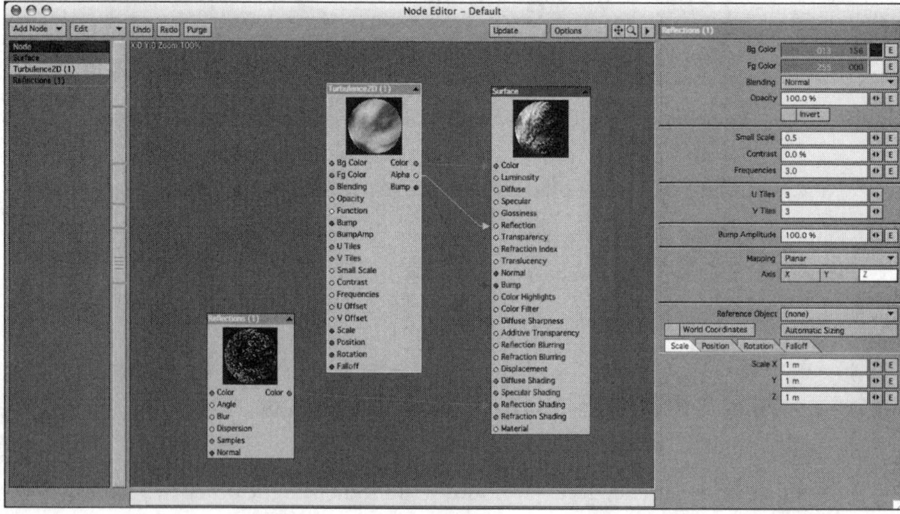

Figure 11.17 Connect the Alpha value from the Turbulence2D node to the Reflection input on the base node.

24. Close the Node Editor and in the Surface Editor, click Smoothing.
25. Move the camera to a position above the torus in Layout to see it better, and press F9 to render. **Figure 11.18** shows the render. There you have it! An object surfaced via the Node Editor!

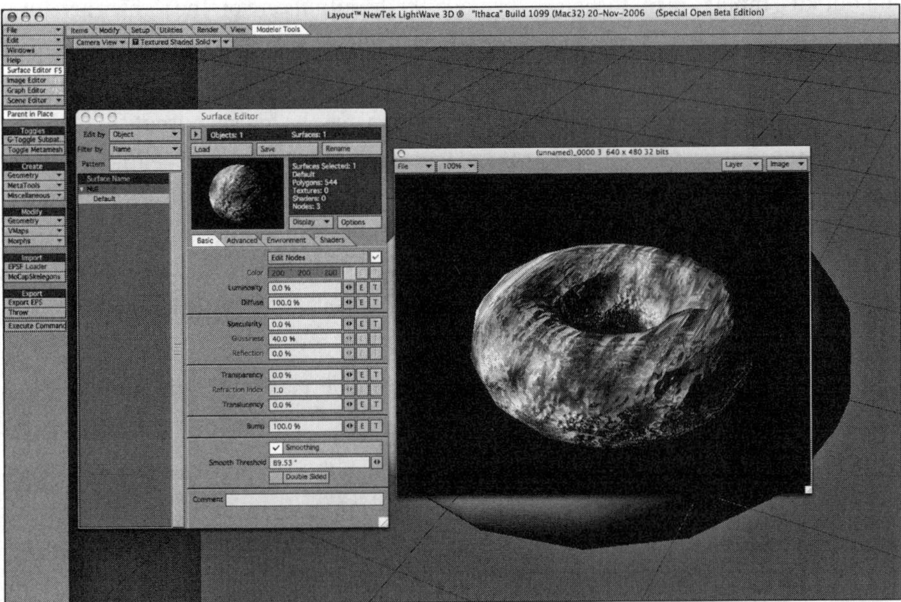

Figure 11.18 Turn on Smoothing for the surface, and then position the camera to see the object.

So what just happened there? Why didn't the reflection show up immediately and why did the Alpha need to be connected? And you're probably wondering what's the deal with all the red, green, and other colored dots? For the Alpha channel you just connected in step 23, you needed to tell the base node to have some sort of value for reflection. Simply adding the shader alone, as you did in step 23, wasn't enough. The data, or information, from the Turbulence2D node's Alpha channel needed be driven into the base destination node. If you went and unhooked the Reflection Shading (the red one), you'd see the change in the surface sample and no reflection at all, even though the Alpha is still connected.

Working with the Node Editor can be confusing at first, but stick with it and read on to learn more. What's important to keep in mind is that there are many different types of nodes, all of which can be connected to build a surface, just as you've done in this exercise. Although you've added only two nodes, you've created a node-based surface just the same. The next section explores the outputs and inputs of nodes, and explains how the colored dots represent the variations.

Outputs and Inputs

Having worked with the Node Editor briefly, you might be annoyed by all the values, settings, and colored dots on the nodes. But don't worry; you'll soon see how it all comes together.

Keep in mind that almost all nodes, except for the final destination node, have both inputs and outputs. Inputs are on the left of the node, while outputs are on the right. Therefore, a good way to work is a "left-to-right" workflow. Although this isn't necessary, it's a good practice as you string together nodes to build your "network." The colored dots are not randomly added for visual appeal, but to help you match the logical outputs of nodes to inputs of other nodes. Using the outputs and inputs properly is what will define and determine your final surface. Here's the breakdown of colors and what they mean:

- Red dots represent color operations.
- Blue dots represent vector operations. Vector operations control attributes such as Scale, Position, or Bumps.
- Green dots represent scalar operations, which govern attributes such as Luminosity, Glossiness, and Alpha channels.
- Yellow dots represent functions. Functions are mathematically based controls for attributes such as Noise; they are used to drive the shape, pattern, or configurations of other nodes. A Noise node might be used to randomize the texture of a Marble or Turbulence node, for instance.
- Purple dots represent integers. Integer operations are used mainly for specifying a choice from a numbered list of node options. Nodes that feature color-blending functions, for instance, offer 14 blending-mode options, numbered 0 to 13, and an integer operation is used to specify the number of the mode that should be applied.

Working through a project will help you understand the use of outputs and inputs, so let's move on to the next exercise, in which you'll build a more complex node network. When that's done, you'll call up the still-life project from Chapter 8 and texture it with the Node Editor.

Exercise 11.2 Working with Outputs and Inputs

1. Save anything you've been working on, and clear LightWave Layout.
2. Load up the Capsules scene from the Projects\Scenes\CH11\Capsules directory of the book's DVD. The scene contains three capsules on a floor, which is a flat polygon. There are four surfaces in the scene and two lights. There are also two large white polygons out of camera view that will act as reflectors. **Figure 11.19** shows the scene loaded, and **Figure 11.20** shows the results of rendering by pressing **F9**.

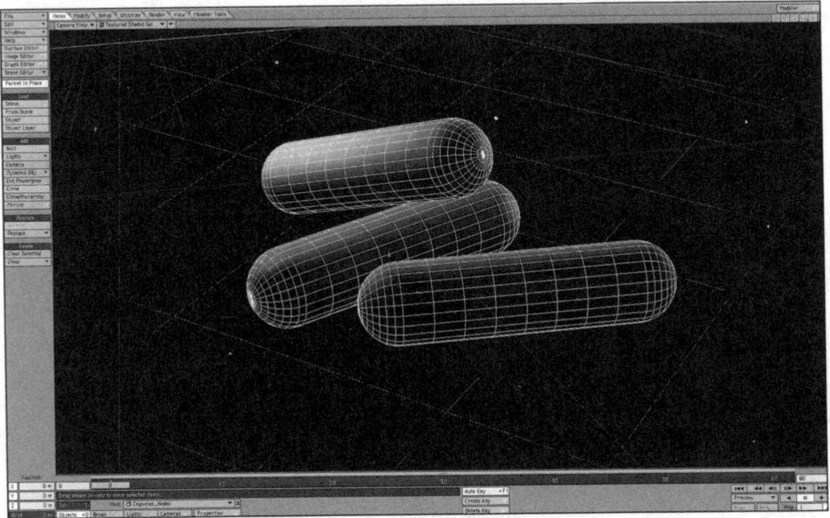

Figure 11.19 The Capsules scene loaded, viewed using the wireframe shade style.

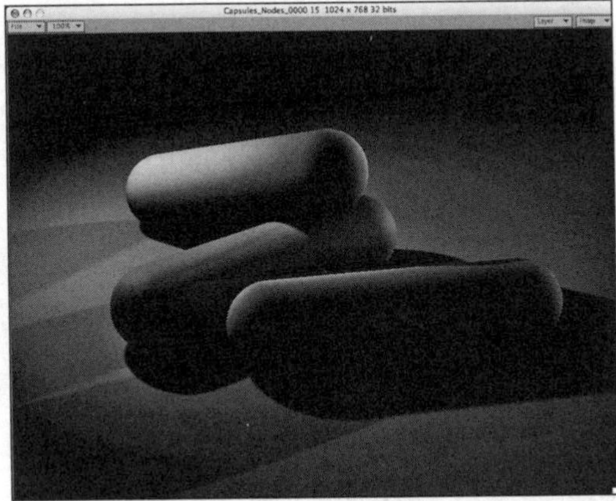

Figure 11.20 After rendering, you can see that, although the objects are well lit, no surface materials are applied to them.

3. Open the Surface Editor and select the Capsule_1 surface. Then, click the Edit Nodes button to open the Node Editor for that surface.
4. Move the base destination node over to the right and resize the Node Editor panel as needed.
5. You're going to create a different surface for each capsule and the ground so that you can see the various possibilities available. From the Add Node drop-down menu, select the Marble node from the 3D Textures listing, as shown in **Figure 11.21** on the next page.

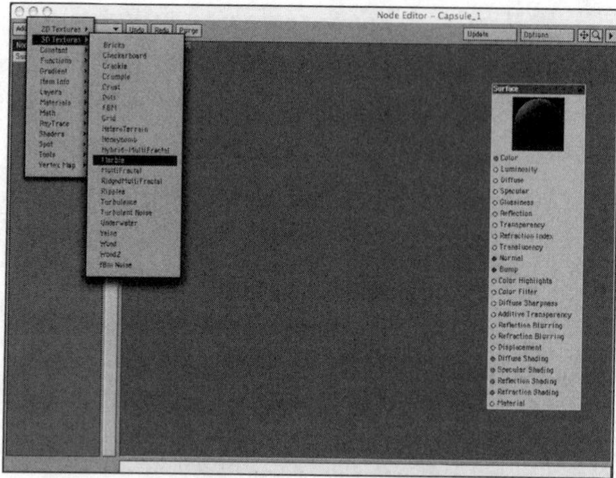

Figure 11.21 Add the first node, a Marble texture.

6. As you did in the previous exercise, hook the Color output from the Marble node to the Color input of the destination node, as in **Figure 11.22**.

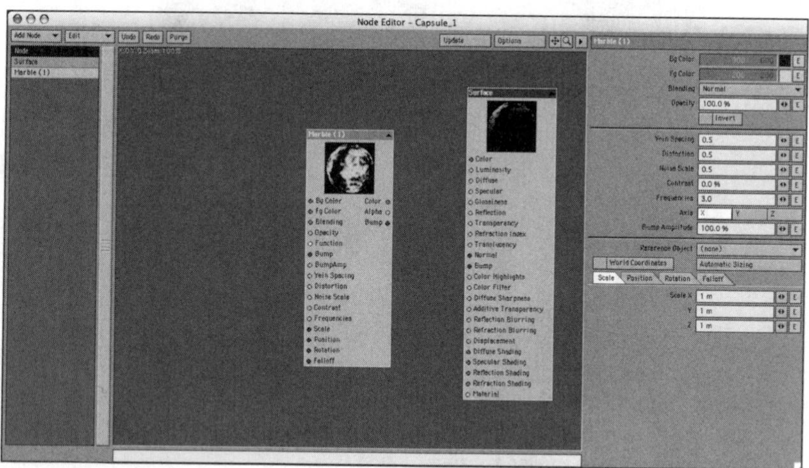

Figure 11.22 Connect the Color output to the Color input.

Note

If you ever need to remove a connection, just click the arrow that you connected and pull it away from the node. If you can't seem to grab the dots to connect from one node to another, there's a good chance your view is not fully zoomed. At the top right of the Node Editor are pan and zoom controls. Use these controls to make sure your Node Editor panel is fully zoomed to connect nodes.

7. Connect the Bump output from the Marble node to the Bump input on the destination node, as shown in **Figure 11.23**.

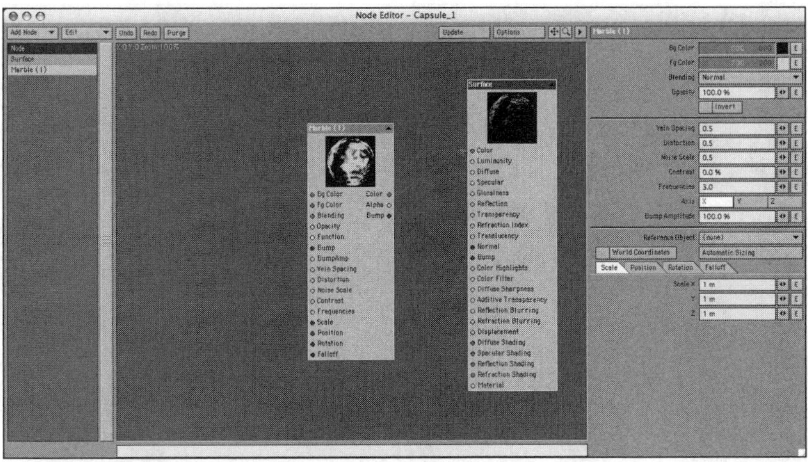

Figure 11.23 Connect the bump from the marble to the destination node.

8. OK, nothing too exciting so far, but wait. Connect the Alpha output of the Marble node to the Specular input of the destination node, as in **Figure 11.24**. Pay attention to the change in the surface sample sphere.

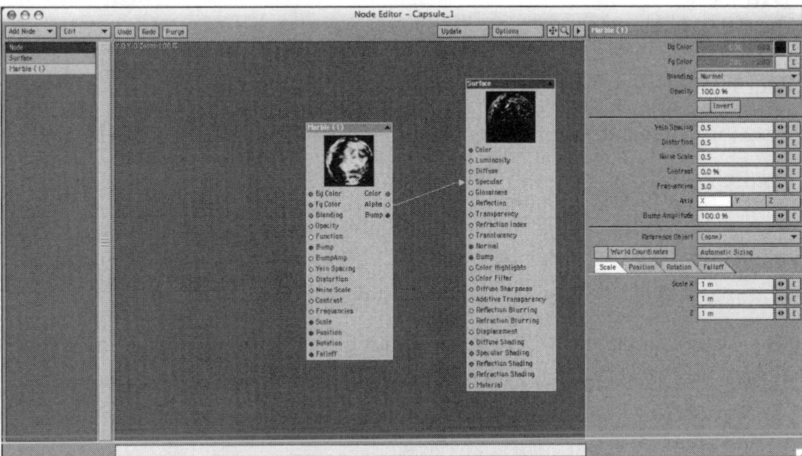

Figure 11.24 Connect the Alpha output to the Specular input.

The Alpha output and the Specular input are identified by green dots, indicating they control scalar values. By connecting them, you give the surface a nice shine. But what happens when you want some gloss too? Can an output on one node connect to more than one input of another node? It sure can!

9. Click and drag from the green dot for the marble Alpha output to the Glossiness destination node input. **Figure 11.25** shows the setup.

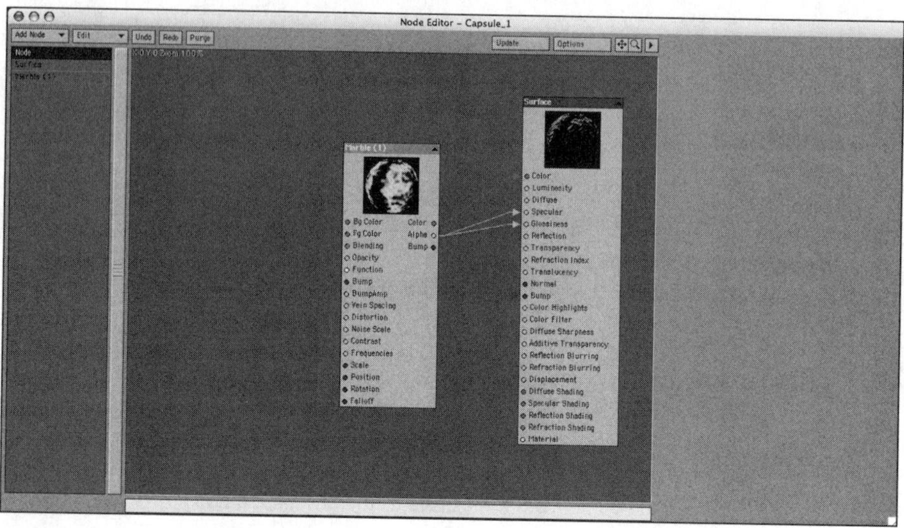

Figure 11.25 You can use an output of a node more than once.

10. There are other ways to bring two outputs together, which you'll see shortly. For now, go to the Add Node menu and add a Crumple node from the 3D Textures list.
11. Click and drag the Crumple node panel to the left of the Marble node in the Node Editor window.
12. Drag the Color output from Crumple to the Bg Color input on the Marble node.
13. Hook the Alpha output from Crumple to the Vein Spacing on the Marble node. Select the Crumple node, and open its Properties panel by clicking the triangle in the upper-right corner of the interface. Note that it is possible to connect the Crumple node directly to the destination node if you like.
14. Set Bg Color to green and Fg Color to orange. Take a look at the sample spheres in the Marble node and destination node to see how the outputs of this node affect everything it's connected to. **Figure 11.26** shows the change.

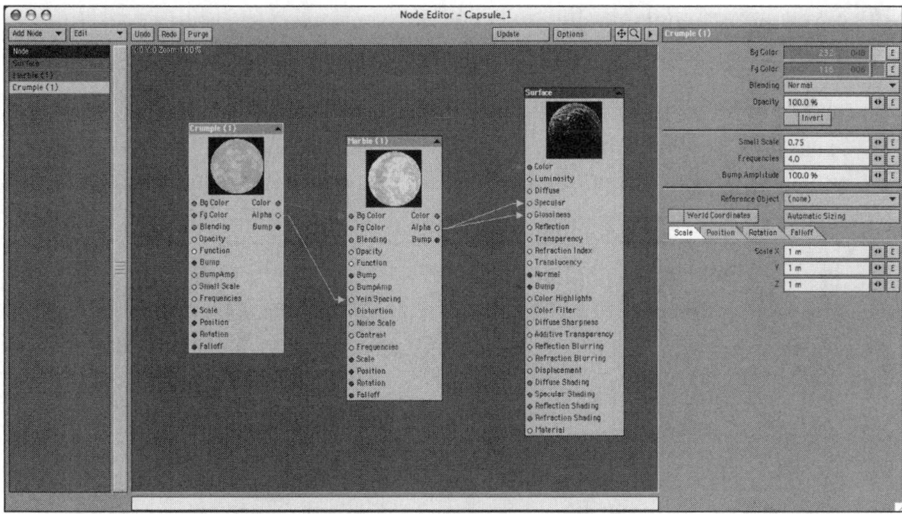

Figure 11.26 Changing the foreground and background colors for the node affect everything it's hooked into in the node network.

15. Go ahead and press **F9** to render a frame to see the change (**Figure 11.27**). What you end up with is a mossy, sort of crystallized surface. Why crystallized when you applied marble? Remember that you took the Alpha from both the Crumple and Marble, and hooked those through to both the specularity and glossiness of the surface. The result is what you see. Pretty cool! But you can adjust any of the values as you like, and see how the changes affect the surface. Remember to select the node, then open the properties for it and make adjustments.

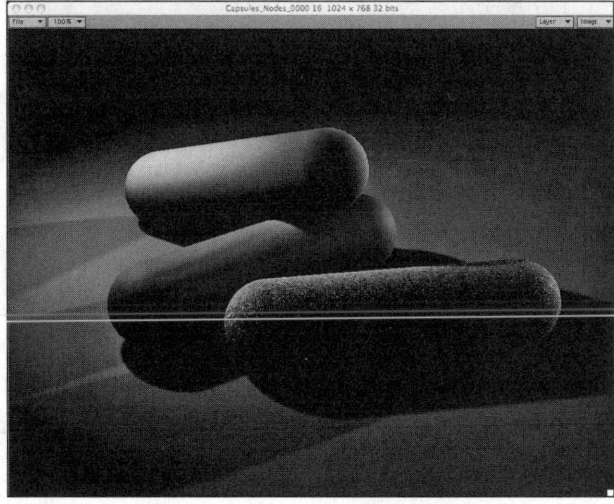

Figure 11.27 Performing an **F9** single-frame render shows the new surface on the first capsule.

16. Save your work and close the Node Editor.
17. Now select the Capsule_2 surface. Open the Node Editor and arrange its window on your screen as you like.
18. From the Add Node drop-down menu, select Shaders, then Diffuse, and choose Minnaert, as shown in **Figure 11.28**.

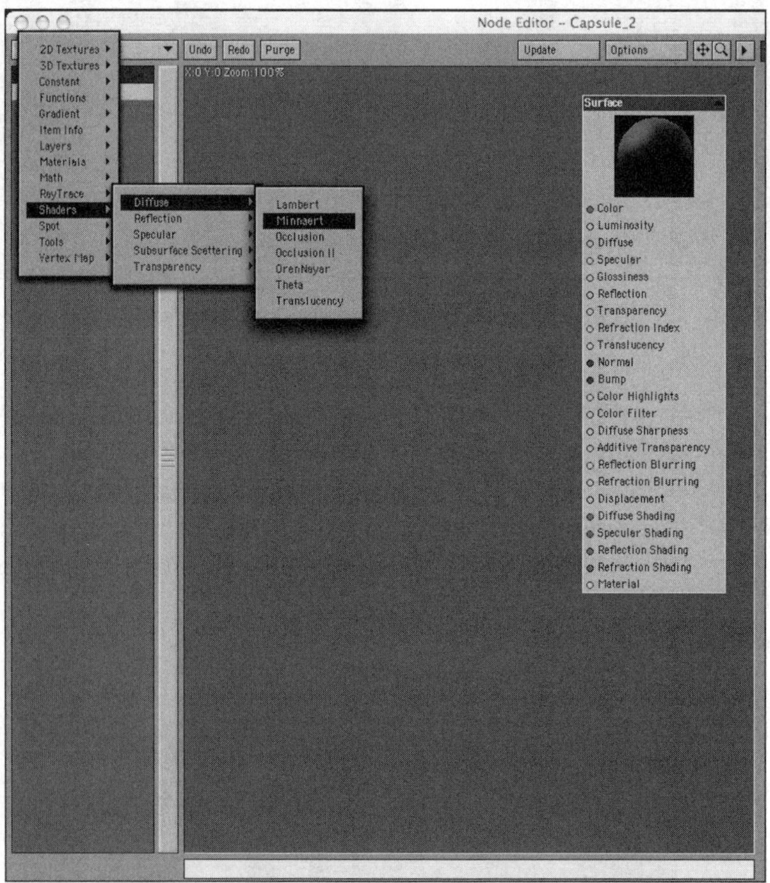

Figure 11.28 Add the Minnaert shader node.

19. The Minnaert is a shader, right? A shader will generate specific surface properties. The Minnaert shader is great for small rough surfaces, like sand, rust, or rocks. So, take the Color output (red dot) and connect it to the Diffuse Shading input, also a red dot, of the destination node. **Figure 11.29** shows the connection.

Figure 11.29 Connect the Color output of the Minnaert shader to the Diffuse Shading input of the destination node.

20. Now, open the Minnaert node properties, and you'll see that this node is simply a shader that allows you to set color, diffuse, and darkening values.

    If you compare a diffuse shader in the Node Editor to the typical Surface Editor diffuse value, you'll see that the Node Editor offers you more control. In the basic Surface Editor, you can set the diffuse value, which tells LightWave how much light your surface accepts from the scene. That's it. But with a Node Editor shader, you are able to apply a slew of different settings for diffuse, with Minnaert being just one of them. This same concept applies to the other Shading models—each is a simple value in the Surface Editor, but you get a lot more control and variation using the Node Editor. You should experiment with each of them to see their effects.

21. Set the color for the Minnaert node to orange. Set Diffuse to 100% and Darkening to 45%, as shown in **Figure 11.30** on the next page. Using this shader the way you've set up here is telling the destination node how the diffuse value for the surface is rendered.

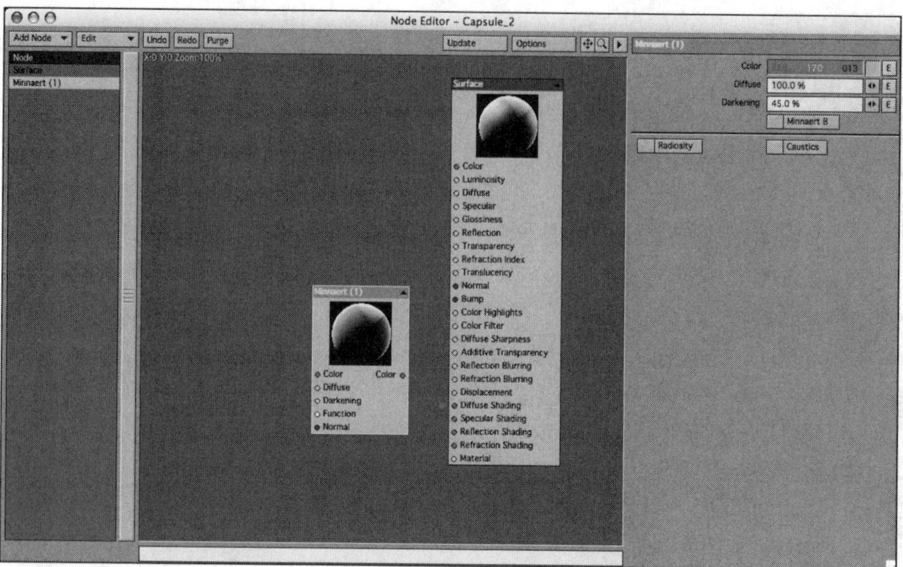

Figure 11.30 Set a few values to make changes to the Minnaert node.

22. Now change how the specularity will differ with another node. From the Add Node drop-down menu, add the Anisotropic shader, as shown in **Figure 11.31**.

23. With the Anisotropic node, you can change the way the surface shines when light hits it. In the properties settings for the Anisotropic node, set Specularity to **85%**.

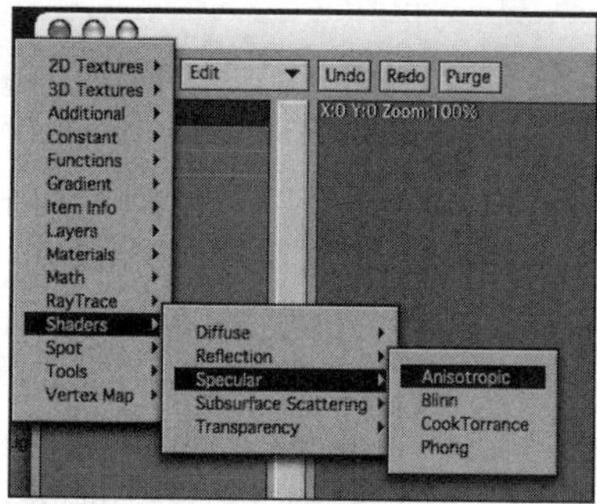

Figure 11.31 Add the Anisotropic shader to the Node Editor.

24. Connect the Color output from the Anisotropic shader to the Specular Shading input on the destination node.

Recall that when we applied Specularity using the the Surface Editor, we could increase and decrease its setting to determine the degree to which a surface exhibited a *hot spot*—a highlight reflecting light source(s) in the scene. In Surface Editor, all specular hot spots are round, but the Node Editor's Anisotropic shader lets you change the shape of a hot spot.

Note

LightWave v9 Specular shaders include Phong, Cook Torrance, Blinn, and Anisotropic. These shaders allow you to create brushed metal surfaces and realistic reflective surfaces.

25. Anisotropy *U* and *V* are coordinate axes used to specify where the specularity shines on the surface; set Anisotropy U to 90% and Anisotropy V to 10% to effectively "pinch" the specular hot spot, as shown in **Figure 11.32**.

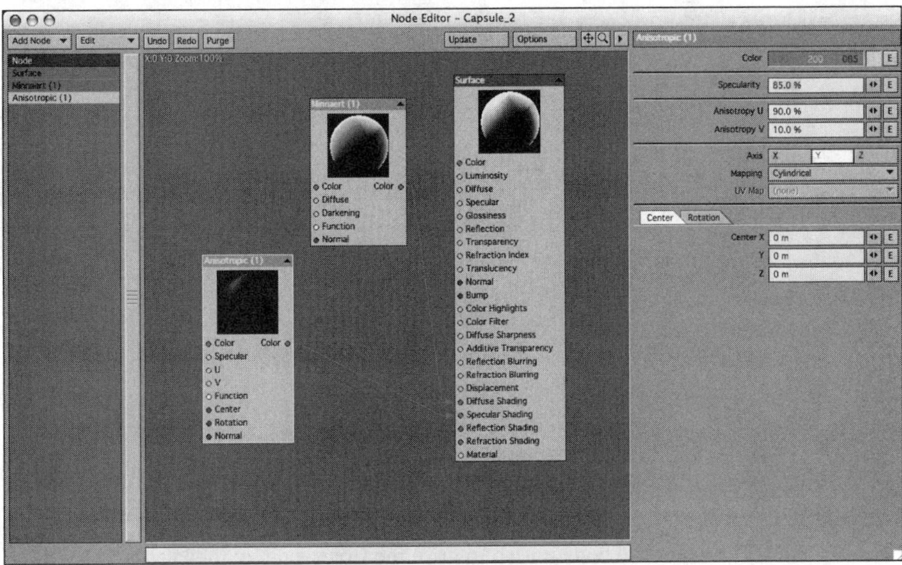

Figure 11.32 Change a few values in the Anisotropic shader and you can see subtle changes in the surface sample preview.

26. Now add another node, but this time for Reflection Shading. Add the Reflection node from the Shaders library, as shown in **Figure 11.33**.

27. Open the properties for the Reflection node. Set Mode to Spherical Map to map the reflection around the surface.

28. For the image, choose the image Glass.jpg image in the Projects\Images\CH11 directory on this book's DVD.

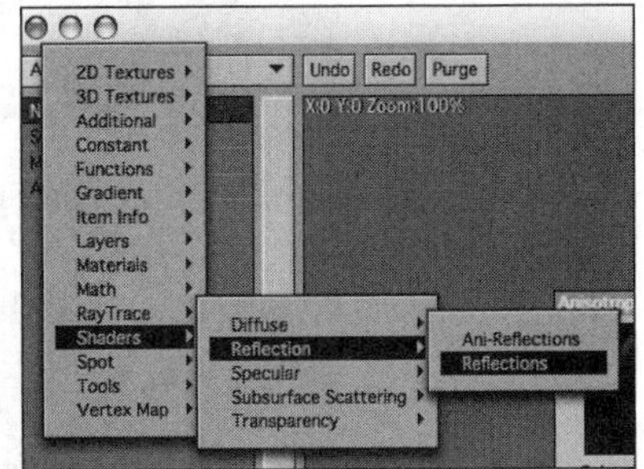

Figure 11.33 Add a reflection shader node.

29. Now, rather than hooking the Color output from the Reflection node to the Reflection Shading input of the destination node, you can control how this reflection is used. First, drag the Color output from the Reflection node to the Color

input of the Minnaert node. **Figure 11.34** shows the Node Editor, and **Figure 11.35** shows the results of a single-frame render produced by pressing **F9**.

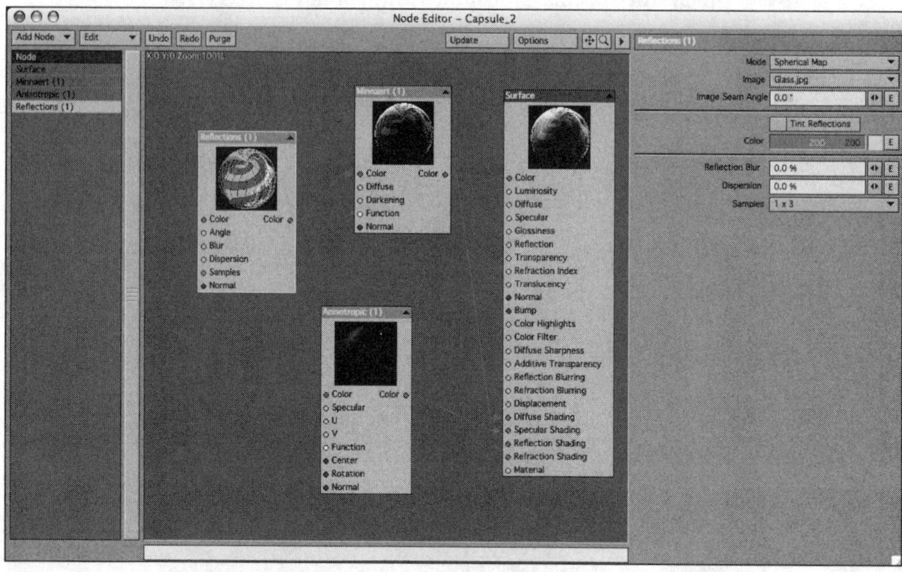

Figure 11.34 The Reflection node is used to drive the Color input of the Minnaert shader.

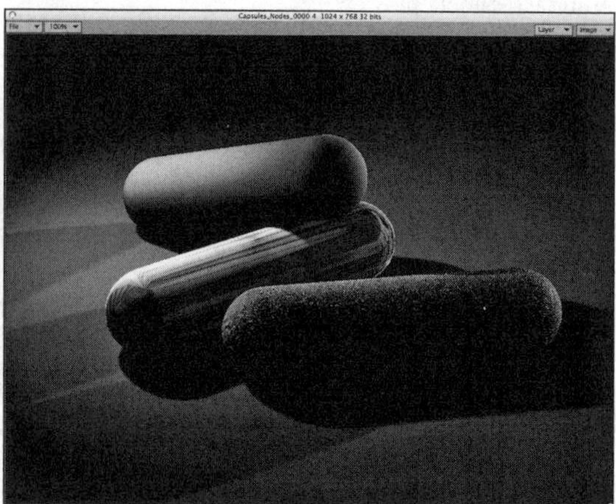

Figure 11.35 By changing the input of the Minnaert shader, you change how the reflection is applied to the surface.

30. Now try something different. Grab the arrow from the connection between the Reflection node Color output and instead of hooking it to the Color input of the Minnaert node, connect it to the Color input of the Anisotropic node.

Figure 11.36 shows the Node Editor setup, while **Figure 11.37** shows a single-frame render of the results.

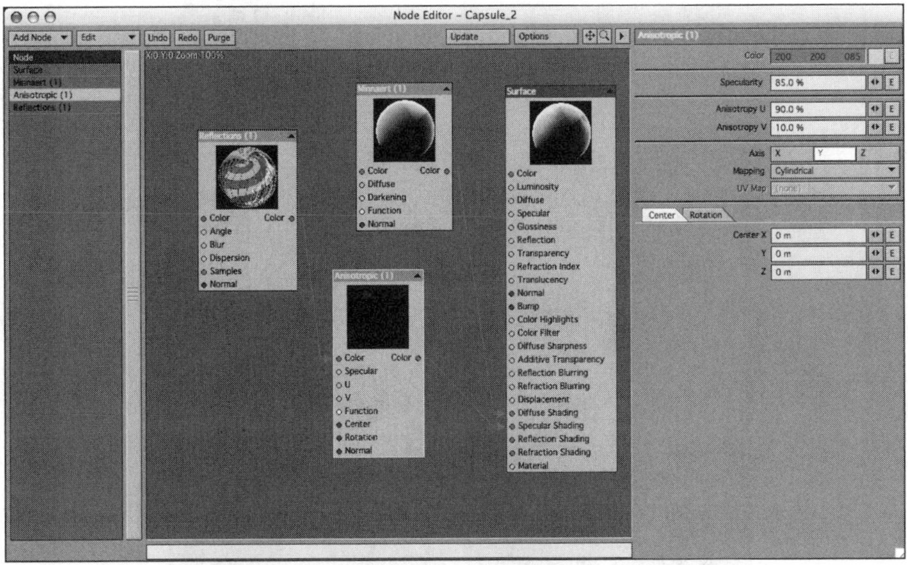

Figure 11.36 Use the Reflection node to drive the Color input of the Anisotropic shader.

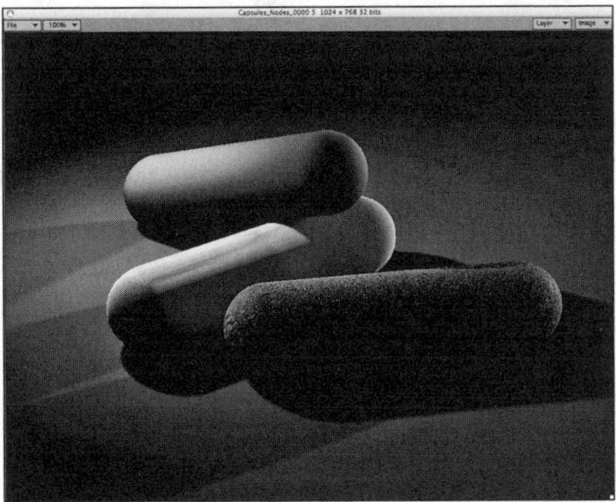

Figure 11.37 By using the reflection as a Color input, the Anisotropic effect shows the reflection.

By using the Reflection node as an input to drive the Anisotropic node, you have changed the look of the specularity shading. This is because the Anisotropic output is driving the destination node's specular shading. So the places where the shader produces hot spots now exhibit reflections. That's pretty cool!

You might be wondering where you could use this technique. How about wheels on a sports car? Or shiny metal objects? Aircrafts, ships, or machinery could all benefit from a simple node setup like this.

31. Open the properties for the Anisotropic node and set Specularity to 200%. Press **F9** to render and see the change, as shown in **Figure 11.38**.

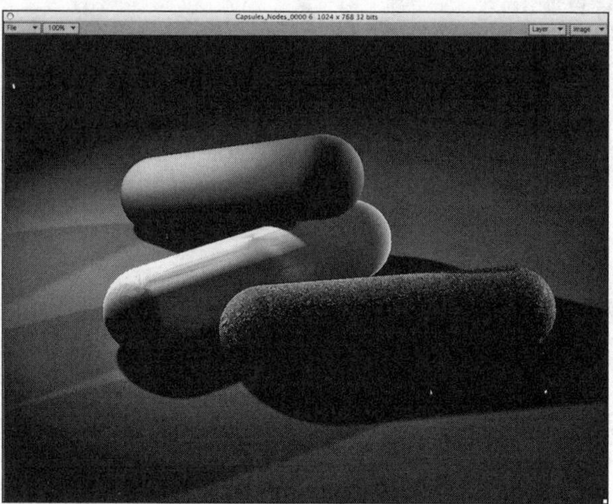

Figure 11.38 Increasing the specularity when the Reflection node is driving it helps show the effects.

32. Play around with the values for the shaders until you find settings you like. When finished, save your work.

Working with the Node Editor is not as complex as you once thought, is it? Sure, there are many nodes that you have yet to explore, and you should know that there are many you might not even use. This next section will show you a few other avenues you can travel down when working with the Node Editor.

Exercise 11.3 Subsurface Scattering with Nodes

The term *subsurface scattering* has been tossed around the 3D community for some time, but it might be a new term to many LightWave 3D users. Put simply, subsurface scattering is an attribute that gives a surface the illusion of thickness or depth. It is rendered based on complex calculations, but it has been made easier to control with the addition of the Node Editor.

A good example is a wax candle: The candle look solid, but toward the top where the flame is, the light from the flame diffuses through the surface. Another good example is skin, or flesh. Go over to your coworker or spouse, grab their ear, and pull it away from their head. (You might want to warn them first…) Look at it in front of a light and what do you see? It's not really translucent like a sheet of paper, and it's certainly not transparent, but light passes through it from behind, more through areas of less thickness than through thicker sections. This is the subsurface scattering effect, and you'll learn to apply it in this exercise.

1. Continuing with the capsules scene from the previous exercise, select the Capsule_3 surface in the Surface Editor. (You've already set up the surfaces for Capsule_1 and Capsule_2.)
2. Click the Edit Nodes button.
3. From the Add Node drop-down menu, head down to the Shaders, then to Subsurface Scattering, and pick Kappa, as shown in **Figure 11.39**.

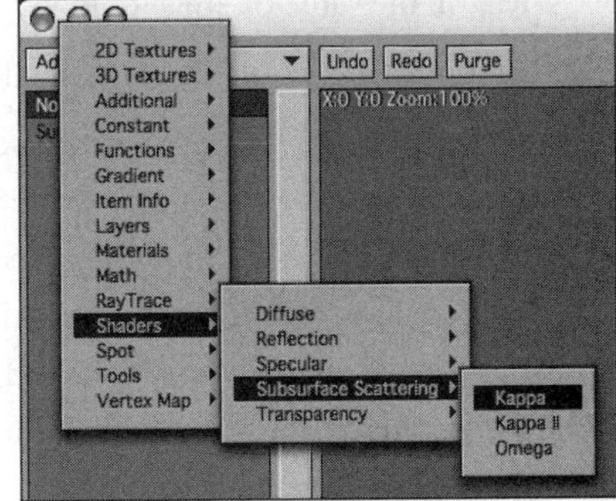

Figure 11.39 Add a subsurface scattering node to the Node Editor

4. Why the Kappa subsurface scattering node? This shader is a simple yet effective way to get subsurface scattering applied to your objects. It's easy to set up and a good stepping-stone to the more advanced subsurface shader, Omega. Double-click the Kappa node to open the properties. You'll see just a few settings, as shown in **Figure 11.40**.

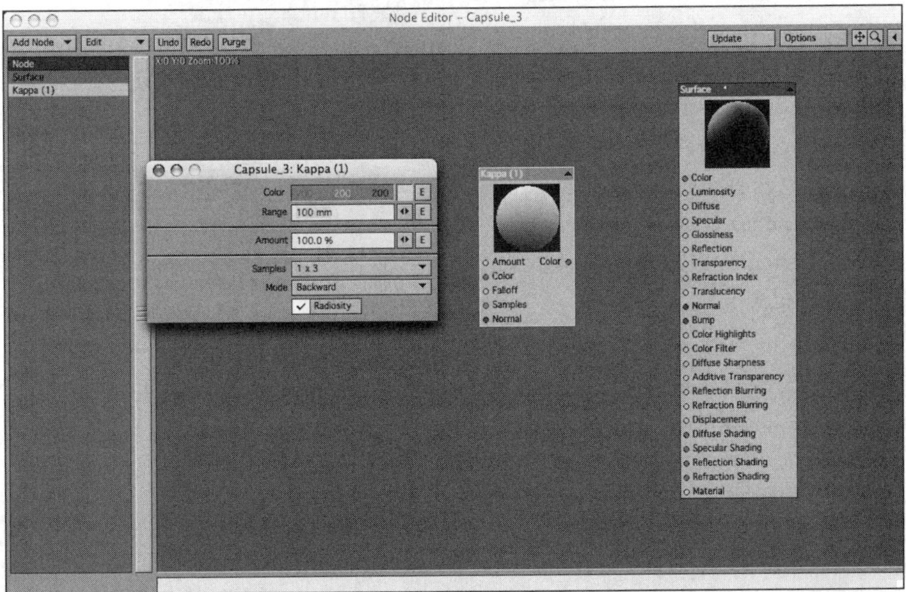

Figure 11.40 Double-click the Kappa subsurface scattering node to open the properties for it.

5. Set the color to a soft yellow. This color is the color you'll see as the subsurface shader is applied. You can also add patterns and colors from other nodes to this via the Color input.
6. Set the range to **2m**. This is the maximum range that the surface will be sampled. Given that the grid square size of your layout is 2m and the capsule is about 3m in length, the value of 2m should work well.
7. Amount sets the extent of the shader's effect. So, set this to **200%**.
8. Set Samples to 11×33. This setting determines the number of directions LightWave calculates for the subsurface scattering shader. Without getting too technical, the higher the value, the more samples LightWave will calculate, and the more exact your shading will be. Of course, this means higher render times. For objects like this capsule (in this project), a mid-range sample is more than fine. For a candle, a mid-range sample is also fine. But for something like a glass statue, which is more intricate, a higher sample would prove more accurate. Testing, of course, is always recommend.
9. Change the scattering Mode setting from its default, Backwards, to Forward. Backwards scattering is best for softer-looking surfaces, such as clouds, plastics, cloth, or skin. The Forward scattering setting is great for glassy or waxy surfaces. On a simple level, you can set this based on your main light's position to the objects: Forward if the object is lit from the front, and backward if it's lit from behind.
10. Ignore the Radiosity check box. Simply, when this is turned on, you're telling the shader to respond to your scene's global illumination settings. If there's no radiosity in your scene (and there isn't any in this one), this setting doesn't really matter. **Figure 11.41** shows the panel.

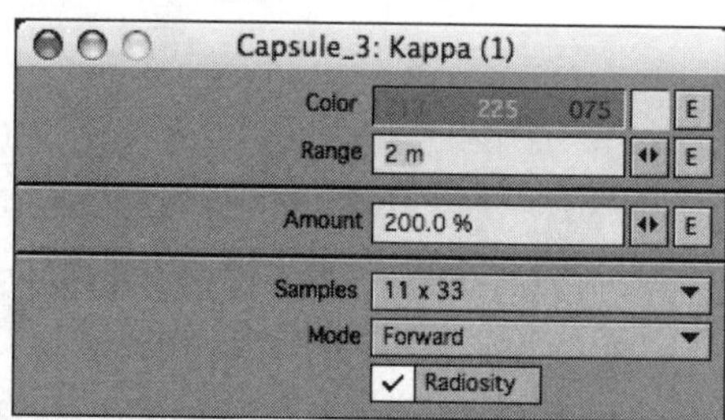

Figure 11.41 A few settings to the Kappa subsurface scattering node and you're ready to go.

11. Close the Properties panel for the node, then drag the Color output and drop it into the Diffuse Shading input of the destination node. **Figure 11.42** shows the connection.

Note

The Kappa subsurface scattering shader works best when connected to the destination node's Diffuse Shading input.

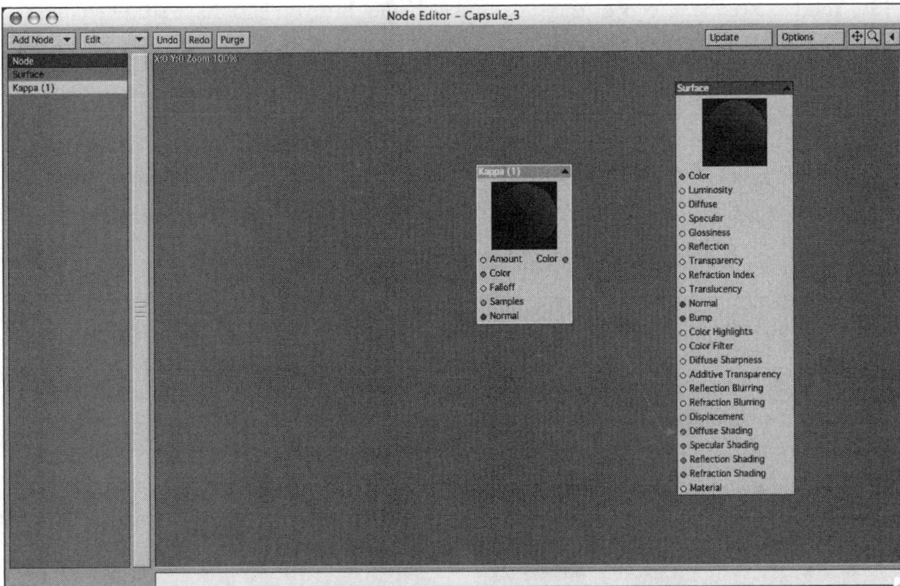

Figure 11.42 Connect the Color output to the Diffuse Shading input.

12. Go ahead and press **F9** to render the current frame. Take a look at the third capsule, the one lying on top of the other two. Notice how it has a sort of inner glow? **Figure 11.43** shows the change.

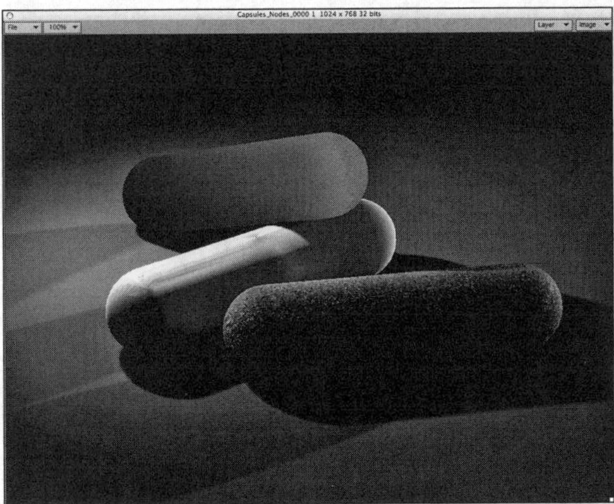

Figure 11.43 Applying subsurface scattering to a surface shows a visible, but not often desirable, result.

13. You can see the effects of the subsurface shader, but you can make some changes to it. You can control this shader (and any other) with a Gradient node. From the Add Node drop-down menu, choose the Gradient entry, then the subentry also called Gradient.
14. Double-click the Gradient node to open its properties. You'll see the gradient panel you might know from LightWave's texture editor, as shown in **Figure 11.44**.

Note

Remember to watch the Node_Intro movie on the book's DVD (3D_Garage_Videos\Chapter_Videos\CH11a_NodeIntro.mov) to become familiar with the navigating Node Editor. You can always right-click a node for more controls such as properties, cut, delete, and more.

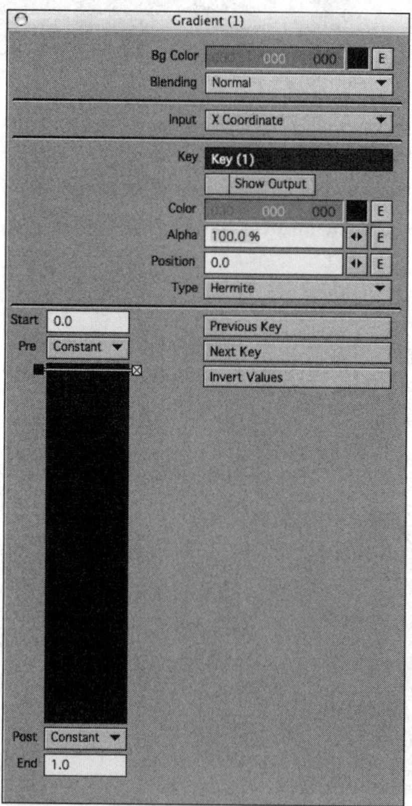

Figure 11.44 Add a gradient node and open the properties for it.

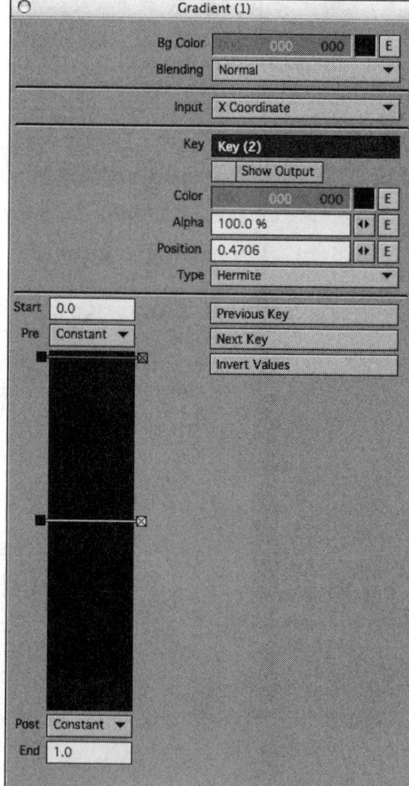

Figure 11.45 Add a key to the gradient by clicking into it.

15. Using the Gradient is simple, and to make things clearer, you can watch the Gradient.mov on the book's DVD (3D_Garage_Videos\Chapter_Videos\CH11b_Gradients.mov), a video project from the 3D Garage LightWave v9 training course. Click into the large vertical black bar, the gradient itself. This will create a key as shown in **Figure 11.45**.
16. Now select the top original key. Set the Alpha value to **0%**, as shown in **Figure 11.46**.
17. Move the Gradient panel out of the way, but don't close it. Take the Alpha (green dot) output from the Gradient and hook it to the Falloff input of the Kappa node, as shown in **Figure 11.47**.
18. Taking a look at the sample spheres in the nodes, it looks as if half of the surface is cut off. Head back to the Gradient panel, and change the Input setting from X Coordinate to Y Coordinate in order to set the gradient from top to bottom.

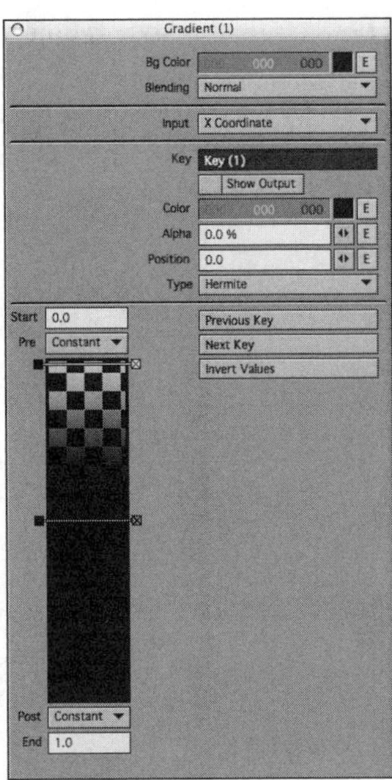

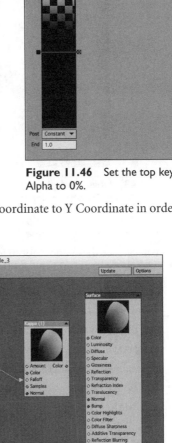

Figure 11.46 Set the top key's Alpha to 0%.

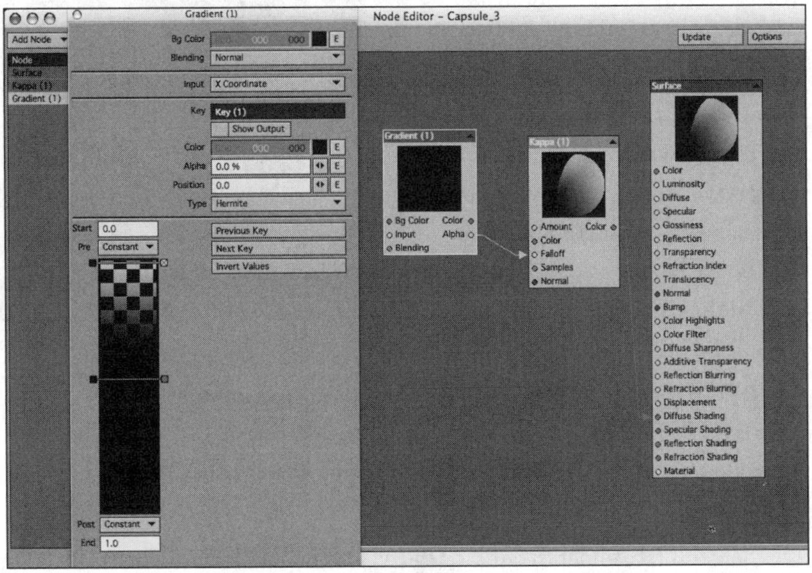

Figure 11.47 Hook the Alpha output from the Gradient to the Falloff input of the Kappa subsurface scattering node.

19. Back in the Node Editor, click the green Gradient node Alpha-output arrowhead, next to the Kappa node's Falloff input, and drag it up to the Kappa node's Amount input, as in **Figure 11.48**.

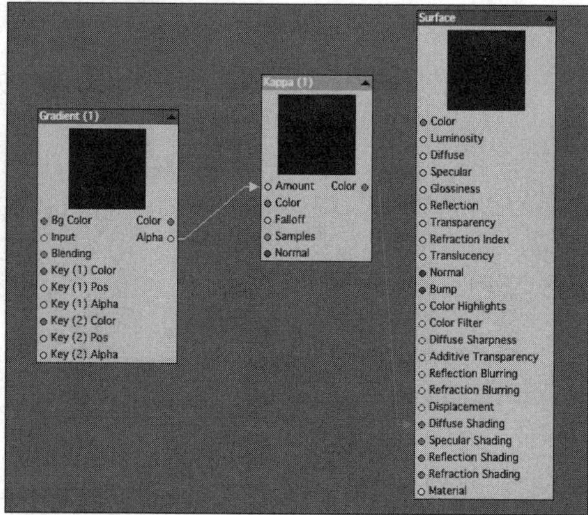

Figure 11.48 Move the Alpha output of the Gradient node from the Kappa ode's Falloff input to its Amount input.

20. Press **F9** to render a frame, and you can see that you've not made the subsurface node's effect fade out toward the bottom of the capsule. It should be noted that when this capsule was created in LightWave Modeler, it was created vertically on the Y-axis. Therefore, LightWave Layout sees the Y-axis toward the right side, because the capsule is lying down on top of the other two capsules. **Figure 11.49** shows the render.

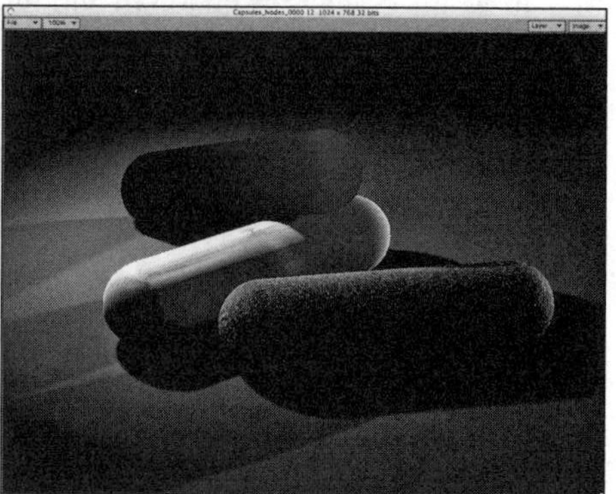

Figure 11.49 Setting the Gradient Input setting to Y Coordinate changes the effect of the subsurface Kappa node.

21. Now, close all of the panels and get into Layout. Or press the Tab key to quickly hide them.

22. On the Items tab, under the Add category, select Spotlight from the Lights drop down menu.

23. Press **5** on your keyboard or numeric keypad to jump to a Light view.
24. Press **t** to select Move, and move the light behind the third capsule. **Figure 11.50** shows the view from the light.

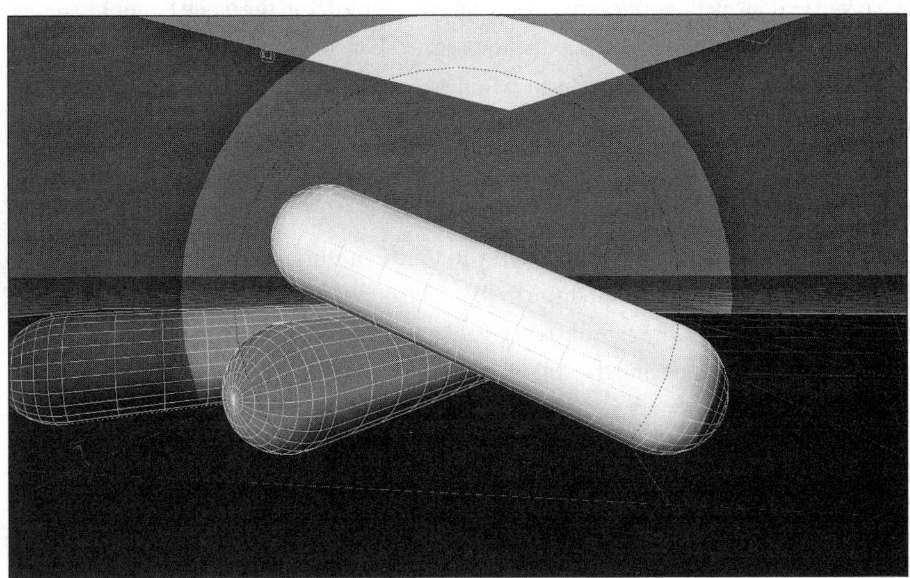

Figure 11.50 Add a spotlight and position it behind the third capsule.

25. Now that you have a light behind the capsule, you might want this to be the primary light. So, open the Node Editor again (if you hid panels in step 21, you can press Tab to unhide). For the Capsule_3 surface, double-click the Kappa node and change Mode from Forward to Backward. This tells LightWave that the primary light is from behind. Press **F9** to render a single frame, and your objects surface will really glow with light. **Figure 11.51** shows the example.

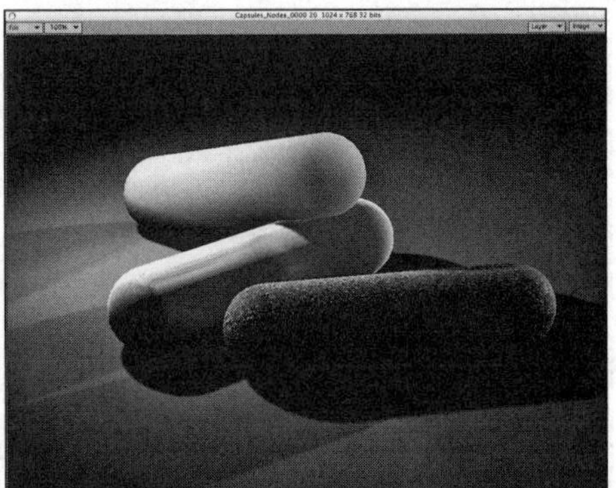

Figure 11.51 Changing the Mode setting for the subsurface scattering node from Forward to Backward uses the new light as its main source for calculation.

26. Change some values, play with inputs, and see what kind of variations you can come up with. Then, save your work.

This brief example of subsurface scattering is just the tip of the iceberg. You might interested to know that glass looks awesome with subsurface nodes. To truly see the effects of this feature, watch the video tutorial on the book's DVD to explain this technique further.

What you've done in this exercise helps strengthen your work in the Node Editor by adding gradients and applying them as inputs. You learned how to change inputs and outputs as well as incorporate scene changes to an existing scene with nodes applied. The next project, in which you create some everyday surfaces, will take you even further with the Node Editor.

Exercise 11.4 Image Mapping with Nodes

The previous exercise briefly introduced you to the subsurface scattering nodes, which you'll see put into further action through the video on the book's DVD. For now, you'll set up another surface for the capsule scene you've been working on, then take your nodes one step beyond by surfacing the still-life scene you modeled in Chapter 8.

1. Continuing from the last exercise, select the Floor surface in the Surface Editor. Then, click the Edit Nodes button to open the Node Editor.
2. You've seen a number of nodes used earlier in the chapter that create computer-generated textures. But what about image maps? No problem! From the Add Node drop-down menu, choose 2D Textures, then Image. **Figure 11.52** shows the added node.

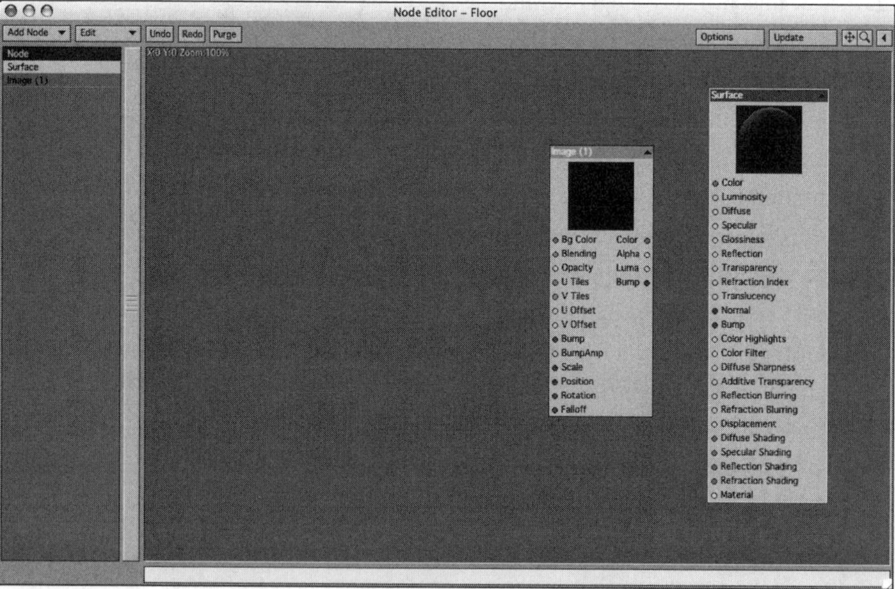

Figure 11.52 Add an Image node to apply an image map to the floor.

3. Double-click the Image node to open the Properties panel. You'll see a large panel with quite a few options, more than any image-mapping feature in previous versions of LightWave. **Figure 11.53** shows the panel.

4. In the Image panel, select Load Image from the Image drop-down. Choose the MetalGrate.jpg image from the Projects\Images\CH11 directory. **Figure 11.54** shows the loaded image.

   The Image node properties allow you to change the blending, rotation, falloff, and more for the image. Blending properties are similar to those found in programs like Adobe Photoshop, such as additive, subtractive, lighten, and more. You can also rotate the image or make the image fade by setting falloff values. You can also edit the image by clicking the Edit Image panel, which brings you right to LightWave's native Image Editor. For now, you don't need to change those settings, but you have to set a few others.

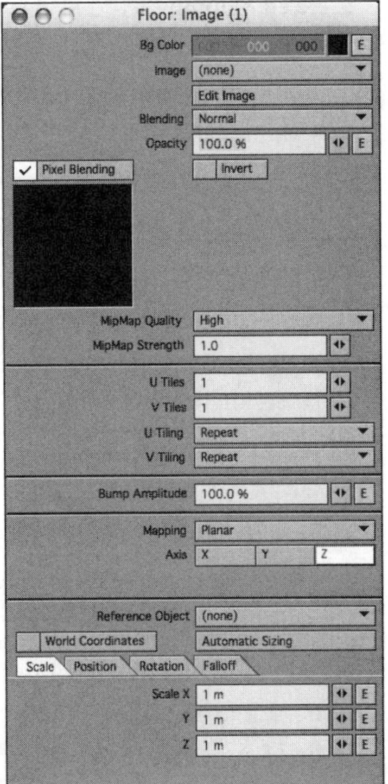

Figure 11.53 Open the Image node properties.

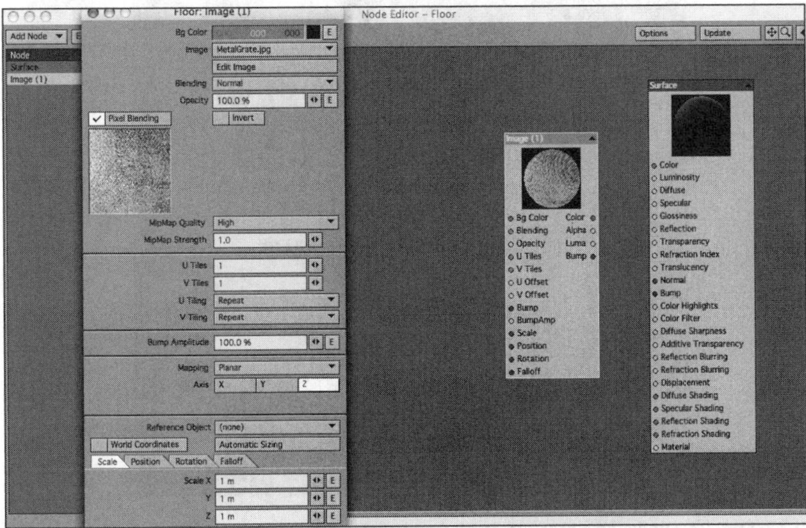

Figure 11.54 Load the MetalGrate image.

5. Keep Mapping set to Planar. You're working with a flat surface (the floor), so neither of the alternative settings, Sphericial nor Cylindrical, applies.
6. For the Axis, choose Y. You want to effectively "drop" the image on the floor, which lies flat on the Y-axis.
7. Click Automatic Sizing and LightWave will scale the image to the geometry. **Figure 11.55** shows the setup.
8. Press **F9** to render a single frame and see the results. What? Nothing there? That's right! You need to place the Image node into your destination node. Begin by closing the Properties panel for the Image node.
9. Take the Color output of the Image node and hook it to the Color input of the destination node, as in **Figure 11.56**.

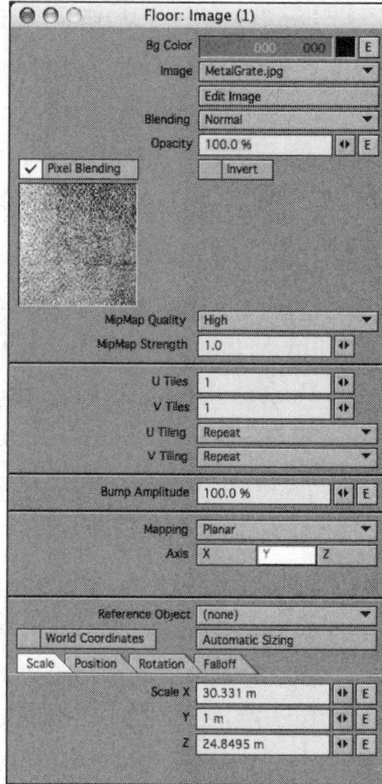

Figure 11.55 Set up the image map with a few changes, all within the Node Editor.

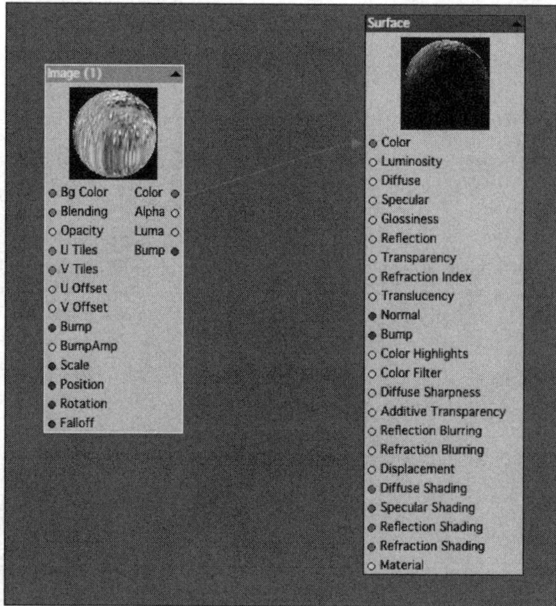

Figure 11.56 To apply the Image node to your surface, hook the Color output to the Color input.

10. Press **F9** and you'll see what you've just done (**Figure 11.57**).
11. The image maps well, but there's a lot more you can do with it now that the node is set up. Right-click the Image node and select Copy, as shown in **Figure 11.58**.
12. Click into the empty Node Editor workspace, then right-click again and choose Paste, as shown in **Figure 11.59**. Now you have two identical image nodes, as shown in **Figure 11.60**.

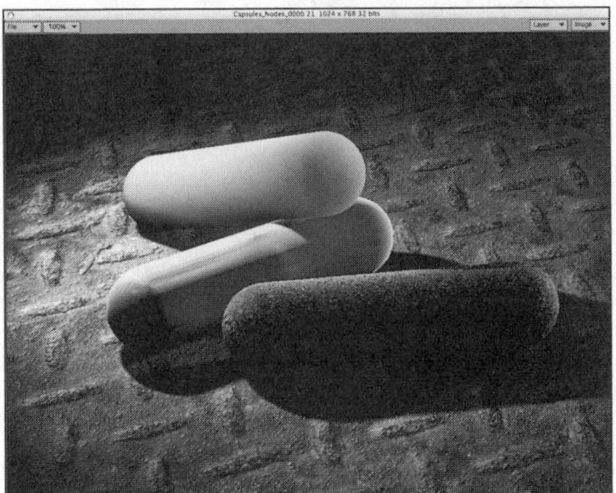

Figure 11.57 A quick frame render shows the image map now applied to the floor.

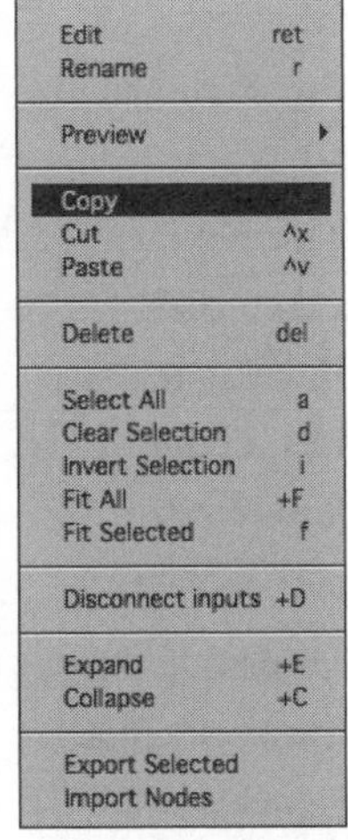

Figure 11.58 Copy the Image node.

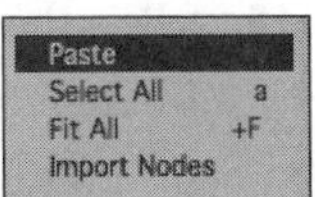

Figure 11.59 Paste the copied node.

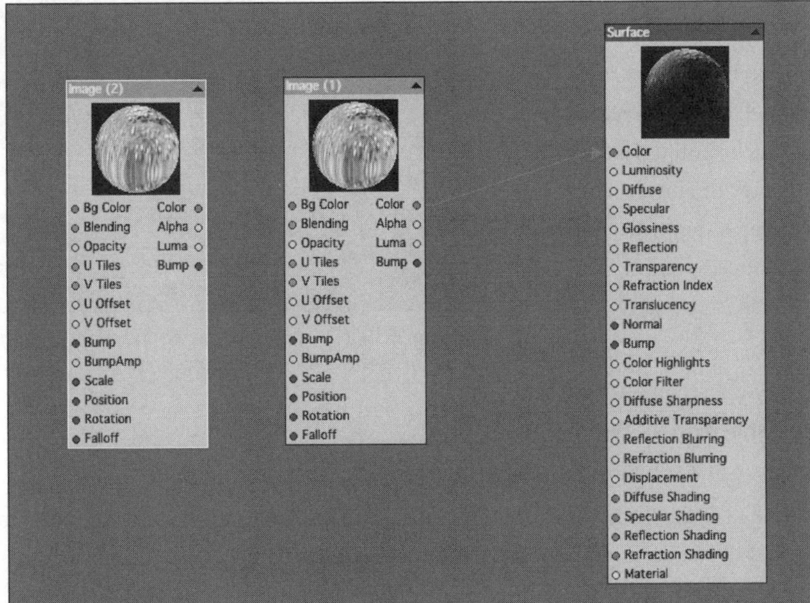

Figure 11.60 Quickly copying and pasting adds an identical copy of the Image node.

13. Double-click the added Image node to open the Properties panel for it. Click the Edit Image button.

14. In the Image Editor, select the MetalGrate image, select the Clone drop-down at the top right of the panel, and choose Instance, as shown in **Figure 11.61**.

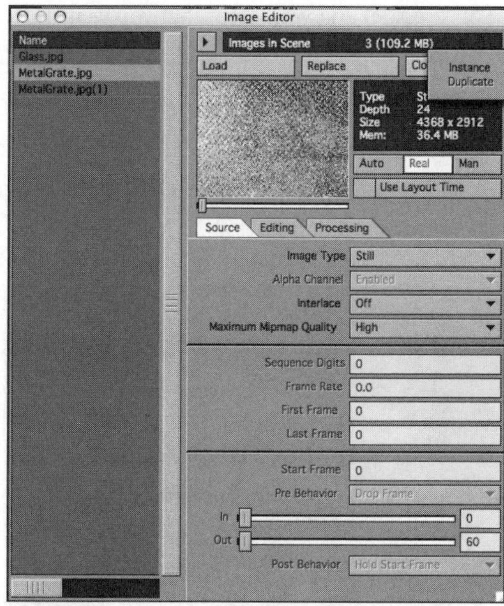

Figure 11.61 Add an instance of the image in the Edit Image panel.

15. Select the instance in the Image Editor, then click the Editing tab. Drag the Saturation slider all the way to the left to remove the color from the image.

16. Bring the Brightness to **-0.35**, with the Contrast set to **0.4**, as shown in **Figure 11.62**.

17. When set, close the Image Editor.

18. Back in the Properties panel for the copied node (which should still be open), change the image from MetalGrate.jpg to the instanced version, MetalGrate.jpg(1).

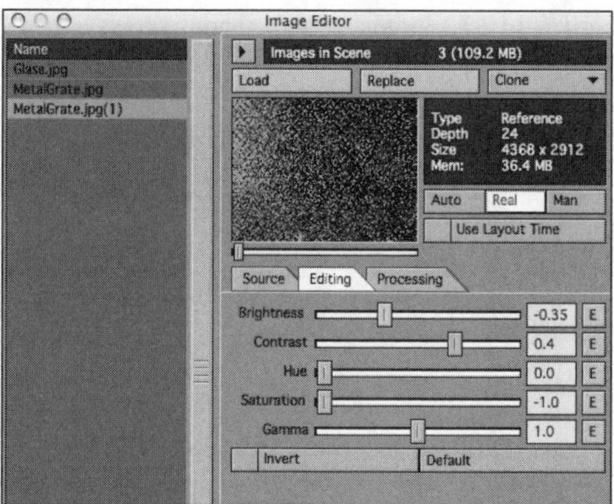

Figure 11.62 Increase the contrast and decrease the brightness for the instanced image.

19. Close the panel—don't make any other changes. Your sample sphere in the nodes should show a black-and-white version and a colored version.

20. Now, take the Bump output of the second Image node and hook it into the Bump input of the destination node, as shown in **Figure 11.63**.

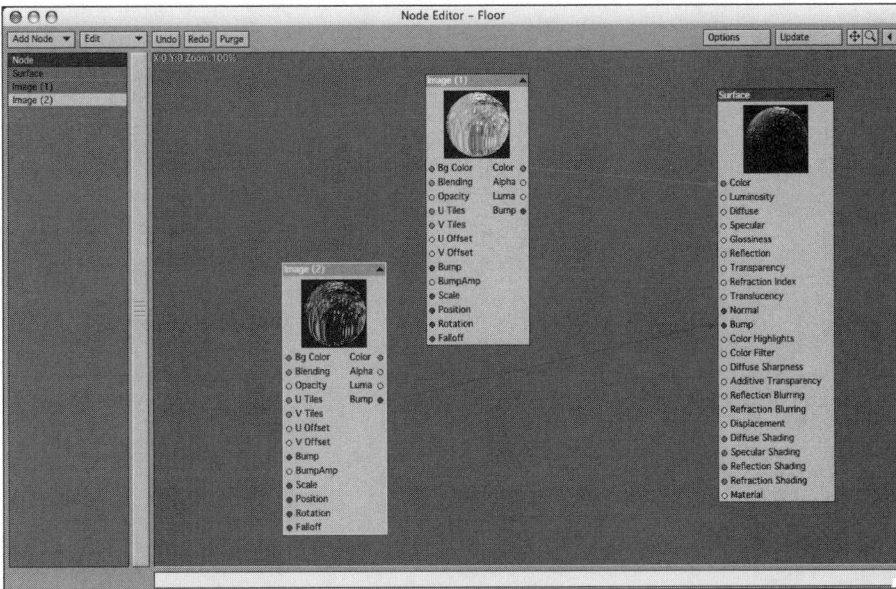

Figure 11.63 Use the black-and-white image, the instanced copy, as the driver for the Bump channel.

21. Go ahead and press **F9** to render a frame. **Figure 11.64** shows the render, now with a bump map applied.

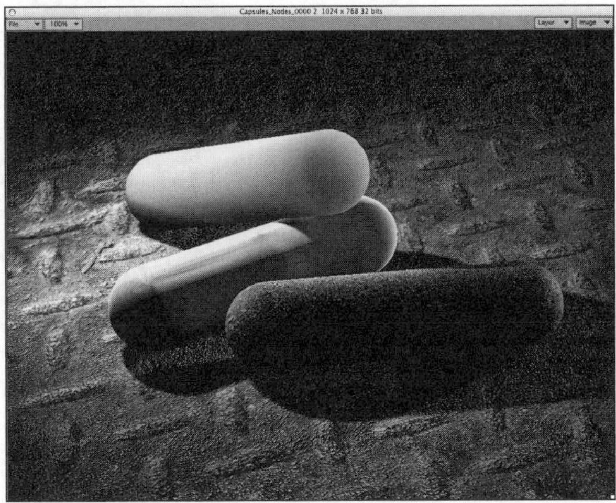

Figure 11.64 Upon setting a bump map to the floor surface from the second image node, you can see a visible difference in the render.

22. You can increase the amount of bump in the Image node Properties panel. The default Bump Amplitude setting is 100%; set it to something like **200%**.

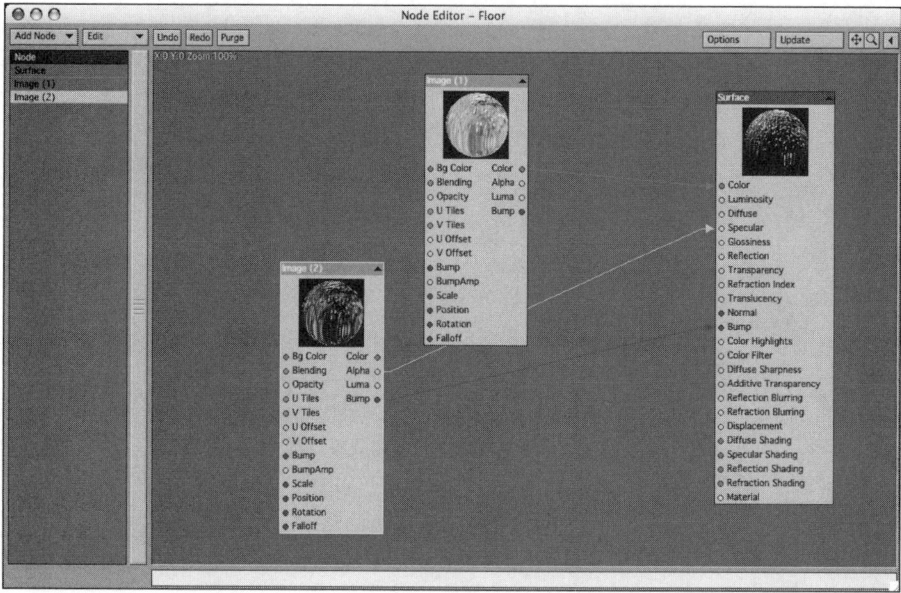

Figure 11.65 The Node Editor set up with a second Image node, attached to multiple inputs on the destination node.

23. Take the Alpha output of the cloned Image node and connect it to the Specular input of the destination node. This takes the high and low values of the black-and-white image and uses them for specularity. The brighter, whiter areas allow more specularity, while the darker areas do not. **Figure 11.65** shows the Node Editor.

24. Open the Camera panel in Layout and turn on Antialiasing. Do this by selecting PLD 9-Pass for the Anitaliasing settings. Set the Reconstruction Filter to Classic. **Figure 11.66** shows the panel.

25. Antialiasing is important to add in this scene now because of the bump map. You'll learn more about the AA settings later in Chapter 15, "Advanced Cameras and Rendering." For now, press **F9** to render a frame. **Figure 11.67** shows the result.

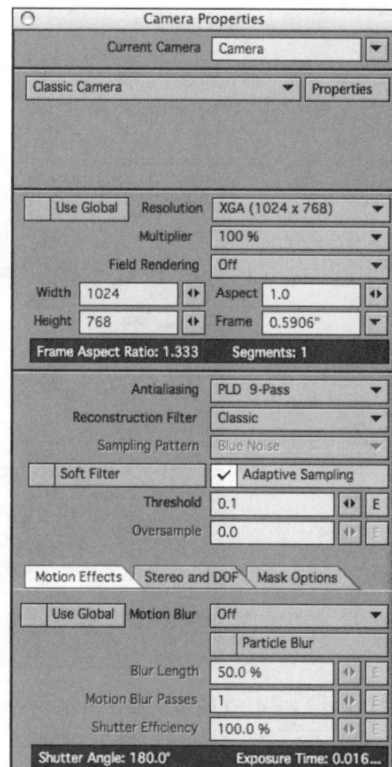

Figure 11.66 Add antialiasing in the Camera panel for the render.

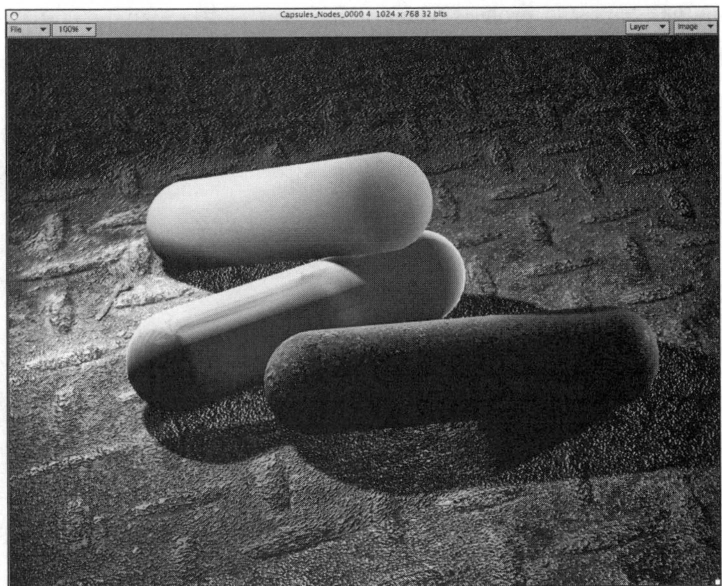

Figure 11.67 A stronger Bump Amplitude setting for the bump map, along with a specularity, enhance the textured floor.

26. Feel free to make some more tweaks and render a few more frames. Then save your work.

Note

Try using this bump technique on the Capsule_1 surface. However, you don't need to make a copy since the texture is computer generated. Just drag the Bump output of the Crumple node to the Bump input of the destination node. Multiple bumps!

Although this scene is nothing too exciting, it gave you a good overview of some basic node setups that you can incorporate into your everyday 3D workflow. Now, read on to the chapter's last project to texture your still-life object from Chapter 8.

Exercise 11.5 Advanced Node Setup

This chapter has covered a number of Node Editor features, and with the videos included on the book's DVD, you should have a strong grasp of this powerful new feature in LightWave v9. So this next project will take you further by applying textures to the still-life model you created in Chapter 8. You'll use techniques presented already, as well as new ones, all within the Node Editor.

1. Save anything you've been working on and clear LightWave Layout.

2. From the Chapter 11 projects folder on the book's DVD, load the FruitBowl scene. **Figure 11.68** shows the interface.

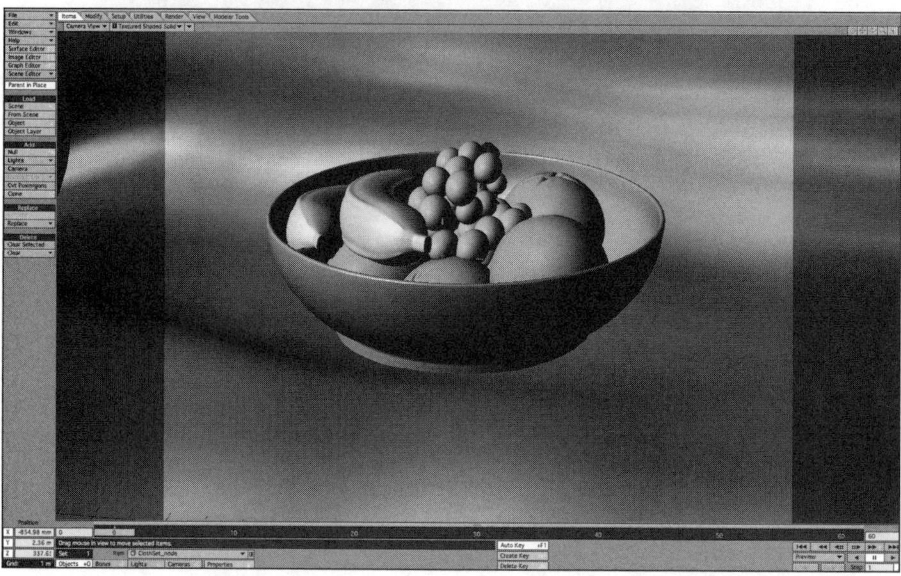

Figure 11.68 The FruitBowl scene loaded and ready for surfacing.

3. Press **F7** to open VIPER, and then press **F9** to run a frame render and to make the scene's rendering data available to VIPER.
4. When the render finishes, click the Render button in the VIPER panel itself. The FruitBowl scene will appear in the VIPER preview window, as in **Figure 11.69**.
5. With VIPER open, you'll be able to see changes to your surfaces from the Node Editor. Open the Surface Editor and select the Banana surface, and then click the Edit Nodes button to open the Node Editor.

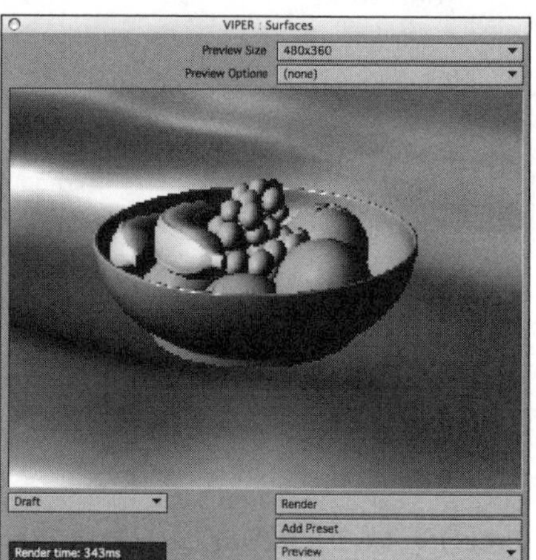

Figure 11.69 After you run a frame render on the scene, click the Render button in the VIPER panel to load the preview data.

6. From the Add Node drop-down menu, select 3D Textures, then Marble. This first surface you'll set up will be similar to one of the capsule surfaces you created earlier but with some changes and additions. **Figure 11.70** shows the added node.

Figure 11.70 Add a Marble node to the Node Editor.

7. Next, add a Crackle node, also from the 3D Textures category. **Figure 11.71** shows it added to the Node Editor.

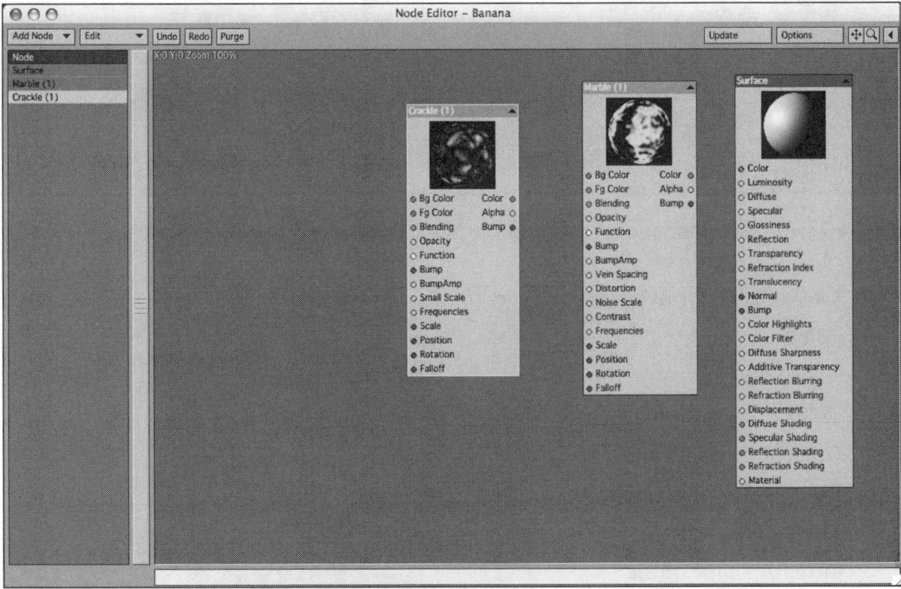

Figure 11.71 Add a Marble node to the Node Editor.

8. Now add something new: a function. From the Add Node drop-down menu, select Functions, then Noise, as shown in **Figure 11.72**. A function node controls the shape or appearance of attributes supplied by another node. **Figure 11.73** shows the Noise node added to the Node Editor.

9. Now that all of the nodes for this surface are added, it's time to hook them together and create the "network." First, double-click the sample sphere on the Crackle node to open its properties.

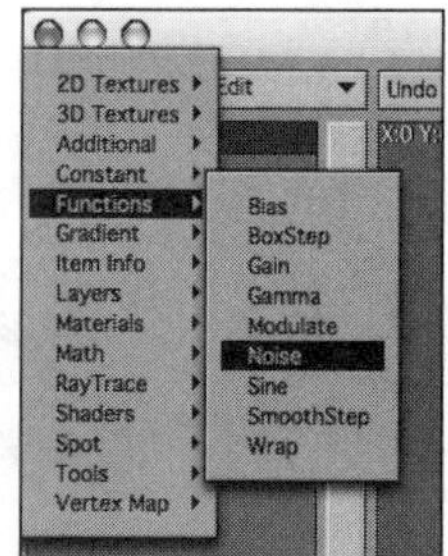

Figure 11.72 Add a Noise node to the Node Editor.

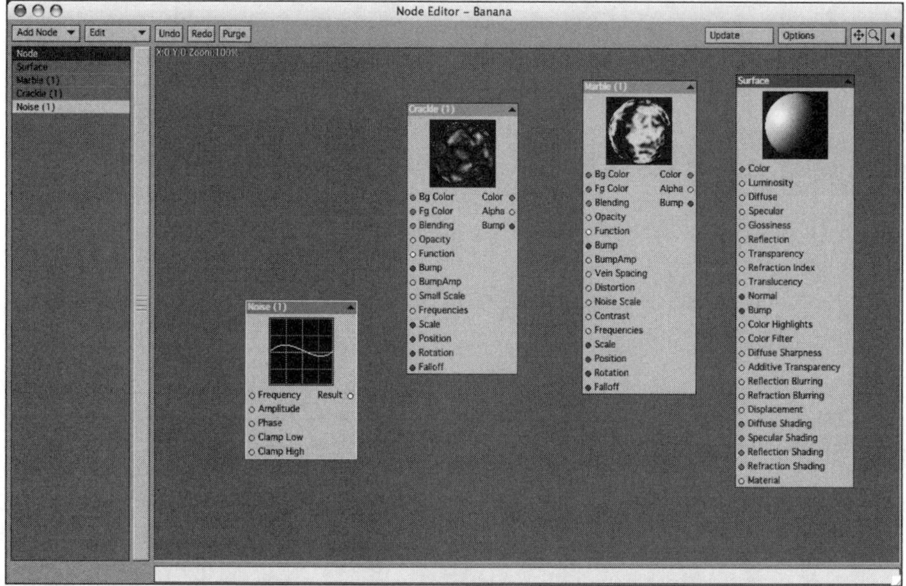

Figure 11.73 Four nodes now added to the Node Editor need to be "networked."

10. Set the Bg Color to a pale yellow, about R: 255, G: 250, B: 235. Set the Fg Color to light brown. Set Small Scale to **0.5** and Frequencies to **1.0** (**Figure 11.74**). This helps set the basic shape of the Crackle node.

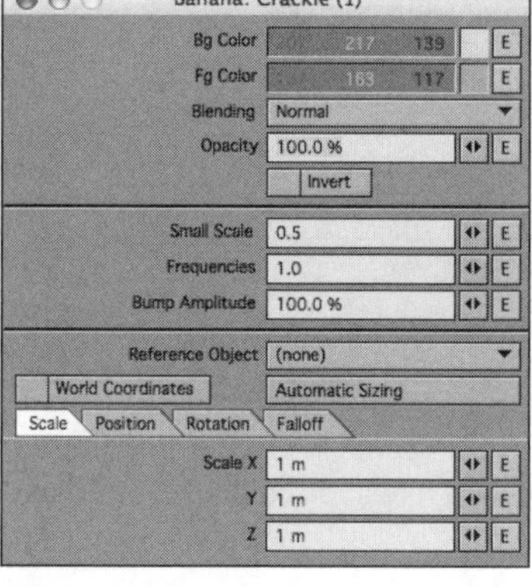

Figure 11.74 Make a few color and property changes to the Crackle node.

11. Close the Properties panel, then drag the Color output of the Crackle node and attach it to the Bg Color input of the Marble node. The yellowish color will be mixed with the second node, as shown in **Figure 11.75**.

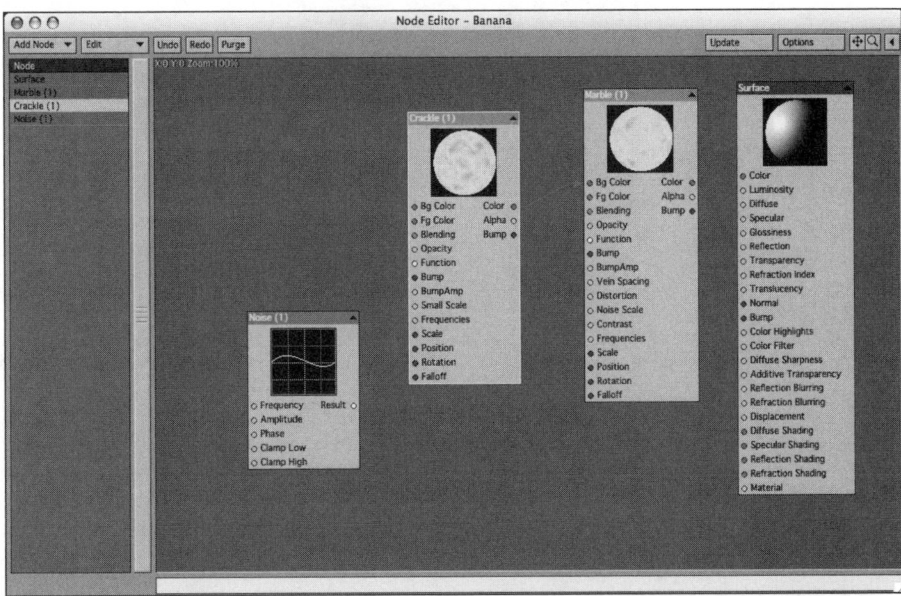

Figure 11.75 Take the Color output of the Crackle node and attach it to the Bg Color input of the Marble node.

12. Double-click the Marble sample sphere to open the Properties panel. You'll see that the Bg Color setting is grayed out, which means you're not able to set the value. This is because you have the Crackle node driving that value. This node replaces Bg Color by generating high and low variations instead. So, change Fg Color to a warm brown, perhaps with a little grayish tone, roughly R: 83, G: 83, B: 22.

13. Leave Opacity at 100%. Set Vein Spacing to **1.0** and Distortion to **1.0**. Opacity represents how much of the node you'll see or how strong its effect is. Vein Spacing sets how close or far apart the marble veins are from each other. The Distortion setting adds an interesting variation to the pattern.

14. Noise Scale should be **1.0**. Then, change the Axis setting to Y. The banana was built in such a way that setting the node value to the Y-axis will make the texture run down the length of the banana. That is, the banana was built in LightWave Modeler in a vertical, or Y-axis, orientation, and then saved. So while the banana is rotated and lying flat on the Y-axis in Layout, LightWave remembers its initial vertical alignment and uses it when applying surface attributes.

15. To increase the size of the node texture, set the X, Y, and Z scales to **6m**. **Figure 11.76** shows the panel and its settings.

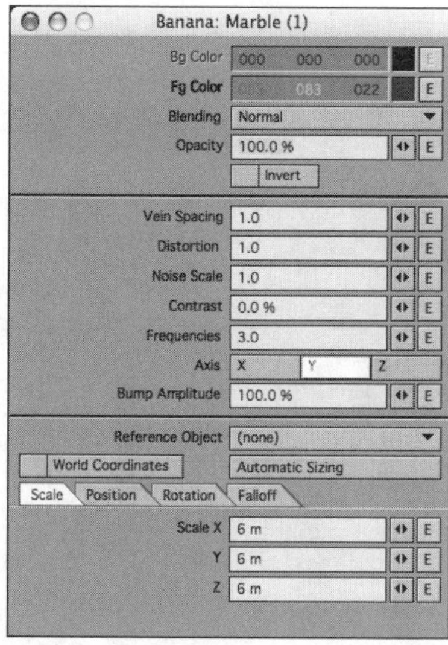

Figure 11.76 A few value changes to the Marble surface and the banana will have some distress and aging.

16. Now, take the Color output of the Marble surface and connect it to the Color input of the destination node, as shown in **Figure 11.77**.

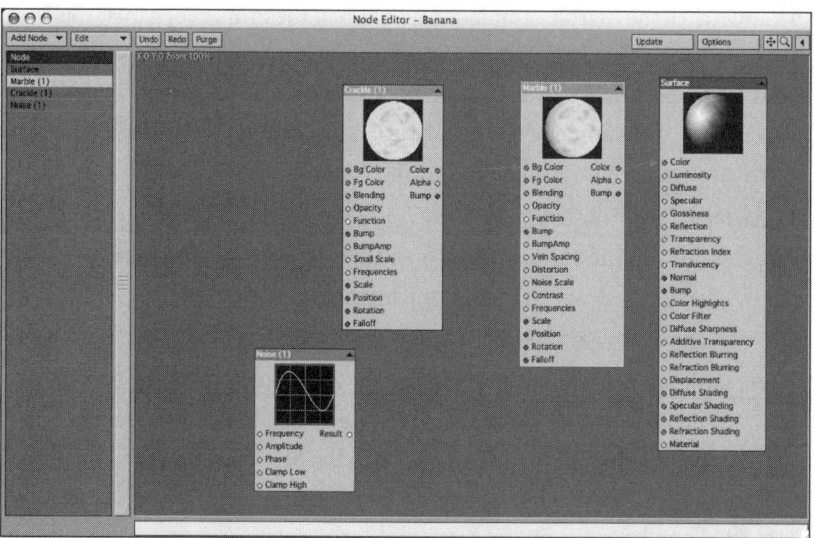

Figure 11.77 Connect the Color output from the Marble node to the Color input of the destination node.

17. Take a look at your VIPER window. The bananas now have some age spots, as shown in **Figure 11.78**. If you were to open the Marble or Crackle properties and make changes now, you'll see them update in the VIPER window because the connection goes through to the destination node.

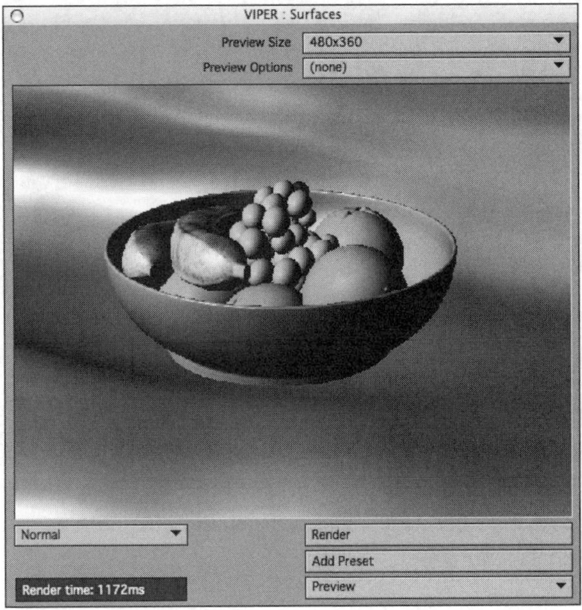

Figure 11.78 VIPER shows the updated surface.

18. To add more variety to the banana-skin texture, double-click the Noise node. Increase the Amplitude setting to **2.0**, as shown in **Figure 11.79**.

Banana: Noise (1)

Frequency	1.0	E
Amplitude	2.0	E
Phase	0.0	E
Clamp Low	0.0	E
Clamp High	1.0	E

Figure 11.79 Increase the amplitude of the Noise node.

19. Increasing the amplitude of the Noise node increases the strength of the noise texture. Close the Properties panel, and then take the Result output of the Noise

node and connect it to the Function input of the Marble node. **Figure 11.80** shows the connection.

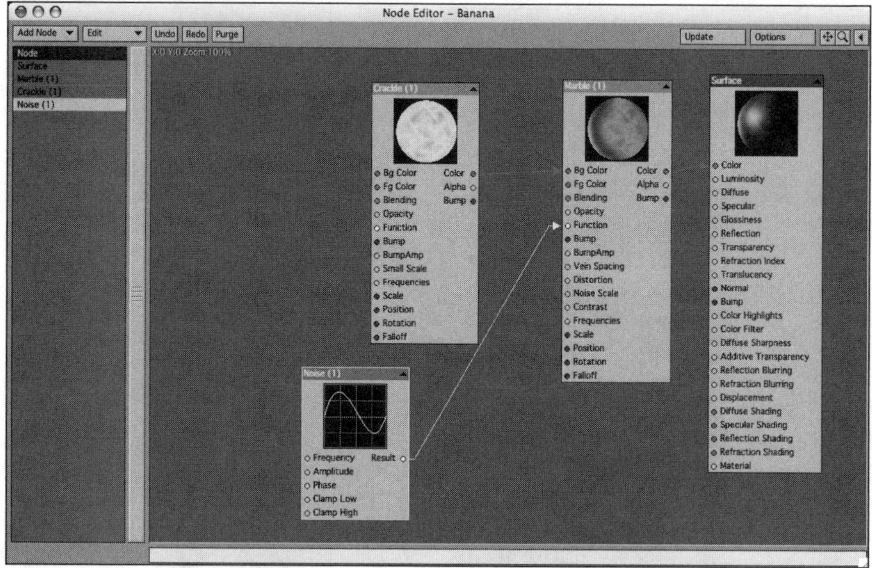

Figure 11.80 Connect the Function output of the Noise node to the Function input of the Marble node.

Note

If you feel that your banana is too dark, open the Marble properties and set the Opacity to 50%. This will reduce the strength of this node by half.

20. Now take a look at your VIPER window, and you'll see that there is now a change in the patterns of the Marble node. It's subtle but effective for this surface. You can experiment with the values and watch the changes in the VIPER window.

21. The last thing to do is bring down the specularity, or shine, of the banana. You can connect the Crackle node's Alpha output to the Specularity input of the destination node. This won't change how shiny the banana is, but it will change the "shape" of the specularity. As you can see in **Figure 11.81**, the specularity is now broken with the Crackle node values. Pretty cool—you're using the same Crackle node to drive the Specularity channel.

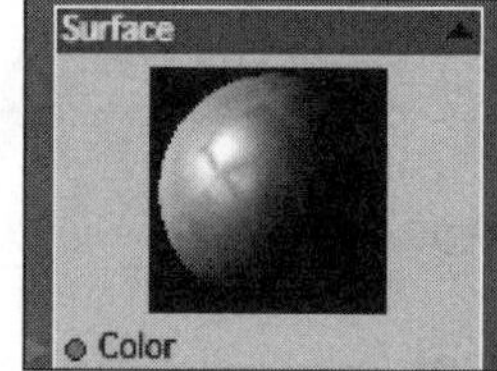

Figure 11.81 The Crackle node can also be used to drive the Specularity channel.

22. From the Add Node menu, select Shaders, then Specular, then Blinn. LightWave traditionally used a variation of Phong shading, built into the Surface Editor's Smoothing option. But with LightWave v9, you have new choices, with Blinn among them. **Figure 11.82** shows the shader.

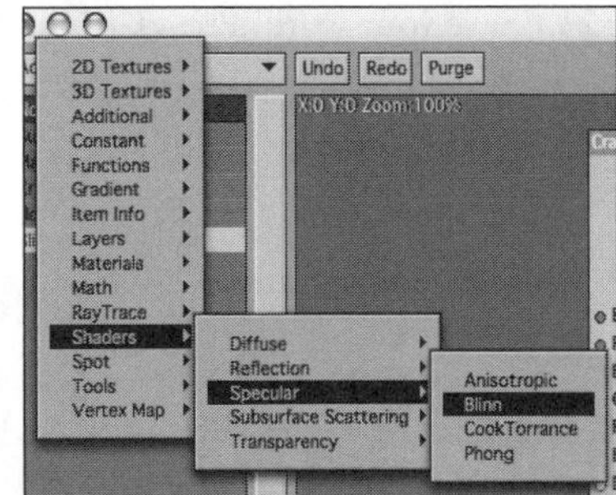

Figure 11.82 Add a Specular shading node, Blinn.

23. After you've added the Blinn node to the Node Editor, take the Color output from it and connect it to the Specular Shading input of the destination node, as shown in **Figure 11.83**.

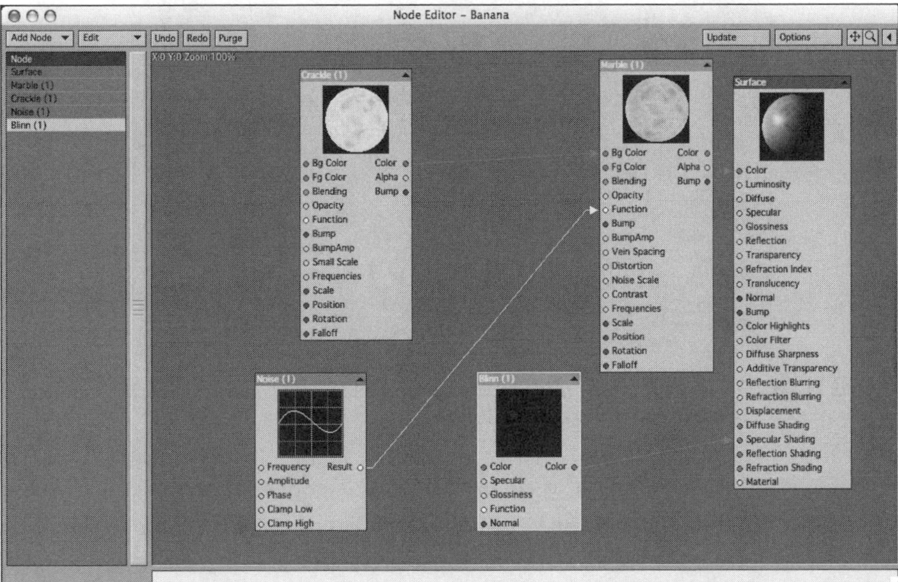

Figure 11.83 Connect the Blinn node output to the Specular Shading input of the destination node.

24. Disconnect the Specular input on the destination node—just click on the arrow to remove it. Then, double-click the Blinn node sample sphere to open the properties for it. Change the Color to a brighter yellow.

25. Set Specularity to **35%** and Glossiness to **10%**, as shown in **Figure 11.84**.

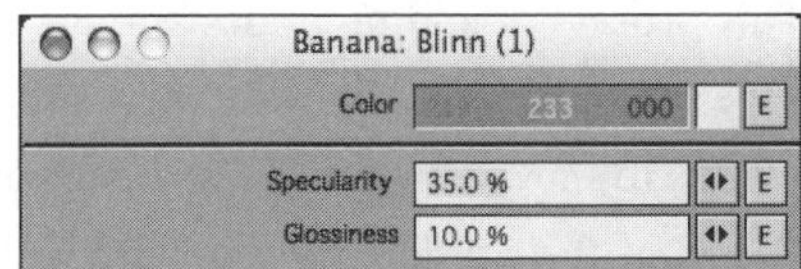

Figure 11.84 A few changes to the Blinn shader and your final banana surface setting is in place.

26. Save your work! Press Ctrl+s to save the scene. Also for safety, from the File drop-down menu in Layout, select Save All Objects. **Figure 11.85** shows the VIPER window displaying the surface changes to the banana.

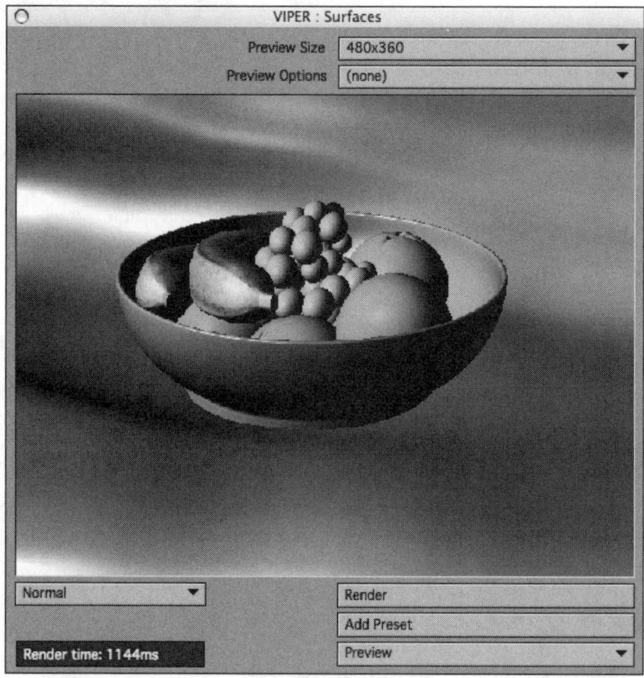

Figure 11.85 By adding the Specular Shading node, the banana no longer has a bright white hot spot but a more natural shine.

If you look at the Node Editor, it almost looks too complex to be something you've created. But think about what you've just done, and you realize that it's not so hard! By creating your "network" of surfaces, or nodes, one step at a time, you can see that the multi-layering texturing capabilities of the Node Editor are very powerful.

The Next Step

This process of adding nodes and experimenting with different results could go on for pages and pages. But because there's so much more to cover in LightWave v9, we created a video to show you how to texture the orange, grapes, and bowl of the still-life scene. Take a look at the StillLife.mov on the book's DVD (3D_Garage_Videos\Chapter_Videos\CH11d_StillLife.mov) to take this project further and learn even more about the Node Editor.

Chapter 12

Bones and Rigging

The focus of this chapter is bones, Skelegons, and proper character setup for animation. As with the previous *Inside LightWave* books, we won't bore you with technical babble about theory and muscle structures; rather, this chapter discusses the following:

- Understanding bones
- Working with Skelegons for character rigs in Modeler
- Weighting characters for precise control
- Rigging characters directly in LightWave Layout

Understanding Bones

Bones are deformation tools; they *deform* your models so they can bend, twist, stretch, and contract realistically, without requiring all of their limbs and other body parts to be modeled and animated as separate objects. Without bones, creation of figures that move naturally in their skin (or in clothing, fur, feathers, and so on) would be virtually impossible, and animated figures would all resemble robots or marionettes. Bones let you model characters as "solid" objects, and then give them movement and life. Given all that, keep the idea in the back of your mind that bones can also be used for other purposes, such as animating billowing curtains or a beating heart. **Figure 12.1** shows a bone in Layout.

Bones aren't difficult to use, but you must follow some rules to make them work properly. First, and most importantly, every bone must be associated with an object. The purpose of a bone is to deform an object, so a bone without an object has no purpose in and of itself. So you must attach every bone to an object, even if it's just a Null object. Exercise 12.1 provides the steps to do just that.

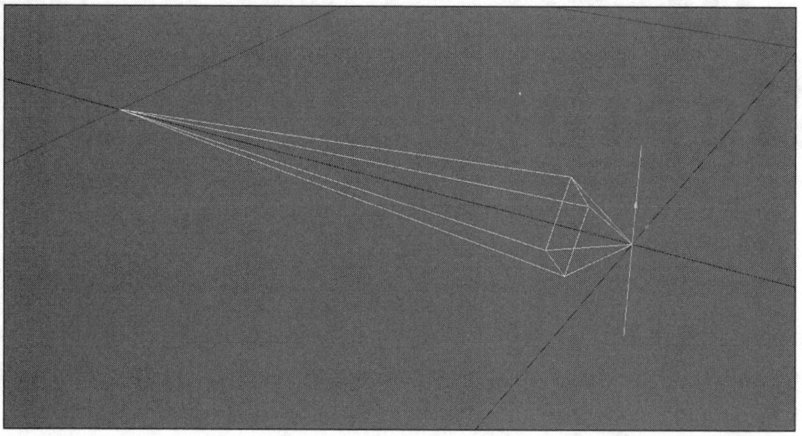

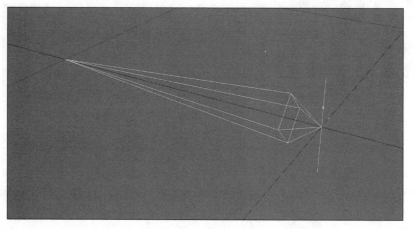

Figure 12.1 A bone in Layout looks like a necktie. It does not render, but it exerts powerful control over its associated object.

Exercise 12.1 Creating Bones in Layout

1. Start Layout, or if it's already running, choose Clear Layout from the File drop-down menu at the top left of the interface. Then click the Setup tab. This is where all of Layout's bone controls are located. If you look to the Add category on the left, you'll see that all the commands are grayed out. You have no objects loaded, so LightWave won't let you add any bones to the scene. Select the Items tab at the top of Layout and, from the Add category, add a Null object to the scene.

   This Null object is your base, or root, object. Even though bones need to be associated with an object, the object can be just a Null object.

Tip

Instead of clicking away from the Setup tab to the Items tab to add a Null object from the Items tab, you can always just press Ctrl+n on your keyboard to quickly add a Null object.

2. Rename the Null object if you like, but the default name "Null" is fine. With the Null object selected (as the only object in the scene, it's selected by default), click the Setup tab. Then from the Add category, select Bone and then Add Bone. LightWave asks you to rename the bone. Just click OK for now.

   You'll see a 1m bone, like the one in Figure 12.1, extending along the Z-axis from the Null object's position at the origin point (**Figure 12.2**).

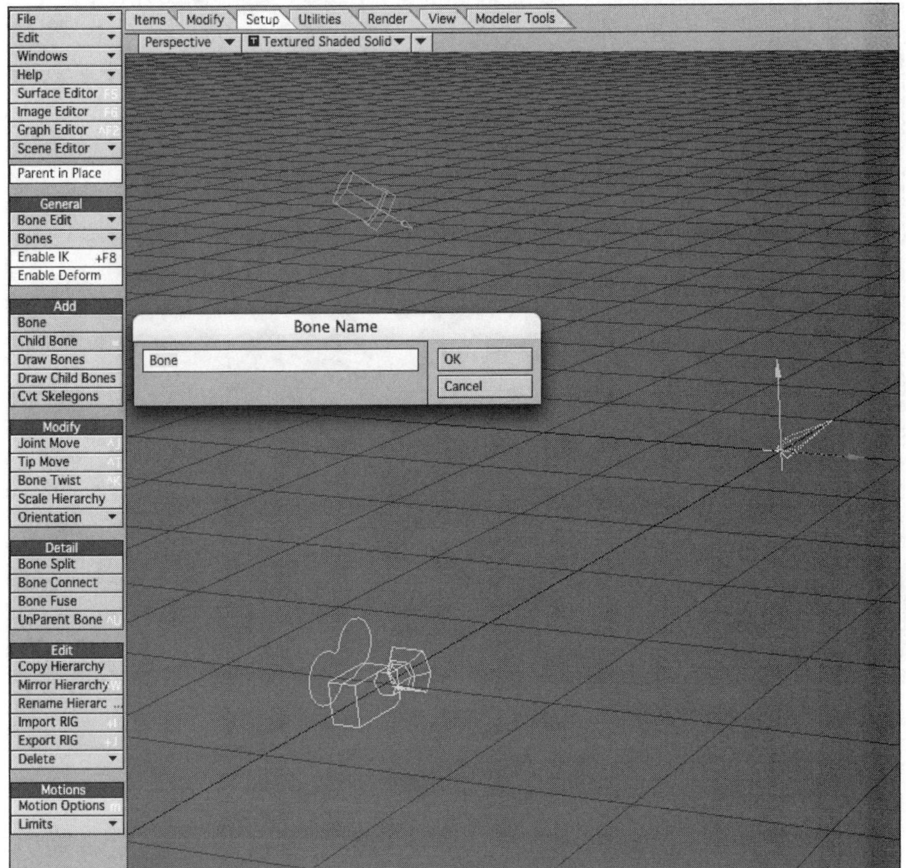

Figure 12.2 Adding a bone to a Null object creates a 1m bone extended along the Z-axis.

Next, you'll set up a chain of bones by adding "child" bones to the one you just made. Just as child objects depend on and move with their parent objects, "child" bones are controlled by parents and can be used to set up subtle or complex object deformations.

3. With the first bone selected, click the Child Bone button. Click OK because you don't need to set a name when the requester asks you to.

   You'll see a bone attached to the end of the previous bone (**Figure 12.3**).

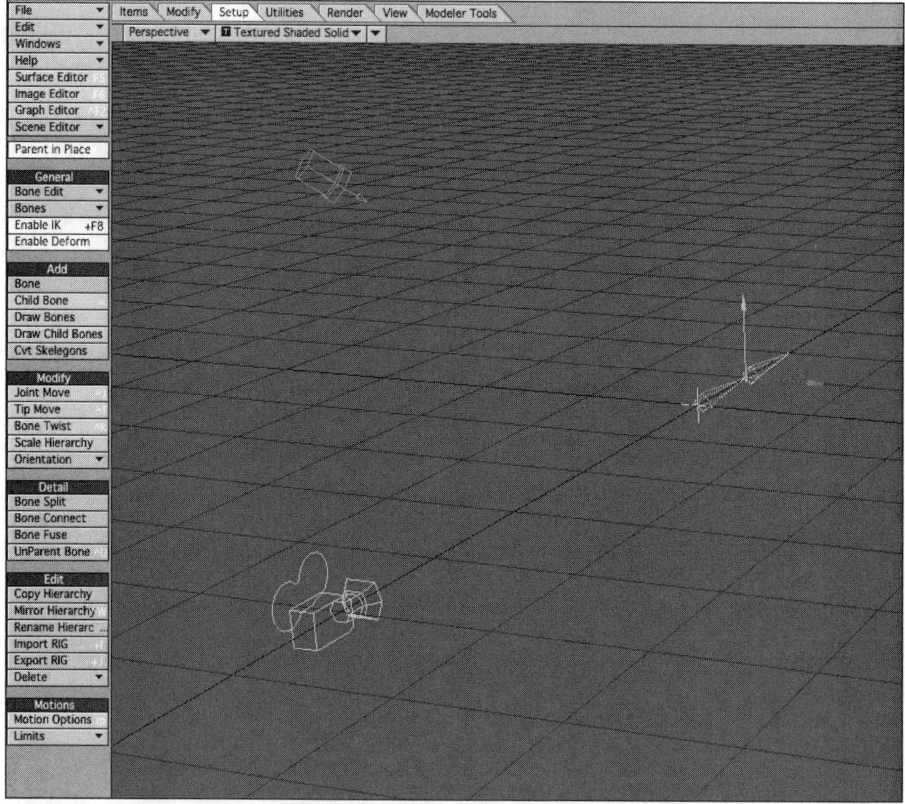

Figure 12.3 You can add child bones to create a hierarchical structure.

4. Add one more child bone as you did in Step 3. A quick way to add child bones is to press = (the equal-sign key). After it is added, select the first bone and rotate it. Press the up-arrow key twice to change the selected bone.

   When the parent bone rotates, you'll see the child bone rotate as well. If you select and rotate the second bone, its child bone rotates, too.

   This hierarchical structure is explained in detail later in the section "Creating Hierarchies." For now, you can think of this structure as similar to your own arm. The shoulder is connected to the upper arm, which is connected to the forearm, which is connected to the hand, and so on. If you move the shoulder, the other parts of your arm move as well.

Tip

Using the LightWave v9 Scene Editor, you can recolor the bones for easier visibility and better organization in Layout. The color change does not affect the bone's function, only its visibility.

This quick-and-dirty example showed you how to create bones in Layout. The base object that you assigned bones to does not have to be null—it can be anything you want, from a character to a snake to a piece of paper. Anything you want to deform can have bones added to it. Granted, this wasn't very exciting, was it? Read on, and we'll see bones in action.

Note

Bones deform objects and their surfaces by repositioning the points that make up their surface polygons. In order for an object to be deformed correctly using bones, therefore, its surfaces must be consist of multiple polygons. A cube with just eight vertices, or points, will not deform well with bones, but if its faces are subpatched or subdivided into multiple squares, the same cube becomes more malleable and can be deformed by bones.

Exercise 12.2 Adding Bones to Objects

This exercise takes you a step further than the previous tutorial by showing how to put bones into an object. From there, you'll see how bones can be used to manipulate the shape of an inanimate object.

1. First, check the bottom of the Layout interface to make sure that Auto Key is enabled. When working with bones, it's good to use this feature because you can concentrate on motions, and LightWave will record the changes. Select Clear Scene from the File drop-down list in Layout. Load the Penguin object from the Projects\Objects\CH12\Penguin.lwo directory this book's DVD. We'll add bones to the character to control its movement. **Figure 12.4** shows the penguin model, as seen in Layout's Perspective view.

Figure 12.4 The Penguin object is loaded into an empty layout, ready for some bones!

2. Press **3** on your keyboard or numeric keypad to switch to the side view (Right).

3. Change the render style to Front Face Wireframe from the top of the viewport interface. This will help you see the placement of bones (**Figure 12.5**).

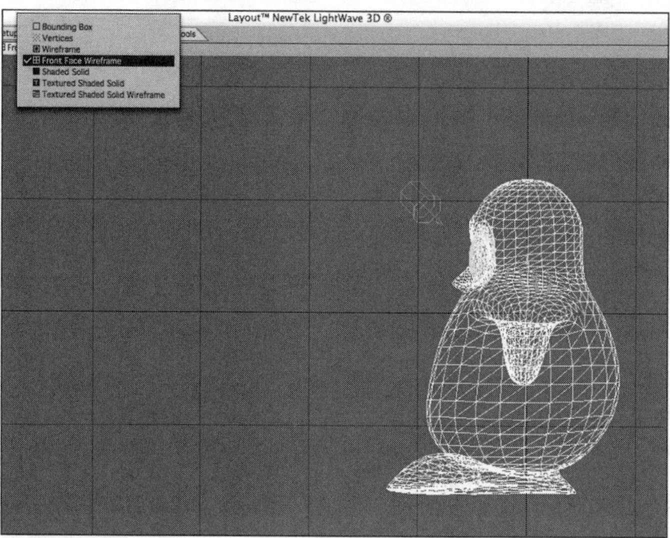

Figure 12.5 Change your view to look at the Right side and switch to a Front Face Wireframe style.

Note

Front Face Wireframe is a good viewing option for bones because LightWave only shows the wireframes visible to your view. This simplifies what you see, making placement of bones much easier. A normal wireframe view will show not only what's in view of the camera, but the other side of the object as well, sometimes making it a bit confusing to determine the shape, size, angle, or position of the object.

4. With the penguin model selected, click the Setup tab and then click Bone in the Add category. Enter the name **Body** for this bone in the panel that appears and click OK. You'll see a bone added to the object at the base of the foot (**Figure 12.6**).

   The bone might be a bit hard to see because its outline is dotted to indicate the bone is not yet active. Also, despite appearances, the bone is not actually added to the bottom of the foot; it's associated with the entire penguin model, aligned along the Z-axis.

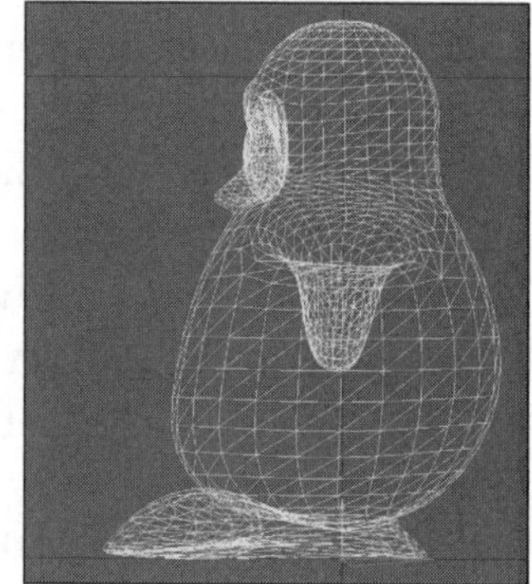

Figure 12.6 After a bone is added, it needs to be put into place.

5. The bone position now needs to be set so that it can properly control the object. Select Move from the Modify tab (or press **t**) and move the bone up to the middle of the body.
6. Click the Rotate tool on the Modify tab (or press **y**) and rotate the bone so that the pointy edge is facing up, with a -90 degree Pitch value, as displayed in the info window at the lower-left corner of the Layout interface (**Figure 12.7**).

Note

When adjusting subpatched objects such as the penguin model, it's sometimes easier to hide surface subdivisions. To do so, set the Display SubPatch Level to 0 in the Object Properties panel: Select the object and press **p**.

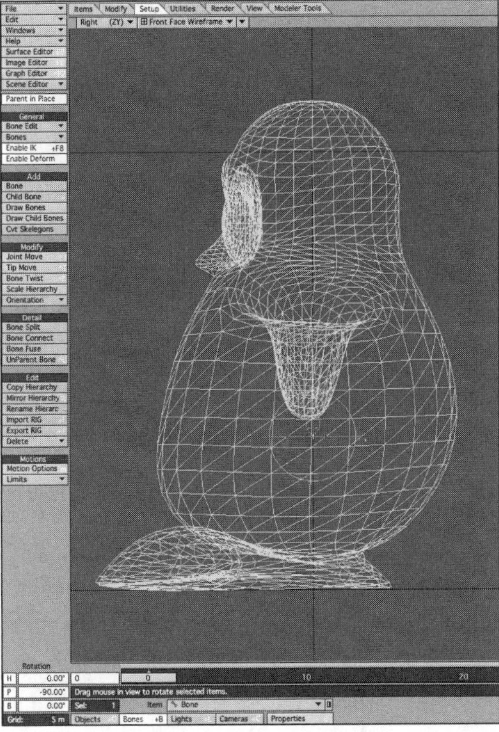

Figure 12.7 Move and rotate the bone so that it rests in position pointing up and in the middle of the penguin.

Note

The object's Render SubPatch Level does not affect way you see in Layout. It can be set higher than the Display SubPatch level, perhaps to 6. When the object is rendered, it will be smooth and subdivided.

7. With the single bone selected, press **p** on your keyboard to open the bone's Properties panel. In the middle of the panel, change the Rest Length to about 1.5m, as shown in **Figure 12.8**. This measurement is representational of your Layout Grid Square Size. Changing the Rest Length tells LightWave to give this bone a larger range of influence—that is, the area or range that the bone is affecting.

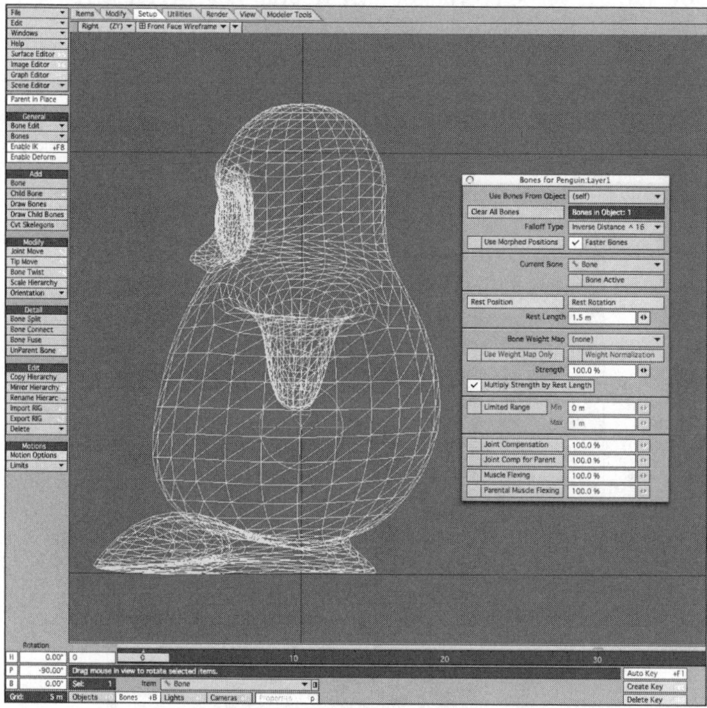

Figure 12.8 Change the rest length of the bone so that it will deform a larger area. Do this from the bone's Properties panel.

When scaling a bone to match the length of a model's limb, spine, or what have you, you must adjust its rest length, not its size. This can't be stressed enough. The Rest Length setting is the final length of the bone before it is made active—in other words, its resting position. The number-one mistake LightWave animators make with bones is to use the Size tool and change the actual size of the bone instead of its rest length.

Once a bone's rest length is set and the bone is activated, resizing the bone will cause a comparable size change in the portion(s) of the model influenced by the bone. A simple application of this would enable an object to "breathe" by expanding and contracting slightly; more advanced applications could allow objects to inflate, characters to shrink, and so on.

What you've done here is create a spine for the Penguin object. These bone techniques can be used for any type of character or object to build arms and legs, tentacles, wings, and so on.

8. Save your scene by selecting File, Save, then Save Scene. You can also just press **s**.

Creating Hierarchies

What exactly is a *hierarchy*? Your fingers are attached to your hand, your hand is attached to your wrist, your wrist is attached to your forearm, and so on. Move the shoulder, and the attached bones move with it. That's a hierarchy! You can create hierarchies of bones and objects in LightWave that work the same way.

Hierarchies of bones and objects in LightWave work according to two distinct but related sets of rules, known as *forward kinematics* and *inverse kinematics*, both of which are essential to realistic movement. Forward kinematics is the process we've just described, whereby moving an object also causes movement of objects below it in a hierarchy: Move a thigh bone, and you also move the shin, ankle, and toes. Inverse kinematics is the reverse effect, in which an object moves those above it in a hierarchy: If something (a bicycle pedal, for example) lifts a model's toes, the attached ankle and knee should rise and bend accordingly. This section demonstrates how to build bones into hierarchical structures that enable both forms of kinematics.

Setting Child Bones

Adding a child bone to an existing bone starts out much like duplicating the parent bone: The new child bone inherits its parent's size, position, and rest length. Setting up that first bone is the hardest part. Once it is in place, you can set child bones. And because they will be "children" of the base bone, their scale will match the penguin better when added, unlike the first bone.

Exercise 12.3 Creating Child Bones

1. This first bone you've created in the previous exercise will begin the hierarchy of the penguin body, meaning that it is the parent bone. Each bone that extends from this one is a child bone. If the parent bone moves, the children move with it. Make sure the Body bone is selected, and on the Setup menu tab in Layout, click Child Bone in the Add category. Note that you can also use the = key. Name this new bone **Neck**.

Note

If you forget to name a bone when you create it, don't worry. Just select the bone, and on the Items tab, select Rename from the Replace category.

2. You can see that an exact duplicate of the Body bone is attached right above it. Change this new bone's Rest Length setting to about 600mm so that its tip meets the base of the head area, as in **Figure 12.9**. Now, if you rotate the Body bone, the new child bone moves with it.

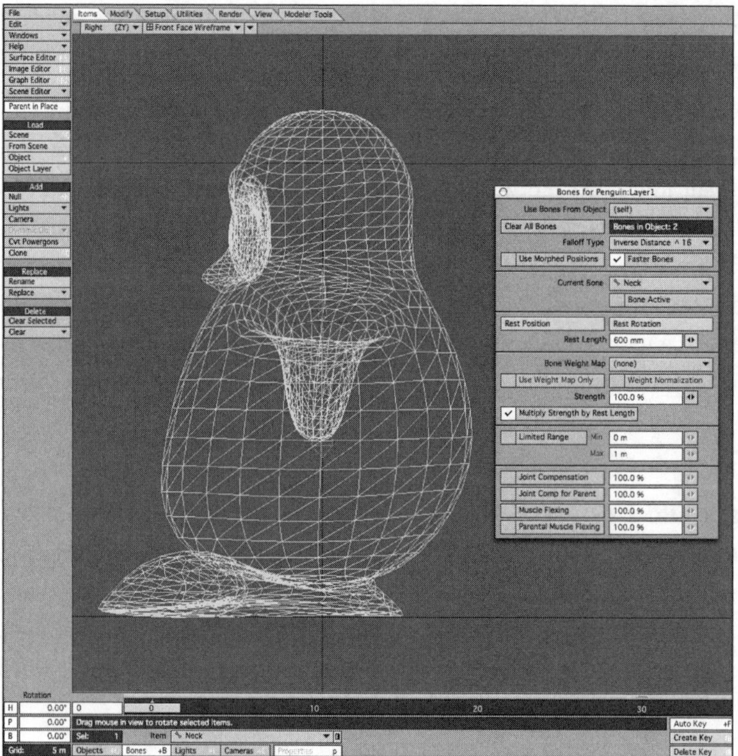

Figure 12.9 A child bone is added to the Body bone, creating a hierarchical duplicate.

3. Now add another child bone, naming it **Head**. Change the Rest Length setting to about 1.6m.

4. Add another child bone, but can also be named **Head**. In Layout, you'll now have Head (1) and Head (2) bones. For this new bone, rotate it on its pitch to point down to the nose, about -148m. You can do this by first pressing **y** on the keyboard and then grabbing the green handle and dragging. Or you can click in the

Numeric panel at the bottom left of the Layout interface and directly enter the value. Change this bone's Rest Length setting to 1.85m so that it encompasses the face. **Figure 12.10** shows the setup.

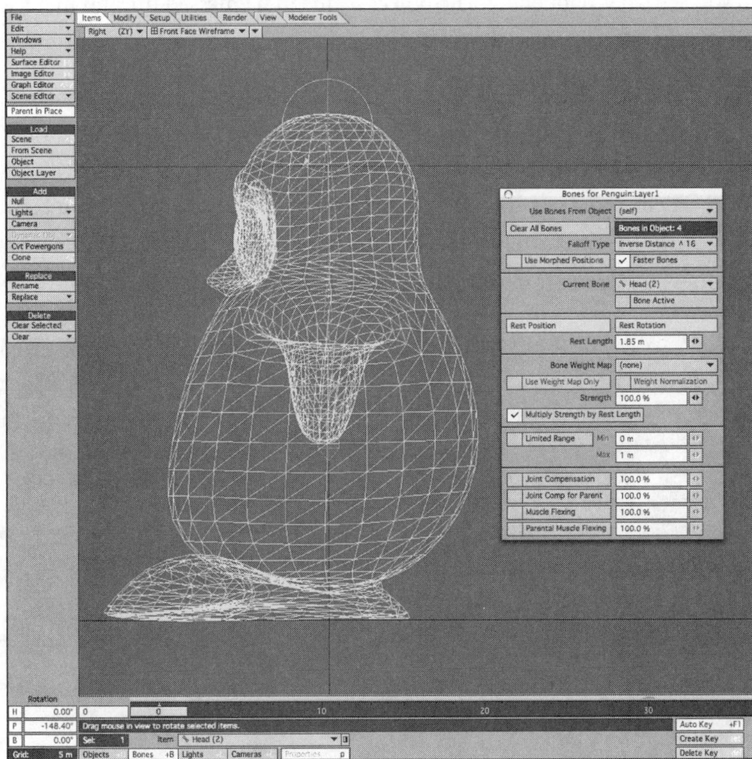

Figure 12.10 A second head bone is added and rotated to fit the face of the penguin.

The reason you created this "face" bone—that is, a second head bone—was to help keep the structure intact as it's deformed. Because the character's head is large, the single head bone deforming it might distort the face. But the added head bone helps hold the face as the Neck bone moves it. You'll see how this works shortly.

The bones are now in place, but they are not yet influencing the model. This is because they are not active. If you rotate say, the Neck bone, the two head bones should follow, but the head of the character won't move. Now you need to activate the bones. Activating tells LightWave where you want the bones to rest and begin working. But here's the thing—people often set their bones to rest, and suddenly, their object disappears or becomes grossly deformed. Try it out and see.

5. First, make sure all of the bones are in their original positions if you've moved them. Select the second head bone and press **r**, the shortcut for Activate Bone. Your object changes positions, essentially falling over, as in **Figure 12.11**.

   Do you see what happened? The object seems to be messed up, and many animators stop here and freak out, usually e-mailing the author of this book! But wait! Read on. You did nothing wrong.

   What's happening at this point is that the bone you've set into position is now active and influencing the model. However, it is the only bone influencing it, so the model is deforming based on the position of *only* this bone. When you activate the other bones, the model returns to its proper shape and position. Start activating the bones, beginning from the base bone, and your object will not distort this way.

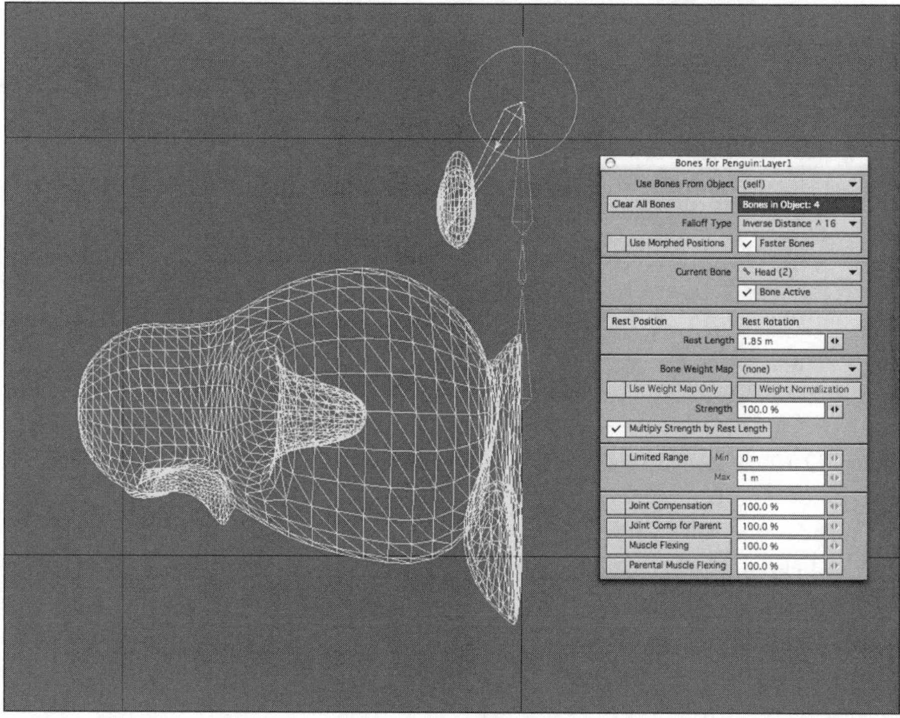

Figure 12.11 Activating a bone by selecting it and pressing **r** key tells the bone to influence the model. When only one bone is influencing the model, the model responds accordingly.

Note

Pressing Ctrl+r deactivates a bone. Press **r** to activate it again.

6. Use the up arrow to select the next bone, press **r**, and repeat the bone activation by pressing **r** for each bone.

   When you activate all the bones, the model returns to its original shape. This is because all bones are now active and properly influencing the deformation of the model. When only one bone was active, such as the last bone for the object, the entire penguin was being influenced by only one bone.

Note

LightWave provides visual cues for differentiating between active and inactive bones. Active bones have solid outlines and inactive bones have dashed outlines. And remember, you can change the color of these lines to make bones easier to see by using the Scene Editor's Visibility commands.

7. Go back to the Perspective view and change the Maximum Render Level setting in the scene to Shaded Solid. Select the Body bone and press the **y** key to rotate the bone. You'll see the object deform, as in **Figure 12.12**.

Figure 12.12 When the bones are in place and active, rotating deforms the object.

8. Make your bones completely visible in your solid shaded object by choosing the Bone X-Ray mode from the top of Layout, as in **Figure 12.13**.

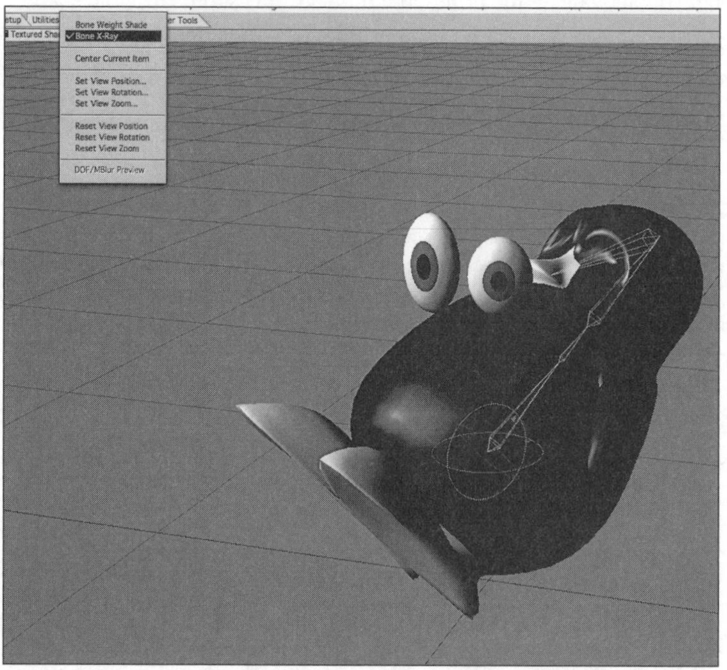

Figure 12.13 Turn on Bone X-Ray mode from the top of Layout to see all the bones in your object.

9. Press Ctrl+z to undo the Body bone rotation so the character is in its original position. Select the Neck bone and rotate it. You'll see the head bend along with the neck. But it's not quite right because the body deforms along with the motion, as in **Figure 12.14**.

Figure 12.14 Rotating the Neck bone deforms the entire object.

When the Body bone rotates, the entire penguin body rotates, but you'll notice that the penguin's eyes don't deform along with it. That's because they are separate objects. As you'll recall from Chapter 10, Character Modeling, you created the penguin eyes in separate layers. The bones that influence the body object do not affect other objects, even those within the same model.

In the next exercise, you'll learn how adding hierarchies to the model will let you deform the eyes and ensure that they move along with the penguin's head. You'll also use additional hierarchies to make the motion of the penguin's lower body independent from that of its upper body and to control the movement of its feet.

Creating Multiple Hierarchies

The body and head bones you've added work very nicely to bend and animate the upper part of this object, but you're not quite seeing the results you want just yet. You might think that because you've already created a hierarchy of bones, you don't need to build onto this existing chain. However, you can create an entirely different hierarchy elsewhere within the object. You created the first hierarchy starting with the Body bone. You rotated it upward so that the rotational pivot point of the bone was at the middle of the body, similar to a hip. Now you'll create a similar hierarchy pointing downward into the base and feet of the penguin.

Exercise 12.4 Setting Up Multiple Hierarchies

1. Select the Penguin object. Then, on the Setup tab, click Bone in the Add category. Name it **Base**. Note that this does not create a child to the Body bone but rather a new individual bone. Move and rotate the Base bone so it rests just below the Body bone, essentially mirroring it, as in **Figure 12.15**.

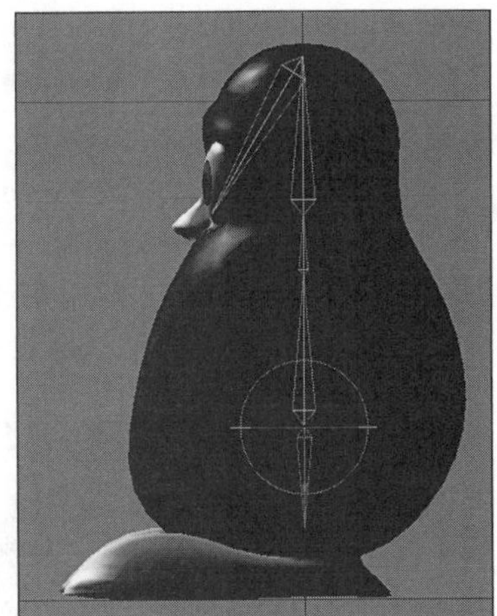

Figure 12.15 Add a bone to the Penguin object, move it up, and rotate it so that it points down into the character.

2. With your new Base bone still selected, choose Child Bone from the Setup tab's Add tool category and enter **RightFoot** as the name for the child bone.
3. Press **1** to switch to a front view. Press **y** to activate the Rotate tool and rotate the child bone (the RightFoot bone) until its heading is -90 degrees. You can do so by dragging the red rotation handle, or by pressing **n** to enter the value numerically at the bottom-left corner of the interface.
4. With the RightFoot bone selected, press **p** to open the Bone Properties panel and set the Rest Length value to about 655mm, so that the tip of the bone is at the center of the right foot (**Figure 12.16** on the next page).

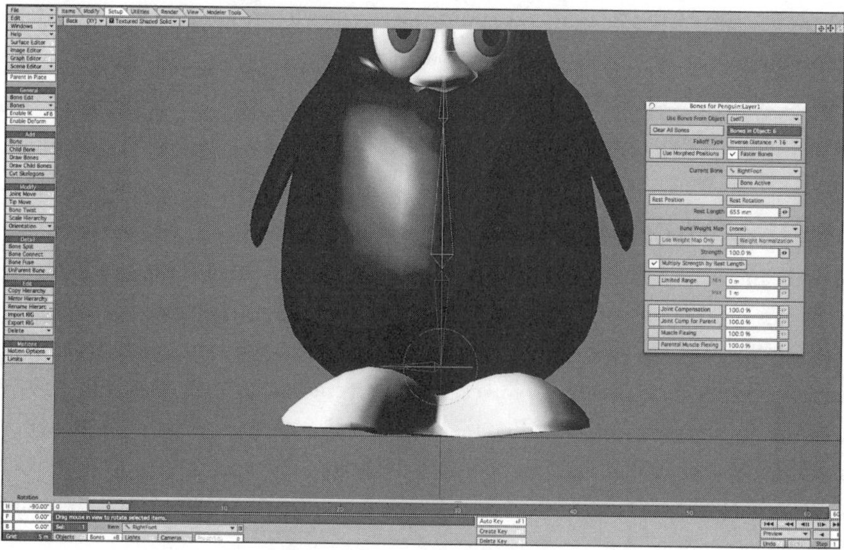

Figure 12.16 Rotate the RightFoot bone 90 degrees and set the Rest Length value so that its tip ends at the center of the right foot.

5. With the RightFoot bone selected, add another child bone (or press **=**, the shortcut for Add Child Bone). Leave the default name, RightFoot (2), unchanged.
6. Rotate this bone, which is the anklebone. Set the bone's Heading value to 90 degrees, so that it's pointed down into the foot. Then, change its Rest Length setting to about 485mm so that the tip of the bone ends in the middle of the foot (**Figure 12.17**). You can check the bone's position by pressing **3** for a side view and then **1** to go back to a front view.

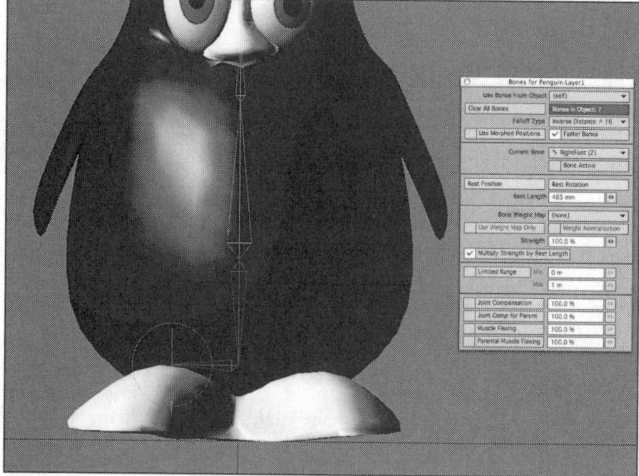

Figure 12.17 Begin creating the bones that will control the foot by adding a bone that acts as an ankle.

The reason you're creating a child bone from the RightFoot bone in this hierarchy is to create a human-like structure. The RightFoot (2) bone will serve as the penguin's anklebone.

7. With RightBone (2) still selected, add another child bone by pressing **=**. Leave the default name, RightBone (3).
8. Set this bone's Pitch value to 90 degrees, so it points down into the foot. Then, set Rest Length to 1m, as in **Figure 12.18**.

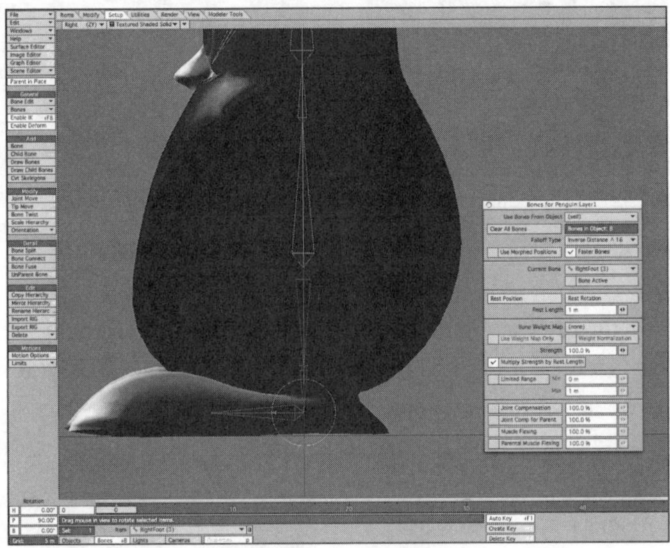

Figure 12.18 Another child bone is added and positioned for the right foot.

9. Add one more child bone and set the Rest Length to about 1.3m, slightly larger than the previous bone, so that it extends to the front of the foot, as in **Figure 12.19**.

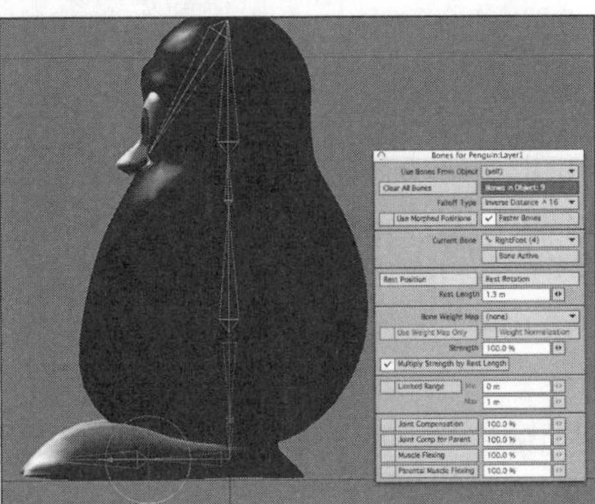

Figure 12.19 One more child bone is added for the front of the foot.

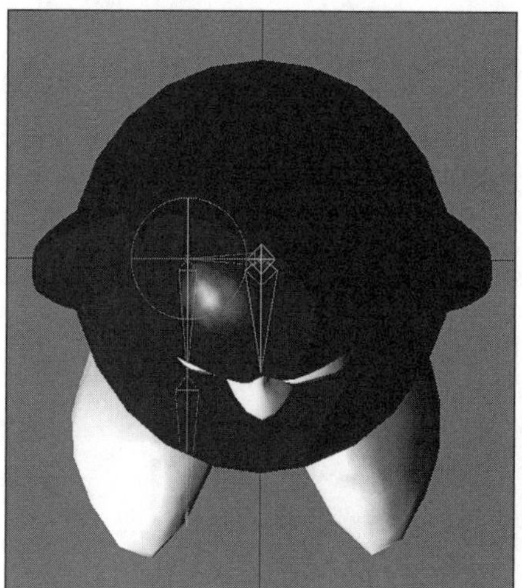

Figure 12.20 While the bones seem to fit the foot in the side view, the Top view shows that their heading is off.

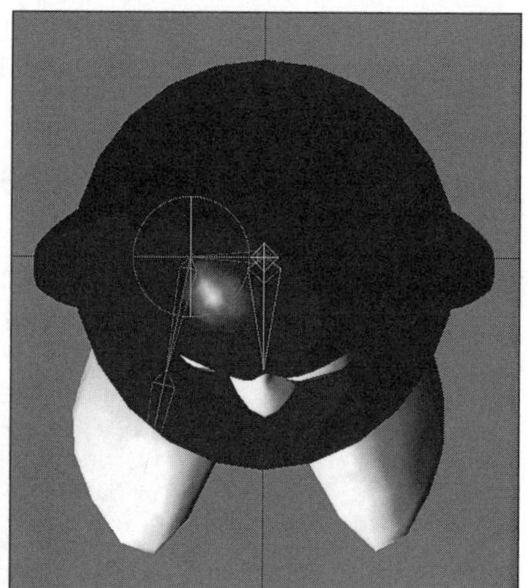

Figure 12.21 By rotating the first bone in the base of the foot, you also rotate its child, easily aligning the foot bones.

10. Press **2** on the keyboard to move to a Top view. Taking a look at **Figure 12.20**, you'll see that the bones in the feet don't quite fit—but they did in the side view. What gives? Just as with anything else you create in 3D, you need to be aware of all axes. So, click RightFoot (3) to select it, and then press **y** to activate the Rotate tool. Rotate the bone until its Heading value is about 76 degrees. **Figure 12.21** shows the change.
11. Save your scene.
12. Now, activate all the bones by selecting each bone and then pressing **r**.
13. After the bones have been activated, select the Neck bone. Press **y** to turn on the Rotate tool, and then use it to rotate the neck. You'll see the head move around, and the body stays in place. Also, there's a nice, smooth flow between the head and the body (**Figure 12.22**).
14. You still need to fix those floating eyes! Select the first eye in Layer 2. Do this by first choosing the Objects

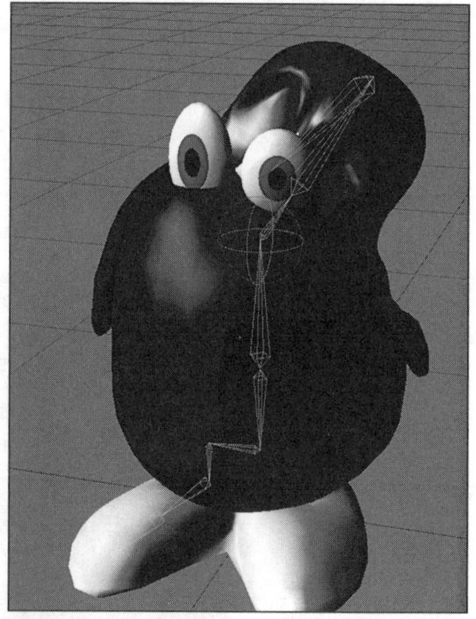

Figure 12.22 Once bones are added to the base of the model, the head can be moved and the body stays put.

button at the bottom of the LightWave interface, telling LightWave that you want to work with Objects. Then, select Layer 2 from the Item drop-down list, also at the bottom of the interface.

15. Click the Bones button at the bottom of the interface. Then, press **p** to open the Bone Properties panel. Since no bones are associated with the selected object (the eye), the panel will show that there are no bones. Click the Use Bones From Object drop-down list at the top of the Properties panel (it says "self" by default) and choose Layer 1, which contains the Penguin-body object (**Figure 12.23**). This tells the eye object to use the bones from the body object.

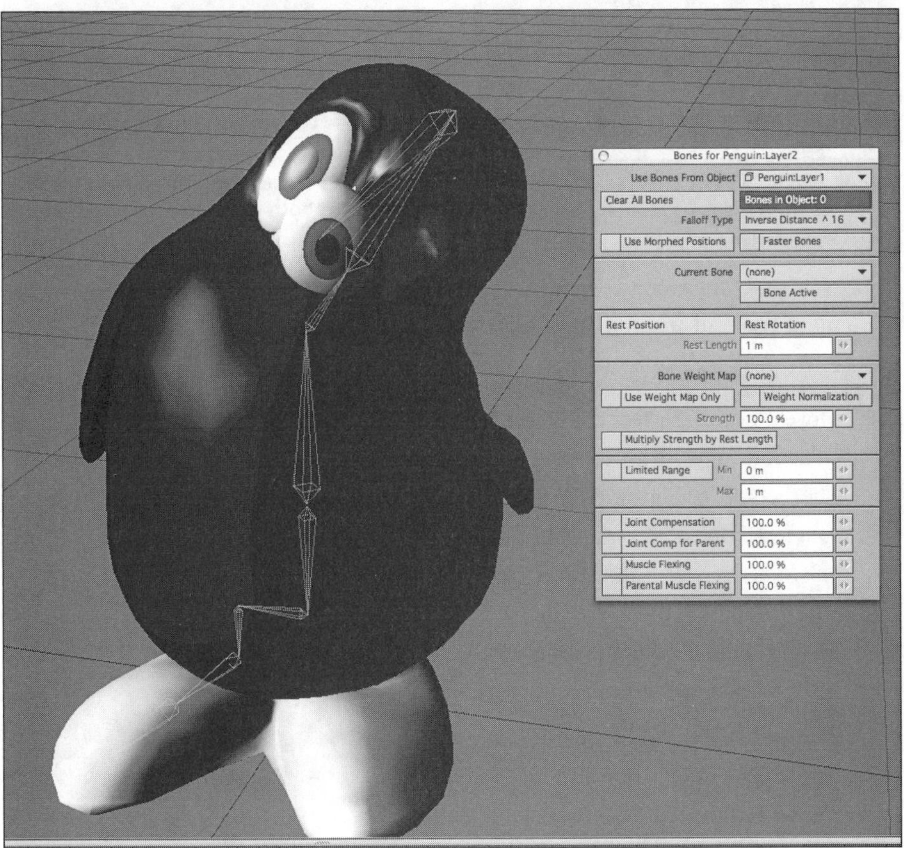

Figure 12.23 Tell the eye object layer to use the bones from the body of the penguin, Layer 1.

Figure 12.24 When the eye objects use the bones from the penguin-body layer, they follow when the penguin body is deformed.

Figure 12.25 Rotating just the right anklebone deforms both feet.

16. Now select the second eye, and repeat the previous step. Select the Neck bone and move the head around. The eyes now follow along (**Figure 12.24**).
17. Save your scene.
18. Move down to the feet and select RightFoot (2), the small bone that serves as an anklebone. Press **y** to activate the Rotate tool and twist the bone. What happens? The feet move (**Figure 12.25**). Yes, *both* feet. You want to move just the one foot. Even though the feet are attached to each other, you should still be able to move each one independently. So, you need to create another hierarchy for the left foot.
19. Before you edit any bones, it's a good idea to deactivate them. You can do this quickly by going to the Setup tab and selecting Bones Off from the Bones menu, under the General category, as shown in **Figure 12.26**. You can also press Ctrl+r to deactivate a selected bone.

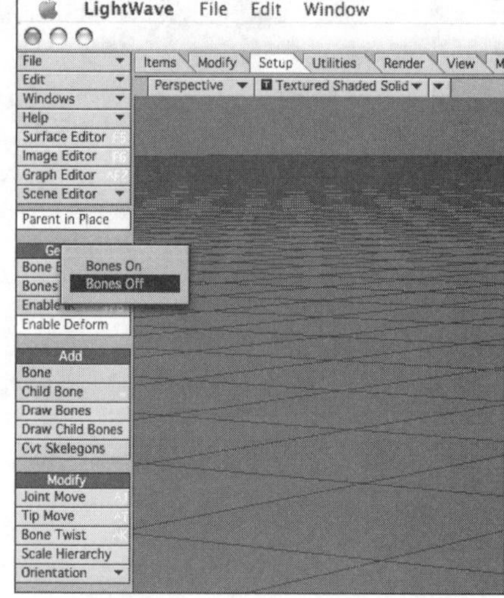

Figure 12.26 Turn the bones off before you edit them.

20. With the bones turned off, click RightFoot (1) to select it (**Figure 12.27**).

Figure 12.27 Select the first RightFoot bone, which is the second bone in the bottom hierarchy.

21. In the Setup tab's Edit tool category, click Mirror Hierarchy. This opens the Bone Setup: MirrorHierarchy panel. You'll see that the selected bone, RightFoot (1), is chosen in the Root of Hierarchy drop-down at the top of the panel.

22. Most of the Bone Setup: MirrorHierarchy panel settings can be left at their default values. In the Axis drop-down list, choose X. You want to mirror this hierarchy of bones across the X-axis.

23. For the Name Edit Method option, choose Replace String. For the Replace This String setting, enter **Right**. For the With This String setting, enter the word **Left**. **Figure 12.28** shows

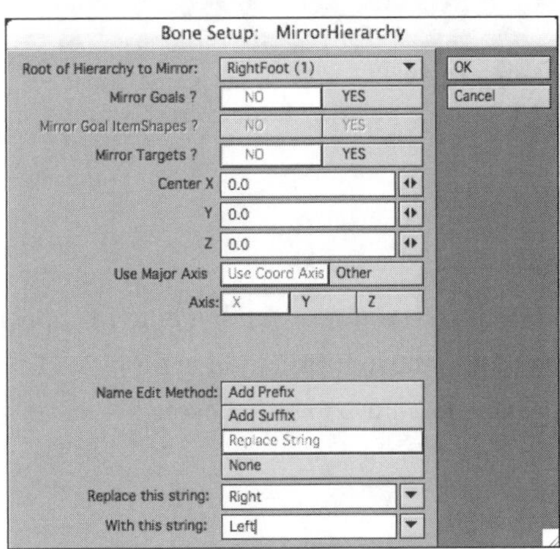

Figure 12.28 The Bone Setup: MirrorHierarchy panel is simple and powerful.

the panel. This tells the Mirror Hierarchy tool to give the new mirrored bones the same names as those in the selected hierarchy, but with "Left" substituted for "Right" in their names.

24. Click OK and the entire bone hierarchy will be mirrored. **Figure 12.29** shows the result.

25. On Layout's Setup tab, click Bones and then click Bones On to reactivate the bones in the model. Select the base bone, which is the parent bone to both sets of legs. Press **y** and rotate this bone. You'll see both sets of legs deform (**Figure 12.30**). OK, they're really just feet—but you get the idea!

Figure 12.29 It's easy to set up the bones for the left leg with the Mirror Hierarchy tool.

Figure 12.30 Rotating the base bone, which is the parent to the bone hierarchies for both legs, causes realistic deformation of the penguin feet.

26. Save your work!

Even though you've added bones to the upper and lower body, moving the feet causes a bit of unwanted deformation in the body. The foot bones aren't deforming the rest of the penguin too much to be annoying to look at, but you can add even more control by using the Bone Weight tool.

Bone Weights

In LightWave, the relative "heft," or resistance to motion, of objects (or portions of objects), is controlled by a special type of UV surface map called a *weight map*, which assigns weight values to points on a model's surface. LightWave provides several methods of generating weight maps, but one of the quickest is Modeler's Bone Weights tool.

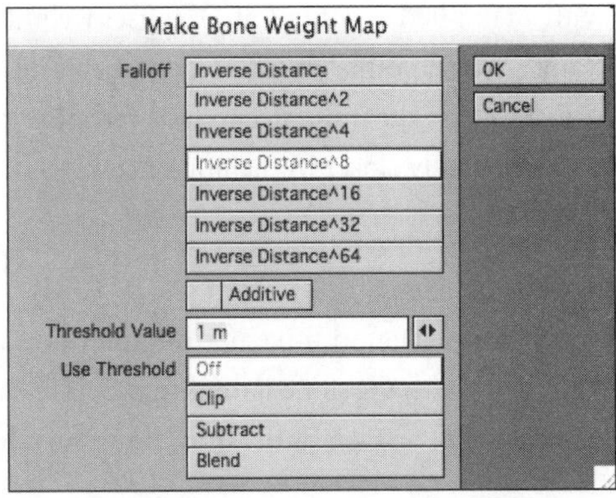

Figure 12.31 The Make Bone Weight Map panel in Modeler.

You activate the Make Bone Weight Map panel (**Figure 12.31**) by selecting a bone or an object associated with a bone and clicking Bone Weight on Modeler's Map tab. The panel lets you use the selected bones to generate weight-map settings for the associated objects, without having to select individual points or polygons on those objects. This tool can be a real time-saver, and often provides a great first step for creating maps that you can fine-tune later by tweaking the settings for individual points. The Bone Weights tool can also be used to make global changes to weight maps you've built the "old-fashioned" way—by specifying weight values for individual points and polygons.

To use the Bone Weights tool, you must first set up Skelegons, which we'll be discussing shortly.

The Make Bone Weight Map Panel

The first step in understanding the use of bone weights is to explore LightWave's weighting features in Modeler. Weight maps enable you to scale the falloff of various tools in LightWave. With a weight map, a bone affects points according to the weight you set. The result is a controlled influence that eliminates the problem you saw in the previous exercise, when the base bone movement deformed some of the body of the Penguin object. The next few sections will help explain some base bone weighting functions so that you better understand how to use them.

Falloff

The Falloff setting in the Bone Weights panel determines the degree to which an applied weight setting is "concentrated" within a bone and how evenly it is distributed over the surface of the associated object. The setting works mathematically and is expressed as one of several preset exponential Inverse Distance values. The default value, Inverse Distance (with an implied exponent of 1), causes weight concentration to fade in direct proportion to any affected points' distance from the bone. Higher exponential settings, ranging from 2 to 128, cause the influence to fade far more rapidly and concentrate the applied weight proportionately closer to the bone itself.

Additive

If you turn on the Additive option, the Bone Weights settings are automatically applied to all bones with the same name—a big time-saver for every bone named "spine" in a sea-urchin model, or even both "shin" bones in a human figure.

Threshold Value

The Threshold Value setting defines a capsule-shaped "border," a fixed distance from a bone, at which the bone's weight settings cease or change. Its setting value is a distance, the radius of influence, expressed in meters (or millimeters).

Use Threshold

The four options for this setting determine how a bone's influence on an object's weight map changes at the edge of the "capsule" defined by its Threshold Value setting. The Off setting means the Threshold Value setting is ignored. The Clip setting sets weight values for all points outside the threshold to 0. The Subtract option causes weight values to fade to 0 at the threshold distance, then continues decreasing weight values (by assigning them negative values) at distances greater than the Threshold Value setting. The Blend option, which is often the most useful, causes weight values to fade steadily to 0 within the "capsule" (like the Subtract setting), but sets all values beyond the threshold distance to 0 (like the Clip setting).

Apply Weight Maps

Exercise 12.5 instructs you on the method of weighting. This process is done in Modeler and enables you to tell a bone to control a specific area rather than the entire object. For example, with weighting, moving the lower leg would not affect the upper area of the penguin, as it did earlier in Figure 12.25.

Bone weights enable you to specify regions of influence. Much of the time when creating character animation you'll be building your model from the ground up, and you can assign weight maps as you go. However, you can also use existing models from a previous project, from another artist, or perhaps from this book's DVD.

Exercise 12.5 Creating Weights

1. Open Modeler and load the Penguin_toWeight object from this book's DVD (Projects\Objects\CH12\Penguin_toWeight.lwo). **Figure 12.32** shows the model loaded. Press **a** to fit the model to the view to match the figure.

Figure 12.32 An existing model is loaded into Modeler and ready to have weights assigned to it.

In Exercise 12.4, you created two four-bone hierarchies, each consisting of a top legbone, an anklebone, and two foot bones. Now you only need to set up some weight maps for these hierarchies, and your model will deform properly in Layout.

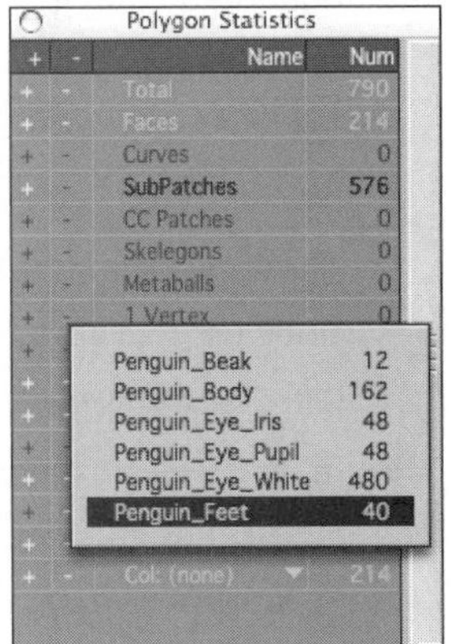

Figure 12.33 Use the Statistics panel to select just the Feet surface of the penguin.

2. Choose Polygons Selection mode by clicking the Polygons button at the bottom of the Modeler interface. Next, press the Tab key to turn off SubPatch mode to make the model easier to work with. You'll turn it back on again when you've finished.
3. Press **w** to open the Statistics panel. Toward the bottom of the panel, click the Surface listing. This will show you all of the penguin's surfaces you created when you built the character in Modeler. Select the Feet surface, as shown in **Figure 12.33**.

4. You want to weight each foot separately, so right-click (Cmd-click on the Mac) and drag to lasso the polygons in the character's left foot and deselect them. **Figure 12.34** shows the selection performed in the Top view.

Figure 12.34 Lasso one of the penguin's feet to deselect its polygons.

5. With the polygons of the right foot selected, click the W button at the bottom of the Modeler interface (next to the T, M, C, and S buttons) to choose Weight mode. In the drop-down list next to these buttons (which reads *(none)*), select [new], as in **Figure 12.35**.

   The Create Weight Map panel appears. You'll use it to assign a weight map to the selected polygons.

6. In the Name box, type **Penguin_RightFoot**. Keep the Initial Value option checked and leave its value at 100%, as shown in **Figure 12.36**.

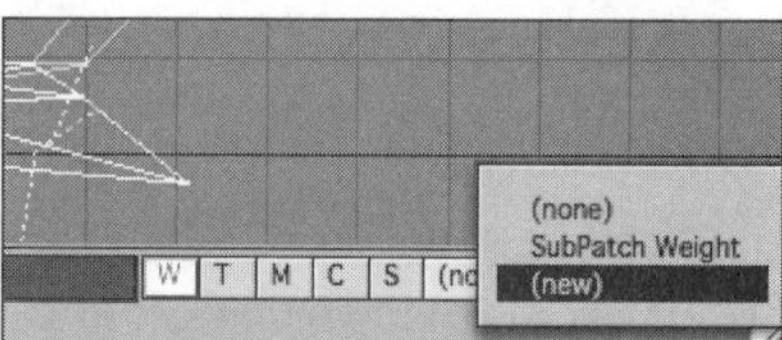

Figure 12.35 Choose Weight mode from the bottom of the Modeler screen, then choose [new] to create a new weight map.

Figure 12.36 Type the name of the new weight map.

You've now created a weight map for the right foot of the Penguin object, but if you remember, there are four bones in the entire leg—well, at least if you can call it a leg... Are you wondering why bones are mentioned here? Good question! While weight maps can be used for many things in LightWave, such as controlling textures, you can also use them to control bone influences. By setting up a weight map in Modeler and giving it the same name as a bone, you tell Layout that the specified bone should only deform the portion of the model defined by that weighted map. For example, a weight map named RightFoot will automatically be associated with the bone named RightFoot. LightWave will automatically apply the weight map in Layout.

This is a good time to change your Perspective view (or any view) to Weight Shade render view mode. When you view your model in Weight Shade mode (selected from the top of each viewport), you can see the weight applied as bright red.

7. Deselect the right foot polygons, and select the left foot polygons. Select [new] again from the drop-down next to the S button to create a weight map for this selection. Enter the name **Penguin_LeftFoot**, as shown in **Figure 12.37**.

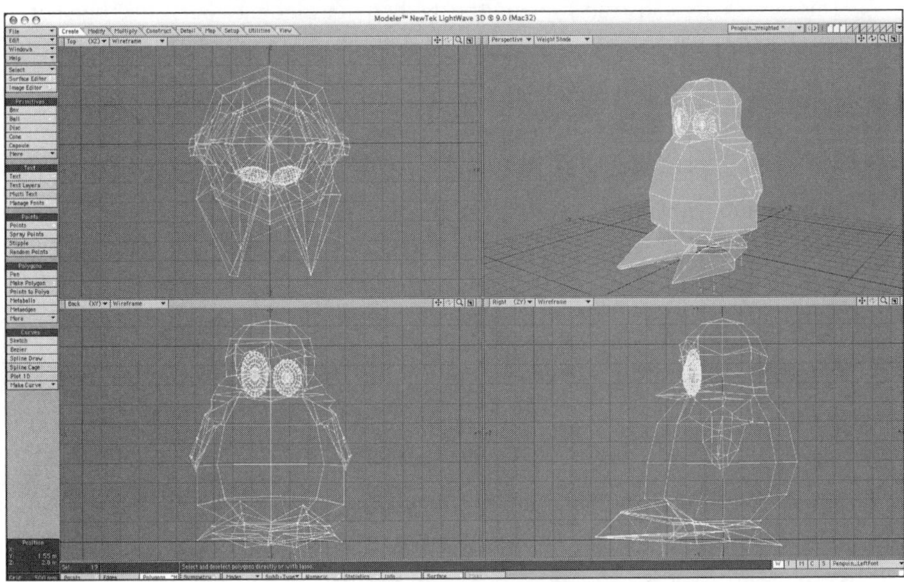

Figure 12.37 Another weight map is added to the left foot of the Penguin object.

You can assign weight maps to selected polygons or points, but if you apply a weight map to selected polygons, you are really applying the weight to the points of the selected polygons. Selecting polygons over points (or vice versa) for setting weight maps is your choice. However, polygons are sometimes a better choice for weight map selection because it is much easier to see what is and (more importantly) what is not selected.

8. Save your model by pressing Ctrl+s (PC) or Cmd+s (Mac). Saving the object saves the weights you've applied.

That's all there is to it! You've identified a range of polygons that is controlled by a bone in Layout. Remember, you use LightWave Modeler to create weight maps. You can adjust them in both Modeler and Layout, but creation is always done in Modeler.

As your models become more complex, you can select points or polygons and weight them as you like. Now, weights are not always needed, but it's important to understand how they work. Often, you don't even need weight maps, and proper bone placement will be more than enough to animate your character.

This next exercise instructs you on the method of assigning a particular bone of your model to the weights you've just created in Layout. As a result, the bone will only influence the weighted area.

Exercise 12.6 Assigning Weights

1. Hop on into LightWave Layout. From this book's DVD, load the Penguin_Bone_Weight scene. You'll find it in the Projects\Scenes\CH12 folder of the Projects directory.
2. Make sure Bone X-Ray mode is on from the top left of Layout to see the bones in the object. This feature is often hard to find, but you access it by clicking the tiny drop-down arrow to the right of the viewport render style button. Then select the RightFoot (3) bone of the Penguin object and press **p**.
3. In the Bone Properties panel, select Penguin_RightFoot as the weight map for the Bone Weight Map option, as shown in **Figure 12.38**.

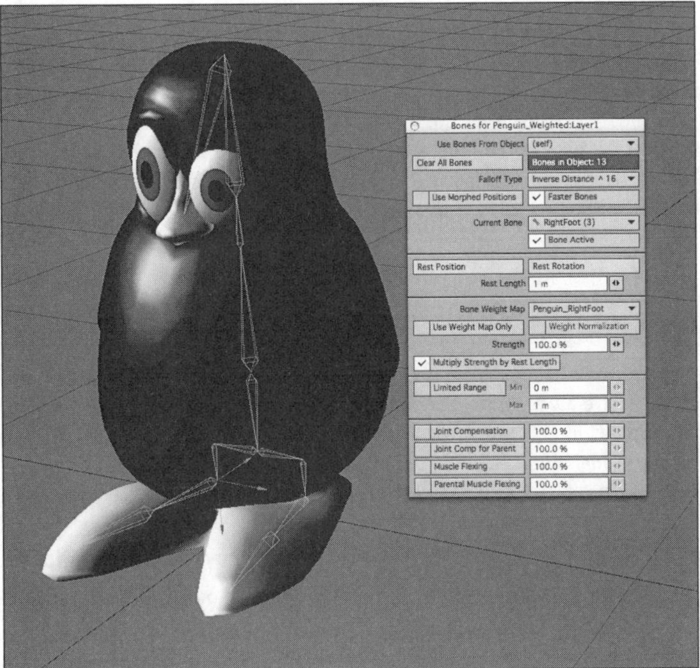

Figure 12.38 Assign a weight map to the RightFoot (3) bone of the object from the Bones Properties panel.

4. Press the down arrow on your keyboard to select the next bone, RightFoot (4), and then also assign the Penguin_RightFoot weight map to it.
5. Close the Bones Properties panel and select the RightFoot (3) bone. Press **y** to rotate the bone around. You'll see, as in **Figure 12.39**, that only the foot reacts. The upper portion of the penguin is not affected at all.
6. Go ahead and repeat the steps for the LeftFoot bones, assigning the appropriate weight map.
7. Save your scene!

Figure 12.39 Assigning weight maps to bones alleviates any problems of bone movements influencing areas of the model they shouldn't.

Note

When working with the Auto Key feature, remember that movements, rotations, and the like are recorded. If you happen to rotate a bone and deform the object when you didn't intend to, you can always undo. LightWave v9 has multiple undos in Layout for actions such as moving or rotating a bone. Just press Ctrl+z (Cmd+z on the Mac), and you're all set. (Just pressing **z** is the shortcut for redo.) You can set the undo levels in the General Options panel by pressing **o**.

Note

There's a little trick in LightWave you can try when setting up additional bones and weights. If you give a weight map created in Modeler exactly the same name as a bone (capitalization included), Layout will apply the map to that bone automatically when you load the model into a scene.

The subtlety of using weight maps with bones is that they confine the influence of bones to the surface regions you want to deform. For a model like our little penguin, a weight map for the feet is ideal because the models parts are so close together, unlike a tall skinny alien or a four-legged animal. If their influence wasn't constrained by weight maps, moving any of those short, tightly packed leg bones could cause unwanted deformations across most or all of the penguin's surface. But as you can see, a simple weight map corrects this problem.

Note that the penguin does not need a weight map for its body or head, because we want that part of its body (unlike its feet and torso) to deform as a single seamless surface, rather than as a set of discrete parts. It would hinder the overall look of the character if its head were clearly articulated from its chest, for instance. When a character like this turns its head, you want its chest and belly to twist as well.

Now that you've completed this exercise, watch the Penguin_FollowUp video in the Chapter 12 folder of this book's DVD to see how you can create weight maps on the points of the arms and create additional bones for them.

Skelegons

As you worked through the setup of just a few bones for the penguin earlier in this chapter, you probably realized that applying bones can be a tedious process. And it can! Skelegons often speed the setup of bone structures, because you build Skelegons along with your model as you work in Modeler.

Skelegons are polygons that resemble bones, and eventually they become bones in Layout. You create and modify Skelegons in Modeler as if they were polygons and then convert them to bones in Layout. The benefit of this is the ability to set up bones for a character in a Perspective view, using modeling tools such as Drag and Rotate. What's more, any Skelegon-based skeletal structure you create for a character is saved with the model. This means you can set up full bone structures for individual characters and load them into a single scene later.

When you create a character with Skelegons, you can adjust its skeletal structure at any time. In addition, you can create one base skeletal structure and use it over and over again for future characters. The next exercise gets you right into it by setting up Skelegons for a full figure.

Note

If you intend to reuse a model's Skelegon-based structure, be sure to save a copy of the model and its Skelegons in Modeler before you move your model into LightWave Layout. Once you convert Skelegons to bones in Layout, they can't be changed back to Skelegons.

Creating Skelegons in Modeler

There are a couple of ways to create Skelegons in Modeler. You can build them point by point or use the Draw Skelegons feature. In the point-by-point approach, you single-line polygons (pairs of points connected by either a line polygon or a curve) to Skelegons. The Draw Skelegons feature is a fast, easy way to create a skeletal structure, and it is the focus of the next exercise.

Exercise 12.7 Creating Skelegons

This exercise uses an existing model to demonstrate how quick and easy it is to set up a full hierarchy for a human character. Using the bone weight information from the previous exercises and the Skelegons information provided here, you'll be moving a fully articulated character in no time. However, you're going to use an automatic feature in LightWave to automatically apply weights to the character. The trick is keeping the Skelegons in the same layer as the geometry. However, for the purpose of providing visual examples, this tutorial shows you the Skelegons in a separate layer.

1. In LightWave v9 Modeler, save any work you might have been doing and create a new object by pressing Shift+n.
2. From this book's DVD, load the BlueGirl object (Projects\Objects\CH12\bluegirl.lwo). This is a killer model that is easy to rig, thanks to our cover creator—William "Proton" Vaughan. Thanks, William!

3. Select a new layer, making BlueGirl a background layer. Bring the bottom right viewport to a full screen and, on the Setup menu tab, click Skelegons (**Figure 12.40**).

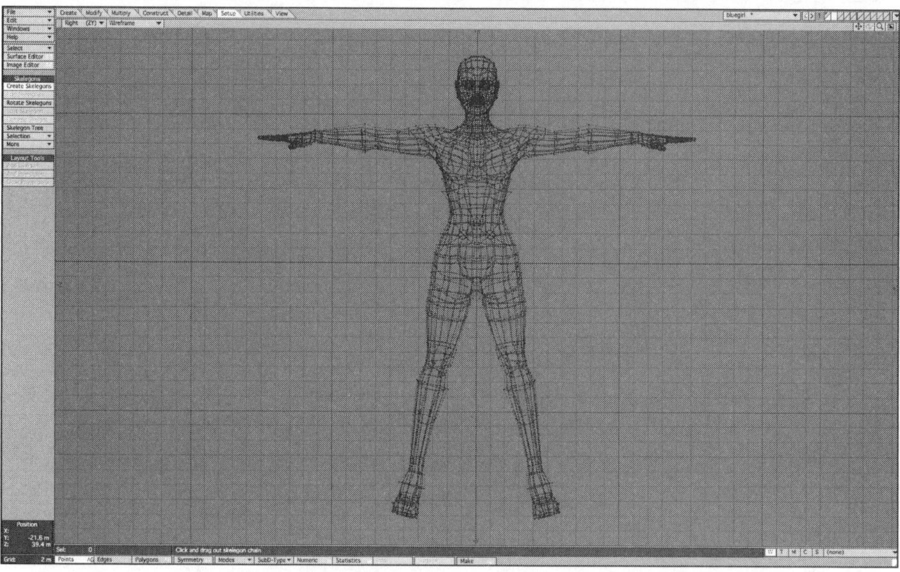

Figure 12.40 To create Skelegons, start with a blank layer but put your model in a background layer for alignment.

Note

The hierarchy you'll create can be used for any type of character, from a human, to an alien creature, or even a four-legged model. You'll soon see how easy it is to create a setup like this using Skelegons. However, do not miss the video portion of this chapter available as a free download from www.3dgarage.com. The video takes you even further into bones and rigging by showing you how to set up a full skeletal structure for a human character, all within Layout. LightWave v9 has more tools than we can write about in this chapter alone!

4. You start building the skeletal structure for BlueGirl's upper body first. Click and drag from the waist of BlueGirl, up to about her chest, as in **Figure 12.41**.

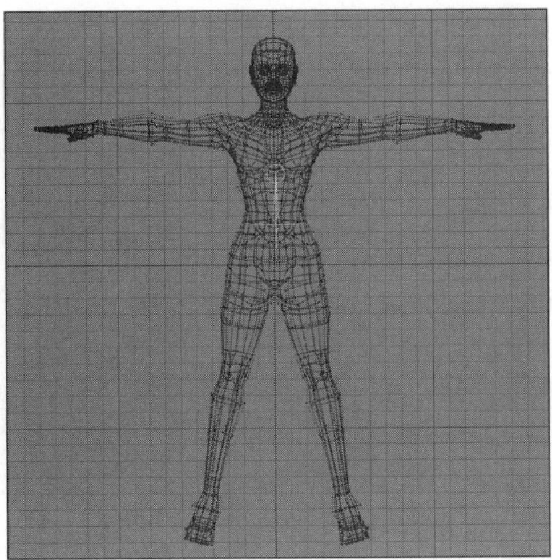

Figure 12.41 Create the first Skelegon, which will be the parent bone of the upper body hierarchy.

Note

Be careful to click and drag just once. It's very common for people to click, let go of the mouse, and then click and drag again. Although you can't see it, doing that creates a tiny little bone that will haunt you later in Layout.

5. With the initial Skelegon still selected, simply click above it to create an additional Skelegon reaching to the base of the neck. This Skelegon will become a child bone later in Layout (**Figure 12.42**).

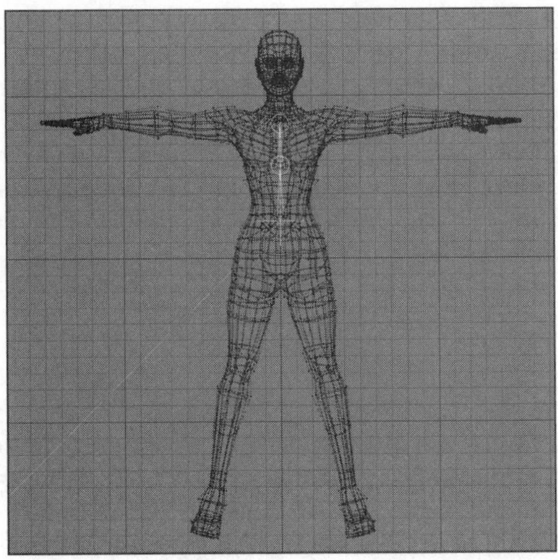

Figure 12.42 Create a second Skelegon that leads to the base of the neck.

6. Now click again, further up the neck, to create yet another Skelegon (**Figure 12.43**).
7. Click once more, at the top of the head, to create one more Skelegon and finish the hierarchy.

   Each Skelegon should start and end at a joint within the character. For example, the Skelegon for the head should begin at the base of the head and end at the crown. When the Skelegon becomes a bone in LightWave Layout and is activated, it will rotate from that base, which will then rotate the head. If it were placed too high, in the middle of the head, rotating it would deform the head in an uncomfortable way, to say the least; placed too low, it would cause the character to wring her own neck.

   The small circles around the ends of the Skelegons are their control handles. If you are in Draw Skelegons mode (which you activate by clicking the Create Skelegons button), clicking outside one of those circles draws a Skelegon between the clicked location and the last handle you made to the one before it. You can adjust a Skelegon in Draw Skelegon mode by clicking within its handle.

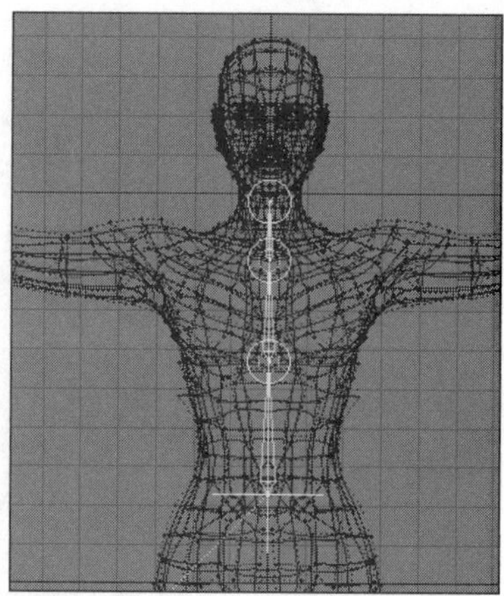

Figure 12.43 Create a Skelegon for the neck.

Note

With the Numeric panel open (press **n**), you can set a name for the Skelegon and create a weight map assignment all at once using the auto weight map feature. In order to do this, you must draw your Skelegons in the same layer as the geometry the Skelegon-based bones will control. The Digits selection in the Numeric panel for Skelegons tells Modeler to sequentially name the Skelegons as you create them. Sometimes, you might not set a name for each Skelegon, so Modeler names them Bone.00, Bone.01, Bone.02, and so on. In addition, these settings (in the Numeric panel) determine how the weight map is applied to the geometry based on the Skelegon you've created (in the same layer as your geometry). This is a real-time implementation of the Bone Weights function.

Note

For a full-body character with full weight maps, it's always good to take advantage of the automatic weight map. The reason is that you'll save time selecting and assigning individual bones in Layout for the full character. With the auto weight map feature, once your Skelegons are active, your weight maps will already be applied.

Now if you screw up while creating Skelegons—accidentally creating too many, for example—don't worry! It's a common mistake. Just press the spacebar to deactivate the Create Skelegons (or Draw Skelegons) tool, and then press the Delete key to get rid of the accidental creation. Select Skelegons and create them again, remembering to name them and set the weights in the Numeric panel if you want. You can also select one Skelegon as you would a polygon and delete it individually. Then select the last polygon in the chain, choose Draw Skelegons, and continue. The next Skelegon you create will be properly added into the hierarchy.

8. Press the spacebar to turn off the Create Skelegons command. Then select the second Skelegon in the middle of the chest and click the Create Skelegons tool again. Doing this tells Modeler to begin creating child Skelegons from the selected Skelegon.
9. Now create four Skelegons for the character's left arm, as shown in **Figure 12.44**.

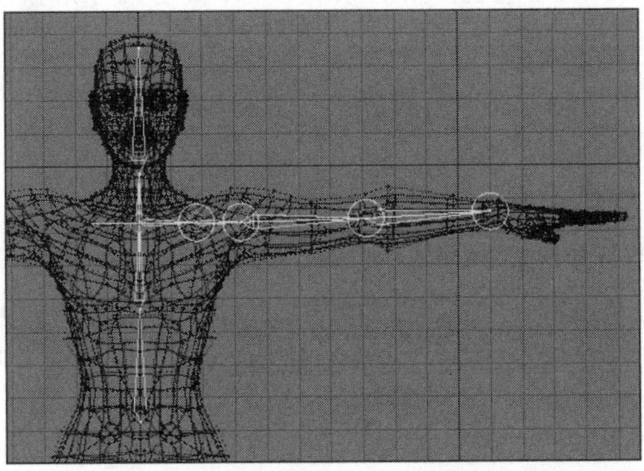

Figure 12.44 Create four more Skelegons for the character's arm.

10. On the Setup menu tab, select Skelegon Tree. When the panel comes up, drag its corner to expand it if necessary to see all its contents.

    You'll see a hierarchy of Skelegons named Bone01 (the first Skelegon you drew), Bone02, and so on (**Figure 12.45**).
11. Double-click the second bone listing under the Skelegons heading. Double-clicking calls up the Rename Skelegon command. Type **Chest**, as it was created in the chest area of the object.

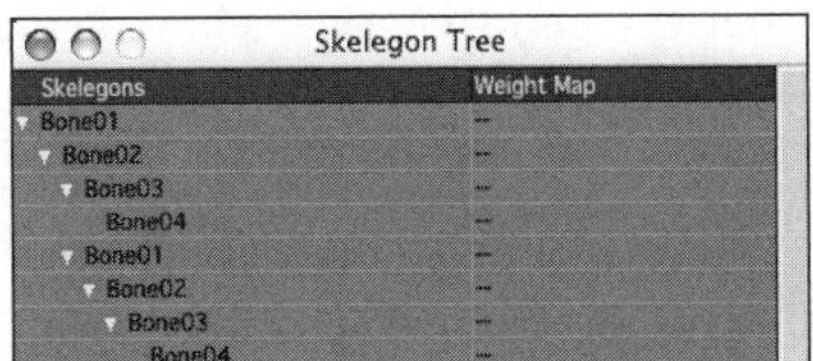

Figure 12.45 The Skelegon Tree panel helps you manage your Skelegon structures. Because no name was applied for the first Skelegon, it simply reads Bone01. Every Skelegon thereafter uses the same name. Remember that you can name each Skelegon as you create it in the Numeric panel. After you name a Skelegon, each one you create from that point takes on that name as well.

Continue renaming Skelegons in this panel. Note that the panel can't stay open while you work, so finish your business and then close it to move on.

12. Save your object. Saving the object also saves the bone structure.

    From here, you can create the Skelegons for the legs. However, you need to build these Skelegons from the original mid-section Skelegon—building Skelegon hierarchies in the opposite direction of those you created for the arms.

Note

If you name the Skelegon and the weight map identically, the weight maps are automatically applied in Layout when the Skelegons are converted to bones. Note that this is case-sensitive.

Creating Skelegons for the legs can be slightly tricky because you need to now build the Skelegons in another layer. To better explain this, we've included a video tutorial available as a free download from www.3dgarage.com. Download the Skelegons tutorial video and continue rigging this baby!

Completing the Skelegon Rig

The process you've just completed puts you on your way to successfully creating a bone structure for bipedal characters. You still would need to build the leg structure of the character for both legs, and there's a little trick or two for the hips, which is explained in the video portion of this chapter. However, the advantage of Skelegons is that you can quickly and easily mirror the structure for the opposite side of the object. You don't have to draw Skelegons again because Skelegons are a polygon type. In the video exercise, you can apply Modeler tools to them and adjust their position, size, and so on.

Here area few extra tips about Skelegons:

- You can use them like polygons, adjusting the points and varying the size.
- Skelegon structures can be loaded back into Modeler and adjusted or added on to at any time.
- If you have created a full structure for a creature but realize later that you need more control, you can split a Skelegon by selecting Split Skelegon from the Construct tab. Also, you can select multiple Skelegons and split them at once. The split will always just slice a selected bone into two equal-sized smaller Skelegons.
- You can define a weight map for a Skelegon, just as you can for a bone, using tools on the Detail tab.

- If you need to separate Skelegons in a hierarchy, you can use the UnWeld command, found on Layout's Detail tab.
- You can instantly create Skelegons from points of an existing object by selecting the points and clicking Convert Skelegon. The command button is tucked in the More drop-down menu within the Skelegons tool category, on Modeler's Setup tab.

Using Skelegons in Layout

Skelegons are Modeler tools that do their most important work in Layout, where you convert them to bones that control your model and assign weight maps created for each Skelegon.

When you're constructing Skelegons in Modeler, it's often convenient to build them on separate layers from the objects they'll control, so you can arrange the Skelegons without disturbing the associated objects. Before you load a Skelegon-containing model into Layout, however, you should cut and paste each finished Skelegon into the layer that contains the associated objects. This ensures that when each Skelegon is converted to a bone in Layout, it will be associated with the correct object.

If you assign a weight map you create in Modeler the same name as a Skelegon, you automatically apply the map to that Skelegon (and to the bone it will become upon conversion in Layout).

Note

LightWave v9's bone tools are too powerful and versatile to cover in just one chapter, so be sure to check out all the cool video tutorials for this chapter (and others) available as a free download from www.3dgarage.com. Learn about new bone tools for LightWave v9 and the new IK Boost tool.

After your model is loaded into Layout with Skelegons, you can simply select the Cvt Skelegons command from the Setup Menu tab. A pop-up window will tell you how many Skelegons were converted to bones. From there, your bones will be visible and usable in Layout.

Note

If Layout has Expert mode set from the General Options tab in the Preferences panel, you don't see a Skelegons to Bones conversion message. Instead, it is highlighted in the status bar underneath the timeline at the bottom of the interface.

Beyond this exercise, you can select portions of the model to assign weight maps just as you did with the Penguin object earlier in this chapter and then apply the bones in Layout.

You can go further and select the regions of points on the full BlueGirl object, assign a weight map, and apply the bone weights. If you remember, applying weights to the feet of the Penguin object enabled you to control the influence of bones—you can do the same throughout the body, for the head, the arms, the legs, and so on. Remember that the Skelegon Tree panel in Modeler shows the name of the weight map that will be used if you've created one. If you've assigned weights in the Numeric panel along with a bone name, your weights should automatically be assigned to the appropriate bone in Layout.

The exercises here are basic and straightforward. However, much of your character work does not need to be more complex than this. It's simply a matter of putting in the time to create bones and Skelegons for your entire model. You can go further by adding Skelegons for BlueGirl's fingers and even her toes. At any time, LightWave enables you to bring this model back to Modeler, make adjustments, and add more Skelegons or weight maps.

The Next Step

To give you the most complete coverage of bones, head over to www.3dgarage.com and you'll find additional video tutorials to accompany this chapter. You'll take the penguin character further and shows you how to edit its existing bone structure directly in Layout for additional control using LightWave v9's new bone tools. You'll be able to view the Skelegons video to further rig the BlueGirl object and apply weight maps. You'll also find a video showing how to use LightWave v9's IK Boost tool, a fast, easy way to create inverse kinematics. You'll find a tutorial video called Layout Bones, which takes you through more of LightWave v9's bone features, including exporting hierarchies, mirroring, and more. And, bones are not just for characters, so there's a video called "Non-bones" that covers nontraditional bone use.

This chapter introduced you to bones and Skelegons and how to create both. You saw how to set bone weights to control the influences of bones. The weighting applies to many areas of LightWave, especially character animation.

With the basic knowledge presented here, you can practice setting up full characters, whether they're full humans, simple characters, or even inanimate objects such as a chrome toaster—the bone and Skelegon information here still applies. Position bones using the Drag tool and use the Mirror tool to copy the Skelegons. See what other kinds of uses you can apply these tools to, such as creating animals, aliens, or your own fascinating creatures.

Skelegons and bones are powerful animation tools in LightWave. Of course, one chapter can't present all the different possible uses of these tools. With the right project and a little time, however, you'll be setting up skeletal structures faster than you could have imagined. But where can you go beyond this? You can turn to the next chapter and learn how to use LightWave v9's powerful particle engine.

Chapter 13
Particles in Motion

Particle animation, collisions, dynamics. What are these terms, so often thrown around in the 3D world? They are your tools for creating cool special effects in LightWave layout. People often equate the term *particle* with 3D animations involving small dots, such as fireworks. Although you can create sparklers and animated dust using particles in LightWave, that's only the beginning. Particles are also used to generate wisps of smoke, fire, snow flurries, and even swarming bees. For many 3D-animation pros, the enhanced particle tools, and the new dynamics capabilities introduced in LightWave v9 (and discussed in detail in this and the next chapter, "Dynamics in Motion"), are enough by themselves to justify the cost of the software. You might hear the term *dynamics* often in computer graphics. Without being too technical, the concept of dynamics in LightWave refers to the ability of animated objects to influence each other's motion and interact naturally. But more than their value, these tools give you control and flexibility over the types of images and animations you can create. That, my friends, is what makes LightWave great!

This chapter takes you into the world of LightWave particle animation. We'll start with the basics so you can familiarize yourself with how the particle tools function in Layout. From there, we'll apply surfacing to particles using HyperVoxels to create smoke, fire, and water effects. Then we'll explore how you can apply dynamics to the particles, such as wind and collisions. In this chapter, you learn how to:

- Work with particles in LightWave v9
- Create surfaces to particles using HyperVoxels
- Use dynamics to change particle motions

Particles In LightWave

Many 3D pros tend to think you need to run out and buy the expensive stand-alone particle creation tools to get decent particle animation. Although dedicated tools have their benefits, you'll see from the following project that you can achieve exceptional particle animation using nothing but Layout. For most everyday animation projects, the robust, easy-to-use particle engine in LightWave v9 is all you need.

Creating a Basic Particle-Motion Scene

In this project, you don't create anything with the particles; you merely apply them to a scene to see how you can interactively adjust parameters for instant feedback.

Using Emitters

The first thing you should know is that for particles to "live" in a scene, they need an *emitter*. You can think of the emitter as a faucet where your particles spill out. The various settings within the particle control panel enable you to adjust how the particles come out, how many, how quickly, and so on. Standard LightWave particle emitters are nonrendering objects you place in your scene, but you can also designate any object as an emitter. A ghostly figure drifting through the air, for instance, might emit a smoke trail consisting of particles with HyperVoxels applied. There aren't any strict rules about when to use an object as an emitter and when to use a standard emitter; the task at hand usually determines your choice.

Note

To make that clear, particles are not objects, points, splines, or curves. However, if you create an emitter as a "Partigon" you will generate single-point polygons.

Note

The LightWave HyperVoxels tool lets you add smoke-like surfaces to particles well as more solid forms for things like water and fluids. HyperVoxels apply to points of an object or particles.

Exercise 13.1 Create a Particle Emitter

1. Open LightWave Layout.
2. On the Items tab under the Add category, click the Dynamic Obj button and choose Particle, as in **Figure 13.1**. When the Add Particle Emitter panel appears, you could type a new name, but for now simply leave the default name, "Emitter" (**Figure 13.2**).
3. Change the Emitter Type selection in the Add Particle Emitter panel from the default, HV Emitter, to Partigon.

   What's the significance of this change? An HV Emitter generates points, which aren't rendered unless HyperVoxels are applied to them (hence the "HV" in the emitter name). HyperVoxels are a type of *volumetric effect*, which simulate fluid, diffuse materials within a defined physical volume, such as the cone of light generated by a streetlamp, or the confines of a room. HyperVoxels and other volumetric effects are used for rendering phenomena such as smoke and fog, which absorb and diffuse light without reflecting it directly—effects that cannot be approximated easily using traditional polygon-based modeling.

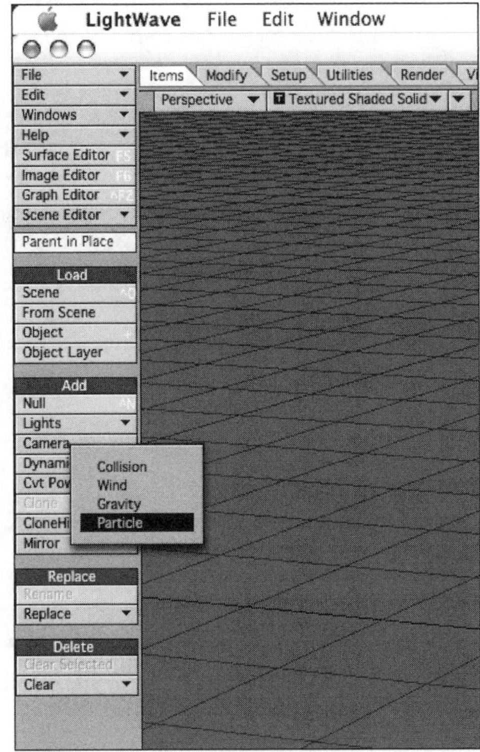

Figure 13.1 You add a particle emitter from the Add category of the Items tab, just as you would with an object, light, or camera.

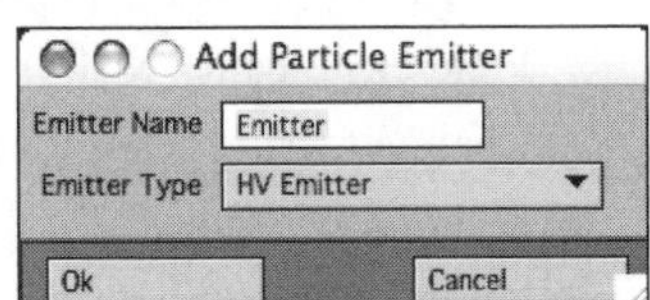

Figure 13.2 After an emitter is added, you can apply a name to it and tell LightWave to make it an HV Emitter or a Partigon Emitter.

   A Partigon Emitter, on the other hand, generates *single-point polygons*, particles that render without HyperVoxels. Partigons can cast and reflect light directly, and you can apply surface characteristics to them. Use Partigons to produce particle systems made up of discrete, tiny objects, such as snow, confetti, or the spray of a sparkler.

4. After the emitter is added, you'll see an outlined box in the Layout view, and the FX_Emitter panel will pop up (**Figure 13.3**). In the timeline at the lower right of the interface, set the last frame of the animation to 200.

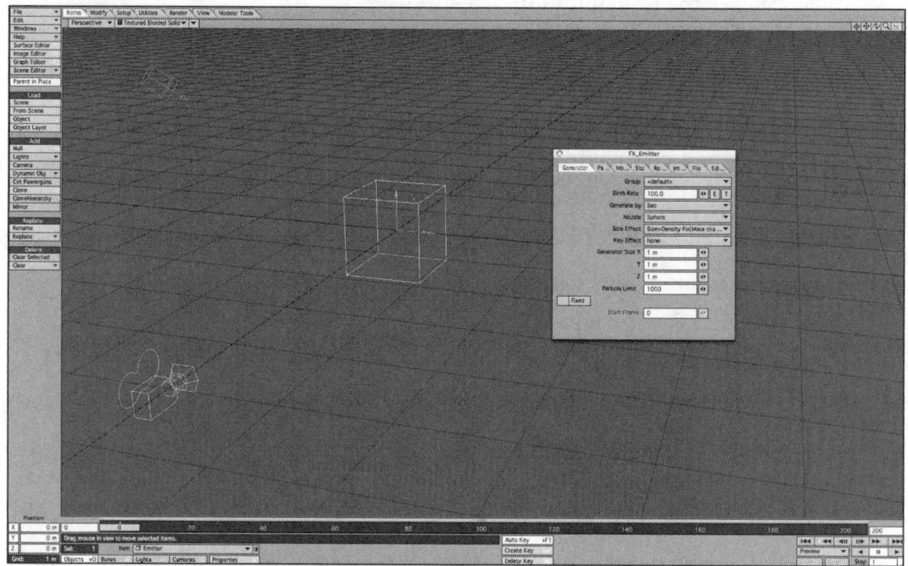

Figure 13.3 After a particle emitter is added to Layout, it is represented by a bounding box, and the FX_Emitter panel appears.

5. Make sure Auto Key is enabled; click the Auto Key button beneath the timeline if it's not.

   Before you move on, press **o** to open the General Options tab within the Preferences panel. Make sure that Auto Key Create drop-down is set to Modified Channels. This means that when Auto Key is turned on, it will automatically generate keyframes as you make positional or rotational changes at different points in time in Layout .

6. Back in Layout, make sure the emitter is selected and then press **t** to activate the Move tool.

7. Press the play button and drag the emitter around in Layout. Look at that—instant particles (**Figure 13.4**)!

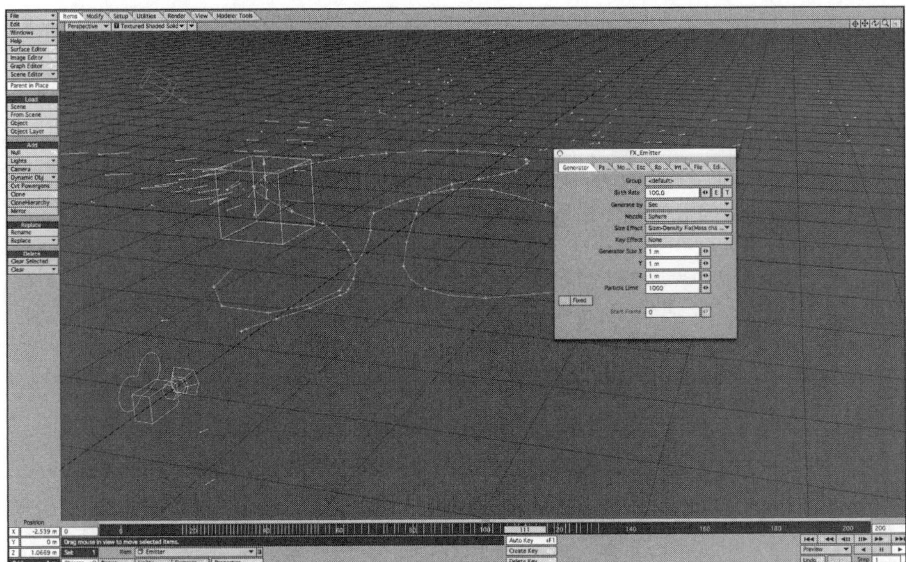

Figure 13.4 By using Auto Key with Auto Key Create set to Modified Channels, you ensure that your motions are recorded in real time in Layout. Moving the particle emitter around shows the spray of particles.

This effect is great for spraying particles in all directions, as you'd see in a sparkler or water shaken from a just-bathed dog, but it lacks control. The particles fall out of the emitter without any rhyme or reason. For most other particle systems, such as a stream of smoke or a running faucet, you'll want your particles to flow in a more controlled fashion. You'll learn how to make that happen in the next exercise.

Controlling Particles

It isn't necessary to always move the particle emitter to see moving particles. The particles can move on their own in a variety of ways. This next section shows you how to create a particle stream to simulate smoke, and with minor modifications, is also good for water fountains, molten lava, gooey chocolate, and more.

Exercise 13.2 Controlling Particle Flow

1. Select Clear Scene from Layout's File drop-down. Make sure Auto Key is active, and then add a new particle emitter as you did in Exercise 13.1. Name it "smoke" when the Add Particle Emitter dialog box appears.
2. For the Emitter Type setting in the Add Particle Emitter dialog box, choose HV Emitter.

You'll notice that the particle emitter (named "smoke") is a set size. You can scale it down to fit objects in your scene. With smoke, such as you'll be creating here, the emitter is often a small, concentrated point of origin, such as a pipe or cigar.

3. When the FX_Emitter panel appears, move it aside as needed, so you can see the emitter in the scene (**Figure 13.5**). Set the last frame of the animation to 300 and move the timeline slider to frame 0.

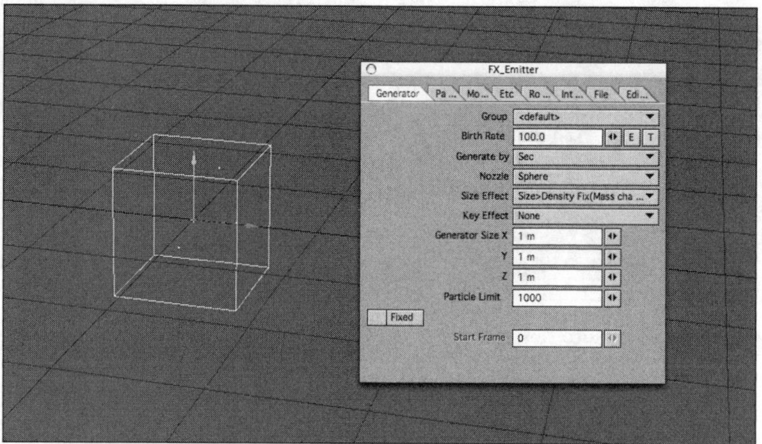

Figure 13.5 Adding a particle emitter to the scene gets you started, but first, you'll need to scale it down.

4. In the Generator tab of the FX_Emitter panel, change the X, Y, and Z size values to 35mm, as shown in **Figure 13.6**.

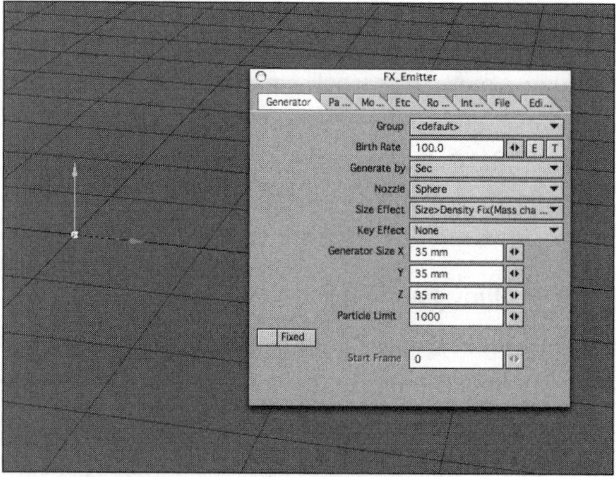

Figure 13.6 Scale the emitter's generator to a tiny 35mm cube to begin creating smoke.

Changing the Generator Size in the FX_Emitter panel tells the emitter to be larger or smaller at the point where particles emerge. Changing the actual size of the emitter in Layout scales the emitter itself, not the area of particle generation.

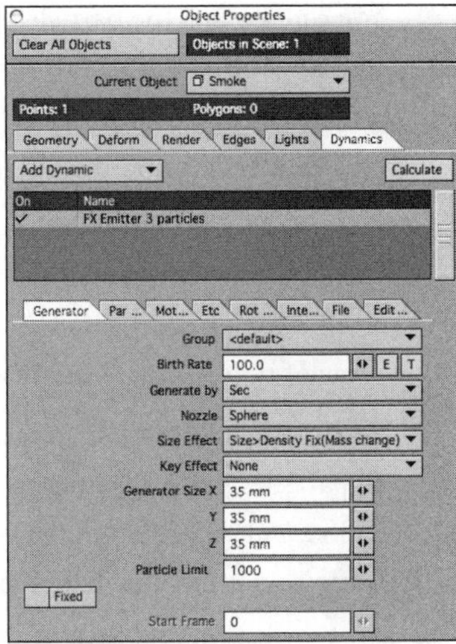

Figure 13.7 In case you accidentally (or on purpose) close the FX_Emitter control panel, you can find the panel again under the Dynamics tab within the Object Properties panel.

> **Note**
>
> Should you accidentally close the FX_Emitter panel, don't worry! Select the emitter item in Layout and press **p** to open the Object Properties panel. Click its Dynamics tab, and then click the item name that begins "FX_Emitter" in the list on that tab. You'll see all the controls, as in **Figure 13.7**. You can also find the FX_Emitter panel in the Additional list of plug-ins, on the Utilities tab.

5. In the FX_Emitter panel, click the Motion tab and bring the Velocity Y value to 400mm, as in **Figure 13.8**. Press the play button in the bottom-right corner of Layout, and you'll see the particles start to stream upward. Note that a negative velocity value on the Y-axis would send the particle stream downward.

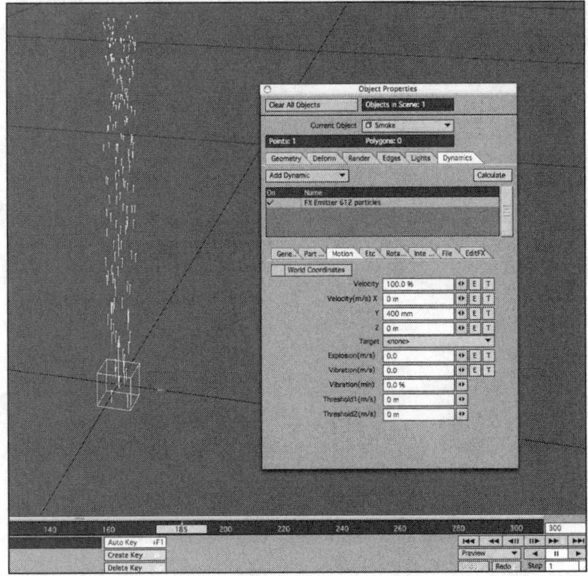

Figure 13.8 Increasing the Velocity value for the Y-axis shoots the particles upward.

You can see that the particle preview updates in real time as you adjust FX_Emitter settings. You can click and drag the arrow buttons to the right of a value for true interactivity. Play around with the Vector values for *X* and *Z* to see how the particles are affected, and then revert to a *Y* velocity of 400mm and *X* and *Z* velocities of 0.

6. Now that the particles are being generated in the right direction, move the camera around for a better view of the particle stream. Right now, we have an upward spray of points—not exactly wispy smoke.
7. Set the Birth Rate value to 60. This tells LightWave to emit, or "give birth" to, 60 particles per *x*, in which *x* represents the unit (second, frame, collision event, wind event) specified in the Generate By drop-down. For now, leave the Generate By unit set to Sec, so that 60 particles are generated every second.
8. Click the Motion tab and bring the Explosion value to 0.105, and you'll see the particles spray outward, as in **Figure 13.9**. Now try adding a little vibration. Set the Vibration (m/s) value to 0.195 and the particles have a bit of randomness—sort of a scattering effect.

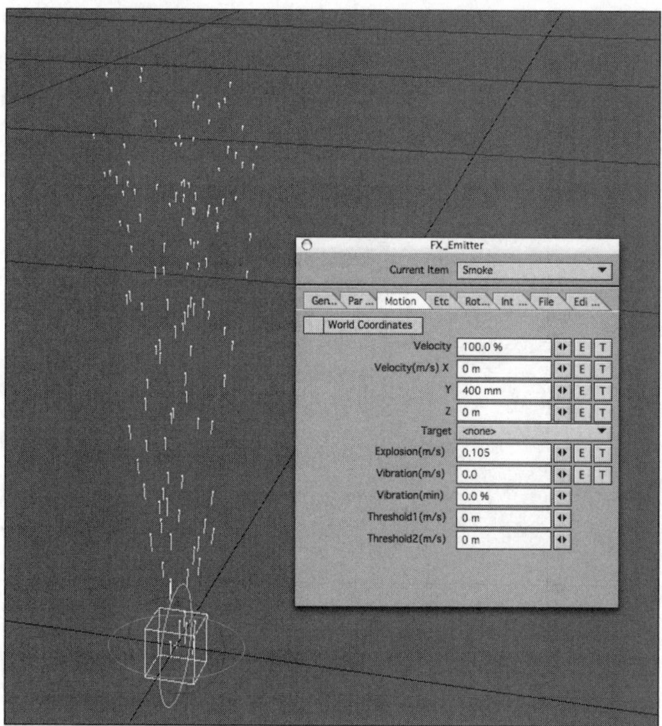

Figure 13.9 Changing the Explosion value makes your particles spray outward, while the Vibration setting adds randomness.

Note

Remember that you can play the animation and make value changes to your particles at the same time. This is the best way to set up particle animations because you can see exactly what your changes are affecting.

9. The second Vibration setting is a minimum percentage that you can apply as well. For now, leave this at 0%. If the first Vibration setting applies the value, or the amount, this second setting determines how much of that amount is used.
10. The particles are moving too fast for smoke. So, up at the top of the Motion tab, set the Velocity value to 20%. This causes the particles move a little slower, more like rising smoke. **Figure 13.10** shows the settings.

    If you watch the particles flow, they seem to be moving evenly at first, but by only setting a Velocity value on the Y-axis, you're sort of pushing the particles. You want them to appear as if they drift upward. Right now, they come out and just hang in midair. You'll also notice that with the Velocity value changed, the particle stream is much shorter.

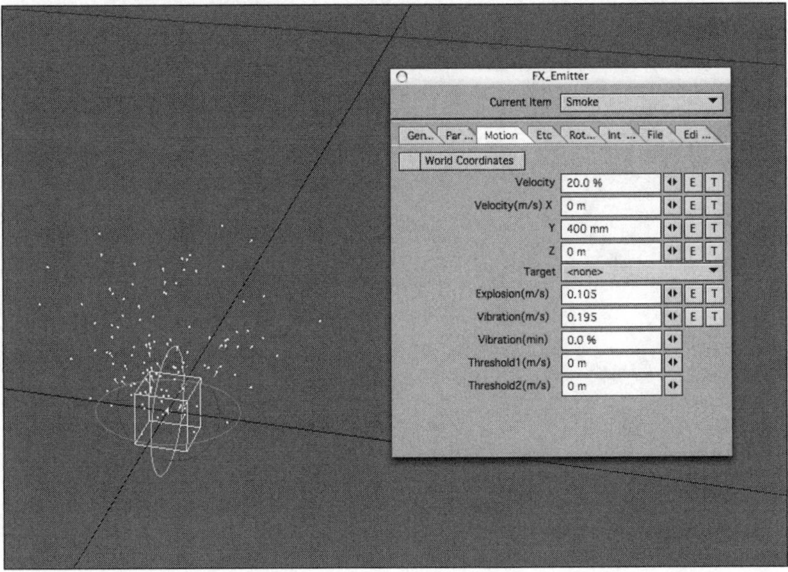

Figure 13.10 Changing the Velocity setting can speed up or slow down your particle stream.

11. Click the Particle tab, and set the Weight value to 3.85 or so. This boosts the particles' momentum so they'll flow a bit farther. Then, on the same tab, set the Life Time value to 120. This tells the particles to "live" for 120 frames, then go away. While you're at it, set the + – setting to 10. This is a plus or minus randomization for the Life Time setting. It's good to use so that the particles don't all die off at the same time but with a variation of up to 10 frames. **Figure 13.11** shows the settings.

Note

If you set the Life Time value to 0 you're telling the particles to flow infinitely. If you leave the value at 60, the particles would only last 60 frames (2 seconds).

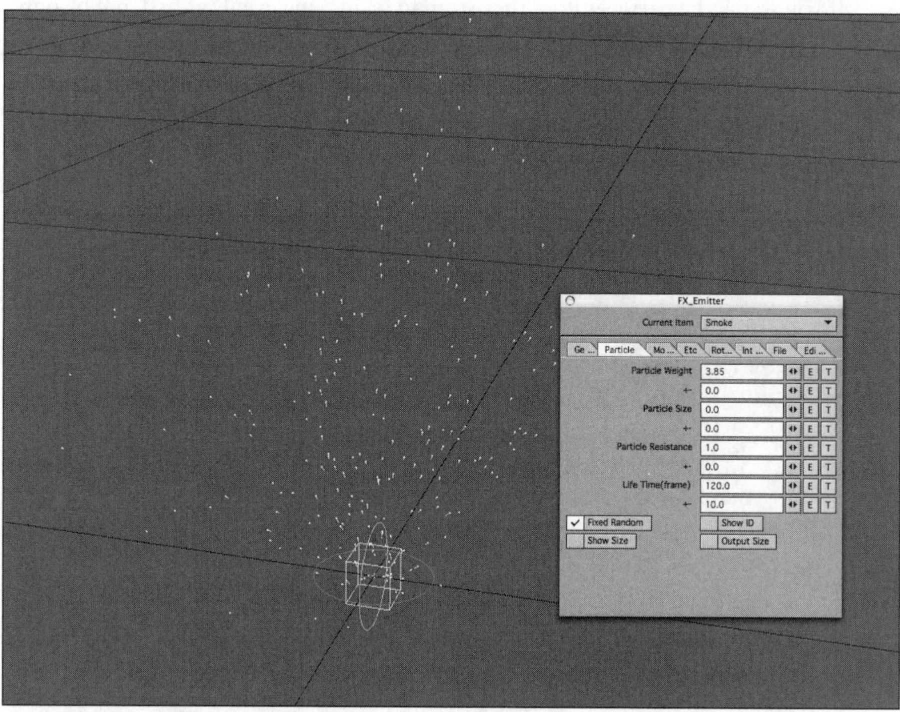

Figure 13.11 Adjusting the Particle Weight and Life Time settings help the particles flow and die a bit more naturally.

12. You might notice now with these changes that the particle stream fans out a bit too much. So, jump back to the Motion tab and decrease the value for Explosion to .0655 and for Vibration to .0385.

13. Finally, save your scene.

Your LightWave 3D manual gives a good description of the numerous settings and values available to you in the Particle FX_Emitter panel. You should reference this as you work through the tools. For now, these first two exercises introduced you to particle emitters and the controls available to them. However, you can do much more with this system, and you can change how this smoke floats through the air.

Working with Particle Wind

Have you ever been visiting a friend and later that night have a craving for a hamburger? So you find the only place open, one of those all-American pub restaurants, and you grab the first available table. Your place your order and sure enough, the old lady with long, dirty, gray hair in the booth next to you lights up a cigarette. What happens? Right! The smoke drifts right over to you as you're trying to eat. While we can't offer a solution for *that* situation in this chapter, it is possible to control the direction of smoke in LightWave. Read on to learn how easy it is to determine where your wind blows.

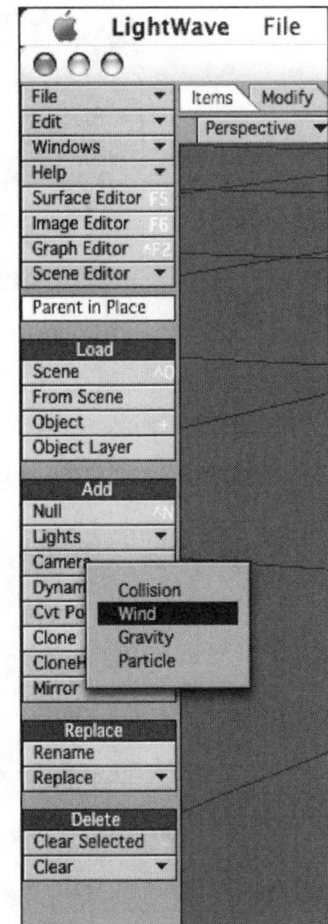

Figure 13.12 Add a Wind effector to the scene, in the same way that you added a particle emitter earlier.

Exercise 13.3 Adding Wind to Particles

1. Continuing from the previous project, make sure your scene is saved. Then, using the Items tab, add a wind effector to the scene by choosing Wind from the Dynamic Obj drop-down menu (**Figure 13.12**).

2. If your FX panel was already open from working with the particle emitter, it will automatically change over to the FX_Wind properties. If the panel does not appear, select the wind effector and then press **p** to open its Properties panel. Click the Dynamics tab and select the FX Wind listing.

3. Because you scaled down the size of the particle emitter in Exercise 13.2, your wind effector is much too large for it. So, in the FX_Wind properties panel, set the Radius to something like 60mm (**Figure 13.13**).

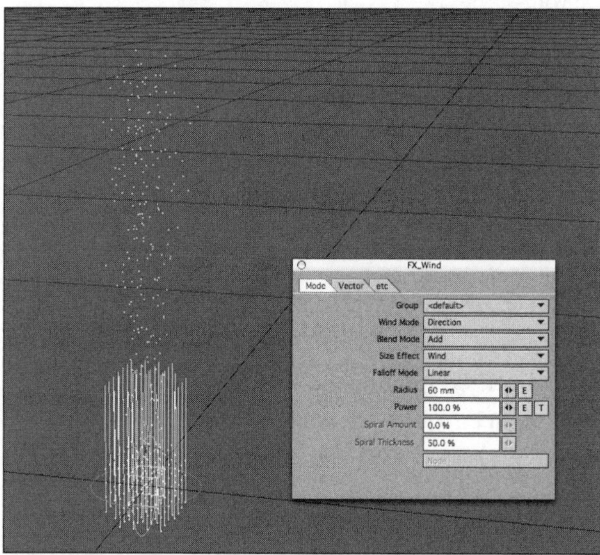

Figure 13.13 Change the radius of the wind to fit the scene.

4. Rotate the wind effector (press **y**, and then click and drag). Look what happens—the particle stream changes direction, as shown in **Figure 13.14**.

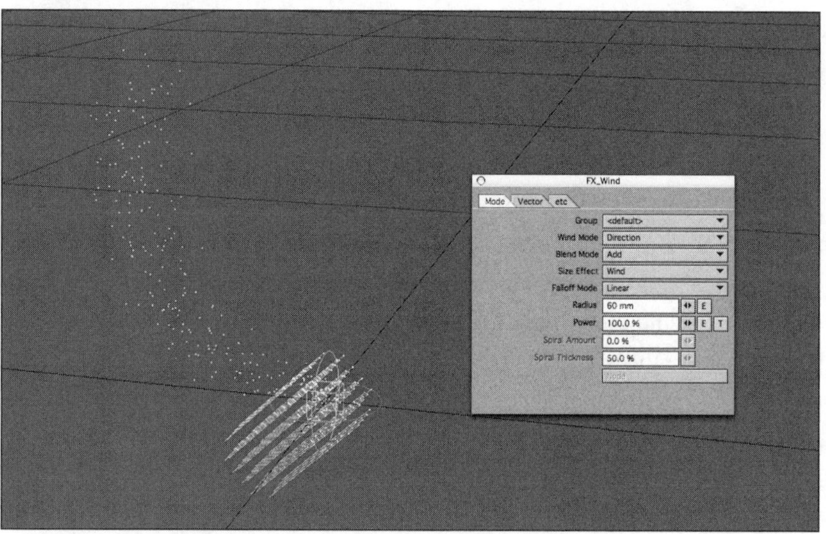

Figure 13.14 Rotating the wind effector has a direct effect on the particle stream.

5. Remember, you can animate the position or rotation of the wind effector to change how the particles flow throughout an animation. For now, reset the wind effector to its original position by pressing Ctrl+z (Cmd+z on the Mac) to undo your rotational changes. The Wind Mode drop-down determines how the effector acts on particles. Change its setting from Direction (the default) to Vortex, as shown in **Figure 13.15**. Now the pulsing of the wind effector causes the particles to emit in bursts, at different speeds, adding a bit more realism to the motion.

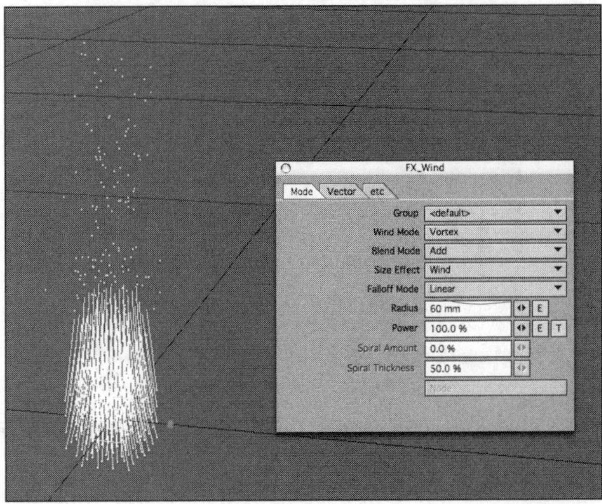

Figure 13.15 Change the Wind Mode setting to Vortex for random emitter control.

Experiment with the various wind modes to see how they affect the particles. If you find a motion value you like, use it. Remember, you can leave the layout animation playback going to see the particles moving while you make changes to the wind.

6. Your scene can contain more than one wind effector, which is pretty cool. So, add another wind effector from the Dynamic Obj drop-down menu on the Items tab.

7. For the second wind effector, set its radius to about 120mm. Then, set Wind Mode to Path, as shown in **Figure 13.16**. The wind will help "steer" the particles to create a stream of smoke.

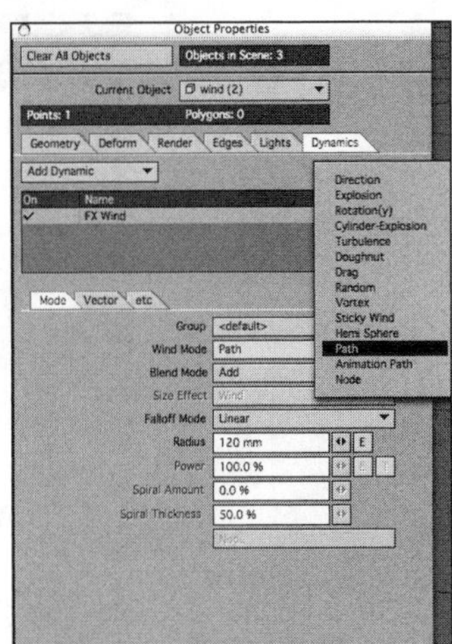

Figure 13.16 A second wind effector is added to the scene, and its wind mode is set to Path.

8. Move the timeline slider to frame 0, and then select the second wind effector. Activate the Move tool (press **t**) and drag the effector down, close to the base of the particle emitter, as shown in **Figure 13.17**.

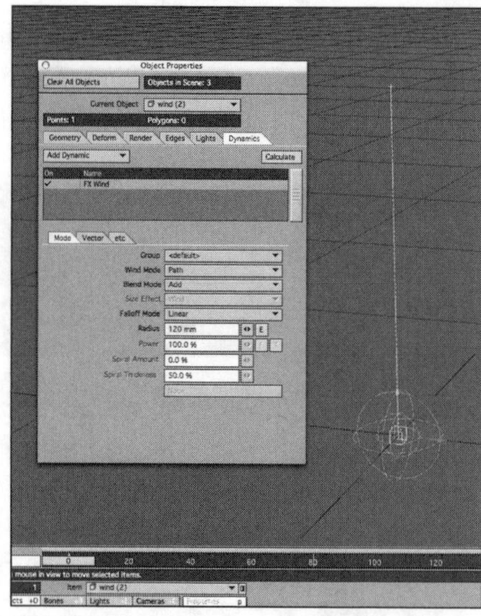

Figure 13.17 Move the second wind effector down toward the base of the particle emitter.

9. Move the timeline slider to frame 80, and then move the wind effector up about 1m along the Y-axis, and slightly to the right along the X-axis (**Figure 13.18**).

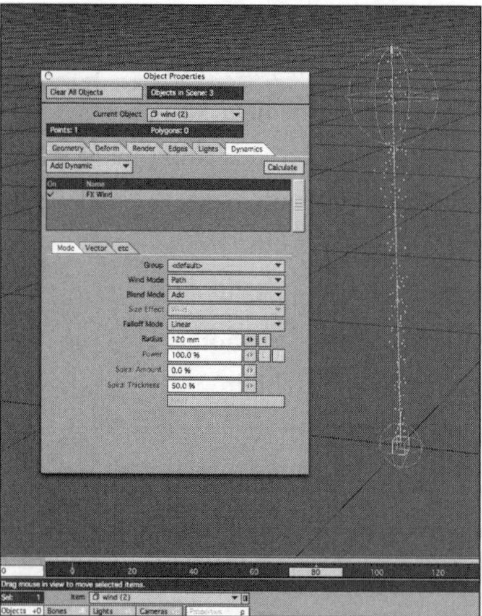

Figure 13.18 Create a second position for the wind effector.

10. Go to frame 160 and move the wind effector again, about 1m over to the right along the X-axis about 1m. **Figure 13.19** shows the position.

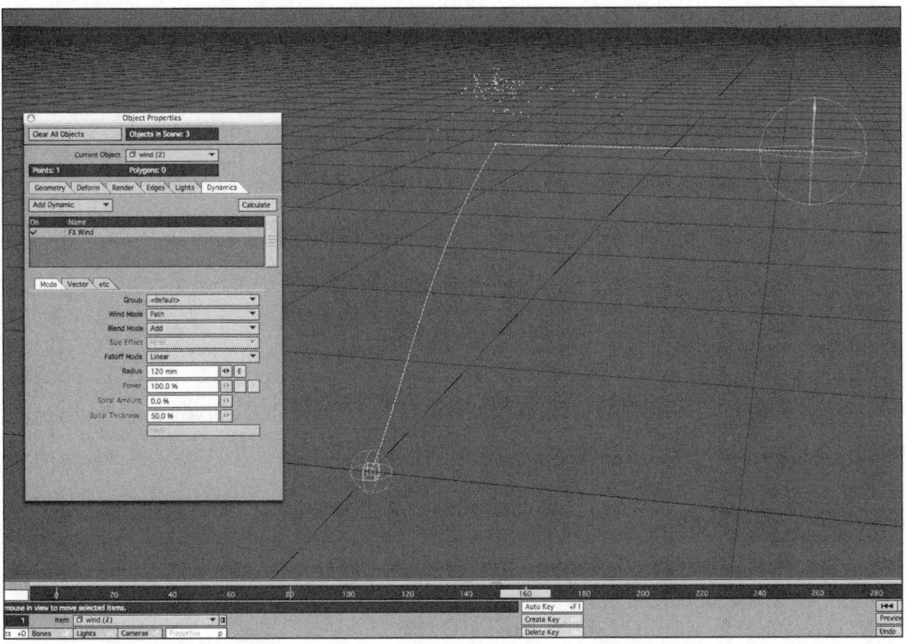

Figure 13.19 Move the wind effector at frame 160, over on the x-axis.

11. At frame 240, move the wind effector up a bit more on the y-axis, about 500mm, and back on the *Z*-axis about 500mm. **Figure 13.20** shows the position.

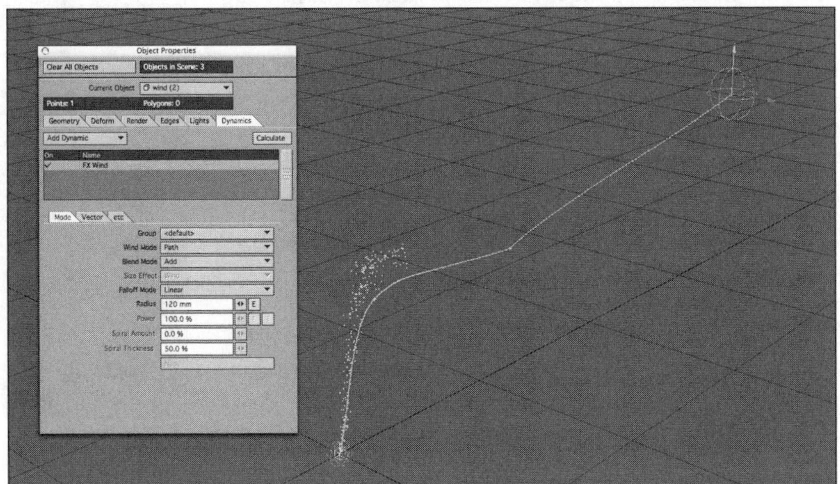

Figure 13.20 Move the wind effector up on the Y-axis for frame 13.20 and back on the Z-axis.

12. Click on the smoke effector to select it, and then change its Life Time setting to 300. Because the path wind is now dragging the particles, you'll want them to live a bit longer.

    You see, the point here is that you can work through your particle animation and make changes to key factors such as lifetime, velocity, and others at any point. Your settings are always adjustable.

13. Finally, if you find that your particles sort of hang around at some point, there's a chance that the path wind is not large enough to carry them all. So, all you need to do is select the second wind effector and then enlarge its radius. If your particles jam up in any area, you can adjust the position of the wind effector.

14. Tweak, adjust, experiment, and then save your scene.

The path wind feature is very powerful. This exercise introduced you to it, but you can go further by rotating the wind at certain keyframes. What would that do, you ask? How about twisting smoke for things like jet exhaust or tornados? Cool stuff. There's a video from 3D Garage.com for this chapter, showing you more about the different particle settings. Be sure to check it out. For now, let's move on to learn about collisions.

Introducing Particle Collisions

This next section will show you how to apply collision behavior to your particles. The goal is to make particle systems behave realistically when they encounter obstacles in their paths. Think of smoke hitting a ceiling before it dissipates, or water splashing as it hits the bottom of a sink. The next exercise takes the basic emitter example discussed in the previous exercises and expands it by changing its particle flow with collisions.

Exercise 13.4 Interactive Particles

1. Use the scene you created in Exercise 13.3 or load the ParticleSmoke scene from the Chapter 13 folder on this book's DVD. Resave the scene as **ParticleCollision**.

2. Choose Collision from the Items tab's Dynamic Obj drop-down (**Figure 13.21**). You can add dynamics to any scene this way.

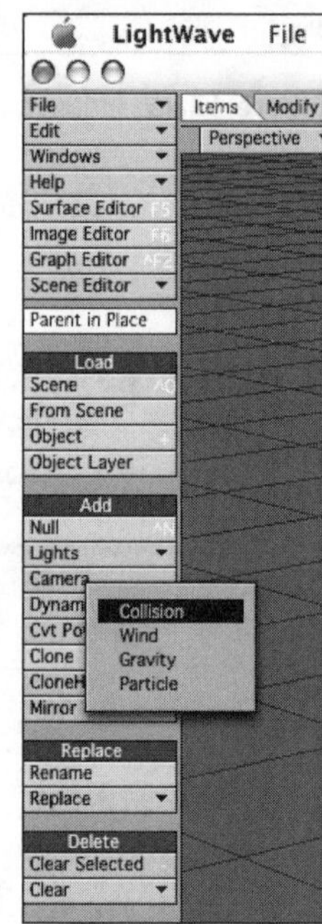

Figure 13.21
Add a collision effector to the scene.

Note

You might have noticed that on the Dynamics tab within the Object Properties panel, you can also add effectors, such as collision. The difference here is that adding an effector here will attach it to an object. Since there are no objects in this particular scene, you've added a collision from the Items tab instead.

3. Take a look at the FX_Collision Properties panel that popped up after you added the collision effector. If you don't see it, in the Object Properties panel select the Collision dynamic on the Dynamics tab and the appropriate controls appear within the panel. Then, check the layout, and note that your particles have sort of exploded all over your scene. It appears that they are already colliding with the collision effector, as you can see in **Figure 13.22**.

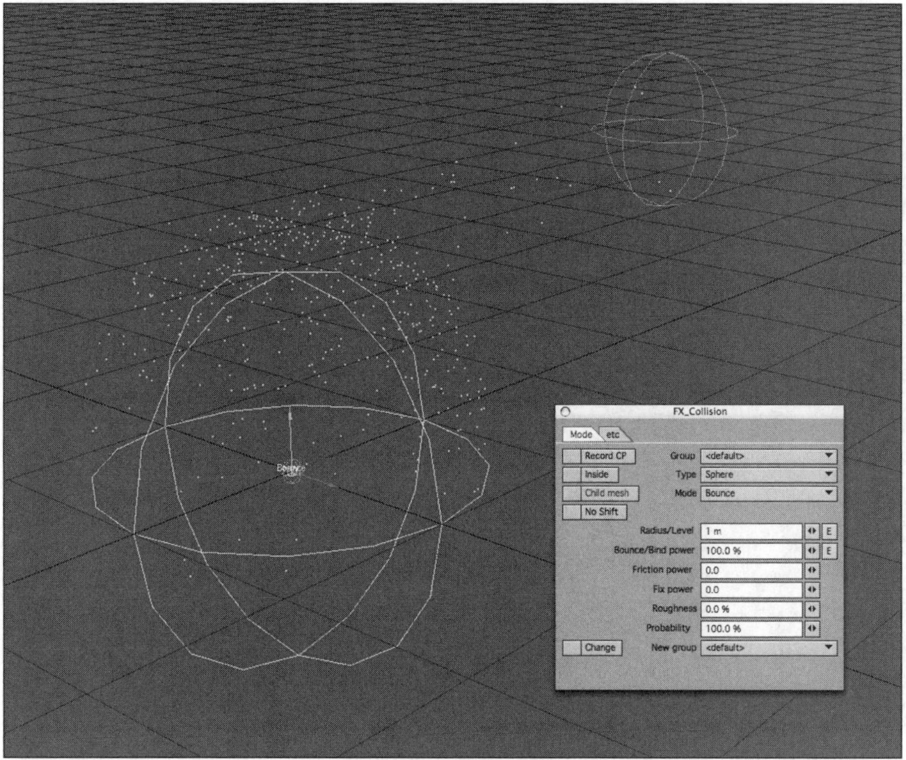

Figure 13.22 Once a collision effector is added to a scene, it immediately goes to work affecting the particles.

4. The default shape of the collision effector, which can be embedded in any object in your scene, is a sphere. We want a flat surface instead for this scene, so in the Properties panel for the collision object, choose Plane from the Type drop-down. Take a look at **Figure 13.23** and you'll see that this creates a collision plane is floating above the Y-axis. This is because the Radius/Level setting for it is set to 1m. Changing the Radius/Level setting is similar to changing the radius of the particle emitter, as you did earlier in the chapter. Set this option to 500mm.

   Setting Type to Plane is good for particles hitting a floor or a wall, and so on, rather than a box or sphere. If you had, say, a building, or a car, you could set Type to Object.

   Remember, this is as basic as it gets, but the collisions work the same no matter what particle scene you're setting up. The difference here is that you're only working with effectors and emitters. You can make any object a collision, and place your particle emitter into any object. Be sure to view the VisualParticle.mov movie file (available as a free download from www.3dgarage.com) to see this in action.

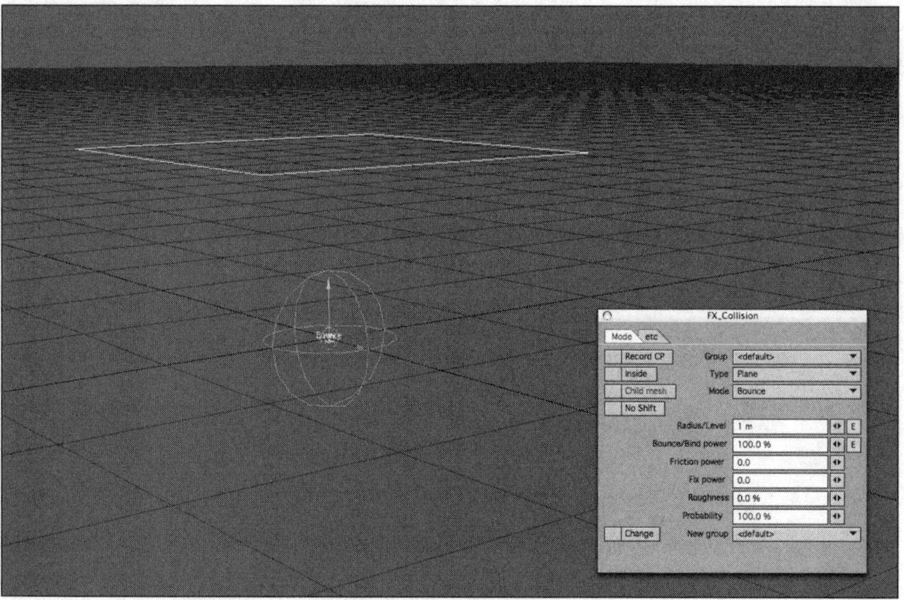

Figure 13.23 New collision planes have a default Radius/Level setting of 1m.

5. Press **t** to activate the Move tool and move the plane up about 1 m along the Y-axis; then create a keyframe at frame 0 to lock it in place.

   Mode is set to Bounce, telling the collision plane to, well, bounce particles that strike it. Alternate settings cause particles to stick to the surface, sink into it, and so on. You'll see that the Bounce/Bind Power option is set to 100% in the Properties panel. This essentially determines the strength of the collision. For now, this value is fine.

6. Save your scene with your changes.
7. Drag your timeline slider or click the play button in the bottom-right corner of the interface to see the particles flow. You'll see them stream up and flow along with the pull of the wind you set up in Exercise 13.3, but now they'll stop and spread out when they hit the collision plane.
8. Click the Inside button in the FX_Collision panel. This tells the particles colliding to be affected in the interior of the collision object, and not just at its surface. Since this object this is a flat plane, and it has no interior, this has the effect of stopping the particles from passing through the collision object, so they stay beneath it (**Figure 13.24**).

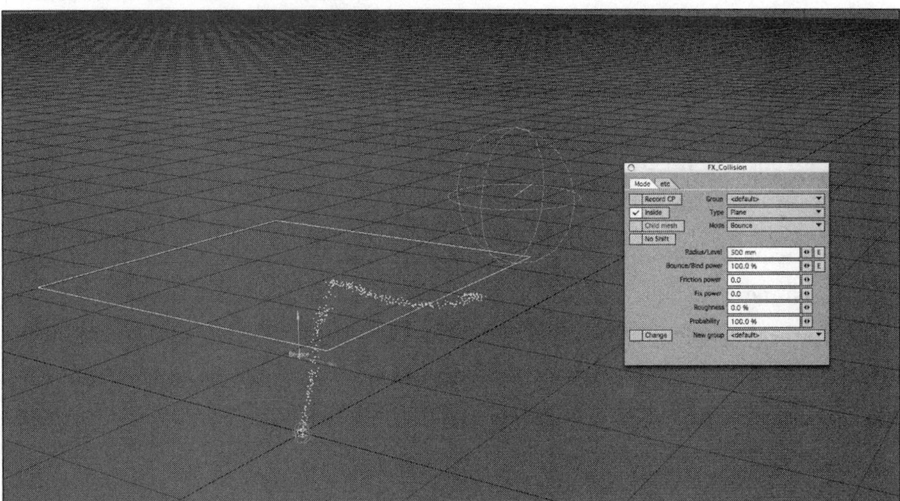

Figure 13.24 Inserting a collision plane in the particle stream does not stop the wind effector that's pulling the particles, but it deflects the particles' motion.

Note

Particles can be hard to see in Layout. So when previewing a particle animation, it may be helpful to select the scene's particle emitter(s) first to highlight them and make them easier to see. While shaping the flow of your particle stream, you may also want to set the emitter's Life Time value to 0 on the FX_Emitter panel's Particle tab, to make the emitter generate particles indefinitely, without "timing out."

As you've seen in these few exercises, making particles interact and applying dynamics is not difficult. You've easily added an emitter, added wind effectors, and included an animation path. You then made those particles interact with an object by adding a collision dynamic. But there's one other thing that might be really helpful: surfacing the particles.

Surfacing Particles

It's possible to exert a ton of control over your particles using things like gravity and collision dynamics, and if you watch the videos for this chapter (available as free downloads from www.3dgarage.com), you'll see more examples. But you can take even the simple particles created here a step further by setting up a cool surface for them. And once the surfaces are set, you can still go back and make changes to the particle emitter and interactively change the parameters with more vibration, less wind, or faster velocity for cooler effects. For now, these particles are cool, but what good are they? If you render a frame, you'll see nothing. If there were objects loaded in the scene, you'd only see those render, and you still wouldn't see the particles. That's because you created an HV Emitter earlier in the chapter, meaning you must apply HyperVoxels to them to make them visible.

Another type of emitter you could add is a Partigon emitter. It works similarly to an HV Emitter, except that it generates single-point polygons that will show during a render. These are great for tiny sparks, water sprays, or even stars.

Three surfacing options are available for HyperVoxels: Surface mode, for solid blobby objects; Volume mode, for 3D clouds and smoke; and Sprite mode. Sprites are like 2D surface maps that emulate the effect of a HyperVoxel when it's applied to a 3D volume. They render much more quickly than true 3D HyperVoxels. These settings have no effect on the particles' motion in Layout, but only their appearance. They are fast, great for smoke effects, easy to set up, and always visible in Layout!

Exercise 13.5 Surfacing Particles for Smoke

1. Load the scene you completed in Exercise 13.4 or load the ParticleCollision scene from the Chapter 13 folder of this book's DVD. Then press Ctrl+F6, or select the Volumetrics and Fog Options from the Window drop-down menu at the top left of the Layout interface. The Effects panel will appear with its Volumetrics tab active (**Figure 13.25**).

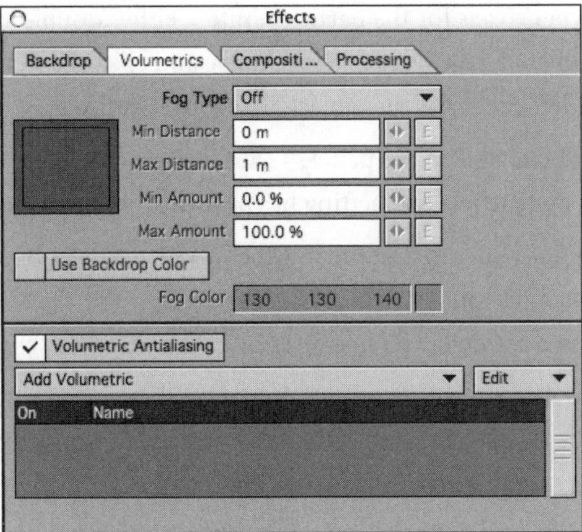

Figure 13.25 Press Ctrl+F6 to open the Volumetrics tab of the Effects panel, home of the HyperVoxels volumetric control.

2. Select HyperVoxels from the Add Volumetric drop-down, and then double-click the name in the object list that appears in the tab. The HyperVoxels panel will open.

   You'll see the name of the HV_Emitter ("Smoke") grayed out in the Object Name list (**Figure 13.26**).

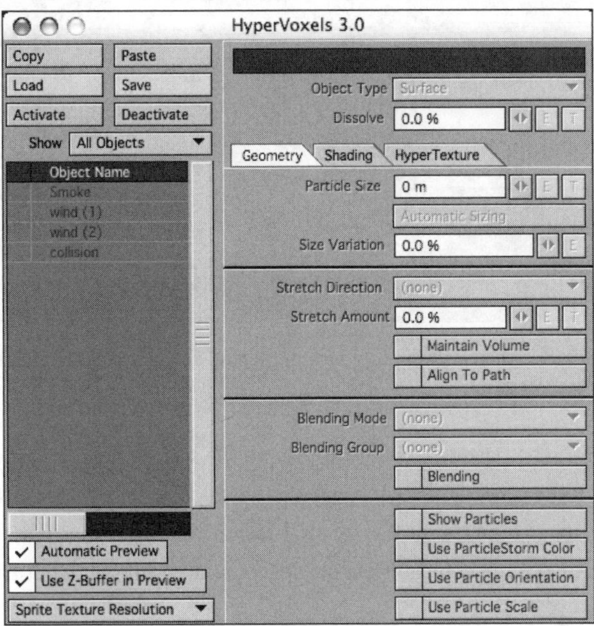

Figure 13.26 As soon as you load up HyperVoxels, your particle emitter is visible in the Object Name list but inactive.

3. To activate HyperVoxels for the particle emitter, either double-click the Smoke entry in the Object Name list, or select it once and click the Activate button just above the top-left corner of the Object Name list window.

   The grayed-out controls in the panel's Geometry tab will become active, and you'll see that the Particle Size setting has been set for you automatically.

4. Move the timeline slider to a frame in which some particles have been emitted. You'll be previewing your particle-surface settings in the VIPER window, so we need to work in a frame in which some particles appear.

5. Now, the best way to begin setting up smoke for these particles is to use VIPER (press **F7**). Because you're using HyperVoxels instead of standard surface attributes, you don't need to run a screen render to load the VIPER buffer before VIPER can preview your effect settings (**Figure 13.27**). You might need to click the Render button directly in the VIPER window to preview the particles.

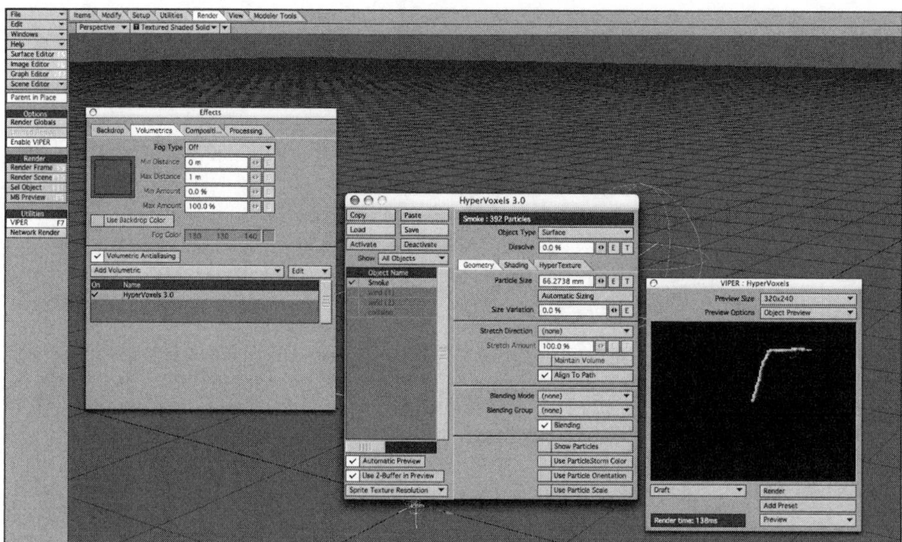

Figure 13.27 VIPER is the only way to go for setting up HyperVoxels interactively on your particles.

6. VIPER shows the particles as they appear to the scene's default camera, so if need be, position the camera in such a way that you can see the particle stream. A quick way to do this is to press the Tab key to hide any open settings panels; select the camera in Layout; switch the view mode to Camera; press **t** to activate the Move

tool; and click and drag in the scene window to move the camera in closer to the particles. When set, create a keyframe at frame 0 to lock the camera in place, and then press Tab to unhide the HyperVoxel and VIPER panels.

7. In the VIPER window, you'll see some white blobs. By default, HyperVoxels uses Surface as the Object Type. This is great for lava, blood, shaving cream, and things of that nature. It's also great for water, and you'd just need to add transparency and reflections for the effect. But if you change the Object Type to Sprite, you can make great-looking smoke. Go ahead and change the Object Type setting in the HyperVoxels panel to Sprite.

8. Now all you need to do is tweak the settings. In the HyperVoxels panel, click the Show Particles button at the bottom of the panel on the Geometry tab. Move the HyperVoxels panel and VIPER aside to see the layout. Your HyperVoxel sprites are now visible in Layout (see **Figure 13.28**).

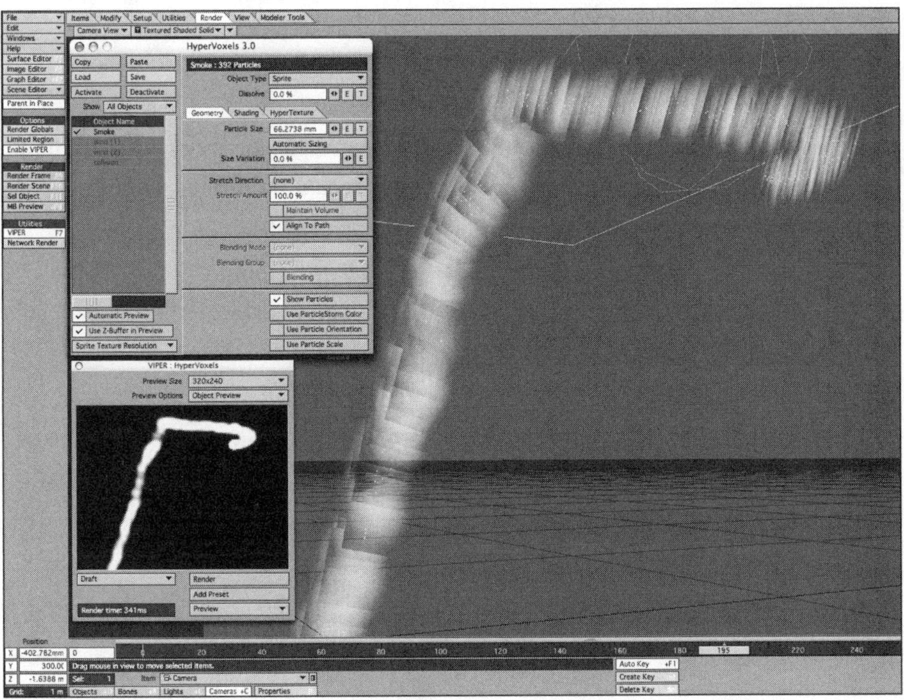

Figure 13.28 Turning on Show Particles in the HyperVoxels panel shows your HyperVoxel surface representation in Layout.

9. Back in the HyperVoxels panel, click and drag the Particle Size mini-slider and change the setting to 40mm.
10. Set Size Variation to 180% to randomize the size of the Sprite particles a bit. Note that although the mini-slider for Size Variation maxes out at 500%, you can manually enter a value much higher than that for added control.
11. Set Stretch Direction to None, so that the particles don't stretch based on their movement. You would use a stretch direction if you were creating fast-moving particles, or perhaps pooling water. Make sure Align to Path is checked.

Note

If you want to see how this setting looks, go ahead and make a preview of your particle animation directly in the VIPER window. From the Preview drop-down menu, click Make Preview. After the preview is generated, play buttons will appear. You can stop the preview generation at any time by pressing the Esc key on your keyboard.

12. Click the Shading tab and then set the particle color to a grayish blue, about R: 172, G: 175, B: 200.

    Just as you set up textures throughout the book using LightWave's Surface Editor, you can do the same here in the HyperVoxels panel. You can apply a texture to the HyperVoxel particles just as you would for an object's surface.
13. Set Luminosity to 70% for a softer look. Set Opacity to about 90%. Making this value lower would add more brightness, almost a glow, to the particles.
14. Set Density to 55% to break up the smoke a bit.
15. Set the number of slices to 7, the maximum. LightWave defaults to 1 slice. As stated, a Sprite is a slice of a HyperVoxel. The more slices, the more detail, but of course, the more rendering time. In some cases, a setting of 1 is all you need, but in this case, 7 gives you the cleanest render. **Figure 13.29** shows the settings.

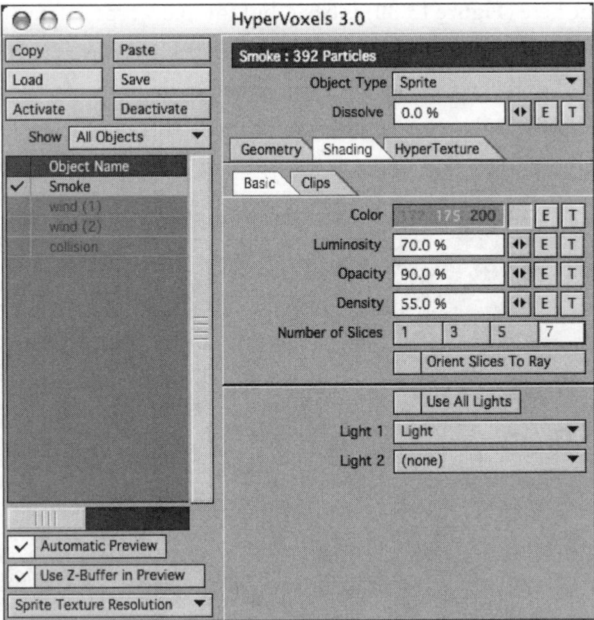

Figure 13.29 Tweak just a few sprite-surface settings and the particles start looking like smoke.

16. Click the HyperTexture tab and choose Turbulence from the Texture drop-down. This applies more variation to the HyperVoxel surfaces. You can experiment with other settings if you like. Set Texture Effect to Billowing and leave the other values at their defaults. Essentially, you're applying an animated texture, characterized by billowing turbulent noise, to the particle surfaces. The results are easier to see than to describe.
17. Make a preview in the VIPER window, and after a moment, you'll see your stream of smoky particles following the path wind.
18. Save your scene, and then experiment. Note that what you see in the VIPER window is not what your final particles really look like. They look much better if you press **F9** for a full frame render.

What you've done here (**Figure 13.30**) is basic, but for many types of particle animations, nothing more complex is necessary. With the power of LightWave's particles, in combination with HyperVoxel surfaces, added textures, and even gradients, the possibilities are endless. Endless how? Read on for another variation on these particles.

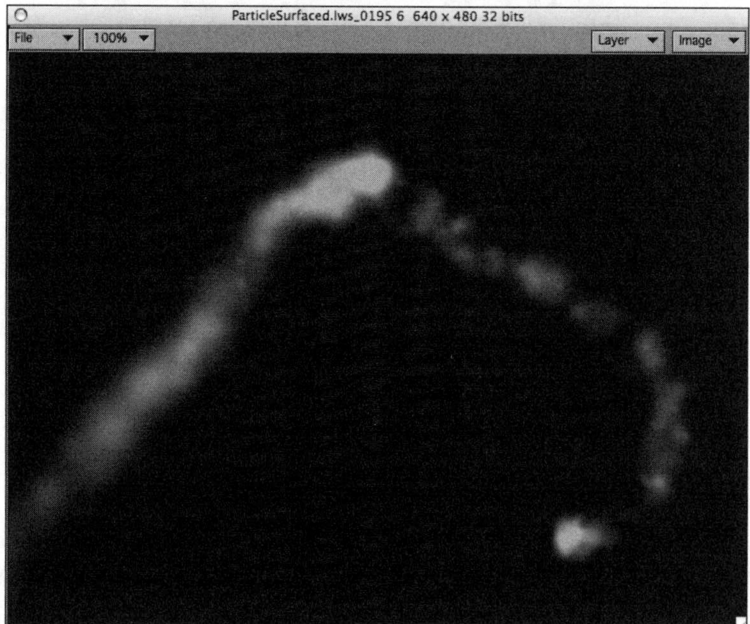

Figure 13.30 As you adjust particle-surface settings, you can press **F9** in Layout to render the scene and see how the particles look.

Note

You can speed up render times slightly by turning off the Volumetric Antialiasing option in the Volumetrics area of the Effects panel (press Ctrl+F6). If you're using Volume-based HyperVoxels, antialiasing will help create a cleaner final render. But for sprites, you can get away with this setting turned off.

Using Images on Particles

Yes, you read that heading correctly—images on particles. Although it sounds odd, it's actually a very handy feature for all sorts of animations—falling snow, falling leaves, bubbles—whatever!

Check this out.

Exercise 13.6 Using Images on Particles

1. With the same scene loaded from the previous exercise, open the Image Editor. Load the MapleLeaf.png image from the Chapter 13 folder of this book's DVD, as shown in **Figure 13.31**.

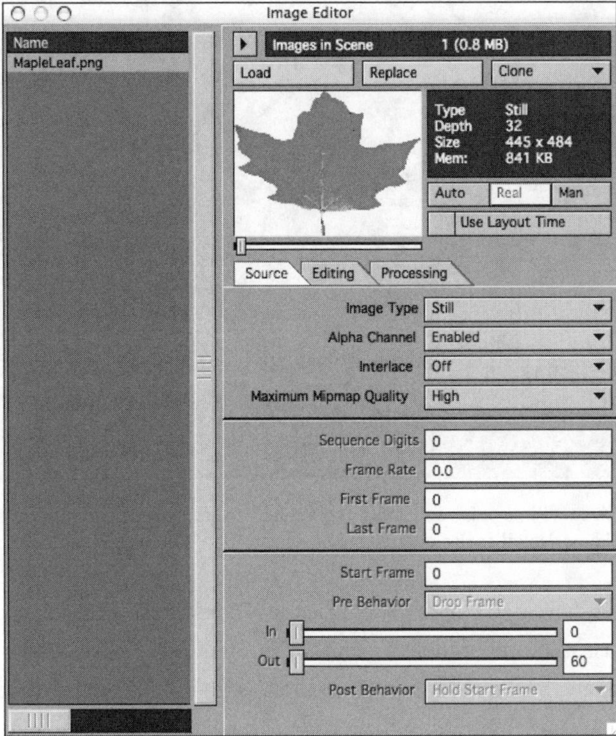

Figure 13.31 Loading a 32-bit image from the Image Editor can make your particle systems flow with pictures!

2. Back in the HyperVoxels panel, make sure you're still using Sprite for Object Type.
3. Next, click the panel's Shading tab, and then select the Clips tab that appears there.
4. Select the MapleLeaf image from the Add Clip drop-down. Watch what happens in Layout—you'll see the leaf image applied to the particles. They grossly overlap each other and probably are showing a white outline, but that's OK.

5. Change the Alpha setting to Embedded. Then, go back to the Geometry tab and set Particle Size to about 15mm and Size Variation to 50%; Stretch Direction should still be set to none. **Figure 13.32** shows Layout with the MapleLeaf image in place.

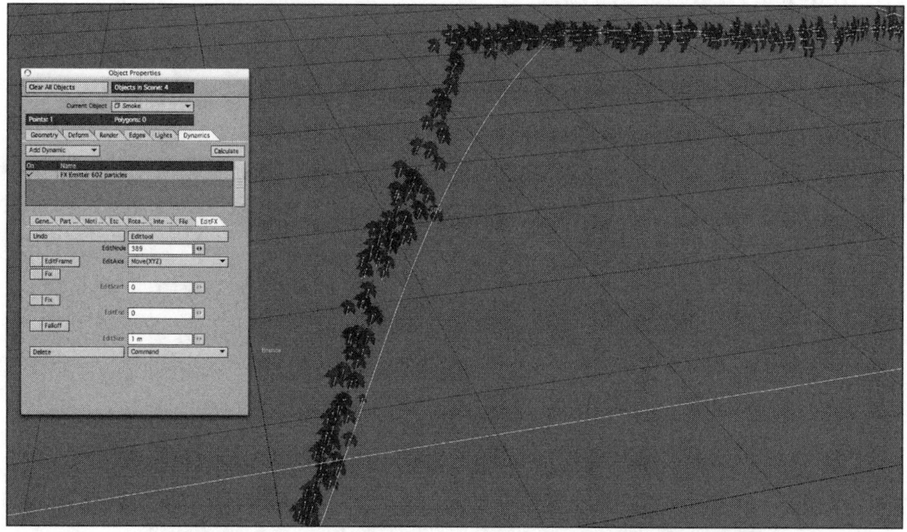

Figure 13.32 A small image is replicated and applied to every particle in the emitter using a HyperVoxel sprite and clips.

That's it! You now have a stream of floating leaves. HyperVoxel sprites with clips are quite useful. As we just saw, one of the reasons they're so useful is because you can take tiny images and animate them quickly based on particles. You can see them directly in Layout, so you know what's happening with their size and color, and they always face the camera.

Of course, you can adjust the motion of the particles, perhaps by adding another wind effector at the top of the path to make the particles spread out as they reach their end. You can also change the emitter to a large, long, flat shape to emit sprite clips such as coins, bubbles, puffs of smoke, and so on. Or how about multiple streams, each with an image of a letter? The examples here should get you started with your own particle animations. All you need to do is create a 32-bit image so that the Alpha channel is embedded. You can do this in Adobe Photoshop. Just load up the image you want, place it on a transparent background, and save.

Editing Particles

You can do a lot to particles within LightWave v9. As you've seen, you can push them, pull them, make them collide with other objects, and so on. They can look like foam, smoke, or leaves. But what happens when you have everything looking just as you like, and then some pesky particle, following the semi-random rules of particle motion, goes astray and gets in the way of your animation? You don't have to just live with it; you can edit your particles. Read on to learn how.

Exercise 13.7 Editing Particles

1. Load the Particle Image scene from the Chapter 13 Scenes folder on this book's DVD.
2. Go to a Perspective view and arrange the viewport so that you can see the majority of the particles.
3. Select the particle emitter named "smoke" and press **p** to open the Properties panel.
4. Click the Dynamics tab in the Properties panel and select the FX_Emitter listing. Click the Calculate button in the middle of the panel.
5. After the calculation is complete, drag the timeline slider, and you'll see the particles moving. There's one or two that are sort of hanging out of the stream, so let's remove them.
6. To fix these crazy particles, click the EditFX tab in the FX_Emitter properties.
7. Click the Edit tool, and then select one of the wayward particles directly in Layout, as shown in **Figure 13.33**. When the particle is selected, you'll see a line appear—that's its motion path, as shown in Figure 13.33. You'll also see a number, which is its ID.

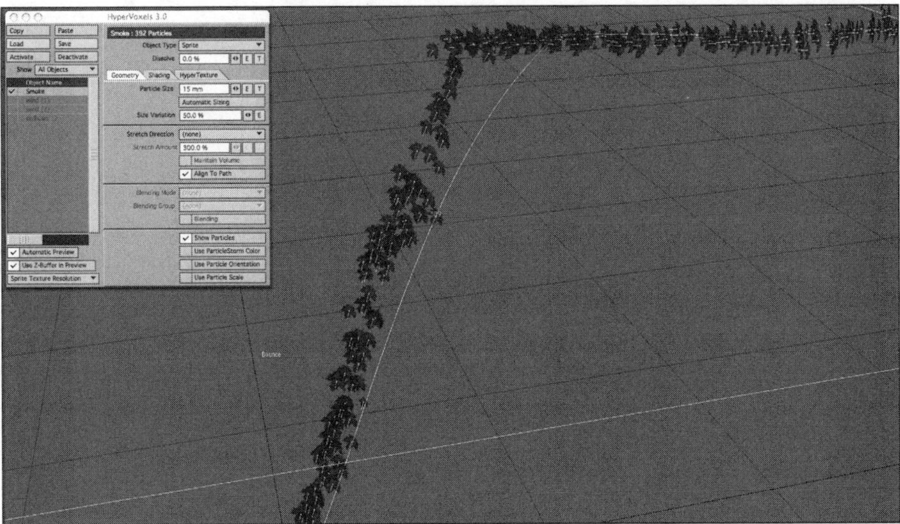

Figure 13.33 Wth the Edit tool in the FX_Emitter properties, you can isolate any particle.

8. When the particle is selected, click the delete button in the FX_Emitter properties and the selected particle will be deleted. You can also just reposition the particle using the Move tool (press **t**).
9. Repeat steps 7 and 8 as needed to remove (or move) any other stray particles in the stream.

Cloning a particle, copying its motion path, and rotating its path are just some of the other things you can do on the EditFX tab.

The Next Step

This chapter introduced you to some of the coolest features in LightWave v9's arsenal. The information in these exercises can easily be applied to projects of your own and ones for your client. You'll find that particles are so fun to use, you'll be looking for projects to use them in. Be careful, though—don't let your client know how easy it is! Go online and visit www.3dgarage.com, and you'll find additional particle tutorial videos. For now, turn the page and learn about more dynamic effects you can create in LightWave v9 beyond particles.

Chapter 14

Dynamics in Motion

In the previous chapter, you were introduced to LightWave v9's particles. This chapter will take you even further by showing how to create various dynamic effects for creative animations. These dynamic effects, which are new in LightWave v9, let you make animations in which objects collide realistically and influence each other's motion in a way that obeys natural laws such as gravity, momentum, and shock absorption. Tools like these will help take your animations to the next level. You will work through various projects so that you can quickly and easily learn how to apply these powerful tools to just about any animation. In this chapter, you'll learn about the following:

- The dynamics-related panels and tools
- Hard-body dynamics, governing solid, rigid objects
- Soft-body dynamics, governing objects that are yielding but resilient
- How to make objects collide and react

Dynamics in LightWave

The word *dynamic* is an adjective that relates to energy or to objects in motion. What puts these objects in motion in LightWave are clever commands that you control. To use any of the dynamics in LightWave, you just need to think about what you want an object to do.

Let's say you have created a fun character with a big, uh, animator's belly. As your character walks, you want his girth to shake a bit. Although you could use bones with a weight map and apply bone dynamics, a simpler and more effective method is to apply a "soft" dynamic to the jelly belly. Or perhaps you're an avid bowler (or aspire to be). Instead of wearing those silly shoes to go bowling, just create some 3D bowling balls and tenpins and use hard dynamics and collisions to send the pins flying—without having to manually keyframe the ball's contact with each pin in its path or each struck pin's contact with other pins around it, and so on. LightWave motion dynamics lets you place objects in your scene, tell them how to move and interact with other objects, and then turn them loose to interact with each other—without manually keyframing all of their collisions and encounters. Once you've learned all the necessary buttons and processes, LightWave dynamics can make your scenes come to life. Now, let's take a quick tour of the dynamics-related panels to familiarize yourself with them.

Understanding Dynamic Controls

Dynamics in LightWave are easy to set up after you understand how the panels work and what the controls mean. **Figure 14.1** shows the SoftFX dynamics panel. This panel is accessed through the Dynamics tab within the Object Properties panel, just as Particle effect controls were in the previous chapter. You can see from the image that there are six tabbed areas within the dynamic controls.

The number of tabbed areas varies depending on which dynamic you apply. As the tutorials progress in this chapter, you'll see how the different areas are used.

The types of dynamics you can apply to objects are as follows:

- Cloth
- Soft
- Hard
- Emitter (for particles)
- Wind
- Collision
- Gravity

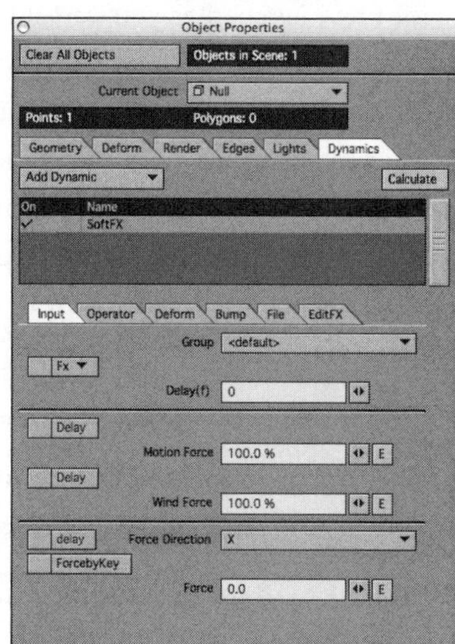

Figure 14.1 When a dynamic is applied, the controls are found within the Object Properties panel.

Each of these dynamic types has a similar set of commands and controls. When you apply a dynamic to an object, you need to think about your process, just as you do when modeling or animating. Think about where you are going with the animation and what you want to do with it. Once you understand that, you can choose the appropriate dynamic for your object and know what tabbed area to access within the controls.

Hard-Body Dynamics

Hard-body dynamics have been around for a while, but few ordinary mortals have been able to take advantage of them. Complex scripting requirements and heavy calculations often made this top-notch feature available only to a few. Now, thanks to some clever programmers at NewTek, this feature is available interactively in LightWave v9.

Hard-body dynamics applies to objects that behave as rigid solids. When hard bodies collide, they retain their shapes without compressing or yielding. Think of marbles, billiard balls, or anvils. Hard-body dynamics control how these objects behave when they run into each other, based on properties such as gravity, weight, and density.

Exercise 14.1 Creating Hard-Body Dynamics

This tutorial will take a few basic objects and show you how to make them interact. From there, you'll change variables to see the how the dynamic toolsets work.

1. Open LightWave Layout.
2. Load the Solids model from the Chapter 14 folder of this book's DVD (**Figure 14.2**). This model has just one layer, containing a few geometric shapes set up as an "obstacle course." Also, load the Ball model from the DVD's Chapter 14 folder. You'll use dynamics to animate the ball object as it rolls around, and interacts with, the Solids model's shapes.

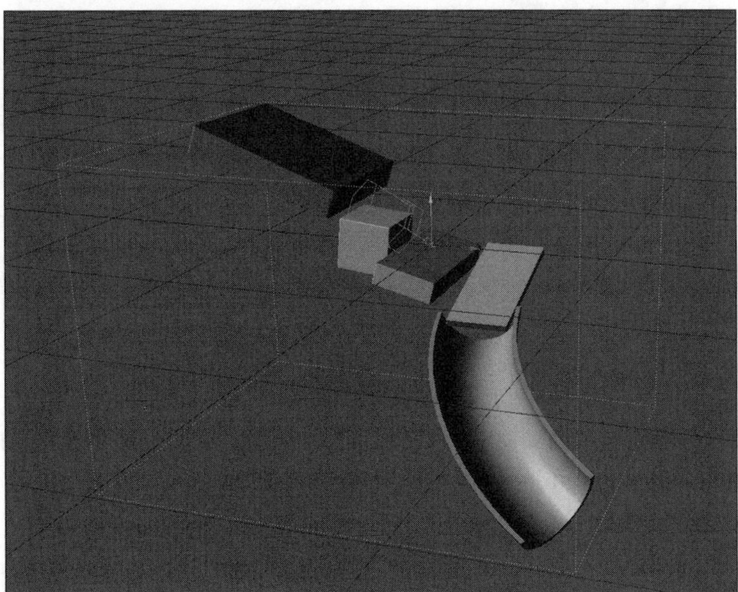

Figure 14.2 The Solids model loaded, ready for some dynamic action. Exciting, isn't it?

3. Select the ball and move it up on the Y-axis so that it's positioned above the top of the highest box. Create a keyframe at 0 to lock it in place, as in **Figure 14.3**.

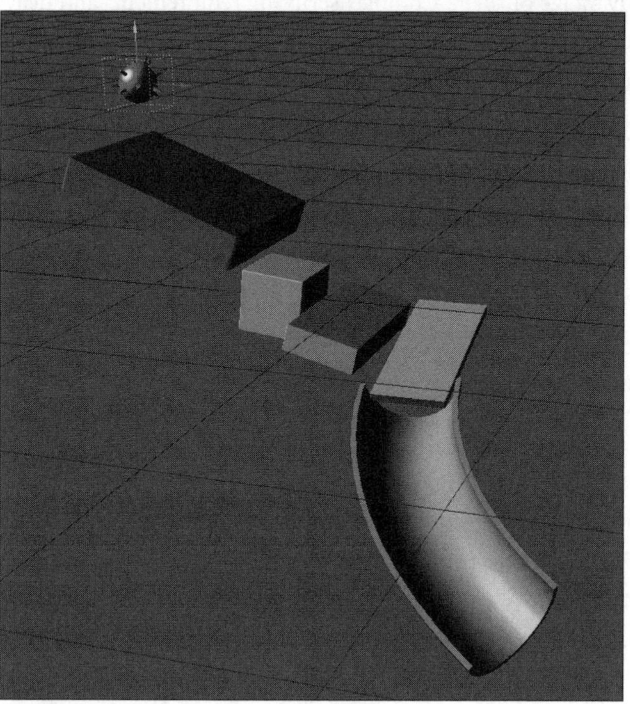

Figure 14.3 Position the ball at the top of the slide.

Note

If either the light or camera icon gets in the way of working, simply move it out of view. This project is a lesson in dynamics and you won't be lighting or rendering.

4. With the ball selected, press **p** to open the Object Properties panel. Although this tutorial is simple, you'll see how cool the dynamic effects can be.
5. Click the panel's Dynamics tab, and select Hard from the Add Dynamic drop-down to apply a HardFX dynamic to the ball object. Position your view similar to **Figure 14.4** so you can see the slide, ball, and Properties panel. Select the HardFX listing to see its controls.
6. Now that you've come this far, it's a good idea to save the scene. Save this scene as **SolidsSetup** and then save it again as **SolidsWorking**, or something similar. The idea behind this is that at any point, you can call up the setup scene and start again.

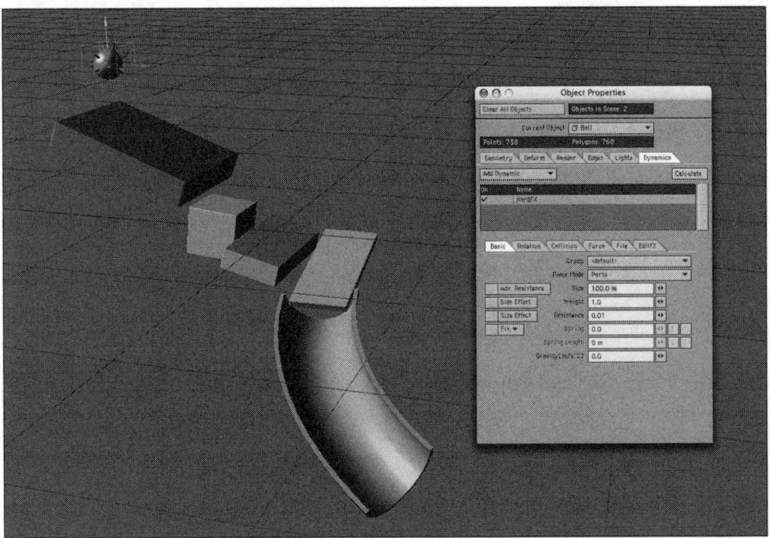

Figure 14.4 Add a hard dynamic to the ball and position the view to see everything.

Note

Don't forget that you can also press Shift+s to save incremental versions of your scenes.

7. In the Object Properties panel, choose the Solids object and add a collision dynamic to it from the drop-down list, as in **Figure 14.5**.

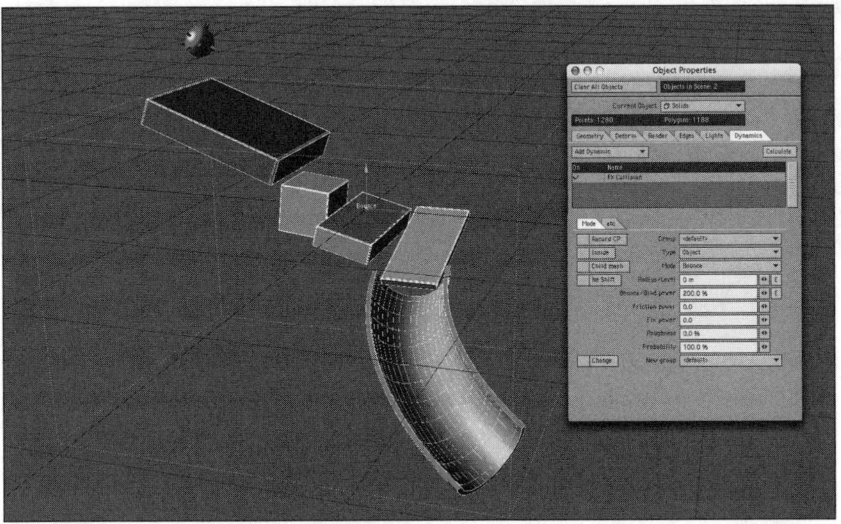

Figure 14.5 Use the Object Properties panel to add a collision dynamic to the slide object.

8. If you click the Calculate button on the Dynamics tab, nothing happens. You've not yet given the dynamics any properties. So, go back to the ball object and select the HardFX listing to access its controls. You only need to click it once for the controls to appear on the Dynamics tab.
9. The first thing you want to do is give the ball some gravity. In the Basic tab of the HardFX controls, set Gravity to –9.8. It's the last setting in the drop-down, and it corresponds to the acceleration due to gravity on Earth, 9.8 meters/second ^{2}. (The negative value reflects the fact that gravity pulls downward, along the negative Y-axis.)
10. Set the last frame of the animation to 400.
11. Click the Calculate button on the Object Properties panel's Dynamics tab. Whoa! The ball falls and bounces down the solid object (**Figure 14.6**)!

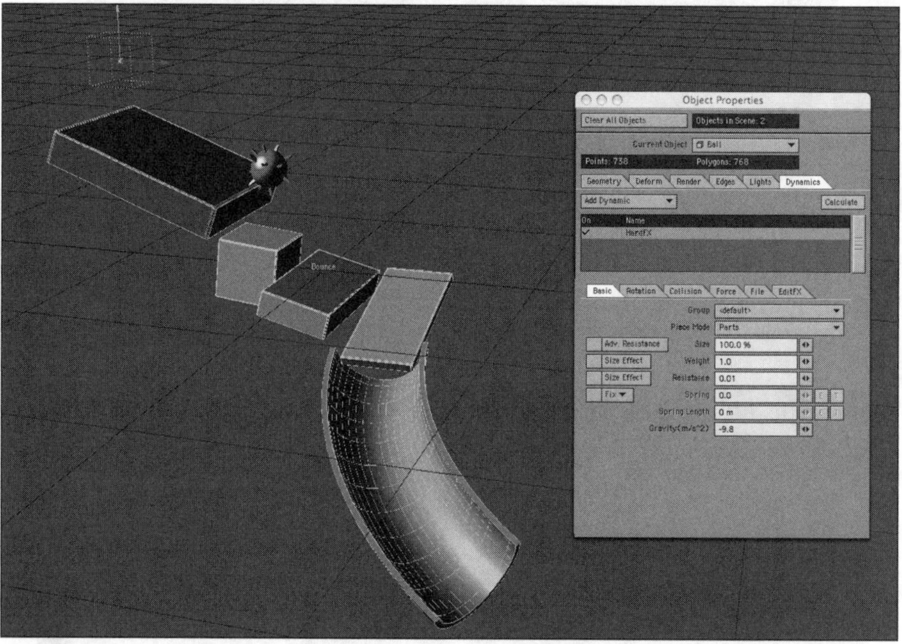

Figure 14.6 With two dynamics applied, your animation starts to have interaction.

Believe it or not, that's all there is to it! You've just created hard-body dynamics. However, there are many more controls to play with, so save the scene and move on to experiment a little.

You might have noticed that the ball doesn't quite fall down through all of the obstacles. A few more adjustments are in order.

12. Back in the Object Properties panel, select the FX Collision listing for the Solids object. Then, set the Bounce/Bind power to 40% (**Figure 14.7**). The default 200% is way too "bouncy," which is why this ball fell, then bounced off into the air.
13. Click the Calculate button again, and the ball now slides down the objects better. But it's still not quite right, is it?
14. Select the Ball object in the Object Properties panel, then select the HardFX listing.
15. Increase the value of the Weight setting to 0.2. This will make the ball heavier. If you calculate again, the ball slides much better. But it *slides*. It should roll, shouldn't it? You can change this too.
16. On the Rotation tab, change the Impact Effect from Force to Roll (**Figure 14.8**).
17. Click the Collision tab and change the Collision by option from Node to Sphere.

    The Node setting tells LightWave to use every point within the object to calculate collision dynamics. That can be significant for complex models and interactions, but in a simple scene like this, containing simple geometric objects, the Node setting simply slows down your animation with excess calculation. Once you've set the Collision by option to Sphere, click the Calculate button.

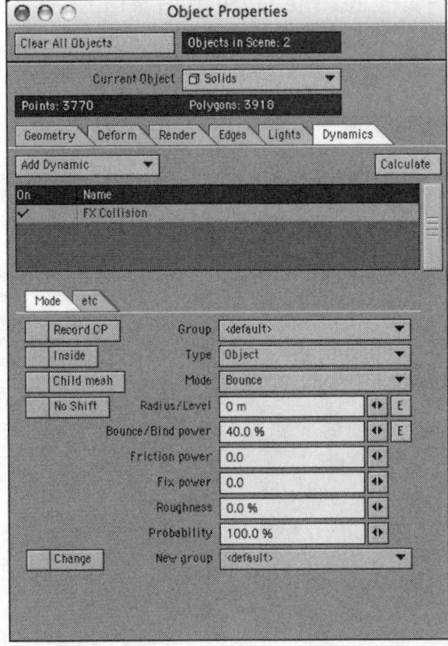

Figure 14.7 Reduce the ball object's Bounce/Bind Power setting to 40% from the default 200% to stop it careening out of the scene.

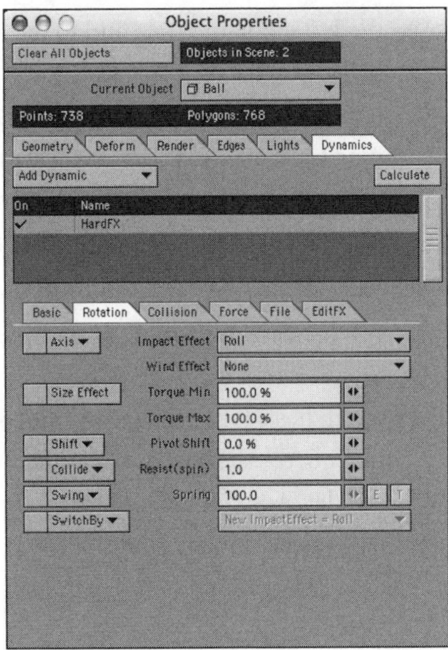

Figure 14.8 Adding weight to the ball and changing the Impact Effect to Roll will change how the ball behaves.

18. Once the calculation is finished, click the play button at the bottom of the interface and you'll see the ball roll smoothly down the solid objects (**Figure 14.9**).

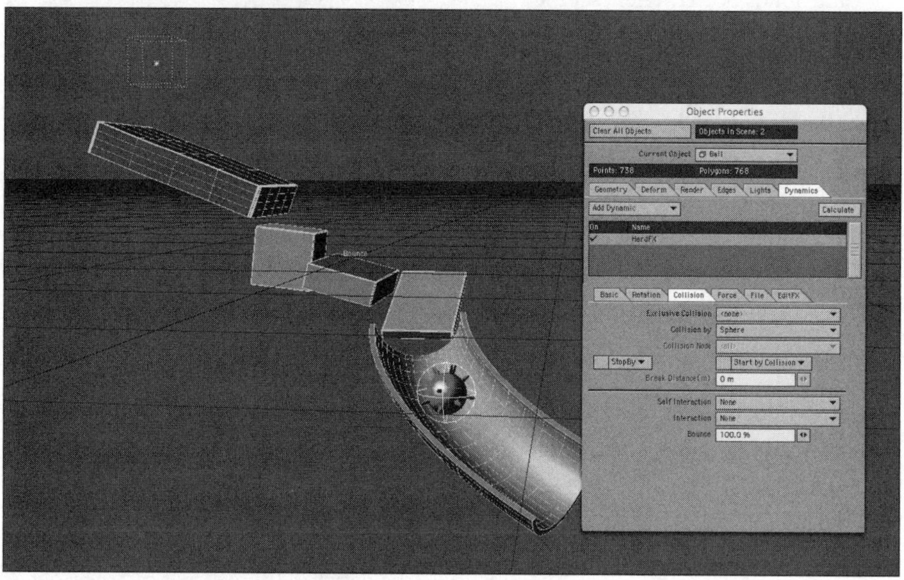

Figure 14.9 Adjusting the Collision by option lets your ball roll down the obstacles.

19. Click the Rotation tab, and to the left of the Impact Effect setting, you can tell the ball to roll on a specific axis only. Click the Axis drop-down list and you can see it's set to Free, but you can change this to the Y-axis (which might apply to a spinning top), or X-axis (for a wheel or yo-yo), and other variations. The Free setting is best for a rolling ball, so you don't need to change anything here, but it's a good idea to familiarize yourself with this important control.

20. You can also change some of the other values, such as Wind Effect and Torque. If you increase the Torque Max value to 300%, for example, the ball will roll faster than it is moving. A good example of this is a children's ball thrown into water, which has a lot of torque coming out of the child's hand. It spins faster than it is moving (or sliding) on the water. Another example is a bowling ball thrown down an alley. Additionally, you can give the ball a Resist (Spin) setting to have it hold back on its spin amount.

- You can see that with just a few changes to the settings, you can make objects interact with each other. However, you might have noticed that there are more controls for collision effects than you've used here. **Figure 14.10** shows these controls, which appear on the Dynamics tab of the Object Properties panel. The following list provides a rundown of its controls and settings.

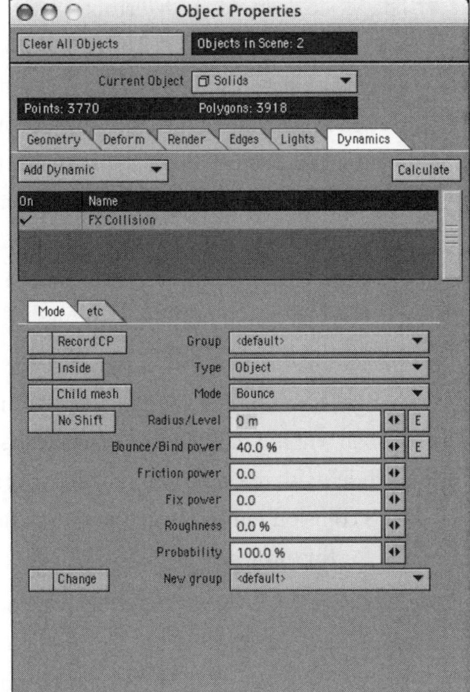

Figure 14.10 The collision controls are located mainly on the Mode tab, part of the Dynamics tab of the Object Properties panel.

- Setting a group through the Group drop-down is useful for times when you are working with larger scenes and multiple objects. For instance, let's say you have three slides going in this scene. You could create a group so that the collision and hard-dynamic objects are tied together and don't react to other objects with dynamics applied. It's a way of separating and isolating dynamics, while maintaining control.
- The Type drop-down specifies the surface shape the selected object "shows" to objects that collide with it, and that is used to calculate the results of that collision, such as the angle at which a given object will ricochet away from its surface. The Object setting uses all the points on an object's surface to calculate collision results; it provides the most realistic dynamics but requires a lot of processing power and rendering time. The Sphere, Box, and Plane settings calculate collisions as if the selected object, no matter how complex in shape, were one of those simpler objects. These options result in collisions that are not as precise, but they suffice in many instances, often appear no different, and can save a lot of rendering time. The Object-Subdiv type setting lets you apply different collision properties to surface subpatches within a single object.

- The Mode drop-down determines how objects will react to the selected object when they collide with it. The default Bounce setting causes objects that strike the selected object to, well, bounce off it. Other options include Stick, Erase, Event, Scatter, and Attract. Stick and Attract have the effects you'd expect on colliding objects. Erase causes objects that strike the selected object to disappear from the scene. The Event setting causes the selected object to act as if it has been struck by another object when a noncollision dynamic events occur, such as the activation of a wind effector. The Scatter option causes colliding objects to bounce off the selected object in a random fashion.
- The Radius/Level setting can change the collision position. For example, if you change this value from 0m to 400mm and then click the Calculate button again, the ball will not fall and drop down the slide like it did before. Instead, it will "collide" with the slide before it actually touches it, because you've made the ball's collision radius larger than its actual physical radius. Keep this setting at 0 for this project.
- The Bounce/Bind Power selector controls the strength of the collision behavior specified in the Mode drop-down—how bouncy a Bounce Mode setting is, how sticky a Stick setting is, and so on. Use the mini-slider or type in a percentage value to adjust this setting.

Note

When setting a Radius/Level or Bounce/Bind Power, you can click the E buttons to the right of the values to change these settings over time. Make your ball bounce hard, and then suddenly stick.

- The Friction Power control, also adjusted via the mini-slider or by typing a number into its requester, determines the amount of resistance the selected object's surface exerts on other objects as they roll or drag across it. Increasing Friction Power for the slide to 20.0 rather than 0, for instance, causes the ball to move down the slide at a slower rate because of the extra friction. You can play with this value to see how the dynamics react, but for this project keep the setting at 0.
- You can increase the Fix Power and Roughness to change how the collision reacts throughout the animation. Let's say you increase Fix Power to 20. The ball will not bounce as much on the collision. It will not slow down, but rather stay attached to the collision object more throughout the calculation. Roughness, on the other hand, will make the ball bounce around, sort of like rough terrain.

Set the value to say, 40%, and you'll see the ball bounce down the slide. Change these values to add variations to see how the ball movement changes as it moves down the slide.

- Finally, you can set the Probability, telling LightWave the percentage of probability that the collision should happen. Right now, it's set to 100%, meaning there's a 100% probability of a collision. Lower this value, calculate again, and see the difference.

Within the HardFX controls, which are located on the Dynamics tab found in the Object Properties panel, click the Collision tab and then click the Start By Collision drop-down selector. Choose Collision in the Start By drop-down, and the ball's dynamic effects will remain turned off until the ball collides with another object. Triggering the effect using this collision-detection method saves processing time. Conversely, you can set a StopBy collision event in the same way as the Start By. Simply click the Stop by drop-down selector and choose Stop by Event. The event would be the collision. In the previous exercise, turning on the Start By Collision option would yield a ball that just sits in the air, that doesn't fall, and that doesn't roll. If something were to hit it, like a 3D hand or baseball bat, this collision would start the effects.

As you can see, setting up hard-body dynamics is not too complicated. You need to just slow down and think about the process. Think about what you're going for, and it'll come together. In this previous exercise, you had a ball, which you told LightWave was a "hard" object. If you calculated after setting this, you might see an error. That's because LightWave doesn't have anything to work with, and you need to set something for this object to interact with. So, you told the ball to collide with the Solids object. The Solids object had a "collision" applied.

So how about going a step further? The next exercise will show you how to shatter glass in 3D.

Exercise 14.2 Modeling for Dynamics

This exercise will show you how you can blow apart a window. The technique can be used for anything, from a creature crashing through a brick wall to a bowling ball knocking down a set of pins. The project you'll do here will show you a quick technique for creating a window in Modeler, then how to use dynamics in Layout to crash an object through it, essentially shattering the window—another hard-body dynamic effect.

1. Open Modeler and select the Box tool from the Create tab. Create a Box in the bottom-left (Back) view, about 10m by 5m, with multiple segments. You can do

this by pressing **n** to open the Numeric panel, then setting the number of segments. Create about 24 segments or so for the X and 14 for the Y. This doesn't have to be exactly like it is here; just make sure your box has many segments so that it can be broken apart. **Figure 14.11** shows the model.

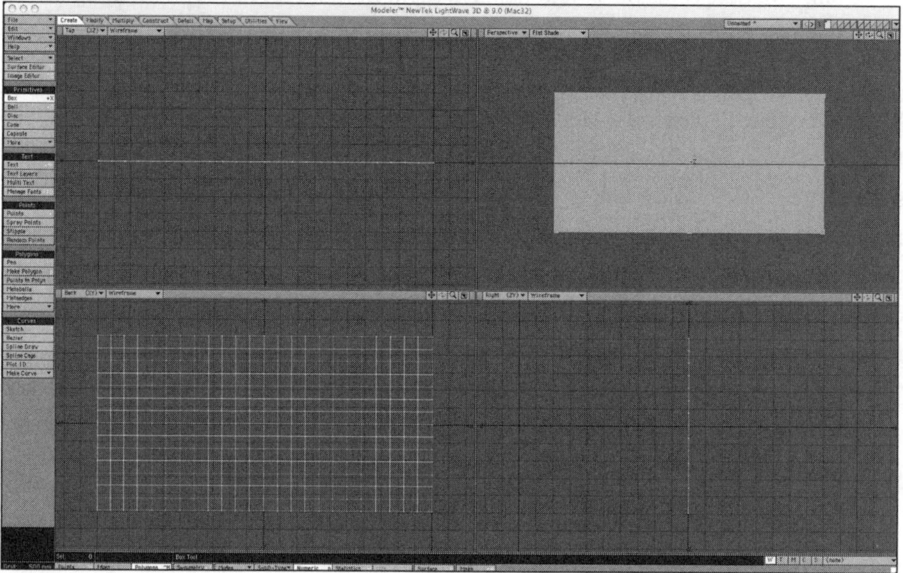

Figure 14.11 Create a box in Modeler that has multiple segments along its X- and Y-axes.

2. If you've created your flat box and can't see it in the Perspective view, press **f** to flip its polygons.
3. Press Shift+j to activate the Jitter tool (also found on the Modify tab).
4. In the Jitter panel that appears (**Figure 14.12**), enter 400mm for both the X and Y values. Leave the Z-axis setting at 0. You're not creating any depth on the Z, as you're creating just a flat window.

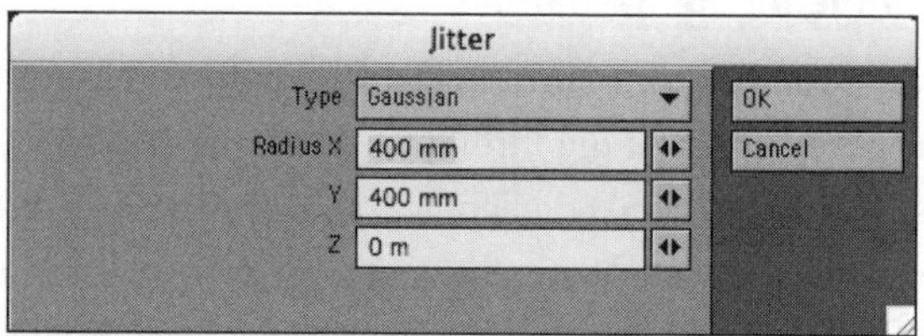

Figure 14.12 Use the Jitter tool to shake up the shape of the polygons.

5. Switch to Points selection mode at the bottom of the interface.

6. Now, carefully select the very bottom-left point of the box, and holding the Shift key, select the point immediately above it, as shown in **Figure 14.13**.

   You're selecting two points sequentially to tell Modeler which way you want your selection to go, for the next step.

7. So, from the Select drop-down at the top left of the interface, choose Select Loop, as shown in **Figure 14.14**.

8. Once you choose Select Loop, LightWave Modeler continues selecting points for you around the entire box, as shown in **Figure 14.15**.

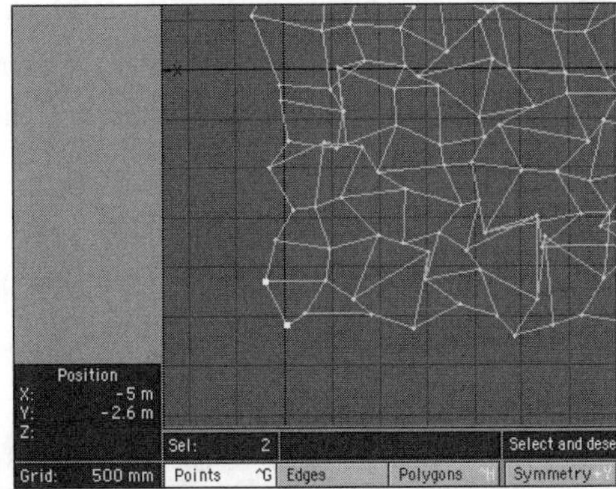

Figure 14.13 Select in order, the bottom-left corner point and the point just above it.

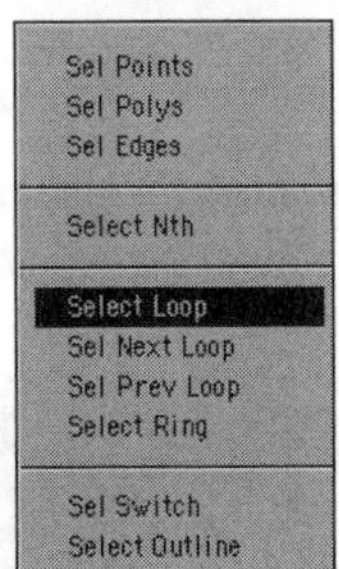

Figure 14.14 Choose Select Loop to automatically continue the selection of points.

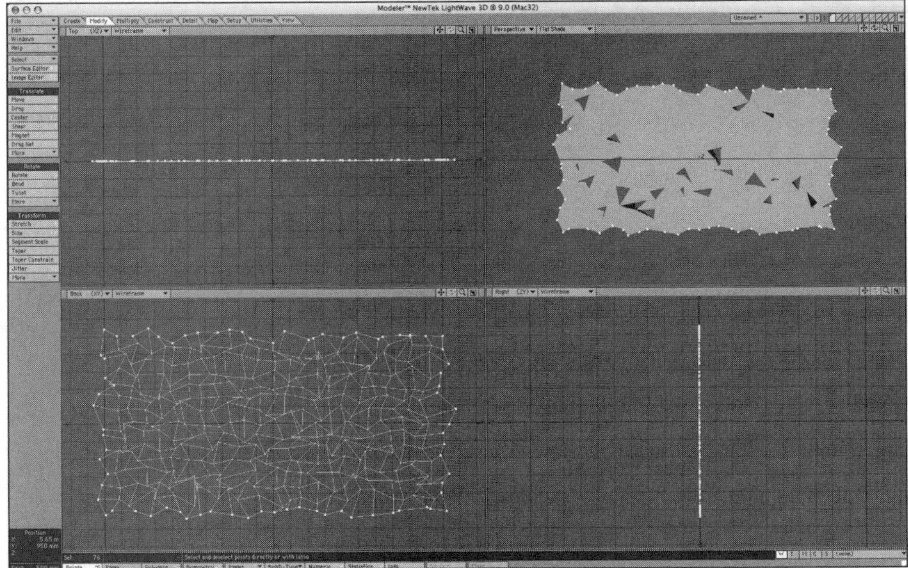

Figure 14.15 Using Select Loop is an easy way to select the points around the entire box.

9. With the entire outer edge of points selected, click the Modify tab, and at the bottom left under the Transform category, click the More drop-down button and then choose Quantize, as shown in **Figure 14.16**.

10. In the Quantize dialog box, leave all axis settings at 500mm, as shown in **Figure 14.17**. You can simply enter **.5** and press the tab key to get a 500mm setting.

BGConform
Pole Evenly Tool
Pole Tool
Spline Guide
Scale Morph
Replicate...
Center Scale
Center Stretch
Smooth... +M
Quantize...
Spherize
Squarize

Figure 14.16 Select Quantize on the Modify tab.

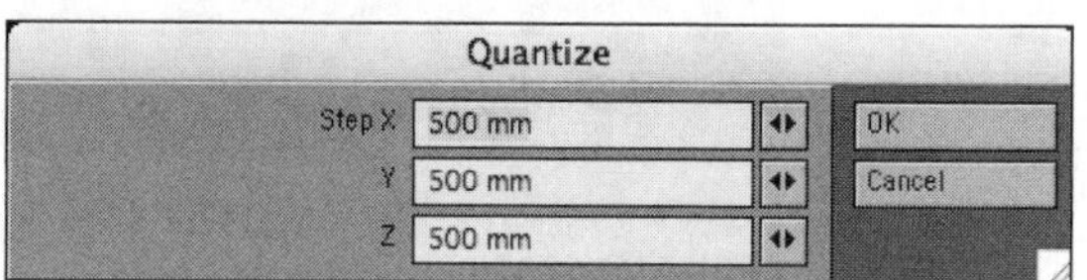

Figure 14.17 Set the Quantize value to 500mm.

11. Click OK to apply the Quantize values, and as you can see from **Figure 14.18**, the selected points even out, except for a few.

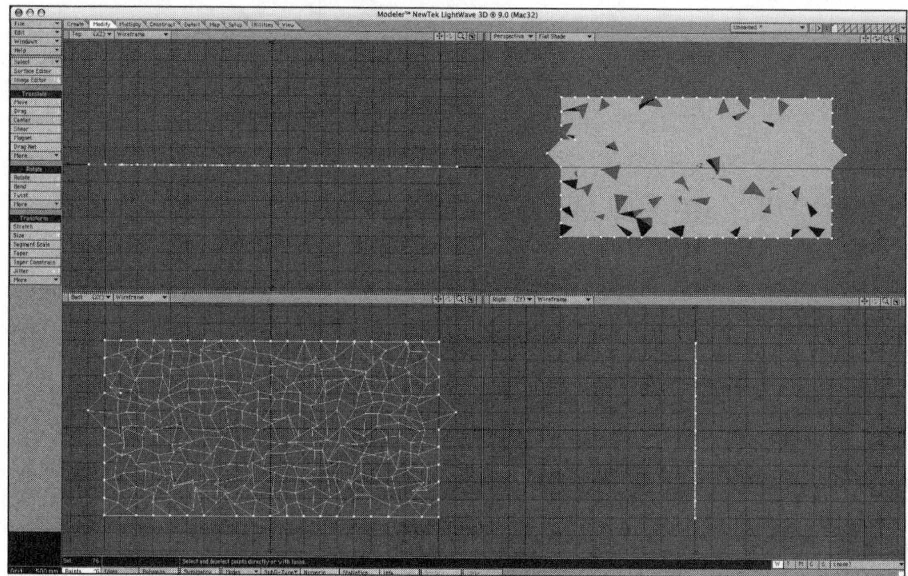

Figure 14.18 Using the Quantize tool, you can even out the selected points.

12. Press Ctrl+t to activate the Drag tool, and then drag the few points that are sticking out of the perimeter back into line with the other points.

13. Save your model as **GlassWindow** or something similar. You're not quite finished.

Note

There's another way you could have created this model to this point. After you had created the segmented box, you could have selected all of the polygons of the model except for those that make up the outer edge. Then, apply the Jitter tool. Only those selected polygons would have Jitter applied, leaving the outer edge nice and even. The reason this exercise showed you another method was simply a way to have you work with a few more of Modeler's tools. So, now you know. The choice is yours for future projects.

14. Switch to Polygons selection mode, and then press **w** to open the Statistics panel. Look to the 4 Vertices listing. Click the plus mark to its left, and all the polygons with more than four vertices will become highlighted, as in **Figure 14.19**.

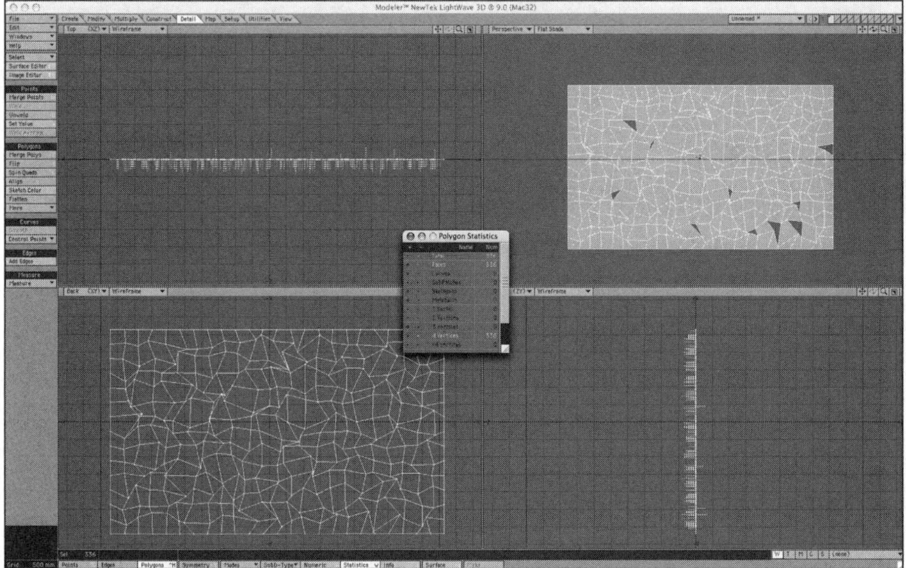

Figure 14.19 Use the Statistics panel to select polygons with more than four vertices.

15. Taking a look at your selection, it pretty much seems that all the polygons have more than four vertices. That's fine, and while you're not going to subpatch these polys, go ahead and press Shift+t to *triple* them—which is LightWave-speak for converting a selected group of polygons into triangles. These triangles will become "shards" of glass in the shattered-window animation.

16. After you've tripled the polygons, click the Align button on the Detail tab. You might get a message saying that 20 polygons have been flipped. The Align tool looks at all the polygons, sees that the majority of them are facing in one direction, and flips the few other polygons that are facing the other direction (**Figure 14.20**).

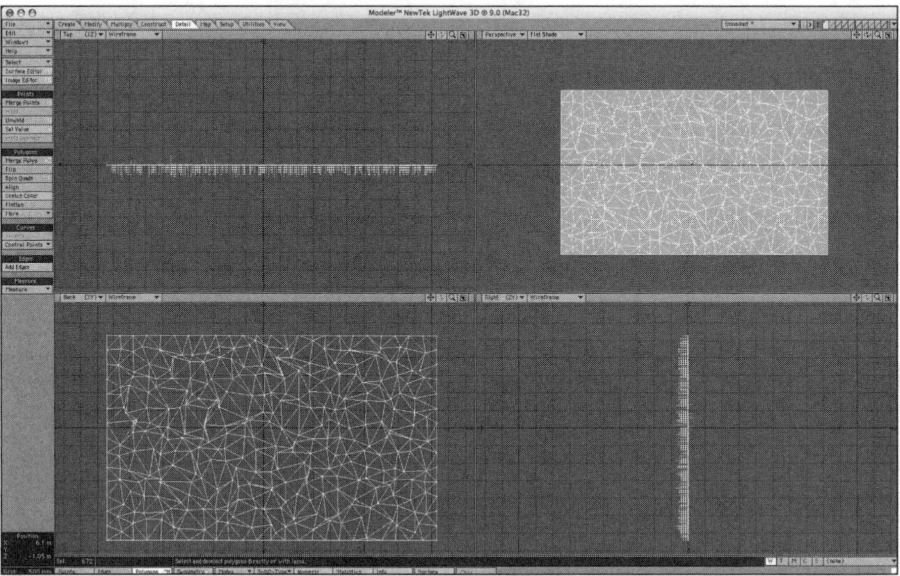

Figure 14.20 Triple the polygons to break them up more, and use the Align tool to make them all face the same direction.

17. We have one last thing to do, and this is probably the most important step. On the Detail tab, select Unweld. The reason this step is important is because in order to have another object break apart this glass window, the multiple polygons you just created can't be attached to each other. **Figure 14.21** shows the tool.

    The adjacent polygons of your model share common points and side segments; in LightWave lingo, these polygons are *welded* together. The Unweld command converts each selected polygon into a discrete, self-contained

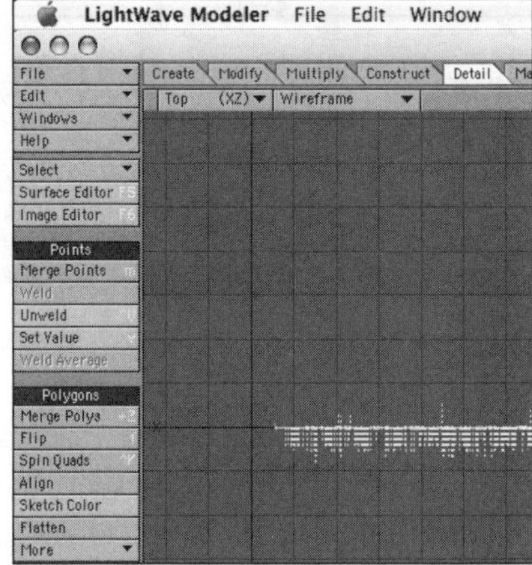

Figure 14.21 Use the Unweld command to disconnect all the polygons.

object with sides and vertices all its own. Applying the Unweld command to the window surface will allow the dynamics engine to shatter the window by animating each triangular segment as an independent "shard." If you did not unweld the points, the dynamics engine could only move or push the entire window object, even though it consisted of multiple segments.

Note

Even though unwelding separates each segment, the window is still one solid object. And, without using dynamics to break up the object, moving the object in Layout will still move the entire object, not the segments.

18. After you've unwelded the points, save the object. That's it! Your window is created.

If you want, select various polygons and apply different surface names to them. Select a few polygons, for example, press **q**, and then give those panes of glass a specific name and color. Deselect, then select some other panes, surface, color, and so on. The Glass object in the Chapter 14 folder of this book's DVD has this already done for you.

Exercise 14.3 Shattering Glass

This next exercise will shatter the glass window object built in the previous exercise. It is similar to the earlier hard-body exercise, but with a few differences in settings.

1. Load the GlassWindow_Setup scene from this book's DVD. This is a glass window, much like the one created in Exercise 14.2, with its surface polygons unwelded. The main difference between this model and the window created in the previous exercise is that it contains a white-to-blue background, which won't appear until you render your scene.

The dynamic collisions that will shatter the window object in this exercise require the window object's polygons to be unwelded—converted to discrete, self-contained polygons that share no points or segments. Recall that we used the Unweld command in Exercise 14.2 to separate the window's surface polygons into "shards" that can be animated independently.

2. Set the scene's final frame number to 200, using the number field at the bottom right of the timeline, and then select Collision from the Dynamic Obj drop-down on Layout's Item tab (**Figure 14.22**).

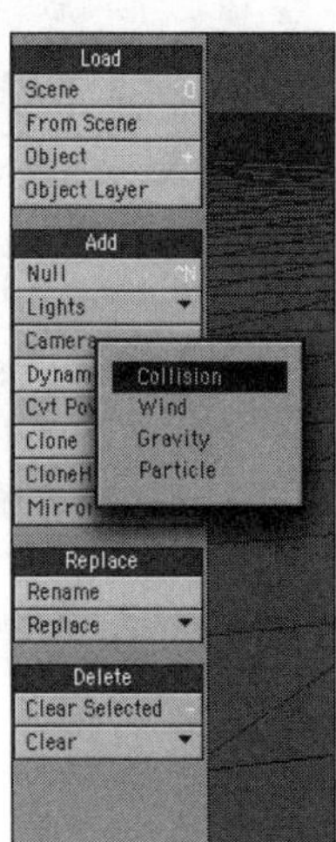

Figure 14.22 Add a dynamic object straight into Layout from the Items tab.

How is this different from the collision you added in Exercise 14.1? In that exercise, you added an object (named Solids) and told LightWave to make it a collision object. In this exercise, you're creating a collision effector, which we'll use to blow apart the GlassWindow object. Instead of building another object, you can just apply a dynamic effect directly. You can then even add a HyperVoxel explosion of particles to the effector to enhance the effect.

3. When you add the collision effector, a panel will appear, inviting you to name the collision. This will be the only collision in scene, so just click OK to keep the default name, bounce. (This name is applied because the default collision mode option is Bounce.) The FX_Collision panel will appear, and you'll see a wireframe sphere appear in the scene, representing the collision effector (**Figure 14.23**).

   Take a look at the FX_Collision control panel, and you'll notice the same controls that appeared on the Object Properties panel's Dynamics tab throughout Exercise 14.1. LightWave often provides multiple locations for its controls.

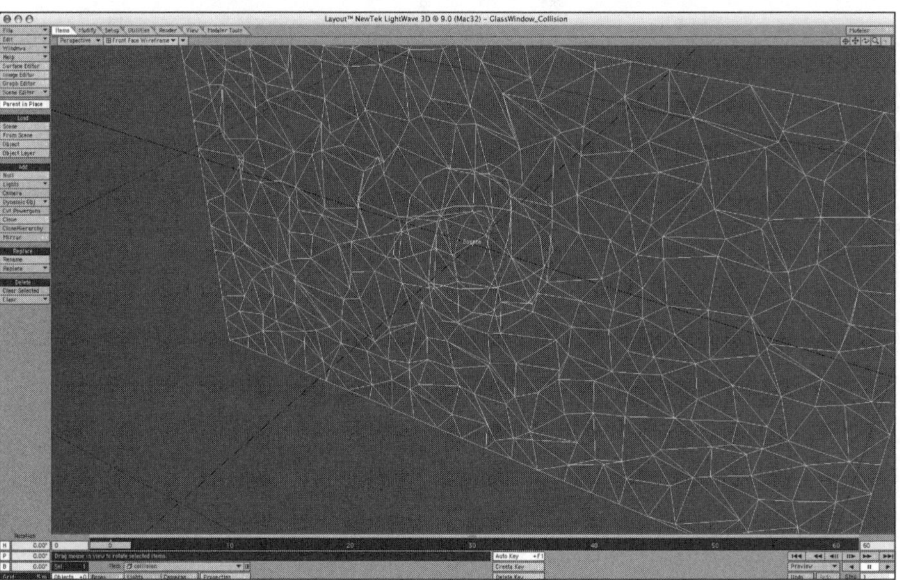

Figure 14.23 Adding a dynamic collision to Layout is represented by a wireframe ball.

4. In the FX_Collision panel, increase the Radius/Level value to 2m, as in **Figure 14.24**.
5. Click the Layout window and press **t** to activate the Move tool. Drag the collision object along the negative Z-axis until its entire volume is behind the GlassWindow object, and then create a keyframe at frame 0 to lock it in place.
6. Move the frame slider to frame 60, and then reposition the collision object along the positive Z-axis, until it is entirely in front of the GlassWindow object, and create a keyframe to lock it in place. **Figure 14.25** shows frame 60 and the motion path the collision object follows between frames 0 and 60.

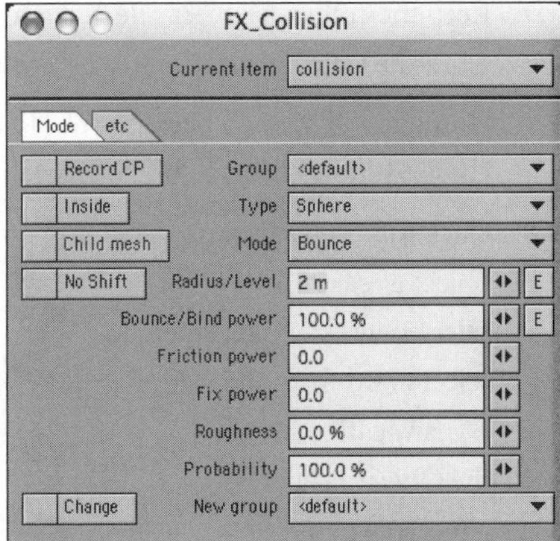

Figure 14.24 Increase the collision dynamic from the FX_Collision control panel.

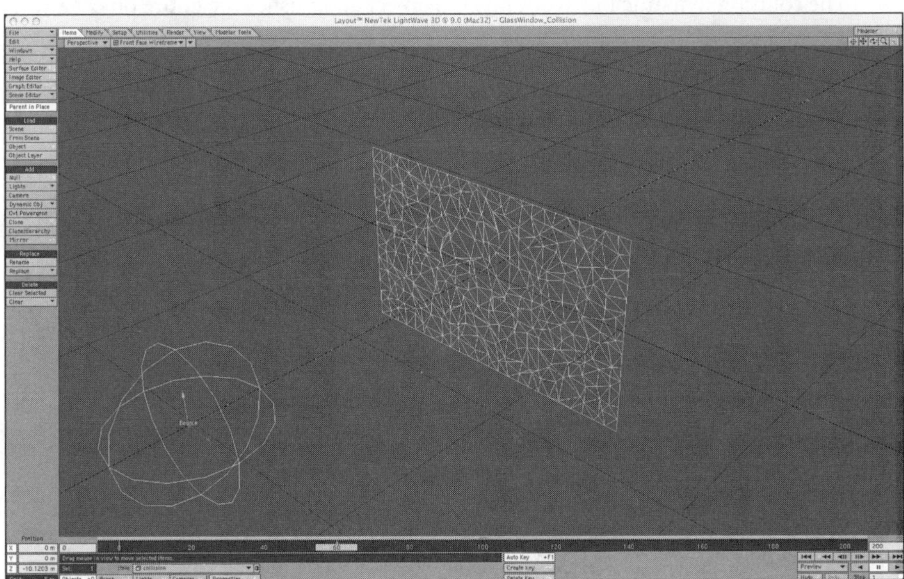

Figure 14.25 A small animation is created with the collision dynamic.

7. Keep the collision object selected and press **p** to open the Object Properties panel. Click the Calculate button on its Dynamics tab.

   Nothing will happen because you do not have anything to calculate. For the GlassWindow object to break apart, you must apply a hard dynamic to it.

8. Click the GlassWindow object to select it (if it isn't selected already), and then select Hard from the Add Dynamic drop-down on the Object Properties panel's Dynamics tab (**Figure 14.26**).

Figure 14.26 Add a hard dynamic to the collision effector.

9. Select the HardFX listing to access the controls, and you'll see that Parts is selected in the Piece Mode drop-down. Change this to 1Piece and click the Calculate button. The collision dynamic in Layout hits the object and pushes the entire object away. This control is important to how your object breaks apart.

10. Change the Piece Mode setting back to Parts and click Calculate. Ahh! There it is; the object breaks apart as the collision dynamic hits it (**Figure 14.27**).

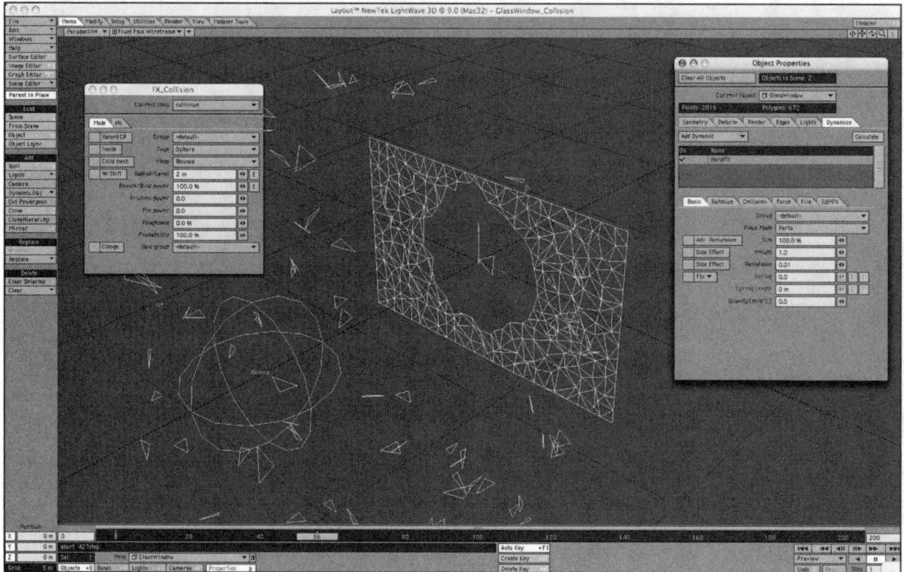

Figure 14.27 Setting the Piece Mode to Parts allows the pane of glass to be shattered.

11. You're probably noticing that the pieces of GlassWindow break apart, but sort of drift off and do not really have any weight or motion of their own. In the HardFX controls for the GlassWindow, choose –9.8 from the Gravity drop-down. Click Calculate, and you'll see the object start to fall before and after the collision. That's better, but you want the gravity to not apply until the collision happens.

12. Click the Collision tab of the HardFX controls and check Start by Collision, as shown in **Figure 14.28**. Then click Calculate again. GlassWindow sits still until the collision effector strikes it, and then its pieces expand and begin to drop.

    From this point on, it's a matter of tweaking the settings and observing the results until the animation looks the way you want it to look. None of the remaining steps in this exercise are essential or strictly "correct." Try them all to acquaint yourself with the effects of the controls they describe, and decide for yourself if you want to keep the suggested settings, apply higher or lower values, or discard the adjustments altogether.

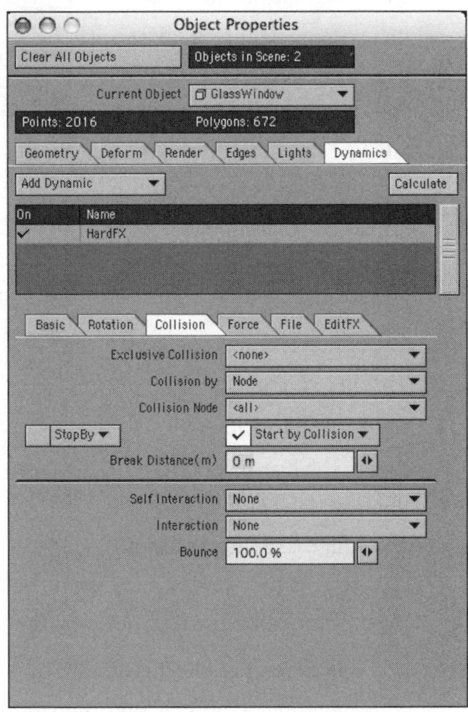

Figure 14.28 Check the collision effector's Start by Collision box to make the GlassWindow object sit still until it breaks apart.

Note

If you want to make sure the exploding pieces do not collide with each other, you can choose Box from the Self Interaction drop-down on the Collision tab of the Object Properties panel's Dynamics tab. Be careful, though, because this will greatly increase calculation times. You can always cancel a calculation by pressing the Ctrl key.

13. Click the Basic tab of the HardFX controls and increase the Weight setting to 35.0. This increases the weight of the pieces when they break up, resulting in heavier parts, which have more inertia and hit the ground faster. If you were animating something like paper, this weight value would be less, about 5 or 10.

14. Click into Layout and select the dynamic collision object. Use the Dope Track to cut the keyframe at frame 60 and paste it at frame 20, and then click Calculate again. This increases the collision effector's rate of acceleration as it collides with GlassWindow, and just like in the real world, that increases the force of the impact. By the same token, pasting the keyframe at, say, frame 120, will reduce the rate of acceleration and lower the force of impact.

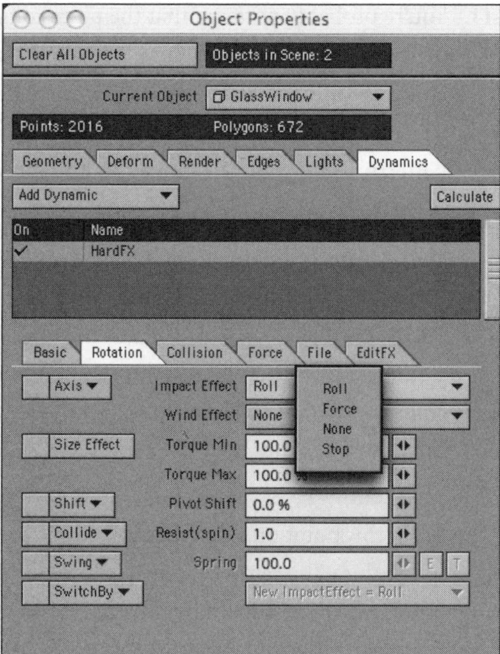

Figure 14.29 Set the Impact Effect to Roll to make the shards spin as they shatter and fall.

15. Set the Impact Effect to Roll in the HardFX panel's Rotation tab (**Figure 14.29**). This will make the shards of glass spin as they spread away from the collision. Try playing with the Min and Max torque values to add more variety.

16. Add one more thing to this animation and then get ready to learn about soft-body dynamics. Choose Collision from the Dynamic Obj drop-down on the Items tab to add another collision object to the scene, and type **Ground** when prompted to give it a name.

17. When the FX_Collision panel opens for the Ground object, choose Plane from the Type drop-down. This makes a flat collision plane.

18. Change the Radius/Level value for the Ground object to –7 m. This tells the collision to happen beneath the GlassWindow object, at –7 m, on the Y-axis. Click the Calculate button and you'll see the exploding parts now fall and hit a ground surface (granted, there is no visible surface).

19. The shards bounce a little too much when they hit the ground, don't you think? So, reduce the Bounce/Bind Power value to 80% in the FX_Collision for the ground plane. Click Calculate again, and you'll see the pieces fall and bounce randomly, as in **Figure 14.30**.

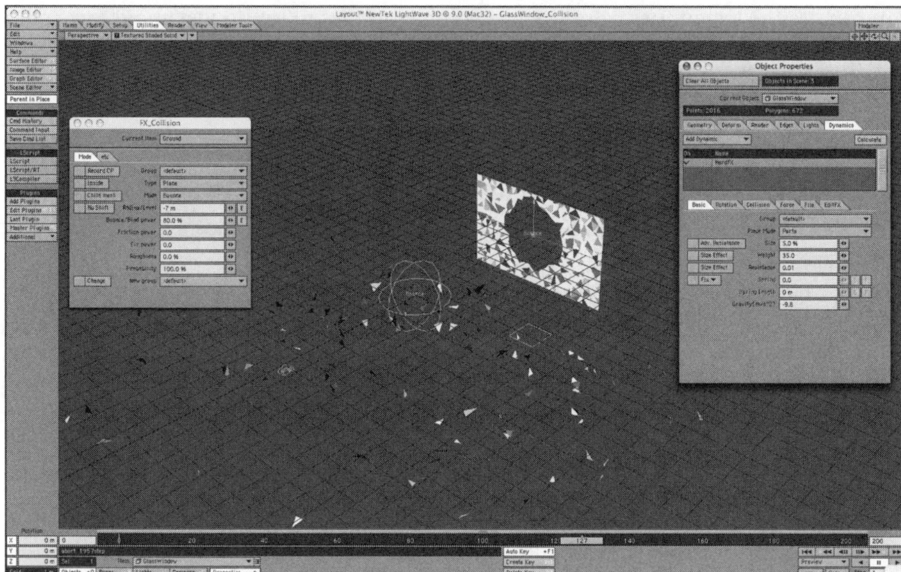

Figure 14.30 A Plane type collision object makes the parts fall and bounce on the ground.

20. Finally, you can use the Camera view to set up a cool moving camera as the glass breaks and flies toward you. **Figure 14.31** shows a render. Save your scene!

Figure 14.31 Once the collisions and motions are set up, you can position your camera to have the shards of glass fly towards you.

You can use the techniques from the preceding examples to set up just about any collision in which rigid objects crash together and break apart or scatter. Here are a few more tips you can try when working with hard-body dynamics:

- On the Rotation tab in the HardFX panel, change Wind Effect to Roll. When your parts are exploded after the collision, they'll roll, as if blown by the force of a shockwave in the air, radiating from the impact point. This adds a nice touch to exploding objects.
- On the Rotation tab of the HardFX panel, change the Torque Min and Torque Max values to balance the amount of initial and ending spin and motion on the exploding parts.
- Try changing the Pivot Shift value so that the exploding pieces rotate differently. At 0%, each part rotates around its own center point. Change this value to 100%, and the parts rotate as a group around a much larger radius, as if you'd moved all of their pivot points individually. You can also set this to just an X Shift, Y Shift, or Z Shift from the drop-down control to the left of the value requester.
- Increase the Resistance setting on the HardFX panel's Basic tab, to slow down the exploding parts.
- If your exploding parts sort of hop like little bugs after they land, try lowering the Ground object's Bounce/Bind Power setting.
- Use the EditFX panel (as you did in Chapter 13, "Particles in Motion") to select and remove or reposition any individual shards as they scatter from the collision.
- Experiment with one setting at a time. Have fun!

What about soft things, like blankets or pillows? How do soft-body dynamics differ from cloth dynamics? When should you use one over the other? Read on to learn about more cool features of the dynamics in LightWave v9.

Soft-Body Dynamics

What is a soft-body dynamic? Is it just for making plump characters move naturally? Well, sure, you can do that. But soft-body dynamics can do much more. A soft-body dynamic applies to any object that is...well, soft! More specifically, it's anything that is soft and resilient; its surface yields when something hits it, but it reverts to its original shape after the collision. Think of a water balloon, a sofa cushion, or perhaps even the pants on a walking character.

Exercise 14.4 Working with Soft-Body Dynamics

1. In LightWave Layout, save any work you've done and clear the scene.
2. Load the Pillow object from the Chapter 14 folder of this book's DVD. Set up the view to a comfortable Perspective view and open the Object Properties panel for the object. **Figure 14.32** shows the scene.
3. On the Dynamics tab in the Object Properties panel, add a soft dynamic from the drop-down list for the Pillow object.
4. Click the Layout window, and choose Collision from the Dynamic Obj drop-down on the Items tab. When prompted, type **Ground** to name the new object, which will provide a ground collision similar to the one you made in Exercise 14.3.

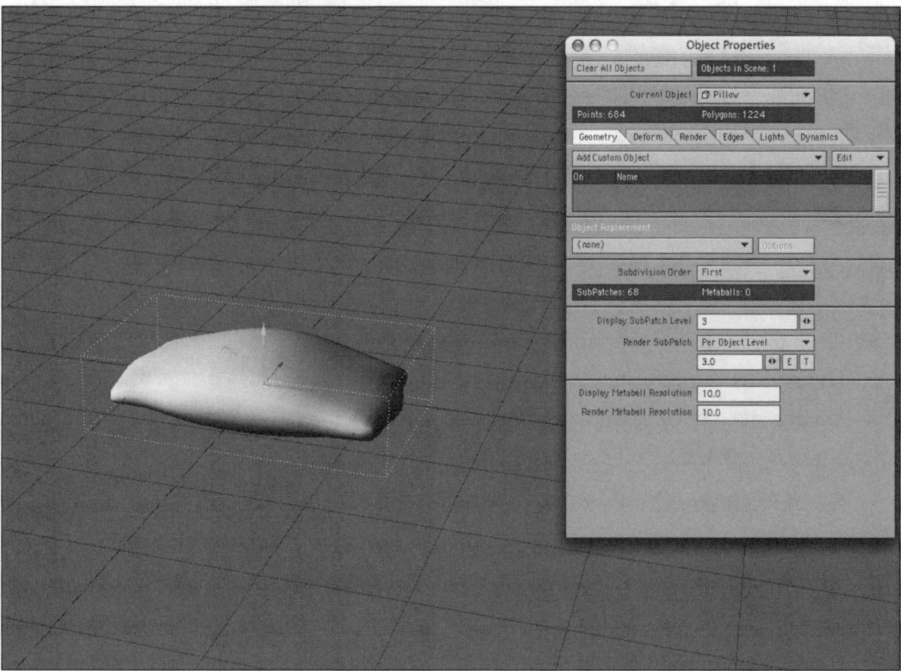

Figure 14.32 Load the Pillow object into Layout and view the scene from a Perspective view.

5. For this collision dynamic, choose Type to Plane and set Radius/Level to 0m.
6. Select the Pillow object and create a keyframe for its current position at frame 15.

7. Use the Move tool (press **t**) to raise the Pillow object up about 20m along the Y-axis (**Figure 14.33**). Create a keyframe at frame 0 to lock it in place.

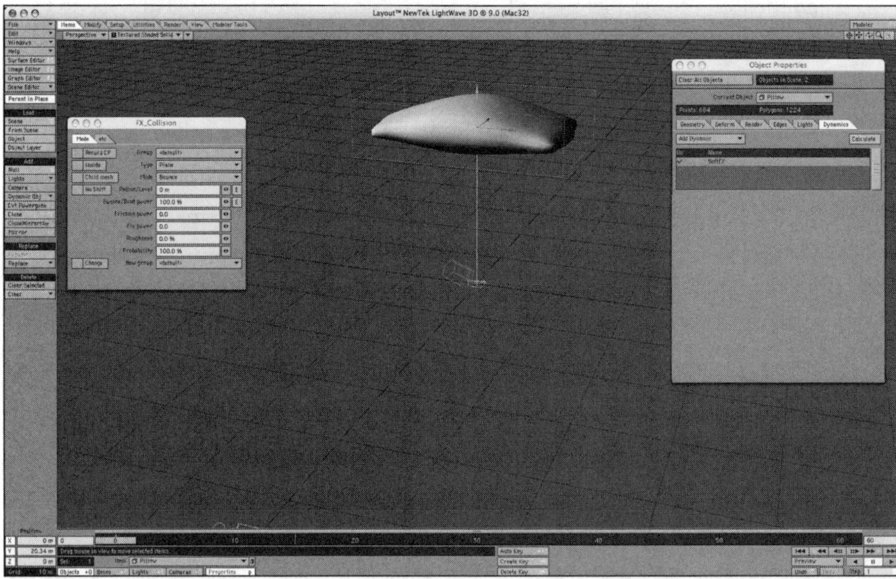

Figure 14.33 Two keyframes are set for the Pillow object.

8. Click the Calculate button in the Dynamics tab and watch the pillow fall. It sort of bounces like gelatin when it strikes the collision object.

   Not very effective for a pillow…

9. Click the Deform tab within the SoftFX controls. Make sure Collision Detect is set to All. Exclusive Collision should be set to None. Increase the Collision Size value to about 6m, as in **Figure 14.34**.

10. Click the Calculate button. The pillow drops and looks better. It still bounces a bit too much, though.

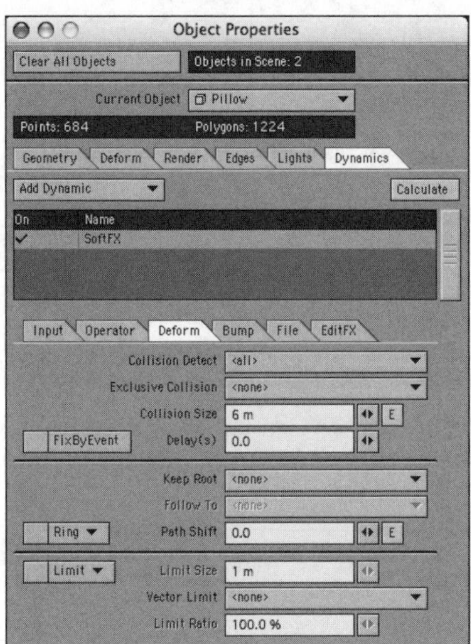

Figure 14.34 Changing the values on the Deform tab tells the pillow how to react to the collision.

11. On the Operator tab for the pillow's SoftFX, set the WaveCycle option for the Operator1 Map to 2.0. Then, set the WaveSize value to 0.2, as shown in **Figure 14.35**. Click Calculate again and your pillow looks more natural dropping into the scene.

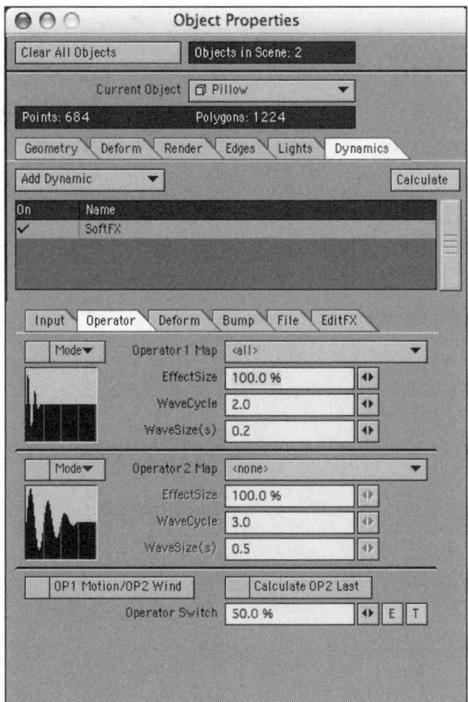

Figure 14.35 Changing the pillow's WaveSize and WaveCycle settings balances the amount the pillow bounces when it hits the ground.

Changing the WaveSize value for the pillow tells LightWave how to calculate the motions after the dynamic is applied. You can even see a small thumbnail window of the wave's motion, starting from more intense on the left and fading off over time to the right.

As you can see from this exercise, setting up objects with soft-body dynamics is easy. What other things can you think of to create with soft-body dynamics? Aside from things like tires hitting the ground or animating gelatin, soft-body dynamics can also be used for characters. You can define a *point set* in Modeler by selecting a group of points and then clicking New for Selection Set (the S button) at the bottom right of the Modeler interface. Then in Layout, use that selection set and the deformer for soft-body dynamics to make a character's body parts jiggle. Fun stuff!

However, as you might have guessed, there is much more you can do with these dynamic settings, and there's a video available showing you how to animate cloth, which is another type of soft body dynamic. Visit www.3dgarage.com and you can find the free video download.

The Next Step

This chapter introduced you to hard- and soft-body dynamics. Even though the tutorials were simple, their methods and results are the same whether you're building New York City in 3D or just a ball and box.

I've said it before, but it can't be emphasized enough: Practice! Experiment! Change a value; see the results. Work with one value at a time, and as always, consult your LightWave 3D manual for any specific technical questions. Now, turn the page and learn about LightWave v9's rendering processes and its new camera tools.

Chapter 15

Advanced Cameras and Rendering

For LightWave v9, NewTek has introduced an entirely new set of cameras as well as a new render panel. For that reason, this chapter encompasses both areas. Without a render, you won't see your final 3D model or animation, and without a camera, you won't see the render. In the past *Inside LightWave* books, rendering pretty much stood on its own, but as you'll learn in this chapter, cameras and rendering go hand-in-hand for LightWave v9.

Throughout this book, you've rendered test frames to see how lights, textures, and various effects look in their final form. But at some point, you'll need to set up a serious render—that is, one that needs to be saved properly, in both the right pixel size and the right format. After you set up your animations, you must ask yourself at some point, "Now what?" This chapter shows you the methods and options available for rendering and outputting your animations. It demonstrates rendering on a single computer and on multiple machines by using LightWave's built-in network rendering engine, ScreamerNet. Specifically, this chapter provides information on the following:

- Enhanced camera tools
- The LightWave rendering engine
- Camera settings for rendering
- Rendering options
- Network render setup

LightWave v9 Cameras

If you're a longtime LightWave user, you know that there is a default camera in Layout (the Classic camera), and that without it properly set up, you can't see your render. You might also know that LightWave has allowed you to add multiple cameras for a few years. Simply put, LightWave allows you to add more than one camera to a scene, sort of like multiple cameras on a photo or video shoot. You've probably mastered this aspect of LightWave. Sure enough, the programmers and NewTek wanted to keep you on your toes, but also wanted to make LightWave v9 more functional. As such, LightWave v9 introduces a new set of cameras that can take your renders further than any previous version of the software. These new camera types were briefly introduced in Chapter 5, "3D Cameras." This section of the book will show you how to set some of them up.

Classic Camera

The Classic Camera, as mentioned in Chapter 5, has been demonstrated throughout this book. It's the default LightWave camera and primarily used for most projects. Use the Classic Camera if you want to render any points or lines in your scene. The reason the Classic Camera is used most often is because it allows you to set a focal length and desired resolution. It's the camera that's always been in LightWave since version 1.0.

Orthographic Camera

The Orthographic Camera is a little tricky to explain. We covered this camera in Chapter 5; however, this section is here to refresh your memory. When you render a scene, LightWave shoots out "rays." These rays are used to calculate all sorts of things, such as shadows, reflections, and so on. You have more control over these rays in LightWave v9 than anytime before, and the Orthographic Camera is just one way to work with different rays. Rather than rays bouncing all over the scene, with the Orthographic Camera their directions are the same. So what does that really mean? It means that you can create a camera with a forced perspective. Perhaps you're a designer working in AutoCAD or Pro/E. You would use the Orthographic Camera for engineering-type renders or for shots in which you need to see more of the model in a single render. If a perspective created from a wider camera might take away from the object or scene you're rendering, the Orthographic Camera might do the trick. Before this camera was implemented in LightWave v9, artists would often pull the camera far away from the scene and then zoom in to create a similar look.

Perspective Camera

The Perspective Camera renders like the Classic Camera, but with a few differences. The Perspective Camera renders the scene from top to bottom. In many cases, more complex scenes will render faster. However, the Perspective Camera will not render points and lines.

So if you're setting up particles, you'd want to render with a Classic Camera, not a Perspective Camera. The new LightWave v9 Perspective Camera is a two-point camera that is most useful for architectural renders, allowing the viewer to see more of the model with less distortion.

Advanced Camera

The Advanced Camera, new to LightWave v9, offers you some really interesting control. It allows you to re-create lenses and real cameras normally not found in 3D applications. With the Advanced Camera, you can define objects (mesh items) as cameras. In addition, you can create spherical cameras with this camera type. This allows you to render an entire scene in a spherical shape, sort of like a severe fish-eye lens. Effects like this weren't possible in LightWave before version 9. The advantage of doing something like this is perhaps for creating high dynamic range (HDR) images. Or, perhaps you want to render a shot of an interior, save it out, and use it later in another scene as a background environment. Using objects as cameras, you can obtain an entirely different look and gain more control than with a normal camera. For example, you can't really distort a camera, but with an object set up as a camera, that object can be bent, distorted, warped, and so forth, thereby distorting what your camera sees. Follow Exercise 15.1 to set up your own Advanced Camera.

Exercise 15.1 Using the Advanced Camera

Take a look at **Figure 15.1**, and you'll see the Advanced Camera panel, which is accessed by choosing the option for the drop-down menu at the top of the Camera Properties panel.

The Advanced Camera tool allows you to create custom camera lenses. While a typical camera in LightWave offers zooms or wide-angle shots, you can't really use an object as a camera unless you parent the camera to the object. For example, let's say you've animated a character who's suddenly getting sleepy. Your main-scene camera sees the character starting to nod off. Then, you switch to an Advanced Camera you've set up from one of the character's eyeballs. The result? You see what the character sees.

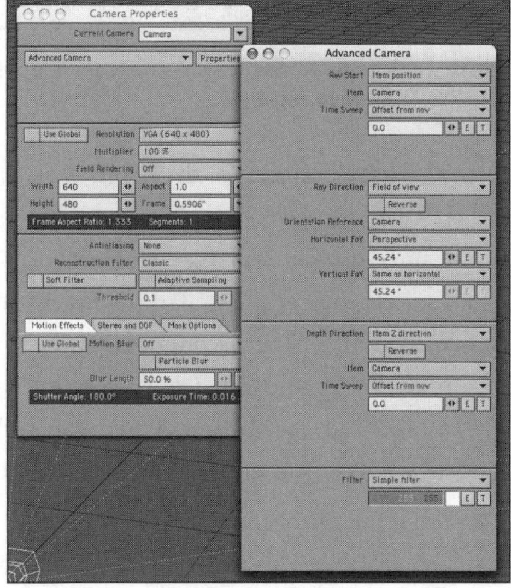

Figure 15.1 The Advanced Camera panel can be found by selecting Advanced Camera from the top of the Camera Properties panel.

And, if you've set up the character's eyelids to close, the eyelids would then cover the camera. Add a little blur to the scene, and you've sold your shot. Pretty cool. To help explain this further, the project here will show you how a simple ball can be used as a camera and allow you to create amazing effects.

1. Load the Room_Balls scene from the Projects\Scenes\CH15 directory on the DVD. **Figure 15.2** shows the scene after loading.

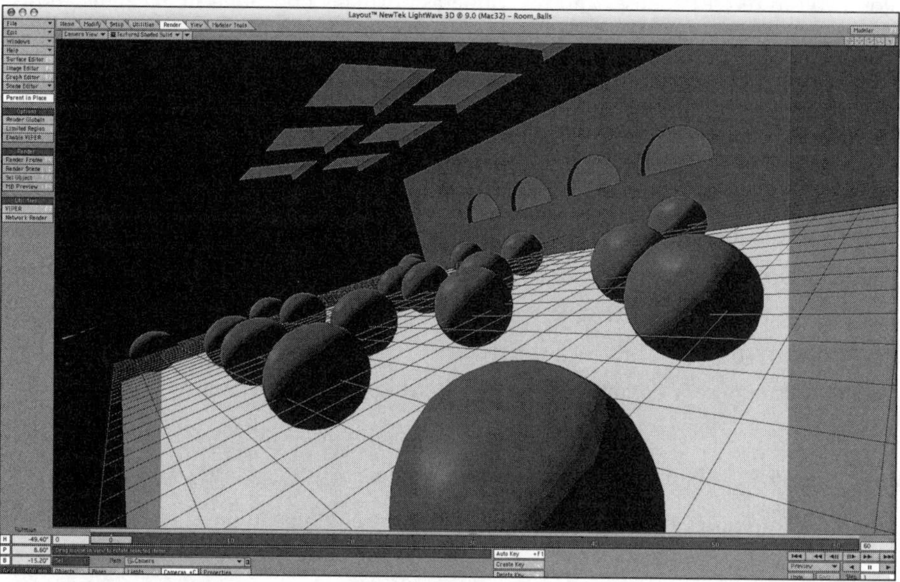

Figure 15.2 The Room_Balls scene loaded looks OK with a standard camera and from a wide angle.

The default camera for the Room_Balls scene has a 13mm Lens Focal Length set in the Camera Properties panel. The lower this value, the wider the shot. But what if you wanted to give the appearance that you're one of the balls in the scene? You can go further using an Advanced Camera than by just placing a wide-angle lens low and near the balls.

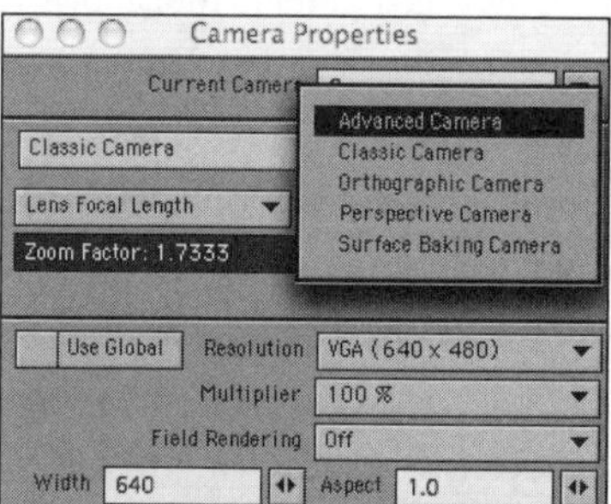

Figure 15.3 Change the default camera in the scene to an Advanced Camera from the top of the Camera Properties panel.

2. From the top of the Camera Properties panel, choose Advanced Camera from the drop-down list, as shown in **Figure 15.3**.

3. In the Advanced Camera panel that appears, there are quite a few options. The first, Ray Start, defaults to Item Position, which gives the appearance of peeking through a pinhole-type camera. This determines the starting point of the rays (when rendering). What's the Item? That's the next setting, which by default is set to Camera. Change this to Room_Balls:CenterBall. This is a single ball that exists in its own layer. **Figure 15.4** shows the panel.

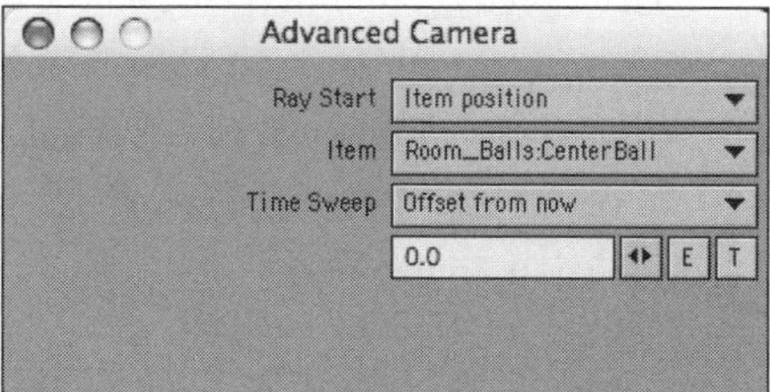

Figure 15.4 To begin using the Advanced Camera, you can tell LightWave to use an object for the camera item.

4. Leave the Time Sweep setting at "Offset from now," the default. This setting will give you the ability to shift the way the rays in the scene are calculated.
5. For Ray Direction, Field of View will work for the current scene. Here, you can tell the Advanced Camera to be rendered toward the item position or toward the UV position, and more.
6. Set the Orientation Reference to Room_Balls:CenterBall. This sets the initial camera position to the same orientation as the ball. After you set this, press **F9** to render a test frame. **Figure 15.5** shows the example.

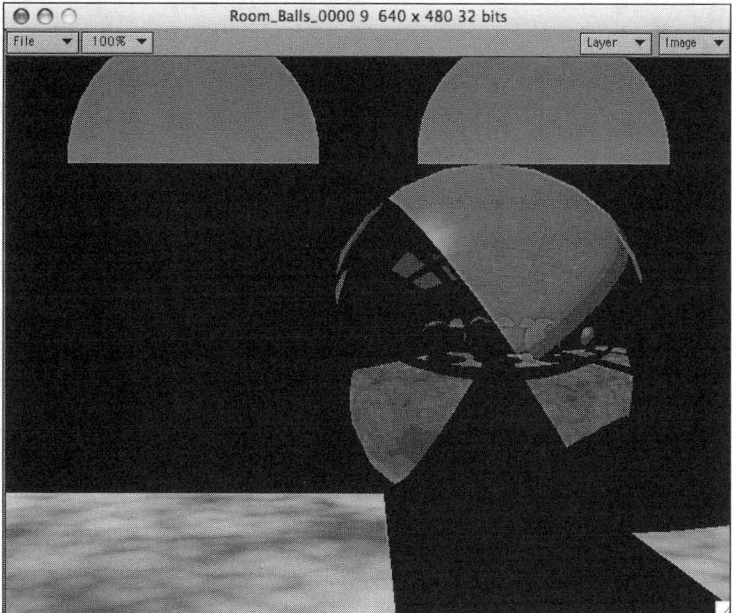

Figure 15.5 With a few simple settings, the center ball in the room becomes a camera!

7. You can see from Figure 15.5 that after inputting a few settings to the Advanced Camera properties, you're rendering your scene from an object's point of view. That's pretty cool! But there's a little more you can do to make the shot better. The Horizontal FOV (field of view) is set to Perspective. This is similar to a default camera view. Change it to Spherical. Then, set the amount to 90 degrees. Press **F9** to render a test frame and you'll see that your shot now has a fish-eye effect, as shown in **Figure 15.6**.

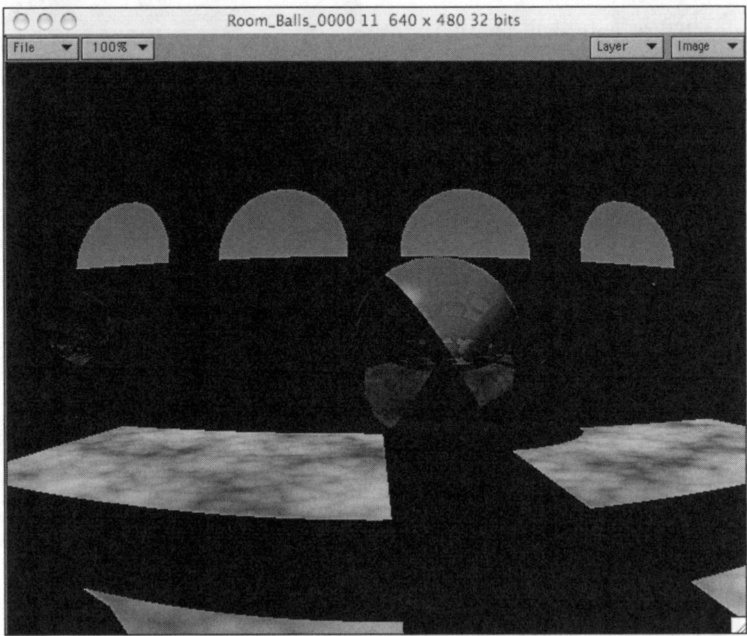

Figure 15.6 Using a Spherical field of view, the camera now has a fish-eye effect, but is still rendered from the ball object.

Note

Figures 15.5 and 15.6 show the scene without global illumination. Later in this chapter you'll learn about this feature to greatly enhance the look of your renders. **Figure 15.7** shows the render with this feature applied.

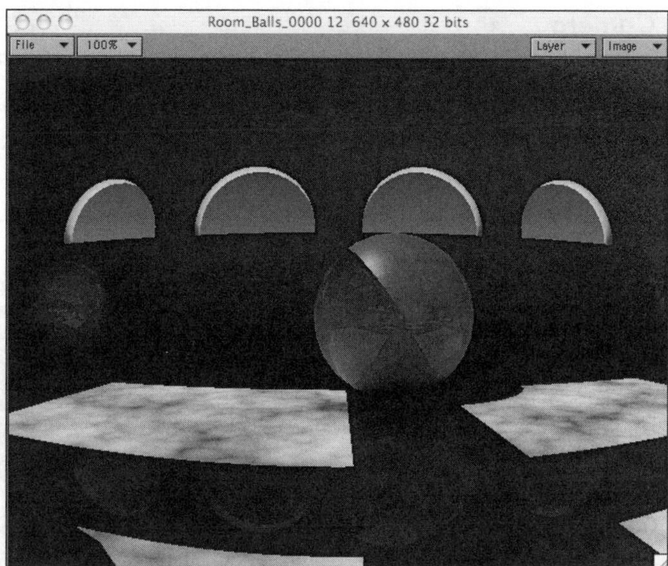

Figure 15.7 The same shot as in Figure 15.6, but with global illumination applied. Global illumination is a cool render feature in LightWave, which you'll learn about later in the chapter.

8. You can experiment with the other field-of-view settings. Depending on what you choose, such as Cylindrical, you'll be able to set the Vertical FOV as well. For now, save the scene.
9. Lastly, you can change the Depth Direction for the camera, and which Item this calculation uses. Experiment by changing the Item to Room_Balls:CenterBall and see what kind of results you get. At the very bottom of the panel, you can also apply a colored filter to the Advanced Camera.

   The Advanced Camera is quite powerful, and these instructions can help you create very cool and interesting renders, even with simple objects. You can go one step further with this project to animate the ball! Roll it across the floor using the instructions from previous chapters regarding dynamics. Or, even just keyframe the ball, and render out a quick movie of it. You'll see that not only are you viewing the scene from an object's point of view, but your camera also takes on the object's motions. Remember, by setting up an Advanced Camera as you've done here, the object *is* the camera. Cool stuff!

Note

When using an Advanced Camera, you won't see the effects in Layout, but you will when you render.

Real Lens Camera

The Real Lens Camera makes mimicking any real-world camera quite easy. **Figure 15.8** shows Layout with the Camera Properties panel opened and changed to a Real Lens. You see that another panel is open, and a Nikon SLR D70 camera has been chosen, along with a 50mm *f*/1.8 Al-S Nikor lens. You'll also see that the icon preview for the camera in Layout changes to a grid. This helps you align your shot based on the real lens setting.

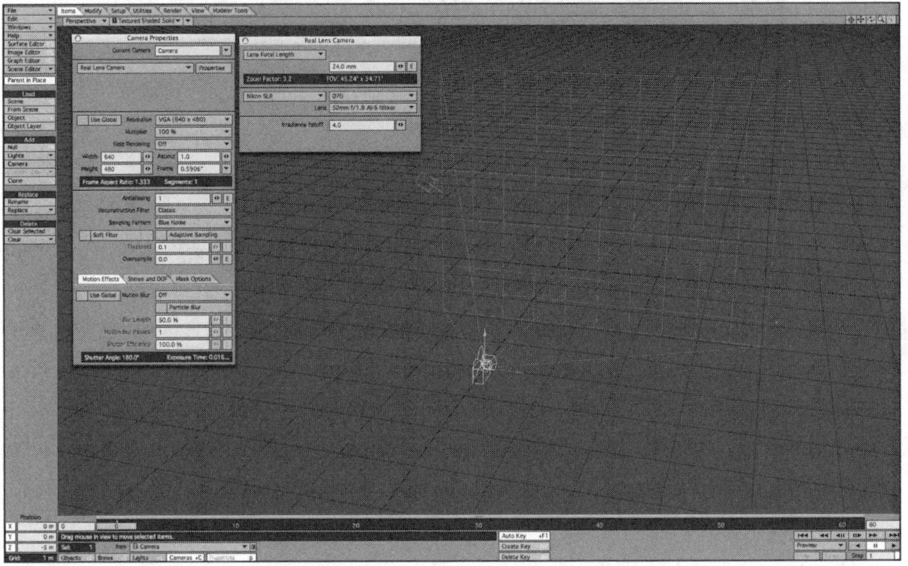

Figure 15.8 The Real Lens Camera offers you the ability to set a number of presets for point-and-shoot and digital SLR cameras and lenses.

Using a Real Lens Camera is ideal for matching still images or moving video clips that have been imported into LightWave. This is useful when compositing 3D objects over images or video, or if the final render will go to a third-party program such as Digital Fusion or After Effects, for compositing. You'll learn about compositing in Chapter 16, "Compositing and Postprocessing Techniques."

Surface Baking Camera

As mentioned in Chapter 5, the Surface Baking Camera will come in very handy for game designers, architectural animators, and anyone who wants to speed up lengthy animations. The Surface Baking Camera allows you to "bake" your textures into one large image map. Say, for example, you have a complex scene with numerous image-mapped textures, procedural textures, ray-traced shadows, radiosity for global illumination, and so on. That would add to your render time, especially if your scene is 30 seconds, 1 minute, or longer. By using the surface baker, you render once, and all of the calculations LightWave needs to perform are saved to an image map you specify. Then, you reload that image and apply it to your entire scene. So, one image map contains all of the other image maps, procedurals, reflections, shadows, and so on. With that, you can turn off advanced ray-tracing features, complex lighting, etc., and LightWave can then crank through the frames for final render output in no time. The Surface Baking Camera looks at each pixel in your render as a UV coordinate. You'll learn more about UVs a bit later in the book, but the UV will allow you to conveniently map a large image around complex shapes. This camera is multithreaded, so if you have more than one processor in your scene, you can take advantage of the extra speed.

The LightWave Render Engine

LightWave provides you with a variety of rendering methods that are easy to set up and use. **Figure 15.9** shows the LightWave Render Globals panel in Layout. You can find this panel by first going to the Render menu tab at the top of Layout and then clicking the Render Globals command on the left side of the interface.

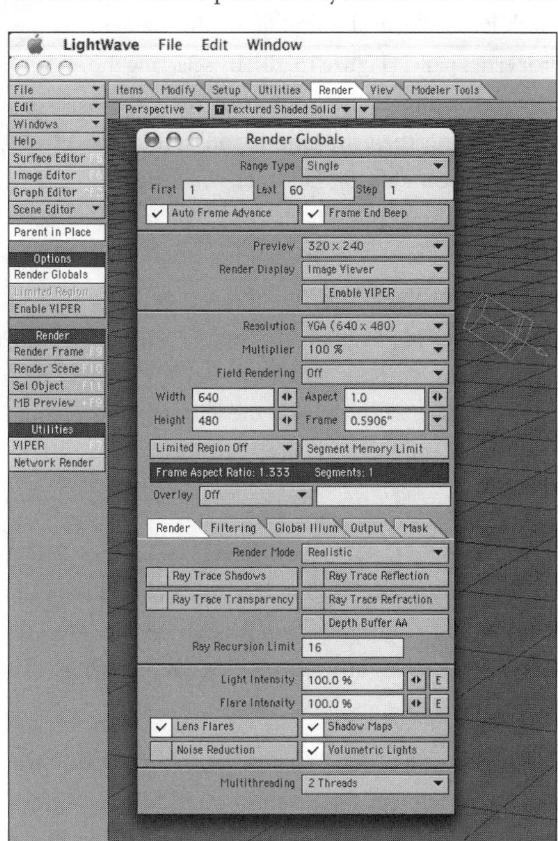

Figure 15.9 The Render Globals panel in Layout.

You will find that the LightWave render engine is one of the best in its class. It's fast, efficient, and, most importantly, good at what it does. As you can see from the images throughout this book and on NewTek's Web site, LightWave produces the highest-quality renders in its class. Through the software's radiosity rendering, area lighting, and shadow options, the LightWave rendering engine can deliver beautifully rendered images and animations. But before you can get to that level of rendering, it's good to know the process of setting up an animation to render.

The Render Globals panel might seem confusing at first. It's a new part of LightWave that houses your camera properties, render options, and saving properties. You can work with the Camera Properties panel as you have throughout this book and in the past, but you can also work in just the Render Globals panel tool. On a simple level, you can set up properties for your Camera, including resolution, for rendering. Then, use the Render Globals panel to save your animation. But you can also tell the Camera Properties panel to "Use Global" and then set your resolution, output settings, and more, all within the Render Globals panel. If you do that, what happens to the Camera Properties panel, you ask? You can still use this panel for various camera controls. All other render-related settings will be done in the Render Globals. The Use Global option is found as a check box right in the middle of the Camera Properties panel (**Figure 15.10**). By selecting the Cameras listing at the bottom of the Layout interface, and then pressing **p** you'll find this panel. In the middle of the panel, you'll see that the Use Globals option is checked. The resolution settings are now ghosted. When you set the resolution in the Render Globals panel, those values will be applied. This alleviates the problem of jumping back and forth between the Camera Properties panel and the Render panel to set up an animation.

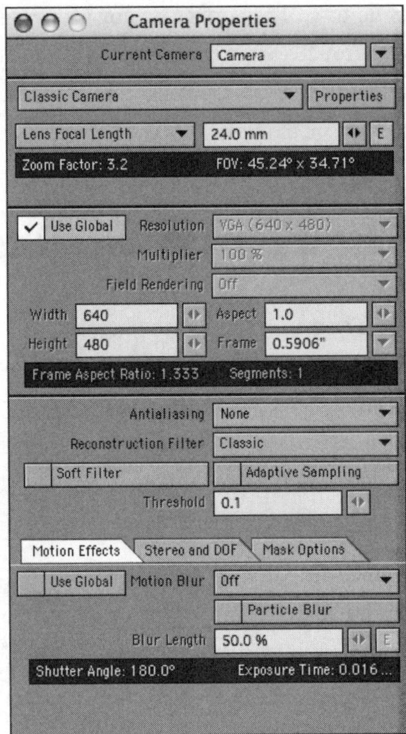

Figure 15.10 The Camera Properties panel.

Setting Up an Animation to Render

Before you can move into rendering an animation (on one machine or across a network), the animation must be set up properly. There are a few details you need to run through first to properly set up an animation for rendering, all of which will be done in the Render Globals panel.

Using the Render Globals panel, you can check out your settings for rendering. For proper camera placement, these values should be set up before you begin animating, and it's always a good idea to double-check them before you render. In addition, you can set up any motion blur, field rendering, or antialiasing here.

Range-Type Rendering

Normally you wouldn't find too much information in this chapter about single-frame rendering, because this is a very old process not often used anymore. This process involved a special cable connected to a broadcast-quality tape recorder. From there, using a single-frame command setting, LightWave would render a frame, then record it directly to tape. Today, animators render to digital movie formats, such as AVI or QuickTime, and also image sequences. Press **F9**, and you've rendered a single current frame. But there's more to this feature in LightWave v9. At the top of the Render Globals panel, you'll see a selection named Range Type. Here, you have three options for rendering:

- **Single.** Setting Range Type to Single tells LightWave to render one frame at a time. Pretty easy, huh?
- **Arbitrary.** This cool setting enables you render a range of frames. Let's say you wanted to render frames 1 through 10, as well as 12, 13, and 20. Set these frames in the panel, and away you go! LightWave renders the specific frames.
- **Keyframe.** Here, you can tell LightWave to render just a specific object on a specific axis. Say you wanted to render the penguin from Chapter 10, "Character Modeling," on just the Z-axis. Set those values next to Range Type and render your animation. The Keyframe option renders the frames on an object's channel that has keyframes. For example, if you had a keyframe on the X channel for a light at 0, 15, 30, 45, and 60, those frames would be rendered with this setting.

General-Purpose Rendering

After you've chosen which range type of rendering you'll use, you'll need to set up the rest of the render options. Most often, to render a full animation, you'll choose Single as the Range Type. This exercise guides you through the kind of rendering most commonly used by LightWave animators: rendering that generates animations for video or computer work. If, however, you are using LightWave for rendering anything other than video or computer work, such as film or print, the information here still applies, and the differences are noted.

Exercise 15.2 Creating a Basic Render

1. In Layout, load the RenderThis scene from this book's DVD.

   This scene is from Chapter 13, "Particles in Motion," with particles and camera motions applied. **Figure 15.11** shows the scene when loaded.

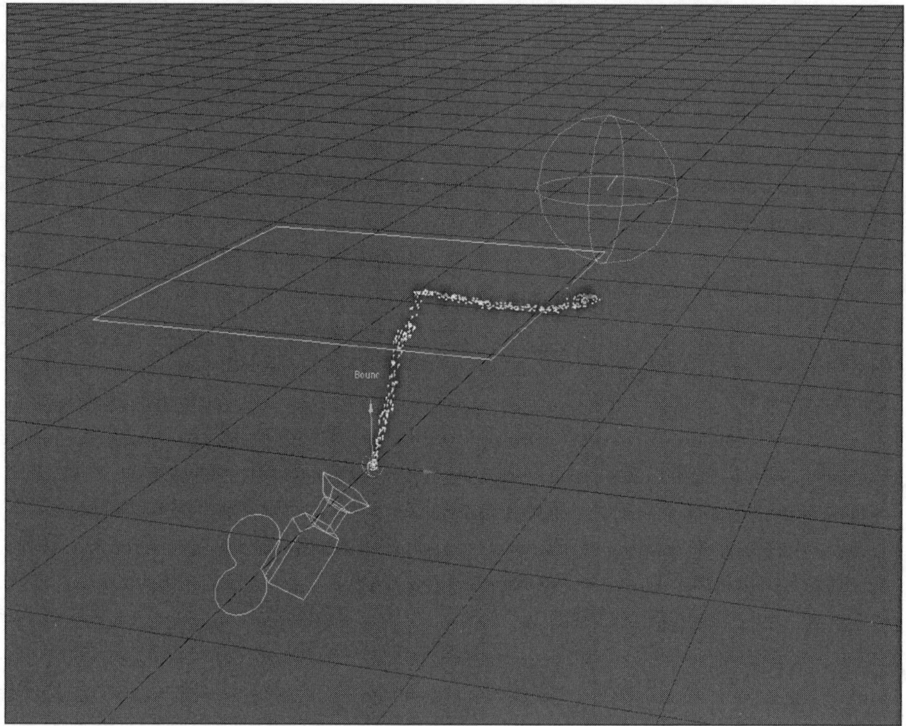

Figure 15.11 For rendering purposes, use the RenderThis scene from this book's DVD.

   Generally, you would have set up your camera when you set up the animation in Layout. You'd do this because a different camera setting can change how your Layout setup looks. The first thing to do when you're ready to render is display the Camera Properties panel. You are ready to render when you have all your lighting, textures, and motions in place. This scene has all these in place.

2. Change your view to a Camera view to see the particles. You can press **6** on your keyboard for a quick change. Select the camera (if it's not already selected) and press **p** to enter the Camera Properties panel. When the panel opens, click the Use Global option.

The Current Camera at the top of the panel should read Camera because only one camera is in the current scene.

3. From the Render tab at the top of Layout, click the Render Globals option on the left of the interface.
4. Set the Resolution to D1 (NTSC) for video resolution. Make sure that the Resolution Multiplier is set to 100% for actual-size output. You'll see the Width and Height values change when you do so.
5. Click the Segment Memory Limit button and make sure the value is set to 32 or higher. The 32 represents 32 MB of memory. The Segment value should change to 1, which means that a rendered frame will be drawn in one pass.

   If you are short on system memory, you can use a RAM setting lower than 32 for rendering. In that case, the Segments value can be greater than 1—say, 3 or 4. Your project won't render as quickly, but your scene will still look great.

   LightWave now has more memory with which to work and will render your frames in single segments.
6. When asked if you want Segment Memory Limit value set to the default, click Yes. LightWave won't use this RAM until it needs it, so you can set it higher than the default 32, perhaps 120. Be careful on how high you set this, though, if you're limited on memory and/or running other programs in the background.
7. Click over to the Filtering tab at the bottom of the panel. Set the Antialiasing to PLD 9-Pass, with a Classic Reconstruction Filter. Then, click Adaptive Sampling.

   Activating this setting tells LightWave to look for the edges to antialias in your scene. The Threshold value compares two neighboring pixels, and a value of 0 sees the entire scene. A good working value is .1. You can set the value higher, which lowers rendering time but performs a less-accurate antialiasing.

Note

While you're working, it's not necessary to have antialiasing on, but you definitely want this on for your final renders. Although you have the choice of Low to Extreme settings, it's recommended that you render all your animations for video in at least Enhanced Low Antialiasing. Medium or Enhanced Medium Antialiasing can provide you with a cleaner render. High Antialiasing is overkill and a waste of render time for video. It might actually make your images look blurry.

8. Set Motion Blur to Photoreal, and then check Particle Blur. Particle Blur is great for this particular scene since you're animating particles. You can leave the Blur Length set to about 50%. With future renders, you can experiment with setting this value higher for more blur, or lower for less.
9. Shutter Effeciency should remain at 100%. This is another option in LightWave to help simulate a real-world camera and the shutters it uses. **Figure 15.12** shows the panel.

   Do not change the Stereo and DOF setting or the Mask Options setting. This scene will not use these. You can read more on these settings in Chapter 5.
10. Save your scene, and all of your settings are saved along with it.

   You should visit the Render Globals panel at least twice during an animation, if not more—once to set up the camera and zoom factors before beginning animation setup, and once before you are ready to render to set up antialiasing, motion blur, field rendering, and proper resolution size. From here, you can set up the other options in the Render Globals panel.

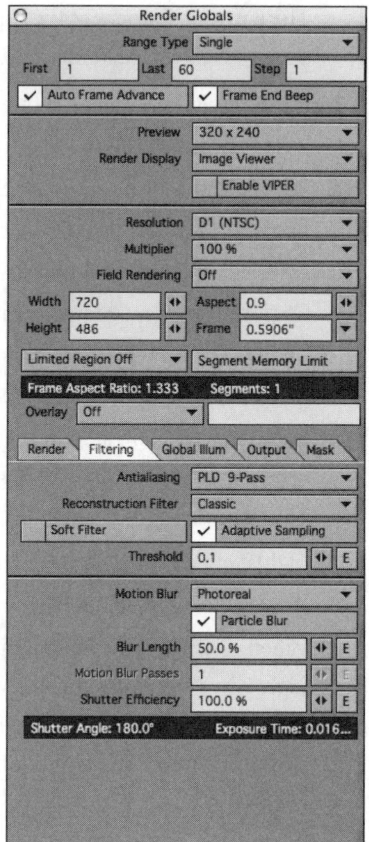

Figure 15.12 New to LightWave v9 is the Render Globals panel, one location to set up your camera and rendering options.

Exercise 15.3 Creating a Render with LightWave

1. With the RenderThis scene from this book's DVD still loaded, open the Render Globals panel.

   Figure 15.12 shows the Render Globals panel. You'll see First (indicating first frame of render) and Last (last frame of render) values at the top of the panel. If your LightWave animation in Layout has a first frame of –30 and a last frame of 300 (or any start or end frames different from the customizable default values of 1 and 60), it will not render those frames unless they are entered here.

   The frame numbers you assign to your timeline in Layout do not automatically apply in the Render Options panel.

Leave First set to 1 and set Last to 300 (10 seconds). LightWave defaults to a last frame of 60; however, you can change this default in the General Options panel (press **o**).

2. Set the Step value to 1 to render every frame. A render frame step of 2 would render every two frames, for example.
3. Click Auto Frame Advance. A crucial setting!

   This tells LightWave to advance to the next frame and continue rendering, which is very important for full animations!

Note

Frame End Beep is useful for monitoring the completion of your rendered frames, but is not necessary. It's kind of annoying after a while.

4. Turn off the Render Display by setting it to "none."

Note

The Image Viewer and Image Viewer FP render display remembers your rendered frames. Turn this on while performing test renders on individual frames (press **F9**) and leave it open. You can select any of your previously rendered images from its Layer list. You also can view the Alpha channel in this viewer and save an image.

5. Click the Render tab at the bottom of the Render Globals panel.
6. Make sure Ray Trace Shadows is on, but not Ray Trace Reflection or Ray Trace Refraction. These options are not needed in this particular case. No refraction is used in this scene, so keeping this option on would only increase render times. If you wanted your object to reflect what's around it, such as other objects, the set, or props, you'd first set a reflection value in the Surface Editor (or Node Editor) and then turn on Ray Trace Reflection. The same applies to Ray Trace Refraction, for instance, if you wanted a transparent object such as a glass to refract light traveling through it.

Note

Be sure to watch the QuickStart video on the book's DVD (3D_Garage_Videos\Please_Start_Here) to make your own glass in LightWave and see the Ray Trace engine in action.

You also can add Ray Trace Transparency for objects that need to have a transparent surface reflect a certain way, such as a car window. For now, this can be left off.

7. The Render Mode is usually set to Realistic and is not often changed. However, you do have the option to render Wireframe or Quickshade versions of your animations here.

8. Click Extra Ray Trace Optimization. Set the Ray Recursion Limit to 6. The higher the value, the longer LightWave takes to render, but the more accurate your Ray Tracing is.

   The Ray Recursion Limit, which doesn't often change, determines the number of times LightWave calculates the bounced rays in your scene. In the real world, this is infinite, but in LightWave, you can set a Ray Recursion Limit up to 24. Changing this setting increases render times. A good working value is 12. However, setting a lower value of 6 or 8 can be a real time-saver when using the Ray Trace Reflection option. For best results, try not to set this value lower than 6. If you find render errors, such as black dots, bring this value back up to 12 or so.

Note

Setting a Ray Recursion Limit too low for scenes that have transparent surfaces may result in a black opaque surface instead of a see-through surface! If this happens, just up the Ray Recursion Limit a bit.

9. If your computer has more than one processor, select 2, 4, 8, or 16 for Multithreading. If you have only one processor, set the Multiprocessing to 1.

Note

This book was written for LightWave 9.2, and a few settings are only available in this version, such as multithreading up to 16.

   If you have multiple processors and have applied pixel filter plug-ins, such as HyperVoxels, make your processors work for you by clicking Multithread Pixel Filters. Some plug-ins might not be compatible with multithreading, so remember to check this setting if you find errors in your render.

10. You can set Overlay to display the Frame Number, SMPTE Time Code, Film Key Code, or Time in Seconds in the bottom-right corner of your animation.

    This is good for reference test renders. In addition, when one of these values is set, you can add a note in the Label area. This is good to do for test renders for clients that have a history of not paying and/or of stealing your work. You can put a copyright notice in the upper corner, for example.

11. After you've set all the render options, be sure to save your scene.

Note

Saving regularly before any render (even a single-frame render) is a good habit to get into.

Those are the main parameters you must set up to render an animation. However, you still need to tell LightWave where to save the files and what type of files to save. The next section discusses the various file formats and procedures for saving your animations.

Saving Renders

Within the Render Globals panel is another tabbed area, titled Output. This area is where you tell LightWave what type of file you want to save, where to save, and in which format it should be saved. **Figure 15.13** shows the Output tab within the Render Options panel.

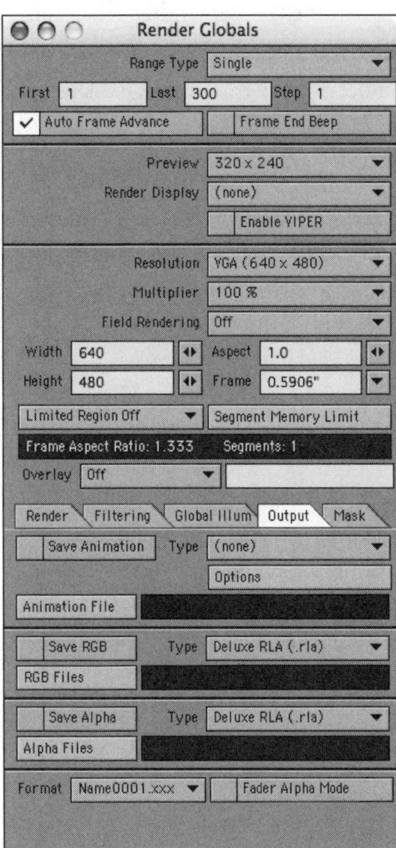

Figure 15.13 The Output tab within the Render Options panel is where you tell LightWave what type of file to save, choose your image format, and specify where to save.

The first area within the Output tab is the Save Animation selection. This confuses many people. You are creating an animation in LightWave, right? Save Animation! Makes sense—but it means something a little different. Clicking Save Animation enables you to save your rendered frames as one animation file, in a format such as AVI, QuickTime, or RTV (Video Toaster). It saves one complete file, as opposed to a series of individual rendered frames. You select different types of animations to save by using the Type selection option. Note that you'll need a Video Toaster board from NewTek for the RTV option.

Using Save Animation is great for previewing QuickTime movies or for using Aura and Video Toaster, but you also can save individual frames—and do so at the same time. If you select the Save RGB button, you're telling LightWave to save the individual frames as they are rendered. Similarly, with Save Animation Type, you select from a variety of RGB formats in which to save your animations by selecting the one you want from the Type drop-down list, as pictured in **Figure 15.14**.

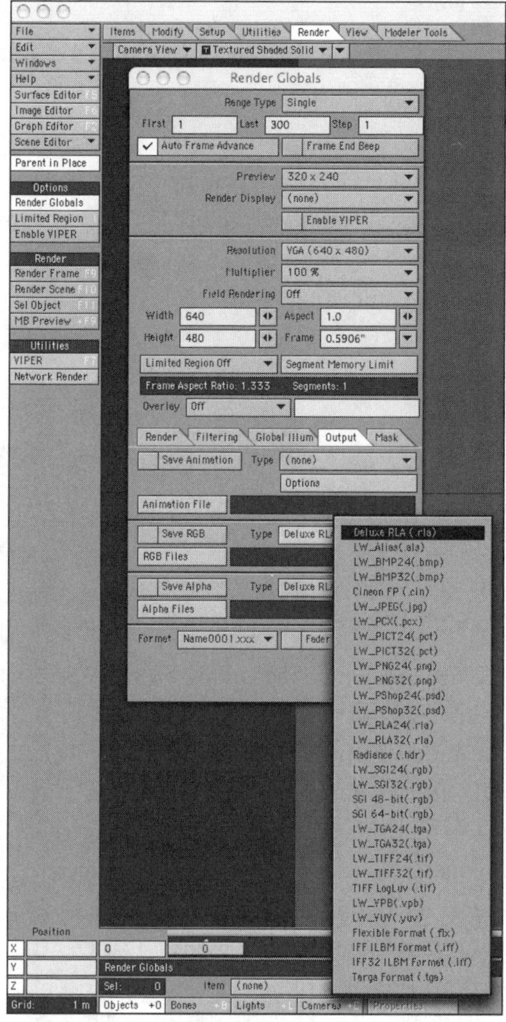

Figure 15.14 LightWave gives you a slew of formats for saving your RGB frames. This is the best way to render your animations if you do not use Video Toaster NT. The individual frames can later be imported into a variety of programs.

Finally, in the Output tab, you also can save the Alpha channels of individual frames. This is great for later compositing in a postproduction environment. Remember that all these file types can be saved with one rendering. You can save a QuickTime or AVI file, plus the RGB and alpha files, all at once. Pretty cool, huh? However, depending on what's in your scene, you can save a sequence of 32-bit files, such as TIF or PNG, and the Alpha channel will be embedded in the RGB frames. Simply load that sequence into your compositing program and you'll instantly be able to blend it into other projects.

When all this is set—the camera resolutions, the rendering information, and the output file information—you're finally ready to render your animation. Pressing the **F10** key renders your animation. Congratulations!

Note

You might have a high-resolution frame that needs to render over a long period of time. You can tell LightWave to automatically save this frame by setting up the Render Options as though you were rendering a full-length animation. Set the RGB format, output filename, and location for saving, and then click Auto Frame Advance. Make the First frame and the Last frame the same frame you want to render—say, frame 10. LightWave renders that frame and saves the RGB, and because it's also the Last frame, rendering then stops.

Render Selected Objects

If you click the Render tab in Layout, you'll see the Sel Object option under the Render category on the left of the interface. Because LightWave enables you to select multiple objects, you can save significant amounts of rendering time with this option. In the Scene Editor or in Layout, you can select all objects at once by holding the Shift key and clicking the objects. Rendering selected objects has two useful functions:

- It saves render time by rendering only the objects you're interested in at the moment.
- It enables you to render multiple passes of the same animation with or without certain objects. This is great for special effects or compositing, or even for rendering before-and-after sorts of animations.

Thoughts on Rendering

You can refer to this section of the book often when it's time to render your animations and images. But then you have to answer the question that arises: "What's next?" When your animations are complete, the next step is to bring them into a digital animation recorder and lay them off to tape or edit your final animations with audio and effects in a nonlinear editor.

The exercises in this chapter have not only introduced you to the new camera tools in LightWave, but they have also given you the knowledge to create your own interesting shots within your 3D scenes. From here, you can build your own 3D objects, such as cars, industrial environments, prototype objects, insects, or people, and experiment with compositing them into real-world images. Whatever you can imagine! Take a look in the Photos folder, and you'll find royalty-free images that you can use in the same manner as the images from the exercises in this chapter. Try using some of the city photographs to fly objects in front of and behind buildings while casting shadows. Use other images to make a 3D character walk down a long sidewalk or a flight of stairs. Try photographing or videotaping your living room and rendering 3D objects on the table! From here, experiment and practice whenever you can. If you have a digital camera, keep it with you at all times to create your own images for compositing. You'll learn all about compositing in Chapter 16.

But no matter what you create in LightWave, unless you export your scene or model to another artist, rendering your scene must be done. Someday, you might not need to render, as processors and video cards become increasingly powerful. For now, though, LightWave still has to render, just like any other 3D application. But you'll find that the rendering engine inside LightWave is one of the best around. It's strong and stable, and most importantly, it produces beautifully rendered images.

NewTek has added many OpenGL enhancements. These speed up your workflow and give the poor **F9** (Render Current Frame) key a break. Work through the exercises in this book and make your own animations anytime you can. You can't be in front of your computer 24 hours a day—well, maybe you can, but you shouldn't. Try going out to a movie, too! When you get ready to take a break, set up a render. Don't just wait until the animation is "perfect." Render often and see how your animation looks. You might find new ways to enhance it and make it even better. Or you might just find that it's perfect the way it is. Now, if they only had a way to do LightWave while driving to work...

Network Rendering

LightWave enables you to render over a network of computers, not just the individual machine on which you're working. Whether you have a few computers or hundreds of computers at your location, you can use all of them for rendering the same animation.

LightWave ships with some important network-rendering software called ScreamerNet. ScreamerNet has been a part of LightWave for years. With ScreamerNet, LightWave needs to be installed on only a single machine. This distributive rendering can send your animations to other networked machines that have a ScreamerNet process running. You don't have to use this feature; it is used more in larger animation studios that want to maximize time by using multiple computer environments. Please refer to your LightWave manuals for proper instruction.

ScreamerNet also is useful on a single machine for batch processing your animations. Think about setting up four versions of your animated logo to render one right after the other. Because LightWave saves the Render Options information within a scene file, ScreamerNet knows where and what to save from your specific animations. You even can run ScreamerNet without running LightWave. Use ScreamerNet to batch-render animations without loading your scenes. The distributed-rendering section of your LightWave manual can instruct you further on the proper command lines needed to set up this process. The following sections provide a complete tutorial on how to set up your own network render farm. **Figure 15.15** shows the Network Rendering panel, found within the Render tab.

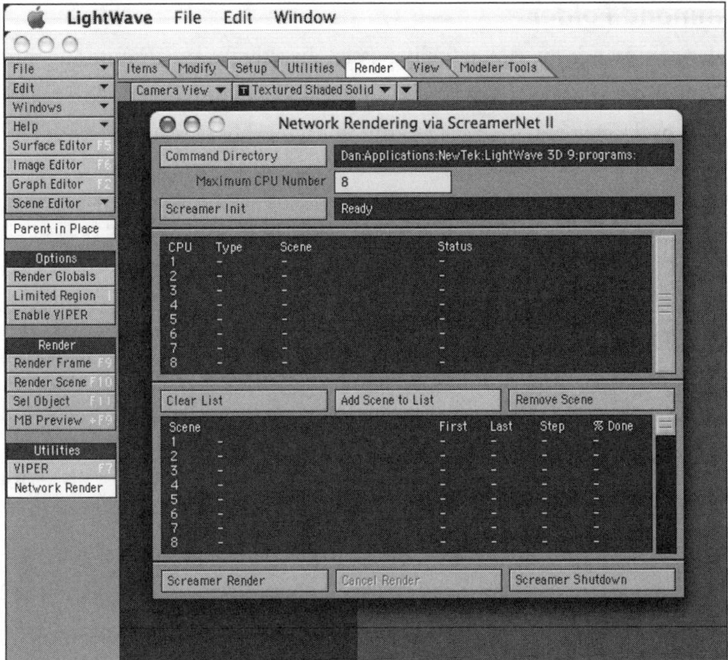

Figure 15.15 The Network Rendering panel is found within the Render tab in Layout.

Overview of ScreamerNet Rendering

The ScreamerNet software has two parts to it; the first resides in the LightWave layout program, found under the Render, Network Rendering pop-up menu. This is the "controller" part of ScreamerNet. The second can be found in the Programs folder, found in the main LightWave install directory. It's a separate program called LWSN; this is the program that is run on the machines that are "controlled."

What Is ScreamerNet and How Does It Work?

The concept is relatively simple. One of the computers on the network is designated the "master" computer. This is usually the computer with the full LightWave installation on it. The master controls the other computers, or "nodes," by passing "render commands" to them. These commands tell the node which scene to load and which frame to render.

When a node has finished rendering a frame, it passes a command back to the master saying it has finished and is ready for the next frame; the process is repeated until all the frames have been rendered.

The Command Folder

These render commands are not actually passed directly from computer to computer—the LightWave program on the master computer isn't talking directly to the LWSN program on each node. Instead, they are talking to each other through a special folder: the command folder.

This is an important folder that the master and all nodes must be able to see somewhere on the network. This is because the render commands are actually text files. Each text file is saved into the command folder with a unique name to separate one node's commands from another. These commands are better known as "job" files. Each job file has a number corresponding to the node it is designed for, so node 1 is passed job1, node 2 is passed job2, and so on.

Likewise, for the nodes to talk back to the master, they too need to save files with unique names so that the master knows which node is talking back to it. These returned commands, or acknowledgments, are known as "ack" files, and like the job files, the ack files have a number to say which node sent it; thus, node 1 returns commands to the ack1 file, node 2 returns commands to the ack2 file, and so on. **Figure 15.16** presents a diagram of the process.

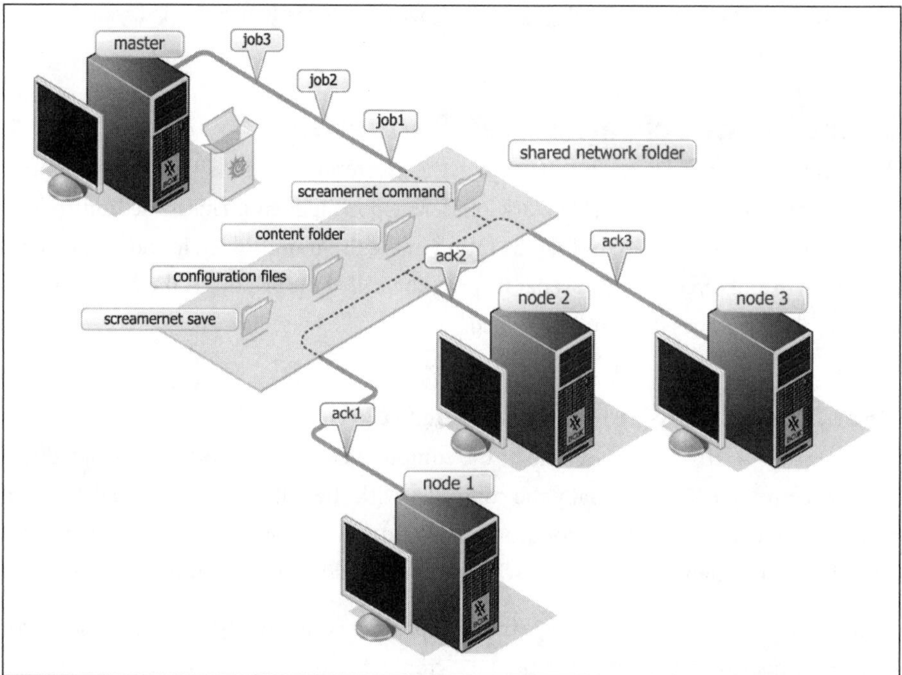

Figure 15.16 Diagram of ScreamerNet command-passing technique.

We know that the master and nodes need to be able to find the command folder in order to "talk" to each other, but the command folder only stores instructions on which scenes and frames to render; it doesn't actually pass any scene data to the nodes. So like the command folder, the render nodes also need to know the location of the scene's content.

The Content Folder

This is where the content folder comes into play. It stores all the objects and images used to make up the scene, as well as the scene file itself. Like the command folder, all the nodes must be able to see this folder so that when told to render a frame from a certain scene, they know where on the network to look for it.

Good Content Organization

Good organization of content is essential if you want to make your life easier in LightWave. Storing files all over your hard drive to make up one scene will just give you headaches, so instead try to organize your LightWave projects in a logical manner. Good content organization is especially important when using ScreamerNet. Before I go into this, you must first understand how LightWave finds content. Bear with me on this; it's long-winded but worth a read!

Ignoring ScreamerNet for a second, start up LightWave Layout and bring up the Options panel (use the **o** key or go to the drop-down menu at the left of the inteface, Edit > General Options). The first setting you'll see is the Content Directory input. This is where you tell LightWave where to look for any content files when it first tries to load anything. When you quit the program, this location is saved, along with other settings, inside the LightWave preference file (LW9.cfg on the PC and LightWave Layout 9 Prefs on the Mac).

If you load the preference file into a text editor (it's just a text file, really), among many other entries, you will find these:

DirectoryType Scenes C:\LightWave\Scenes
DirectoryType Objects C:\LightWave\Objects
DirectoryType Surfaces C:\LightWave\Surfaces
DirectoryType Images C:\LightWave\Images
DirectoryType Previews C:\LightWave\Previews
DirectoryType Motions C:\LightWave\Motions

Note

Mac users, your LightWave directory will be found in Applications > NewTek > LightWave 3D 9.

These are search locations added by LightWave that are scanned when you try to load anything. For example, if you try to load an object, LightWave looks in C:\LightWave\Objects first. If you're on a Mac, it'll search Applications:\NewTek\LightWave. It looks in C:\LightWave because that is where the content directory has been set. If you were to set your content folder in your preferences to D:\Somewhere\on\my\harddrive, LightWave would automatically change the entries in this list:

DirectoryType Scenes D:\Somewhere\on\my\harddrive\Scenes
DirectoryType Objects D:\Somewhere\on\my\harddrive\Objects
DirectoryType Surfaces D:\Somewhere\on\my\harddrive\Surfaces
DirectoryType Images D:\Somewhere\on\my\harddrive\Images
DirectoryType Previews D:\Somewhere\on\my\harddrive\Previews
DirectoryType Motions D:\Somewhere\on\my\harddrive\Motions

LightWave takes the content directory setting and adds those subdirectories. If they don't exist, LightWave uses only the content directory you set, in this case D:\Somewhere\on\my\harddrive.

The point is, LightWave expects to find these subdirectories within the content directory. Taking this into account, when you save a scene (which is also a text file you can read), LightWave saves the location of any items in the scene file without the content directory part of the location. For example, if your content folder were set to C:\Program Files\LightWave\Content, and in your scene you had loaded an object called final_object.lwo that was stored in a folder called My Objects and then in a subfolder called "Final Versions," the scene file would have an entry that loads the object from disk like this:

LoadObjectLayer 1 My Objects\Final Versions\final_object.lwo

The LightWave program knows the top-level location of the content directory (taken from the LW9.cfg or LightWave Layout 9 Prefs file), and the scene file knows the rest (see **Figure 15.17**).

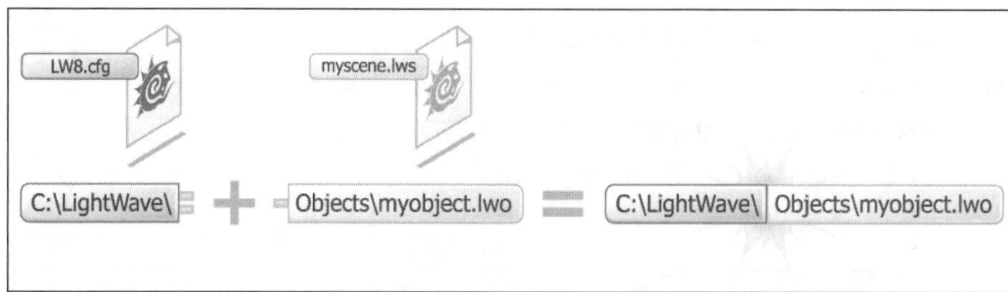

Figure 15.17 This diagram shows how the path works when a scene file is saved.

There is a reason for this, and it's important! Let's imagine LightWave didn't have a content directory preference, and instead it saved the full location of any objects, images, and so on with the scene file. Thus, it would be C:\Program Files\LightWave3D 9\Content\My Objects\Final Versions\final_object.lwo. If you were to give that scene to someone else to work on, or if you wanted to work on a different computer, unless you copied the files into exactly the same directory structure, LightWave would complain about missing files.

This is because LightWave tries to load the files using the locations from the original computer, which might not match the current computer. Hard-coding file locations isn't a good idea, which is why LightWave doesn't work this way.

So what is the best way to organize content files? Well, that depends on how you work with your files. The favored method is to have a folder with the project name, and inside that are the objects, scenes, and images folders. You would then set your content directory to the top-level folder before trying to load anything. This method is great if you constantly work on a project in various places, or if several people are working on it and it needs to be passed around because everything needed for the scene is in a self-contained set of folders.

However, if you are the sole user and you work from one machine, this method can be a pain when working on several projects because you must keep setting your content directory to each project before loading. This is shown more clearly in **Figure 15.18**.

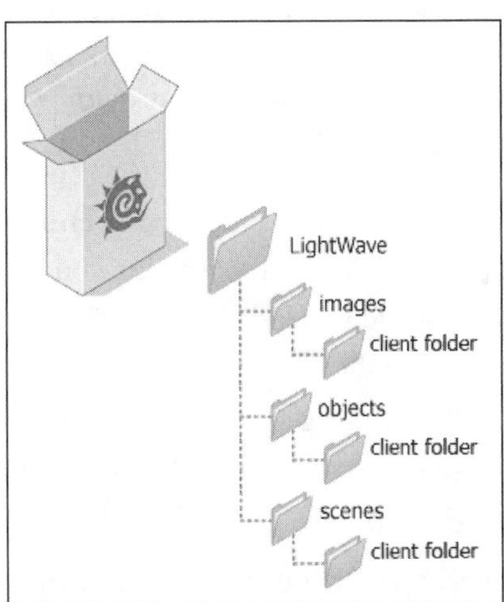

Figure 15.18 A good content directory within LightWave could work something like this.

Personally, I find that it's easier to organize content files as shown in the figure. The benefit of doing it this way is that you must point your content directory to one folder only once. This is essentially a reworked version of the first method. It is still portable because you just have to collect items for a scene in several places, and if you don't move your content around much, I find this to be a better way of organizing content files.

If none of that made any sense, don't worry. As far as ScreamerNet is concerned, it doesn't matter how you store your files as long as it can find them, but it is good practice to organize your files logically.

Another very important fact to remember when saving scenes, objects, and textures is that spaces in file and folder names can sometimes cause problems with ScreamerNet, such as the program being unable to find certain elements of the scene file. Instead of a space, use the underscore symbol (_) or a hyphen (<->).

Back to ScreamerNet; let's recap. We've learned so far that for the master computer to "talk" to the nodes, they all must be able to see the command folder because they use this to pass messages to each other. The nodes must also be able to see the content folder because it stores all the files needed for rendering. Thus, the content folder holds the files for rendering, while the command folder stores the instructions on what to render.

Configuration Files

In addition to the content and command folders, a third item must also be accessible to the nodes: plug-ins. Any plug-ins you've used to create effects in your scene must also be available on the network. For example, if you've used Sasquatch to create hair on a character or a motion plug-in to move an object (LightWave itself uses plug-ins to load and save files), or even if you haven't used any FX plug-ins, ScreamerNet still needs to know where they are to save files after it has rendered them. All these plug-ins are separate files that need to be loaded by the LWSN program, just as LightWave did when you created your scene.

When you think about it, if the ScreamerNet program needed to know the location of all the plug-ins you have installed, you would need to type the location of every single one! That would be a lot of typing! The way LightWave deals with this is by storing the location of all the plug-ins in a configuration file. When you scan your plug-ins, LightWave is "writing down" where they all are; it then saves them to a configuration file. This file is called LWEXT9.cfg (LightWave EXTensions). So to tell ScreamerNet where all your plug-ins are, all you need do is tell it where the LWEXT9.cfg file is on the network.

There is another config file ScreamerNet needs to find in order to work: LW9.cfg. As we mentioned earlier, this is the LightWave Layout configuration file. It stores a whole bunch of settings, but most importantly, it stores the location of the content folder we mentioned earlier.

Let's review. **Table 15.1** presents a breakdown of what ScreamerNet needs to be able to find on a network in order to run.

Table 15.1 ScreamerNet Needs

Needs to Find	Needed for...	Information Stored in...
Command folder	Master computer to "talk" to render nodes	Nodes told at initialization time
Plug-ins	Plug-ins used in the scene and for file saving	LWEXT9.cfg
Scene content	All objects, images, and scene files Nodes told at initialization time	LW9.cfg

Technically, these items don't need to be in one place; they don't need to be in the same building or even the same country! As long as ScreamerNet can find them, they could be anywhere. However, for the sake of simplicity, it makes sense to group these items in one place: a shared network folder (see **Figure 15.19**).

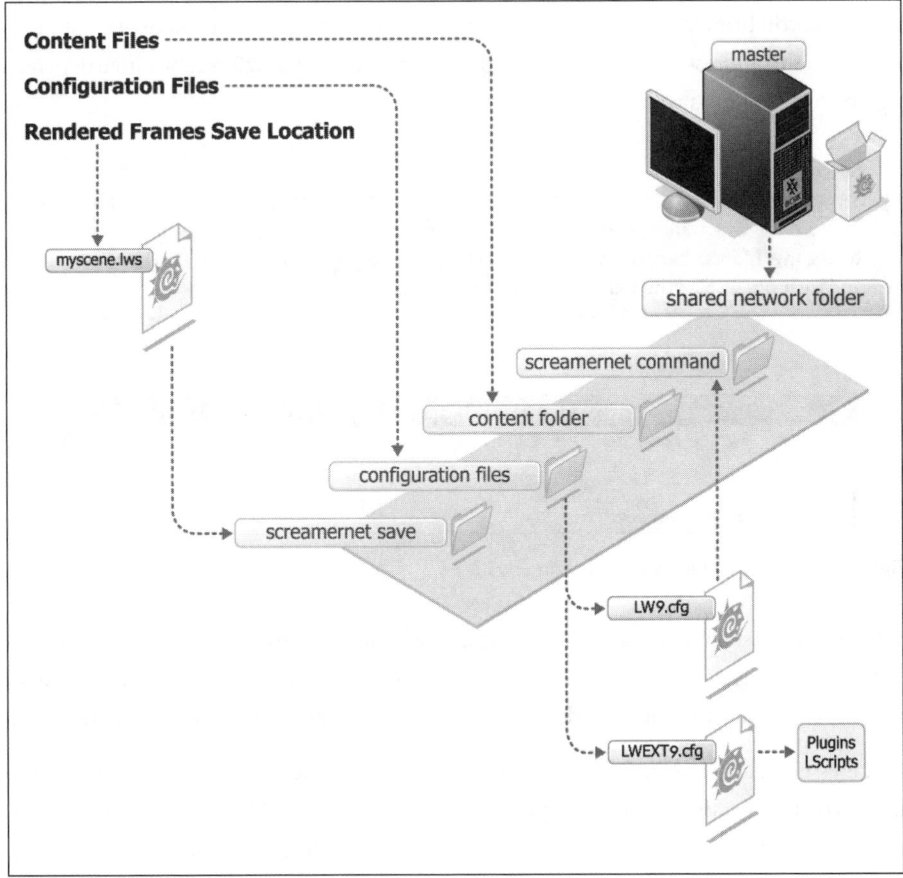

Figure 15.19 This diagram shows files that ScreamerNet needs on a shared network.

There are many methods of physically networking computers together, but because there are so many variables to consider—too many for this book—I'm going to assume that you already have a network up and running. If not, the Internet is your best resource, or your computer administrator if you have access to one.

Sharing files across a network obviously means you are going to refer to locations using pathnames. As far as ScreamerNet is concerned, there are two main methods for doing this. The first is using Universal Naming Convention (UNC), while the other is using drive mapping. They ultimately do the same thing but differ very slightly.

UNC Naming

This is the simpler method of the two. UNC naming is exactly as it sounds—it's a standard naming convention for finding drives or folders on a network.

Whenever you browse through folders using Windows, the address or network path can be seen in the address bar (the screen shot shown in **Figure 15.20** might differ depending on your Windows version).

Note

In the Windows 2000 and Windows XP versions of Internet Explorer, you might need to set the address bar to display the path by going to Tools > Folder Options > View and turn on Display the full path in the address bar.

Figure 15.20 An address path in Windows.

In the example shown in Figure 15.20, the address path tells us that the computer name on the network is dansboxx, and on that computer is a folder (which has to be shared to be seen) called screamernet. Inside that folder is another called screamernet_command.

That is essentially it! Locating folders and files for ScreamerNet using this method requires us to type the location of the shared network folder, kind of like the address for your house. So as long as you can see the computers, drives, and folders you are trying to access on the network, it's very easy to work out the network path by simply looking at it in the address bar, as shown in Figure 15.20.

Drive Mapping

This technique is favored by a lot of the ScreamerNet tutorials I've read, but I could never understand why, because it takes more time to set up than UNC naming and can be confusing.

Drive mapping is the process of replacing a network path to a folder with a letter. Imagine we had a folder on a computer on a network, and its pathname was something like \\my_computer\documents\excel\timesheets\2007. You could substitute all that with a letter, T, for example. Then whenever you accessed the T: drive, it would take you straight to the folder 2003.

Sounds great, doesn't it! Well, not quite. If we were to use this method for ScreamerNet, we would have to map the path to the shared ScreamerNet folder to a letter on each computer. The problem arises when a node computer tries to access a mapped drive on a computer that is switched off or unavailable; the node computer complains that the path can no longer be found.

Figure 15.21 Right-click on My Network Places and select Map Network Drive.

This can be a problem if you are setting up ScreamerNet in an office using your colleagues' computers, especially if they don't know what the error message means! They will soon tell you about it!

However, if you are intent on using this method for resolving pathnames, here's how to map a letter to a pathname. I won't be using this method for this tutorial because it offers no benefits over UNC naming that I'm aware of.

Right-click on the My Network Places icon (again this will differ depending on the version of Windows you are using; if in doubt as to where the option is, do a search in Windows Help). See **Figure 15.21**.

There will be an option called Map Network Drive. Clicking the option invokes another window, as shown in **Figure 15.22**.

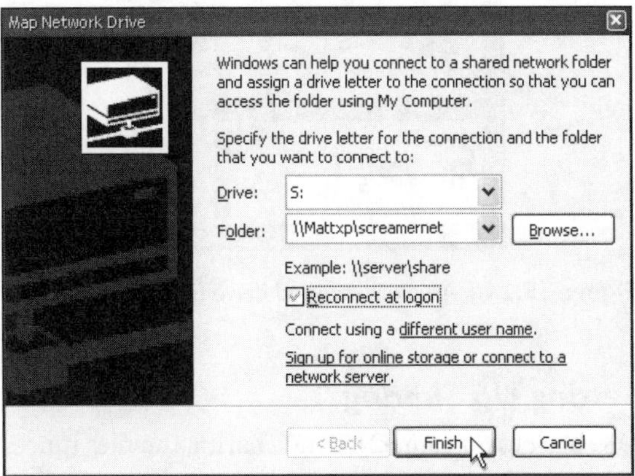

Figure 15.22 The Map Network Drive dialog box is where you can configure drives from your network.

The Map Network Drive dialog box is where you set which letter you want to assign; in our ScreamerNet example, S: seems to makes sense. After a letter is selected, you can then set the path to map the letter to in the Folder pull-down menu. Alternatively, you can click the Browse button and browse the network for the folder (see **Figure 15.23**).

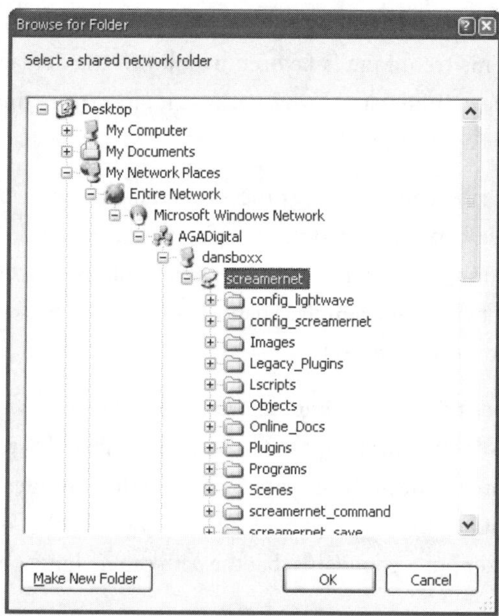

Figure 15.23 The Browse for Folder panel lets you point to a specific folder.

When done, click the Finish button. If you now look in My Computer, you see a new drive called S:, which points to the folder you specified. Any reference to the S: drive goes straight to that folder, as shown in **Figure 15.24**.

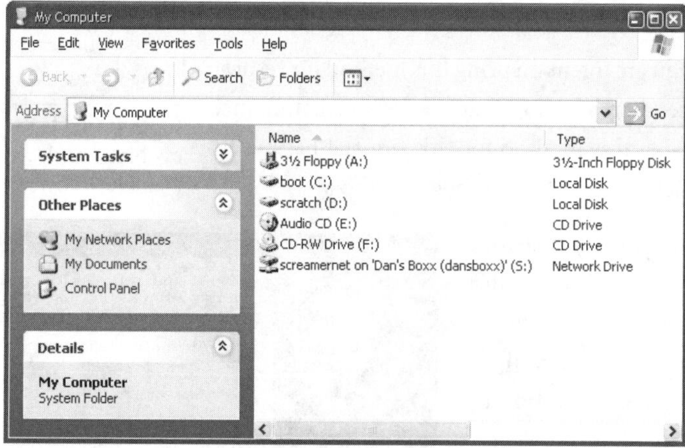

Figure 15.24 A newly mapped drive from your network.

Setting Up Sharing

OK, back to ScreamerNet and sharing the files it needs.

We know what ScreamerNet needs to be able to find. Now is the time to figure out where to put these files. By default, LightWave stores most of its files in one folder, usually found on the main hard drive in a folder called LightWave. If yours is different from this, don't worry.

When I say "most files," this is because Windows steps in here and interferes a little! If a program is written to conform with Windows protocol, it stores its preference files in user-specific folders. The idea is that many people using one machine can have their own preferences and setups, and technically this is a good idea, but it can cause problems with ScreamerNet if you're not sure which preference files LightWave is using. To avoid confusion, either use one set of preference files or "point" LightWave to the right files when it starts up—more on this later.

The location of these preferences depends on which version of Windows you are using, but it is either in C:\WinNT\Profiles\WhichUser or C:\Documents & Settings\WhichUser. If in doubt, do a search for LW9.cfg and see where they are.

The content files are also usually stored within the main LightWave folder, but again these can moved anywhere you like as long as you tell LightWave and ScreamerNet where the new location is.

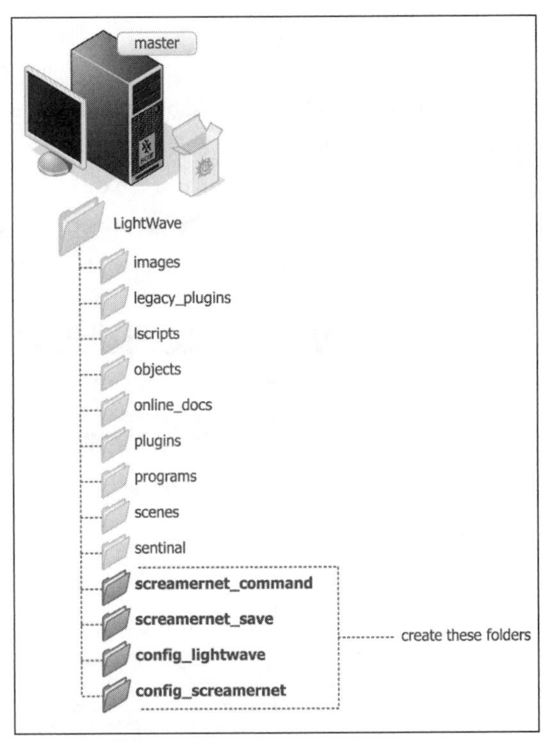

Figure 15.25 Here is a typical LightWave directory showing the folders created during installation and the new ones you must create.

To make this tutorial the same for all users, I'm going to suggest that the LightWave content, config files, and command folder all be stored in the main LightWave folder (on the master computer). If you don't want to do this, just make sure you replace all pathnames to these items with the new location you've decided on.

Before we start sharing these files, you must create some new folders in your LightWave directory. **Figure 15.25** shows the folder structure for a typical LightWave installation and the new folders you need to create.

The new folders are screamernet_command, screamernet_save, config_lightwave, and config_screamernet. These are in the command folder, a folder to which to save the rendered frames, the regular LightWave config folder, and a config folder specifically for ScreamerNet use.

OK, we now have placeholder locations for all the items ScreamerNet needs. They are all in one place, and all we need to do now is share the folder across the network so all the computers can see it.

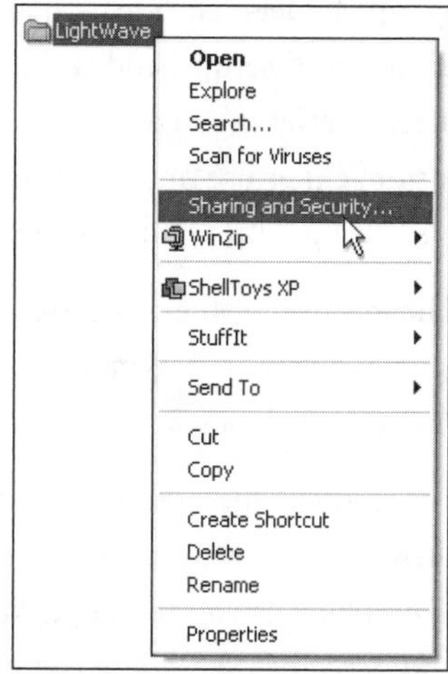

Figure 15.26 Right-click your LightWave folder to view the Sharing and Security option.

The process for this might differ slightly depending on which version of Windows you are using. I use Windows XP Professional, but the principles are the same for nearly all versions of Windows.

Locate your main LightWave folder on the master computer and right-click it to bring up the context-sensitive menu. In the list, there should be a Sharing and Security option (see **Figure 15.26**); if not, select the Properties option and find the Sharing tab.

You should now be presented with another window. Under the Sharing tab, there should be an option to turn on sharing for that folder. When activated, you can enter a name in the Share name box. You can call this anything you like, but something succinct like "screamernet" is all that is needed, and just to be safe, make sure it's all lowercase with no spaces, as in **Figure 15.27**.

Figure 15.27 The Sharing option for the LightWave folder.

While you're in there, make sure you set the Share Permissions for the folder to Full Control so that any computer (or render node) can read from and write to the LightWave folder. See **Figure 15.28**.

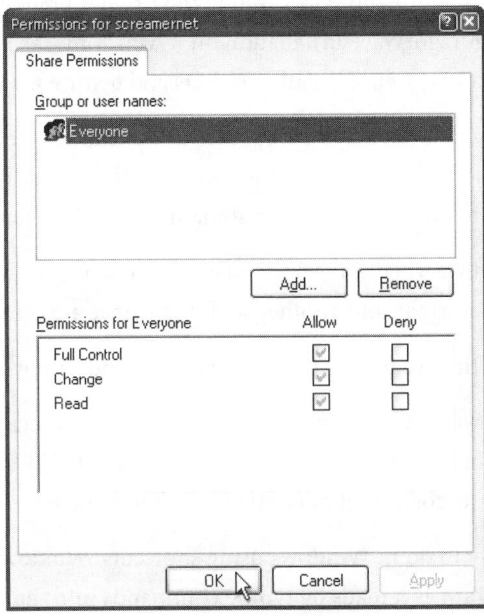

Figure 15.28 When accessed, you'll find the Share Permissions dialog box.

Now if you browse your Windows network, you should be able to see the folder you've just shared (see **Figure 15.29**).

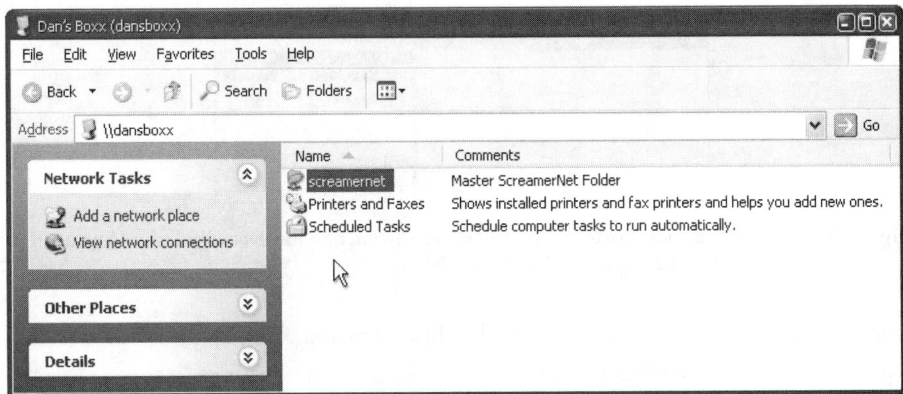

Figure 15.29 After you set up the folders for sharing, you can view them.

Setting Up the Master Computer

Now that all the folders are in place and are accessible across the network, we can begin to set up the computers.

Setting up the master is a little more involved than setting up render nodes because this computer has the main LightWave installation on it, which means it's the computer that is normally used for editing scenes, creating objects and texture maps, and so on.

As mentioned earlier, LightWave uses config files to determine where certain things are. The pathnames to these items are local to the computer they reside on. This causes problems for ScreamerNet because it needs the pathnames to be "network-aware."

What this means is that we will need two sets of config files: one set for when we are working with LightWave as normal, and another set for when we are using ScreamerNet.

This is why we created the two folders (config_lightwave and config_screamernet) earlier.

By default, LightWave won't know anything about these folders because we created them, so we need to tell LightWave to use them. The easiest way to do this in Windows is to "point" LightWave to the correct set of config files when it loads.

Fortunately, this is easy to do in Windows using shortcuts. Windows shortcuts can pass information to a program as it loads by typing commands into the Target box. To locate this box, you'll need to find the existing shortcut to LightWave Layout in your Start Menu or create some new ones from scratch in the usual manner.

You'll need to create two shortcuts to the LightWave Layout program, one for regular LightWave use and one for ScreamerNet use (see **Figure 15.30**).

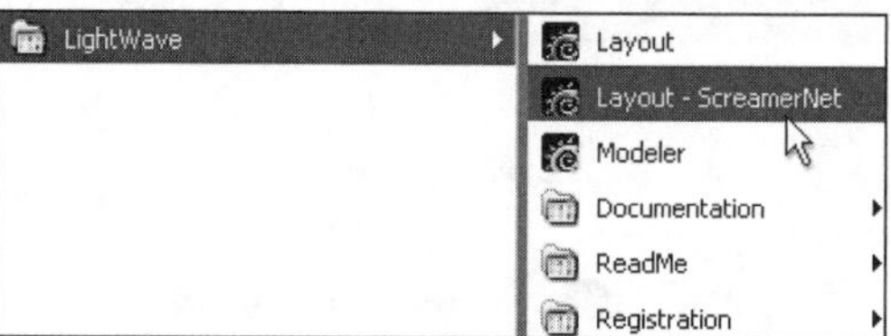

Figure 15.30 Create two shortcuts to LightWave Layout, one for everyday LightWave use and the other just for ScreamerNet.

After you've created the two shortcuts, right-click them and bring up the Properties dialog box for each one (see **Figure 15.31**).

Find the box called Target.

For normal LightWave use, enter the following:

```
C:\LightWave\Programs\lightwav.exe -cc:\LightWave\config_lightwave
```

For ScreamerNet use, enter the following:

```
C:\LightWave\Programs\lightwav.exe -0 -cc:\LightWave\config_screamernet
```

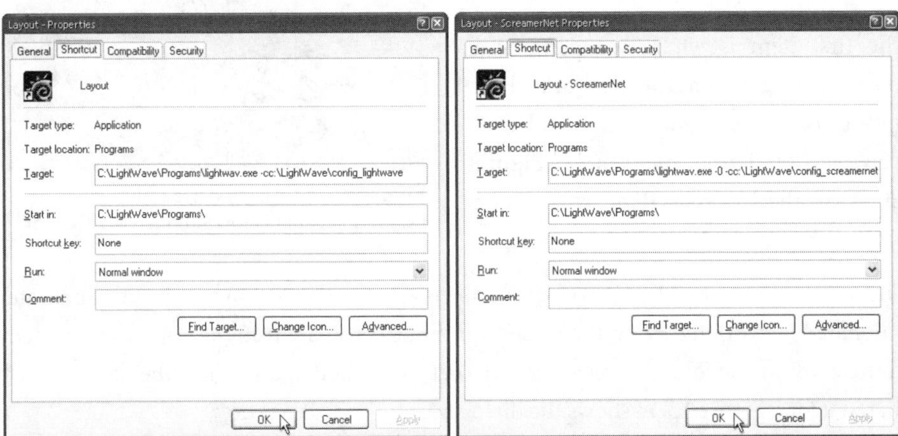

Figure 15.31 Right-click on the shortcuts you've created to bring up the Properties dialog box.

The first part, C:\LightWave\Programs\lightwav.exe, has to do with the shortcut, and it's simply a path to the LightWave Layout program. The second part is the bit we're interested in, –cc:\LightWave\config_screamernet, where the –c switch tells LightWave you are providing the location of the config files, and c:\LightWave\config_screamernet is the path to where the config files are located. Note there is no space between the –c and c:\LightWave\config_screamernet.

We don't need these paths to be network-aware because they are not used by ScreamerNet; they simply point LightWave to the files that do contain the information ScreamerNet needs.

Now that we have the shortcuts for LightWave pointing to the correct config files, you need to actually copy your existing config files to both the config_lightwave and config_screamernet folders so that any custom menus, color settings, plug-ins you've added, and so on are loaded when you run LightWave. As mentioned earlier, these config files might be located in different places, depending on your version of Windows, so simply do a search for LW9.cfg. When found, copy the files LW9.cfg and LWEXT9.cfg into the two config folders you've created.

OK, now everything is in place to run the version of LightWave Layout that will be using the ScreamerNet config files.

You need to set up a few things in this version of LightWave so that the settings are saved to the ScreamerNet version of the config files when you quit the program.

The first item is where the command folder is located on the network. This option is found under the Render > Network Rendering menu (see **Figure 15.32**) in the Network Rendering dialog box (see **Figure 15.33**).

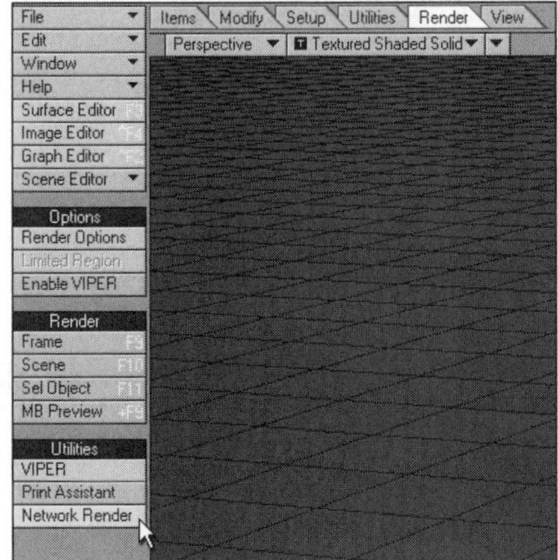

Figure 15.32 LightWave's Network Rendering panel is found under the Render tab in Layout.

Clicking the Command Directory button opens another window in which you can locate the shared network folder on the master machine. If you are using the names suggested in this tutorial, the folder is called screamernet_command and is inside the screamernet shared folder. **Figure 15.34** shows the dialog box.

Whenever you browse for anything in the screamernet shared folder like this, make sure you browse from Entire Network. If you added screamernet as a Network Place shortcut

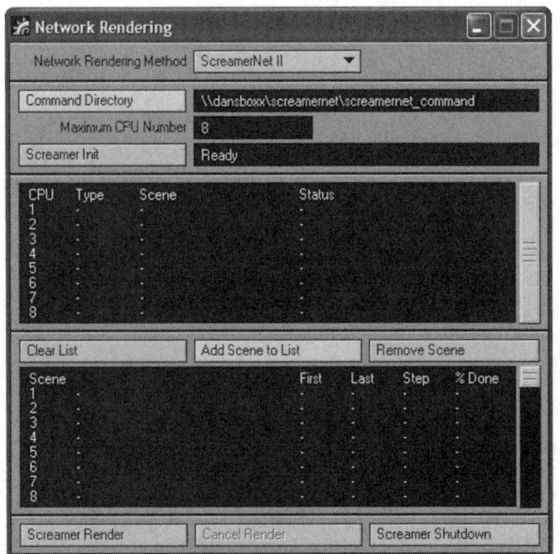

Figure 15.33 LightWave's Network Rendering panel, where you can set up multiple renders and network rendering.

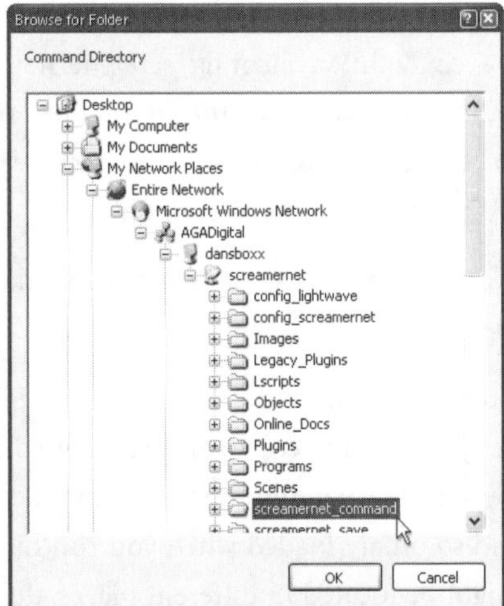

Figure 15.34 The Browse for Folder panel, shown accessing the screamernet_command and other folders.

and used that, it seems Windows resolves to a local pathname, which causes problems because the path is no longer network-aware. I learned the hard way!

The next item to set is the content directory. This is found under the General Options panel (press the **o** key), as shown in **Figure 15.35**. Click the Content Directory button and locate the screamernet shared network folder again. Select the top-level screamernet folder and click OK (see **Figure 15.36**).

Almost done! The last thing we need to set up is the location of the plug-ins on the network. Some tutorials tell you to open the LWEXT9.cfg file and perform a search and replace on the pathnames. You could do it that way, but it's easier (and less error-prone) to rescan your plug-ins using the shared network path location.

The option to scan your plug-ins can be found under Layout > Plugins > Edit Plug-ins menu (or Alt+F11), as shown in **Figure 15.37**.

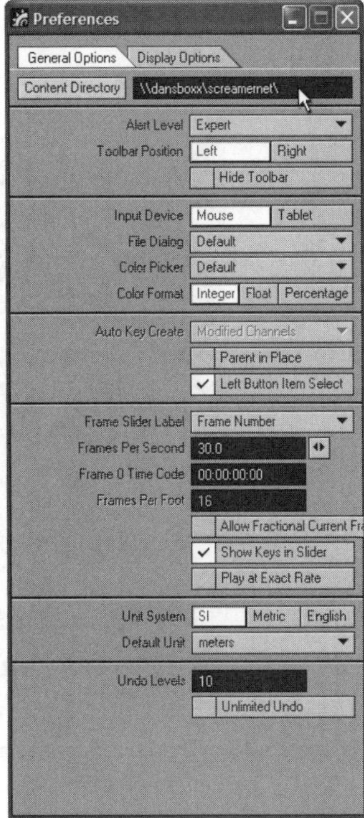

Figure 15.35 LightWave's General Options panel, accessible by pressing **o** on the keyboard.

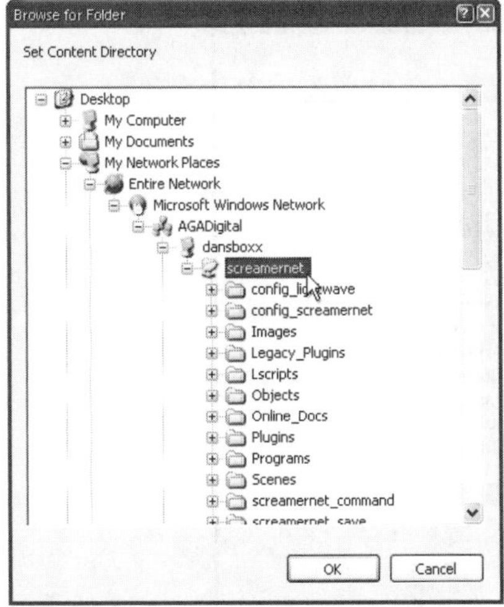

Figure 15.36 The Browse for Folder panel used again.

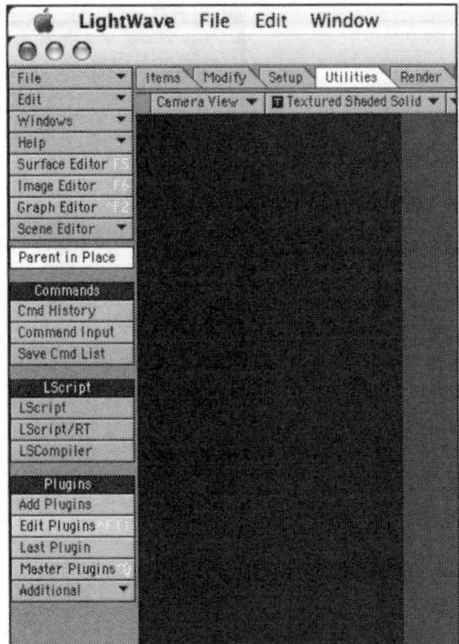

Figure 15.37 LightWave's Edit Plugins panel is found under the Utilities tab in Layout and Modeler.

This opens the Edit Plug-ins window, where you will find the option to Scan Directory (see **Figure 15.38**).

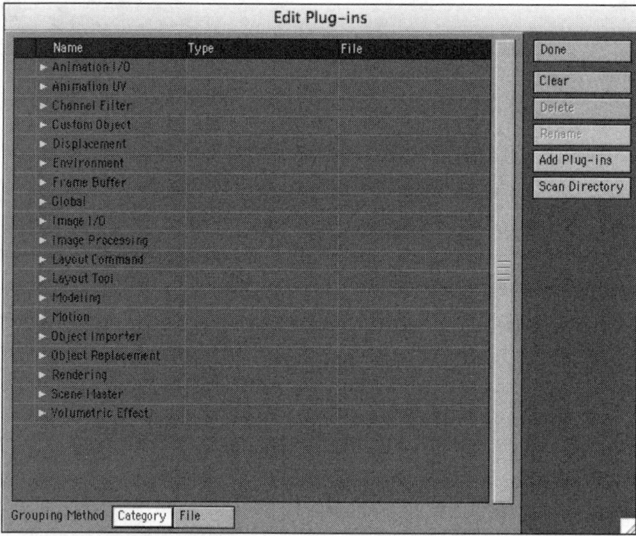

Figure 15.38 The Edit Plug-ins panel enables you to scan for multiple plug-ins or to simply add one at a time.

Click the Scan Directory button, locate the Plugins folder on the shared network, and click OK to scan the folder (see **Figure 15.39**).

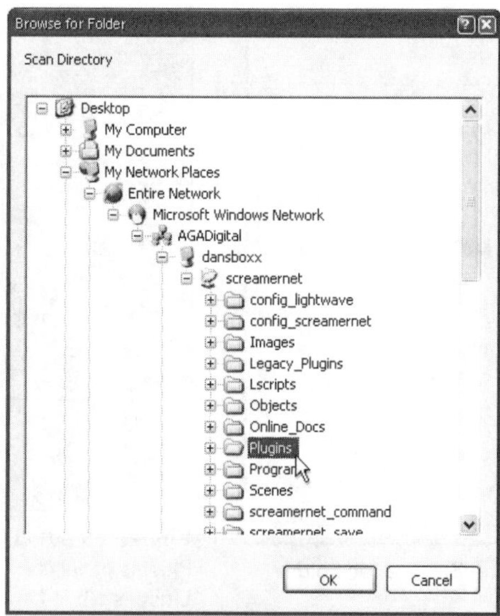

Figure 15.39 When scanning for plug-ins, you can also scan across your network.

Repeat this process and locate the Lscripts folder. That's the master computer setup (see **Figure 15.40**)!

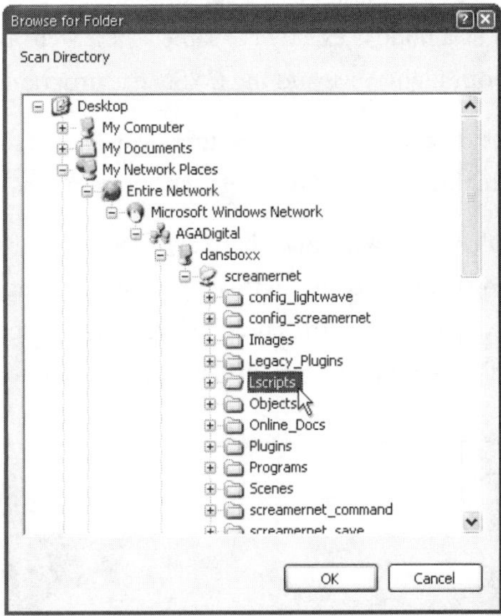

Figure 15.40 The Browse for Folder panel again, used for adding plug-ins.

To recap, you created two shortcuts to the LightWave Layout program. Each shortcut pointed to a different set of config files, one for normal LightWave usage and the other for ScreamerNet use.

You then copied the existing config files into the config_lightwave and config_screamernet folders. When done, you loaded the version of LightWave pointing to the ScreamerNet config files.

Next, you set up the content folder and the command folder, and rescanned the plug-in list. This saved the network-aware pathnames for each item into the ScreamerNet config files.

Setting Up the Render Nodes

Setting up the nodes is relatively simple compared to setting up the master computer because you can set up one node and then simply copy the same set of files to the other nodes, changing only a few bits of information.

At this point, you need to decide whether your master computer itself is a render node. When ScreamerNet is up and running, the master computer isn't doing anything more than passing commands around, and it's certainly not doing any rendering. So unless you plan to do some work while the other computers are rendering, you could make the master a render node, too.

Whether you decide to use your master computer as node 1 is up to you, but the process of setting up the master as a node is exactly the same as if it were a totally different computer. You simply run both LightWave and the LWSN.exe program.

Before you start with the detailed stuff, the first thing you'll need to do is copy some files from the master computer onto the hard drive of each computer that will be a render node.

Create a folder called LightWave on the main hard drive (usually the C: drive) of each node computer (obviously, you don't need to do this on the master because it should already have LightWave installed). Now copy the entire folder called Programs from the master computer into the LightWave folder you've just created on each node (see **Figure 15.41**).

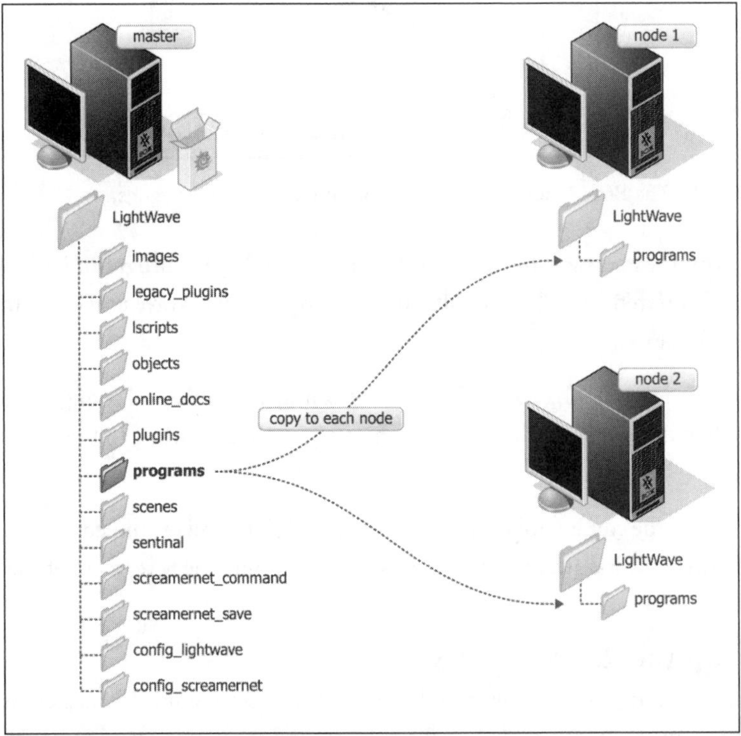

Figure 15.41 Copy the LightWave programs folder to each node, as shown here.

The last part of setting up a node requires a little explanation. If you are unfortunate enough to remember computers in the days of MS-DOS, you'll be familiar with running programs through a command line. MS-DOS didn't have a lovely GUI with icons for programs, so you had to type the name of the program to run it, along with any "commands" the program needed after its name.

Well, nostalgia is back! Despite the lovely Windows XP interface, some programs still require you to run them through the command line, and LWSN.exe is one of them!

The LWSN.exe program needs to know a few things at runtime: where the config files are stored, where the content directory is located, and which job and ack number it is going to be in order to distinguish itself from the other render nodes.

Having to type all this information for each node every time you needed to run ScreamerNet would be a pain. Fortunately, Windows enables you to create a text file that acts as a stored command line. This text file has a special name—a batch file. It has the .bat file extension, but really it's just a plain text file.

To create a render batch file, open up a text editor. (Notepad is fine.) Type the following text, replacing any reference to \\Dansboxx\screamernet with the network path to your own shared folder you set up earlier.

```
echo "LightWave ScreamerNet Node 1 Initialisation..."
cd c:\lightwave\programs\
LWSN -2 -c\\Dansboxx\screamernet\config_screamernet -d
➥\\Dansboxx\screamernet\ \\Dansboxx\screamernet\screamer_command\job1
➥\\Dansboxx\screamernet\screamer_command\ack1
```

Now save the file (as a text file) with the .bat extension and place it inside the LightWave folder of the computer that will be node 1. You can call the batch file sn_init_1.bat, for example, although you can call it anything you like.

The render batch file script might look complicated to users unfamiliar with MS-DOS, but it's pretty straightforward when broken down, so let's do it.

echo "LightWave ScreamerNet Node 1 Initialisation…"

This line has nothing to do with ScreamerNet whatsoever; it's just a little text that is echoed to the screen to tell you to which node number the batch file has been assigned. You can leave this out if you want.

cd c:\lightwave\programs\

This line changes the current directory to the Programs directory on the main hard drive so that the next line knows where to find the LWSN.exe program. If you installed LightWave somewhere else, then change this line to reflect where you put it.

LWSN –2

This runs the LightWave ScreamerNet program. The -2 sets up which mode ScreamerNet will run in. The -2 basically says you're accepting commands from the master computer on which scene or frame to render. There is a -3 mode, which enables you to specify the scene and the start/end frames, but this mode defeats the point of using several computers to render a scene because -3 mode only enables you to pass it one scene. Basically, you'll never need to use -3 mode!

–c\\Dansboxx\screamernet\config_screamernet

This command tells LWSN.exe where the config files are kept on the network. The -c is the switch that says the following text is the path to the config files. If you have your config files elsewhere, now is the time to tell ScreamerNet where they are. Remember, LWSN.exe needs to know the location of the config files in order to find the location of the plug-ins, the paths to which are stored in the LWEXT9.cfg file. Note that it's important that there is no space between -c and the pathname after it.

–d\\Dansboxx\screamernet\

This command tells LWSN.exe where the content directory is on the network. The -d is the switch that says the following text is the path to the content directory. I've never quite understood why you need to tell ScreamerNet this because it should be stored in the LW9.cfg. I guess it's just in case you want to store them somewhere else. Again, if your content directory is not in the shared network folder, replace \\Dansboxx\screamernet\ with the path to where you put the shared network folder containing these items.

\\Dansboxx\screamernet\screamer_command\job1

No switch this time, but this is where you tell LWSN.exe where to look for job commands and which job number it is to be allocated.

\\Dansboxx\screamernet\screamer_command\ack1

This is almost the same as the previous line, but instead of a job number, an acknowledgement number is provided. The number must be the same as the job number.

The diagram in **Figure 15.42** shows how this all links up with the shared network folder you set up earlier.

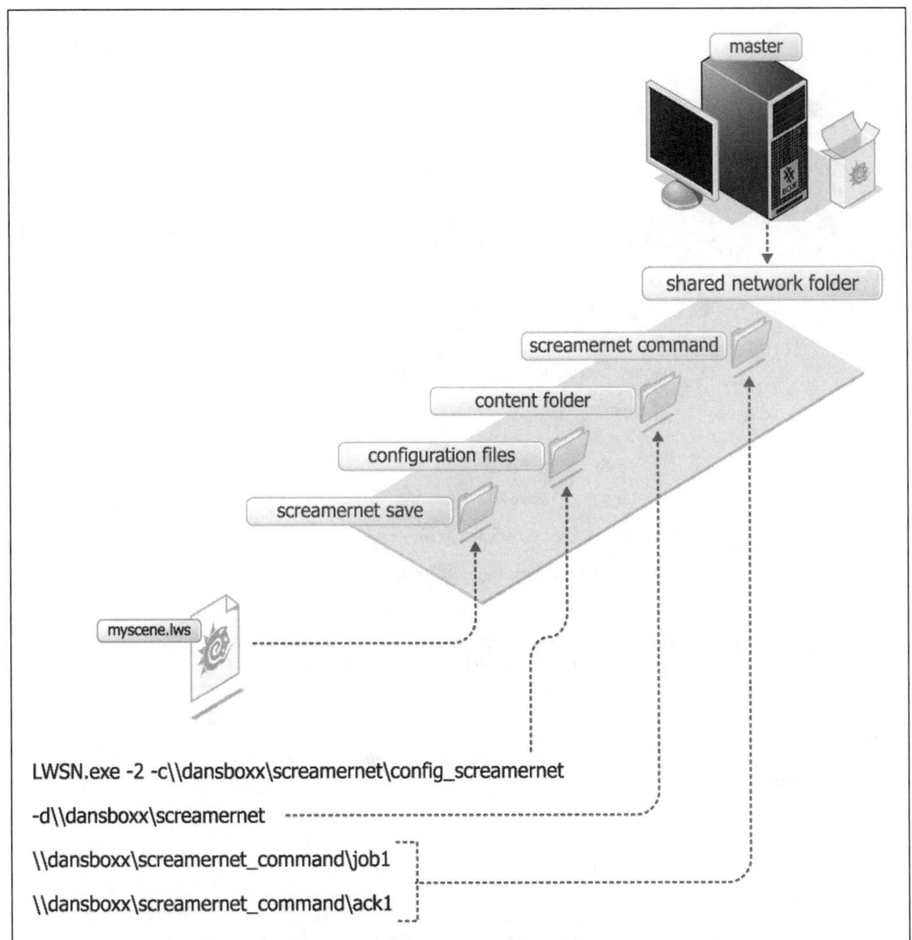

Figure 15.42 A batch file matches shared folder locations.

That's the node 1 setup. To set up the other nodes, simply copy the sn_init_1.bat file (or whatever you named it) to the LightWave folder on all the other nodes.

After copying, you need to rename the file to reflect the render node it is going to be. You also need to edit the job and ack numbers to reflect the node number. Depending on how many nodes you have, you should have something like what is shown in **Figure 15.43**.

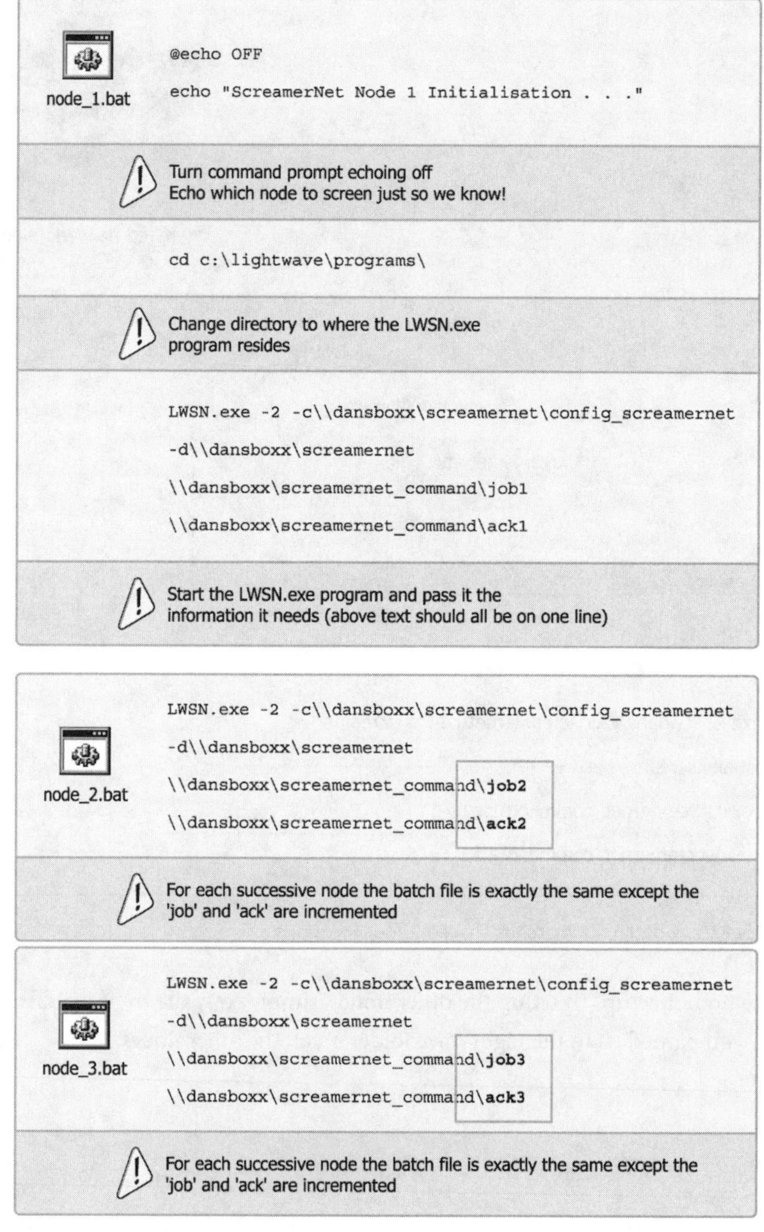

Figure 15.43 Successive nodes are set up as shown here.

Before you run ScreamerNet through its paces, **Figure 15.44** presents an overview of what's been set up.

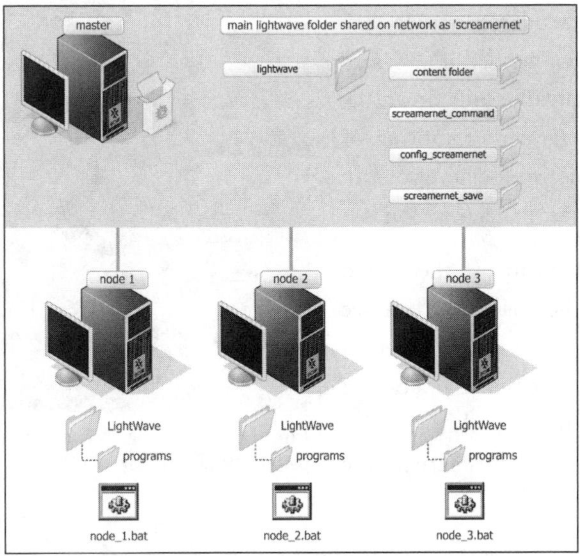

Figure 15.44 Here's an overview of what's been set up for ScreamerNet.

If you decided to set up the master computer as a node, it should look like **Figure 15.45**.

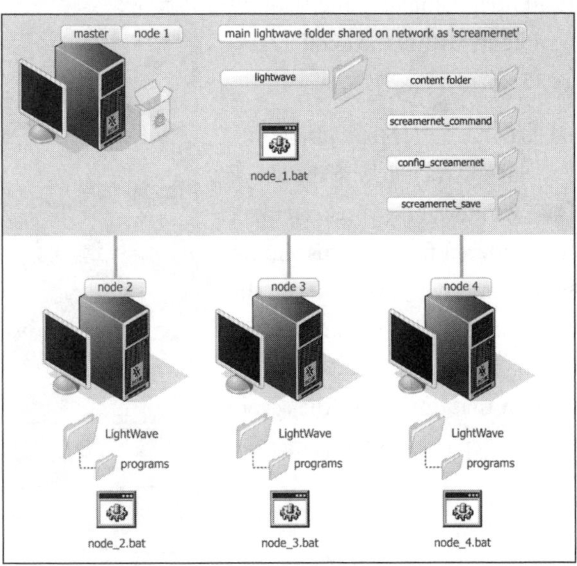

Figure 15.45 The master node setup for ScreamerNet.

Setting the Save Location

You need to do one last thing before you run ScreamerNet, and that is set the save location for the rendered frames. You could have all the render nodes save their frames locally; the only downside to this is that you have to go hunting for them across the network before you can build them into the final animation.

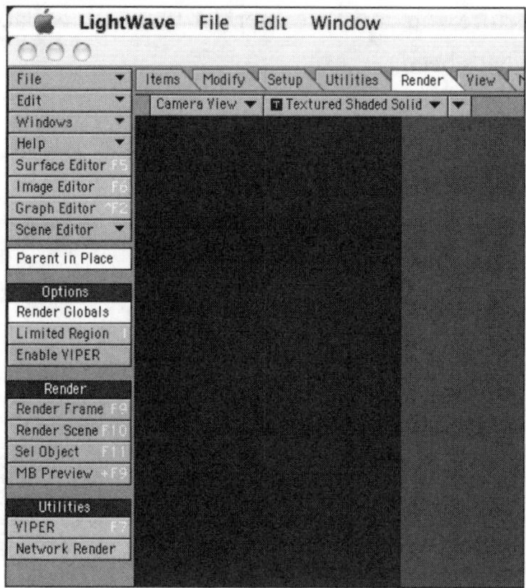

Figure 15.46 LightWave's Render Globals panel is found under the Render tab in Layout.

It makes sense then to use the shared folder that all the machines can see because all the frames can be saved in one place, making them nice and easy to find. As I'm sure you guessed already, this is why you created the screamernet_save folder earlier.

The only place you can set the save location for the rendered frames is within the scene file itself. So run the version of LightWave using the normal config files, open up the scene you want to render, and bring up the Render Globals panel (found under the Options category within the Render tab), as shown in **Figure 15.46**.

In the Render Globals panel under the Output tab, there is an option to Save RGB. Clicking the check box invokes a file-save window; here you need to set the location for the rendered frames. This should ideally point to the screamernet_save folder in the shared network folder, although this can be anywhere you like, as long as *all* render nodes can see it on the network. With that done, save the scene, and you're ready to render it using ScreamerNet (see **Figure 15.47**).

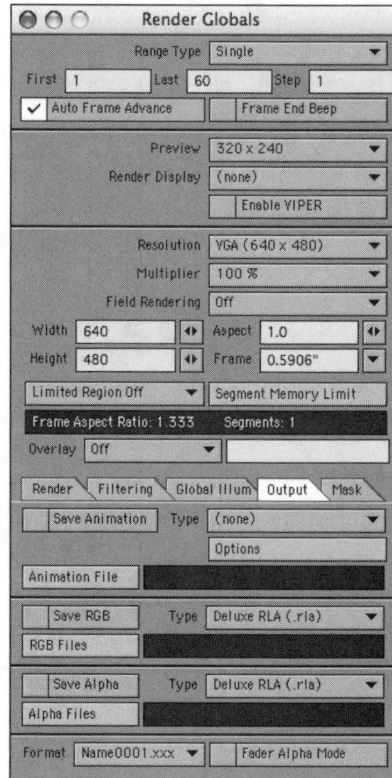

Figure 15.47 LightWave's Render Globals panel enables you to set a save path for renders.

Rendering Using ScreamerNet

You're almost there, but first let's run through a quick checklist:

- Master Computer
- Created new folders in main LightWave folder: config_lightwave, config_screamernet, screamernet_command, screamernet_save
- Copied existing config files to new config_lightwave and config_screamernet folders
- Set main LightWave folder to share across network using the name screamernet
- Created two shortcuts to LightWave Layout
- Pointed one shortcut to the config files in the folder config_lightwave, the other shortcut to config_screamernet
- Ran LightWave Layout using the config_screamernet config files
- Set the command directory to the folder screamernet_command in the shared network folder
- Set the content directory to the shared network folder screamernet
- Rescanned the plug-in list from the shared network folder screamernet location
- Render Nodes
- Created folder called LightWave on the main hard drive
- Copied programs folder from LightWave folder on the main computer to the LightWave folder on the render node
- Set up render batch file using config_screamernet as config folder, shared network folder as content directory, and each with unique job/ack numbers
- Scene Files
- Set the save folder to screamernet_save in the shared network folder

OK? Let's go!

If you can remember that far back, I mentioned that ScreamerNet had two "parts" to it; the first is the controller part that is the Network Rendering panel in LightWave, while the second part is the LWSN.exe program sitting on each node.

When a node is activated, it looks for its first job file. However, there won't be any there until you initialize ScreamerNet in the Network Rendering panel, but it's pointless initializing it until you've activated all the nodes!

When you run ScreamerNet, a node does two things: It looks for job files and sticks its hand in the air, saying "I'm here, I'm over here!" Well, not quite, but it's waiting to be found by the controller part of ScreamerNet. This is where some confusion lies with

ScreamerNet. Nodes complain they can't find job files when they're first run. This is perfectly normal. Bearing this in mind, double-click each render batch file to activate it. You'll see output like that shown in **Figure 15.48**.

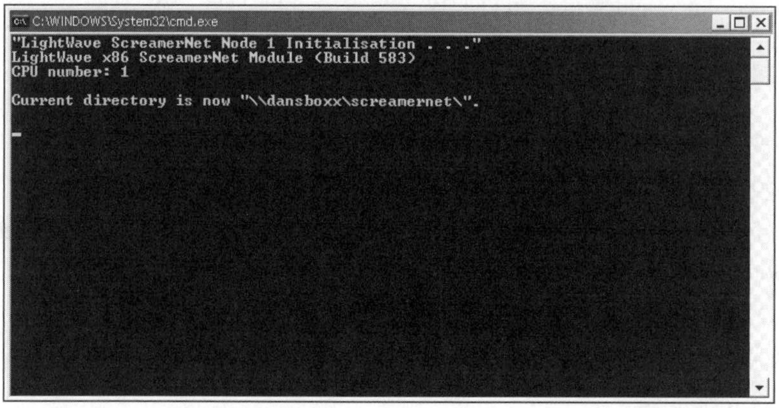

```
C:\WINDOWS\System32\cmd.exe
"LightWave ScreamerNet Node 1 Initialisation . . ."
LightWave x86 ScreamerNet Module (Build 583)
CPU number: 1

Current directory is now "\\dansboxx\screamernet\".

_
```

Figure 15.48 The current directory is identified.

The first thing the node should tell you is where it's looking for the content files. If this is wrong or if it comes up with an error, close it down and check the script for errors in the pathnames.

The next thing you should see is the node complaining that it can't open a job file (see **Figure 15.49**). This is perfectly normal because there isn't one to open, but the important thing to note is that the node is running. If the render nodes still repeat the line "Can't open job file" after you have initialized ScreamerNet, then they can't find the command folder. Close them down and check the path in the script to the command folder. Make sure it's visible on the network.

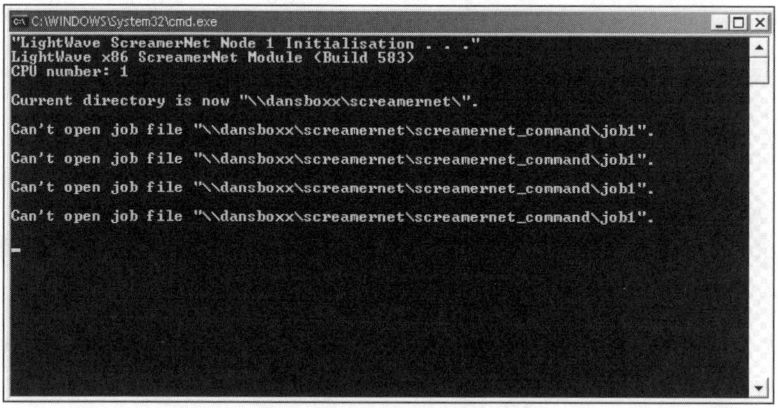

```
C:\WINDOWS\System32\cmd.exe
"LightWave ScreamerNet Node 1 Initialisation . . ."
LightWave x86 ScreamerNet Module (Build 583)
CPU number: 1

Current directory is now "\\dansboxx\screamernet\".

Can't open job file "\\dansboxx\screamernet\screamernet_command\job1".

Can't open job file "\\dansboxx\screamernet\screamernet_command\job1".

Can't open job file "\\dansboxx\screamernet\screamernet_command\job1".

Can't open job file "\\dansboxx\screamernet\screamernet_command\job1".

_
```

Figure 15.49 The node complains that it can't open a job file.

Returning to the master machine, run the version of LightWave that uses the configuration files in config_screamernet and bring up the Network Rendering panel (see **Figure 15.50**).

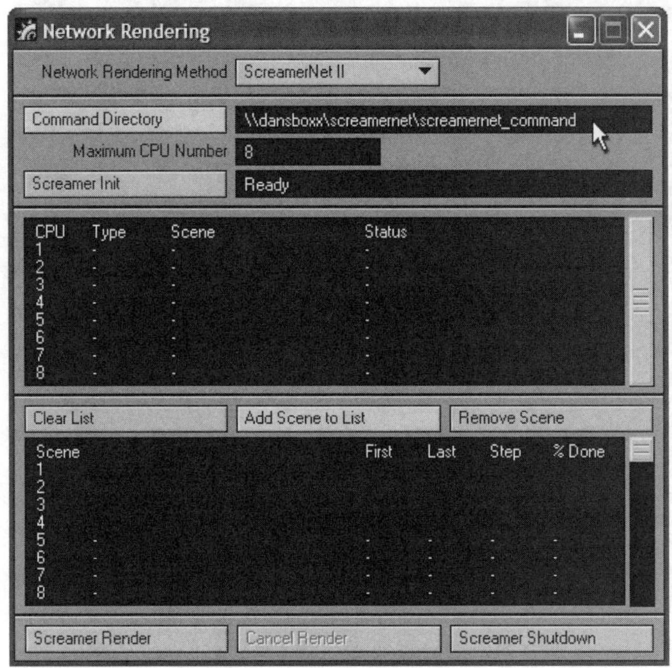

Figure 15.50 LightWave's Network Rendering panel.

The box called Maximum CPU Number requires you to enter the number of the highest-numbered node you have set up on your network. Here, there are 8 nodes, numbered 1 through 8, but you should put in the highest number of nodes you might have, such as 3. Nodes can be numbered from 1 to 1000; they don't even have to be in sequence. You could have nodes 1, 7, and 68 running, but if you do this, you would have to put 68 as your maximum CPU number, not 3 as you might think.

Now click the Screamer Init button. ScreamerNet checks for nodes that are sitting there complaining about job files! If successful, you are told how many CPUs (or render nodes) it has found. If the number isn't correct, then check the job/ack numbering in the render script files and try again. If no CPUs are found, check that the nodes and Network Rendering panel are both looking for the same command folder, which should be visible on the network. Also, check that all machines have access rights to read/write to that folder.

If everything has gone well, the nodes should now be happily repeating, as in **Figure 15.51**.

```
LightWave x86 ScreamerNet Module (Build 571)
CPU number: 1
Current directory is now "C:\Projects\inDreams\lw".
Can't open job file "C:\WUTemp\sn\job1".
Can't open job file "C:\WUTemp\sn\job1".
Can't open job file "C:\WUTemp\sn\job1".
Can't open job file "C:\WUTemp\sn\job1".
Can't open job file "C:\WUTemp\sn\job1".
Can't open job file "C:\WUTemp\sn\job1".
Can't open job file "C:\WUTemp\sn\job1".
Can't open job file "C:\WUTemp\sn\job1".
Can't open job file "C:\WUTemp\sn\job1".
Can't open job file "C:\WUTemp\sn\job1".
Can't open job file "C:\WUTemp\sn\job1".
Can't open job file "C:\WUTemp\sn\job1".
Can't open job file "C:\WUTemp\sn\job1".
LightWave command: init.
LightWave command: wait.
LightWave command: wait.
LightWave command: wait.
LightWave command: wait.
LightWave command: wait.
LightWave command: wait.
LightWave command: wait.
LightWave command: wait.
LightWave command: wait.
LightWave command: wait.
```

Figure 15.51 Here is what the LWSN.exe output looks like if all goes well.

This means they have successfully found a job file with a command inside saying "wait there and do nothing!"

All that's left to do now is to fill the Network Rendering panel with scenes, click Render, and watch it fly! So click the Add Scene to List button and browse to the projects you want to render. After you've added them all, you can click the button you have been waiting to click for a while now—Screamer Render (see **Figure 15.52**)!

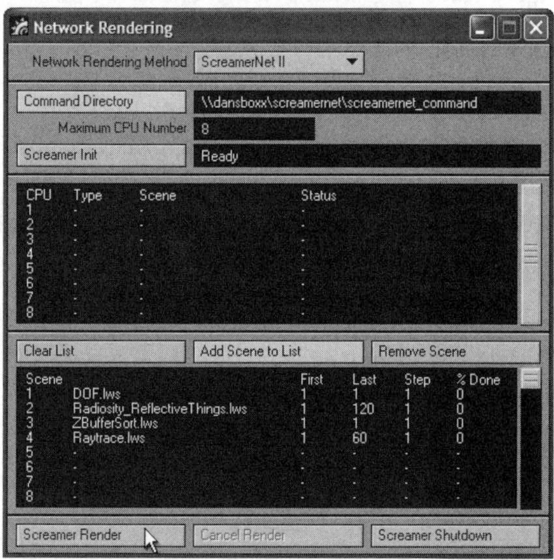

Figure 15.52 When rendering, LightWave's Network Rendering panel displays the current status.

The panel tells you what's going on as it renders, such as which node is rendering which frame and how far through the rendering it is.

When all the frames have rendered, the render nodes sit there repeating the "LightWave command: wait" line. At this point, you can click the Screamer Shutdown button. This closes all the node windows. You should now have lots of frames in the save folder you specified earlier, ready for building into an animation.

Batch Rendering on One Machine

As mentioned in the early pages of this tutorial, ScreamerNet is also useful for batch rendering on one machine. You may find this to be more valuable than networking multiple computers. This is for users who don't have a network but who need to render multiple scenes. This is extremely helpful for, say, rendering multiple camera angles or rendering multiple scenes over a long weekend. Maximize that time!

The good news is the process is no different from rendering with 1,000 computers. There is no bad news!

The overview of the folder structure for a batch render would look like that shown in **Figure 15.53**.

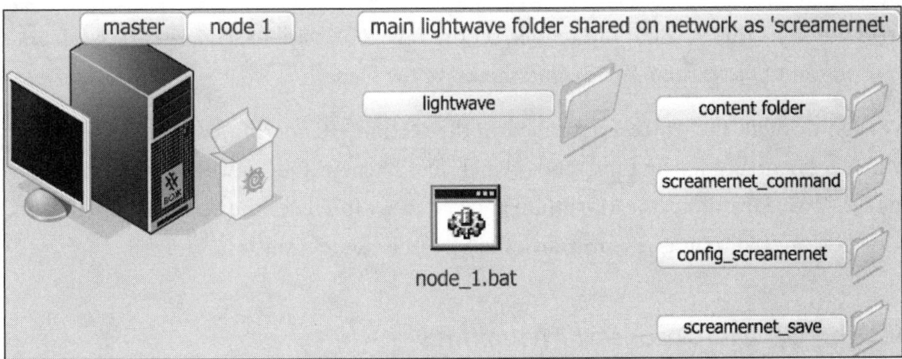

Figure 15.53 For batch rendering on a single machine, the node setup should look like this.

This setup assumes that all your content files are located in the main LightWave folder, that you copied all your config files to the new folder config_lightwave, and that you set the LightWave shortcut to point to that folder.

The only difference between batch rendering on one machine and network rendering is that all the pathnames to the config, content, and command folders can be local. You don't need to rescan your plug-ins, either, because they are already set up for normal LightWave use.

Setting Up Batch Rendering on One Machine

Before attempting this, it is probably a good idea to read all the previous material in this chapter (if you haven't already) so that you are familiar with the terminology and concepts. We're mentioning this just in case you've nipped straight to this section!

Note

When batch rendering on a single machine, be sure that each scene file knows where the objects are located and that the objects know where the texture maps are located. This is one area where a proper content directory is crucial. Another important issue is to set up so that your scenes will save files. Do this from the Render Options panel and then save the scene. When ScreamerNet calls up the scene to render, it will know where to save the rendered images.

If you haven't already created the folders screamer_command and screamer_save, do so now. Then create a batch file (node1) with the following text (replacing c:\lightwave\programs\ with the path to your LightWave installation):

```
@echo OFF
echo "LightWave ScreamerNet Node 1 Initialisation..."
cd c:\lightwave\programs\
LWSN -2 -cc:\lightwave\programs\config_lightwave -dc:\lightwave
c:\lightwave\screamer_command\job1 c:\lightwave\screamer_command\ack1
```

Load the scene files you want to render, set the Save RGB path to screamer_save (assuming you want to save them there), and then save the scene.

Now go through the process described in the section "Rendering Using ScreamerNet," which is essentially starting the render batch file. Then, in the Network Rendering panel in LightWave Layout, set the Maximum CPU Number to 1, click the Screamer Init button, add the scenes for rendering, and click the Screamer Render button.

Setting Up Multiprocessor Machines

If you have multiprocessor machines available on your network or if you want to batch-render on one multiprocessor machine, the process is the same and very simple!

All you have to do is treat each processor as a separate render node. We know that each render node has a batch script file that is run to identify that it is render node "X." So if a machine has more than one processor, it simply has more than one batch script but with different job/ack numbers. An overview of the setup for a batch render on a multiprocessor machine would look like what is shown in **Figure 15.54.**

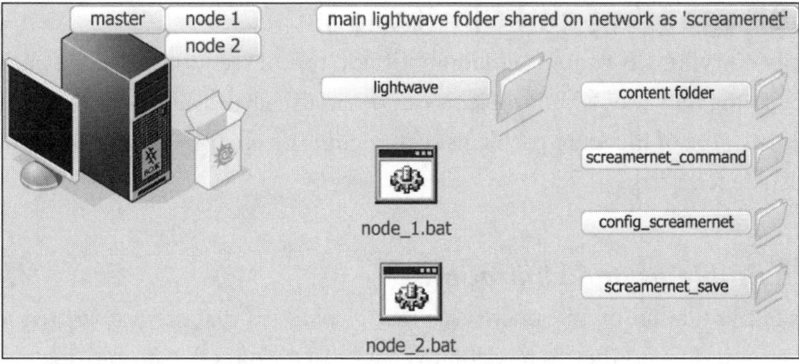

Figure 15.54 A batch render for dual processors would look something like this.

Figure 15.55 shows what the setup for a network render involving multiprocessor machines would look like.

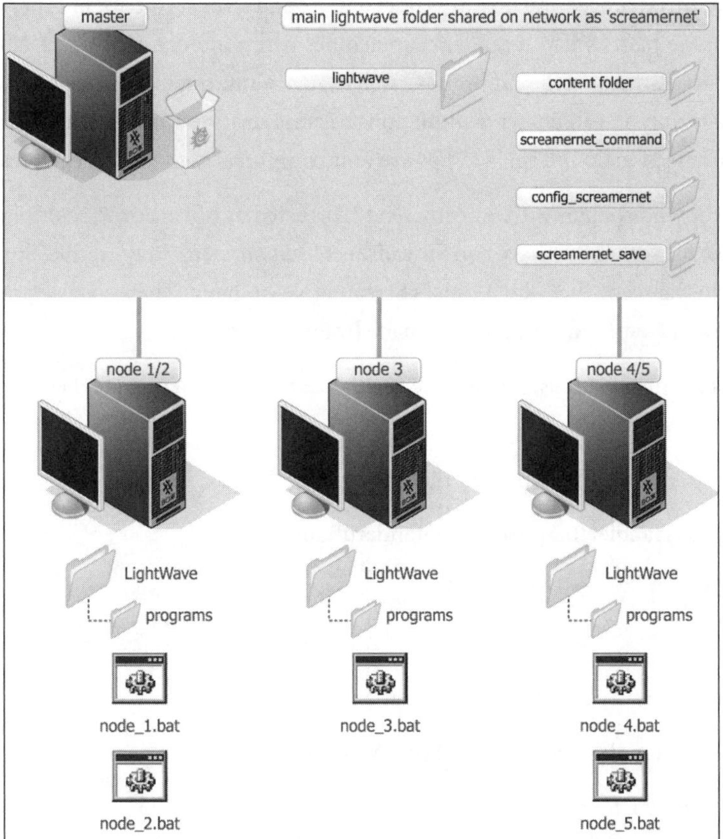

Figure 15.55 A setup for dual processors on a network would look something like this.

Troubleshooting and Limitations

Hopefully everything is running smoothly (if not, reread sections that don't click until they do; it's the only way!), but problems can occur, usually because something is set up incorrectly. Some of the main problems that might arise are listed in this section, along with possible remedies.

Plug-in Problems and Limitations

The biggest limitation of ScreamerNet is that of plug-ins that are not written to take advantage of it. To date, there is no definitive list of all the ones that do and don't work. If in doubt, read the documentation that came with the plug-in; it should say whether it has problems. If it doesn't say, but the plug-in still does not seem to be working, rescan your plug-ins to update the LWEXT9.cfg file. If it still doesn't work, then chances are it's not compatible with ScreamerNet.

If your scene uses procedural textures (fractal noise and so on), you might experience differences in the pattern if you render on machines with different processors. Mixing old and new processors or different brands, such as AMD and Intel, could lead to problems. This is really only a problem with animations because textures can suddenly change from frame to frame. If in doubt, run a test or use only computers with the same processor type.

Another known problem with ScreamerNet (corrected as of version 7.5c of LightWave) is its dislike for scenes that have had Spreadsheet used on them. Plug-ins like Spreadsheet save data to the scene file, which causes ScreamerNet to hang. The only way around this is to remove the entry in the scene file made by Spreadsheet.

Scene files are just text files; if you force-load a scene file into a plain text editor, you can read it!

Near the top, you will find an entry that says:

Plugin MasterHandler 1 .SpreadsheetStandardBanks

followed by:

EndPlugin

There will be another entry right after that entry that starts with:

Plugin MasterHandler 2 SpreadsheetSceneManager

If you scroll down, there will be another:

EndPlugin

Highlight all the text between the first Plugin MasterHandler and the last EndPlugin, delete it, and then save the file. It should now render without problems.

Other Common Problems

This section covers other problems that you might run into and offers solutions for each.

Problem:

"My nodes can't find the job files."

Possible solution:

The nodes can't find the job files because they can't see the command folder. The command folder holds the job files, so open up the batch file and check the script lines that end in "job" and "ack." Make sure that the pathname before these words points to your command folder. Also, check that all the render node computers have access to read and write to the folder.

Problem:

"My nodes seem fine, but when I press Screamer Init, it can't find any CPUs."

Possible solution:

Again this is a command folder problem; check that the Network Rendering panel has the same command directory path set that the nodes are pointing to. Also, check that the master computer has access to read and write to the folder.

Problem:

"Rendering seems to be working, but no files are saved."

Possible solution:

First, make sure your scene file is saving RGB files and not an animation (MOV, AVI, and so on) in the Output tab of the Render Options panel. ScreamerNet can only save RGB image sequences.

Next, check that your plug-ins file (LWEXT9.cfg) is up-to-date by rescanning your plug-ins using the pathname all the nodes use to find them on the network.

Finally, check that the render batch files are looking in the correct place for the config files and that they can access the folder on the network.

Problem:

"Rendering seems to work OK, but all my saved files are in FLX format."

Possible solution:

There are two possible reasons. The first is that ScreamerNet can't find the plug-in to save in the format you've specified, so check that your plug-ins file (LWEXT9.cfg) is up-to-date by rescanning your plug-ins using the pathname all the nodes use to find them on the network. Also, check that the render batch files are looking in the correct place for the config files and that they can access the folder on the network.

The second reason is that the render node that saved the file ran out of memory to load the saver plug-in, so ScreamerNet used the last-resort, built-in FLX saver.

To convert them, you can use LightWave as a converter; load the FLX images into LightWave using the Images panel, highlight the image in question, and double-click the preview to open it up in the image view. Now you can save in the format you need.

Problem:

"My particles aren't working."

Possible solution:

ScreamerNet can have problems with particle FX. The best way to address this is to save the particle FX calculation to disk (as a PFX file) in the folder with the scene file.

Problem:

"Dynamics aren't working."

Possible solution:

ScreamerNet might have problems with certain dynamics. The best way to address this is to save the dynamics calculation to disk from the File tab within the Dynamics tab under the Object Properties folder. Save this in the folder with the scene file.

The Next Step

As you've seen, LightWave has plenty of rendering power. These examples can help you maximize your use of your computer and network, as well as your time. There's not much more to it, other than using moving images rather than stills. Use programs like NewTek's VT3, Eyeon's Digital Fusion, or Adobe's After Effects, even Apple's Motion for compositing final rendered images, and make your work really stand out! Now, read on to Chapter 16 to learn how LightWave can be used for compositing all on its own! Thank you to Matt Gorner for his informative ScreamerNet information and illustrations.

Chapter 16

Compositing and Postprocessing Techniques

Some of the coolest 3D animation you see is work you don't even notice. That's right, animators and compositors spend months in front of computers creating visual effects that you aren't aware of. For example, in the movie *Hart's War* starring Bruce Willis, animators used LightWave to add snow outside a moving train. If you saw the movie, you wouldn't even think twice that the snow wasn't real. Or how about the movie *A Beautiful Mind* starring Russell Crowe? There's a scene where a little girl is running around a park, surrounded by pigeons. If you've ever run toward a pigeon, you'd know that as soon as you get close enough, it flies away. But in *A Beautiful Mind*, director Ron Howard needed the girl to be a figment of the main character's imagination. Because she's not real, the birds do not notice her and don't fly away. This too was done in 3D. However, achieving this movie magic took more than modeling, texturing, and animation; it all comes down to compositing.

If you took a movie of a street and then brought it into LightWave, you could easily place a 3D object, such as a car, into the shot. After you've taken your shots with your camera and set up your 3D objects, you need to composite them to match the scene—to look as if they're integrated into the footage. This, my friends, is an art all its own. Do it correctly, and no one will notice your work. That is the mark of a good composite—it's seamless! Read on to learn more about compositing in LightWave.

In this chapter, you will examine several different compositing techniques and learn the methods used to blend 3D objects with real images. You can use LightWave's compositing tools to do the following:

- Place a 3D object against a still background
- Place and move a 3D object in front of and behind a photograph
- Import moving footage and track LightWave's camera
- Examine the basic techniques for doing two-pass compositing

Understanding Compositing

When we talk about compositing, we're talking about seamlessly blending 3D computer-generated images either with other 3D computer-generated images or with 2D images, such as photographs of real settings or people. Most of the visual effects created for film and video consist of 3D animation and digital effects composited over or, more accurately, into live-action footage. The live action can include photography, video, and film, as well as AVI or QuickTime movies. Using compositing, you can make it seem as though a 3D object is there when it actually isn't.

An important aspect of compositing with LightWave is that it enables you to expand your creativity, especially if your system is not as fast as you'd like it to be. Compositing in this sense enables you to blend multiple images together. Of course, before you can complete a composite in LightWave, you'll need to render! Later in this chapter, you'll learn about the steps needed to render your composite animations for many types of applications, taking what you learned in Chapter 15, "Advanced Cameras and Rendering," a step further. Production houses often have entire departments devoted to the task and thousands of dollars invested in the software. From the optically composited spaceships of *Star Wars* (the first three original films) to the digital, computer-generated people of *The Matrix* trilogy, compositing has come a long way. Over the years, compositing technology has evolved from purely optical techniques, such as matte paintings and frame-by-frame painting, to completely digital methods, but compositing will always be an important part of animation and visual effects. It is its own unique art and takes a lot of skill. That is the core of success for most Hollywood production studios.

Indeed, the enormous importance of compositing has led to the development of many high-powered, complex, and expensive programs dedicated to the task. But LightWave comes with its own, rather extensive set of tools, both for compositing within the program and for exporting images to be composited in other software packages.

Compositing Basics: Background and Foreground Images

Compositing can be an extraordinarily complicated process, combining hundreds of separate 2D and 3D elements into one final image. However, many times, it's just as simple as placing a 3D object against a background image. A background image, or *background plate*, as it is commonly called, is a 2D image. It is usually a digitized photograph or sequence of film, though not necessarily; sometimes, other rendered 3D footage is used as the background image. A 3D object is placed against the background image to make it appear as though the 3D object was always a part of the background. An example of this is the creatures in *Jurassic Park III*. Real settings were filmed with a regular camera, the footage was digitized, and then the 3D dinosaurs were composited into the footage to make them appear to be part of the picture.

Of course, compositing can be more complex than the preceding simple example. Regardless of how complex the composite, it all begins with the background, be it a still image or moving video.

In LightWave, the background image or movie has its place in the Effects panel under the Compositing tab (see **Figure 16.1**). This is where you begin the first exercise.

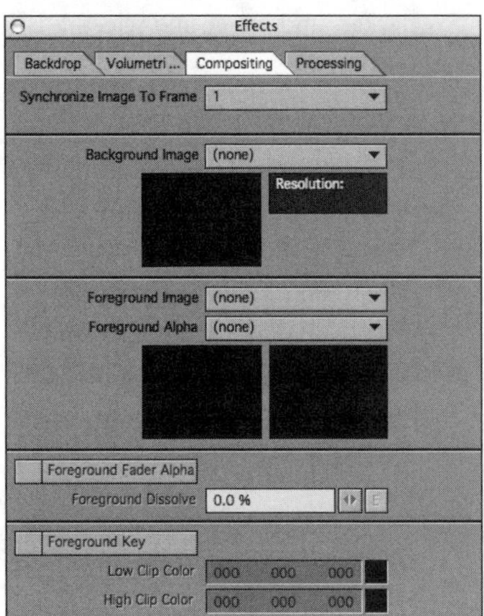

Figure 16.1 The Compositing tab is located within the Effects panel. Most everything needed for compositing in LightWave can be found here. You can open this directly from the Window drop-down menu at the top left of Layout or by pressing Ctrl+F7.

Exercise 16.1 Adding a 3D Object to a Still Image

In this first exercise, you'll learn the basics for setting up just about any composited scene. You'll find out how to load a background plate, as well as a 3D object, and marry the two seamlessly. Study this process because it will be the same for any composite you do in LightWave, including those involving video footage.

1. From Layout, press Ctrl+F7 to open the Compositing tab of the Effects panel.

Note

At the top of the Compositing tab, there is a setting labeled Synchronize To Frame with a choice of 1 or 0. This is useful for sequences and movie clips. LightWave defaults to 1.

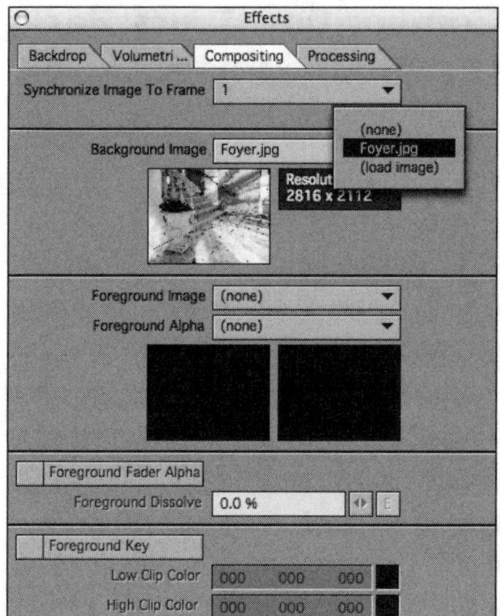

Figure 16.2 A shot of an outdoor foyer loaded into Layout.

2. Click the drop-down menu for Background Image and select Load Image.
3. Load the Foyer.jpg image fromthe Projects\Images\CH16 directory on the DVD, as shown in **Figure 16.2**. You can do this from the Image Editor panel, or select Load Image from the Background Image drop-down in the Compositing tab of the Effects panel.

Note

In addition to loading images directly from the Compositing tab, you also can go directly to the Image Editor (press **F6**) and select Load Image. This enables you to load your image or sequence while having access to image-editing features.

4. Render a frame by pressing the **F9** key. You'll see the Foyer image and nothing else. Exciting, isn't it?

   Only the image is displayed in the render because nothing else has been added to the scene. There are a few important things to note at this point that apply to both still and moving images:

   - When you use a background image, it overrides any backdrop color or gradient backdrop.
   - The background image is not affected by fog, though it can be used as the fog color instead of a solid color.
   - By default, the background image is not refracted by transparent objects. However, you can set this option for each surface in the Surface Editor.

- The background image is always centered and stretches itself to fill the camera's entire field of view. (This also is true of the foreground image, which you'll get to shortly.)
- The background image can be seen directly in Layout through Camera view if the Camera View Background is set to Background Image in the Display Options tab (press **d**).
- Even though the Foyer image used here is over 2000×2000 pixels in size, it will only render in the size you specify in the render options.

The next step involves adding a 3D object into the scene.

5. Load the Vase object from this book's DVD (Chapter 16 projects folder). This is a 3D vase, similar to the one in the photo.
6. Select the Camera in Layout and press **6** on the numeric keypad to switch to Camera view. Make sure that Camera View Background is set to Background Image in the Display Options tab (press **d**).
7. Move the camera so that the LightWave grid is roughly in line with the floor in the Foyer background image, as in **Figure 16.3**. Start by moving the camera up and then rotating it.

Figure 16.3 To make your compositing job easier, first move the camera into a position that more closely matches the position of the real-world camera that took the original photograph. You can align the camera easily by using LightWave Layout's grid as a guideline.

8. Move the Vase object back into the frame and rotate it so that it is resting on the ground plane. Create a keyframe at frame 0 for the vase to lock it into its new position, as shown in **Figure 16.4**.

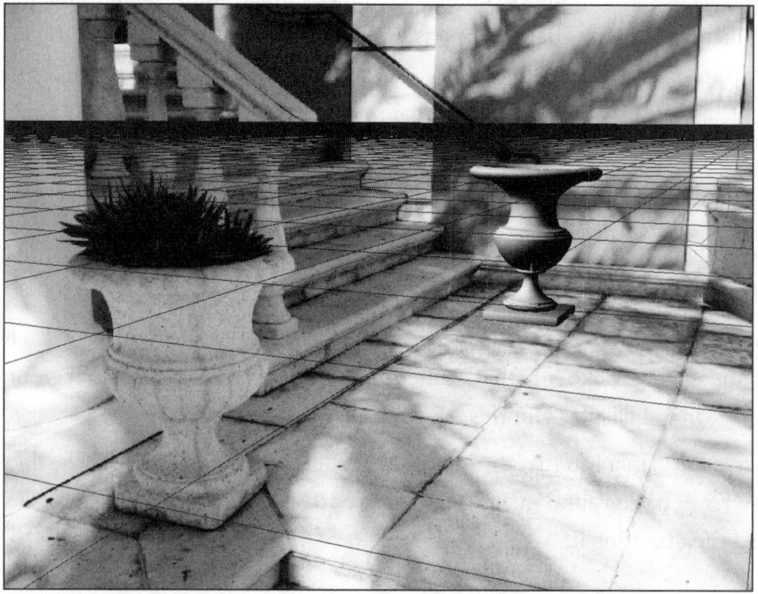

Figure 16.4 To composite the vase, move it into position so that it rests in front of the stairs.

Now, the 3D object is composited against the background image, the most basic of all compositing situations. By moving the camera into a similar position as the camera that took the photograph, positioning the vase was not too difficult. The LightWave grid helps you align to the background image.

This technique works for any situation in which a 3D object does not need to go behind a 2D image. You can also render, say, a logo background as its own animation. That rendered animation then can be applied back into LightWave as a background image. The 3D letters would then be animated on top. The benefit of this is control—not only do you have control over what you deliver your client, but you also have control over shadows, reflections, lights, shaders, and more. Rendering in passes is vital to proper compositing, and it is covered more fully later in this chapter. LightWave v9's Real Lens Camera settings can help isolate the view.

9. Open the Camera Properties panel. At the top of the panel, click the camera selector, which currently reads Classic Camera, and choose the Real Lens Camera.

10. In the panel that opens, choose Nikon SLR, then D70, with a 12–24mm lens, as shown in **Figure 16.5**.

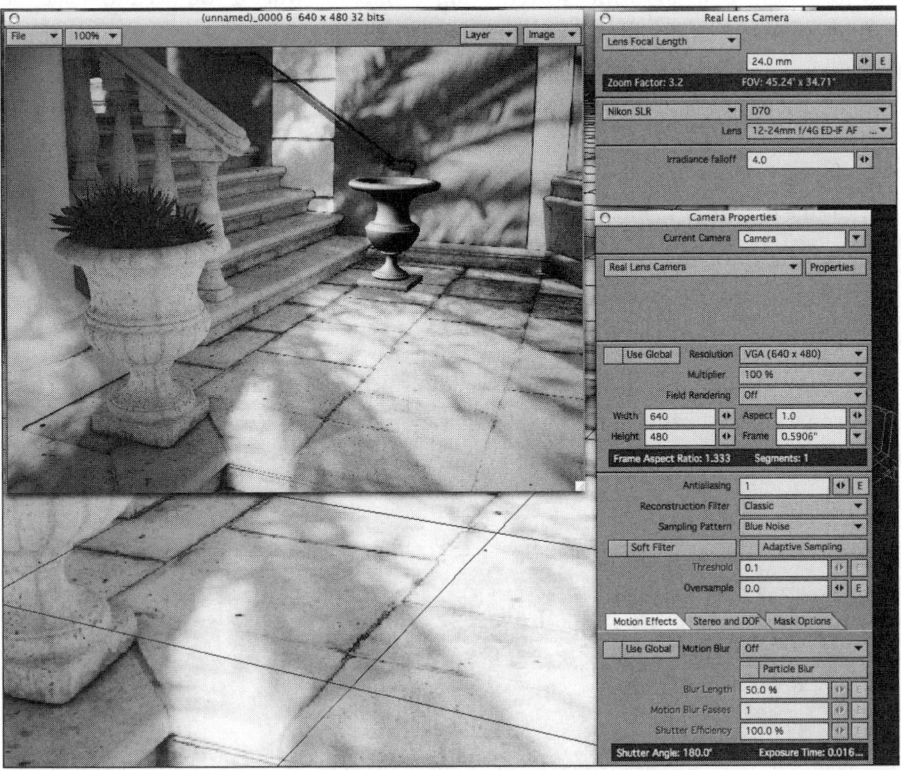

Figure 16.5 Using the Real Lens Camera settings, you can enhance LightWave's compositing efforts even further by instantly matching the camera lens that shot the image.

Often, you'll need to use a foreground image for situations in which a 3D object needs to go behind a 2D image. For example, suppose that a 3D car driving down the street needs to pull up behind other cars that are in the footage. Using a combination of foreground images (the cars) and a background image (the other parts of the footage), you can literally put a 3D element "into" your still or moving imagery.

The foreground image behaves in most ways like the background image. The main difference is that whereas the background image appears behind the 3D objects in the scene, the foreground image is applied on top of the 3D objects.

Exercise 16.2 Applying Front Projections

You've seen how easy it is to place a 3D object in front of a photograph. The look is convincing, and you can go further with moving images. But what if you need to make the Vase image blend more with the photograph? What if it needs to peek out from behind the other parts of the image? This exercise shows you how to do just that.

1. Continue in Layout from the previous exercise.
2. In the Compositing tab of the Effects panel, make sure the Foyer image is still set as the background image.
3. Be sure you're in Camera view so that you can see the backdrop image (press **d** for Display Options to view backdrop images). You should see the background image pop up into the Layout screen when you select Camera view.
4. In the position the vase rests in now, it only needs a shadow and lighting, which you'll create shortly. But for now, you want to make the Vase object appear behind other objects. Move the vase to the closer side of the foyer behind the larger planter, as in **Figure 16.6**.

Figure 16.6 Position the vase on the front side of the foyer so that it's behind the planter, or at least it will be shortly!

5. Press **F9** to render a frame.

   You'll see that as in Exercise 16.1, the 3D object is pasted over the background image. But in this case, it needs to be *behind* the planter! You might think that's a problem. Most compositing programs show you how to composite behind a solid object, like a rock or building, but what about something with an odd shape like the planter? LightWave makes it easy.

   Now you add the foreground image and see how that changes your final output. You just need to create a mask for the vase in Modeler.

6. Jump into LightWave Modeler and press **d** for Display Options. Go to the Backdrop tab and load the same Foyer image as a background image for the bottom-left view. Increase the size to 5 m. **Figure 16.7** shows the Modeler setup.

Note

You can make the Image Resolution 1024 for better display in your backdrop images. Do this within the Display Options panel, under the OpenGL tab.

7. Expand the bottom-left view and then zoom into the image, as shown in Figure 16.7.

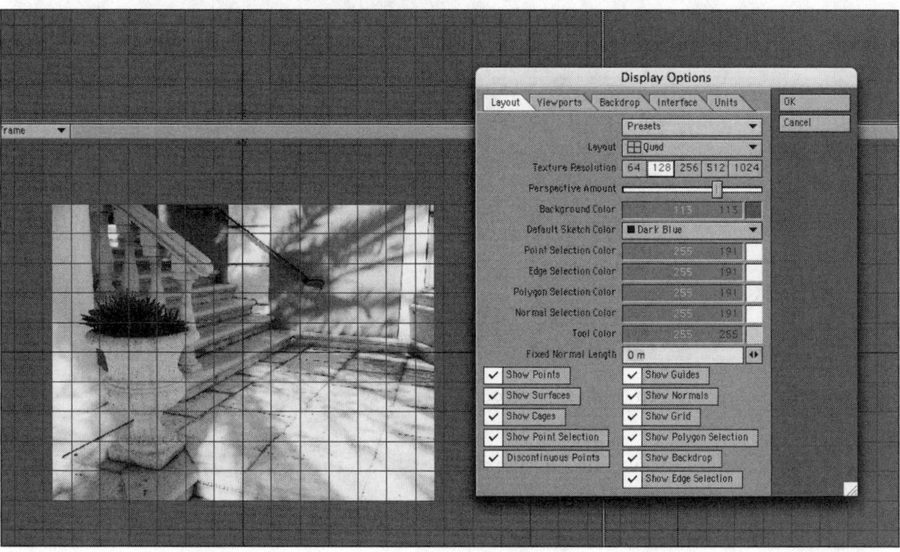

Figure 16.7 Place the Foyer image in the background display in Modeler to create mask objects.

8. Using the Pen tool from the Create tab, create a polygon in the shape of the planter, as shown in **Figure 16.8**. Just click to create points around the planter in the image. Feel free to zoom into the view, and make it full frame to easily align the Pen tool.

Note

When building this mask (or any mask), you only need to create enough of an object to meet your needs. For example, in the current exercise, you do not need to create a mask for the stairs, columns, or floors. You're building a mask so that a vase can pass behind it. Therefore, you only need to create a polygonal mask for the planter that is big enough to make the Vase object appear to be behind it. If, however, you had a moving object, you would then need to build a larger mask.

Figure 16.8 Using the Pen tool, you can quickly create a mask for any area of an image.

9. After you've laid down the necessary points with the Pen tool, press the spacebar to turn off the Pen tool. Then, using the Drag tool (Ctrl+t), shape the points to better fit the image, if needed.

10. Press **q** (or the Surface button at the bottom of the Modeler interface) and name this new polygon **PlanterMask**. Then save the object.

11. After the object has been saved, send it to Layout from the drop-down arrow at the very top right of the Modeler interface, as shown in **Figure 16.9**.

Figure 16.9 Use the Send Object to Layout command at the top right of the Modeler interface.

12. After the object has been sent to Layout, move and position it so that it rests in front of the planter in the image. You'll need to do this from the Camera view, as that is the only way to see the image in Layout. Note that a bit of sizing might be needed to properly place the mask. You can press Shift+h for Size. Press **t** for Move.
13. When the object is in place, create a keyframe at frame 0 to lock it down. **Figure 16.10** shows the mask in place. You might find that a Wireframe view of the scene helps with aligning the mask.

Figure 16.10 A little bit of positioning in Layout puts the mask object in place.

14. Be sure to save the scene at this point. Don't forget that pressing Shift+s saves incremental versions.

15. Press the **F9** key to see how the scene looks. You should see something like **Figure 16.11**. The mask you made for the planter does indeed block the vase behind it, but the object is just gray.

Figure 16.11 Rendering a frame shows the mask in place blocking the vase but not really looking like part of the scene.

Note

If your render doesn't show any object mask, the polygons might be flipped. Back in Modeler, make sure the surface normal is facing forward toward the positive Z-axis. At worst, you can try clicking Double Sided in the Surface Editor panel directly in Layout.

16. Open the Surface Editor and select the PlanterMask surface. Then, open the Node Editor. You're going to apply an image map to the mask.
17. Choose 2D Texture and then Image from the Node Editors Add Node drop-down. This creates an Image node (**Figure 16.12**).

Figure 16.12 Begin surfacing the polygon mask with a 2D Image node.

18. Double-click the newly added node to open its Properties panel.
19. At the top of the Properties panel, select the Foyer as the image. The other settings can all remain at their defaults, except for one—Mapping. Change this to Front, for front projection mapping, as shown in **Figure 16.13**.

    Front projection image mapping is one of the most powerful compositing tools LightWave has to offer. It enables your 3D objects to interact with your 2D images in almost every way that they can interact with other 3D objects.

    Front projection image mapping works by—you guessed it—projecting an image onto an object. The image is "projected" from the camera's point of view such that it would appear exactly as though it were a background or foreground image.

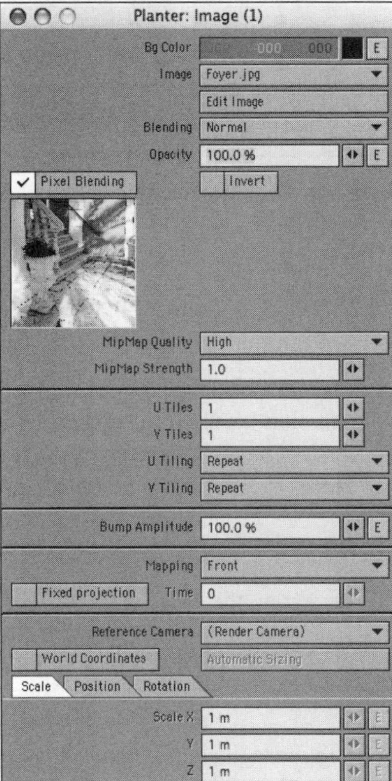

Figure 16.13 The Image node with a front projection map applied.

20. Now all you need to do is hook the Image node into the destination node to apply it to the PlanterMask. Drag the Color output of the Image node to the Color input of the destination node, as shown in **Figure 16.14**.

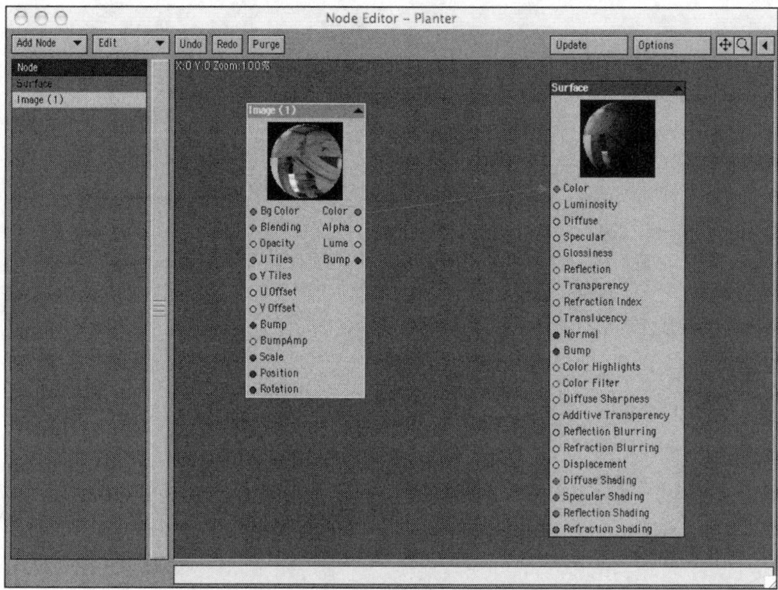

Figure 16.14 The Image node is hooked into the Color input of the destination node.

In most cases, you'll need to adjust the Luminosity and Diffuse values for the front projection–mapped surface. Because of the lighting in the scene, you need to carefully balance these two values so that the polygons that make up the mask perfectly blend and match the background image. In this particular tutorial, the mask is small, so making it blend is not too difficult.

Note

Remember to move, rotate, size, and stretch the mask object. Render a frame. It will always show a portion of the image, no matter where you place it or what its angle is. Remember that by using OpenGL Textured Shaded Solid view, you'll be able to see your textures applied in real time, directly in Layout. Rendering an image gives you a more accurate idea of the setup with surface values.

21. To make the mask blend a bit better, close the Node Editor. Then, back in the Surface Editor, set Luminosity to 40% and Diffuse to 70%. Render a frame again (press **F9**), and you'll see that the front projection mask is easier to see, but the lighting needs to change.

22. Select the light, which currently is a default distant light, and rotate it so that it's above, behind, and to the right of the camera. **Figure 16.15** shows the Perspective view with the light position change.

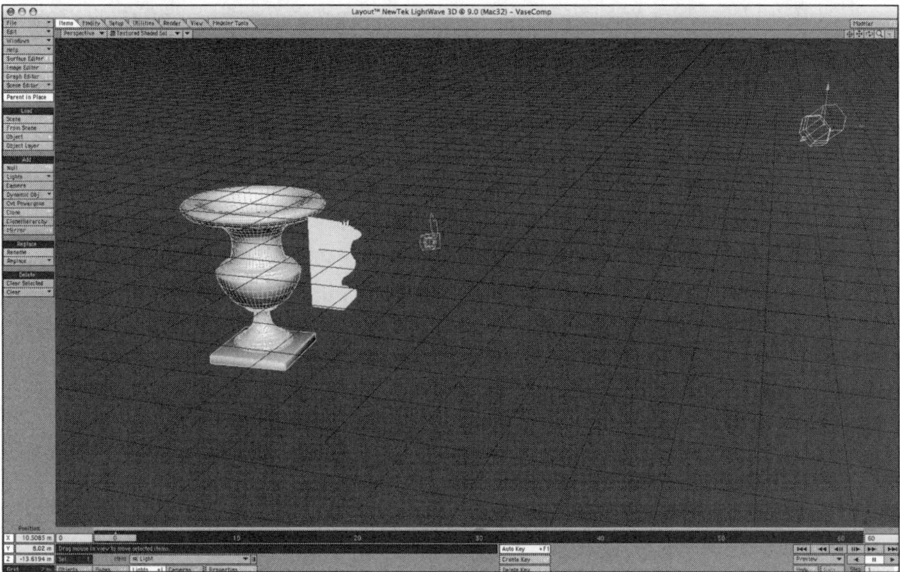

Figure 16.15 Position the light so that it is behind and to the upper right of the camera.

23. After the light has been changed, press **F9** to render a single frame. You'll now see that there is little difference between the polygon mask and the background image. **Figure 16.16** shows the example.

Figure 16.16 After the light has been rotated and positioned, the render shows a better blend between the front projection mask and the background image.

Note

The way a distant light, such as the one used here, affects a scene is independent of its distance from the lit object. (Only its angle relative to the object affects shadows, reflections, and the like.) But it's still a good idea to move the distant light anyway. That way, if you decide to change it to a different light type, it will be positioned correctly in the scene.

24. Oh, and did you save? Yep, gotta save all objects to save the surface changes, and be sure of course to save the scene.

However, the vase itself still looks like it's floating, and it's not textured. This is because all the elements in the background image have shadows, but your 3D vase does not. Shortly, you'll learn how to create matching shadows to finish off your composite. But first, read on to the next section, which takes a different approach on compositing in LightWave using foreground images.

Foreground Key and Foreground Alpha

In the next exercise, you'll learn about the Foreground Key. The Foreground Key is nothing more than a color-keying system, such as the blue- and green-screen systems used by TV meteorologists and in visual effects throughout the industry. It works by *keying out*, or removing a range of colors that you specify. LightWave gives you two colors: a Low Clip Color and a High Clip Color.

The Low Clip Color is generally the darkest, most saturated color you would want to remove from your foreground image. The High Clip Color is the brightest, least saturated color you'd want to take out. Any colors between these two colors are removed from the foreground image before it's pasted over the rendering. For Exercise 16.3, you'll take out the sky to reveal a new background. There's no Adobe Photoshop involved—it's all done directly within LightWave.

Exercise 16.3 Setting Up a Foreground Key

In this exercise, you key out the sky and leave the buildings of the Fountain image found on the book's DVD. To do this, you want to pick the darkest, most saturated color in the sky and set this to be the Low Clip Color, and you'll set the brightest, least saturated color for the High Clip Color.

1. Load the Fountain image from the book's projects folder. In the Compositing tab of the Effects panel, apply the loaded image as a Foreground Image, as shown in **Figure 16.17**. Then, check Foreground Key.

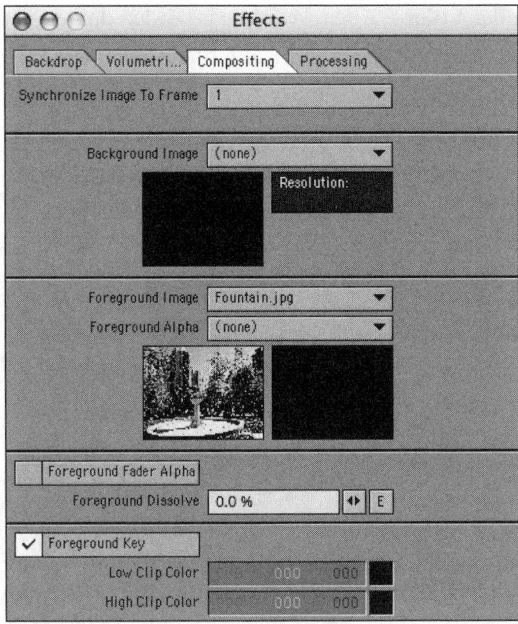

Figure 16.17 Load the Fountain image as the Foreground Image in the Compositing tab of the Effects panel.

2. Set the Low Clip Color to R:118 G:168 B:239. Set the High Clip Color to R:180 G:218 B:254.

   Now, you're probably wondering where these values come from. Although you can use another image-editing program to determine the color value of the Low Clip (the sky in the fountain image), you can do it directly in LightWave. The following steps show you how.

3. From the Render tab at the top of Layout, select Render Globals. In the Render Globals panel, set the Render Display to Image Viewer. You'll see two options there: Image Viewer and Image Viewer FP ("FP" stands for "floating point"). The FP version is useful for determining values for high dynamic range (HDR) imagery.

   For this project, you want to use just the Image Viewer for RGB images (not Image Viewer FP). You can simply select a color based on your own eye. Remember, this is a range of color, high and low—it's not specific.

4. Press **F9** to render a frame. After the frame is rendered, the Image Viewer opens. Move the mouse over to the sky. Click and hold the mouse and look at the title bar of the Image Viewer panel. **Figure 16.18** shows the Image Viewer.

Figure 16.18 Using LightWave's Image Viewer from the Render Globals panel, you can easily find RGB color values of your background image.

Values appear there! Those are the RGB values of the image where the mouse is. You'll see four values—Red, Green, Blue, and Alpha. The first two sets of numbers before the dashed line are the pixel number of the image.

The RGB values (118, 168, and 239, respectively) for the Low Clip Color setting were determined using the Image Viewer. Cool, huh?

Note

You can set color values quickly by clicking and dragging each of the color values to the desired color, in the Foreground Key settings.

5. Back in Layout, load the Moon object from this book's DVD. This is a simple flat polygon, or plane, with a moon mapped onto it that you can use for compositing in this exercise. Move the plane back into the frame and position it so that it's rising up from behind the buildings, as in **Figure 16.19**.

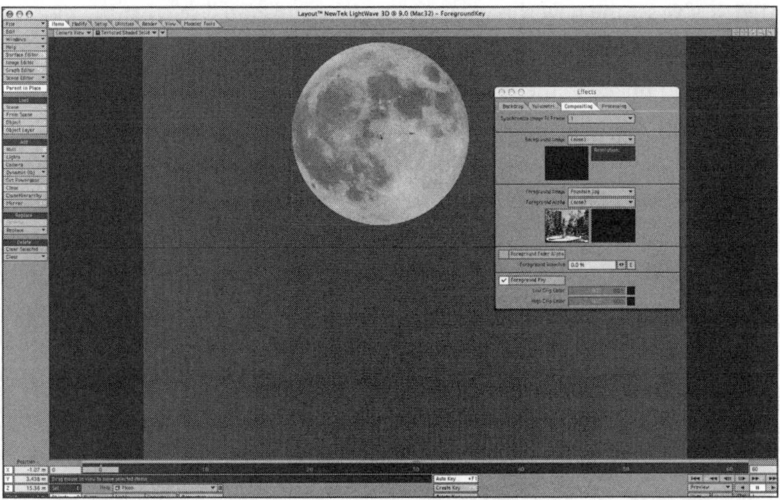

Figure 16.19 Load the Moon object.

6. Press **F9** to render a frame, and you'll see the moon scattered through the trees, sky, and building, as in **Figure 16.20**.

Figure 16.20 Even though you've set the High and Low Clip colors, the range is too small for LightWave to key out the sky, so the moon is partially obscured.

7. Often, the color values you set for the Low and High Clip values aren't enough. So, hike the High Clip Color values to R:195 G:235 B:255 in the Compositing tab of the Effects panel. Reduce the Low Clip Color values to R:110 G:150 B:220.

8. After you've set the new clip colors, press **F9** again. You'll see that the moon is clearly visible, but the area behind it is black. So, in the Compositing tab, set the Background Image to the Fountain.jpg as well. Then, render again by pressing **F9**. **Figure 16.21** shows the moon now rising up from behind the buildings.

Figure 16.21 With a slight change in the High Clip Color, the moon now appears to be rising out from behind the buildings.

This is a good technique to use when your foreground image can support it. The example here can use a little tweaking in the High Clip Color area, which you can experiment with on your own. The less variation between the High and Low Clip colors, the better. And, the less area to be keyed out, the better. While this is not the best keying method you could choose, it is a quick way to consolidate operations and software, while maximizing time. In this case, the image was a good candidate for this technique because the area you needed to key out was a large bright area with little variation in color, and it was significantly different in color than the rest of the picture. For the sky, this image was good to use because there is a clear distinction between the buildings and the sky. There is little haze and a strong variation in brightness and color.

Foreground Keying

Not all images are easy to use for keying and compositing. For images that are more complex, or for those times when you want more control, LightWave offers you the Foreground Alpha.

An *alpha* is a grayscale image that is used to tell a program where certain things should happen. In the case of a surface texture, an alpha image tells the surface where to apply a texture map. It could, for example, tell a surface where to be transparent and where to be opaque. And in the case of a foreground image, the alpha image determines where the image appears and where it doesn't.

Exercise 16.4 Using Foreground Alpha

This exercise uses a feature available in LightWave that enables you to key out portions of an image for foreground compositing. This technique uses the Foreground key features to remove parts of an image.

1. Using the Image Editor, continue from Exercise 16.3 and load the Fountain_Alpha.psd image from this book's DVD. Uncheck Foreground Key in the Compositing tab if it's still active.
2. In the Compositing tab of the Effects panel, next to the Foreground Alpha image, click the selector and choose the Fountain_Alpha.psd image. If you want, you can load a standard (non-grayscale) image from here as well.
3. Click the check box below Foreground Fader Alpha.

   This tells LightWave to ignore the areas of the foreground image that are pure black. The white areas of the image are dropped out.
4. Move the moon so that it's more centered in the shot, which will align it between the tall building on the left and the trees on the right.
5. Press **F9** to render a frame. **Figure 16.22** shows the rendered image and scene setup.

Figure 16.22 Using a Foreground Alpha image gives you precise control over where the composited foreground image will be clipped.

Obviously, the moon might not belong in the image like this; however, other objects could, and that's the point. Using a Foreground Alpha image provides the control you might need for specific keying purposes.

The alpha image you used was created in Adobe Photoshop from the original Fountain image. It has had its sky painted black, while everything else is painted white. The white areas block the objects from rendering, enabling the foreground image to show, thereby making it look as if the moon is behind the buildings and trees.

Now you can see that the rendered image appears much as it did with the Foreground Key, but this time using an alpha image, which is a bit more precise. Using an alpha image gives you much more flexibility in determining where your foreground image appears. It is also more accurate than using a range of colors to clip the image. However, both methods are suitable depending on the project and the images at hand.

Using alpha images when compositing gives you the most control over your scene because the alpha image can be used to shape the foreground image into any shape you desire.

The situation outlined in the previous exercise would be fine if your 3D object needed only to be placed behind the buildings and in front of the sky. But if your object needed to start out behind the trees, rise up above them, and then swoop down in front of them, it wouldn't work. The foreground image would be pasted on top, no matter what.

Another, more common situation is that of having a 3D object cast shadows and otherwise interact with your 2D images. Earlier in this chapter you put the Vase object on the Foyer image and created a mask so that the planter appeared to be in front of the vase. It now needs some shadows. This kind of seamless compositing is the mainstay of the visual-effects industry. Without it, the movies and television shows you watch every day would be tremendously different.

As you might have guessed, LightWave has the answer to compositing and casting shadows.

Shadows

Adding shadows to your 3D objects helps you move one step closer to creating a perfect composite.

Exercise 16.5 Creating Shadows for Compositing

Front projection image mapping is unique in the way it maps the texture image, but in every other way it's just a normal surface texture. It can receive shadows, reflect other objects, and be transparent. By using these characteristics, you can make the objects appear to interact with the scene.

1. Load your scene created from Exercise 16.2 or load the VaseComp scene from this book's DVD. This is the background image, with the PlanterMask and Vase object loaded.
2. Back in LightWave Modeler, create a large flat polygon about 25m in size, as shown in **Figure 16.23**.

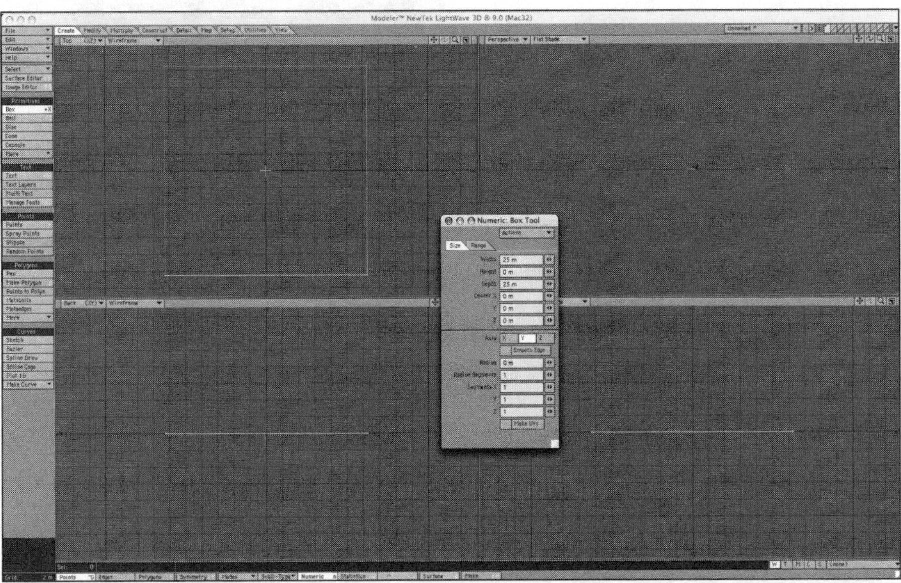

Figure 16.23 You can create a simple large flat polygon to catch the shadows of the vase in Layout.

3. When created, press **q** to set the name of the new polygon foyer_shadow or something similar. Save the object and send it to Layout.
4. In Layout, move and position this new object so that it's aligned with the grid in LightWave. Make sure it's placed beneath the vase, as in **Figure 16.24**. You can change your views to a Top or Side view to help align the polygon.

Figure 16.24 Position the large flat polygon so that the Vase object rests right on top of it.

5. Just as you did with the planter in Exercise 16.2, apply a Front type projection image onto the large polygon representing the concrete ground. You can do this with a Texture map, or within the Node Editor, as in Exercise 16.2.

6. Increase the Luminosity to about 40% for the surface, as shown in **Figure 16.25**.

   At this point, you need to set up the lighting so that you can match the real-world lighting and cast shadows.

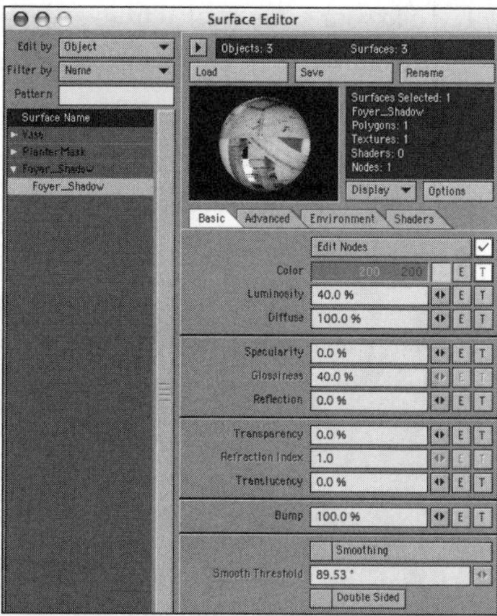

Figure 16.25 Be sure to make the front projection map blend with the background image by increasing the luminosity of the surface.

7. Select the light in the scene. While still in Camera view, press **y** to rotate the light so that it casts light onto the vase matching the rest of the image. Looking from the Camera view, this light's position is to the upper left. **Figure 16.26** shows the light from three angles.

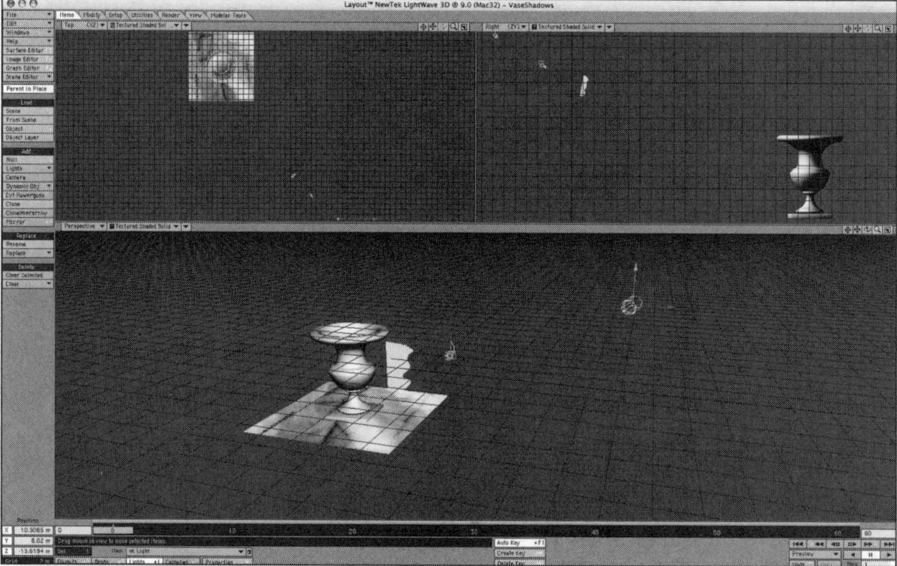

Figure 16.26 A single distant light is used to light the composited scene. Its position is not important—but its rotation is. However, moving it into a key location helps you visualize its effect on the scene.

8. Be sure to create a keyframe for the light at frame 0 to lock it in place. Then, from the Render Globals panel under the Render menu tab, turn on Ray Trace Shadows. Press **F9**. **Figure 16.27** shows the vase on the concrete ground with shadows now visible.

   As you can see, it's not very difficult to cast shadows in composited images. There are a few more things that will help integrate the vase into the background image.

Figure 16.27 After the light is in place and shadows are turned on, the Vase object is now more closely integrated into the background image.

9. Add another distant light to the scene. Name it **fill light** or something similar.

10. Make sure the new light is selected, and press the **p** key to call up the Light Properties panel. Change the Light Type to Area Light. Then, set the Light Intensity to 60%. Change the Light Color to a soft blue, about R: 220, G: 225, B: 240—something along the lines of the sky. The lower light intensity is important because area lights are much brighter than distant lights.

11. Reposition the light so that it casts shadows on the top and front side of the vase, as in **Figure 16.28**. Be sure to create a keyframe for the light to lock it in place. Then, press Shift+h for the size tool, and resize the light to about 8.5. You can reference the numeric values in the lower left of the interface. Increasing the light's size creates a softer shadow when using an area light.

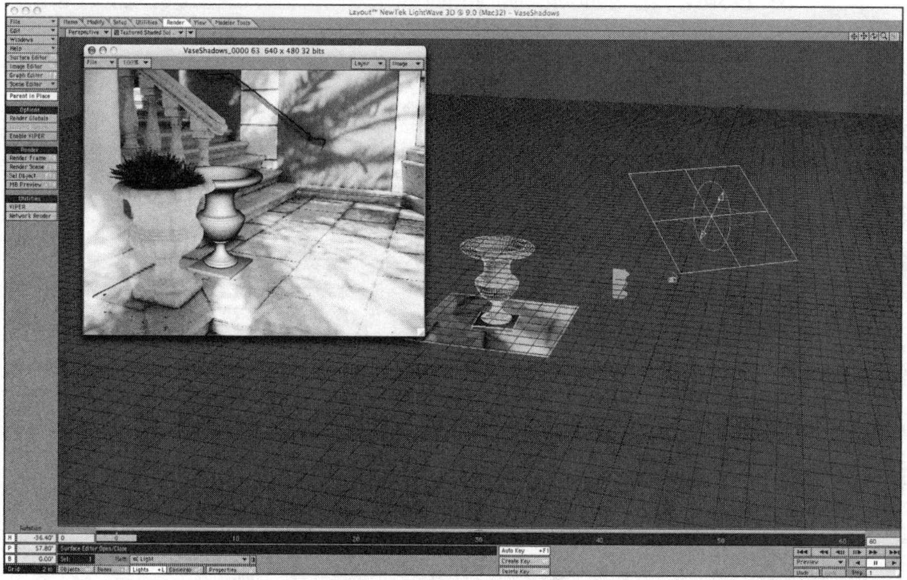

Figure 16.28 A repositioned area light helps create softer shadows.

12. You might have noticed that changing the light also changes the ground polygon that you made to catch the shadow. So, in the Surface Editor, add more luminosity to the foyer_shadow surface, about 45%.

13. Save the scene.

14. Select the PlanterMask object you made in Exercise 16.2. Press **p** to open the Object Properties panel (if it's not already open). Selecting an object after a light with a Properties panel open simply makes the panel change over.

15. In the Object Properties panel for the planter mask object, select the Render tab. At the bottom of the panel, turn off Self Shadow, Cast Shadow, and Receive Shadow. This object needs none of these, and keeping them checked on might cause an accidental shadow on the vase. **Figure 16.29** shows the panel.

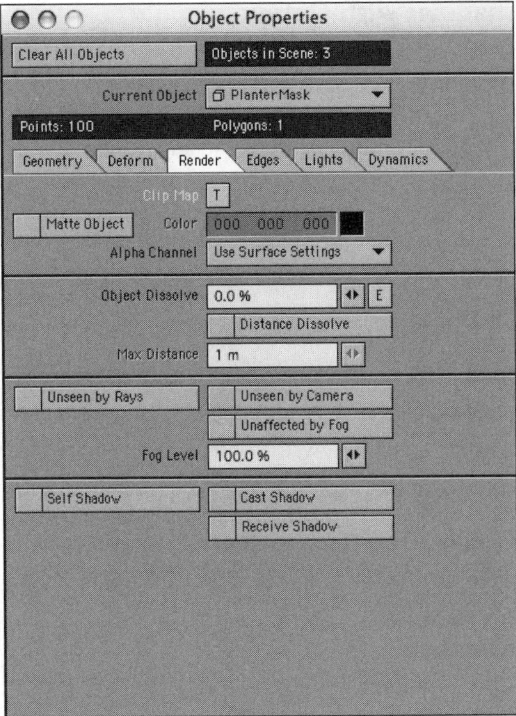

Figure 16.29 Make sure that only the objects that are supposed to be casting shadows are doing so. Here, the shadows are turned off for the PlanterMask object in the Object Properties panel.

16. Press **F9** again to render a frame. The vase casts a soft, gentle shadow on the ground.
17. Save the scene!

Many times, animators are looking for a magic variable to set up composite shots. In actuality, nothing is better than your own eye and sense of judgment. Does the 3D object look too big for its environment? If so, make it smaller. Does the object look out of perspective? If it does, rotate and reposition it. The same goes for lighting.

The shadow cast from the vase has a pretty nice value, closely matching the shadows in the image. This is as far as you're going to take this project, but you could do a lot more with it to flesh it out, such as adding textures and surfacing to the vase. Use the techniques you've learned in the previous surfacing chapters. Then, you can add even more objects, and have them case shadows onto front project planes as well. From there, you can use a *gobo*, or cookie on a light to give the effect of light casting shadows through trees.

Creating Cast Shadows with Gobos

This technique is simply a black and white blurred image applied to a Spotlight. The light cast onto the scene through the image. Cool stuff.

- Set other objects, such as more planters or characters, in place to receive shadows.
- Model the stairs and back wall to receive not just shadows. If your shot has a window, model a polygon, apply a front projection image, and turn on reflections.
- Add more lights to more fully simulate the light in the scene, such as a light on underside of the vase.
- Add a bit of fog or some blur to help blend the vase into the background.
- Add postprocessing filters, such as film grain. A bit of film grain usually helps to really set in the objects. Right now, the object might be too clean for the image.
- Instead of a single image, replace it with an AVI or MOV file in the Image Editor.

This was a simple example with a single frame, but everything in it applies properly to image sequences and movies as well. Situations like you've just seen—casting shadows on flat surfaces—are fairly common.

The Next Step

This chapter gave you a good working knowledge of using images and 3D objects together. You can see that the possibilities are endless, using a combination of backdrop images, front projection mapping, and 3D objects. It is very possible for you to make your own robots, monsters, or characters come to life in photographs and moving footage. LightWave's compositing tools are all you need for working with moving footage as well. Be sure to try out some ideas on your own, and don't forget to experiment!

Appendix A

Plug-ins and Resources

LightWave v9's architecture is built around plug-ins. It would be cool if there were a book covering just the plug-ins, because there are so many. Add to that the crazy amount of third-party plug-ins available to you—some for purchase, many for free—and you can be in plug-in heaven. You've used LightWave plug-ins throughout the book already. Many of the tools and commands used in Modeler and in Layout, are plug-ins! This appendix will give you a better understanding of where the plug-ins are located and how to work with them.

Plug-in Categories

You'll find plug-ins throughout LightWave Modeler and Layout. These plug-ins are necessary and have various purposes. They are divided into the following categories:

- **Animation I/O.** Plug-ins used for input and output.
- **Animation UV.** Plug-ins used for animated UV maps.
- **Channel Filter.** Plug-ins that perform direct control over channels, such as expressions and Motion Mixer.
- **Custom Object.** Plug-ins that are used for object control, such as particle effects.
- **Displacement.** Plug-ins that can shape and deform objects, be they points or polygons.

- **Environment.** Plug-ins that add functionality to Layout environment variables, such as SkyTracer2.
- **Frame Buffer.** Plug-ins used for certain types of render display, such as the new DV View, found within the Render Options.
- **Global.** Plug-ins that look at the entire scene, such as the Spreadsheet Scene Manager.
- **Image I/O.** Plug-ins for loading and saving images. Generally, you won't access these plug-ins directly, but you'll use their functions when loading or saving in both Layout and Modeler.
- **Image Processing.** Plug-ins that control the various image-related functions, such as pixel calculations for SasLite for fur and Image Filters for things like Bloom and Corona.
- **Layout Command.** Plug-ins used in Layout to control the interaction of other plug-ins that use representation in Layout.
- **Layout Tool.** Plug-ins used for specific Layout tools, such as Bone Twist, Bone Scale Hierarchy, IK Boost Tool, Sliders, and more.
- **Modeling.** Plug-ins and tools used throughout LightWave Modeler.
- **Motion.** Plug-ins for various motion operations, such as Jolt! or Gravity.
- **Object Importer.** Plug-ins for importing object formats other than just LightWave.
- **Object Replacement.** Plug-ins used to replace objects during the course of an animation.
- **Rendering.** Plug-ins used for textures and shaders.
- **Scene Master.** Plug-ins for various scene-related functions, like Proxy Pic for item selection.
- **Volumetric Effect.** Plug-ins used for effects like ground fog.

Where to Find LightWave's Plug-ins

In Layout, finding the various plug-ins is easier than it is in Modeler. Modeler's plug-ins are accessible usually via a button added within the interface, or a selection in a list. In Layout, most plug-ins can be accessed from the various areas throughout the program. Those areas are as follows:

- Object Properties panel, for Custom Object plug-ins and Displacement Map plug-ins.
- Motion Options panel, for a selected item's motion plug-ins.

- Effects panel, which is home to the plug-ins for the Environment (Backdrop tab), Volumetrics (Volumetrics tab), and Pixel Filter and Image Filter plug-ins (Processing tab).
- Graph Editor, under the Modifiers tab for plug-ins like Oscillator.
- Master plug-in list, found under the Utilities tab.
- Additional, which is a drop-down list found within the Utilities tab. These plug-ins range from basic system tools to key functions to third-party plug-ins.

Loading Plug-ins

When you install LightWave, your plug-ins are already loaded for you. However, there may come a time when you might want to reload certain plug-ins or add third-party plug-ins. You can do this through Layout or Modeler, regardless of the plug-in. The information within the plug-in file is read by LightWave, and it is installed in the proper place to one of the areas in the preceding list.

Loading plug-ins is very easy, and only needs to be done one time. LightWave writes the information to a configuration file when you close the programs. In Layout, you can click to the Utilities tab, and you'll find a Plugins category. There, you can access various plug-in commands, such as Add Plugins, Edit Plugins, Last Plugin, Master Plugin, or select from the Additional list. **Figure A.1** shows the Plugins category within the Utilities tab in Layout. **Figure A.2** shows the Plug-ins category within the Utilities tab in Modeler.

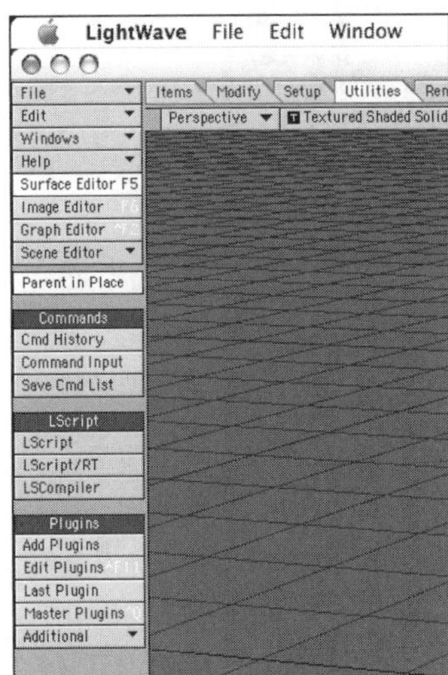

Figure A.1 Plug-in options and controls in Layout are accessible from within the Utilities tab.

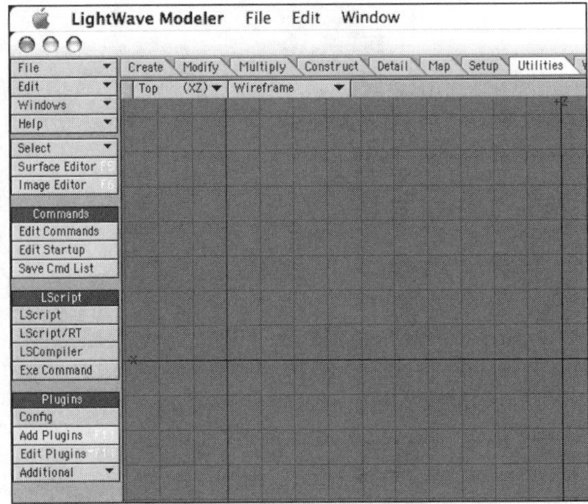

Figure A.2 Plug-in options and controls in Modeler are also accessible from within the Utilities tab.

The easiest way to add plug-ins in LightWave is to use the Edit Plug-ins panel and select Scan Directory. Click this, and point your system to the Plug-Ins folder. Select OK, and in a moment, a small dialog box appears telling you how many plug-ins were added, as in **Figure A.3**.

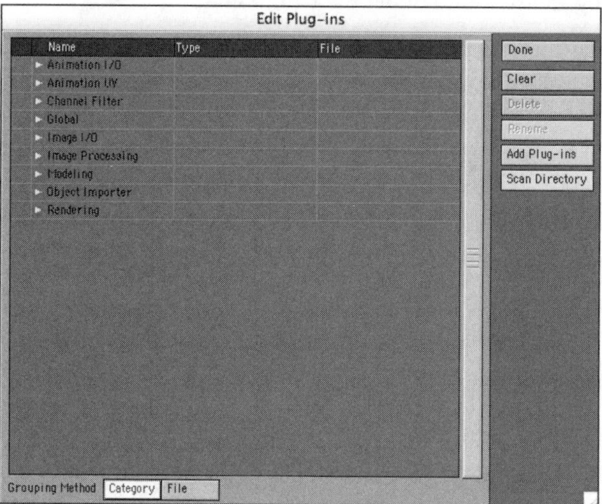

Figure A.3 The Scan Directory option in the Edit Plug-ins panel allows you to load all plug-ins in one click for both Layout and Modeler.

Clicking OK displays the plug-ins loaded, as in **Figure A.4**.

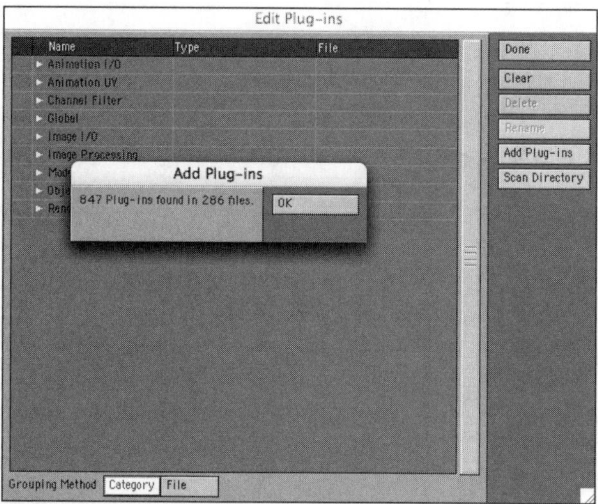

Figure A.4 When loaded, the plug-ins are displayed within their appropriate groupings. And after a scan, the total plug-ins added are listed.

To add more than one plug-in, you can use the Scan Directory option. To add just a single plug-in file, click Add Plug-ins, point your system to the plug-in, and click OK. You can also delete or rename plug-ins in the Edit Plug-in panel. Image Filters are available in the Effects panel, as well as the Image Editor, and so on. Other plug-ins, however, are only available in specific locations, such as Pixel Filter, or Modeler plug-ins. You'll also notice that plug-ins vary in name, based on their usage, such as a modifier, tool, command, or generic plug-in.

LScripts

LScripts, custom "mini-programs" written in LightWave's custom scripting language, are also loaded as plug-ins, although they are slightly different. If you have an LScript you've written or have one compiled from a third-party source, you can load it the same way you do a regular plug-in. Select Add Plug-in, and then select the LScript. Certain plug-ins, such as LScript, are available in more than one location.

Learn Your Tools

LightWave's Layout and Modeler are extremely powerful creation tools. The tools within LightWave require a lot of time and experimentation. Hopefully, the information in this book has given you a good indication of what can be accomplished. There's nothing better than knowing the tools that are available to you. To expand even further on the powerful plug-ins throughout LightWave, here are a few more references for you when creating surfaces and rendering.

Technical Reference

This section of the appendix consists of various charts and tables that come in handy when you're trying to find that particular property or specification that you swore you knew but just can't seem to remember. It consists of the following:

- RGB color values
- Reflection properties
- Refraction properties
- Color temperatures of light
- Film output resolutions
- Video output resolutions

It can't be stressed enough that the following information should be used as a guideline only! The scientific world routinely deals in absolutes. However, animators do not. The information presented here should be used as a starting point only. Feel free to adjust anything as necessary to achieve the look you are going for. Don't worry that your diamond doesn't have the exact refraction value of a real diamond. If it looks better tweaked higher or lower, do it! If your banana looks kind of funky with the "proper" banana color, change it! There are no hard and fast rules, and in the end, the only thing that really matters is that you and your client are happy with the end result.

RGB Color Values

In Table A.1, we provide a good mix of various RGB color values. The diffusion value and lighting scheme you use in a particular scene can have a pronounced effect on the visible color of an object, so keep that in mind. Also, there are very few things in this world that have a 100% diffusion value. For most objects, except metals, 70% to 80% is a good starting point if you don't know an object's diffusion value.

Table A.1 RGB Color Values for Common Colors

Base Color	R	G	B
Black, True	0	0	0
Base Color: Blue			
Blue, Cobalt	61	90	170
Blue, Dodger	30	144	255
Blue, Indigo	8	46	84
Blue, Manganese	3	168	158
Blue, Midnight	25	25	112
Blue, Navy	0	0	128
Blue, Pastel	131	147	202
Blue, Peacock	50	160	200
Blue, Powder	176	224	230
Blue, Royal	65	105	225
Blue, Slate	106	90	205
Blue, Sky	135	206	235
Blue, Steel	70	130	180
Blue, True	0	0	255
Blue, Turquoise	0	200	140
Blue, Ultramarine	20	10	143
Base Color: Brown			
Brown, Beige	163	148	128
Brown, Burnt Sienna	138	54	15
Brown, Burnt Umber	138	51	36
Brown, Chocolate	210	105	30
Brown, Flesh	255	125	64
Brown, Khaki	240	230	140

Base Color	R	G	B
Brown, Raw Sienna	199	97	20
Brown, Raw Umber	115	74	18
Brown, Rosy	188	143	143
Brown, Saddle	139	69	19
Brown, Sandy	244	164	96
Brown, Sepia	94	38	18
Brown, Sienna	160	82	45
Brown, Tan	210	180	140
Brown, True	128	42	42
Base Color: Cyan			
Cyan, Aquamarine	127	255	212
Cyan, Pastel	109	207	246
Cyan, True	0	255	255
Cyan, Turquoise	64	224	208
Base Color: Gray			
Gray, Cold	128	138	135
Gray, Slate	112	128	144
Gray, True, Medium	128	128	128
Gray, Warm	128	128	105
Base Color: Green			
Green, Chartreuse	127	255	0
Green, Cobalt	61	145	64
Green, Emerald	0	201	87
Green, Forest	34	139	34
Green, Lawn	124	252	0
Green, Lime	50	205	50
Green, Mint	189	252	200
Green, Olive Drab	107	142	35
Green, Pastel	130	202	156
Green, Sap	48	128	20
Green, Sea	45	140	87
Green, Spring	0	255	127
Green, Terre Verde	56	94	15
Green, True	0	255	0
Base Color: Magenta			
Magenta, Blue	138	43	226
Magenta, Orchid	218	112	214
Magenta, Pastel	244	154	193
Magenta, Plum	221	160	221
Magenta, Purple	160	32	240
Magenta, True	255	0	255
Magenta, Violet	143	94	153

Table A.1 Continued

Base Color	R	G	B
Base Color: Orange			
Orange, Cadmium	255	97	3
Orange, Carrot	237	145	33
Orange, Red	255	69	0
Orange, True	255	128	0
Base Color: Red			
Red, Brick	156	102	31
Red, Cadmium	227	23	13
Red, Coral	255	127	80
Red, Firebrick	178	34	34
Red, Indian	176	23	31
Red, Maroon	176	48	96
Red, Pastel	246	150	121
Red, Pink	255	192	203
Red, Raspberry	135	38	87
Red, Salmon	250	128	114
Red, Tomato	255	99	71
Red, True	255	0	0
Base Color: White			
White, Antique	250	235	215
White, Azure	240	255	255
White, Bisque	255	228	196
White, Blanch	255	235	205
White, Corn Silk	255	248	220
White, Eggshell	252	230	201
White, Floral	255	250	240
White, Gainesboro	220	220	220
White, Ghost	248	248	255
White, Honeydew	240	255	240
White, Ivory	255	255	240
White, Linen	250	240	230
White, Navajo	255	222	173
White, Old Lace	253	245	230
White, Seashell	255	245	238
White, Smoke	245	245	245
White, Snow	255	250	250
White, True (White is all colors combined!)	255	255	255
White, Wheat	245	222	179

Base Color	R	G	B
Base Color:Yellow			
Yellow, Banana	227	207	87
Yellow, Cadmium	255	153	18
Yellow, Gold	255	215	0
Yellow, Goldenrod	218	165	32
Yellow, Melon	227	255	0
Yellow, Orange	247	148	29
Yellow, Pastel	255	247	153
Yellow, True	255	255	0
Metals			
Aluminum	220	223	227
Brass	191	173	111
Copper	186	110	64
Gold	218	178	115
Graphite	87	33	77
Iron	115	115	120
Silver	230	230	215
Stainless Steel	125	125	120

Reflection Properties

Table A.2 presents a good mix of materials and their basic reflective properties. There are many factors that affect an item's reflectivity, so use these values as a starting point.

Table A.2 Percentage of Incident Light Reflected by Various Materials

Material	%
Aluminum	45
Aluminum Foil	65
Asphalt	14
Brass	40
Brick	30
Bronze	10
Chrome	70
Copper	71
Earth, Moist	08
Gold	84
Graphite	20
Green Leaf	21

Table A.2 Continued

Material	%
Iron	15
Linen	81
Marble, White	53
Mercury	69
Paper, Newsprint	61
Paper, White	71
Pewter	20
Platinum	64
Porcelain, White	72
Quartz	81
Rubber	02
Silicon	28
Silver	90
Slate	06
Stainless Steel	37
Steel	55
Tin Can	40
Vinyl	15
Wood, Pine	40

Refraction Properties

Table A.3 provides a rather extensive list of items. Chances are you won't need most of them until someone comes along from a scientific institution wanting work done that has to be scientifically accurate. You'll be glad you have this list then!

Indices of refraction for various elements, materials, liquids, and gases at Standard Temperature and Pressure (STP) in visible light are listed.

Table A.3 Indices of Refraction

Material	Index
Vacuum	1.000 (Exactly)
Acetone	1.360
Actinolite	1.618
Agalmatoite	1.550
Agate	1.544
Agate, Moss	1.540
Air	1.000
Alcohol	1.329
Alexandrite	1.745
Aluminum	1.440

Material	Index
Amber	1.546
Amblygonite	1.611
Amethyst	1.544
Amorphous Selenium	2.920
Anatase	2.490
Andalusite	1.641
Anhydrite	1.571
Apatite	1.632
Apophyllite	1.536
Aquamarine	1.577
Aragonite	1.530
Argon	1.000
Asphalt	1.635
Augelite	1.574
Axinite	1.675
Azurite	1.730
Barite	1.636
Barytocalcite	1.684
Benitoite	1.757
Benzene	1.501
Beryl	1.577
Beryllonite	1.553
Brazilianite	1.603
Bromine (liquid)	1.661
Bronze	1.180
Brownite	1.567
Calcite	1.486
Calspar1	1.660
Calspar2	1.486
Cancrinite	1.491
Carbon Dioxide (gas)	1.000
Carbon Dioxide (liquid)	1.200
Carbon Disulfide	1.628
Carbon Tetrachloride	1.460
Cassiterite	1.997
Celestite	1.622
Cerussite	1.804
Ceylanite	1.770
Chalcedony	1.530
Chalk	1.510
Chalybite	1.630
Chlorine (gas)	1.000
Chlorine (liquid)	1.385

Material	Index
Chrome Green	2.400
Chrome Red	2.420
Chrome Yellow	2.310
Chromium	2.970
Chromium Oxide	2.705
Chrysoberyl	1.745
Chrysocolla	1.500
Chrysoprase	1.534
Citrine	1.550
Clinozoisite	1.724
Cobalt Blue	1.740
Cobalt Green	1.970
Cobalt Violet	1.710
Colemanite	1.586
Copper	1.100
Copper Oxide	2.705
Coral	1.486
Cordierite	1.540
Corundum	1.766
Crocoite	2.310
Crown Glass	1.520
Crystal	2.000
Cuprite	2.850
Danburite	1.633
Diamond	2.417
Diopside	1.680
Dolomite	1.503
Dumortierite	1.686
Ebonite	1.660
Ekanite	1.600
Elaeolite	1.532
Emerald	1.576
Emerald, Synth flux	1.561
Emerald, Synth hydro	1.568
Enstatite	1.663
Epidote	1.733
Ethyl Alcohol (Ethanol)	1.360
Euclase	1.652
Fabulite	2.409
Feldspar, Adventurine	1.532
Feldspar, Albite	1.525
Feldspar, Amazonite	1.525
Feldspar, Labradorite	1.565

Table A.3 Continued

Material	Index	Material	Index
Feldspar, Microcline	1.525	Iolite	1.548
Feldspar, Oligoclase	1.539	Iron	1.510
Feldspar, Orthoclase	1.525	Ivory	1.540
Fluoride	1.560	Jade, Nephrite	1.610
Fluorite	1.434	Jadeite	1.665
Formica	1.470	Jasper	1.540
Garnet, Almandine	1.760	Jet	1.660
Garnet, Almandite	1.790	Kornerupine	1.665
Garnet, Andradite	1.820	Kunzite	1.655
Garnet, Demantoid	1.880	Kyanite	1.715
Garnet, Grossular	1.738	Lapis Gem	1.500
Garnet, Hessonite	1.745	Lapis Lazuli	1.610
Garnet, Rhodolite	1.760	Lazulite	1.615
Garnet, Spessartite	1.810	Lead	2.010
Gaylussite	1.517	Leucite	1.509
Glass	1.517	Magnesite	1.515
Glass, Albite	1.489	Malachite	1.655
Glass, Crown	1.520	Meerschaum	1.530
Glass, Crown, Zinc	1.517	Mercury (liquid)	1.620
Glass, Flint, Dense	1.660	Methanol	1.329
Glass, Flint, Heaviest	1.890	Moldavite	1.500
Glass, Flint, Heavy	1.655	Moonstone, Adularia	1.525
Glass, Flint, Lanthanum	1.800	Moonstone, Albite	1.535
Glass, Flint, Light	1.580	Natrolite	1.480
Glass, Flint, Medium	1.627	Nephrite	1.600
Glycerine	1.473	Nitrogen (gas)	1.000
Gold	0.470	Nitrogen (liquid)	1.205
Hambergite	1.559	Nylon	1.530
Hauynite	1.502	Obsidian	1.489
Helium	1.000	Olivine	1.670
Hematite	2.940	Onyx	1.486
Hemimorphite	1.614	Opal	1.450
Hiddenite	1.655	Oxygen (gas)	1.000
Howlite	1.586	Oxygen (liquid)	1.221
Hydrogen (gas)	1.000	Painite	1.787
Hydrogen (liquid)	1.097	Pearl	1.530
Hypersthene	1.670	Periclase	1.740
Ice	1.309	Peridot	1.654
Idocrase	1.713	Peristerite	1.525
Iodine Crystal	3.340	Petalite	1.502

Material	Index	Material	Index
Phenakite	1.650	Steatite	1.539
Phosgenite	2.117	Steel	2.500
Plastic	1.460	Stichtite	1.520
Plexiglas	1.500	Strontium Titanate	2.410
Polystyrene	1.550	Styrofoam	1.595
Prase	1.540	Sugar Solution (30%)	1.380
Prasiolite	1.540	Sugar Solution (80%)	1.490
Prehnite	1.610	Sulphur	1.960
Proustite	2.790	Synthetic Spinel	1.730
Purpurite	1.840	Taaffeite	1.720
Pyrite	1.810	Tantalite	2.240
Pyrope	1.740	Tanzanite	1.691
Quartz	1.544	Teflon	1.350
Quartz, Fused	1.458	Thomsonite	1.530
Rhodizite	1.690	Tiger Eye	1.544
Rhodochrisite	1.600	Topaz	1.620
Rhodonite	1.735	Topaz, Blue	1.610
Rock Salt	1.544	Topaz, Pink	1.620
Rubber, Natural	1.519	Topaz, White	1.630
Ruby	1.760	Topaz, Yellow	1.620
Rutile	2.610	Tourmaline	1.624
Sanidine	1.522	Tremolite	1.600
Sapphire	1.760	Tugtupite	1.496
Scapolite	1.540	Turpentine	1.472
Scapolite, Yellow	1.555	Turquoise	1.610
Scheelite	1.920	Ulexite	1.490
Selenium, Amorphous	2.920	Uvarovite	1.870
Serpentine	1.560	Variscite	1.550
Shell	1.530	Vivianite	1.580
Silicon	4.240	Wardite	1.590
Sillimanite	1.658	Water (gas)	1.000
Silver	0.180	Water (100°C)	1.318
Sinhalite	1.699	Water (20°C)	1.333
Smaragdite	1.608	Water (35°C, room temperature)	1.331
Smithsonite	1.621	Willemite	1.690
Sodalite	1.483	Witherite	1.532
Sodium Chloride	1.544	Wulfenite	2.300
Sphalerite	2.368	Zinc Crown Glass	1.517
Sphene	1.885	Zincite	2.010
Spinel	1.712	Zircon, High	1.960
Spodumene	1.650	Zircon, Low	1.800
Staurolite	1.739	Zirconia, Cubic	2.170

Color Temperatures of Light

The color temperature of light is the temperature to which you would have to heat an object (a black body) to produce light of similar spectral characteristics. Low color temperatures produce warmer (yellow/red) light, whereas higher temperatures produce colder (bluer) light.

The color of light is measured in Kelvins. LightWave has a handy Kelvin scale on its color picker, which makes it easy to plug in these values when you want an accurate starting point. For example, if you want to light your gunfight scene from *High Noon*, you would select a starting temperature of 6000 to 6500 degrees Kelvin (noontime) for your skylight and adjust from there. Table A.4 presents various temperatures and the type of light they represent.

Table A.4 Kelvin Temperatures for Various Light Sources

Temperature	Light Source
1400–1930	Candlelight
2000–2500	Sunrise
2680	40W incandescent lamp
2800–2850	100W household (tungsten) bulb
2950	500W tungsten lamp
2960–3200	Tungsten studio lamp
3000	Fluorescent light (warm white) 200W incandescent lamp
	1000W tungsten lamp
3200	Halogen bulb, Nitraphot B
3400	Photoflood (floodlamp) Halogen bulb, Nitraphot A
3800–4000	Clear flashbulb
4000	Moonlight
4400	Sun two hours after rising
5000	Fluorescent light
5000–6000	Daylight sun at midday to noon
5500	Daylight (for photography) Electronic flash tube
5500–6000	Blue flashbulb
6000–7000	Electronic flash
6500	Daylight (sun and sky averaged)
7000	Overcast sky
8000	Cloudy sky, light shade
9000	Hazy sky, light shade
11000	Sky light without direct sun
13000	Blue sky, thin white clouds
16000	Average blue sky, medium shade
18000–19000	Clear blue sky, deep shade

Film Output Resolutions

Table A.5 represents the most common resolutions you are likely to run into when working with film. These numbers are not absolute, however. There are many factors that could change the final output resolution. The second rows under some of the formats represent alternate resolutions asked for by some postproduction facilities. Some facilities may also ask for rendered output resolutions not on this chart. It all depends on the particular needs of the project.

Table A.5 Common Film Resolutions

Film Resolutions	Image Aspect	Pixel Aspect	<1K	1K	1.5K	2K	4K
35mm Full Aperture	1.33	1.00	768×576 1024×778	1024×768 1556×1182	1536×1152 2048×1556	2048×1536 4096×3112	4096×3072
35mm Academy	1.37	1.00	1024×747	1556×1134 1536×1119	2048×1494 1828×1332	4096×2987 3656×2664	914×666
35mm Academy Projection	1.66	1.00	512×307 914×551	1024×614	1536×921 1556×938	2048×1229 1828×1102	4096×2458 3656×2202
35mm 1.75:1	1.75	1.00	560×320	1120×640	1575×900	2048×1170	4096×2340
35mm 1.85:1	1.85	1.00	512×277	1024×554 914×494	1536×830 1556×841	2048×1107 1828×988	4096×2214 3656×1976
35mm 2.35:1	2.35	1.00	512×218	1024×436	1536×654	2048×871	4096×1743
35mm Anamorphic 2.35:1	2.35	2.00	512×436	1024×871	1536×1307	2048×1743	4096×3486
70mm Panavision	2.20	1.00	880×400	1024×465	1536×698	2048×931	4096×1862
Panavision	2.35	1.00			1536×653	2048×871 1828×777	4096×1742 3656×1555
70mm IMAX	1.36	1.00	512×375	1024×751	1536×1126	2048×1501	4096×3003
VistaVision	1.50	1.00	512×341	1024×683	1536×1024	2048×1365 1828×1219	4096×2731 3072×2048
CinemaScope	1.17	1.00		1024×872	1536×1307	2048×1743 1828×1556	4096×3487 3656×3112
CinemaScope	2.35	1.00			1536×653	2048×871 1828×777	4096×1742 3656×1555
35mm (24mmx36mm) slide	1.50	1.00	512×341	1024×683	1536×1024	2048×1365	4096×2731
6cmx6cm slide	1.00	1.00	512×512	1024×1024	1536×1536	2048×2048	4096×4096
4"×5" or 8"×10" slide	1.33	1.00	768×576	1024×768	1536×1152	2048×1536	4096×3072

Video Output Resolutions

Table A.6 represents the most common video and computer resolutions for working with video. Although NTSC and PAL are interlaced formats, it is a common practice today to render final output as frames rather than fields. It should also be noted that HDTV formats are still far from being standardized across various industries. Always find out from your clients which format they are using.

Table A.6 Common Video and Computer Resolutions

Video Resolutions	Image Aspect	Pixel Aspect	Resolution	Frames/Sec.
D1 NTSC	1.33	0.90	720×486	30i
D1 NTSC Widescreen	1.78 (16:9)	1.20	720×486	30i
D2 NTSC	1.35	0.86	752×480	30i
D2 NTSC Widescreen	1.87	1.15	752×480	30i
D1 PAL	1.33	1.07	720×576	25i
D1 PAL Widescreen	1.78 (16:9)	1.42	720×576	25i
D2 PAL	1.33	1.02	752×576	25i
HDTV	16:9	1.00	1920×1080	60i,30p,24p
	16:9	1.00	1280×720	60p,30p,24p
	16:9 (4:3)	1.00	704×480	60p,60i,30p,24p
	4:3	1.00	640×480	60p,60i,30p,24p
VGA	1.33	1.00	640×480	
SVGA	1.33	1.00	800×600	
XGA	1.33	1.00	1024×768	
SXGA*	1.25	1.00	1280×1024	
SXGA	1.33	1.00	1280×960	
UXGA	1.33	1.00	1600×1200	

*Note: 1280×1024 should be avoided, as it is not the correct aspect ratio for video or computer monitors.

More References You Can Use

The tables listed in this appendix are tremendous assets when creating the various surfaces and resolutions available to you in LightWave.

Now, we wanted to be the be-all end-all to LightWave learning, but that's not fair. Not fair to you, that is! There are so many resources out there, it'll make your head spin. Because of that, we've included a comprehensive list of other LightWave learning resources, as well as books and videos related to the art of 3D modeling and animation.

Reading References

Some might say that books are becoming a thing of the past, because of the Internet and various learning videos on the market. Not so! In fact, book production is greater than it ever has been! So here are some great books that you can use to help learn the art of 3D. There are so many out there, so search online, at your library, and at your local bookstore.

- Birn, Jeremy. *Digital Lighting & Rendering*. 2nd ed. New Riders, 2006.
- Maestri, George. *Digital Character Animation 3*. New Riders, 2006.
- Ablan, Dan. *Digital Photography for 3D Imaging and Animation*. Wiley Publishing, 2007
- Ablan, Dan. *Digital Cinematography & Directing*. New Riders, 2003.
- Kerlow, Isaac V. *The Art of 3D: Computer Animation and Imaging*. 2nd ed. John Wiley and Sons, 2000.
- White, Tony. *The Animator's Workbook*. Watson-Guptill Publications, 1988.
- Lord, Peter. *Creating 3D Animation*. Harry N. Abrams, 1998.
- Thomas, Frank, and Ollie Johnston. *The Illusion of Life: Disney Animation*. Disney Editions, 1995.
- Culhane, Shamus. *Animation: From Script to Screen*. St. Martin's Press, 1990.

These are just a few books of interest, and there are more emerging every day. Browse online, read reviews, and check around to see who's used a book you're interested in. Get feedback and see if it's right for you. Often, one simple tip or idea is worth the price of a book alone, especially during a project! What's better, head on down to your local bookseller and browse the shelves yourself. Often getting your hands on a book before you buy it gives you the opportunity to review it and see if the info you need is in there.

Audiovisual References

Like most people, you enjoy a good, thick LightWave book. You can read it on the train, in bed, even while in the bathroom! But sometimes, you want to see something being done. You want to hear the click of the mouse. If that's the case, there are plenty of visual reference materials out there to help you learn LightWave, as well as many other applications. Below is a list of great learning resources:

- **3D Garage** (`www.3dgarage.com`). 3D Garage has become the number-one site for visual LightWave learning. This DVD-ROM-based LightWave learning course comes direct from this book's author, Dan Ablan. It is a course that Dan has taught for years, and a brand-new course is available for LightWave v9. It is a very high-quality, high-impact learning course, with completely different projects than what's shown in this book. If you're a student or teacher looking to learn LightWave from the ground up, the Signature Courseware is for you. Visit the site for free downloads and examples.
- **Class On Demand** (`www.classondemand.net`). Class On Demand sells not only LightWave training videos and DVDs, but also Video Toaster, Speed Razor, and many others. If you're not looking for a course but rather an inexpensive spot tutorial, you've come to the right place. Visit the site to check out the full list of topics, and check with your local reseller for pricing.
- **Desktop Images** (`www.desktopimages.com`). Desktop Images has been around for years, teaching cool LightWave techniques to students around the globe. Visit the site for updates and information on products.
- **Motion Blur Artwork** (`www.mba-studios.de`). MBA sells LightWave training DVDs of excellent quality through Carnera 3D Seminars. Clear and concise, the tutorials are very complete.
- **Kurv Studios** (`www.kurvstudios.com`). Kurv sells LightWave training DVDs with specific topics of interest.

Web Resources

Often the best place for information is right on your computer! The Internet is a terrific place where you'll find not only information on the latest version of LightWave but tutorials as well. While many tutorials need a little figuring out on your part, there are a ton of freebies that can help you pick up a quick tip or technique. Here is a list of just a few LightWave-related Web sites you can check out:

- **NewTek, Inc.** (`www.newtek.com`). The home of the makers of LightWave, this is a great place to begin learning with many online tutorials, free of charge.
- LightWave Tutorials on the Web (`http://members.shaw.ca/lightwavetutorials/Main_Menu.htm`). Plenty of resources can be found here.
- **Flay** (`www.flay.com`). Hands down, this is the single best online reference for LightWave, be it tutorials, plug-ins, and more.
- **3D Links** (`www.3dlinks.com/tutorials_lightwave.cfm`). This is another user-based site that is a great resource.
- **LightWave Oz** (`www.lightwaveoz.org`). Our friends from down under set up this killer LightWave resource page.
- **3D Palace** (`www.3d-palace.com`). This site includes information for LightWave and other applications.
- **3D Buzz** (`www.3dbuzz.com`) A leader in free 3D training, 3D Buzz offers LightWave tutorials, links, and references.
- **MD Arts** (`www.md-arts.com`). This is simply a great LightWave tutorial page.
- **Creative Cow** (`www.creativecow.net`). The Cow has forums set up where you can discuss LightWave and many other related applications. Find links to more information there.
- **LightWave Group** (`www.lwg3d.org`). The LightWave Group is a cool site for forums, links, and tutorials.
- **Simply LightWave** (`www.simplylightwave.com`). What more can you say? Simply LightWave! Check it out for some great tutorials.
- **Dan Ablan** (`www.danablan.com`). The author's site has more links to LightWave information and training.

These are just a few sites, but a search on Google.com, Lycos.com, or Yahoo.com yields a plethora of wonderful resources. Some may or may not be helpful in your situation or project, but it doesn't hurt to check them out. You never know what you can pick up!

Be sure to also cruise the forums, which are great places to view, discuss, and critique 3D work. Try these:

- **NewTek Forums** (`www.newtek.com`)
- **CG Talk** (`http://forums.cgsociety.org`)
- **3D World** (`www.3dworldmag.com`)
- **LightWave Group** (`www.lwg3d.com`)
- **SpinQuad Forums** (`www.spinquad.com`)

And there is much more out there. Search, and you shall find. Happy learning!

Appendix B

What's on the DVD

The accompanying DVD is full of resources. It contains all the exercise files to help you work with this book and with LightWave v9. The following sections contain descriptions of the DVD's contents and how to use the content included for the tutorials in this book. In addition, exclusive video tutorials have been included just for this book, direct from 3D Garage (`www.3dgarage.com`). These quick-start tutorials help you get up to speed quickly and easily with LightWave v9.

For specific information about the use of this DVD, please review the ReadMe.txt file in the DVD's root directory. This file includes important disclaimer information as well as information about installation, system requirements, troubleshooting, and technical support.

Technical Support Issues

If you have any difficulties with this DVD, please check out our tech support website at `www.peachpit.com`. Go to Customer Support and choose Contact Us, then select Defective Products Support under Select Your Type of Question.

DVD Contents

We've literally packed the DVD with hours of video and cool resources to enhance your learning. On the DVD, you'll find:

- Hours of additional video tutorials to complement the chapters, exclusively from 3D Garage
- High-quality color JPEGs of the book's screen shots
- All the scene files for the book's projects and tutorials
- A full working demo of LightWave v9 from NewTek
- Royalty-free textures and backgrounds from 3D Garage

Using the Video Files

In order to play the 3D Garage video tutorials supplied on the book's DVD, you'll only need to use QuickTime. They were recorded with the H.264 codec and work on both PC and Mac. The video tutorials are supplements to the chapters, some of which coincide with the tutorials in the book and some that stand on their own. Be sure to check out all of them for additional tips and tricks. And be sure to watch the Quick-Start videos first to get you up and running with LightWave v9 quickly. Be sure to vew the read-me files on the disc to see a rundown of the videos included. Be careful, there's a lot of video tutorials! These videos won't be found anywhere else. They were created exclusively for this book.

For more video training and LightWave courseware, visit `www.3dgarage.com`.

System Requirements

This DVD was configured for use on systems running Windows NT Workstation, Windows 98, Windows 2000, Windows XP, and Macintosh OS X or OS9. It should work without issue in Windows Vista, and Mac OS X 10.5.

Loading the DVD Files

To load the files from the DVD, insert the disc into your DVD/CD-ROM drive. If autoplay is enabled on your machine, the DVD setup program starts automatically the first time you insert the disc. You can copy the files to your hard drive or use them right off the disc.

Note

This DVD uses long and mixed-case filenames, requiring the use of a protected mode CD-ROM driver.

Project Files

This DVD contains all the files you need to complete the exercises in *Inside LightWave v9*. These files can be found in the root directory's Projects folder. To properly access the project files, do the following:

1. In LightWave's Layout, press the **o** key to call up the General Options panel.
2. At the top of the panel, select the Content Directory button.
3. A system file dialog box titled Set Content Directory opens. Select your DVD/CD-ROM drive, go to the Projects folder, and click Open.

   If you'd like to use the files directly from your own hard drive, simply copy the Projects folder from the book's DVD to your drive.
4. Your Content Directory is now set for working through the exercises. The Content Directory path should look something like \X:\Projects\, where X is your DVD/CD-ROM drive.

When you select Load Scene, LightWave opens the Projects folder. There, you'll see folders named Scene, Objects, and Images. Within these folders are the individual chapter folders. Selecting Load Object within LightWave points to the Objects folder within the Projects folder.

Index

Symbols and numbers

A

C

D

E

F

G

J

K

L

M

N

O

P

S

T